THE RUSSIAN REVOLUTION

STALIN

THE RUSSIAN REVOLUTION 1917–1921

BY

WILLIAM HENRY CHAMBERLIN

VOLUME TWO

WITH A SELECTED BIBLIOGRAPHY OF RECENT WORKS ON THE CIVIL WAR BY DIANE KOENKER

PRINCETON UNIVERSITY PRESS
PRINCETON, NEW JERSEY

Published by Princeton University Press, 41 William Street, Princeton, New Jersey 08540
In the United Kingdom: Princeton University Press, Guildford, Surrey

Library of Congress Cataloging in Publication Data will be found
on the last printed page of this book

Reissued with a new introduction, February, 1952

First Princeton Paperback printing, 1987
LCC 87-3719
ISBN 0-691-05493-2
ISBN 0-691-00815-9 (pbk.)

This edition is reprinted by arrangement with Macmillan Publishing Company,
a division of Macmillan, Inc.

Clothbound editions of Princeton University Press books are printed on acid-free paper,
and binding materials are chosen for strength and durability. Paperbacks, while
satisfactory for personal collections, are not usually suitable for library rebinding.

Printed in the United States of America by Princeton University Press,
Princeton, New Jersey

CONTENTS

ILLUSTRATIONS

MAPS

SELECTED BIBLIOGRAPHY OF RECENT WORKS ON THE CIVIL WAR

BY DIANE KOENKER

MANY monographs, memoirs, and collections of documents have been published since the original edition of Chamberlin's work, although none has completely replaced his synthesis. Nor can this updated bibliography be as comprehensive as the one published at the end of this volume. The works listed below represent a small selection of studies on the Russian Civil War that deserve mention, both because of their contribution to the historical understanding of the civil war and for their value as further bibliographic guides. For reference to many other important studies and collections, in Russian, English, and other languages, the reader is encouraged to consult the bibliographies in the works cited here.

ADAMS, ARTHUR. *Bolsheviks in the Ukraine, 1918–1919: The Second Campaign.* New Haven, Yale University Press, 1963. Political history.

ANWEILER, OSKAR. *The Soviets: The Russian Workers, Peasants, and Soldiers Councils, 1905–1921.* Trans. of *Die Ratebewegung in Russlands 1905–1921* by Ruth Heil. New York, Pantheon, 1974.

AVRICH, PAUL. *Kronstadt 1921.* New York, Norton, 1970. Superb study of the rebellion by radical sailors against Bolshevik rule; lucid and sympathetic.

BETTELHEIM, CHARLES. *Class Struggles in the USSR: First Period, 1917–1923.* New York, Monthly Review Press, 1976. Brian Pearce, trans. Theoretical work by a noted French Marxist economist.

BORYS, JURIJ. *The Sovietization of Ukraine, 1917–1923.* Edmonton, Canadian Institute of Ukrainian Studies, 1980 (rev. ed.).

BRINKLEY, G. A. *The Volunteer Army and Allied Intervention in South Russia, 1917–1921.* South Bend, Ind., Notre Dame University Press, 1966. Solid, well researched.

CARLEY, MICHAEL JABARA. *Revolution and Intervention: The French Government and the Russian Civil War 1917–1919.* Montreal, McGill/Queens University Press, 1983.

CARR, E. H. *The Bolshevik Revolution, 1917–1923.* Baltimore, Penguin,

1966. 3 vols. Fundamental study of the development of the Soviet state, using state sources and an institutional perspective.

COHEN, STEPHEN F. *Bukharin and the Bolshevik Revolution*. New York, Knopf, 1973. Important study of a leading Bolshevik intellectual for whom the civil war was a critical turning point.

DANIELS, ROBERT V. *The Conscience of the Revolution*. New York, Simon and Schuster, 1960. Thorough study of the Bolshevik oppositions.

DEUTSCHER, ISAAC. *The Prophet Armed: Trotsky, 1879–1921*. New York, Vintage, 1954. First volume of the classic trilogy; Trotsky as commander of the Red Army.

FITZPATRICK, SHEILA. *The Commissariat of Enlightenment: Soviet Organization of Education and the Arts under Lunacharsky*. Cambridge, Cambridge University Press, 1970. Pioneering study of government, politics of culture, and the formation of the Soviet state.

GETZLER, ISRAEL. *Kronstadt, 1917–1921: The Fate of a Soviet Democracy*. Cambridge, Cambridge University Press, 1983. Compelling survey of the path from 1917 to the rebellion of 1921 among radical sailors.

HAUPT, GEORGES, AND JEAN-JACQUES MARIE. *Makers of the Russian Revolution*. Ithaca, Cornell University Press, 1969. Translated autobiographies of Bolshevik leaders.

HOVANNISIAN, RICHARD G. *Armenia on the Road to Independence, 1918*. Berkeley, University of California Press, 1967.

———. *The Republic of Armenia: The First Year, 1918–1919*. Berkeley, University of California Press, 1971. Careful studies of the Transcaucasian republic.

HUNCZAK, TARAS (editor). *The Ukraine, 1917–1921: A Study in Revolution*. Cambridge, Harvard University Press, 1977. Essays.

KAZEMZADEH, FIRUZ. *Struggle for the Trans-Caucasus, 1917–1922*. New York, Philosophical Library, 1951.

KENEZ, PETER, *Civil War in South Russia, 1918*. Berkeley, University of California Press, 1971.

———. *Civil War in South Russia, 1919–1920*. Berkeley, University of California Press, 1977. Major studies of the military side of the civil war, using extensive archival materials.

———. *The Birth of the Propaganda State: Soviet Methods of Mass Mobilization 1917–1929*. Cambridge, Cambridge University Press, 1985. Extensive coverage of the press and propaganda efforts during the civil war.

KENNAN, GEORGE F. *Soviet-American Relations 1917–1920: Russia Leaves the War*. New York, Atheneum, 1967.

———. *Soviet-American Relations 1917–1920: The Decision to Intervene*.

New York, Atheneum, 1967. Well-written and solid history by a scholar-diplomat.

LEGGETT, GEORGE. *The Cheka: Lenin's Political Police*. Oxford, Clarendon Press, 1981.

MALLE, SYLVANA. *The Economic Organisation of War Communism 1918–1921*. Cambridge, Cambridge University Press, 1985.

PALIJ, MICHAEL. *The Anarchism of Nester Makhno, 1918–1921*. Seattle, University of Washington Press, 1976. Intellectual history of the anarchist freebooting leader.

PIPES, RICHARD. *The Formation of the Soviet Union: Communism and Nationalism, 1917–1923*. New York, Atheneum, 1968. The civil war in Russia's borderlands; meticulous, comprehensive, critical.

RADKEY, OLIVER HENRY. *The Sickle under the Hammer: The Russian Socialist Revolutionaries in the Early Months of Soviet Rule*. New York, Columbia University Press, 1963. The further decline of the Socialist Revolutionary Party.

———. *The Unknown Civil War in Soviet Russia: A Study of the Green Movement in the Tambov Region 1920–21*. Stanford, Hoover Institution Press, 1976. Uneven study of anti-Bolshevik peasant movements.

REMINGTON, THOMAS F. *Building Socialism in Bolshevik Russia: Ideology and Industrial Organization 1917–1921*. Pittsburgh, University of Pittsburgh Press, 1984. Institutional history, well conceived and well researched.

RIGBY, T. H. *Lenin's Government: Sovnarkom 1917–1922*. Cambridge, Cambridge University Press, 1979. Major study of the central government in formation.

ROSENBERG, WILLIAM G. *Liberals in the Russian Revolution: The Constitutional Democratic Party, 1917–1921*. Princeton, Princeton University Press, 1974. Important and comprehensive study of the Kadet party and its political role during the civil war.

SCHAPIRO, LEONARD. *The Origin of the Communist Autocracy: Political Opposition in the Soviet State 1917–1922*. Cambridge, Harvard University Press, 1977 (2nd ed.). How Leninism crushed its rivals, by a leading British Sovietologist.

SERVICE, ROBERT. *The Bolshevik Party in Revolution 1917–1923: A Study in Organizational Change*. New York, Barnes and Noble, 1979. Focuses on grass-roots party organization and structure.

SHKLOVSKY, VIKTOR. *A Sentimental Journey: Memoirs 1917–1922*. Ithaca, Cornell University Press, 1970. Richard Sheldon, trans. Episodic but valuable account by a major formalist writer.

SIRIANI, CARMEN. *Workers' Control and Socialist Democracy: The Soviet Experience*. London, Verso Editions, 1982. Written from a theoretical, sociological perspective, with relevance to workers' self-management elsewhere.

STITES, RICHARD, ABBOTT GLEASON, AND PETER KENEZ (editors). *Bolshevik Culture: Experiment and Order in the Russian Revolution*. Bloomington, Indiana University Press, 1985. Essays; "culture" here is used in a broad sense, including daily life as well as arts and literature.

TROTSKII, LEV. *The Trotsky Papers, 1917–1922*. The Hague, 1964. In English and Russian, well annotated.

ULLMAN, RICHARD H. *Anglo-Soviet Relations 1917–21*. Princeton, Princeton University Press, 1968–1973. 3 vols. Major diplomatic studies, well researched.

VOLINE. *The Unknown Revolution*. New York, Free Life Editions, 1974. Important anarchist perspective.

THE RUSSIAN REVOLUTION

VOLUME TWO

CHAPTER XX

THE CLASH WITH THE CZECHS AND THE DEMOCRATIC COUNTERREVOLUTION

By one of the curious accidents of history a small force of Czecho-Slovaks, former war prisoners and deserters from the Austro-Hungarian Army, citizens of a state which in 1918 still existed only in the imagination of its nationalist leaders, played a most significant rôle in Russia's civil war and made possible the temporary overthrow of the Soviets in vast, although sparsely populated, Siberia, and also in the Middle Volga and in part of the Ural Regions.

Despite the seething discontent which was described in the last chapter, the Soviet regime in May, 1918, seemed stronger than any force that could be arrayed against it in Northern and Central Russia or in Siberia. The Germans seemed satisfied with the acquisitions of Brest-Litovsk and with the occupation of Ukraina, the overthrow of the Red Government in Finland and the possibilities of indefinite expansion in the Caucasus. They showed no disposition to penetrate farther into Russia or to bring about the downfall of the Soviet Government. A Japanese naval descent in Vladivostok on April 6, ostensibly to protect the lives of Japanese subjects, had not been followed by more serious measures of intervention. A Far Eastern Cossack Ataman, or chieftain, Semyenov, was making occasional raids into Eastern Siberia from Manchuria; but the local Far Eastern Soviet forces seemed able to cope with him. The Allies were so absorbed in meeting the great German onslaughts of the spring and summer of 1918 that there was little reasonable prospect of large-scale intervention, except perhaps, on the part of Japan.

While the Soviet regime in many parts of the country was so weak and poorly organized that it scarcely seemed able to withstand the pressure of even a small body of disciplined hostile troops it was not clear where those troops would emerge. The logic of developments seemed to favor the opponents of anti-Soviet intervention, the unofficial British diplomatic representative, Lockhart, the head of the American Red Cross Mission, Robins, and the French Captain Jacques Sadoul.

The situation changed with dramatic suddenness as a result of the clash between the Czecho-Slovak and the Soviet forces in the latter part of May and the rapid and sweeping victories of the former. Intervention, from a theory yearned for by hostile foreign Ambassadors and anti-Soviet Russians, became a fact. Within a few weeks an enormous territory was wrested from Soviet control. The action of the Czecho-Slovaks made possible the establishment of anti-Bolshevik Governments on the Volga and in Siberia; the organization of anti-Bolshevik armies.

The nucleus of the future Czecho-Slovak Army was a brigade, recruited from Czecho-Slovaks resident in Russia and attached to the Russian Army immediately after the outbreak of the War. The Czech Nationalist leaders, Professor Thomas G. Masaryk and Eduard Beneš, were eager to enlarge this brigade as rapidly as possible by enlisting Czecho-Slovak war prisoners and deserters. They encountered a good deal of chilliness and reserve on the part of the Tsarist military authorities, who looked on nationalist rebels, even when they were rebels against Austria-Hungary, a country with which Russia was at war, with instinctive disapproval. Only after the March Revolution Masaryk, going to Russia, obtained permission to carry on recruiting among Czecho-Slovak war prisoners, with the result that about 30,000 volunteers flowed into this new nationalist force and it attained the status of an independent corps in the autumn of 1917.[1]

Realizing that Russia was definitely out of the War and eager to strengthen his people's claim for national independence by furnishing tangible aid to the Allied cause, Masaryk conceived the idea of transporting the Czecho-Slovak forces to France. Small numbers of Czechs were transported to France by way of Archangel.

At the time of the Bolshevik Revolution the main forces of the corps were concentrated around Kiev. General Alekseev and other anti-Soviet Russians looked hopefully to this corps, which had maintained its discipline and fighting capacity at a time when the whole Russian Army was in a state of complete demoralization and hasty self-demobilization, as an ally against the Bolsheviki. But Masaryk firmly declined any suggestions that pointed to an interference of the Czechs in internal Russian affairs.[2] In view of the lack of shipping at Archangel and the danger of submarine attacks it was decided to send the Czecho-Slovaks almost around the world, despatching them by sea from Vladivostok and through the Panama Canal to the battlefields of France. On January 25, 1918, Masaryk publicly proclaimed the corps a part of the Czech Army in France.[3] On March 7 he left Moscow for Vladivostok, with a view to proceeding to America and Europe, partly in the hope of hastening the provision of the shipping which was needed for the transportation of the troops from Vladivostok.[4]

Up to this time the relations between the Czecho-Slovak Corps and the Soviet forces had been quite friendly. The Czechs had withdrawn from their positions around Kiev when the Germans began to occupy Ukraina. Side by side with the more steadfast of the Soviet Red Guards they had fought delaying skirmishes with the Germans, of which the hottest was around the railroad station Bakhmach. The commander of the Soviet forces in Ukraina, Antonov-Ovseenko, spoke quite warmly of the services of the Czechs, declaring in an army order: [5] "The Revolutionary armies of South Russia will never forget the brotherly aid which was granted by the Czech Corps in the struggle of the laboring people against the hordes of base imperialism." On leaving Ukraina the Czechs handed over to the Red armies a part of their weapons.

However, despite this auspicious beginning, clouds soon appeared on the horizon of the Soviet-Czech relations. As soon as the Corps crossed the frontier from Ukraina into Russia, Czech Communist propagandists began to appear in its ranks, agitating against the officers and endeavoring to persuade the soldiers to join the Red Army. If this was a ground for complaint on the part of the Czech leaders, the Soviet officials, on their side, took exception to the presence with the corps of a considerable number of Russian officers of the higher grades,[6] whose attitude toward the Soviet regime was naturally anything but friendly.

On March 26 an agreement which aimed to remove some of the causes of friction and to insure the unobstructed passage of the Czech Corps across Siberia was signed by Soviet and Czech representatives and by the French Colonel Vergé, as a representative of the Entente, at Penza. Under the terms of this agreement [7] the Czechs were to travel "not as fighting units, but as groups of free citizens, who carry with them a specified number of weapons for defense against counterrevolutionary attacks." Every trainload of troops was to have with it an armed company of Czech soldiers, to the number of 168, with one machine-gun. Three hundred bullets were to be allowed for every rifle, 1,200 for every machine-gun. The remainder of the arms were to be turned over to the Soviet authorities in Penza and some of the Russian officers were to be dismissed. Had this agreement been faithfully adhered to by both sides and had normal transportation conditions prevailed in Siberia, the Czecho-Slovaks might have gone to France, and the history of the civil war in eastern Russia and Siberia would have been appreciably different.

But between the Czech leaders and the Soviet authorities there was a wall of mutual distrust, and neither side observed either the spirit or the letter of the Penza agreement. Some of the Czech detachments concealed arms in excess of the permitted quota, hiding them beneath the straw and behind the double walls in their cars. On the other hand local Soviets, which at that time sometimes paid little regard to instructions from Moscow, often delayed the movement of the Czechs and demanded the surrender of more arms than the Penza agreement had prescribed. The efforts of the Soviet authorities to break up the Corps through propaganda carried on by Czech Communists continued.[8] The more conservative Czech officers and those Russian officers who remained carried on counter-propaganda to the effect that the Bolsheviki were German agents and suggested that attempts to disarm them might be only the prelude to handing them over to the Austrian Government, which would give them short shrift as traitors and deserters. An atmosphere of suspicion and hostility grew up, and was intensified by the disorderly condition of the country and by the breakdown of transportation and supply. Although it was obviously in the interest of the Soviet Government to get the Czechs out of Russia as soon as possible, their trains moved at a snail's pace. Some detachments spent two months in covering a distance which a train should normally travel in two days. The provision of food in a hungry country raised new difficulties and furnished other occasions for quarrels with unfriendly local Soviets.

Many Soviet historians are inclined to represent the clash with the Czechs as part of a prepared scheme of Allied intervention. Documentary proofs of this are lacking; [9] and the weight of available evidence indicates that the Allied Governments, while they were quick to welcome and utilize the Czechs as an anti-Bolshevik force after their clash with the Soviets had led to rapid and overwhelming victory in Siberia and in a considerable part of Eastern Russia, did not provoke or instigate this clash.

It is true that the British War Ministry on April 1 suggested that the Czech troops should not leave Russia, but should concentrate in Eastern Siberia and coöperate with the anti-Bolshevik leader, Semyenov.[10] But both the Czech nationalist leaders in Paris and the French Government rejected this scheme, and it was dropped. The Czecho-Slovaks were more dependent upon France than upon any other power; their nationalist headquarters were in Paris; their young army was regarded as part of the French army, and French discipline had been introduced in it. The wishes of the French Government were, therefore, of decisive importance in determining the policy of the Czech leaders. And the primary desire of the French Government in the spring of 1918 was to place as many fresh troops on the Western Front as possible, in order to resist the onslaught of Ludendorff. That the French Government sincerely desired to transport the Czechs to the Western Front is evident from the following message which Clemenceau addressed to the French Foreign Minister, Pichon, on April 26: [11]

"All detachments of the Czech Corps should be transported with the swiftest means to the Western Front, where the presence of these excellent troops is very important; for this purpose I have taken suitable steps with the British Government, in order to obtain sea transportation for a part of these troops by way of Archangel."

And on May 2 the Supreme Allied War Council approved the suggestion that all the Czech forces west of Omsk should be despatched to France by way of Archangel. This resolution was followed by negotiations in Moscow between the head of the French Military Mission, General Lavergne, and Trotzky, who agreed to permit this change of route for a part of the Czechs; he also promised to turn over to them a part of the considerable stocks of war material which the Allies had shipped to Russia and which had piled up in Archangel and in Murmansk for lack of adequate transportation. The theory of a deliberate Allied plot to promote intervention through the Czechs can scarcely be squared with the evident willingness of the Allied military representative to split the Corps, already strung out over thousands of miles of the Trans-Siberian Railroad, and thereby weaken it further for offensive purposes in Russia.

But this decision to divide the Corps and to send part of it by way of Archangel unexpectedly and accidentally played a considerable part in increasing the estrangement between the Czech leaders and the Soviet authorities. As a result of defective communication the Czechs gained the impression that the initiative in deciding to transport some of their forces through Archangel had emanated not from the Allies, but from the Soviet Government. They immediately suspected a scheme to divide them with a view to forcibly disarming and perhaps interning them. While the civilian commissars attached to the Czech Corps, Maxa and Czermak, were anxious to carry out Masaryk's policy of sending the Czech troops to France without becoming involved in internal Russian affairs the Czech military leaders, especially the restless and ambitious Captain Gaida, who was soon to rise to the rank of a general, were already aggressively disposed against the Soviets and inclined to favor the policy of making their way through to the Far East by force of arms, if necessary. Gaida and other Czech officers were apparently already in touch with some of the underground Socialist Revolutionary and officers' organizations which existed in Siberia and perhaps already foresaw the rôle which the Czechs might play in helping the anti-Bolshevik Russians to rebel.

Under these circumstances a small incident led to big consequences. On May 14 a group of Hungarian war prisoners came into contact with a number of Czech soldiers in one of their trains. Nationalist antipathy soon flared up; one of the Hungarians threw a piece of iron at the Czechs and hit one of the soldiers; a scuffle followed and the Hungarian who threw the missile was killed. This obscure brawl between representatives of the unfriendly races of the Austro-Hungarian Empire in an Ural railroad junction was the spark that ignited a blaze of civil war over a vast expanse of Russian territory. The Cheliabinsk Soviet, investigating the incident on May 17, arrested several Czech soldiers. Their comrades demanded their release; and when this was not forthcoming they marched with arms into the town, forcibly released the prisoners, occupied the station and disarmed the Red Guards—apparently no very difficult task. This affair was not followed by any immediate outbreak of hostilities; but it strained the already unsatisfactory Soviet-Czech relations to the breaking-point.

As soon as the news of the Cheliabinsk incident reached Moscow (telegraphic as well as postal communication at this time was slow and irregular) the Soviet authorities resolved to take vigorous action. The civilian commissars, Maxa and Czermak, were arrested on the night of May 20 and induced, under threat of being tried before a courtmartial, to send a telegram to the Czech troops demanding that they give up their arms to the Soviet authorities.[12]

This telegram reached Cheliabinsk at the time when a military congress, attended by officers and representatives of a number of the Czech detachments, was taking place.

Suspecting that Maxa and Czermak, being in Moscow, were no longer free agents, the delegates to the congress rejected the proposal to give up their arms, elected an executive committee to supervise the transportation of the troops to Vladivostok, refused to sanction the alteration of the route to Archangel and decided that movement toward Vladivostok should be continued with all available means. This clearly indicated a determination to resort to force, if the local Soviets attempted to delay the transportation or to disarm the troop-trains.

Trotzky's assistant in the War Commissariat, Aralov, despatched two telegrams to the Soviets along the line of movement of the Czech troops which showed that the Soviet Government also was prepared to resort to warlike measures. The first telegram, dated May 21st, instructed the Soviets to request the Czechs to create trade-union organizations and to enter the ranks of the Red Army. The second, dated May 23, was couched in much stronger language and called for "swift measures for the detention, disarming and dissolution of all trains and detachments of the Czecho-Slovak Corps," [13] This was followed on May 25 by a still sharper order from Trotzky which began as follows:

"All Soviets on the railroad line are instructed, under heavy responsibility, to disarm the Czecho-Slovaks. Every Czech who is found armed on the railroad is to be shot on the spot."

The order also instructed railroad workers not to permit a single train with Czechs to move eastward, and added: "Any delay is equivalent to treason and brings with it the severest punishment for the guilty. Simultaneously reliable forces are to be sent in the rear of the Czech troop trains, which are commanded to suppress the insurgents." [14]

Simultaneously with the publication of Trotzky's drastic order, which it was not in the power of the local Soviets to carry out, the first clashes between the Czechs and Soviet forces occurred on May 25 at Marianovka, near Omsk and at Marinsk, farther east on the Trans-Siberian Railroad. The Czech leaders had doubtless prepared plans for the eventuality of a military clash at the congress in Cheliabinsk; and one town after another passed into their hands with amazing rapidity. Novo-Nikolaevsk, in Central Siberia, and Cheliabinsk, where the first serious clash had occurred a few days earlier, were occupied on May 26; Penza and Syzran, farther to the west, on May 28 and 29; Tomsk on the 31st; Omsk, the largest town in Western Siberia, on June 7; Samara, the central point of the Middle Volga, on June 8.

At the time of the outbreak of hostilities the Czechs were divided into six groups, with a distance of more than five thousand miles between the westernmost of these groups, at Penza, and the easternmost, at Vladivostok. The largest of these groups, under the Russian General Diederichs, numbering about 14,000, was in and around Vladivostok. The Czech General Chechek commanded a force of about 8,000 at Penza; the Russian Voitzekhovsky had a slightly larger detachment at Cheliabinsk; while the Czech forces in Central Siberia, under the general command of Gaida, were divided into three small detachments, one of 2,000 at Novo-Nikolaevsk, a second of 1,000 at Kansk and a third of 800 at Marinsk.[15] So the total strength of the Czech Corps was a little less than 35,000, of whom only about 20,000 were in a position to go into immediate action in Central and Western Siberia and on the Volga.

Several causes contributed to the swift and in some cases almost bloodless victories of the Czechs. The Soviets were caught almost completely unprepared, without trained and reliable troops. The Siberian towns were honeycombed with secret organizations of Socialist Revolutionaries and of officers, which were preparing for an uprising in any case and which found their task very much eased by the appearance of the Czechs. In Western Siberia alone it was estimated that about 7,000 men with military experience were organized in anti-Bolshevik groups in May.[16] In some towns, such as Semipalatinsk, Biisk, Omsk and Krasnoyarsk, the Bolsheviki were overthrown before the Czechs actually arrived, as a result of uprisings from within. Some of the Soviets showed a good deal of cowardice, running away at the first signs of danger. In other cases the workers displayed an indifferent or even hostile attitude toward the Soviets. In Omsk, for instance, the railroad workers tore up the rails, in order to prevent the Soviet from evacuating in the eastern direction, and the Soviet leaders had to escape on boats on the Irtish River.[17]

Here and there Red detachments offered more serious resistance; the town of Barnaul, south of the Trans-Siberian line, beat off the first attack of the Czechs; and there was sharp fighting around Lake Baikal, where the cliffs, pierced only by railroad tunnels, offered good natural means of defense. But the general

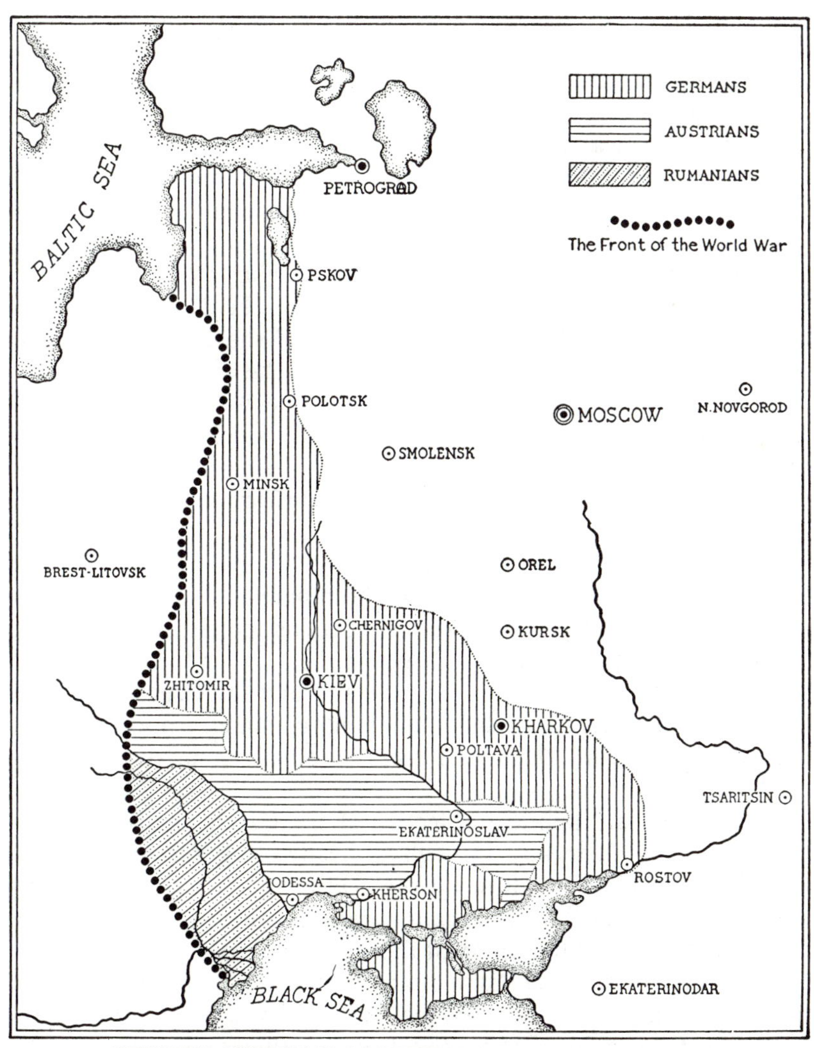

GERMAN-AUSTRIAN OCCUPATION OF RUSSIA IN 1918

course of civil war throughout the summer months was distinctly in favor of the Czechs and of the Russian anti-Bolshevik armies which grew up in Siberia and on the Volga. The idea of transporting the Czechs to France was abandoned as soon as the scope of their victory was realized in the Allied capitals. On June 20 the French General Lavergne in Moscow, received instructions from Paris to the following effect: The Czech regiments, "immobilized through Russian events," should remain where they were; they were to carry out no intervention, but to do nothing that would make future intervention difficult. A week later, on the 27th, the instructions become more clearcut and positive; all the Russian elements that desire the restoration of order are to be rallied around the Czechs; the Trans-Siberian Railroad is to be completely occupied. And on July 12 Clemenceau, who at the end of April had been anxious to expedite the movement of the Czechs to France, wrote to his Foreign Minister, Pichon: "All our efforts must now be directed to diverting the action of the Czechs to the restoration of order in Siberia and to the complete occupation of the Siberian Railroad, in order thus to prepare quick progress for Japanese intervention."[18] On July 7 the western portion of the Czech Corps declared itself the vanguard of a new eastern front to be organized by the Allies. Intervention was in the air; and the Czechs imagined that large Allied forces would soon enter the country and coöperate with them and with the anti-Bolshevik Russians in overthrowing the Soviets.

The immediate military objective of the Czechs, as soon as the idea of forcing their way through to Vladivostok for embarkation was abandoned, was to link up the scattered units of their Corps and to obtain control of the Trans-Siberian Railroad. Ufa was captured on July 4, and the union of those Czech forces which had been west of the Volga at the time of the outbreak of hostilities and of those which had been in Cheliabinsk was achieved on July 6. Meanwhile the Czechs in Vladivostok had overthown the local Soviet on June 29 and commenced to march back to rejoin the units of Gaida which were pushing eastward. The Bolshevik resistance in Eastern Siberia was stronger than in Western Siberia; and it was only about the end of August that the last Soviet towns in Eastern Siberia were taken and the Red forces either dispersed or scattered in the forests and broke up into partisan bands. By this time the struggle in the Far East had acquired an international character. For on August 3 Japanese and British troops had landed in

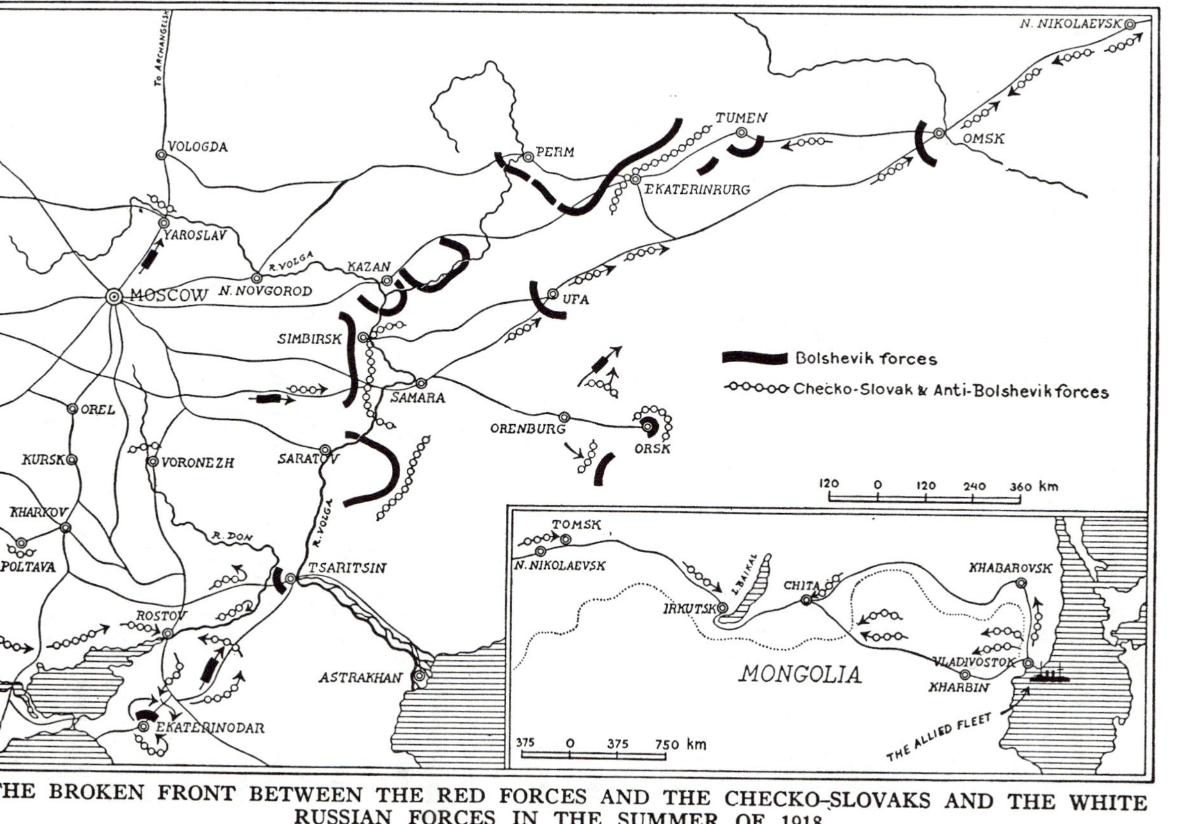

THE BROKEN FRONT BETWEEN THE RED FORCES AND THE CHECKO-SLOVAKS AND THE WHITE RUSSIAN FORCES IN THE SUMMER OF 1918

Vladivostok, to be followed in a short time by two American regiments from the Philippines and by a small French force from Indo-China. President Wilson had finally yielded to the pressure for intervention, although the tone of the American communication which was issued in this connection on August 3, 1918, indicates that the decision was taken rather reluctantly. The communication limited the objectives of the American action to "the occupation of Vladivostok and safeguarding the country to the rear of the westward-moving Czecho-Slovaks." [19] The Allied forces, with the exception of the Japanese, rendered passive rather than active aid to the anti-Bolshevik armies; the Japanese, at the height of the intervention, displayed definite territorial aspirations in regard to that part of Siberia which lies east of Lake Baikal, and sent about 70,000 troops into the country.

Experience soon showed that it was much easier to overthrow the Soviets than to replace them with governments which would win the united support of the population. Two governments emerged as a result of the first successes of the Czechs: the West Siberian Commissariat and the Government of the Committee of Members of the Constituent Assembly in Samara.

The West Siberian Commissariat announced its existence on June 1, after the first victories of the Czechs. It derived its claim to authority from the Government, headed by a Socialist Revolutionary named Derber, which had been elected in February by the Siberian Regional Duma, a body which had been chosen on the basis of universal suffrage and which, like the Constituent Assembly, had been dispersed by the Bolsheviki. Derber himself, an obscure personality who played no particular rôle in the subsequent development of events, was in the Far East at the time of the Czech action; but the initiative in setting up a new government was taken by three men, Markov, Mikhailov and Lindberg, who described themselves as representatives of the Siberian Government and members of the All-Russian Constituent Assembly, and by the head of the Tomsk Zemstvo, Sidorov. They proclaimed as the first objectives of their Government the reëstablishment of democratic organs of local government, the restoration of normal goods exchange, the guarantying of the population with food, the resumption at the earliest possible moment of the work of the All-Russian Constituent Assembly. They announced that autonomous Siberia was to have a white and green flag, symbol of the snows and forests of the country.

Siberia in the early summer of 1918 was much less torn up with civil strife and consequent passion and hatred than were many parts of European Russia. The ease with which most of the Siberian Soviets were overthrown shows that they had no wide measure of mass support. At the same time it would be inaccurate to describe the majority of the Siberian population as violently anti-Bolshevik. As a shrewd writer and participant in the Siberian anti-Bolshevik movement, G. K. Gins, remarks: [20]

> "All the things that excited the indignation of wide circles of the population in European Russia were little felt in Siberia. There was no hunger. There were few savage cruelties; in any case Siberia scarcely experienced terror. The Kronstadt sailors visited only Tyumen and Omsk. The severity of the Brest-Litovsk Peace was scarcely understandable to Siberia. The food detachments had still not penetrated into the Siberian village. . . .
>
> "In general, in the summer of 1918 Siberia was not prepared for the overthrow of the Bolsheviki. Neither the peasants nor the workers could cherish hostile sentiments toward Bolshevism. The Cossacks, who in Siberia differed little from old established peasants, also could not feel hostility. . . . The strength of the anti-Bolsheviki lay mainly in the weakness of the Bolsheviki."

A similar impression of passivity on the part of the majority of the population is to be found in the description of the overthrow of the Soviet regime in Siberia by a Communist historian, Parfenov, who writes: [21]

> "In most cases the village was passive and did not react to the overturn, which touched it only externally, with the replacement of Soviet signs by zemstvo signs. A further explanation is to be found in the fact that the overthrow of the Soviets coincided with the spring field work, which was more intense after the demobilization."

If the majority of the population, in the beginning at least, took little interest in the change of the regime, a lively struggle soon began between the more radical and more conservative groups of Siberian politicians, in which the latter, assured of the support of the army officers, invariably gained the upper hand. The first sign of a swing to the right was the replacement of the Commissariat, which had been guided in its activities by the programme of the Socialist Revolutionary Party, by a group of Ministers of the Derber Government, headed by Peter Vologodsky, a jurist with the reputation of a moderate liberal.

The Commissariat had been inclined to tolerate the existence of Soviets, not as agencies of government, but as workingclass organizations, to go slowly in denationalizing the larger factories and to preserve the land committees which originated in the time of Kerensky. The new Government took a firmer conservative stand, calculated to appeal to the middle classes and to the army officers and to disillusion the Socialist Revolutionaries, who had hoped that the sequel to the Soviet regime would be a radical form of democracy, with a considerable infusion of socialism. The change of regime occurred on June 30. On July 4th the Siberian Government proclaimed itself the sole authority in Siberia, with the right to maintain independent relations with foreign powers, and annulled all Soviet decrees. On the 6th it ordered the suppression of all existing Soviets and forbade the election of new ones, simultaneously authorizing the organization of "trade-union organizations which do not pursue political aims."[22] Throughout July and August the policy of the Siberian Government was directed to the restoration of private property in every form. The swing away not only from Bolshevism but also from moderate socialism was very marked. In the beginning the Siberian Government relied on volunteer armed forces and on the aid of the Czechs. In Siberia itself, where there was little resistance, this was sufficient. But the struggle with the stronger Bolshevik forces in the Ural Territory (the Siberian Government was inclined to extend its frontiers westward into European Russia) demanded more troops, and on July 31st two classes of recruits were called up on the basis of general mobilization. The War Minister, Grishin-Almazov, a young officer who had played a leading rôle in organizing the revolt against the Soviets, on August 17 described the new army as "without any committees, congresses and meetings, without limitation of the rights of the officers."

While a conservatism that would ultimately deepen into reaction characterized the anti-Bolshevik regime in Siberia a government of a more radical type, dominated entirely by Socialist Revolutionaries, had emerged in Samara and was in fairly effective control of a large area in the Middle Volga. In Samara, as in most other towns of Eastern Russia and Siberia, the Socialist Revolutionaries in the spring of 1918 had their secret organization. When news of the clash between the Czechs and the Soviets in Penza reached Samara one of the local Socialist Revolutionary leaders, Brushvit, went to meet the Czechs, who at first received him somewhat coldly and distrustfully. However, he persuaded them to occupy Samara, which they did on June 8 after a trifling brush with the local Red Guard, in which seven Czechs and thirty Red Guards were killed.

A committee of five members of the dissolved Constituent Assembly, all Socialist Revolutionaries, Brushvit, Fortunatov, Klimushkin, Volsky and Nesterov, thereupon assumed civil and military power in Samara City and Province. The new government decreed the dissolution of the existing Soviets, the reëstablishment of the zemstvos and city councils and proclaimed as its slogans: "United Independent Free Russia! All Power to the Constituent Assembly!" It also announced the reëstablishment of "freedom of speech, press and assembly," a principle which, however, was not and could not be observed in the heat of fierce civil war. In actual practise Bolshevik activity on the territory of the Samara Government was proscribed; thousands of real or suspected Bolsheviki crowded the prisons of the small provincial towns; and Bolshevik uprisings were put down with pitiless severity.

At first the enterprise of the members of the Constituent Assembly seemed almost hopeless. There was little organized popular support; the members of the Committee went to their first session under a guard of Czech soldiers. In the immediate vicinity of Samara were a number of roving Red partisan bands. However, the absence of any strong Red striking force gave the Socialist Revolutionaries a breathing-space. A few daring and talented military commanders appeared, such as Colonel Kappel, who developed a technique of disorganizing the Red armies by making raids far behind their rear and Colonel Makhin, a Socialist Revolutionary who entered the Red Army with the purpose of disorganizing it, and passed over to the troops of the Constituent Assembly after he had made the defense of the town of Ufa by the Reds impossible.

Contact was established with the Ural Cossacks, who had been carrying on an intermittent guerrilla war with the Reds for several months. The territory acknowledging the authority of the Constituent Assembly gradually expanded; Ufa was taken on July 4; Simbirsk, Lenin's birthplace, was seized by Kappel after one of his raids on July 21; the area of the new regime was extended to the south by the capture of Volsk. The high point of the military success of the Samara Government was achieved on August 6, when the old Tartar town of Kazan, with its minarets and its picturesque Kremlin, passed into the hands of the Constituent Assembly troops as a result of a combined attack from the land and from the Volga River. The loss of Kazan was an especially severe blow to the Soviets because gold to the value of 651,500,000 rubles, the former reserve of the Imperial Government, had been transferred there from Petrograd for safety, and was captured along with the town. Later this gold came into the possession of the Siberian dictator, Kolchak; part of it was spent in buying munitions and other supplies abroad; part of it leaked out of the country in various ways when Kolchak fell; some of the gold was recovered by the Red troops.

On the day after the fall of Kazan an uprising against the Bolsheviki broke out among the workers of the state munitions factory in Izhevsk, northeast of Kazan, in the valley of the main tributary of the Volga, the Kama.[23] Apparently these workers had been better off as regards pay and living conditions than the majority of their fellows before the War; and many of them were small proprietors, with cottages and gardens. They resented the rough methods of Soviet requisitioning detachments and were ready to listen to the appeals of local Mensheviki and Socialist Revolutionaries, who called for the tearing up of the Brest-Litovsk Peace, the overthrow of the Soviets and the establishment of a democratic government. It is also noteworthy that, whereas the average Russian worker looked back on the World War with utter disgust and was grateful to the Bolsheviki for having stopped it, there was a strong organization of former front soldiers in Izhevsk—many of them, doubtless, men of the type who are recruits for Fascism in other countries.

So, when the Bolsheviki attempted to carry out a mobilization for the Red Army in Izhevsk an uprising, headed by the front soldiers, broke out on August 7 and resulted in the overthrow of the Soviet. Some leading Bolsheviki were killed; many others were imprisoned; and the insurgents quickly organized a local military force. Their sentiments are reflected in one of the appeals which they issued to the workers:

> "Comrade workers! Bolshevism promised you bread. It gives an eighth of a pound of bread to the Petrograd and Moscow workers,—and thousands of carloads to Germany under the Brest-Litovsk Treaty. . . . Comrade peasants! You know how bread is being taken away from you. You get bayonets and machine guns for it instead of money."

The uprising spread to the neighboring Votkinsk factory and to the town of Sarapul; and this stretch of territory was held by the insurgents until November, when they were obliged to retreat to the east under the pressure of the general Red advance. Izhevsk and

Votkinsk deserve mention as among the very few workingclass centres which furnished large numbers of voluntary recruits to the anti-Bolshevik armies. These workers were certainly firm in their anti-Soviet convictions, for they continued to fight stubbornly for Kolchak when his regime was already in a state of progressing disintegration.

The opposing fronts which grew up during the summer of 1918 from Perm, in the Northern Urals, to Orenburg, where the steppes of Asia begin, presented a curious checkerboard appearance in August. The forces engaged were very small in proportion to the area; there were apparently about 65,000 Red troops as against approximately 50,000 Czechs and anti-Bolshevik Russians. In some cases the troops of one side were wedged in between armies of their opponents; and there was no regular connection or coördinated action between some of the armies. At the southern end of the vague battleline the Orenburg Cossacks, under their Ataman, Dutov, fought against the Turkestan Red Army, which was commanded by Zinoviev, who should not be confused with the well-known Bolshevik leader who adopted the name Zinoviev as a pseudonym. At the northern end the Third Red Army, under the Lettish Bolshevik, Berzin, grouped around Perm, fought on one side against the combined anti-Bolshevik and Czech forces under Voitzekhovsky, which had occupied the main Ural centre, Ekaterinburg, on the other against the Izhevsk insurgents. Red forces strung out along the right bank of the Volga covered such points as Sviazhsk, near Kazan, Penza and Saratov and were preparing to launch a counteroffensive against the troops of the Constituent Assembly.

Despite the extension of territory and the victories which ended with the occupation of Kazan the outlook for the Samara Government was far from hopeful. It had aroused no upsurge of popular enthusiasm, no flow of eager volunteers into the ranks of its army, such as would have made possible a victorious march on Moscow and a triumphant reopening of the Constituent Assembly. The early successes of the "People's Army," as the troops of the Constituent Assembly were called, were attributable largely to the confusion and disorganization of the Reds and to the effort of the first Soviet Commander of the Volga Front, Muraviev, who was a Left Socialist Revolutionary himself, to turn his troops against Moscow at the time of the uprising of the Left Socialist Revolutionaries in the Soviet capital early in July. The attempt failed and Muraviev was soon shot. But his action naturally did not conduce to the stability of the Red front. By August the troops of the Constituent Assembly were already meeting stiffer resistance; and it was evident that as soon as the discipline and morale of the Red Army were fully established it would be extremely difficult to advance farther, or even to hold what had already been gained.

The reasons for the failure of the Socialist Revolutionaries, who had the majority of members in Russia's one freely elected parliament, the Constituent Assembly, to vindicate their claim to rule the country by force of arms are varied. First of all, their regime, in the majority of cases (Izhevsk was a striking exception) completely failed to win the support of the masses of the workers. Both the Soviet which they tolerated in Samara for a time and the trade-unions were very much under the influence of the Bosheviki, who continued to operate surreptitiously in the guise of "nonpartisans" or "Menshevik Internationalists." [24]

On the other hand the middle classes and many of the army officers were inclined to be at best lukewarm in their support of the new regime. If many of the workers, despite the hardships which had existed under the Soviet regime, still felt that it was their own government and wanted to restore it, the outraged merchants, property-owners, Tsarist officials, private traders wanted to stamp out any semblance of Bolshevism and to bring back what they regarded as normal pre-revolutionary conditions. They hated the red flag which was still the emblem of the Socialist Revolutionary Government and the radical phraseology of the Constituent Assembly leaders. General Petrov, a participant in the armed struggle on the Volga, points out a serious weakness in the position of the Government: [25]

> "The Government was Socialist Revolutionary, Party, unconciliatory even with the Cadets, and the armed force, in its majority, consisted of right-wing elements, hostile to the Socialist Revolutionaries."

So the Constituent Assembly Government was unpopular with one part of the Volga town population because it was not considered sufficiently revolutionary, with another part because it was considered too radical. Its supporters consisted largely of radical and liberal provincial intellectuals, with a sprinkling of the better paid workers who were disgusted with the excesses of the Bolsheviki. But this basis of support was not broad enough to pave the way for victory.

One might have imagined that the peasants would have given the

Samara regime hearty support. The Socialist Revolutionaries were against any return of the land to the landlords and also against the Bolshevik policy of armed requisitions and stirring up the poorest peasants against all the others. But the villages gave little evidence of enthusiasm for the new government. Few peasant recruits appeared voluntarily; the mobilization which the Committee decreed on June 30 proceeded with indifferent success and, in the words of Maisky,[26] "immediately spoiled the relations between the village and the new government."

The peasants certainly had no love for the Soviet regime; the numerous uprisings and riots, large and small, reported in the Soviet press during the spring and summer of 1918, leave no doubt on this score. But it was the tragedy of the Socialist Revolutionaries, who always regarded themselves as a peasant party, that most of the Russian peasants were too ignorant and backward to act consciously on behalf of their own interests. Throughout the civil war one is repeatedly impressed by the fact that the peasants, the great majority of the population, were quite unable to make their influence felt, except in purely negative ways. When the Whites began to bring back the landlords, the peasants organized guerrilla bands and fell on them. When Red requisitioning bands became too intolerable the peasants, when they had the opportunity, cut them to pieces. But the idea of actively supporting and creating their own government, which would permit neither the return of the landlords nor requisitions was quite beyond the mental capacity of the average peasant. His instinct was that of a primitive anarchist, to pay no taxes and to give no soldiers to any government, whether it called itself Red, White or democratic.

The fact that the base of the Constituent Assembly regime was an obscure provincial town, with no great reserves of arms and munitions, was another unfavorable factor. Still another was the chronic antagonism between the Samara regime and the Siberian Government at Omsk. Instead of coöperating wholeheartedly against the common enemy, the Bolsheviki, the Omsk and Samara Governments bickered incessantly, refused to transship freight to each other and at one time declared a customs war along their somewhat indefinite frontier. There were several causes for this antagonism; Samara claimed for itself, at least in the future, an All-Russian significance which Omsk, which had declared itself the sole authority in Siberia, was unwilling to admit. Moreover, Omsk was "right" and Samara was "left" in political orientation.

A third regional anti-Bolshevik government arose in the capital of the Urals, Ekaterinburg; its head, rather significantly, was the president of the Ekaterinburg stock-exchange, Ivanov. This Ural Government gravitated toward Omsk, not towards Samara, in its political allegiance.

Partly under pressure from the Czechs, who were becoming impatient at the inability of the anti-Bolshevik Russians, whom they had been aiding, to help themselves, a state conference, attended by representatives of the Omsk and Samara Governments and of other numerous political organizations and regional authorities, opened in Ufa on September 8 for the purpose of working out some scheme of political and military unity. There is a curious similarity between this Ufa State Conference and the Moscow gathering which met under the same name in August, 1917. The setting in provincial Ufa was less ornate than in the Moscow State Opera-House; and no doubt many of the delegates to the Ufa assembly appeared in shabbier clothes; almost a year of Bolshevism had not passed for nothing.

But the figures on the little stage at Ufa were in many cases the same as those who had declaimed their rôles on the larger stage at Moscow; one could see the venerable "Grandmother of the Revolution," Breshko-Breshkovskaya, bitterly grieved and disillusioned by the course the Revolution had taken; there were Socialist Revolutionaries and Mensheviki who spoke about the need for democracy and socialism; and military officers and Cadets who emphasized the need for order and authority. And there was the same fundamental hopeless divergence of viewpoint and psychology between the right wing and the left wing of non-Bolshevik Russia. The victory of Bolshevism in the main centres of Russia had brought no formula of unity to its enemies.

The Ufa State conference opened under an unlucky star; on September 10 the Red Army, whipped into shape by the feverish efforts of Trotzky, recaptured Kazan. This was an especially severe blow to the left wing of the assembly, represented by the Samara Socialist Revolutionaries, and weakened their position in the subsequent negotiations. Simbirsk fell into the hands of the Reds soon after Kazan; Samara itself was clearly threatened.

The radicals at Ufa wished to make the new government, which was to be created, responsible before the original Constituent Assembly; the conservatives wanted to make it as authoritarian and as free from external control as possible; they contended that the Constituent Assembly, elected at a time when Bolshevism enjoyed its greatest popularity, was no longer representative of the mood of the country. Ultimately an unreal and unworkable compromise was reached; the new Government, which was to assume the form of a Directory of five persons, was not to be responsible before the Constituent Assembly, but the latter was to resume its activity if 250 of its members could be gathered by January 1, 1919, or 170 by February 1, 1919. The personnel of the Directory represented another compromise, which satisfied neither the Right nor the Left. It was made up of two moderate Socialist Revolutionaries, Avksentiev and Zenzinov, two non-Socialists, the Siberian Premier Vologodsky and a Cadet lawyer, Vinogradov, and a liberal General, Boldirev.

The Directory regarded itself as the successor of the fallen Provisional Government, as an all-Russian authority. Vologodsky went to Eastern Siberia and obtained the abdication of the phantom Derber Cabinet in Vladivostok and the acknowledgment of the power of the Directory by General Horvath, former manager of the Chinese Eastern Railroad, who was another pretender to power in the Far East.

But the Directory was the merest shadow of a government. It had neither an administrative apparatus, nor financial means, nor an official organ. For lack of any other available place it was obliged to take up its residence in Omsk, already a centre of militarist reaction. From the very beginning it lived under the shadow of a *coup d'état* and forcible dissolution.

How far the militarist reaction had gone in Siberia was evident from some events which occurred in Omsk shortly before the creation of the Directory. There had been chronic antagonism between the conservative Siberian Government in Omsk and the radical Siberian Regional Duma in Tomsk. The President of the Duma, Yakushev, and two of the left-wing Ministers of the Government, Shatilov and Krutovsky, conceived the idea of coöpting for the Cabinet one of their sympathizers, Novoselov, who had been elected a member of the Derber Cabinet and had just arrived in Omsk from the Far East. Colonel Volkov, the commandant of Omsk, promptly arrested Yakushev, Shatilov, Krutovsky and Novoselov. Krutovsky and Shatilov offered their resignations when they were told they would be shot if they did not do so. Novoselov was murdered—the first in a long series of outrages by the irresponsible Siberian military chieftains. At the same time, on September 21st, the conservative members of the Siberian Cabinet decreed the dissolution of the Regional Duma. The latter body attempted to resist, refused to recognize the order for its dissolution and dismissed the Siberian Minister for Finance, Ivan Mikhailov, son of a famous revolutionist, but himself regarded as the moving spirit of the reactionary group in the Government.

But real power was in the hands of Mikhailov and his military friends. The Tomsk provincial commissar, Hattenberger, dissolved the Duma, closed its headquarters and arrested some of its more prominent representatives. All this boded little good to the Socialist Revolutionaries west of the Urals who had coöperated in the establishment of the Directory. These luckless champions of democracy on the uncongenial Russian soil were between the hammer of the advancing Red Army, which was bringing with it the Cheka and Communist dictatorship on one side and the ruthless Omsk officers, many of whom were ready to kill any socialist, however moderate, on sight, on the other.

The Czechs might have come to the aid of the Socialist Revolutionaries; their sympathies were democratic and they regarded the growth of reaction with aversion. But the Socialist Revolutionaries, perhaps convinced of the hopelessness of a struggle against dictatorship on two fronts, refused to assume the responsibility of appealing to the Czechs for strong action; they hoped in the face of all probability that the rough methods which had been employed at Omsk and at Tomsk were the result of misunderstanding and that the Directory would succeed in coming to an agreement with the Siberian authorities and curbing militarist excesses.

From the autumn of 1918 the Czechs ceased to play an active part in the Russian civil war. They were disappointed by the failure of the Allies to intervene on a large scale and were increasingly disinclined to shed their blood in a Russian civil war which was becoming increasingly severe as the Red Army grew in organized strength. They had struck the Soviets a hard blow just when they were weakest and had made possible the establishment of anti-Bolshevik rule over a huge territory. But they did not succeed in creating in the place of the Soviets the democratic regime with which most of them sympathized, and to which they would some day return in their native Czecho-Slovakia.

By the autumn of 1918 the "democratic counterrevolution" was already at its last gasp, with the Red Army driving the troops of the Constituent Assembly back from the Volga and with Siberia obviously ripe for a military dictatorship. There were several reasons for the failure of the anti-Bolshevik movement to assume a democratic form. The very conditions of a ruthless class civil war tended to push off the stage humane and kindly intellectuals like Avksentiev and Zenzinov and to bring to the fore the hard and pitiless type of officer, who was as ready to hang Bolsheviki as the Bolshevik Chekist was to shoot counterrevolutionists. Moreover, Russia, for a number of reasons, of which the backwardness and illiteracy of a large part of its peasantry was perhaps the most important, was quite unsuited for democratic methods of government. The democratic phase of the counterrevolution was bound to be futile and shortlived; the main burden of the struggle against Bolshevism fell on conservative nationalist military dictators of the type of General Denikin and Admiral Kolchak.

The clash with the Czechs and the upsurge of Russian counterrevolution which accompanied it placed the Bolshevik leaders before a grim alternative: to create without too much delay an army that would fight and obey orders instead of debating them or to go down in a welter of sanguinary defeat and fierce revenge on the part of the classes which they had driven from property and power and trampled on so mercilessly.

NOTES

[1] *Cf.* Thomas G. Masaryk, "Die Weltrevolution," p. 173, and Henry Baerlein, "The March of the Seventy Thousand," pp. 77, 78.

[2] Masaryk, *op. cit.*, p. 198.

[3] Baerlein, *op. cit.*, pp. 98ff.

[4] Masaryk, *op. cit.*, p. 208.

[5] Margarethe Klanthe, "Von der Volga zum Amur," p. 135.

[6] The Czechs had a number of Russian officers of higher ranks, because they lacked trained senior officers of their own nationality.

[7] Klanthe, *op. cit.*, pp. 137, 138, and Baerlein, *op. cit.*, pp. 109ff.

[8] For a detailed discussion of the activity of the Czech Communist agitators *cf.* Yaroslav Papoushek, "The Czecho-Slovaks and the Soviets."

[9] The Soviet historian, P. S. Parfenov, for instance, makes the assertion that the offensive of the Czecho-Slovaks against the Soviets was planned at a secret meeting in the headquarters of the French Military Mission in Moscow on April 14. Inasmuch, however, as he cites no authority for this statement it must be regarded with considerable reserve, especially as the head of the French Military Mission, General Lavergne, some time later made what were apparently sincere efforts to evacuate a part of the Czecho-Slovak Corps through Archangel.

[10] Eduard Beneš, "Die Aufstand der Nationen," p. 466.

[11] *Ibid.*, pp. 470, 471.

[12] Papoushek, *op. cit.*, pp. 52ff.

[13] Klanthe, *op. cit.*, pp. 149ff.

[14] P. S. Parfenov, "The Civil War in Siberia," pp. 25, 26.

[15] Captain V. Golochek, "The Czecho-Slovak Troops in Russia," pp. 32ff.

[16] Professor S. P. Melgunov, "The Tragedy of Admiral Kolchak," Vol. I, p. 71.

[17] A. Anishev, "Sketches of the History of the Civil War," p. 138.

[18] Beneš, *op. cit.*, pp. 513ff.

[19] The Allied intervention in Russia will be treated in detail in another chapter.

[20] *Cf.* his book, "Siberia, the Allies and Kolchak," Vol. I, p. 60.

[21] "The Civil War in Siberia," p. 35.

[22] V. Maksakov and A. Turunov, "The Chronicle of the Civil War in Siberia, 1917–1918," p. 199.

[23] *Cf.* the article of N. Sapozhnikov, "The Izhevsk-Votkinsk Uprising, August–November, 1918," in *Proletarian Revolution,* No. 8–9, for 1924.

[24] *Cf.* I. Maisky, "The Democratic Counterrevolution," pp. 127ff.

[25] *Cf.* his book, "From the Volga to the Pacific Ocean," p. 17.

[26] "The Democratic Counterrevolution," p. 134.

CHAPTER XXI

THE REVOLUTION ARMS ITSELF

FROM the first days of the Bolshevik Revolution its leaders recognized the necessity of creating an armed force which would defend the new regime, crush its enemies within the country and beat off attacks from outside. To preserve the old army in any form was obviously impossible; the enormous mass of peasant soldiers were making for their homes as fast as the overloaded trains would carry them.

The first soldiers of the Revolution consisted of Red Guards, largely recruited in workingclass districts, and of sailors. Any attempt to carry out compulsory mobilization in the first months of the Revolution would have been foredoomed to failure; the country was utterly sick of the war; and the main appeal of the Bolsheviki was that they were bringing peace. So it was proposed to bring more order and unity into the revolutionary military operations by raising a Red Army on a voluntary basis. A Soviet decree of January 28, 1918, laid down the conditions of recruiting for this army. Any Soviet citizen who had reached the age of eighteen could join, provided that he was vouched for by a trade-union organization or by an army committee. The volunteers signed up for a period of three months' service, received a salary of 150 rubles a month, along with a promise of some privileges and exemptions for members of their families. More than 100,000 recruits joined the newly formed Red Army during the following two and a half months.

The technical efficiency and fighting quality of the Red Army during these first months of its existence were extremely low. The recruits put on uniforms of varied kinds, and sometimes kept civilian clothing. The condition of the arms was poor; there was little training. Discipline was extremely loose; the soldiers often held meetings, debated orders, made impossible demands in regard to pay, food and clothing.[1]

This early Red Army, like the Red Guard detachments from which it could scarcely be distinguished, was effective only against anti-Soviet Russian forces which were equally weak in organization and discipline and less numerous and well-armed. Against a regular army, such as the Germans in Ukraina or the Czechs in Siberia and on the Volga, they were about as helpless as Chinese troops against Europeans or Japanese. The spirit of many of the recruits was expressed by a delegate to a conference of Red Army soldiers which was held in Petrograd late in March who stood up and bellowed, shaking a threatening fist: "Either give us 300 rubles a month with food, clothing and lodging, or we will show the Council of People's Commissars that we are able to defend our interests." [2]

A good many criminals and bandits joined the first units of the Red Army, despite the theoretical requirement of a character voucher from a trade-union or some other organization; the speedy collapse of any semblance of discipline and fighting capacity is evident from some of the official army reports, which are preserved in the Soviet archives. So the army of Petrov, which retreated from Ukraina before the Germans and took up quarters in Voronezh, is described as "engaged only in plundering, by which it aroused the whole population against the Soviet Government." Another Red Army unit, under the command of Remnev, according to a telegram of April 18, "is retreating in disorder before patrols of Ukrainians and Germans, carrying out acts of robbery and violence, terrorizing the railroad workers. The army now does not represent a real force." On April 8 the military leader Sitin telegraphed to the Supreme War Council that "the majority of the volunteer units which arrive in Briansk are distinguished by complete lack of organization and by absence of the most elementary military training. . . . The people absolutely do not recognize their officers or execute their commands." [3]

The Bolshevik leaders, and especially War Commissar Trotzky recognized the weaknesses of their armed forces and the necessity for creating a regular army. As early as April 22 Trotzky was publicly advocating a new kind of army, based on the principles of the art of war and built up with the coöperation of military experts.[4]

Trotzky's main objectives were the substitution of conscription for voluntary service, the creation of a central military authority which would be powerful enough to make its authority respected, the rooting out of the Red Guard partisan spirit and the substitution of the traditions of a regular army, the enlistment of a sufficient number of the old officers to give the Soviet military forces intelligent direction, the restoration of discipline in the ranks by meting out

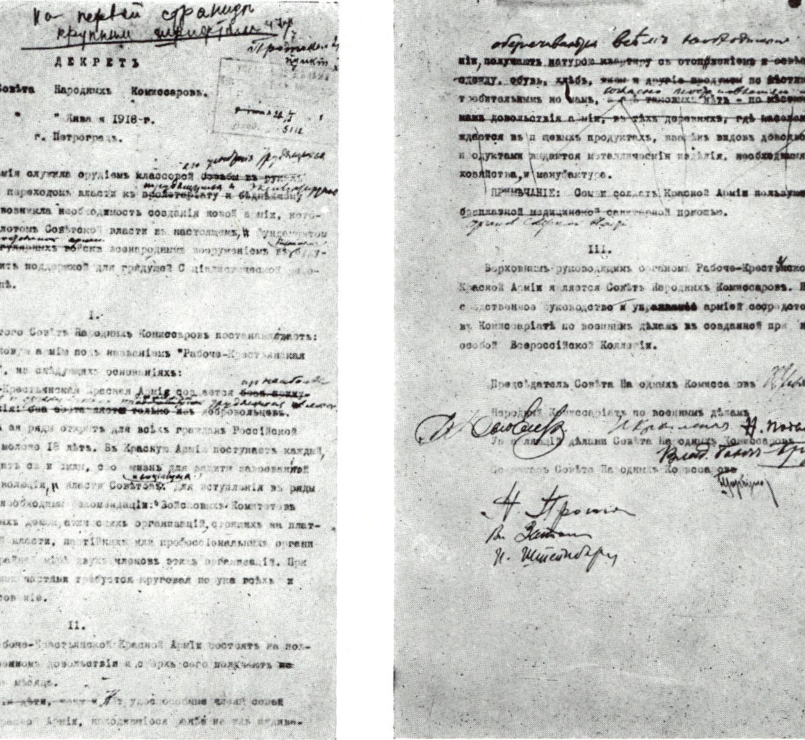

ДЕКРЕТЪ

Совѣта Народныхъ Комиссаровъ.

г. Петроградъ.

I.

II.

III.

Original text of the decree creating the Red Army, with corrections in Lenin's handwriting

stern punishment to cowards, mutineers and deserters. On the success of his effort to create disciplined armies out of the armed bands which were originally at his disposal depended the prospects of survival of the Soviet regime. In the early months of the year Trotzky seemed to have plenty of time for his task; disorganized and undisciplined as the Soviet troops were, there was no hostile force within the country which could defeat them. The situation changed when the Czechs appeared on the horizon; and by August, when the Soviet regime, more through its own weakness than through the strength of its enemies, had lost Siberia, a large part of the Ural Territory and the Valley of the Middle Volga, Trotzky's attempt to create a revolutionary army that could hold its own on the battlefield had become a desperate race against time. With the Czechs and the People's Army in Kazan a further collapse of the Red front would have opened the way to Nizhni Novgorod and then to Moscow.

A Supreme War Council was created in Petrograd on March 1; it took over the organization of the Red Army. Decrees of April 8 and April 20 set up all over Soviet territory provincial, county and township war commissariats; these bodies were responsible for the general military training of the population.

An important step forward toward the creation of a regular army was taken when the Soviet Government on April 22 decreed compulsory military training for all workers and for peasants who did not employ hired labor.[5] The training was to be for a period of twelve hours a week over a period of eight weeks a year; the age limits for mobilization were from eighteen to forty. The employing and propertied classes in the towns and the richer peasants were excluded from the new army; the Soviet leaders realized that to admit them to active service would be to place arms in the hands of enemies of the new regime.

Although the members of the more well-to-do classes were not to be armed there was no intention on the part of the Soviet leaders to release them from the burdens of the war. Trotzky announced on July 10 that the bourgeoisie would be mobilized for hard and dirty noncombatant tasks in the rear, and, with his genius for dramatic effect and also for appealing to mob psychology, he cried:[6]

"Our grandfathers and fathers served your grandfathers and fathers, cleaned up dirt and filth, and we will compel you to clean up dirt."

A decree of July 20 formally established the liability of members of the bourgeois classes between the ages of eighteen and forty-five to service in the rear and laid down the following list of the pariah castes of Soviet society who would be liable to this hard and humiliating service. Among those who were to be forced, in Trotzky's words, "to clean up dirt" were persons living on income not derived from work, employers of hired labor, directors of stock companies, former lawyers (the Bar had been abolished in the early months of the Revolution), stock-exchange brokers, bourgeois journalists, priests, monks, former officers and officials.

Carried out with little organization or plan these mobilizations of the propertied for hard labor brought less positive advantage to the Soviet cause than physical pain to the victims of the mobilizations, and this was probably their purpose. Serious mistakes, even from the Soviet standpoint, were often made in carrying out this measure. In some cases simpleminded proletarian officials seized anyone who wore a coat as a "bourgeois." Artists, actors and scientists were sometimes rounded up in the mobilizations, which were carried out without distinction of age or sex and without medical examination of the fitness of the persons mobilized for the work to which they were assigned.[7]

Simultaneously with the introduction of compulsory military training for the workers and poorer peasants the practise of electing officers was abolished. The Bolshevik military authorities now began to talk about the harmful and disruptive influence of army committees very much as Kornilov, Denikin and the old officers had spoken in 1917; and strict obedience to the orders of the officers gradually became embedded in the discipline of the Red Army.

Immediately after the clash with the Czecho-Slovaks the Soviet Government decided to make a decisive break with the volunteer system and to resort to at least a partial mobilization. The mood of the country made it doubtful whether a general mobilization would be successful, so it was decided to begin by conscripting the workers in Moscow and Petrograd, where the influence of the Revolution was strongest, and at the same time to carry out compulsory mobilizations in the regions which were most directly threatened by the victory of counterrevolution, in the Don and Kuban, in fifty-one counties of Siberia, the Ural Territory and the Volga provinces.

There is no reliable information as to the effect of the mobilization in the provinces; it certainly did not arrest the rapid progress of the Czechs and their Russian allies during the summer months. But there was a good response to the workingclass mobilization in Moscow and Petrograd; half starved though they were, the majority of the workers, especially those of the younger generation, were still ready to take up arms for the Soviet regime.

As the authority of the Soviet regime became more established the principle of mobilization was extended to the whole population of the Soviet Republic. The formerly well-to-do classes in the towns and the kulaks in the villages were forbidden to bear arms; but all other Soviet citizens were liable to service. As the civil war grew in scope and intensity (the White armies of Kolchak and Denikin in 1919 were far more numerous and better organized than the anti-Soviet forces in 1918) the Red Army steadily increased in numbers; and by the summer of 1919, when the civil war was at its height, the categories of recruits were almost exhausted, and the Soviet authorities decided to call up eighteen-year-old boys. Later they abandoned this project.[8]

The Red Army on August 1, 1918, numbered 331,000; this figure increased to 550,000 on September 5 and to 800,000 by the end of the year. On October 4, 1918, Lenin, foreseeing that the approaching end of the War and the probable revolution in Germany might increase both the defensive and the offensive tasks of the Red Army (the end of the War might free large Allied forces for intervention, while revolution in Central Europe would open up alluring prospects for the westward expansion of Bolshevism), proclaimed: "We decided to have an army of a million men in the spring. Now we need an army of three million. We can have it and we will have it."[9]

Lenin's desired figure of 3,000,000 was reached on January 1, 1920; and during 1920 the Army continued to grow until it amounted to about five and a half million.[10] This figure in reality was far less impressive than it seems on paper, because only a very small proportion of the Red soldiers were actually on the fronts. About half the Army was in interior districts of the country, where large forces were required to deal with the little insurrections which were perpetually breaking out and to hunt down roving bands of so-called "greens," peasant guerrillas who had often deserted from the Red or White armies, or from both, and had taken to a roving bandit existence, their hand against every government and every government's hand against them. Shortage of arms and equipment and defective transportation also tended to keep an abnormally large proportion of the Red soldiers in the rear depots and concentration points.

Desertion was a chronic problem in the Red Army, even more in the White Armies. The enormous majority of the peasants, who necessarily constituted the main source of recruits for both sides in the civil war, had experienced all the fighting they desired during the World War. When any government was sufficiently established to carry out mobilization with threats of concentration camps, confiscation of property and shooting for recalcitrant recruits and deserters the peasants perforce went as soldiers; but they often took the first opportunity to run away and return to their homes. The amount of desertion naturally depended a good deal on the fortunes of war (it increased when the Red Army was losing ground and decreased when it was advancing).

According to official Soviet figures[11] there were 2,846,000 deserters during the years 1919 and 1920. Of these 1,543,000 appeared "voluntarily" in response to proclamations promising them immunity if they joined the ranks before specified dates, while about a million were caught in raids which were regularly organized in towns and on the railroads. The main causes of desertion, apart from the peasants' general disinclination to fight, seem to have been the rapid changes of government in some parts of the country, especially in Ukraina, which bred disregard for authority of any kind in the population; concern of the deserters for the well-being of their families; and the bad physical conditions in the rear barracks, where the bread ration was small and the soldiers' quarters were often overcrowded and unheated. In some cases there were "desertions" from these barracks,—to the front, where rations were more plentiful and the chance of being killed was considerably less than it had been during the World War.

Committees to combat desertion were created in all districts. To shoot such enormous numbers of people would, of course, have been impossible, and a general infliction of the death penalty would have turned every deserter into a rebel and a potential recruit for the Whites. The Soviet authorities, therefore, as a general rule, shot only the main instigators of desertion or the leaders of bands which sometimes took refuge in the woods. During the last seven months of 1919, 4,112 deserters were sentenced to death, but only 612 were actually executed, according to official figures. During the same period 55,000 deserters were sent to punishment units, where they were subjected to a very severe disciplinary regime.[12]

Perhaps the most serious problem which confronted the organizers of the Red Army was that of creating an officers' corps which would be at once technically competent and politically reliable. There were pronounced differences of opinion on this question between War Commissar Trotzky, who from the beginning was a strong advocate of the general employment of veteran officers in the Red Army, and local Communist military chieftains, especially in the North Caucasus, who hated and distrusted "bourgeois" military experts and preferred the irregular methods of partisan warfare, with commanders chosen from among the more energetic workers and soldiers and discipline of an informal type.

Trotzky insisted that without the old officers no regular army worthy of the name could be formed. His opponents argued that the majority of these officers were hostile to the Soviet regime and would betray it at the first opportunity. There was truth in both contentions. There were not nearly enough Communists with professional military experience or self-made military leaders, trained in the school of partisan war, to provide officers for a force of the size of the Red Army. The need for specialists was especially great in the artillery and in the technical branches of the service. On the other hand, cases of sabotage and desertion to the Whites among the officers were not uncommon; if one considers the ferocity of the class war and the outrages which many relatives and friends of the officers experienced it is surprising that there were not more such cases.

However, Trotzky insured the loyalty of the majority of the former officers by an adroit mixture of cajolery and terrorism. He did not resort to the coarse abuse of the officers with which some of the cruder Petrograd Communists, such as Zinoviev, Volodarsky and Lashevitch, endeavored to reconcile the proletariat to the necessity of employing them.[13] In his personal relations with the old military specialists he was courteous and tactful, quick to praise and reward distinguished service, ready to make it easier for the old officer to feel at home in the revolutionary army.

On the other hand the officer who refused to serve in the Red Army, or who joined it and subsequently ran over to the Whites had to expect the most merciless punishment not only for himself, but also for his family. On July 29, 1918, Trotzky announced that former officers who refused to serve would be placed in concentration camps; as the Red Terror increased such officers were not infrequently shot. An order issued by Trotzky on September 30, 1918, illustrates the cruel hostage system which held some wavering officers on the side of the Reds.[14] It read in part as follows:

"Let the deserters know that they betray their own families: fathers, mothers, sisters, brothers, wives and children. I order the staffs of all armies of the Republic, and also regional commissars to communicate by telegraph to the member of the Revolutionary Military Council Aralov lists of all officers who have run over to the hostile camp, with all necessary information about their family position. I order Comrade Aralov, in agreement with the suitable institutions, to take the necessary measures for the detention of the families of deserters and traitors."

Under these circumstances the Russian officers tended to fall into three classes. The uncompromising enemies of Bolshevism, at whatever risk to themselves and their families, made their way into the forces of Denikin, Kolchak, Yudenitch and other White leaders. Others, especially those who had been promoted to the officer's rank during the War and who did not come from wealthy or aristocratic families, became absorbed in spirit in the Red Army and were loyal fighters in its ranks. Still a third type of officer, weak in will and character, responded mechanically to the pressure of his environment, joining the Red Army when the alternative was death or a concentration camp, passing over to the Whites, perhaps, in periods of panic and retreat.

Between June 12, 1918 and August 15, 1920,[14a] 48,409 former officers were taken into the Red Army. This exceeded the number of thoroughly "red" officers, or commanders, as they were called, in an effort to differentiate between the new army and its Tsarist predecessor, who received their training in short-term courses during 1918, 1919 and 1920; the number of graduates of the Soviet military schools during those years was 39,914.[15] Besides these two sources of recruiting military specialists, the pre-revolutionary officers and the graduates of the new military schools, the Red Army obtained many commanders from the noncommissioned officers of the old army, who were mobilized along with the officers and who generally belonged to classes which, from the Soviet standpoint, were politically more reliable.

Trotzky seems to have been unquestionably correct in his contention that without the approximately fifty thousand pre-revolutionary officers who were persuaded or forced to serve in the Red Army, victory in the civil war would have been impossible or at least difficult. In the section of the country where the partisan tradition was strongest and where military specialists sent from Moscow were treated with contempt and rejected, the North Caucasus, the Red Armies, despite their considerable numerical superiority, went down in the end to overwhelming defeat before the smaller, but better organized and better disciplined forces of the Volunteer Army and the Kuban Cossacks.

A very important rôle in the Red Army was played by the

political commissars, who were supposed simultaneously to watch out for the political loyalty of the officers, to take charge of Party work in the units and to carry on political propaganda and educational work among the peasant recruits. The commissar was not supposed to interfere with the operative orders of the commander; but he was empowered to take drastic action if he suspected treason. As the civil war went on, an elaborate Communist Party organization was built up in the Army; so-called political departments were formed on every front and in every army (at the height of the civil war there were sixteen armies on the farflung sections of the Red front) and these departments appointed and removed commissars and exercised very authoritative supervision over the work of the Communist Party groups in the army. This apparatus of Party control and organization was the best guaranty against Bonapartist dreams on the part of successful leaders of the Red armies. Here and there, especially in turbulent, anarchistic Ukraina, local chieftains, such as Grigoriev, rebelled against the central government in Moscow, and carried their troops with them. But in the main the centralized organization was sufficiently strong to keep the Soviet Government master of the army and to keep the army loyal. A dreaded institution in the Red Army was the Special Department, headed by agents of the Cheka, which dealt summarily with cases of real or suspected disloyalty.[16]

A high proportion, at least a third, perhaps a half, of the Communist Party members were in the Red Army. In October, 1919, there were 180,000 Communists in the Army; this figure had increased to 278,000 in August, 1920. Their effect as a stiffening leaven in the raw mass of peasant soldiers was very marked; and it sometimes happened that old officers would ask for Communist reinforcements as a means of strengthening the positions which they were holding. The sincere Communists were fanatically devoted to their cause; and all of them realized that if they fell into the hands of the Whites and were recognized as Party members death in decidedly unpleasant forms was likely to be their portion. So they fought with desperate courage and instilled something of their spirit into the nonparty soldiers in their regiments. The practise of forming purely Communist detachments was not favored; it was felt that this would lead to a lowering of morale in the rest of the Army. So the Communists were sprinkled in among the other troops and, under the direction of the commissars and political departments, acted as the eyes and ears of the Government, reporting any symptoms of disaffection. Trotzky, always a master of the brilliant phrase, in one speech [17] likened the Communists to Japanese samurai, saying:

"We once heard with interest of the Japanese caste of samurai, who did not hesitate to die for the sake of collective, national interests. I must say that in our commissars, our leading Communist fighters, we obtained a new Communist Order of samurai who—without caste privileges—are able to die and to teach others to die for the cause of the working class."

Not all Communists, of course, conformed to Trotzky's samurai ideal; it was necessary more than once to sound a warning that membership in the Communist Party should convey no special privileges or advantages. But the fact that the Communists proved a fighting Party, prepared to take up arms in such numbers, was a very important factor in determining the issue of the civil war. It was not only on the battlefield that the Communists made their influence felt; when territory had to be abandoned and cities given up to the Whites there was always a group of Communists that remained behind to carry out underground work and propaganda, to take advantage of any stirrings of discontent among the workers and peasants. Not one of the White regimes had such a close-knit organized body of sympathizers.

Intensive educational propaganda was a feature of the organization of the Red Army. Amateur plays and Communist lectures were given in the soldiers' clubs which were established wherever circumstances permitted. Vivid posters endeavored to bring home to the worker and the peasant what would happen to them if the factory-owner recovered his factory, the landlord took back his land and the old Tsarist officials and Cossacks returned to rule. If one looks through a collection of civil war posters one is impressed by the effort to represent the conflict to the peasants as a struggle for land, and to the poorer classes generally as a war to the death against the aristocrats and the propertied classes.

As the Red Army increased in size and the fronts extended in distance a more complex apparatus of administration came into existence. The Revolutionary Military Council of the Republic, headed by Trotzky in his capacity as War Commissar and combining administrative and operative functions in directing all the armed forces of the Republic, came into existence on September 2, 1918; and on November 1 of the same year a Field Staff was organized as an executive operative department of the Revolutionary Military

Council.[18] A dominant rôle in the latter body was played by its Bureau, which consisted of Trotzky, one of his most trusted assistants, Aralov, and the Commander-in-chief.

For the Soviet Republic, as for every power engaged in war, the conduct of hostilities demanded far-reaching coördination of the national productive resources. The supply of the army with food, clothing and munitions raised many difficulties. With a view to establishing close collaboration between the Revolutionary Military Council and other agencies of the Soviet Government the Council of Workers' and Peasants' Defense was established under the presidency of Lenin on November 30, 1918. There were five other members: Trotzky, the Commissar for Transport, Nevsky, the assistant Commissar for Food, Brukhanov, the President of the Extraordinary Commission for Supply, Krassin, and Stalin, as representative of the Soviet Central Executive Committee. The functions of this institution were "to mobilize the forces and resources of the country in the interest of defense."[19]

The organization of regular and adequate supply of the Red Army was extremely difficult for several reasons: the tremendous decline in industrial production, the frequent separation of Soviet territory from important sources of minerals and raw materials, the disorganization of railroad transportation. The situation would have been still worse if the Soviet Government had not inherited considerable stocks of war material from its predecessors. By the summer of 1919 there was an acute shortage of bullets; the armies on the Southern Front, where the fighting at this time was especially severe, were obliged to lead a hand-to-mouth existence, with stocks of bullets which would not have been regarded as sufficient for a regiment in a single day of heavy fighting during the World War.[20]

An Extraordinary Commission for the Supply of the Red Army was created under the direction of Leonid Krassin, one of the few prominent Communists with practical business experience, on November 10, 1918. It was to control the output of the existing munition works, to place munition orders, where this was practicable, with plants which ordinarily worked on nonmilitary production and to place orders for munitions abroad. This last function, incidentally, was purely theoretical, because the blockade and the universally hostile attitude of foreign powers made it impossible for the Soviet regime to obtain military aid from foreign sources.

On July 8, 1919, the office of Extraordinary Plenipotentiary of the Council of Defense for the Supply of the Red Army was created and entrusted to the veteran Communist, A. I. Rykov. He was given sweeping powers to reorganize the organizations of supply, to change, remove and arrest undesirable officials. Rykov went about the country, seizing what he could for the needs of the Army and exposed to a crossfire of criticism from the Army commanders, who were never satisfied with what they could get, and from the directors of local industrial and supply organizations, who constantly complained that too much was being taken away from them.

Every soldier in the Red Army was supposed to take the following "socialist oath," which was confirmed by the Soviet Central Executive Committee on April 22, 1918:

"1. I, son of the toiling people, citizen of the Soviet Republic, take on myself the name of warrior in the Workers' and Peasants' army.

"2. Before the working classes of Russia and of the whole world I vow to bear this name with honor, to study military affairs conscientiously and to guard the people's and military property, as the apple of my eye, against spoiling and theft.

"3. I vow strictly and undeviatingly to observe revolutionary discipline and unquestioningly to fulfill all the orders of the commanders who are appointed by the power of the Workers' and Peasants' Government.

"4. I vow to refrain myself and to restrain my comrades from any offenses which would bring disgrace and humiliation on the dignity of a citizen of the Soviet Republic, and to direct all my activities and thoughts to the great goal of liberation of all the workers.

"5. I vow to come out in defense of the Soviet Republic against all dangers and attacks by all its enemies at the first summons of the Workers' and Peasants' Government, and in the struggle for the Soviet Republic, for the cause of socialism and brotherhood of peoples, not to spare either my strength or life itself.

"6. If from bad will I break this, my solemn pledge, may general contempt be my lot and may the stern hand of revolutionary law punish me."

An important factor in some of the victories of the Red Army, especially in the later stages of the civil war, was the *kursanti*, the graduates of the Soviet military schools. An energetic New York Jewish trade-union organizer, Goldfarb-Petrovsky, who went back to Russia, was at the head of a network of these training-schools, which extended all over the country and supplied not only commanders, but also picked shock troops for the Red Army. The courses were very short, from four to six months; and when the civil war was at its height and every front was calling for reinforcements, in 1919, they were shortened to a period of from two to four months.[21] Repeatedly these Red cadets were interrupted in their studies by an outbreak of counterrevolution in the neighborhood of their schools; they particularly distinguished themselves against Wrangel, in 1920, in suppressing the Kronstadt uprising, when many of them perished storming the fortress over the ice of the Baltic Sea, and put down many of the isolated peasant uprisings which flared up here and there after the regular civil war was ended. These short-term officers' courses were most useful to men who had already been on the front; those who entered without previous military experience often did not come out as satisfactory commanders.

The civil war may be said to have begun on a large scale with the movement of the Czecho-Slovaks and to have ended with the defeat of Wrangel in November, 1920. During this two and a half years the Red Army, fighting on a score of fronts all over the enormous Russian territory, naturally produced its heroes and outstanding leaders, although the strictly military figures in Russia's civil war are overshadowed by the colorful figure of their chief, a Jewish revolutionary who, without any technical military experience, drove the heterogeneous masses of the Red Army to final victory by a combination of ruthless fanaticism, abounding energy and never failing resourcefulness.

No general of Napoleonic stature or genius emerged in the course of the struggle. After Muraviev's futile uprising a Lettish officer named Vatzetis took over the command of the Red Army. He was displaced (it is not altogether clear whether because of dissatisfaction with his strategy or because of suspicion as to his full loyalty to the Soviet regime) by Sergei Kamenev, a former officer of the Russian General Staff, who held the post until the end of the civil war. Among the outstanding individual generals or "commanders" in the Red Army were Mikhail Frunze, a veteran Bolshevik who displayed a natural gift for military leadership, although his previous experience in this field had been confined to firing a shot at a Tsarist chief of police; M. N. Tukhachevsky, a young officer who led the triumphant forward sweep of the Red Army against Kolchak in Siberia and later was in command of the invasion of Poland, which barely failed to capture Warsaw; and Sergei Budenny, a former cavalry sergeant of the Tsarist Army, who led the Cavalry Army that finally wrested from the Whites the advantage which they had long possessed in this branch of the service. More than anyone else, perhaps, Budenny, with his big frame, his impressive moustaches and his reputation for personal courage, was a popular hero of the civil war. He was of peasant stock in Southeastern Russia and originally fought on the side of the Reds largely because of the traditional feud between the peasants of that part of Russia and the Cossacks.

But it was Leon Trotzky who made by far the greatest individual contribution to the victory of the Red Army. The systematic campaign of defamation and ignoring which has been carried on against him in the decidedly colored works about the civil war which were written in Russia after his fall cannot obscure this fact. What Trotzky did in rallying the demoralized Red forces at Sviazhsk, the little town to which they had retreated after the fall of Kazan is vividly summarized by a subsequent political enemy and critic, who was with him at the time, as follows: [22]

"The general condition of the Sviazhsk group of troops at the beginning of August could be briefly described as lack of confidence in their own strength, absence of initiative, passivity in all work and absence of discipline from top to bottom. The arrival of Trotzky brought a decisive change into the state of affairs. In the train of Trotzky arrived at the backwoods station Sviazhsk firm will to victory, initiative and decisive exertion in all sides of army work."

This trip to Sviazhsk was only the first of thirty-six long journeys to the widely separated fronts of the civil war which Trotzky made in the special train from which he guided much of the conduct of the civil war and which was a symbol of his restless, consuming physical and mental energy. On the train, which was so heavy that it had to be pulled by two locomotives, were a library, a printing-press, an electrical station, a radio and telegraph station and a small garage for the automobiles in which the indefatigable War Commissar sometimes dashed off over the muddy steppe roads in order to visit places far away from the railroad. A detachment of machine-gunners and sharpshooters accompanied the train; it was never quite safe from attack by roving guerrilla bands, especially near the front.

At the time when the White General Yudenitch made a dash for Petrograd and very nearly captured it, in the autumn of 1919, the guards on Trotzky's train took an active part in the fighting and the train received the Order of the Red Banner, the newly created highest Soviet military decoration. In the few spare moments which remained from receiving reports, dictating orders, inspecting units, making speeches, awarding gold watches and other signs of distinction to officers and soldiers who had distinguished themselves,

Trotzky dashed off articles for the little newspaper, *On the Road,* which was published on the train. Many of these articles referred to phases of the political and military struggle through which Russia was passing, denouncing Mensheviki and Socialist Revolutionaries, defending pre-revolutionary officers against the violent attacks of unreconciled Communists, threatening deserters and mutineers that they would be "wiped off the face of the earth" if they did not immediately submit, analyzing the weaknesses in the position of the Whites. On one occasion, in a dreary little station in Southeastern Russia, Trotzky gave his revolutionary fantasy free play and wrote an article predicting the triumph of Bolshevism all over Europe, to be followed by a triumphant onset of the European workers on the last stronghold of capitalism, the United States.

Trotzky was not an infallible leader. He was not, and did not imagine that he was, a Napoleon or a Marlborough; he left matters of strategy to the judgment of military experts. Some defects of his character and temperament left their impression on his work as War Commissar. In the autumn of 1918 two Communist members of the revolutionary military council of the Third Army, Smilga and Lashevitch, protested to the Party Central Committee against "Trotzky's extremely lighthearted attitude toward such things as shooting."[23] The occasion for this protest was a peremptory demand from Trotzky that the commissars attached to a division from which some officers had deserted to the Whites should be promptly shot. Among these commissars were old Bolsheviki with long revolutionary records, and Smilga and Lashevitch flatly refused to carry out the order, declaring that there were cases of treachery in every division, and that there would be no end of executions if the death penalty were applied in every such case.

To say that Trotzky was cruel is merely to say that the Revolution was cruel. Every Bolshevik leader, from Lenin down, was prepared to use as much "frightfulness" as was necessary to win the war and to confirm the new regime in power. But Trotzky's passionate, impetuous nature sometimes led him to order measures, such as the shooting of the commissars, which would have been not only inhuman, but inexpedient.

The War Commissar's habit of racing from front to front had its disadvantages as well as its advantages; it upset the regular functioning of the administrative apparatus to some extent. Trotzky's intense individualism made him a difficult man to work with; in the summer of 1919 he resigned his post as War Commissar as a result of sharp differences of opinion with the Party Central Committee; [24] he was finally induced to withdraw it, however.

But when one has made all allowances for the weak sides of Trotzky's military activity, he still remains the outstanding hero of the civil war, from the Soviet standpoint. All the conditions of Russian life at that time tended to eliminate the possibility of a precise, mechanically perfect functioning of the improvised Soviet war machine; what was necessary above everything else was to galvanize the huge amorphous body of the Red Army with spirit and will to victory, to stiffen morale, to give new drive to the nucleus of Communists which was driving into action the wavering and uncertain peasant masses of soldiers. Here Trotzky's service was unique and unquestionable. And, so far as one can judge from the imperfect available evidence, his judgment on military matters was at least as good as Lenin's. If Trotzky was wrong in his desire to stop the offensive against Kolchak in the summer of 1919 he was certainly right in opposing the drive on Warsaw, which Lenin favored, and in rejecting Lenin's hasty suggestion that Petrograd should be abandoned before the drive of Yudenitch in October, 1919.

The Russian civil war differed very greatly in character both from the World War and from the American Civil War. It was a struggle not so much between sections of the country as between classes of the population, and it took place in a country which was already exhausted and warweary after the years of unequal struggle against the technically superior German armies. Consequently its history is full of revolts behind the lines on both sides, of wholesale desertion, of mutinies, of spectacularly successful raids, of sudden breakdowns on the fronts which are attributable more to political than to military causes. In that vast panorama of confusion and disorder the cometlike figure of Trotzky, storming up and down the Red lines, distributing new revolutionary military honors and orders for execution with equal prodigality, exhorting and denouncing, always organizing for victory, was certainly one of the decisive factors in finally bringing the whole Russian land under the red flag of the Soviets.

NOTES

[1] "The Civil War, 1918–1921," p. 51.

[2] A. F. Ilin-Zhenevsky, "The Bolsheviki in Power," pp. 61ff. The soldier who made this demand held a card of membership in the Communist Party. At that time Party discipline was considerably looser than it became in the later period of the civil war.

[3] N. Kakurin, "How the Revolution Was Fought," Vol. I, pp. 141, 142.

[4] L. D. Trotzky, "How the Revolution Armed Itself," Vol. I, p. 105.

[5] *Cf.* S. A. Piontkovsky, "The Civil War in Russia: Documents," pp. 98–100, for the full text of this decree.

[6] Trotzky, *op. cit.*, Vol. I, p. 310.

[7] Ilin-Zhenevsky, *op. cit.*, pp. 166, 167.

[8] N. Movchin, "The Recruiting of the Red Army," pp. 88, 89.

[9] V. I. Lenin, "Collected Works," Vol. XV, p. 422.

[10] "The Civil War, 1918–1921," Vol. II, pp. 87, 89.

[11] *Ibid.*, Vol. II, p. 83.

[12] Movchin, *op. cit.*, pp. 140, 141.

[13] *Cf.* Ilin-Zhenevsky, *op. cit.*, pp. 88, 89. Zinoviev, Volodarsky and Lashevitch spoke of the former officers as "serfs, orderlies and squeezed lemons."

[14] Trotzky, *op. cit.*, Vol. I, p. 151.

[14a] One method which was employed to safeguard the Red Army against accepting officers of extreme monarchist or conservative views, or men who had been especially unpopular with the soldiers under their command was to publish lists of officers who were candidates for acceptance, along with invitations to persons who had any criticisms of these officers to communicate them to the Soviet military authorities.

[15] "The Civil War, 1918–1921," Vol. II, p. 96.

[16] A firsthand description, from the standpoint of a hostile foreigner, of how the organization of the Red Army worked out in practise is to be found in "Red Dusk and the Morrow," by Sir Paul Dukes, pp. 225–261. Engaged in espionage work, Dukes lived incognito in Petrograd for some time in 1919 and was even able to join a unit of the Red Army.

[17] Trotzky, *op. cit.*, Vol. II, Book II, p. 7.

[18] Kakurin, *op. cit.*, Vol. I, pp. 138, 139.

[19] Trotzky, *op. cit.*, Vol. I, p. 343.

[20] Kakurin, *op. cit.*, Vol. I, p. 148.

[21] D. A. Petrovsky, "The Military School in the Years of Revolution," p. 103.

[22] S. Gusev, "The Civil War and the Red Army," p. 14.

[23] *Ibid.*, p. 214.

[24] One difference of opinion was about the desirability of continuing the offensive against Kolchak. Trotzky, foreseeing that Denikin in the South was becoming a grave military menace, advocated a stoppage of the drive into Siberia, the adoption of a defensive position against Kolchak and the throwing of all available forces against Denikin. The Red Army leaders on the Kolchak front objected, insisting that Kolchak's forces were so demoralized that only slight pressure was required to complete their defeat; and this view prevailed. *Cf.* in this connection Trotzky, "Mein Leben," p. 435. A result of this disagreement was the replacement of the Commander-in-chief, Vatzetis, who had advocated the stoppage of the offensive, by the Commander of the Eastern Front, Kamenev.

CHAPTER XXII

THE MOST CRITICAL PERIOD

THE Bolshevik Revolution passed through three major crises, three periods when the existence of the Soviet regime was seriously threatened. The first and the greatest of these crises was during the summer months of 1918, when the area of the Soviet Republic was restricted to a territory which roughly corresponded with that of the Muscovite principality in the fifteenth century, when the Soviet regime possessed neither a trained army nor an organized apparatus of administration, when the bony hand of hunger clutched the country more and more tightly, when the Soviet provinces flamed with peasant uprisings and foreign intervention had set in, when the loyalty of a considerable part of the workers was wavering and uncertain.

The Soviet Republic would still witness difficult days, in the fall of 1919, when Denikin was threatening Tula, the first large town south of Moscow, and Yudenitch had reached the suburbs of Petrograd, and in the spring of 1921, when the continued application of outworn and unworkable economic polities had led to widespread discontent, even in the ranks of the Communists. But neither of these subsequent crises equalled in grim severity the situation in the summer of 1918. Lenin, who was one of the greatest realists, as well as one of the greatest fanatics among the world's political leaders, who might deceive himself as to the possibility of the world revolution, but who never shut his eyes to the dark sides of his own regime, declared quite openly toward the end of July: [1]

"The time before the new harvest is the most difficult and critical period for the Russian socialist revolution. Now, I think, we must say that the highest point of this critical situation has been reached."

The main element in the crisis was the sheer lack of bread. A very high proportion of the speeches of Soviet leaders and the decrees of the Soviet Government at this time are devoted to the problem of how to extract from the country districts enough food to save the towns from perishing of starvation. The numerous uprisings, big and small, are mostly riots of hungry people or protests of people whose bread has been taken away. The ferocity of the terror in which this critical period reached its culmination is partly explained by the fact that the Soviet regime was fighting for its existence, its back to the wall, in an atmosphere of stark hunger.

"The more the famine surges up on us the clearer it becomes that against this desperate need desperate measures of struggle are necessary," Lenin cried on another occasion. "To get bread,—that is the basis of socialism to-day." [2]

One of the first of these "desperate measures" was the creation of a centralized dictatorship in the form of the Food Commissariat. By a decree adopted on May 27 the Food Commissariat was recognized as the sole organization responsible for supplying the population with objects of primary necessity. The Commissar for Food was given the right to remove local commissars, to change decisions of local Soviets and, in special cases, to institute court proceedings against the disobedient representatives of local Soviets. The Food Commissariat was empowered to delegate its representatives into all local food committees, with the right to cancel their decisions.

Throughout the decree one sees the effort to mobilize the representatives of the hungry "consuming" provinces (those provinces in Russia which did not produce enough grain for their own needs were referred to as "consuming," as against the "producing" provinces, which raised a surplus) for energetic collection of the hoarded stocks of food in the "producing" provinces. So special detachments, recruited predominantly in the consuming regions, were to be attached to the local food committees; "their main task must be the organization of the working peasants against the kulaks." Moreover, the Food Commissar is to nominate up to half the members of the county food committees in the producing provinces from candidates recommended by the Soviets and the trade-unions of the consuming provinces.

A still more important decision, fraught with possibilities of civil war, was taken on June 11, when it was decided to set up all over the country "Committees of the Poor." [3] These Committees were to exercise two functions: to distribute grain, products of primary necessity and agricultural machines, and to coöperate with the local food organizations in taking surplus grain away from the kulaks and richer peasants. As a bribe to the poorer peasants to take an active part in the work of the Committees they were promised a share in the grain and other products which would be requisitioned from the kulaks; and they were to be given this requisitioned grain on more favorable conditions if they carried out their levies on the kulaks promptly.

The qualification for membership in these Committees was made rather broad; Lenin was aware of the danger of setting only the poorest peasants and farm laborers against all the other peasants. So it was provided that persons who employed hired labor for farming holdings which raised products mainly for the peasant's own needs could be members. Excluded from membership in the Committees were "kulaks and rich peasants, owners of surplus grain or other food products, possessing trade or industrial significance, employers of farmhands or hired labor." The line of demarcation between the kulaks who were to be despoiled and the other peasants was thin and indefinite; a good deal was left to local initiative.

In many cases the Committees took into membership only the poorest peasants and thereby exasperated all the others. This is evident from a circular letter [4] which Lenin and the Commissar for Food, Tsurupa, sent to all the provincial Soviets and food committees on August 18, 1918, stating that "very often the interests of the middleclass peasants are violated in the organization of the poor" and concluding: "The Committees of the Poor must be revolutionary organizations of the whole peasantry against former landlords, kulaks, merchants and priests and not organizations only of the village proletarians against all the rest of the village population."

Despite this injunction the Committees of the Poor, with their arbitrary and undefined powers and their sweeping requisitions, often excited the bitter hatred not only of the kulaks, but also of the middleclass peasants. Their task of tearing grain away from the peasants who possessed it without giving them any fair equivalent would have been hard and thankless at best. Moreover, both the Committees of the Poor and the workers' food detachments which were despatched into the villages to use force, if necessary, in taking the grain, attracted into their ranks some criminals and bandits, who took advantage of the situation to rob and commit all kinds of violence. In many cases the peasants protested that they were all equally poor, and that there was no need for organizing such Committees.

Besides coöperating with the city food detachments in requisitioning grain the Committees of the Poor not infrequently pushed out the local Soviets and took over their most important functions, such as levying taxes and collecting food. They sometimes took away from the richer peasants not only their grain, but also their cattle and agricultural implements, dividing these up among their own members. The Committees seem to have been especially active in the more fertile black-earth provinces which were still under Soviet control, such as Tambov, Tula, Penza and parts of Voronezh and Kursk. It was in this region that the class war against the landlords had been most violent and ruthless; and after the owners of big and small estates had been driven away there still remained scores to settle between the more prosperous peasants and the considerable mass of their poorer neighbors who lived in these over-populated regions. In the more industrial provinces around Moscow, Petrograd, Tver and Ivanovo-Vosnessensk the Committees seem to have been more moderate.

How fierce was the struggle that raged around the Committees of the Poor may be judged from the fact that the archives of the Commissariat for Internal Affairs record twenty-six peasant uprisings in July, forty-seven in August and thirty-five in September.[5] The greatest ferocity was displayed on both sides; people were cut to pieces, beaten to death, burned alive in these unknown battles over the country's last crusts of bread.

But, bitterly as the Committees were hated by those peasants who had any surplus food or property that tempted requisitioning, much as they added to the difficulties of maintaining order, they fulfilled the purpose for which they had been created. They split the village into two hostile camps and they made much easier the activities of the workers' food detachments, which by the end of July numbered over ten thousand members. In an article entitled "The Dictatorship of the Poor" a Soviet writer[6] triumphantly asks, referring to the spoliation carried out by the Committees: "Where and in what other country could you have such requisitioning, such dividing up, carried out by the poor against the rich?"

Certainly there are few, if any West European countries where such an agrarian policy could have been carried out with any prospect of success; the ability of the Communists to split the united front of the village against the requisitioning city is only explained by the extreme poverty of many of the Russian peasants, who were as short of bread as the city workers and, like the latter, felt that the best way to get it was to plunder the stocks of their richer fellows. Occasionally a voice of protest made itself heard; an anonymous letter which, for some reason, was printed in the Soviet peasant newspaper, *Byednota,*[7] reads in part as follows:

> "Lenin says the peasants are to give to the city the bread they got by sweat and blood. Comrade Lenin then calls some peasants to go against others, against their brothers, with bayonets and take away from them what they have produced, calling them 'the village bourgeoisie.' Who is to blame that there is no bread for Petrograd and Moscow? You had better talk less and do more; you must give the peasants textiles and iron, and then ask for bread from him, and not call on one to kill another. For if you kill off the peasant, the plougher, the hungry workers will be still worse off. Lenin had better allow that products and goods be carried freely on the railroads; then the cities would have bread."

On one occasion there was an effort to obtain grain by more conciliatory means; a trainload of manufactured goods was sent into the villages, accompanied by Lunacharsky, Commissar for Education, who delivered lectures to the gaping peasants. But lectures were not especially efficacious and manufactured goods were scarce; most of the grain in that hungry summer of 1918 was taken at the point of the bayonet, with the aid of the Committees of the Poor. The latter, at the height of their development, in August and September, numbered several tens of thousands.

Important as emergency organizations, as a means of organizing a part of the peasantry along Communist lines, the Committees of the Poor in their original form had a comparatively short existence. They obviously carried on many of the functions which normally belonged to the village Soviets. It was a question whether the Committees or the Soviets should be preserved. It was solved in November by abolishing the Committees as separate organizations, but simultaneously providing for general reëlection of the village Soviets and for including in the latter the outstanding representatives of the village poor. "We shall fuse the Committees of the Poor with the Soviets; we shall act so that the Committees of the Poor shall become Soviets," Lenin declared at a meeting of representatives of the Committees on November 8. And at the same time he laid down as the formula of Soviet policy in the village: "To reach an agreement with the middleclass peasantry, not relaxing for a moment the struggle against the kulak and relying firmly only on the poor." [8]

To have left the Committee of the Poor as the ruling power in the village would have been too hard a blow at the middleclass peasants; but the last part of Lenin's injunction, "to rely firmly on the poor," was put into practise by recruiting the new leaders of the Soviets largely among the former active members of the Committees. A very considerable proportion of the leaders of the Committees of the Poor were not peasants at all, but city workers, many of them, no doubt, of the common Russian migratory type who drifted from farm to factory and back again with changing seasons and changing possibilities of employment. Subsequent investigation of the make-up of the Committees of the Poor in certain districts shows that about a quarter of the presidents and about half the treasurers of these organizations were former workers and thus belonged to a class which was considered more reliable from the Communist standpoint.[9]

A symptom of the growing tenseness of the political situation was the declaration of martial law in Moscow on May 29. The commandant of the city, Muralov, soon afterwards announced the rules of this new state of affairs. All former officers under sixty had to register with district war commissariats. All citizens must register with their house committees. Private movement of automobiles was forbidden, and all privately owned cars had to be registered. Persons guilty of concealing arms and of using forged documents were to be shot; and the same penalty was to be meted out to "all robbers, bandits, pogrom agitators, to persons guilty of arson, to bribetakers, to all who call for pogroms and the overthrow of the Soviet regime." [10]

The immediate occasion for the declaration of martial law was the discovery by the Cheka of traces of Savinkov's conspirative organization, "The Union for the Defense of the Motherland and Freedom." [11] Doubtful of the possibility of holding out in Moscow, even if a sudden revolt should bring temporary success, Savinkov was engaged in evacuating the ex-officers who constituted the major part of the membership of the organization to Kazan, where he hoped to raise an uprising and thereby help the Czecho-Slovaks and the anti-Soviet Russian forces on the Volga. However, this scheme was thwarted by the Cheka; about a hundred arrests were made in Moscow; and General Popov, the head of the Kazan branch of the organization, with a number of his assistants, was arrested.[12] Savinkov, who, as an old conspirator, knew how to disguise himself, and two of his chief lieutenants, Colonel Perkhurov and Doctor Grigoriev, remained at liberty; his organization would still be able to strike a blow at the Soviet regime in the following month.

The strained atmosphere of the spring persisted during June.

The most serious among a number of local disturbances during this time occurred in the town of Tambov, where an unsuccessful attempt to carry out a military mobilization led to an uprising and to a brief downfall of the Soviet. The uprising took place on June 17; the insurgents killed several Communists, restored the authority of the former town council and established a "Military Committee," which proclaimed that "the power of the robbers and usurpers who tore Russia asunder and betrayed it to the Germans has fallen."[13] The victory of the anti-Soviet rebels was shortlived; Tambov was retaken on June 19 and fifty of the insurgents were put to death.

Two centres of disaffection developed in Petrograd: the Obukhov Factory, where the workers were very much under the influence of the Socialist Revolutionaries and held continual meetings, denouncing the food shortage and various measures of the Soviet regime; and the torpedo-boat squadron of the Baltic Fleet, where officers and men were enraged by rumors that the Soviet Government, at the demand of the Germans, intended to destroy the Fleet. This discontent, however, assumed passive, rather than active forms; the closing of the Obukhov Factory and the disarming of the torpedo-boat squadron took place without bloodshed. Admiral Stchastny, who was accused of having fomented dissatisfaction among the sailors, was shot by sentence of a Revolutionary Tribunal after a fierce speech of accusation by Trotzky; his death marked the beginning of what was to be a long series of political executions. Another sign of the increasing bitterness was the killing of Volodarsky, a Jewish trade-unionist from Philadelphia who had come back to Russia and become one of the most active figures in the Petrograd Committee of the Communist Party, by a Socialist Revolutionary named Sergeev.

While there was no mass uprising of the workers against the Soviet regime a number of incidents, even as reported in the naturally partial Soviet press of this period, indicates that the enthusiastic support which the majority of the workers had given the Bolsheviki in November was vanishing along with the country's bread supply. In Tula and Sormovo (near Nizhni Novgorod) there were bitter strikes, characterized by the use of firearms against the workers. The Cheka arrested a number of strikers in a plant at Lublino, a suburb of Moscow.

The most serious difficulties occurred with the railroad workers. Shots were fired and several people were wounded at a stormy meeting in the workshops of the Alexandrovsk railroad line, in Moscow, on the evening of June 19. A little later a state of emergency was declared on the Nikolai Railroad, which connects Moscow with Petrograd; a "central revolutionary committee" took over the management of the railroad and absolutely forbade "incitement to nonfulfilment of the orders of the existing authorities, to the organization of strike committees, declaration of strikes and arbitrary stoppage of work," threatening violators of this order with deprivation of wages and food rations and immediate discharge. The fear of the Soviet authorities that a general strike might break out on the railroads is reflected in a telegram which an official of the Commissariat for Transportation, Byelyakov, sent to all the railroads: [14]

> "In connection with the attempts of counterrevolutionists to provoke a strike on the railroads I instruct all guard detachments to increase watchfulness, to arrest all agitators who appeal for stoppage, and I instruct all forces to coöperate with the railroad organizations in the struggle against the stoppage of movement. Besides this, strengthen the guard of food trains and warehouses, paying special attention to the impermissibility of uncoupling trains with food."

That the railroad workers had genuine grievances against the Soviet authorities is evident from a telegram of June 26, signed by Lenin and by the Commissar for Transportation, Nevsky, which frankly stated that "some agents of the central and local authorities exceeded their powers and took measures which were hostile to workingclass interests," mentioning among such measures: "firing on the railroad workers, threats coupled with violence, extra-legal shootings."

The Mensheviki and Socialist Revolutionaries endeavored to take advantage of the disillusionment among many of the workers and here and there played a leading part in stirring up local strikes. But their attempts to give the discontent of the workers a nationwide form of expression by creating a conference of nonparty workers met with little success, apparently for two main reasons. In the first place, so far as one can judge from the confused records of the time, the masses of the workers were not politically opposed to the Soviet system. They might grumble or even strike as a protest against almost intolerable food conditions. But they had no desire for a violent overthrow of the Soviet Government, no idea of what could be put in its place. Then the chances of anything remotely suggesting free agitation against the Soviet regime were steadily being curtailed. The Cheka was becoming continually more active and was carrying out arrests not only among officers and other classes which might be regarded as counterrevolutionary, but also among leading Mensheviki and Socialist Revolutionaries, who were consequently obliged to lead a harassed underground existence, very much as in Tsarist times. Typical of the repression was the arrest on July 23 of thirty-nine moderate Socialists who had met in the club of the Moscow coöperatives on July 23 to discuss a programme of action.[15]

Any chance of oppositionist activity in the Soviets had been cut off still earlier. For on June 14 the All-Russian Soviet Executive Committee decided to expel all Socialist Revolutionaries of the Right and Centre and Mensheviki from its membership and to instruct all local Soviets to do likewise. The reasons for this step were that the Soviet regime was living through an exceptionally difficult moment, that Socialist Revolutionaries and Mensheviki were in contact with leaders of the counterrevolution and that "the presence in Soviet organizations of representatives of parties which are clearly attempting to discredit and overthrow the power of the Soviets is quite intolerable."

This purge left only one legal Soviet party, the Left Socialist Revolutionaries, along with the Communists. But events were rapidly driving toward a breach with the Left Socialist Revolutionaries also; and this occurred in dramatic fashion during the sessions of the Fifth All-Russian Soviet Congress early in July. The Left Socialist Revolutionaries were in disagreement with Lenin's policies on three points. They wanted to tear up the Treaty of Brest-Litovsk and to resume the war with Germany; they were opposed to the Committees of the Poor; and they were against granting to the courts the right to impose the death penalty. It was typical of the semi-anarchist romanticism of the Left Socialist Revolutionaries that they included individual terrorism in their programme and were willing to participate in the work of the Cheka, where capital punishment was meted out with scant formality, but objected to the infliction of capital punishment by court trial as a "bourgeois relic."

The Congress opened on July 4. Among the 1,035 delegates elected with a right to vote there were 678 Communists and 269 Left Socialist Revolutionaries. The Left Socialist Revolutionaries, amateurs with little political experience, could not compete with the President of the Soviet Executive Committee, Sverdlov, in manipulating votes and the allocation of seats; the Bolshevik majority was apparently achieved, at least in part, by giving the representatives of the Committees of the Poor a disproportionately large share of the seats reserved for peasant delegates.[16]

The Great Theatre in Moscow, where the Congress was held, had very different inmates from the gentlemen in evening dress and the ladies in gowns and jewels who had attended performances of "Boris Godunov" and "Sadko" in pre-revolutionary days. In the orchestra sat the mass of the Congress delegates, workers predominating among the Bolsheviki, peasants among the Socialist Revolutionaries. The intellectual leaders of the two parties sat on the stage as members of the presidium; the keen-eyed British unofficial diplomatic representative, Lockhart, who was present, along with a few other foreign diplomats and journalists, noticed the predominance of Jews among the leaders of the two parties which were soon to dispute the mastery of that part of Russia which was still under the Soviets.[17] Among the Communists were Trotzky; Sverdlov, a dark man with black beard and fierce black eyes; Zinoviev, with his enormous forehead; Steklov-Nakhamkes, now editor of *Izvestia,* who always contrived to stay on the winning side amid the political changes; Afanasiev, the Secretary of the Soviet Central Executive Committee. Among the Jewish leaders of the Socialist Revolutionaries were Kamkov, Karelin and Steinberg, who for a short time had been Commissar for Justice.

As their first spokesman the Socialist Revolutionaries put forward a picturesque and appealing figure in a bright red and blue peasant shirt. He was an Ukrainian named Alexandrov and he brought to the Congress the greetings of an illegal peasant congress in Ukraina. He elicited roars of applause, especially from the Socialist Revolutionaries, when he described, perhaps with some exaggeration, the guerrilla warfare which the Ukrainian peasants and workers were carrying on against the German forces of occupation. "The peasants rise spontaneously against the Germans. The latter have no artillery warehouses; they are all blown up. The Germans tried to use an airplane factory in Odessa; it was burned." Finally he appealed to the Congress for help, shouting: "We shall drive the generals out of Kiev all the sooner if you will drive the German Ambassador out of Moscow."

Trotzky endeavored to pour cold water on the outbursts of enthusiasm which the Ukrainian's speech aroused. He complained that irresponsible agitators were endeavoring to incite an offensive of the Soviet troops in Kursk against the Germans. A commissar had been killed and a commander wounded as a result of this. He read the text of a proposed order denouncing "the agents of German militarism and Anglo-French imperialism" who wished to provoke a Russo-German war and threatening agitators with a revolutionary tribunal.

Kamkov was speedily on his feet retorting that the things of which Trotzky complained reflected "the healthy revolutionary psychology of those who do not want to serve German capital." Rising to an oratorical climax, he strode across the stage and shook his fist at the box where the German Ambassador, Count Mirbach, was sitting, shouting: "Do you think our peasant soldiers will stand by idly and see their brothers murdered by the agents of this bandit, this hangman?" This was the signal for a violent demonstration of the Socialist Revolutionaries against Mirbach; and some time elapsed before Sverdlov could be heard drily calling Kamkov to order for "using an improper expression to a guest of the Congress."

On the following day Maria Spiridonova and Kamkov debated with Lenin on the agrarian question. Behind Spiridonova, who was still in her early thirties, was a tragic revolutionary past. When she was a young girl she had killed a Tsarist governor and had been subsequently raped by the soldiers of his guard. Her delivery was monotonous, but occasionally rose to a hysterical note, which showed that her sufferings had affected her mind. The main point of her speech was that on the peasant question the Socialist Revolutionaries would fight against the Bolsheviki to the end. Kamkov put the case against the Bolshevik agrarian policy more concretely and in greater detail he characterized the Committees of the Poor as committees of village loafers and announced that the Socialist Revolutionaries would fight against them as against any other counterrevolutionary measure. As for the food detachments, these were made up not of the more advanced and classconscious workers, but of those who wished to rob the village.

Lenin replied that against desperate need desperate measures were required. Socialists who deserted at a time when thousands were starving were enemies of the people. The fight in the village was to save socialism and to divide bread in Russia justly. Only the union of the proletariat and the village poor could save the Revolution until the next harvest. Striking at the agitation of the Socialist Revolutionaries for war with Germany, he declared that the people were grateful for peace and that those who talked of the "Brest-Litovsk noose" themselves wanted to cast over the peasants a landlords' noose.

The Communist majority of the Congress passed a resolution approving the food policy of the Government and declaring that mass terror should be the answer to counterrevolutionary attempts to organize food riots and strikes.

But the issue between the Communists and the Left Socialist Revolutionaries would not be decided by a packed congress. A session of the Central Committee of the latter party on June 24 had sanctioned the "organization of terrorist acts against the most prominent representatives of German imperialism" on the ground that "it was necessary within the shortest period of time to put an end to the so-called breathing-space created by the ratification of the Treaty of Brest-Litovsk." [18]

On the basis of this resolution the Left Socialist Revolutionaries set to work on two schemes: a quite definite plan to assassinate the German Ambassador, Count Mirbach, and a much vaguer design to overthrow the rule of the Bolsheviki, or at least to resist any repressive measures which the Soviet authorities might take after Mirbach was killed. The preparation of Mirbach's assassination was facilitated because the Left Socialist Revolutionaries were still coöperating with the Bolsheviki in the Cheka and had access to its stamps.

About 2.30 on the afternoon of July 6 two conspirators, Jacob Blumkin and Nikolai Andreev, called at the German Embassy. Blumkin had worked in the Cheka and had provided himself and his companion with a document worded as follows and attested by the forged signatures of the head of the Cheka, Dzerzhinsky, and its Secretary, Ksenofontov: [19]

> "The Cheka empowers its member, Jacob Blumkin, and the representative of the Revolutionary Tribunal, Nikolai Andreev, to enter into discussion with the German Ambassador in Moscow on a matter of direct concern to the Ambassador."

Mirbach, it seems, had already received warning about possible attempts on his life, and thought the emissaries of the Cheka might be bringing him information. He received them in the presence of the Counsellor of the Embassy, Dr. Rietzler, and the military attaché, Lieutenant Moeller. Blumkin, a dark man with a bushy shock of hair, in a black shirt, began to talk about the case of an arrested Austrian officer named Robert Mirbach, who was supposed to be a relative of the Ambassador. Count Mirbach professed indifference, whereupon Andreev said: "It seems that it would be good for the Ambassador to know what measures may be taken against him." This was a signal; Blumkin leaped on a table and began to fire at all three Germans. Mirbach was hit, staggered into an adjoining room and fell with a wound in the neck; the two revolutionaries followed him and Andreev hurled a bomb which exploded with a tremendous detonation and inflicted on the Ambassador a mortal wound. Blumkin and Andreev then jumped out of a window, Blumkin breaking his leg, and fled to the Socialist Revolutionary staff, which was in the Pokrovsky Barracks.

The Central Committee of the Left Socialist Revolutionary Party immediately announced its responsibility for the assassination. It published a bulletin accusing Mirbach of concentrating stores of arms in Moscow City and Province for the purpose of arming German war prisoners and Whites and declaring: "The Soviet Government was helpless before Mirbach's band and the Central Committee was compelled to remove this agent of foreign imperialism and obvious counterrevolutionary, who enjoyed immunity."

Maria Spiridonova testified before a commission which investigated the affair: [20] "I organized the matter of killing Mirbach from beginning to end. Learning about the assassination, I went with a report about it to the Congress of Soviets, in order to explain this act and in order to assume responsibility before all the workers and before the International. I indignantly reject the accusation of willing or unwilling union with the British, French or any other bourgeoisie." Spiridonova, whose rather naïve fanaticism predisposes one to believe in her frankness, insisted that the Central Committee of her Party had not planned to overthrow the Bolshevik Government. All that subsequently happened she attributed "to the vigorous defense of the slain agents of German imperialism by the Soviet Government and to the selfdefense of the Socialist Revolutionary Central Committee."

The news of Mirbach's assassination naturally aroused consternation and indignation among the Bolshevik leaders. They certainly had no liking or regard for the German diplomat; but his killing exposed them to the danger of a German occupation at a time when they were hard pressed from all sides. Felix Dzerzhinsky, head of the Cheka, after paying a flying call to the German Embassy and obtaining details about the murder, rushed off, quite indifferent to personal danger, to the headquarters of Popov's Socialist Revolutionary detachment of Cheka troops, convinced that Blumkin had taken refuge there. This detachment, which numbered about 600, was the main, almost the sole, military force on which the Left Socialist Revolutionaries could rely. Its chief, Popov, had systematically filled it up with Left Socialist Revolutionaries and had recently recruited a number of turbulent Black Sea sailors, who were against the Bolsheviki. When Dzerzhinsky demanded that Blumkin be given up two members of the Left Socialist Revolutionary Central Committee, Proshian and Karelin, intervened, saying that the Central Committee alone was responsible for the act. Dzerzhinsky thereupon declared them under arrest and threatened to shoot Popov if he did not give them up. Then the sailors disarmed Dzerzhinsky and held him as a prisoner; and some of the Socialist Revolutionary leaders, gathering around Dzerzhinsky, triumphantly shouted: [21]

"You have before you an accomplished fact; the Brest-Litovsk Treaty is torn up; war with Germany is unavoidable. We don't want power; let it be here as in Ukraina: we will go underground. You can remain in power; but you must stop being lackeys of Mirbach. Let Germany occupy Russia up to the Volga."

In this outburst one can see all the confused, unrealistic political psychology of the Left Socialist Revolutionaries. They had no clear-cut, conscious plan for ousting the Bolsheviki and seizing governmental power themselves; they were willing to let the Bolsheviki go on ruling, provided that the war with Germany was resumed. And this war they envisaged not as a struggle between organized armies, but as a partisan war, in which individual terrorists like Blumkin and peasant guerrilla bands would play a large part.

The Left Socialist Revolutionaries succeeded in capturing Latzis, Dzerzhinsky's assistant in the Cheka, and about eight in the evening a force of some forty of them seized the Moscow post and telegraph office and sent to all Soviets two telegraphic messages. One forbade the transmission of messages signed by Lenin, Trotzky and Sverdlov and also of despatches sent by "the counter-revolutionary parties of Right Socialist Revolutionaries and Mensheviki" and referred to the Left Socialist Revolutionaries as "the Party now in power." The other message began with the statement, "The representative of German imperialism, Count Mirbach, has been killed according to the resolution of the Central Committee of the Party of Left Socialist Revolutionaries," and ended: "Long live the revolt against imperialism! Long live the power of the Soviets!" Automobiles in the vicinity of the postoffice were stopped and a few prominent Communists were placed under arrest.

But here the success of this very amateurish play at a *coup d'état* ceased. There was no attempt to move on the Kremlin, to push the offensive further. The Bolsheviki reacted vigorously to the threat to their power. The Great Theatre was encircled by reliable troops, including some of the famous Lettish Sharpshooters, and Maria Spiridonova had no opportunity to deliver her dramatic speech announcing the death of Mirbach to the Congress. Along with all the other Socialist Revolutionary delegates she was arrested and confined in the basement of the Great Theatre.

The Bolshevik delegates to the Congress scattered among the workingclass districts to act as agitators. Podvoisky, one of the active leaders in Leningrad during the November Revolution, and Muralov, the commandant of Moscow, were entrusted with the suppression of the movement. They concentrated troops in the neighborhood of the Cathedral and around the Strastnoi Monastery, in the centre of the city. A very slight "whiff of grapeshot" on the morning of the 7th was enough to put Popov's disorderly force to rout. Some of the first shells, whether from luck or from good marksmanship, struck the building of his Staff, and the Left Socialist Revolutionaries broke and fled. They first went to the Kursk Railroad Station; but, finding this occupied, retreated from the city altogether in the direction of the neighboring town of Bogorodsk. About four hundred of them were captured; thirteen, including an old revolutionist and prominent Party leader, Alexandrovitch, were shot. The time of relative leniency toward former fellow-revolutionists was over. Executions in general began to be much more frequent; on July 13 it was announced that the Cheka had shot ten officers, members of Savinkov's "Committee for the Defense of the Motherland and Freedom," headed by General Popov. A statement accompanying the notice of this execution declared that imprisonment was useless as a deterrent to such people, because they organized escapes and resumed their activity.

With the successful assassination and the abortive uprising, if it may be so called, of July 6, the Left Socialist Revolutionaries passed from the Russian political stage. Some of them, who had acquired the habit of working in coöperation with the Communists, repudiated their Central Committee and joined the Communist Party. Others went "underground" and constituted another anti-Bolshevik grouping. A Left Socialist Revolutionary, Donskoy, followed up the tradition set by the assassination of Count Mirbach and assassinated General Eichhorn, Commander of the German forces in Ukraina, in Kiev.

The Left Socialist Revolutionaries, of course, were no longer tolerated as members of the Soviets; from this time the Soviet regime became a pure and undiluted dictatorship of the Communist Party. Philips Price, a foreign observer who was, in the main, very sympathetic with the Bolsheviki, felt that an element of revolutionary enthusiasm disappeared from the Soviets when they were eliminated. Certainly they incarnated much that was striking and picturesque in early Russian revolutionary practise: the hatred for a strongly organized state, even a so-called proletarian state, the preference for individual terror, the doctrinaire impracticality, the love for grandiloquent and melodramatic phrases.

Blumkin escaped punishment for the murder of Mirbach. He hid for a time under an assumed name; after his leg was healed he went to Ukraina and took part in the reëstablishment of the Soviet regime there. On May 16, 1919, when no more diplomatic consequences were to be apprehended, the All-Russian Central Executive Committee pardoned him. But he met his end at the hand of a Soviet executioner more than a decade later for quite a different reason. Working in the Gay-Pay-Oo, the successor to the Cheka, Blumkin was accused of carrying out commissions for the exiled Trotzky, found guilty by a secret tribunal and summarily put to death.

The 6th of July 1918 was marked by another serious outbreak against the Bolshevik regime; the town of Yaroslavl, on the upper Volga, was seized by a surprise attack of a group of conspirators enrolled in Savinkov's organization under the command of Colonel Perkhurov. The capture of Yaroslavl, which was followed by a struggle of almost two weeks before the Soviet forces retook the town, the shortlived seizure of Murom, taken by Savinkov's organization on the night of the 8th and retaken by the Reds on the 10th, and an unsuccessful attack, in which Savinkov himself participated, on the Volga town of Rybinsk, near Yaroslavl, on the night of the 7th were all, if one may believe Savinkov's testimony before a Soviet court,[22] inspired by the French Ambassador in Russia, Noulens, who seems to have been the leading figure among the advocates of intervention. According to Savinkov, his organization was always in close contact with the French representatives in Moscow, Consul Grenard and General Lavergne, who supplied him with funds, at first meagrely, and later, when there was prospect of an uprising, more generously.

The French proposed to Savinkov that his organization should seize four towns in the Upper Volga region, Yaroslavl, Rybinsk, Kostroma and Murom. An Allied descent in Archangel would then support the insurgents and make possible a victorious advance on Moscow. But one very essential factor in the success of this scheme was lacking: the Allied descent in Archangel did not take place until the following month; and then the forces which were landed were too small to exert any influence on the course of the Russian civil war. The repulse in Rybinsk also condemned the enterprise to failure; there were much larger artillery stores in Rybinsk than in Yaroslavl.

The lax guard which the Soviet troops maintained at the artillery base in Yaroslavl (which Perkhurov was able to seize on the morning of the 6th with a small company of men), the indifferent quality of most of the Red soldiers in the town, the hostility of at least some of the workers to the Soviet regime (some of the factory and railroad workers promised Savinkov to join in the insurrection, and, although they did not keep this promise, they seem to have remained neutral, giving no support to the Soviet side), all helped to place Yaroslavl in the hands of the insurgents. The Reds, however, held the western outskirts of the town, along with the railroad station, which was some distance from the centre, and stubborn fighting set in and lasted for thirteen days. Perkhurov announced himself as a representative of the Northern Volunteer Army, operating under the orders of General Alekseev, and declared in one of his appeals: "God will help us and Yaroslavl, with its holy shrines, and from it health and strength will proceed into the body of our unhappy motherland. Long live the legally elected Constituent Assembly."

The reaction of the population of the town and of the surrounding countryside was varied. The workers did not keep their original promises of support; however much they may have disliked the Soviet regime and the hunger which it had brought, they apparently could not bring themselves to fight side by side with old officers. As for the other classes of the Yaroslavl population, "they rejoiced as if it were a holiday and crowds of people from morning besieged our staff, wishing to enter our detachments as volunteers," according to one participant in the uprising.[23] Not all these volunteers, however, proved reliable when they learned that the uprising was not a completed success and that heavy fighting was still ahead. The "front" of this little episode in the civil war stretched to some neighboring villages; but it was impossible to train and drill those peasants who were sympathetic with the insurgents amid the continual fighting.

Although the Red forces besieging the town were considerably superior in numbers to the few hundred ex-officers and their hastily recruited supporters, the recapture of Yaroslavl was delayed by the lack of capable leaders. The Whites had killed the President of the Soviet, Zakheim, the district military commissar, Nahimson, who was particularly hated by the officers because he had been an active agitator on the Front in 1917, and several others. Finally the "Extraordinary Staff," which was directing the operations against the insurrection, issued a stern warning to the population, worded as follows:

> "It is recommended to all to whom life is dear to leave the town within twenty-four hours after the date of this declaration and to go to the American Bridge. Those who remain in the city after the specified time will be regarded as partisans of the rebels. After the expiration of twenty-four hours there will be quarter for no one; the most pitiless, hurricane fire will be opened on the city from heavy guns, and also with chemical shells. All who remain will perish under the ruins of the town along with the rebels, traitors, enemies of the revolution of the workers and poorest peasants."

After this threat had been carried out and a considerable part of the city, along with several beautiful Russian medieval churches, had been smashed to pieces by the bombardment, in which airplanes took an active part, the Red troops entered the town on July 19. Perkhurov escaped on a boat on the Volga; he was captured and shot only in 1922. Savinkov also escaped and made his way to Kazan, which was soon to pass into the hands of the Czechs. The Whites who remained endeavored to save their lives by surrendering to a German lieutenant who, with a number of war prisoners, was in the town; but the Reds forced the Germans to hand over fifty-seven of the active Whites who had been placed in the town theatre and shot them all. An investigating commission then picked out 350 more alleged participants in the uprising and put them all to death.[24] "Mass Red Terror" was becoming a reality.

Curiously enough, although the uprising of the Left Socialist Revolutionaries and the seizure of Yaroslavl by Savinkov's organization occurred on the same day, there is no evidence that there was any connection between the two. It does not seem that the two groups of conspirators even knew of each other's plans. Although the fanatical enthusiasts of revolt among the Left Socialist

Revolutionaries and the ex-officers who constituted the backbone of Savinkov's organization were in agreement in demanding a renewal of the war with Germany, their views on political and social questions were so far apart that there was no possibility of effective coöperation between them. The Left Socialist Revolutionaries wanted to preserve the Soviets; they were quite willing to work with the Communists, if the latter would break with Germany. Savinkov's followers were officially in favor of the Constituent Assembly; what many of them doubtless wanted was a return to pre-War social conditions, whether with or without a Tsar. With the crushing of the Yaroslavl outbreak the Committee for the Defense of the Motherland and Freedom ceased to function on Soviet territory; those members who escaped the Cheka mostly made their way eastward and joined the anti-Bolshevik forces on the Volga.

The Left Socialist Revolutionary movement had its effect on the Volga Front, where the Soviet commander, Muraviev, was himself a member of that party. Taking some troops with him Muraviev moved from Kazan to Simbirsk and sent out telegrams in which he "declared war on Germany" and urged the Soviet troops which were moving to the east to turn back to Moscow. He endeavored to take the control of Simbirsk out of the hands of the local Soviet. But the majority of the troops remained loyal to the Communists; and in a scuffle which broke out Muraviev either shot himself or was killed by the troops.

Amid the general hunger and the excitement created by the outbreaks in Moscow and in Yaroslavl and by the numerous smaller clashes all over Soviet territory, two events of July aroused less popular attention than might have otherwise been the case. One was the killing of the former Tsar with his wife and children in Ekaterinburg,[25] the other was the formal promulgation, on July 19, of the Soviet Constitution, with its preamble, "The Declaration of the Rights of the Working and Exploited People." Many provisions of the Constitution were of purely theoretical interest, because they were not carried out in practise. Real power rested not with the Soviets, but with the Communist Party; and those provisions of the Constitution which prescribed the methods of election, the frequency of convening Soviet Congresses, etc., were neglected or violated. One interesting feature of the Constitution was the granting of as much representation to 25,000 town dwellers as to 125,000 country dwellers; the framers of the Constitution wished to parry the considerable preponderance which the peasants would have enjoyed over the workers if free and equal suffrage had prevailed under the Soviet system.

The Constitution excluded the following classes of persons from voting: persons employing hired labor for the purpose of extracting profit; persons living on income not derived from work; private traders; monks, priests and ministers of all religious faiths; employees and agents of the former police, of the Special Corps of Gendarmes and of espionage departments; members of the former ruling family; persons recognized as feebleminded or insane; and persons condemned for selfish and disgraceful crimes.

It is noteworthy that while guaranties of personal liberty and of freedom of expressing opinion are weaker and vaguer in the Soviet Constitution than in most other such documents (and those guaranties which are given—for instance, "the right of Soviet citizens to hold meetings and processions freely"—were most consistently not observed), there is very strong emphasis on the economic and social ideals and purposes of the new regime. The Constitution describes as the basic problems: "the destruction of any exploitation of man by man, the complete elimination of the division of society into classes, the pitiless suppression of exploiters, the socialist organization of society and the victory of socialism in all countries." [26]

A disillusioned former Bolshevik wrote a book about Russia in 1918 under the title: "The Kingdom of Famine and Hatred." The title seems justified in the light of the records of the time, as preserved in reminiscences and newspapers. The resolutions which the Communists propose in central and local Soviet gatherings fairly drip with hatred for the "bourgeoisie," which is held responsible for all the miseries of the country. Hunger, the Committees of the Poor, the food requisitions sowed bitter hatred between the workers and the peasants, and between different classes of the peasants. A typical incident, reported in a newspaper, took place in one of the Moscow markets, when a working woman argued with a peasant woman about the price of a glass of milk; when the working woman called a policeman the peasant woman threw the glass on the ground and broke it. Ferocious lynchings of thieves by mobs, which were often half crazed by hunger, occurred not only in remote villages, but in the heart of Moscow. Crushed and impoverished, living in growing fear of being arrested and shot by the ever more ruthless agents of the Cheka, the former well-to-do and middle classes also lived in impotent hatred, dreaming of the day when they would be revenged by a general massacre of Communists and Jews. (To conservative Russians the terms were often almost synonymous.)

More than one government appeal testifies to the wide circulation of anti-Semitic propaganda at this time. There were no pogroms, such as occurred on an appalling scale in Ukraina in 1919; but in cases when the anti-Bolsheviki gained the upper hand for a short time in rebellions, Jews among the Communists were apt to be killed first.

By the end of July Lenin publicly admitted that the most critical period of the Revolution had arrived. A big meeting, attended by representatives of the Soviets, the factory committees and the trade-unions, was held and Trotzky harangued it with his unfailing fiery eloquence, ending: "The working class cannot suffer defeat. We are sons of the working class; we have made our pact with death and, therefore, with victory." The meeting, which was held on July 29, declared "the socialist fatherland in danger" and recognized as the basic problems of the moment "the driving back of the Czecho-Slovaks and the successful collection and transportation of grain." [27] There was to be intensified propaganda among the workers, and "mass terror in practise" was to be used against the bourgeoisie.

Not only was the war on the Eastern Front going badly at this time (Ekaterinburg had just fallen and Kazan would soon follow); not only did "the bony hand of hunger" show no sign of relaxing its grip; but clouds were thickening from another quarter. The French had been premature in assuring Savinkov that an Allied descent would take place in North Russia; but plans for such a move were being seriously weighed. At least as early as May 24 the British War Office had in mind the sending to North Russia of a strong military mission and a small expeditionary force [28] which hoped to train the Czechs and a Russian force, in order to reopen the Eastern Front against Germany. (Presumably the plan, as regards the Czechs, was based on the idea that they would be partly evacuated through Archangel and Murmansk.)

A small mixed force under British command had been in Murmansk for some time, guarding military stores against a possible attack by the Germans from Finland. So long as this force was defensive in character the Soviet Government had no objection to its presence, although it felt obliged, under pressure from Germany, to send occasional notes of protest to the British unofficial representative in Moscow, Lockhart. But toward the end of June the British force of occupation in Murmansk began to play a more aggressive rôle, concluding a separate agreement with the Murmansk Soviet, which was not loyal to Moscow, and extending the sphere of occupation as far to the south as Kem. There was a clear probability that Archangel, the chief Russian port on the White Sea, would soon be occupied; and on July 23 Trotzky issued an order forbidding Soviet citizens to go to Archangel, Murmansk or into "the region of the Czecho-Slovak revolt" without written permission from the War Commissariat, and threatening with death "anyone who sells himself to foreign imperialists for participation in revolt or for occupation of Russian territory."

By some strange accident, which probably indicated that one British governmental department did not always know what another was doing, a British economic mission arrived in Moscow on July 22, with the avowed purpose of discussing possibilities of trade relations with the Bolsheviki. This mission very quickly departed, realizing the futility of its errand; and on the night of the 24th the missions of the Allied powers, which had taken up their residence in Vologda at the time when Petrograd was threatened by German occupation, departed for Archangel, declining Chicherin's pressing invitation to come to Moscow, where their members might easily have been held as hostages in the event of intervention. A British officer, Captain McGrath, had warned the American Ambassador that the presence of the Allied missions in Vologda, which was under Soviet control, might embarrass the military plans of General Poole, commander of the expeditionary force which was destined for Archangel.[29]

Archangel was occupied on the night of August 2, a British naval descent being timed to coincide with an uprising headed by anti-Bolshevik officers within the city. This marked the loss of the last Soviet port. The British and American force at Archangel was much too small to undertake any large-scale southward offensive against Moscow. But the symbolic effect of the intervention, which occurred simultaneously with the announcement of the intention of America and the Allied powers to intervene in the Far East, was considerable; it aroused exaggerated hopes of aid from outside in the anti-Bolshevik Russians and indicated the complete isolation of the Soviet regime.

August passed in an atmosphere of deadlock on the front, of sanguinary class war in the villages, of raids on the homes of real or suspected conspirators. A decree published on August 8 [30] declared kulaks and rich peasants who refused to give up their surplus grain enemies of the people, liable to be punished by confiscation of all their property, imprisonment for not less than ten years and perpetual banishment from their homes. The same penalties were prescribed for peasants who used grain to make liquor; while "shooting on the spot" was to be the fate of any peasants or bagmen who offered armed resistance.

Amid all the stark human misery of that period, faced with difficulties and problems which might well have broken a less resolute and fanatical leader, Lenin remained unshaken in his faith in the fundamental rightness of his cause and in its ultimate victory. His spirit during those dark days was vividly reflected in the following passage in a letter which he wrote on August 20 and addressed to the workers of America, few of whom, it may be suggested, ever learned of it or were affected by it: [31]

> "For every hundred of our mistakes . . . there are 10,000 great and heroic acts. . . . But if the situation were reversed, if there were 10,000 mistakes to every hundred of our correct acts, all the same our Revolution would be and will be great and unconquerable in the eyes of world history, because for the first time not a minority, not only the rich, not only the educated, but the real mass, the enormous majority of the workers themselves build up a new life, with their own experience decide the most difficult problems of socialist organization."

August 30 was a fateful day which perhaps marked the climax of "the most critical period." On the morning of that day a young officer named Kenigiesser shot down and killed the head of the Petrograd Cheka, Uritzky, as the latter was going to his office. On the evening of the same day Lenin had been addressing a meeting of workers in the Michelson factory. As he was leaving the meeting and was near his automobile two women came up to him and complained about the actions of the search detachments which took away food from passengers on the railroads. As Lenin was saying that abuses would be remedied three shots rang out; Lenin fell, with one bullet in the chest and one in the left shoulder. His assailant, who threw away her revolver and fled, but was soon caught, and promptly shot by the Cheka on the following morning, was a Jewish woman named Fanya Kaplan, who had served a prison sentence in Siberia under the Tsar as an Anarchist. Later she had become a Socialist Revolutionary; and when she was examined she declared herself a sympathizer with the Constituent Assembly.

There was no coördination between her act and that of Kenigiesser; [32] but the two terrorist acts, coming together at a moment of the greatest strain and hardship, furnished the psychological stimulus for one of the most ferocious outbursts of organized revolutionary terrorism since the French Revolution.

NOTES

[1] V. I. Lenin, "Collected Works," Vol. XV, p. 390.
[2] *Ibid.*, Vol. XV, pp. 375, 376.
[3] For the text of the decree *cf.* V. Averev, "The Committees of the Poor," Vol. I, pp. 52–54.
[4] The full text is published by Professor A. V. Shestakov, "The Committees of the Poor in the Russian Socialist Federative Soviet Republic," pp. 55–57.
[5] Vera Vladimirova, "A Year of Service of 'Socialists' to Capitalists," p. 291.
[6] *Pravda,* for July 23, 1918.
[7] *Cf.* its issue for July 2, 1918.
[8] Lenin, "Collected Works" (later edition), Vol. XXIII, p. 294.
[9] Averev, *op. cit.*, p. 22.
[10] *Izvestia,* for May 31, 1918.
[11] *Cf.* Chapter XIX, pp. 421, 422.
[12] Popov and a number of his associates were executed in July.
[13] *Cf. Izvestia,* for June 22, 1918.
[14] *Ibid.*, for July 3, 1918.
[15] Vladimirova, *op. cit.*, pp. 198, 199.
[16] M. Philips Price, "Reminiscences of the Russian Revolution," p. 315.
[17] R. H. Bruce Lockhart, "Memoirs of a British Agent," p. 295.
[18] Mackintzian, "The Red Book of the Cheka," Vol. I, p. 129.
[19] *Ibid.*, pp. 137, 138.
[20] *Cf.* her testimony as reproduced in "The Red Book of the Cheka," Vol. I, pp. 200, 201.
[21] Vladimirova, *op. cit.*, p. 273, citing *Pravda.*
[22] *Cf.* "The Case of Boris Savinkov," pp. 37, 38.
[23] *Cf.* the translated excerpts from General Gopper's book, "Four Defeats," published in the book, "The Beginning of Civil War," in the series, "Revolution and Civil War in the Descriptions of the White Guards," p. 312.
[24] *Cf.* Mackintzian, *op. cit.*, pp. 114, 115.
[25] The details of the slaughter of the imperial family are given in Chapter XXIV.
[26] *Cf.* S. A. Piontkovsky, "Civil War in Russia: Documents," p. 18.
[27] The complete text is to be found in L. D. Trotzky's "How the Revolution Armed Itself," Vol. I, p. 229.
[28] General Sir C. Maynard, "The Murmansk Venture," pp. 12ff.
[29] David Francis, "Russia from the American Embassy," pp. 250ff.
[30] *Cf. Pravda,* for August 8.
[31] Lenin, "Collected Works," Vol. XV, p. 412.
[32] The question of whether Fanya Kaplan had the sanction of the Central Committee of the Socialist Revolutionary Party for her act was vigorously disputed during the trial of a number of prominent Socialist Revolutionaries in Moscow in 1922. A certain Semyenov, who testified that he had committed terrorist acts against the Soviet regime at the order of the Central Committee of the Socialist Revolutionary Party, turned state's evidence at the trial and made the most sweeping statements, calculated to incriminate the Party Central Committee in authorizing the assassination of Volodarsky and the attack on Lenin. This was vigorously denied by Gotz, Donskoy and other members of the Socialist Revolutionary Central Committee who were on trial. In any case there seems to have been no link between Kaplan's attack on Lenin and the shooting of Uritzky by Kenigiesser, although they occurred on the same day, because Kenigiesser belonged to another grouping, "The Union of Regeneration." Just as in the case of the armed outbreaks in Moscow and Yaroslavl on July 6, the two terrorist acts of August 30 coincided by pure accident.

CHAPTER XXIII

TERROR, RED AND WHITE

THE reaction to the assassination of Uritzky and the attack on Lenin (who was in a critical condition for a few days, but by September 19 had sufficiently recovered to be able to resume work) was swift and ruthless. On September 3 it was officially announced that more than five hundred persons had been shot in Petrograd as a reprisal for the killing of Uritzky.[1] And on the next day the Commissar for Internal Affairs, Petrovsky, issued a proclamation of terror in the form of the following telegraphic order to all Soviets: [2]

"The murder of Volodarsky, the murder of Uritzky, the attempted murder and wounding of the President of the Council of People's Commissars, V. I. Lenin, the mass shooting of tens of thousands of our comrades in Finland, Ukraina and finally in the Don and in Czecho-Slavia,[3] the continually exposed plots in the rear of our armies, the open participation of Right Socialist Revolutionaries and other counterrevolutionary scoundrels in these plots and at the same time the extraordinarily negligible number of serious repressions and mass shootings of White Guards and bourgeoisie by the Soviets show that, notwithstanding continual talk about mass terror against Socialist Revolutionaries, White Guards and bourgeoisie, this terror really does not exist.

"There must be a decisive end of this situation. There must be an end of laxity and weakness. All Right Socialist Revolutionaries known to local Soviets must be immediately arrested. A considerable number of hostages must be taken from among the bourgeoisie and the officers. Mass shooting must be applied upon the least attempts at resistance or the least movement in the midst of the White Guards. Local Provincial Executive Committees must show special initiative in this respect.

"Administrative departments through the militia and the Extraordinary Commissions must take all measures to detect and arrest all who hide under foreign names and surnames, with unconditional shooting of all who are involved in White Guard activity.

"All the above mentioned measures must be carried out immediately.

"The Commissariat for Internal Affairs must be immediately informed of any indecisive activities of local Soviets in this direction.

"Last of all, the rear of our armies must be finally cleared of all White Guardism and all scoundrelly conspirators against the power of the working class and the poorest peasants. Not the least wavering, not the least indecision in the application of mass terror.

"Confirm the receipt of this telegram. Transmit it to the county Soviets."

This order sanctioned and spurred on a wave of sanguinary terror that was already going on all over the country and that, according to Soviet official figures, took many thousands of victims. The revolver replaced the guillotine of the French Revolution as the favored weapon of execution; executions were carried out secretly, not openly. The organization which carried out the mass terror was the Cheka, or All-Russian Extraordinary Commission, which developed into one of the most formidable institutions for the perpetration of state-organized homicide that the world has ever seen.

Petrovsky's statement about the "extraordinarily negligible numbers of repressions and mass shootings" up to the time of his order is scarcely borne out by the facts; actually centralized mass terror may be said to have set in after the uprisings of the Left Socialist Revolutionaries in Moscow and of Savinkov's organization in Yaroslavl on July 6. The shooting of over four hundred people in Yaroslavl was a definite start in this direction.

As a matter of fact terrorism, although of a different type, for which the central government could not be held directly responsible, had existed much earlier. The case in Sevastopol in February, 1918, when the sailors of the Black Sea Fleet ran amuck through the town, killing hundreds of "bourgeoisie," men, women and children, may have been one of the worst of its kind, but certainly was not unique. Red Guards and Bolshevik sailors carried out many acts of unauthorized violence, such as the lynching of General Dukhonin in Moghilev and the murder in hospital of the Cadet leaders, Shingarev and Kokoshkin. The progress of Antonov's partisan army through Ukraina was marked by a good deal of robbing and killing; and the Red regime in outlying districts, far away from the centre, such as the Urals and the North Caucasus, was a sanguinary one almost from the beginning.

But the terrorism which reached perhaps its greatest height during the late summer and autumn of 1918 and continued, with varying degrees of intensity, throughout the period of the civil war, differed from the lynch law of revolutionary mobs or undisciplined Red Guards because it was sanctioned by the Soviet Government and carried out by an organization which was part of the

Government administrative apparatus, the Extraordinary Commission.

The psychology of fear and hatred which lay behind the intensified terror was further stimulated when the Cheka on September 3 published a sensational communiqué to the effect that the British unofficial representative in Russia, Lockhart, a Lieutenant of the British Intelligence Service, Reilly, the French Consul, Grenard, and the head of the French Military Mission, General Lavergne, were implicated in an elaborate plot which aimed at the overthrow of the Soviet Government. Lockhart was singled out for special attack, and it was stated that the plot included the subornation of the loyalty of Soviet troops, the arrest of Lenin and Trotzky and the aggravation of the food difficulties in Moscow and Petrograd through the blowing up of railroad bridges and the destruction of food warehouses.

A good deal of doubt about the genuineness of this "plot" is cast by an incautious statement of Peters, a Lett who played a prominent rôle in the Cheka,[4] who declared in an interview that the Cheka, having become convinced that the threads of various plots led to the British Mission, "arranged a fictitious plot," sending old Communists, whose loyalty to the Soviets was unquestioned, to Lockhart in the guise of discontented men who wished to betray the Soviets.

Lockhart's own account of the matter [5] bears out Peters's statement, inasmuch as it describes how, on August 15, he received a visit from two Letts, Berzin, commander of one of the Lettish regiments in the Red Army, and Smidchen, who brought a letter of recommendation from the British naval attaché, Captain Cromie, who was in Leningrad. Berzin, who was an old and thoroughly loyal Bolshevik, the *agent provocateur* selected by the Cheka, suggested to Lockhart that the Letts were tired of fighting for the Soviets and would surrender if they were sent to the northern front against the British.

Lockhart gave them a paper, requesting that they be admitted through the British lines, and put them in touch with Sidney Reilly, who, despite his Irish name, was an Odessa Jew, and something of an international adventurer, who seems to have met his death in Russia under mysterious circumstances, in 1926.[6] Reilly was an agent of the British Intelligence Service and was supposed to stay on after the departure of Lockhart and other British military and civilian representatives, whose status had become decidedly anomalous after the British intervention in Archangel and Murmansk had placed Great Britain in a state of actual if undeclared war with Soviet Russia.

Apparently Berzin and Smidchen laid tempting plans of counterrevolution before Reilly, for the latter suggested to Lockhart that he "might be able to stage a counterrevolution in Moscow." This suggestion, according to Lockhart, "was categorically turned down by General Lavergne, Grenard and myself, and Reilly was warned to have nothing to do with so dangerous and doubtful a move."

While it is difficult, of course, to distinguish with absolute certainty between the genuine plots, the suspected plots and the fictitious "plots," organized by the Cheka itself, which occurred during that dark and confused period, it seems intrinsically improbable that Lockhart, who always took a realistic view of the Russian situation and who had personally vigorously opposed the policy of intervention against the will of the Bolsheviki, was implicated in such far-reaching conspiracies as the Cheka communiqué asserted. By his own admission, he had been subsidizing anti-Bolshevik groups after his Government had decided irrevocably on the policy of intervention; and it would seem that the "Lockhart Plot" was a compound of actual advances of money, of which the Cheka probably found some trace, and of fanciful schemes which the Cheka agents laid before the too credulous and too imaginative Reilly.

Naturally the publication of alleged facts about a huge conspiracy, in which representatives of the Allied powers were involved, coming immediately after the shooting of Uritzky and Lenin, created a vast stir; Lockhart and a number of other British and French military and diplomatic representatives were arrested. There were sharp exchanges of communications between the French and British Foreign Offices and the Soviet Commissariat for Foreign Affairs on this question. Ultimately, when Lenin's recovery and the improving situation on the Volga Front had produced a calmer atmosphere, a process of exchange was arranged; and Lockhart, with a number of British and French officials, left Russia while Litvinov, who had occupied in England an unofficial representative capacity similar to that of Lockhart in Russia, along with some other Bolsheviki was permitted to return to Russia, where he became Assistant Commissar for Foreign Affairs. The British naval attaché in Russia, Captain Cromie, had been killed in an exchange of shots with agents of the Cheka who had come to search the building of the Embassy.

While elementary prudential considerations led the Soviet authorities to exempt foreign diplomatic representatives from the scope of "mass Red terror," the toll of victims among Russians mounted from day to day. The largest single batch of shootings was in Petrograd, where more than 500 people, including the former Tsarist Ministers, A. N. Khvostov, A. D. Protopopov, I. D. Stcheglivitov and N. A. Maklakov, were slaughtered in revenge for the killing of Uritzky and the attempt on Lenin. Yaroslavl seems to have come second, with more than 400 victims. A description of what must have been a grim massacre in a sleepy provincial town is contained in the following laconic message from Penza, dated September 25: [7]

"The White Guard plot and attempt to break into the prison and free the hostages has been liquidated. For the murder from ambush of one comrade, Egorov, a Petrograd worker, the Whites paid with 152 lives. In the future firmer measures will be taken in regard to the Whites.

"President of the Provincial Soviet Turlo"

On a single day, October 3, almost 200 killings are reported from various parts of the country. The Cheka of the Front in Kotelnich led the list with 61 executions; the Chembar County Cheka put to death 48, as "hostages for Egorov"; Rybinsk killed 30 hostages; the little town of Klin executed 8 for "counterrevolutionary agitation" (several of these were former landlords); the Astrakhan Cheka put to death 12 who were accused of participating in an unsuccessful uprising in that town on August 15. The Cheka recognized no sex distinctions; one often finds the names of women among its victims; and sometimes it seems that whole families were wiped out, especially in the country districts.

That persons arrested by the Cheka were often subjected to torture of revolting cruelty is plainly indicated by an extraordinary letter which was printed in No. 3 of the *Bulletin of the Cheka,* dated October 6, 1918.[8] The letter was signed by Communist and Cheka officials of the town of Nolinsk, in Vyatka Province, and was published under the heading: "Why Are You Soft?" The authors express great indignation at the fact that Lockhart, according to a newspaper report, was permitted to leave the building of the Cheka in Moscow in great confusion. How Lockhart or anyone suspected of counterrevolution would have been treated by the Nolinsk Chekists is evident from the following excerpts from the letter:

"The Cheka has still not got away from petty-bourgeois ideology, the cursed inheritance of the pre-revolutionary past. Tell us, why didn't you subject Lockhart to the most refined tortures, in order to get information and addresses, of which such a bird must have had very many? Tell us why you permitted him to leave the building of the Cheka 'in great confusion,' instead of subjecting him to tortures, the very description of which would have filled counterrevolutionaries with cold terror?

"Enough of being soft; give up this unworthy play at 'diplomacy' and 'representation.'

"A dangerous scoundrel has been caught. Get out of him what you can and send him to the other world."

The reply, for which the central organization of the Cheka is responsible, is even more significant than the outburst of a remote country Cheka, which was apparently well versed in the practise of "refined tortures." It read: "Not at all objecting in substance to this letter, we only want to point out to the comrades who sent it and reproached us with mildness that the 'sending to the other world' of 'base intriguers' representing 'foreign peoples' is not at all in our interest."

The Cheka acquired a sinister reputation not only for inhuman cruelty, but also for blackmail and corruption. Its real or self-styled agents not infrequently took bribes from friends or relatives of prisoners. In the matter of corruption there is also interesting evidence in the *Bulletin of the Cheka.*[9] So there is a statement to the effect that "into the provincial and especially into the county Chekas people who are not only unworthy, but who are actually criminal are trying to make their way." The wholesale arrests carried out by the Cheka were accompanied by extensive confiscations of property, which was often taken without any account. Another candid article in the *Bulletin* suggests that "it is necessary to stop forever the giving out of goods in a lump; such a method leads to a good deal of corruption and to the spreading of all sorts of reproaches against the Chekas. Some ordinary citizens say that the Chekists 'divide everything among themselves'!"

The reproach of corruption certainly would not have applied to the majority of the men at the top, to such figures as the head of the Cheka, Felix Dzerzhinsky, a fanatical idealist who had suffered many years of imprisonment under Tsarism for his political convictions and activities. But, especially in little provincial towns, where there were few pre-revolutionary Communists, the unlimited powers which were vested in the Cheka attracted into its service not only men of a very brutal type from the poorer classes, who delighted in the opportunity to "send to the other world" representatives of the hated aristocracy and middle classes, but also many rogues and adventurers, quick to scent the opportunity for illegal loot. Sometimes such men were caught and executed; but more often they escaped detection, because the fear which the Cheka inspired in the masses of the population was so great that few people, especially if they belonged to the proscribed "bourgeoisie," ventured to complain of its activities.

The Red Terror was intended to be and was, in the main, at least in the towns, a class terror, directed against the formerly powerful and well-to-do classes. While numerically probably the largest number of persons executed were peasants who rose up against requisitions or abuses on the part of the local authorities, the men and women who were picked out for slaughter in the towns were, as a rule, people of wealth, education or former social standing: pre-War officers and officials, with members of their families, former factory owners and country squires, priests and merchants. Typical news items in the chronicle of the Cheka for the autumn of 1918 [10] were the execution of thirty-nine "prominent landlords of the Western Region" by the Smolensk Cheka and the decision of the Nizhni Novgorod Cheka to shoot "forty-one people from the hostile camp." In the list of names one finds five colonels, five captains, several capitalists, former police agents, etc. Every member of the Romanov family who fell into the hands of the Bolsheviki was put to death.

That the terror sometimes deviated from its main object, the former propertied classes, and struck at quite ordinary people, and even at workers, is apparent if one reads the few copies of the Menshevik newspaper, *Always Forward,* which were permitted to appear during the civil war. A woman named Frumkina, then a member of the Bund, later a Communist, testified to the Ural Committee of the Communist Party that she had been arrested in the little Ural town of Krasnoufimsk and taken as a hostage to Perm. Among the persons whom she reported as shot were an old revolutionary, Dmitry Vershinin, a Labor member of the Second Duma, Ershov, a dentist named Kleshelsky and a notary, Meder, and his wife, the latter because their stepson had fled. Goldin, the chief figure in the local Cheka, had said, while examining the wife of Meder: "If you don't give up your son we will break your arms and legs, and then finish with you." [11] After a hunger riot in Ozeri, near Kolomna, a Menshevik worker named Gorbatov, along with eight other workers, was shot, although Gorbatov is said to have taken no active part in the riot.[12]

The rule of terror which was incarnated in the Cheka, with its right to execute without formal trial, did not cease throughout the whole period of the civil war; indeed, it has continued under various forms up to the present time. But the intensity of the Red Terror varied appreciably with time and circumstances. It was at its height during the months immediately after the assassination of Uritzky and the attack on Lenin. Then the collapse of the anti-Bolshevik front on the Volga and the German Revolution, with the consequent cessation of the German occupation of Ukraina, greatly eased the internal position and led to relaxation of the terror. One sign of this was the substitution of political departments, attached to the militia, for the county Chekas, which had committed some of the worst atrocities, on January 24, 1919.[13] Another was the temporary and fitful legalization of newspapers published by the Mensheviki and Socialist Revolutionaries,—a grudging concession which was quickly withdrawn when the situation became more serious with the rise of the strongest White armies, those of Admiral Kolchak in Siberia and of General Denikin in South Russia.

After the defeat of Kolchak and Denikin there was a short-lived tendency toward mildness, which found expression in the decree of January 19, 1920, when the death penalty was abolished, except on the fronts. This decree, however, seems to have been observed for a very short time, if at all; the war with Poland, the continued resistance of the last of the White leaders, General Baron Wrangel, in the Crimea and the difficulty of subduing the unruly Ukrainian peasantry all tended to preserve a system of ruthless severity. Only after the civil war was definitely ended the Cheka was reorganized and renamed as the OGPU, or United State Political Administration.

The number of persons who were put to death by the Cheka cannot be established with any degree of certainty. In the first flush of the terror, in the summer and autumn of 1918, the Soviet authorities, wishing to create as much fear as possible in the hearts of their enemies, pursued the policy of publishing fairly regular figures, accompanied by names in some instances, of the numbers of victims of Cheka shootings. Later the opinion apparently prevailed that too great frankness in this matter was injurious to the prestige of the Soviet regime abroad, and that secrecy in regard to the numbers of executions might perhaps create still greater terror. It is a fact of common knowledge among Russians that one of the most sweeping outbursts of terrorism occurred in the Crimea after the defeat and evacuation of Wrangel. Immense numbers of persons suspected of having had any connection with Wrangel's regime were rounded up and shot in Sevastopol and other towns. On this point I have the testimony of a number of Russians who were resident in the Crimea at this time. But one searches the Soviet newspapers of the time in vain for any reference to this massacre, which was carried out under the direction of Bela Kun, the defeated Soviet dictator of Hungary, who had escaped to Russia after the collapse of the Hungarian Soviet Republic, and of Zemlyachka, a fanatical woman veteran Bolshevik.

M. Y. Latzis, a prominent Chekist, states [14] that 12,733 persons were shot in all Russia by the Cheka during the first three years of its existence, which would cover the whole period of the civil war. But there are very strong reasons for regarding this figure as a gross underestimate. The same Latzis, in another work,[15] asserts that the Cheka, during 1918 and the first seven months of 1919, shot 8,389 people *only in twenty provinces of Central Russia* (my italics). Now there were other parts of Russia where the civil war was much more protracted and fierce than in Central Russia, and where the number of victims of terrorism must have been far greater. There was Ukraina, where the peasantry, being more well-to-do and more attached to the homestead system, fought much more stubbornly against Bolshevism than the poorer peasants of Central Russia. There was the Ural Territory, where, by general agreement, there was a savage struggle, marked by wholesale killings on both sides. There were the Don and Kuban Territories, strongholds of the White movement, where the dissatisfaction of the Cossacks certainly created an abundance of work for the local Chekas. Many Russians are convinced that the victims of Bela Kun and Zemlyachka in the Crimea run into tens of thousands. There is certainly every probability that they were numbered in thousands.[16] As has been pointed out, large-scale organized terror began only in July, 1918. With the Cheka admitting 8,389 executions in twenty provinces of Central Russia during the first year of a struggle that lasted for approximately two and a half years, and with the struggle often most bitter just in outlying parts of the country, it is simply impossible to believe that the Cheka only put to death 12,733 people in all Russia up to the end of the civil war. While any estimate, in view of the lack of reliable data, must be highly conjectural and approximate, I should consider it probable that about fifty thousand persons were put to death in the course of the Red Terror during the period of the civil war. This, of course, would not include insurgents who were shot down with arms in their hands or people who were killed by mobs or by uncontrolled bands of soldiers and sailors.

Some confirmation of the probability of my approximate estimate of fifty thousand as the number of persons put to death by the Cheka and definite refutation of Latzis's much lower figure are furnished by an interesting document in the possession of the Russian Foreign Archive in Prague. This document bears the title: "Otchet Tsentralnogo Upravlenie Chrezvichainnikh Komissii pri Sovnarkome Ukraini za 1920 God" (Report of the Extraordinary Commissions under the Council of People's Commissars of Ukraina for 1920) and was published in Kharkov in 1921. This report states that, during 1920, 3,879 persons were shot by the Extraordinary Commissions in Ukraina, the Odessa Cheka making the most sanguinary record with 1,418 executions and the Kiev Cheka following with 538. If almost four thousand persons are officially stated to have been put to death by the Cheka in Ukraina in one of the three years of civil war (Ukraina contains about a fifth of the population of the entire area affected by civil war), it would seem that fifty thousand is a reasonable and probably moderate estimate of the total number of victims of Red Terror.

Some time after the civil war was over a story began to circulate that the Bolsheviki had put to death over 1,700,000 persons during the Terror. It was not supported by any documentary proof; and, on the basis of the available evidence, it would seem to be a wild exaggeration, just as the statement of Latzis, the Cheka official and apologist, is, in all probability, a substantial understatement. In general, it should be noted that, while an abundance of ghastly and revolting atrocities were certainly committed on both sides, Red and White authors alike, with a few exceptions, display a tendency greatly to exaggerate the numbers of persons killed by their opponents, while minimizing or glossing over the terroristic activities of their own side.

The figures for executions in twenty provinces of Central Russia classify the causes of the shootings as follows: participation in uprisings, 3,082; membership in counterrevolutionary organizations, 2,024; appeals to revolt, 455; banditism, 643; espionage, 102; desertion, 102; crimes in office, 206; other causes, 1,704. Among the "others" were presumably many who were shot as hostages or simply because they belonged to the richer classes.

By one of the curious ironies of the Revolution the head of the Cheka, an organization which certainly attracted into its service many brutal and sadistic individuals and which was associated not only with appalling bloodshed, but also with a good deal of corruption, was an old revolutionary of the most unimpeachable idealism. This was Felix Dzerzhinsky, who had spent a quarter of his life before the Revolution in prison and who remarked to a British woman sculptor, Clare Sheridan, who came to Moscow to make busts of the Soviet leaders and who spoke of his extraordinary patience during the sitting: "One learns patience in prison." In contrast to the majority of his collaborators, who came from the grim industrial slums and sordid ghettoes of Eastern Europe, Dzerzhinsky was of an old, although poor, aristocratic Polish family. His colleagues, after his death in 1926, paid the highest tributes to his personal modesty and austerity, his absolute fearlessness, his intense concentration on his work.[17] Dzerzhinsky slept in the building of the Cheka and often remained there for days at a time without taking a breath of fresh air. So severe was his austerity that he resented it when his employees tried to procure him bacon and potatoes as a substitute for the horseflesh which was the general fare in those hungry years.

Perhaps if Dzerzhinsky, in his student days, before he had definitely become an extremist Social Democrat, could have seen in anticipation his future subordinates of the Nolinsk Cheka, with their preference for "refined tortures," he might have hesitated before embarking on his revolutionary career. But long years in prison and in harassed underground work had hardened him, as it had hardened many other old Bolsheviki. Convinced that in a period of civil war and many internal plots and uprisings a punitive organization which would strike hard and ruthlessly was absolutely necessary, he gave himself entirely to the work of building up the Cheka, repressing its abuses when they were brought to his attention, doubtless realizing that many acts of ferocity and corruption went unpunished, but discounting these with the argument, ever beloved of fanatics, that the end justifies the means.

The theoretical justification of the Red Terror was that the

Soviet regime could not survive without it. As Lenin wrote on one occasion: "When a revolutionary class struggles against the propertied classes, which resist it, it must crush this resistance; and we will suppress the resistance of the propertied with the same means by which the propertied suppressed the proletariat; other means have not been invented."

Lenin expressed his view still more strongly in his letter to the American workers, written when the crisis of 1918 was in its height. In that letter is the following passage: [18]

> "The bourgeoisie of international imperialism killed ten million and mutilated twenty million human beings in 'its' war, a war to decide whether British or German robbers should rule the whole world.
>
> "If our war, the war of the oppressed and exploited against the oppressors and exploiters, will cost half a million or a million victims in all countries the bourgeoisie will say that the former sacrifices were justified, the latter criminal.
>
> "The proletariat will say something quite different."

A vehement and declamatory exaltation of Red Terror is to be found in a note of reply which Chicherin on September 12, 1918, addressed to the diplomatic representatives of the neutral powers in Petrograd, who had officially expressed "deep indignation against the regime of terror established in Petrograd, Moscow and other cities." The concluding passages of Chicherin's reply read as follows: [19]

> "In all the capitalist world rules the regime of White Terror against the working class. The working class of Russia destroyed the Tsarist Government, the sanguinary regime of which called forth no protests of the neutral powers. The working class destroyed in Russia the rule of the bourgeoisie, which, under the banner of revolution, amid the silence of the neutral powers, shot down soldiers who no longer desired to shed their blood for the interests of war speculators. They shot down peasants because they proclaimed as their own property land which they had sowed for hundreds of years and which they fertilized with their sweat. The overwhelming majority of the Russian people, in the form of the Second Congress of Workers', Peasants', Soldiers' and Cossacks' Deputies, transferred power into the hands of the Workers' and Peasants' Government. A handful of capitalists, who wished to get back the factories and the banks which were taken away from them for the benefit of the whole people, a handful of landlords, who desired to take away from the peasants their land, a handful of generals, who desired to teach the workers and peasants submission again with the whip, did not recognize this decision of the Russian people. With the help of the money of foreign capital they mobilize counterrevolutionary bands, with the help of which they cut

Russia off from bread, so that the bony hand of hunger may throttle the Russian Revolution. Convinced of the impossibility of overthrowing the Workers' Government, which is supported by the masses of the people, by the hands of these masses, they organize counterrevolutionary uprisings, in order to tear the Workers' and Peasants' Government away from constructive work, to prevent it from bringing the country out of the anarchy into which the criminal policy of former governments pushed it. They sold Russia in the South, in the North, in the East, to foreign imperialist states, summoning foreign bayonets from wherever they could get them. From behind the forest of foreign bayonets they send hired murderers, in order to remove the leaders of the working class, in whom not only the proletariat of Russia, but all tortured humanity sees the incarnation of its hopes.

"The Russian working people will mercilessly suppress this counterrevolutionary clique, which enjoys the support of foreign capital and of the Russian bourgeoisie, which desires to cast around the neck of the Russian people the noose of slavery and war. We say before the proletariat of the whole world that no hypocritical protests and pleas will hold back the hand which will punish those who take up arms against the workers and poorest peasants of Russia, who want to starve them, to drive them into new wars for the sake of the interests of capital. We guaranty equal rights and freedom to all who loyally carry out all the obligations which rest on citizens of the Workers' and Peasants' Socialist Russian Republic. To them we bring peace, to our enemies merciless war, and we are convinced that the masses of all countries, oppressed and terrorized by little cliques of exploiters, will understand that in Russia violence is employed only for the sake of the sacred interests of liberation of the masses, that they will not only understand us, but will follow our example.

"We most vigorously decline the interference of the neutral capitalist powers in favor of the Russian bourgeoisie and we state that we shall regard any attempt of the representatives of these powers to go beyond the legal defense of the interests of their citizens as an attempt to support the Russian counterrevolution."

So much for the theory of Soviet terrorism. In regard to its practise and technique one finds interesting observations in the booklet of Latzis, who, along with Peters and Boki, was one of the most dreaded of Ozerzhinsky's lieutenants: [20]

"It is necessary to show the greatest strictness, pitilessness, directness in the very beginning; deserved punishment must follow the crime; then many fewer victims fall on both sides. This is the wisdom which three years of civil war taught us. . . . The highest measure of punishment was applied most of all for the purpose of influencing the counterrevolutionary element, of producing the necessary effect, terrorization. . . . Shooting must be applied when the work of counterrevolutionists finds expression in open armed activity, when plots are revealed, when there are uprisings. . . . But it is very often necessary to resort to this measure when there is still no direct danger."

The Cheka, which started out with a small staff of workers, expanded rapidly and at one time numbered 31,000 employees. The provincial Chekas had their own detachments of troops, for self-protection and for the suppression of the continual little uprisings within the country. It had several departments: a secret operative department for "struggle with counterrevolution," a special department for work in the Armies, a transport department for control of the railroads, an organization-administrative department, which attended to technical office work and kept up communication with the provinces. Extraordinary Commissions in provincial towns were supposed to have four branches: (1) for combating counter-revolution; (2) for combating speculation; (3) for combating crimes committed by officials; (4) an External Department, which maintained communication with other towns and with the centre.[21]

As might have been expected, there was a good deal of friction between the Chekas, with their sweeping and practically unlimited powers and the local Soviet authorities. An example of such friction was a case which occurred in Kursk in the autumn of 1918. The local Cheka had arrested a military instructor named Zunblat, whereupon the provincial military Commissar, Mazalov, announced that he would liberate by armed force any of his employees who were arrested without his knowledge or consent.

The Cheka was successful in guarding its position as a special and privileged organization. Dzerzhinsky on August 29, 1918, sent out a circular order, pointing out that there had been many disputes between the Chekas and the Soviets and instructing the former to preserve the closest relations with the latter, simultaneously informing the Soviets that they might not change or cancel the orders which emanated from the All-Russian Extraordinary Commission. Peters later defined the rights of the Cheka still more vigorously: "In its activity the Cheka is completely independent, carrying out searches, arrests, shootings, afterwards making a report to the Council of People's Commissars and the Soviet Central Executive Committee."[22]

Lockhart, who could base his opinion on a good deal of personal experience, describes the Cheka as "terrifying, but far from clever,"[23] and gives several instances of how he and his assistants were able to destroy compromising documents almost under the eyes of the Cheka search agents. This was quite natural, because the Cheka had to build up its organization from the bottom with inexperienced and untrained people. Such successes as it achieved in exposing genuine plots were attributable not to any detective finesse on its part, but to its complete lack of restriction in such matters as arresting whom it pleased, and threatening its prisoners with torture or death; and also to the clumsiness of some of the anti-Soviet plotters.

Terror was by no means a characteristic exclusively of the Soviet regime. The White Governments which arose in opposition to it gave short shrift to real or suspected Bolsheviki; and not a few of the wilder military chieftains who raised bands of followers and fought on the White side (Pokrovsky and Shkuro in the Kuban, Annenkov and Ivanov-Rinov in Siberia, Semyenov and Kalmykov in the Far East, to mention a few of the more notorious) rolled up atrocity records that would compare fairly with those of the worst provincial Chekas.

It is far more difficult to gain even an approximate idea of the number of victims of the White Terror than of those of the Red Terror. The Cheka, the main instrument of the Red Terror, was a centralized organization which kept some account, although not, one suspects, a very complete or regular one, of its killings. The White Governments had their *kontrarazvyedka* (counter-espionage), which, like the Cheka, acquired a bad reputation both for indiscriminate killing and for blackmailing the relatives of its victims. But by far the largest number of persons who met a violent end under the regime of the Whites seem to have come to their death not as a result of any regular trial, or even of a summary verdict by a drumhead courtmartial, but were simply slaughtered by more or less irresponsible bands of soldiers whose leaders certainly kept no records of their actions.

A few excerpts from the reminiscences of White leaders and of observers on their territory, however, convey a fair idea of the ruthlessness which characterized the White, as well as the Red movement. "I had 370 Bolshevik officers and non-commissioned officers shot on the spot," writes Wrangel.[24] Drozdovsky, who marched across Ukraina with an officers' detachment to join Denikin in the spring of 1918, tells how in the village Maleevka his men "beat everyone hard with bayonets," while in Melitopol "they caught and liquidated forty-two Bolsheviki." General Denisov, one of Krasnov's chief lieutenants in the Don, writing of the early days of the White regime, says: "It was necessary to exterminate without any mercy persons who were detected in coöperation with the Bolsheviki." In Siberia under Kolchak many political prisoners were killed with the internationally familiar, and highly suspicious explanation that they were shot "while trying to escape"; among the victims of Kolchak's terror, some of the worst acts of which were probably carried out without the knowledge or desire of the Admiral, by the chiefs of Cossack detachments, who often acted without waiting for orders, were many Socialist Revolutionaries, who had taken part in overthrowing the Siberian Soviets in the summer.

One of Kolchak's Generals, Rozanov, proved an apt pupil of the Bolsheviki in the matter of taking and shooting hostages; he ordered in the spring of 1919 that local Bolsheviki in prison should be regarded as hostages for the security of the railroad; and that any attacks on the railroad line by Red partisan bands should be followed by the execution of from three to twenty hostages.[25]

Instances of White, as of Red, atrocities could be multiplied indefinitely; only a blind partisan would endeavor to deny that the civil war which followed the Russian Revolution was fought on both sides with extraordinary ferocity. The fiercest episodes of the British Civil War of the seventeenth century or of the American Civil War seem mild compared with the regular practise of the contending sides in Russia. Indeed it is not improbable that the numbers of people killed by the Cheka, by the White military executioners, by the punitive expeditions which both sides employed very freely against recalcitrant peasants, may have very easily exceeded the losses in the civil war battles, which, measured by the standards of the World War, were extremely light, largely as a result of the lack of will to fight on the part of the masses of peasant troops on both sides.

One reason why no government could have survived in Russia in those years without the use of terrorism was that the national morale was completely shattered by the World War. No one, except under extreme compulsion, was willing to perform any state obligation. The old order had simply crumbled away; a new order, with new habits and standards of conduct, had not yet formed; very often the only way in which a governmental representative, whether he was a Bolshevik commissar or a White officer, could get his orders obeyed was by flourishing a revolver.

At least equally important as a factor which determined the fierceness of the struggle was the greatness of the social stakes involved. To the Bolsheviki victory meant the first successful blow for the world revolution, the first overthrow of the hated power of capital. This was the idealistic side of the case. Looked at from the more personal angle, the victory of the Red Army meant that the conglomeration of new rulers who had thrust out of power the old aristocracy and the old bureaucracy, and also the soft liberal and radical intelligentsia who had come to the fore under Kerensky, —such types as the veteran Bolshevik with his years of exile and prison and his dogmatic faith, the worker from the Putilov factory who had become the President of a Soviet, the ex-sailor or soldier who was now a Red commander, the Jew from the small town who was now a commissar—would stay in power. Defeat meant for them, at the worst, death, perhaps in painful forms, at the best, a dreary return to a bare and forlorn round of life. Decidedly Red Terror seemed a cheap price to pay for victory.

A corresponding feeling that the civil war must be won at any cost, that Bolshevism must be smashed, prevailed, quite naturally, among the Whites. To them victory meant a return of what had been to them a comfortable, natural and reasonable social order which had suddenly tumbled to bits about their ears. Defeat might well mean death at the hands of the Cheka or a hunted existence in Russia, or the dreary life of the *émigré* in Paris or Belgrade or Harbin. If "firm measures" were necessary to open the road to Moscow they were glad to see them applied. One side regarded itself as fighting for the establishment of a new civilization; the other considered itself the champion of an old one. And both were quite ready to employ the most barbarous measures to promote their cause. So Russia's great revolution of the twentieth century, in its course of development, proved grimly reminiscent of the vast upheavals associated with the names of Stenka Razin or Pugachev, in which Russia's "Reds" and "Whites" of the seventeenth and eighteenth centuries vied with each other in ferocity.

NOTES

[1] *Izvestia,* for September 3, 1918.

[2] *Ibid.,* for September 4.

[3] Presumably Petrovsky meant by "Czecho-Slavia" the territory occupied by the Czecho-Slovaks.

[4] *Cf. Pravda,* for September 5, 1918.

[5] "Memories of a British Agent," pp. 314ff.

[6] While no official statement in regard to this curious case was ever published, it would seem that Reilly was lured into Russia by Gay-Pay-Oo agents, masquerading as monarchists, and then arrested and shot.

[7] *Izvestia,* for September 29, 1918.

[8] There are six extant numbers of this weekly organ of the Cheka, the first one being dated September 22, 1918. It is not clear whether the *Bulletin* ceased to be published after its sixth issue or whether it was deemed expedient to withdraw it

from general circulation. However this may be, the *Bulletin* is one of the most valuable of the few available sources of official information about the Cheka.

[9] *Cf. Bulletin of the Cheka,* No. 4, for October 13, 1918.

[10] *Ibid.,* No. 6, for October 27.

[11] *Cf. Vsyegda Vperyed* (Always Forward), No. 1, for January 22, 1919. The Mensheviki were able to issue a few copies of this newspaper during the time when they enjoyed a semi-legal status.

[12] *Ibid.,* for January 29.

[13] M. Y. Latzis, "The Extraordinary Commissions for Struggle with Counterrevolution," pp. 28, 29.

[14] *Ibid.,* p. 9.

[15] *Cf.* his "Two Years of Struggle on the Internal Front," p. 74.

[16] Among the major mass killings by the Cheka, of which there is no official or numerical record, but of which I have obtained what I consider convincing testimony from persons resident in the towns at the times, were those in the prisons of Kiev and on the eve of the evacuation of these cities before the advance of General Denikin in the summer of 1919; in the prison of Ekaterinodar in the summer of 1920, when this town was threatened with recapture from the Reds by the forces of General Wrangel; and in Tashkent, after an officer named Ossipov had made an unsuccessful effort to overthrow the Soviet regime in Turkestan in January, 1919.

[17] *Cf.* the contributions of Y. Peters and M. Y. Latzis in "Felix Dzerzhinsky," pp. 144–177.

[18] "Collected Works," Vol. XV, p. 411.

[19] *Cf.* Professor U. V. Kluchnikov and Andrei Sabanin, "Recent International Policy in Treaties, Notes and Declarations," Part II, pp. 167ff., for the complete texts of this diplomatic interchange of notes.

[20] "The Extraordinary Commissions for Struggle with Counterrevolution," pp. 9ff.

[21] *Cf. Bulletin of the Cheka,* No. 1, p. 9.

[22] *Ibid.,* No. 2, pp. 11, 12.

[23] "Memoirs of a British Agent," p. 309.

[24] "Memoirs of General Wrangel," p. 59.

[25] *Cf.* the Siberian newspaper, *Golos Rabochego* ("The Voice of the Worker"), for May 25, 1919.

CHAPTER XXIV

THE END OF THE TSARIST FAMILY

THE captivity of the former Tsar Nicholas II and his family passed through three phases, each of which was affected by the changing political conditions in the country. The first part of the captivity was spent in the former imperial palace of Tsarskoe Syelo, where the family suffered few deprivations, apart from the limitations placed on its liberty. The second phase was in the remote Siberian town of Tobolsk, where, after the Bolshevik Revolution, living conditions became much harder and the attitude of the guards more hostile. The last phase was spent in the Ural industrial town of Ekaterinburg, where rough Bolshevik workers kept the Tsar and his family under the closest observation and where, as the front of the civil war rolled closer and closer to the town, the shadow of approaching doom became constantly darker and more imminent.

The subnormal passivity of the Tsar's character made him bear his deposition and confinement with less visible chafing than a more active sovereign might have shown. If one reads through the pages of his diary during the period of his captivity [1] one sees no evidence of a desire to take up the burdens of state from which he had been forcibly relieved. On his forty-ninth birthday, on May 19th, he notes: "Much more with my dear family than in ordinary years."

Nicholas II was notably devoted to his wife and children; and he seems to have enjoyed the new possibility of spending more time with them, teaching his incurably sick son, Aleksei, history and geography, playing cards with his wife and daughters. In June he writes: "It is hard to be without news of dear mama; as for the rest, it is of no consequence." He often records birthdays, name-days, anniversaries in his diaries, sometimes with prayers. So on August 1 one finds the entry: "Three years ago Germany declared war on us; it seems that we have lived through a whole existence during those three years. Lord, help and save Russia"

His comments on political affairs are very much what might be expected, in view of his background and views. He rejoices at the few Russian victories. On one occasion he remarks, in regard to Kerensky: "This man is advantageous in his place at the present moment; the more power he will have, the better." He greets the restoration of the death penalty at the front, observing: "if only this measure wasn't taken too late."

In the latter part of July Kerensky paid a visit to the Tsar and informed him that he would soon be sent away from Tsarskoe Syelo. And on the morning of August 14 the imperial family, accompanied by a suite of thirty-five persons, tutors, attendants and servants, left Tsarskoe Syelo for Tobolsk, an isolated Siberian provincial town, which lies on the Irtish River, some distance to the north of the main line of the Trans-Siberian Railroad.

The trip was carried out with the greatest secrecy. Two comfortable trains, marked as belonging to the Japanese Red Cross, were used for the transportation of the family; and a guard of 330 picked soldiers, under the command of Colonel Kobilinsky, an officer who had been disabled for active service at the front, and who enjoyed the confidence and friendship of the family, accompanied them to Tobolsk.

The disorderly fighting which had taken place on the streets of Petrograd in mid-July apparently was a main factor in causing the Provisional Government to send the imperial family to a more tranquil place. New disturbances in the capital were regarded as not improbable, especially in the event of a clash between the Government and the Petrograd Soviet; and a riotous mob might have easily attacked the palace at Tsarskoe Syelo. The Tsar would have preferred his palace at Livadia, on the beautiful southern coast of the Crimea, as a residence; but the Provisional Government preferred Tobolsk for two reasons: it seemed less exposed than the Crimea, where the Black Sea Fleet was stationed, to outbursts of disorder; and less criticism was to be apprehended from the Soviets and from the radical groups in the population if the Tsar were not despatched to a well-known palace. By sending the Tsar, the Tsarina and their children to a place far away from any seaport the Provisional Government, quite unconsciously and unintentionally, sealed their death warrants in the event that the Revolution should take a more violent turn to the left. It is difficult to say with certainty what would have happened to the imperial family if they had been permitted to proceed to the

Crimea. They might have been slaughtered even earlier by the Black Sea sailors or they might have been rescued by the Germans.

As the Tsar and the Tsarina travelled by boat on the last stage of the journey to Tobolsk they could see Pokrovskoe, the native village of Rasputin, who had played such a disastrous rôle in their lives. Curiously enough, the fatal link with Rasputin was not broken even by the death of the latter. An adventurer named Soloviev, who married one of Rasputin's daughters, settled in Tyumen, the nearest large town in the vicinity of Tobolsk. He won the confidence of the highstrung, credulous Tsarina, who apparently believed that he shared some of Rasputin's supposed mystical powers, and acted as an agent in forwarding letters and messages to and from the former court favorite, Virubova, and others in Petrograd and Moscow. Soloviev seems to have told the Tsarina all sorts of fantastic tales and persuaded her to believe that in Tyumen there were hundreds of monarchist officers, waiting for the first opportunity to rescue the family. She was brought to such a point of delusion that when Red Guards arrived from Omsk, the administrative centre of Western Siberia, she believed that among them were devoted monarchists in disguise.[2] Soloviev and some confederates created around the family a secret wall against the outside world and permitted no monarchist agent to visit them unless he came to terms with them. In this way they secured most of the money which monarchist groups collected and sent for the relief of the family and thwarted the activities of some officers who came from Petrograd and Moscow.

In the beginning the stay of the Tsar in Tobolsk, where he was lodged in the former governor's home, while it was dull, was not unpleasant. In this quiet town many probably believed that the monarchy would return and retained their respect for the former autocrat. When people passed the house they often took off their caps. The nuns in a neighboring monastery brought gifts of eggs, sugar and whipped cream.

At first the family was under the very mild tutelage of Colonel Kobilinsky. In September a political commissar arrived, a man named Pankratov, a Socialist Revolutionary who had served a term of some years in the fortress-prison of Schlüsselburg, on account of his revolutionary activities. Despite his own sufferings Pankratov seems to have been quite free from any spirit of petty revengefulness. There were a few cases of minor friction; but as a rule he exercised his power tactfully and humanely.[3] The placid family life of Tsarskoe Syelo continued; the Tsar habitually read aloud in the evenings, while his daughters sewed and the Tsarina played bezique with General Tatishev, a member of the suite.

The situation for the prisoners changed definitely for the worse after the Bolshevik Revolution. The news of what had happened in Moscow and Petrograd reached Tobolsk with a delay of about two weeks; and several months elapsed before a local Soviet regime was set up in Tobolsk. But the vast social upheaval all over Russia found its reflection in the conduct of the detachment of soldiers which was guarding the Tsar. They became more insubordinate to their commander, Colonel Kobilinsky, and to the commissar, Pankratov; a corporal named Matveev took the initiative in organizing a soldiers' committee, which adopted a much more hostile and suspicious attitude toward the imperial family. After an incident when the Tsar was greeted by one of the officiating ecclesiastics in the Tobolsk church with his old titles the soldiers decided that members of the family could worship only in private and could not attend church any longer. About the same time, in December, the members of the suite were transferred from a separate house which they had formerly occupied and were placed in the dwelling of the imperial family, which consequently became uncomfortably crowded. After a jolly party in which the Tsar, in a Cossack uniform, went to the room of the English tutor of the Tsarevitch, Gibbs, the soldiers organized a search and took away sabres from the Tsar, from Dolgorukov, a member of the suite, and from Gilliard, a French tutor.

Apart from the general revolutionary mood of the country, the soldiers were exasperated by the nonreceipt of their pay; the Provisional Government, in the last weeks of its existence, apparently forgot about the maintenance of the imperial family; and Kobilinsky had to raise funds by borrowing wherever he could. After the Bolshevik Revolution the imperial family began to experience genuine deprivations; butter and coffee were excluded from their table as articles of luxury; they were obliged to dismiss ten servants and were forbidden to spend more than six hundred rubles a month apiece.[4]

A detachment of Red Guards from Omsk appeared in Tobolsk in March under the command of a Lett named Dutzman; it behaved quietly and did not molest the prisoners. In the following month a much more aggressive detachment of Ural workers under the command of a certain Zaslavsky arrived from Ekaterinburg; Zaslavsky wanted to put the whole family in the local prison; but Kobilinsky parried this demand by suggesting that in that case the soldiers would also have to be lodged in the prison, in order to guard them,—a proposal which did not commend itself to the Red Guards. Pankratov had been deposed some time before; Kobilinsky also wanted to leave, feeling that he no longer possessed any influence over the soldiers, but had stayed on at the request of the Tsar.

A decisive turn in the fate of the imperial family occurred on April 22, when a commissar named Yakovlev, provided with credentials from the Soviet Central Executive Committee, arrived with a detachment of mounted Red Guards and proposed to take away the family to an unknown destination. It was impossible to move the boy, Aleksei, who, as often happened, was ailing; but the Tsar, the Tsarina and one of the princesses, Maria, left Tobolsk under the escort of Yakovlev and his guard on April 26 and reached Tyumen on the 27th.

The figure of Yakovlev is a decidedly enigmatical one in the whole tragedy of the Romanov family. Apparently he was a man of education and knew several foreign languages. That he was not a reliable Bolshevik is evident from the fact that during the civil war he passed over from the Red Army to the Whites. What he intended to do, after having taken charge of the person of the Tsar, is obscure. Apparently he was supposed to bring the imperial family to Ekaterinburg, an industrial town in the heart of the Urals, which the higher Soviet authorities regarded as a safer place of confinement than remote Tobolsk. But instead of taking the Tsar and Tsarina directly to Ekaterinburg, Yakovlev started on a train eastward, in the direction of Omsk. When the Ural Soviet learned of this it proclaimed him a traitor to the Revolution and an outlaw and sent instructions to the Omsk Soviet to stop him.

Yakovlev's train was surrounded with Soviet troops at Kolumzino, a station on the way to Omsk; he yielded to the superior force and turned back to Ekaterinburg. Why he acted contrary to his own original instructions is a matter of conjecture. N. Sokolov, the judicial investigator who made the most complete study of the circumstances attending the killing of the Tsar, expresses the view, for which, however, definite proof is certainly lacking, that Yakovlev was acting in the interest of the Germans.[5] P. Bikov,

President of the Ekaterinburg Soviet in 1918, who has written the most complete Soviet account of the affair, states: [6]

> "Later it was revealed that Yakovlev, knowing that the Romanovs would be shot in the Ural Territory, decided to save them and planned to take them out of the train on the way to Samara and to hide them for a time in the mountains."

Whatever may be the truth of the matter, Yakovlev was apparently able to give a satisfactory explanation to the authorities in Moscow, because, notwithstanding his sharp dispute with the Ural Soviet, which suspected him of double dealing, he was subsequently employed in a responsible military capacity in the Red Army, until the time of his desertion to the Whites.

According to one of his guards, Corporal Matveev, the Tsar declared that he would rather go anywhere than to the Urals "because the workers were apparently very hostile to him." His apprehensions were fully justified; and the rough treatment which was accorded to the imperial family in the Ipatiev House, a two-story dwelling in the centre of the town which was assigned to them in Ekaterinburg, was a plain intimation of their impending fate.

The guards, who were mostly Bolshevik workers from the Ural factories, watched every move of the prisoners and took every opportunity to show rudeness. When the princesses (the other members of the family followed the Tsar, the Tsarina and the Princess Maria to Ekaterinburg as soon as the Tsarevitch had recovered sufficiently to travel) went to the toilet the guards followed them to the door, making coarse observations. The food became much worse than it had been in Tobolsk; the family received tea and black bread in the morning; their dinner in the afternoon was sent in from a Soviet restaurant and was served to them on a table without a cloth. The Princesses slept on the floor for lack of beds.[7]

The Soviet and Communist leaders originally desired to hold a public trial of the Romanovs in Ekaterinburg, with Trotzky in the rôle of public prosecutor.[8] Judged from the example of earlier revolutions this trial would certainly have resulted in a verdict of death for the Tsar, most probably also for the Tsarina. It is easy to imagine how Trotzky would have excelled himself in bitter revolutionary denunciation, making the Tsar responsible for all Russia's miseries, from the accidental trampling to death of many people who attended his coronation in Moscow to the wholesale carnage of the World War.

The unforeseen course of the civil war, however, led to a simpler, more expeditious and more ruthless decision: to exterminate the entire family. No court could well have passed capital sentences on young children; but they could easily be disposed of in a secret and more or less unofficial killing. Early in July Ekaterinburg was threatened from two sides by the advancing Czechs and the Russian anti-Bolshevik forces who were fighting on their side. At this time the Ural Soviet Military Commissar, a veteran Bolshevik named Goleschekin, went to Moscow and conferred with the President of the Soviet Executive Committee, Sverdlov, who probably authorized the Ural leaders to take whatever steps the changing situation might require. Although the uprising against the Bolsheviki in Siberia, in the Volga and Ural Regions had not put forward the restoration of monarchy as its aim, although Socialist Revolutionaries were prominently identified with this movement in its first stages, there was potential political danger, from the Bolshevik standpoint, in a rescue of the imperial family by their enemies.

The decision to kill all the members of the family, together with the Tsar's personal physician, Botkin, and three servants, was taken at a meeting of the Ural Territorial Soviet on July 12. The military authorities reported that Ekaterinburg could not hold out more than three days.[9] As Bikov writes: [10] "In connection with this fact the Territorial Soviet decided to shoot the Romanovs without awaiting trial. It was proposed that the commanders of the guard, with the aid of some reliable Communist workers, should carry out the shooting and the destruction of the corpses." The decision to destroy the corpses was taken because of fear that the anti-Soviet leaders might arouse the peasants by displaying the bones of the Tsar as sacred relics.

The man who was commissioned to carry out the killing was a Jew named Jacob Yurovsky, who had been born in Siberia, who had subsequently lived for a time abroad, in Berlin, where he became converted to Lutheranism, and then returned to Russia and kept a photographer's shop. Yurovsky was one of the countless obscure people whom the Revolution for a time brought into historical notoriety. He had been a hospital assistant in the War, took an active part in stirring up the soldiers against the officers and became a member of the Ural Soviet.

The factory workers who had originally acted as guards in the Ipatiev House were replaced by special men from the Cheka, among whom there were a number of Letts. About midnight on the night of July 16 Yurovsky awakened the members of the Tsarist family and told them to dress and come into the basement of the house, as there was danger of shooting in the town. Their preparations were completed in about an hour and the doomed family, with the physician, Botkin, the cook, Kharitonov, the waiter, Trupp, and the chambermaid, Demidova, walked down the staircase and went into the basement. They were quite calm and apparently had no apprehension of what was to happen. The Tsar carried the Tsarevitch in his arms.[11]

The Tsar stood in the middle of the room, at his side the Tsarevitch sat in a chair; on his right stood Doctor Botkin. The Tsarina and her daughters stood behind them near the wall; the three servants stood in corners of the room. Yurovsky told the Tsar (there is no clear record of the precise words which he used) that he was to be put to death. The Tsar did not understand and began to say "What?" whereupon Yurovsky shot him down with his revolver. This was the signal for the general massacre. The other executioners, seven Letts and two agents from the Cheka, emptied their revolvers into the bodies of the victims. The Tsar fell first, followed by his son. The room was filled with shrieks and groans; blood poured in streams on the floor. The chambermaid, Demidova, tried to protect herself with a pillow, and delayed her death for a short time. The slaughter was soon ended; Yurovsky fired two additional bullets into the body of the Tsarevitch, who was still groaning and the Letts thrust bayonets into any of the victims who still showed signs of life.[12]

Yurovsky was a methodical man. On the 15th he had ordered peasant women to bring him a basket of eggs; [13] this was to be part of his food during the time when he supervised the destruction of the bodies. Stripped of their precious ornaments, these were placed on an automobile and taken to an abandoned mine in the neighborhood of the little village Koptyaki, about thirteen miles away from Ekaterinburg. The mine was surrounded with troops and during two days all movement was stopped on the Koptyaki highway. Great quantities of benzine and sulphuric acid were brought from Ekaterinburg; and the bodies were destroyed as completely as possible.

Extremely anxious to prevent any traces of the bodies from

falling into the hands of the Whites, Yurovsky and his associates, after the burning of the bodies, took the remains and carried them to a swamp a considerable distance from the mine. The investigators who set to work endeavoring to learn the circumstances of the killing of the family and to find, if possible, the corpses, made no search in the swamp; and, in the words of Bikov, the President of the Ekaterinburg Soviet, "the corpses remained and have now happily rotted." [14]

The manner in which the Tsar, the Tsarina and their children were done to death in this Ekaterinburg cellar was very symbolic of the spirit of the Bolshevik Revolution. Here was no parade of a public trial, no chance for dramatic exchange of speeches between prosecutor and accused; there was just a plain, unadorned, unsentimental, utilitarian massacre. The family of the last Tsar died very much as many Jewish families had perished during the pogroms of 1905, as many Lettish peasant families had been cut down during the "pacification" which followed the agrarian upheaval in the Baltic Provinces at that time. There was grim, although probably quite accidental, retribution in the fact that the chief executioner was a Jew and that most of his assistants were Letts.

The news of the death of the Tsar aroused singularly little interest in Moscow. It was announced to the Council of People's Commissars by Sverdlov, who, according to the testimony of a participant in the session,[15] entered a meeting of the Council of People's Commissars, which was engaged in discussing a measure for health protection proposed by the Commissar for Health, Semashko, and said: "Nicholas was shot in Ekaterinburg, according to a decision of the Territorial Soviet. Nicholas wanted to flee. The Czechs were approaching. The presidium of the All-Russian Soviet Executive Committee decided to approve." There was general silence until Lenin suggested that the Council go on reading Semashko's project by paragraphs.

The official statement on the killing read as follows: [16]

> "Lately the approach of the Czecho-Slovak bands seriously threatened the capital of the Red Urals, Ekaterinburg. At the same time a new plot of counterrevolutionists, which had as its objective the taking of the royal hangman out of the hands of the Soviet Government, was disclosed. In view of this the presidium of the Ural Territorial Soviet decided to shoot Nicholas Romanov, which was done on July 16. The wife and son of Nicholas Romanov were sent to a safe place. The All-Russian Soviet Executive Committee, through its presidium, recognizes as correct the decisions of the Ural Territorial Soviet."

The statement about the sending of the wife and son of the former Tsar to a safe place was, of course, quite untrue; and the allegation of a plot was highly questionable. No doubt there were Tsarist sympathizers in Ekaterinburg; but there is no evidence that they had made any concrete plan for a rescue. Sverdlov was in all probability informed immediately of everything that happened in the cellar of the Ipatiev House; quite possibly he had agreed with Goloschekin as to the desirability of annihilating the entire family in the event that Ekaterinburg was threatened with capture. The ambiguous and inaccurate wording of the statement was probably dictated by the desire to avoid official admission of the killing of the children.

In Ekaterinburg, as in Moscow, the execution of the Tsar was announced without reference to the fate of his family. The announcement in the Ekaterinburg newspaper appeared on July 22, three days later than in Moscow. On the preceding evening a workers' meeting in the town theatre greeted the news with applause and passed a resolution to the following effect:

"The execution of Nicholas the Bloody serves as an answer and threatening warning to the bourgeois-monarchist counterrevolution, which attempts to drown in blood the workers' and peasants' revolution."

On the night of July 17th, some twenty-four hours after the killing of Nicholas II, the Tsarina and their children, another tragedy in the annals of the Romanov family occurred near Alapaevsk, a little mining town in the Northern Urals. Six members of the former ruling house, the Grand Duke Sergei Mikhailovitch, who had been chief of the Artillery Department during the World War, the Grand Duchess Elizaveta Fyodorovna, well known because of her fervent piety, the Princes John Constantinovitch, Constantine Constantinovitch and Igor Constantinovitch and the Prince Vladimir Pavlovitch Paley, had been banished some time before to this remote place. Since June 21 they had been placed under an intensified prison regime. On the night of the 17th the six, along with a nun named Varvara Yakovleva, a companion of Elizaveta Fyodorovna and an attendant of Sergei Mikhailovitch, Remez, vanished. For some reason the local Soviet authorities resorted to an absurd mystification, causing some shots to be fired off in the neighborhood of the school building in which they were confined and then announcing that they had been carried off by an unknown band. Actually they had been killed by Bolshevik agents, who threw them into a deep mine-shaft about eight miles from Alapaevsk. The bodies were recovered after the Whites occupied Alapaevsk (there had been no such elaborate attempt at destruction as in the case of the Tsarist family). They were taken to Peking after the collapse of the anti-Bolshevik forces in Siberia and ultimately given solemn interment in Jerusalem.

The former Tsar's brother, Michael, had been put to death still earlier. He had been banished to the town of Perm, on the Kama River, in the Ural Territory and lived here under surveillance in the former Noblemen's Club. The President of the Motovilikh Soviet, G. I. Myasnikov, who seems by general testimony to have been an uncommonly bloodthirsty individual, even measured by the standards of Russian civil war, was impatient at the slowness of the Soviets in executing Michael; and on the night of June 12, accompanied by four workers, he called at Michael's quarters, forced him and his English secretary, Johnson, to accompany them and shot both in the woods between Perm and Motovilikh. Other members of the Romanov House, including the scholarly Grand Duke, Nikolai Mikhailovitch, who was a member of the French Academy and who had made substantial contributions to Russian history, were executed during the Red Terror in Petrograd. The Romanovs had come into power in 1613, at the end of a period of anarchical chaos which is generally known as "The Troubled Times"; they lost their power, and a considerable number of them lost their lives during a new convulsive spasm of Russian historical development, which reproduced in the twentieth century not a few of the characteristics of the Troubled Times of more than three hundred years ago.

In noteworthy distinction to the English and French Revolutions, there was no strong avowed monarchist anti-revolutionary movement in Russia. The Grand Duke Nicholas Nicholaevitch lived for a time in the Crimea while the Whites were in occupation of that part of the country; but he made no attempt to take any part in political life, much less to assert a claim to the vacant throne and, long before the end of the civil war, he left Russia altogether. The old Russian national hymn, "God Save the Tsar," was popular at gatherings of White officers; but no anti-Bolshevik leader openly avowed as his objective the restoration of the Romanovs. The recent scandal associated with the name of Rasputin, the absence of a striking personality among the Romanov princes, the fear of alienating public opinion in France, Great Britain and America, where absolute monarchy was not regarded with favor,—all these considerations prevented the anti-Bolshevik regimes of Admiral Kolchak and General Denikin, conservative, restorationist and dictatorial as they were, from raising the flag of reëstablishment of the autocracy. The Revolution physically destroyed many of the Romanovs. More than that, its course clearly indicated that the idea which the Romanovs incarnated, the idea of autocratic sovereignty, was dead, so far as the Russian masses were concerned. There would have been no lack of leaders if any strong popular movement had developed among the peasants for the restoration of the Tsar. But there was no such movement; there was no recurrence of the pretenders who sprang up during the Troubled Times.[17] The rattle of the revolvers of Yurovsky and his Letts could only kill individuals. But the spirit of dynastic loyalty, of devotion to the Romanov House, which had ruled Russia for more than three hundred years, was already dead, except among a negligible fraction of the Russian people.

NOTES

[1] *Cf. Krasny Arkhiv* (Red Archives), Vol. XXI, pp. 79ff.

[2] For an account of the career of Soloviev *cf.* N. Sokolov, "The Murder of the Tsarist Family," pp. 88ff.

[3] Pankratov has written a brief account of his experiences as commissar attached to the imperial family, entitled, "With the Tsar in Tobolsk," in the magazine, *Biloe* (The Past), No. 24, pp. 217, 218.

[4] P. Bikov, "The Last Days of the Romanovs," pp. 75ff.

[5] The German Ambassador, Count Mirbach, perhaps convinced of the futility of any intercession on his part, manifested an attitude of cool indifference when he was requested to take some action on behalf of the imperial family by the Russian monarchists. In this connection *cf.* Sokolov, *op. cit.*, pp. 107, 108.

[6] P. Bikov, *op. cit.*, p. 96.

[7] Sokolov, *op. cit.*, pp. 127ff.

[8] Bikov, *op. cit.*, pp. 106ff.

[9] Ekaterinburg actually fell about two weeks later, on July 25.

[10] Bikov, *op. cit.*, p. 114.

[11] The best collection of evidence furnished by persons who witnessed the killing or who were intimately acquainted with its details is to be found in Sokolov, *op. cit.*, pp. 211ff.

[12] The careful and thorough manner in which the slaughter was carried out practically excludes the possibility that Anastasia might have escaped.

[13] *Cf.* Sokolov, *op. cit.*, p. 241.

[14] Bikov, *op. cit.*, p. 126.

[15] *Cf.* V. Milyutin, "Pages from a Diary," published in the magazine, *Prozhektor* (Projector), No. 4.

[16] *Izvestia,* for July 19, 1918.

[17] Toward the end of Kolchak's regime one such pretender arose in a little town in Siberia. He was arrested and exposed, however, before he acquired any considerable following.

CHAPTER XXV

WAR COMMUNISM

THE economic system which prevailed in Soviet Russia from 1918 until 1921 has gone into history under the name: war communism. And the name accurately reflects the double nature of the system, which was a compound of war emergency and socialist dogmatism.

As convinced disciples of Karl Marx the Bolshevik leaders were convinced that state ownership must replace private ownership of the means of production. One of their first decrees was the nationalization of the land; and quite early in their regime they nationalized the banks and the country's shipping and declared foreign trade a state monopoly. But Lenin himself recognized quite clearly that the Soviets were technically unprepared to take over the management of the entire economic life of the country; and during the short breathing-space between the signing of the Peace of Brest-Litovsk and the beginning of hostilities with the Czechs he laid stress not on rapid expropriation of the capitalists, but on inculcating among the workers a spirit of conscious labor discipline and a will to work. During this period he seems to have played with the idea of establishing some kind of *modus vivendi* with those factory owners who were willing to carry on operations, of setting up a system under which the state, while it retained control over industrial life, would utilize the managerial and technical experience of the factory-owners.

Whether Lenin would have been able or would have desired, in the long run, to resist the impulse of the more aggressive Soviets and local labor organizations to drive away the employers and take over the management of the plants is a hypothetical question. For the outbreak of civil war on a large scale, combined with the acute food crisis, tended to sharpen class antagonism to such a degree that any idea of peaceful coöperation with the capitalists was discarded.

The sugar industry was nationalized on May 2 and the petroleum industry on June 17. Soon after this, on June 28, a very important decree indicated that Soviet economic policy was set definitely in the direction of the complete expropriation of the private capitalists. This decree [1] called for the nationalization of the largest undertakings in the mining, metallurgical, metal-working, textile, electrotechnical, pottery, tanning and cement industries. It set in motion a huge process of confiscation which continued until all the large factories in Soviet territory had been taken over by the state and reached its culminating point when a decree of November 29, 1920, declared nationalized all plants which employed more than ten workers, or more than five workers if motor power were employed. The Soviet census of 1920 showed that 37,000 undertakings were in the hands of the state; many of these were the smallest kind of workshops or enterprises where sometimes only a single worker was employed.[2]

The crushing of private or even of coöperative economic initiative, the concentration of all economic authority in the hands of the state marched relentlessly forward in every branch of national life. A decree of November 21, 1918, abolished legal internal trade, making the Food Commissariat the sole institution authorized to supply the population with articles of consumption and giving it the right to confiscate all stocks of goods which might still be in private hands.[3] A decree of March 20, 1919, abolished the autonomy which the coöperatives had formerly enjoyed and fused them with the huge apparatus of the Food Commissariat, bringing them under the strictest state control.

War communism as a system was characterized by six main principles, which were more and more rigorously and intensively applied as the system early in 1921 approached its final crisis, which led to the substitution of the entirely different New Economic Policy.[4] The first of these was that the state through its central or local organs took over all means of production and reduced the sphere of private ownership to the narrowest possible limits. Not only factories, railroads and banks, but private houses of any size, large libraries, privately owned objects of value, such as gold and jewels, were confiscated and taken from their owners.

The second principle of war communism was state control over the labor of every citizen. Especially in the later phase of the system, which began early in 1920, after the defeat of the chief leaders of the Whites, Kolchak and Denikin, compulsory labor was applied on a very wide scale. Armies which had no further military occupation were kept as "labor armies" and set to such mass tasks as felling trees, building roads, loading and unloading freightcars. Different categories of workers were mobilized under threat of punishment and assigned to the places where they were most needed. The peasants were subjected to a number of compulsory labor duties, such as supplying teams for carting wood and clearing snow from the railroad tracks. A decree of February 5, 1920, established in more concrete and definite form the obligation, already written into the Soviet Constitution, of every Soviet citizen to work. Typical of the numerous labor mobilizations of 1920 was an order to all women between the ages of eighteen and forty-five to sew underwear for the Red Army.

A third feature of the system was the effort of the state to produce everything in its own undertakings. With the nationalization even of the smaller workshops and the legal prohibition of private trade (which, incidentally, was continually disregarded and evaded) all production in the towns, on paper at least, was brought under state control. A logical extension of this system, decreed just on the eve of its final collapse, was the effort to control and direct from above the agricultural activities of millions of peasant households. The Eighth Congress of Soviets, which was held in December, 1920, passed a resolution which read in part as follows: [5]

"Demanding the exertion of all the forces of the state to help the peasant farms with cattle and machinery, with the establishment of repair workshops, etc., the Workers' and Peasants' Government simultaneously demands from all agriculturists the complete sowing of the fields according to the instructions of the state and proper cultivation of the fields, according to the example of the best and most industrious farms of the middleclass and poor peasants."

With a view to carrying out this decree, sowing committees were set up in every province, county and township, for the purpose of supervising the work of the peasants and inducing or compelling them to plant as much as was required.

A fourth characteristic of the system was extreme centralization. There was an effort, quite unprecedented in history, to place the entire regulation of the economic life of a vast country, with a population of well over a hundred millions, in the hands of a few hastily improvised state bureaucratic organizations. Prominent among these was the Supreme Economic Council, created by a decree of December 15, 1917,[6] which described as the function of the new body "the organization of national economic life and of state finances." Originally it was supposed to possess wide powers in various branches of economic life, another clause in the decree granting it the right of "confiscation, requisition, sequestration and compulsory trustification of different branches of industry and trade and of taking other measures in the field of production, distribution and state finances."

In actual functioning, however, the Supreme Economic Council became a specialized department for the management of industry. As constituted in 1918 it consisted of sixty-eight members, of whom ten were nominated by the Soviet Central Executive Committee, thirty by the industrial trade-unions, twenty by the local Supreme Economic Councils and the remainder by various Commissariats and by the Workers' Coöperative Organization.[7] Actual executive power rested in the hands of its presidium, which was made up of ten or twelve members. Typical of the activity of the presidium in taking away the property of individual owners is a partial record of its decisions in the month of November, 1918, which includes the following items: [8]

"To nationalize thirteen paper factories. (November 14.)

"To nationalize all metals and metal products in wholesale warehouses in Russia. (November 19.)

"To nationalize all the cloth goods in Moscow. (November 5.)

"To nationalize the automobile factories, 'Russian Renaud,' 'Amo' and the factory of Lebedev. (November 26.)

"To nationalize all the property of the chemical-bacteriological laboratory of Professor M. N. Ostromislensky in Moscow. (November 16.)"

For the direct administration of the nationalized industries the Supreme Economic Council created over forty "*glavki,*" or head departments, each charged with the management of a single industry. These *glavki* were unwieldy, cumbersome bodies; some of them were theoretically managing many hundreds and even thousands of plants.[9] They were organized on a strictly vertical basis, without any adequate means of coördination with each other; and they were distinguished, even among other Soviet institutions of the time, by their extreme bureaucratism and their inability to coördinate their activities in a rational way. There were continual disputes of functional jurisdiction between the *glavki* and the local Supreme Economic Councils.

The management of the individual factories, after the original owners or directors had been driven away, passed through several stages of organization. In the first process of nationalization, in 1918, authority was usually vested in a collegium, or committee, of workers. The activity of such a collegium was usually characterized by much talk and little concrete action; and with the passing of time there was a tendency first to limit the numbers of the collegia and finally to pass over to a system of one-man management. A. I. Rykov, President of the Supreme Economic Council, declared in the autumn of 1920[10] that in the great majority of cases there was definite improvement as soon as full authority and responsibility were vested in a single manager. The heads of factories were nominated by the *glavki,* in agreement with the trade-union concerned.

As the Supreme Economic Council became more and more the sole authority in the field of industrial production, the Food Commissariat became the exclusive authorized provider of food and manufactured goods. The Commissariat for Transportation managed the railways and water transport along semi-military lines, especially when the energetic Trotzky for a time took over the operation of the railroads and endeavored, without much success, to apply in economic life the principles of ruthless discipline which he had instilled into the Red Army. The Commissariat for Agriculture endeavored to direct and regulate the production of the peasants; but here the attempts at state regulation were far less effective than in the industrial sphere. It was possible, at the point of the bayonet, to extort from the peasants year after year a growing quantity of grain and of other food products. But it was not possible to make them work efficiently or to arrest the natural tendency of the peasant to plant less as he saw that his surplus grain would be taken away from him without compensation; and this was the most important of several rocks on which the whole experiment in war communism finally foundered.

The fifth principle of war communism was that the state attempted to assume the functions not only of the sole producer, but of the sole distributor. The all-powerful Food Commissariat took from industry whatever it produced for distribution among the population and took from agriculture, mainly on the basis of forced levies, whatever could be extracted from the peasants and distributed it among the town population, which was placed on ration cards. The "class principle" was rigidly applied in the allotment of rations. The Moscow Soviet in September, 1918, divided the population into four categories. The first consisted of manual workers engaged in harmful trades; the second, of workers who were obliged to perform heavy physical labor; the third, of workers at light tasks, employees, housewives; the fourth, of professional men and women and persons living on income or without employment. Such food supplies as were available were doled out to these four categories in the ratio: 4;3;2;1. Inasmuch as even the favored class, the manual workers, received so little food in those years that great masses of them fled from the cities to the villages, the persons in the fourth category received practically nothing, and were likely to die of malnutrition or starvation unless they were able to barter some of their former possessions for extra supplies of food on the illegal free market, which existed all through these years, although it was subjected to periodic raids and confiscations.

How straitened the food situation was may be judged from the fact that persons in the first category in Petrograd during the month of May, 1919, received the following allotments: 15½ pounds of bread, one pound of sugar, half a pound of vegetable oil butter, four pounds of herrings, two pounds of fish, one pound of salt and a quarter of a pound of mustard.[11] Those in the less favored categories, of course, did not receive even this meagre ration. If the population had depended exclusively on the efforts of the Food Commissariat the death toll from hunger would have been far greater than it actually was. Taking the whole period of war communism, it would seem that about half the general supply of the population with articles of consumption and considerably more than half of the food supply were obtained either through purchases on the private market or through trips to the villages for direct purchase of food,[12] often through barter or through the relaxations which the Soviet authorities themselves occasionally permitted when the hunger became too acute. So in the autumn of 1918 people were allowed to carry forty-eight pounds of food products on the railroads; in the summer of 1919 workers' organizations were permitted to buy food in Simbirsk Province, where there was a good harvest, independently of the Food Commissariat; in the spring of 1919 town dwellers were authorized to receive not more than two food parcels of a content of not more than twenty pounds each a month. It was forbidden to send flour, grain, meat, fowl or sugar in these parcels; baked bread, sausage and salt could be sent.

But the Food Commissariat protested against these encroachments on its monopoly; and toward the end of the system, in the latter part of 1920 and the beginning of 1921, the possibilities of free trade were being constantly curtailed. So the second All-Russian food conference, which took place in July, 1920, demanded that all food collection in the future should be based "on the obligation to surrender all surplus agricultural products to the state." That the system of compulsory collection of grain yielded appreciably more from year to year is evident from the following figures in regard to the state collections of food and bread grains for four years, each year running from October 1 to October 1: [13]

1917–1918	47,500,000 poods*
1918–1919	107,900,000 poods
1919–1920	212,500,000 poods
1920–1921	367,000,000 poods

* A pood is thirty-six pounds.

This shows an increase from about 850,000 tons to about 6,600,000 tons. Of course it must be borne in mind that between the summer of 1918, when Soviet territory was restricted to the provinces around Moscow and Petrograd, and the summer of 1921, when almost all the present area of the Soviet Union had been conquered, both the need for food and the possibilities of obtaining it had greatly increased. That even the last figure of approximately six million tons was far below the requirements of the city population is evident from the fact that in 1932 and 1933, when bread rationing was again found necessary in the Soviet Union, the annual grain collections ranged between twenty and twenty-five million tons. But the unmistakable tendency in the last months of war communism was to press on with the policy of centralized distribution, to plug up, so far as possible, the leaks of the private market and of purchases outside the agency of the Food Commissariat, which even extended its monopolistic control to such objects as honey and mushrooms.

The sixth outstanding feature of war communism was the attempt to abolish money altogether as a means of exchange, to go over to a system of natural economy, in which all transactions were carried out in kind. As in the case of the other features of the system, this attempt was not made all at once. The whole trend of Soviet policy, the complete concentration of production and distribution in the hands of the state, the substitution of requisitions for free purchases from the peasants, the tendency to pay a larger part of wages and salaries in allotments of food and clothing was in the direction of making money superfluous. Communist economists of that period, far from deploring the visible shrinkage in the value of Soviet currency, welcomed it as a step toward a new and higher economic stage. Larin, an economist of rather fantastic views, who had a good deal of influence at this time, wrote as follows toward the end of 1920, when money was visibly losing all value and significance: [14]

"The constant decline of money will increase in accordance with the growth of the organized character of Soviet economy . . . Money, as a sole measure of value, does not exist at all. Money as a means of circulation can already be abolished to a considerable degree. Money as a means of payment will end its existence when the Soviet state will free the workers from the necessity of running to the Sukharevka [*i.e.*, the markets, so called because the Sukharevka market in Moscow was one of the largest and most famous]. Both these developments may be foreseen and will be practically realized within the next years. And then," Larin triumphantly concluded, "money will lose its significance as a treasure and remain what it really is: colored paper." Another Communist economist, Eugene Preobrazhensky, dedicated a book which he published in 1920 to "the printing-press of the People's Commissariat of Finance," which he described as "that machine-gun which attacked the bourgeois regime in its rear—its monetary system—by converting the bourgeois economic law of money circulation into a means of destruction of that same regime and into a source of financing the revolution." The Soviet Central Executive Committee, in a resolution of June 18, 1920, announced as the goal of Soviet financial policy "the establishment of moneyless accounts for the destruction of the money system."

The Soviet regime inherited a financial system that had been badly shattered by the War, which both the Tsarist and the Provisional Government had financed to a considerable extent by the printing of new currency. The 1,630,400,000 rubles which were in circulation in Russia on July 1, 1914, increased to 10,044,000,000 rubles on March 1, 1917, and to 19,477,900,000 rubles on November 1, 1917. The Soviet Government soon went over to a policy of completely uncontrolled inflation, under which the value of the rubles declined as their volume grew until the ruble became as worthless as the German paper mark became, as a result of a similar process, in 1923. The tremendous growth in the issue of paper rubles and the simultaneous decline in their real value, measured in pre-War gold rubles is illustrated by the following comparative tables: [15]

	Paper rubles	*Value in gold rubles*
January 1, 1918	27,650,000,000	1,331,900,000
January 1, 1919	61,326,000,000	379,300,000
January 1, 1920	225,015,000,000	93,000,000
January 1, 1921	1,168,596,000,000	69,600,000

The printing of paper money became an important industry; its factories in Moscow, Petrograd, Penza, Perm and Rostov-on-the-Don employed 13,616 men on January 1, 1921. During the first years of the Soviet regime the unlimited issue of money helped slightly in procuring grain and other products from the peasants. But as time went on the stupidest peasant in the most backwoods village began to assess Soviet money for what it was, "colored paper," in Larin's phrase. The taking of food from the peasants, whose homes were stuffed with the paper money which had practically no purchasing power, became a matter of sheer compulsion, sweetened occasionally and slightly by the distribution of meagre supplies of manufactured products of very bad quality in the villages.

Under the uncontrolled inflation prices rose even faster than money could be printed. This was a natural consequence of the fact that the number of commodities for which money could be paid was continually narrowing. How far the Soviet Government had proceeded in the direction of the destruction of a money economy is indicated by such decrees as one of December 4, 1920, which provided that food was to be distributed to the population without charge beginning with January 1, 1921, and one of February 3, 1921, which stopped the levying of all taxes, except, of course, the requisitions in kind from the peasants. Payments of rent and of charges for such communal services as water and electricity (services, incidentally, which functioned with considerable irregularity under the regime of war communism) were abolished; travel on the railroads was free and postal charges were abandoned. The last bank in the country, the People's Bank of the Russian Socialist Federative Soviet Republic, was liquidated on January 19, 1920, and fused with the Commissariat for Finance under the new title of "budget-accounting department."

With the endless flow of new paper money and the complete abolition of large incomes taxation lost all significance. The sole large tax which the Soviet Government levied was the so-called "extraordinary revolutionary tax," the conditions of which were announced on November 2, 1918. This tax was supposed to extract from the well-to-do classes of the cities and the villages ten billion rubles, which at that time was still a considerable sum. The tax bore the character of an act of revolutionary expropriation, rather than of a financial measure; there was no clear specification as to how much each citizen was expected to pay; and the levying of the tax was entrusted to the local Soviets and the Committees of the Poor, who were to be guided by the following principle: "that the city and village poor should be completely exempted from the extraordinary tax; that the middle classes should be subjected only to small levies and that the whole weight of the tax should fall on the rich part of the city population and on the rich peasants." The collection of the tax was stopped after about a billion and half rubles had been realized; the instructions about sparing the middle-class peasants were not always observed and this was leading to a good deal of discontent.

So the economic system which had grown up in Russia until the roar of cannon during the Kronstadt uprising and the ominous rumble of peasant insurrections in many parts of the country brought about a sharp change in the spring of 1921 was one in which the state aspired to the rôle of sole producer and sole distributor, in which labor under state direction and regimentation was compulsory, in which payments were in kind, in which both the need for and the use of money had largely disappeared. What were the practical results of this system?

Considered purely as an economic experiment, without regard for the highly relevant circumstances which helped to inaugurate it and which prevailed while it was carried on, such as the civil war and the blockade enforced against Soviet Russia by the outside world, war communism may fairly be considered one of the greatest and most overwhelming failures in history. Every main branch of economic life, industry, agriculture, transportation, experienced conspicuous deterioration and fell far below the pre-War levels of output. The quality of the goods that were produced was indescribably bad; productivity of labor declined enormously; agriculture reverted to the most primitive type of subsistence economy because of the breakdown of normal exchange with the towns. The cultivation of such crops as cotton and flax, sugar-beets and tobacco almost ceased; the tendency was to cultivate only crops with an immediate food value.

The collapse of the productive forces of the country brought on the Soviet population a state of misery far greater than that experienced by the civilian population in West European countries during the worst years of the War. A Soviet author calculates [16] that the food card system in Moscow gave the population about one seventh of the calories which the Germans received on ration cards during the War and about one tenth of the calories which the

British obtained. Even if one makes allowance for the fact that the Russians may have been able to purchase more food outside the rationing system through the private market it is evident that malnutrition and in some cases downright starvation were far more prevalent in Russia than in wartime Germany or England.

The most dreaded epidemic scourges, typhus and cholera, stalked hand in hand with cold and hunger through the dreary and forlorn cities of Soviet Russia. With the most essential industries and the transportation system chronically short of fuel, little was assigned for heating the private homes in which hungry people shivered or the offices in which they sat huddled up in overcoats during the cold Russian winters and prepared endless futile reports and charts of largely non-existent production. In the summer of 1919 it was decided that the maximum temperature during the winter months in Soviet institutions must not exceed fifty degrees Fahrenheit.[17] Abandoned houses, barges, sheds were torn to pieces by those people who had strength enough for such activity and the wood was used for heating.

During those years it seemed as if some malicious demon were mocking Lenin's dreams of a powerful socialist industrialized state and turning every Communist aspiration into its precise opposite. Communism presupposed an urban civilization, a drawing of large numbers of the peasants into expanding city industries and the organization of agriculture along modern mechanical lines.

Between 1916 and 1920 the cities and towns of Northern and Central Russia lost over a third of their population; [18] there was a wholesale flight from the starving towns to the country districts where there was more chance of getting food. The number of workers in industry appears to have declined by about fifty percent under war communism; many of them returned to their native villages and those who remained in the factories were driven by hunger in many cases to become petty speculators, leaving their work for days at a time, despite the threats of drastic punishment, in order to get food, stealing material and selling it on the market, making cigarette lighters and articles of household use during the time when they were supposed to be turning out engines and machines. The qualitative degradation of agriculture was tremendous; the landlord estates, some of which had introduced modern methods of farming and stockbreeding, were destroyed and the peasants, crushed under the burden of requisitions and unable to obtain new machinery, scratched a living out of the soil as best as they could.

Communism wished to substitute large-scale for small industry and to replace private trade by state and coöperative distribution. Actually the smaller industries survived the acute crisis of war communism better than such big plants as the Putilov works in Petrograd, where production was almost completely paralyzed by the simultaneous shortage of food and fuel, of metal and skilled workers. And it was one of the paradoxes of the period that, while private trade was illegal, more people, under the spur of hunger, were engaged in it than at any time in Russian history before or since. The few trains that crawled slowly from station to station were packed with "speculators," big and little, recruited from all classes of society, who were prepared to run the gantlet of the brutal search detachments which were posted at the main stations,[19] some in the hope of gain, some because they saw no other means of feeding themselves and their hungry wives and children.

Agriculture, as the most self-sufficient branch of national economic life, suffered less than industry or transportation. Even here, however, the decline of production was severe enough to be called critical. By 1920 the planted acreage, by comparison with 1913, had declined by 12½ percent; the yield per acre by 30 percent.[20] The average Russian harvest of the main food and fodder crops during the ten years before the War had been about 80,000,000 tons. In 1920 it was a bare 50,000,000. There was a notable decline in livestock. By 1920 Russia possessed 75 percent of the horses, 79 percent of the big horned cattle, 55 percent of the sheep and goats and 72 percent of the pigs which it had possessed in 1916, when the War had already made some inroads on the country's supply of livestock, especially of horses. Nonfood crops suffered especially severely. Taking 1913 as a basis of comparison the area under flax by 1920 declined by 50 percent; the area under sugar-beets, by 74 percent; the area under cotton, by 87 percent; the area under tobacco, by 90 percent.

The output of small industry declined proportionately more than that of agriculture; the output of big industry suffered still more; the situation in railroad transportation was nothing short of catastrophic. Small industry in 1920 produced 43 percent and big industry 18 percent of the pre-War figure. Every branch of industry was affected by this tremendous decline; the output of pigiron was 2.4 percent, that of iron ore 1.7 percent of the pre-War figure, while the production of copper stopped altogether The production of coal was 27 percent of the 1913 figure; the production of engines 14.8 percent and that of cars 4.2 percent.

There was a tremendous decline of rollingstock on the Russian railroads as a result of the civil war; and the locomotives and cars which remained in Soviet possession showed an increasing percentage of damage and unfitness for use. In January, 1917, Russia possessed 537,328 freightcars, of which 4.2 percent were out of commission; by the end of 1919 the number of freightcars had sunk to 244,443 and the percentage of damaged ones had risen to 16.6. There was a similar decline in the condition of the locomotives, of which there were 20,394 (of which 16.5 percent were unfit for use) in January, 1917; and 8,955 (47.8 percent of which were unfit for use) by the end of 1918.[21] Despite the most strenuous measures it proved impossible to check the decline in the number of fit locomotives; the percentage of unfit in 1920 was 57. A prominent railroad engineer, Professor Lomonosov, declared at a Congress of Supreme Economic Councils in the winter of 1919–1920:

"It is useless to shut our eyes to reality. However badly the Tsarist Ministers may have managed, however destructive the imperialist War may have been, in the last account it was the Revolution and the civil war that destroyed our railroads."

There was a very great fall both in real wages and in productivity of labor during the period of war communism. The average Russian worker earned 22 rubles a month in 1913. According to the estimate of a prominent Soviet statistician this very meagre wage, which helps to explain the readiness of the Russian workers under Tsarism to follow extremist leadership, declined to 10.49 rubles a month in 1918, to 8.47 rubles in 1919 and to 8.30 rubles in 1920. If the majority of the Russian workers before the War were living under conditions which would have been regarded as below the minimum required for proper health and nourishment, it is easy to appreciate what their condition was when the low pre-War wages declined by almost two thirds. Productivity of labor, which had increased during the War years, sank to 44 percent of the 1913 level in 1918, to 21.6 percent in 1919 and to 26 percent in 1920.[22] The slight rise in 1920 was apparently attributable to the more widespread and thoroughgoing introduction of piecework and to the measures of semi-military discipline and compulsion which were applied to the factories. No considerable rise was possible, however, until the workers could be given enough nourishment to sustain their physical strength.

The question naturally arises: how did the industrial workers, in whose name the Bolshevik Revolution had been made and who certainly, in the majority of cases, supported Lenin in his seizure of power in 1917, react to the unprecedented hardships of this period? Those who were convinced Communists listened to their leaders who told them that all their sufferings could be ascribed to international capitalism and to the Whites, to the blockade and the civil war. Those who were not Communists in many cases dispersed to the villages. There were occasional strikes throughout the period of war communism; but, so far as one can judge from the fragmentary and incomplete information on this subject, labor discontent with the Soviet regime found less frequent expression in strikes in 1919 and in 1920 than in 1918; the Cheka had struck its stride, and active Mensheviki and Socialist Revolutionaries who could lead the strikes were mostly under arrest. There was a new upsurge of workingclass discontent in the winter of 1920–1921, when it became evident that the defeat of the Whites and the end of the blockade did not mean an immediate end of the appalling economic sufferings which were associated with war communism; and this was one of the causes of the modification of the system.

In judging the mentality of the industrial workers during the period of war communism several circumstances must be borne in mind. Many of the more active workers were at the front or were promoted to posts in the Soviet administration and consequently felt themselves a part of the new ruling system. So bitter was the class hatred engendered by the Revolution, so fierce and numerous were the cruelties practised on both sides that the majority of the workers, even amid all the hardships which they were undergoing, certainly did not desire to see a victory of the Whites. Finally, conditions in the areas which the Whites conquered from the Bolsheviki were far from attractive.

Under the Soviet regime the workers, hungry as they were, enjoyed some of the social benefits which went with their theoretical position as the ruling classes. In many cases they moved from their poorer quarters into the abandoned or confiscated homes of the well-to-do classes. A number of protective features were introduced in Soviet labor legislation; pregnant women workers, for instance, were assured sixteen weeks' holiday; children under the age of sixteen were not taken as factory workers without special permission. However, a writer in *Economic Life,* for January 1, 1920, points out that the Soviet labor laws were often violated, partly as a result of the shortage of labor. So "overtime work assumed very broad proportions; night work, hitherto exceptional, became habitual in many places; the basic provisions of the labor laws and the wage rules are violated under the most varied motives and pretexts."

Had Kolchak, Denikin or any other White leader been able, in the territory under his control, to give the masses as good living conditions as they had enjoyed under Tsarism it is quite probable that the Soviet regime would have gone down in the struggle; the contrast in material wellbeing would have been too much to its disadvantage. But the Whites took over regions which were utterly disorganized politically and economically; they suffered as much as the Reds from the fact that the civil war, with its frequent shifts of military fortune and sudden transfers of wide expanses of territory from one side to the other, completely broke up Russia's old economic unity and made orderly exchange between different parts of the country quite impossible. The food situation was not as desperate in the White regions as in Soviet territory, if only because the bases of Kolchak and Denikin, Siberia and the North Caucasus, were far richer in agricultural products than the regions which remained permanently under Soviet rule. But the Whites had few industrial plants at their disposal (except for the few months when Denikin occupied Ukraina) and showed little capacity to operate those which they did possess. They also financed themselves with an endless flow of increasingly worthless paper currency; and wholesale speculation, accompanied by endless debauches in the towns under White control, exasperated the poorer classes and the officers and soldiers who were fighting at the front. In the country districts the Whites, like the Reds, pillaged the peasants and made requisitions on them. In the South the situation was further aggravated because the victory of the Whites meant the return of the landlords.

Most historical developments are relative; and one can only understand the survival and the ultimate victory of the Soviet regime, despite the tremendous decline in every branch of economic life under war communism, if the weaknesses and failures of the White regimes are steadily borne in mind.

The Communist economist and historian of war communism, L. Kritzman, after analyzing the economic collapse of the country, makes the frank and indisputable assertion: "Such a decline in the productive forces not of a little community, but of an enormous society of a hundred million people . . . is unprecedented in the history of humanity."[23]

For this unprecedented decline there were three main causes, which were more or less interwoven. These causes were the civil war, the blockade of the country by the outside world and the inherent defects of the system itself. It is quite impossible with any degree of certainty or definiteness to apportion the shares of responsibility as between these three causes; the first and the third, however, seem to have been much more important than the second.

The civil war tore the economic body of Russia asunder. The most important industrial regions of Northern and Central Russia remained under Soviet control throughout the whole period of hostilities. But these factories, together with the railroad transportation system, were dependent upon sources of fuel and raw materials which were often cut off for long periods of time. The textile mills of Moscow and of the ring of factory towns around it, for instance, depended on cotton from Turkestan. And Turkestan, as a result first of the Czech onslaught on the Volga and later of Kolchak's advance, combined with the activities of the anti-Bolshevik Ural Cossacks, was completely cut off from Soviet Russia until the latter part of 1919. By that time the primitive Central Asian peasants of Turkestan had largely given up planting cotton and had substituted crops which would yield something to eat.

In the same way the machine-building, metallurgical and munitions works of Petrograd, Briansk, Tula, Kolomna and other Soviet industrial towns needed coal from the Donetz Basin and iron from the Urals and from Ukraina. The Ural region was lost from the summer of 1918 until the summer of 1919, when Kolchak was driven back into Siberia. The engineers and some of the skilled workers left the mines and factories as Kolchak retreated; military operations caused some damage; and the Ural production could be restored only slowly and with great difficulty. As for the Donetz Basin, it was entirely separated from Russia from the time of the German occupation of Ukraina in the spring of 1918 until the retreat of Denikin's army in the last months of 1919, with the exception of a brief period when part of it was occupied early in 1919. But this period was too short and too disturbed with military operations to bring about any perceptible relief. There was no chance of obtaining Baku oil from the time when the Turks occupied Baku in the summer of 1918 until the Red Army entered Azerbaidjan in the spring of 1920; the secondary oil source in Grozny, in the North Caucasus, was cut off by Denikin. One could proceed indefinitely with examples of how Soviet industry was crippled and handicapped by the loss for varying periods of time of important sources of fuel and raw materials.

Besides completely breaking up Russia's natural economic connections the civil war demanded an enormous share of the country's depleted resources for the needs of the Red Army. In 1920 the Army was taking from the centralized stores of the country all the tobacco, 90 percent of the dried fruits, 60 percent of the meat, fish and sugar, etc.[24] In 1919 the state industries produced 4,600,000 pairs of shoes for the Army, as against 2,100,000 pairs for the civilian population. The corresponding figures for 1920 were 5,800,000 pairs and 1,800,000 pairs.

Foreign blockade, along with civil war, helped to shatter the Soviet economic structure. Throughout the period of war communism foreign trade, so far as Soviet Russia was concerned, practically ceased to exist. The country was formally blockaded by the Allies from the beginning of active intervention in the summer of 1918 until the Allied Supreme Council decided to lift the blockade on November 16, 1920; and no international trade of any importance took place during the first months of the Soviet regime. The effects of the blockade and of the general prostration of Soviet economic life (even if there had been no blockade little trade could have been carried on, in view of the collapse of production and the breakdown of the transportation system) is vividly reflected in the following figures on the volume of Russian exports and imports: [25]

	Exports	*Imports*
1913	1,472,100,000 poods	936,600,000 poods
1917	59,600,000	178,000,000
1918	1,800,000	11,500,000
1919	109	500,000
1920	700,000	5,200,000

In some respects Russia was less susceptible to the effects of blockade than a more urbanized country might have been. In pre-War times it had been a heavy exporter of food products; and the appalling hunger which descended on the towns during the years from 1918 until 1921 was the result not of a withholding of accustomed foreign food supplies, but of the loss of rich grain regions which were under White rule, the breakdown of transportation, the wellnigh complete cessation of normal exchange between city and village. Of course the blockade did make its effect felt in depriving the country of foreign equipment, machinery and raw materials and in making impossible any replacement from foreign sources of the supplies which were cut off as a result of the civil war. In this respect the Whites were in a more favorable position; they received supplies from the Allied countries.

When one has made full allowance for the disastrous effects of civil war and blockade a vast number of inherent defects remain in the system of war communism itself. The fact that it was abandoned after the civil war had been won and after the blockade had been raised is the best possible proof that the Soviet leaders had recognized that it was not calculated to promote the economic reconstruction of the country.

The attempt to nationalize everything from locomotive works to public baths and to provision the population through state agencies with everything from bread to mushrooms inevitably led to the creation of an enormous, unwieldy and incompetent bureaucracy, which stifled all creative initiative and often led to bungling misuse and neglect of the slender resources which the country possessed. A Soviet commentator on the system summed up its characteristics vigorously and succinctly in the following terms: [26]

"There can be no two opinions as to the fact that bureaucratism really eats us up and destroys all initiative. Whoever is acquainted with the activity of our institutions, whoever knows how endless interdepartmental quarrels and disputes make all work difficult will not deny that the most insistent problem of the day is the struggle against bureaucratism. . . . Small industry and small trade cannot be administered from one centre without creating a bureaucratic apparatus, which not only swallows up all the income from them, but directly throttles them."

On another occasion the leading economic organ of the Soviet Government at that time, the newspaper *Economic Life,* complains: "One of the sins of the economic organizations of Soviet Russia is not that there were no plans, but that there were too many of them, while scarcely one of the plans was fulfilled."

The enormous system of universal state control and operation was largely a paper system; the officials at the top, hopelessly entangled in the red tape of long reports and endless conferences, had little idea of the condition of the enterprises which were under their management. The simplest act of distribution, the provision of matches for the Moscow population, for instance, might be held up for weeks or even months as a result of endless quarrels in regard to departmental jurisdiction.

No doubt there was some conscious sabotage among the engineers and among the members of the educated classes who worked in

Soviet institutions. The course of the proletarian revolution in those years was certainly not calculated to inspire the intelligentsia, to say nothing of the former well-to-do classes, with sentiments of enthusiastic loyalty. Severe as was the decline in the standard of living for the manual workers, the position of the office worker was relatively much worse.

But there was so much inevitable incompetence and mismanagement, as a result of the sudden influx of uneducated and untrained men into the higher posts of state administration and because of the nature of the stiff, inefficient bureaucratic system, that the practise of deliberate sabotage might well seem a matter of carrying coals to Newcastle. The virtual abolition of money removed a powerful stimulus to individual productivity and also a means of estimating the efficiency of the state undertakings.

The town population had become so docile as a result of long years of undernourishment and of the terrorist regime of the Cheka that the costly experiment in war communism might have been carried still further without provoking any overwhelming outburst of revolt. The Achilles heel of the system lay in the fact that it represented systematic robbery and exploitation of the peasants. So long as White armies were in the field it was possible for the Communists to make a propagandist appeal to the peasants on the ground that sacrifices were necessary to sustain the Red Army and that the fall of the Soviet regime would mean the restoration of the landlords and the institution of a regime of cruel vengeance against the peasants who had plundered the estates. But when the last White Army of General Wrangel was driven into the Black Sea this argument lost its avail; and ominous rumblings of discontent, which took the form of fierce uprisings and small guerrilla wars in Tambov, in Ukraina and in Western Siberia, together with the mutiny of the predominantly peasant sailors in Kronstadt, warned Lenin, whose ear was always closely attuned to political reality, that the system of war communism had been carried as far as the political safety of the Soviet regime permitted. The growing mood of peasant discontent was further accentuated because, along with the general impoverishment of agriculture, indicated by the decline of the planted area and the reduction in the number of livestock, there had been a levelling among the peasants, which tended to obscure the old antagonism between rich and poor which the Communists had always been adept in exploiting.[27] It was no longer possible for the poorer peasants of a village to buy themselves off from requisitions by seizing the grain stocks of a few of the richer families. Moreover, the practise under war communism of dealing with the whole village community, demanding from it a given amount of grain and other products and giving it for distribution a certain quantity of city products, was utterly unsuited to stimulating the individual peasant to greater effort, because he had no assurance that if he raised more grain he would receive a proportionately larger share of the goods.

Among the many causes which made war communism (some features of which were probably inevitable during the period of hostilities) quite ineffective as a system of peace-time reconstruction, perhaps the most decisive was the fact that the overwhelming majority of the Russian peasants emerged from the Revolution with the status and the psychology of individual property owners. Neither the state farms which were set up here and there on former estates nor the communes and artels, or coöperative groups for tilling the land which were formed sometimes among the poorer peasants, played a large enough rôle in agricultural production to form the basis for a new socialist agriculture. And neither state farms nor collective farms were looked on with favor by the majority of the peasants. As a writer in *Economic Life* observed: [28]

> "The middleclass peasant knows the commune, with rare exceptions, as a group of lazy fellows who have seized on all the objects in the landlords' estates which he dreamed of owning himself. The middleclass peasant knows the state farm, with rare exceptions, as a piece of vacant land which the Land Department did not give him, but which it cannot manage itself, as an estate where the former owner's cattle die from lack of food and mismanagement."

With a ruined industry which would require years of patient reconstruction and an exhausted country, the Soviet leaders could not in 1921 inaugurate the policy which they launched in 1929: forcible collectivization of the peasant households on a basis of tractors and other large farm machines. There was nothing to do but to retreat before the small peasant proprietor; and this meant scrapping the whole edifice of war communism just after it had acquired its last touches in the form of general compulsion to work, virtual abolition of money, free dispensation of food, housing and communal services and committees which were to undertake the formidable task of compelling the peasant to plant just what the state wanted him to plant. Compulsion had been stretched almost to the breaking point before the Soviet Government agreed to give up war communism as a permanent economic system and to revert, for a term of years, to a compromise arrangement, under which the state would retain the railroads and large factories, the banks and the monopoly of foreign trade, while pacifying the peasants by permitting them to keep the products of their labor and to sell them on the free market.

NOTES

[1] "Collection of Government Acts for 1918," No. 47, Article 559.

[2] *Cf.* an article by Naumov, The Organization of Industry, in the symposium, "Russian National Economy for 1921–1922," p. 325.

[3] "Collection of Decrees, 1917–1918," pp. 186ff.

[4] L. N. Yurovsky, in his book, "The Monetary Policy of the Soviet Government," pp. 52–79, gives an interesting illustrative description of these principles and of their practical application.

[5] Cited in Yurovsky, *op. cit.*, p. 55.

[6] *Cf.* "Decrees of the October Revolution," Vol. I, pp. 224, 225.

[7] *Narodnoe Khozaestvo* (National Economy), No. 4, for June, 1918.

[8] *Ibid.*, Nos. 1–2, for 1919.

[9] Y. S. Rosenfeld, "Industrial Policy of the Soviet Union," pp. 123ff.

[10] *Ekonomicheskaya Zhizn* (Economic Life), for October 7, 1920.

[11] *Ibid.*, for July 3, 1919.

[12] Various estimates regarding the means by which the population was supplied under war communism are to be found in L. Kritzman, "The Heroic Period of the Great Russian Revolution," p. 134.

[13] *Cf.* "Soviet Policy in Public Finance," by Gregory Y. Sokolnikov and associates, p. 93.

[14] *Economic Life,* for November 7, 1920.

[15] Yurovsky, *op. cit.*, pp. 71–73.

[16] N. Orlov, "The Provisioning Activity of the Soviet Government," p. 350.

[17] *Economic Life,* for July 10, 1919.

[18] Kritzman, *op. cit.*, p. 51.

[19] Complaints about the rough and arbitrary conduct of the search detachments often came to the attention of the Soviet authorities. So a ruling of the All-Russian Soviet Central Executive Committee, published in *Izvestia* of January 3, 1919, refers to "information from various railroad districts about the unlawful actions of the search detachments, which stop trains at every half-station, treat roughly the passengers whom they search, especially women, take away their things and produce for their own personal use, etc." And on April 3, 1919, *Economic Life* publishes a circular order from the Food Commissar Tsurupa to all provincial and county food committees, in which it is stated that the detachments sometimes take away everything, including unrationed products, and keep their booty for themselves, instead of turning it over to the state for the feeding of children, as they were supposed to do. Tsurupa directs that the detachments which cannot be reformed should be sent to the front.

[20] The best compact analysis of the decline of production under war communism is to be found in Kritzman, *op. cit.*, pp. 149–162.

[21] *Cf.* article by Nekrasov, "The Work of the Railroads in 1918," in *Economic Life,* for January 1, 1919.

[22] *Cf.* S. G. Strumilin, "Wages and Productivity of Labor in Russian Industry, 1913–1922," p. 56.

[23] Kritzman, *op. cit.*, p. 162.

[24] "Provisioning Activity," p. 236.

[25] Kritzman, *op. cit.*, p. 49.

[26] *Cf.* article by "Spectator," in *Economic Life,* for July 18, 1919.

[27] A comparative study carried out in thirty-two provinces (*cf.* A. Khryashov, "Groups and Classes in the Peasantry," pp. 53, 54), showed that the proportion of peasant households which were unable to sow any land diminished from 10.6 percent in

1917 to 4.7 percent in 1920. On the other hand the percentage of holdings which exceeded 10.8 acres (four desyatinas), fell from 28.9 to 15.8. A similar process of levelling was found in the distribution of working animals. In 1917, 29 percent of the peasant families had no working animals; in 1920, only 7.6 percent. At the same time the percentage of farms with three or more horses shrunk from 4.8 percent to 0.9 percent.

[28] *Cf.* the article by Bogdanov in *Economic Life,* for April 27, 1919.

CHAPTER XXVI

THE TURN OF THE TIDE AND THE GERMAN REVOLUTION

THERE was a time when the further existence of the Russian Revolution hung on a hair. Just as in the French Revolution, the new regime was confronted by the insistent questions: Could it defend itself? Could it substitute a new revolutionary discipline for the disorganization and chaos which followed the overthrow of the old regime? The answer of the French Revolution was given at Valmy, when the invading foreign armies which wished to restore the fallen monarchy were first decisively checked by the French revolutionary troops.

The Valmy of the Russian Revolution was Sviazhsk, an obscure little town near Kazan where Trotzky took up his headquarters in August, 1918. When Trotzky on August 7 left Moscow on the special train which was to carry him from front to front during the civil war he did not know that Kazan was already in the hands of the Whites. And this gloomy news only intensified the picture of wellnigh hopeless demoralization which he found among the Red troops, which had retreated in disorder and taken up a position around Sviazhsk. He describes the spirit which he found as follows: [1]

> "Every detachment led its own life. The one common desire was for retreat. . . . The earth itself was seized by panic. Fresh Red detachments, which arrived in good sentiment, were immediately caught up by the mood of retreat. . . . Everything was breaking in pieces; there was no longer any firm point. The situation seemed hopeless."

Out of this panic-stricken, undisciplined mob Trotzky within a few weeks created a genuine fighting force, which, as the Fifth Army, was one of the best of the sixteen armies which were organized during the civil war. Indefatigable propaganda and tireless organization work, combined with ruthless methods against cowards and deserters, achieved the transformation. As not infrequently happens in history, a struggle that was very big in its ultimate significance for the fate of Russia, and even of the world, was decided by the efforts of very small forces. At the beginning of the series of indecisive skirmishes which preceded the final drive on Kazan the Reds had between three or four thousand troops in action on the two sides of the Volga, while the Whites had little over 2,000.[2] These numbers probably increased, especially on the side of the Reds, in the course of the operation; but the struggle for Kazan, which may be considered as one of the most decisive battles of the civil war, if not the most decisive of all,[3] was fought out by negligibly small forces, with very slight technical equipment. The Whites had one airplane; the Reds had five or six.

It was during his stay in Sviazhsk that Trotzky issued his Draconian order, announcing that commissars and commander of regiments which fled would be shot. He was quick to put his threat into action, when a regiment recruited from Petrograd workers, inexperienced in action, took to their heels when they were attacked by a raiding party of Whites, seized a ship and proposed to sail up the Volga to Nizhni Novgorod. Trotzky had the ship surrounded by loyal vessels of the Volga river flotilla, forced the mutineers to evacuate it and had the commander and commissar of the regiment, along with every tenth soldier, shot on the spot.[4]

It is difficult to set with absolute certainty the decisive moment of this protracted skirmish of small forces. Perhaps it was on the night of August 28, when Colonel Kappel, the most gifted leader of the Volga White forces, made an unsuccessful attempt to capture Sviazhsk by means of a raid in the rear. With the first days of September fortune inclined more and more clearly to the side of the Reds; and on the 10th Kazan fell, as a result of the combined pressure of the forces advancing from Sviazhsk, of the Second Red Army which advanced on Kazan from the East and of the Volga river flotilla. Some torpedo-boats and other small warcraft had been brought to the Volga from Petrograd through the Marinsky canal system, and played a considerable part not only at Kazan, but in subsequent operations along the banks of the Volga and its large tributary, the Kama.

Trotzky celebrated the capture of Kazan with an order to the Red Army and Fleet which began as follows:[5] "The 10th of September will go as a holiday into the history of the socialist Revolution. The forces of the Fifth Army have torn Kazan out of the hands of the Whites and the Czecho-Slovaks. This is the turningpoint. The pressure of the bourgeois army has finally met proper resistance. The spirit of the enemy is broken."

The tide really had turned on this sector of the front. The power of the Samara Government, shaky at best, could not stand before military defeat and the pressure of a reorganized and far more efficient Red Army. Simbirsk fell on the 12th, only two days after Kazan. The demoralization which had characterized the Red Army before Trotzky whipped it into shape now began to manifest itself on the side of the Whites. A report of the Fifth Army of September 14 mentions "a mass of deserters from the side of the enemy," and states that 200 men passed over to the Reds in a single day.[6]

On October 3 the Red Army occupied Syzran, with its bridge over the Volga, and on the 8th the capital of the Constituent Assembly Government, Samara, fell. On the night of the evacuation the Menshevik Minister for Labor, Maisky, entered the hall where sessions of the Government were held and found the Premier, Volsky, and some other prominent Socialist Revolutionaries sitting around a table which was covered with bottles, glasses and *hors d'œuvres*. Volsky, already somewhat intoxicated, lifted a glass of vodka and drank demonstratively "to the dead Samara"[7] bursting out in loud and bitter guffaws of laughter. What Samara stood for, a struggle against Bolshevism on democratic lines, was indeed dead. The Government of the Constituent Assembly dragged out the last days of its existence in Ufa, farther to the east, until it was swept out of existence as a result of Admiral Kolchak's *coup d'état* in Omsk in November.

Except in the neighborhood of Ekaterinburg, where fairly strong White forces were concentrated, the Red Armies continued to advance east of the Volga until the end of the year. The insurgent workers' centre, Izhevsk, was captured on the anniversary of the Bolshevik Revolution, on November 7; and during the last days of the year the Red troops occupied Ufa and Sterlitamak. Further large-scale advance was checked by the diversion of considerable forces to new promising lines of advance in the South and the West; and much of the ground which had been gained east of the Volga was temporarily lost during Kolchak's advance in the spring of 1919.

The capture of Kazan and the subsequent clearing of the Volga from anti-Soviet forces had important material consequences, apart from its symbolic significance as the first victorious campaign of the new Red Army. It opened up for requisitioning forays from hungry Moscow and Petrograd a number of rich grain-producing provinces. It also reopened for the Soviets the important Volga water artery of transportation; while the chronic difficulties with transportation, of course, limited the achievements in this respect, some grain could be shipped up the Volga from Tsaritsin, and oil which had been stored in Astrakhan, at the mouth of the Volga, could also be despatched up the river.

While the Bolshevik regime was thus conquering for itself an outlet to the East and crushing one of its first enemies, the Socialist Revolutionaries in Samara, the retreat of the German armies and the subsequent German Revolution were opening up even more promising possibilities of expansion in the vast territories of Eastern and Southern Russia which had been subjected to German occupation.

As early as the beginning of October, Lenin, not yet fully recovered from his wounds, pointed out in a letter to the Soviet Central Executive Committee that Russia must be prepared to play an active part in helping the German workers in their struggle "with their own and British imperialism." [8] He demanded specifically that reserves of grain should be prepared with a view to aiding the German workers [9] and that the Red Army be brought up to a strength of three million by spring, observing: "World history during the last days has remarkably hastened its course toward the world workers' revolution."

On October 22 he set forth very clearly and vividly the hopes and the fears which the visibly impending revolution in Germany were calculated to inspire.[10] "First, we were never so near to international proletarian revolution as we are now. Second, we were never in a more dangerous position than at the present time."

Developing these ideas Lenin declared that a popular, and perhaps a proletarian, revolution was inevitable in Germany. This, of course, would enormously strengthen the international appeal of Bolshevism. But at the same time he regarded the situation for the Soviet regime as dangerous because the victorious Allies would now be free to turn their attention to Russia and would be inclined to regard Bolshevism as a dangerous enemy that must be crushed. He suggested that Allied forces would attack Russia from the Dardanelles, from the Black Sea, or through Bulgaria and Rumania. He sounded a warning against overconfidence, declaring that those Communists who believed the struggle was over when the Russian counterrevolutionists were defeated did not take account of the fact that "there is a new enemy who is much more terrible,—Anglo-French imperialism."

Trotzky, who always inclined to exalt the international at the expense of the purely Russian Revolution, who at Brest-Litovsk had been much more willing than Lenin to risk the newly established Soviet Republic in an effort to cast sparks of rebellion into Germany and Austria, seems to have based greater hopes than Lenin on the prospects of the German Revolution. As early as October 3 he was publicly predicting the creation of "a mighty block of Russia and Germany, with 200,000,000 inhabitants, on which all the waves of imperialism will break." He furnished a clue to the new direction of Soviet military strategy when he told the Sixth Congress of Soviets on November 9: [11]

> "We must slip in between departing German militarism and approaching Anglo-French militarism. We must occupy the Don, the North Caucasus and the Caspian, support the workers and peasants of Ukraina, crush their enemies and enter into our Soviet house, in which we include the North Caucasus, the Don and Ukraina, go into our own Soviet dwelling and say that there is no entrance there for British or for German scoundrels."

This westward and southward extension of the Soviet frontiers was a marked feature of Soviet strategy until a new wave of peasant revolts, especially in Ukraina, in the spring of 1919 and the emergence of the relatively well organized White armies of Kolchak and Denikin forced the Soviet military leaders to abandon dreams of expansion to the West and to concentrate on the defense of the main centres of the interior of Russia. How far Trotzky's dreams of the spread of international revolution soared is indicated by the following excerpt from another speech which he delivered on October 30: [12]

> "Free Latvia, free Poland and Lithuania, free Finland, on the other side, free Ukraina will be not a wedge, but a uniting link between Soviet Russia and the future Soviet Germany and Austria-Hungary. This is the beginning of a European Communist federation,—a union of the proletarian republics of Europe."

The prospects, both political and strategic, which the breakdown of the German Empire opened up before the Bolsheviki were certainly alluring. A vast cordon of territory, stretching for about two thousand miles along Russia's western and southern frontiers, from the lakes and forests of Finland to the open steppes of the

Red sailors of the Black Sea Fleet under the command of the partisan leader Mokrovsov, displaying a banner skull and crossbones for the bourgeoisie

Red troops near Kazan in the summer of 1918. One of the banners bears the inscription, "All Power to the Soviets"

"tranquil Don," inhabited by fifty or sixty million people, was propped up by German military power. The avowedly anti-Bolshevik Mr. Winston Churchill describes the Germans in Ukraina at that time as "the only strong, sane, effective element by which the daily life of twenty or thirty million people was maintained."[13] In Finland, at the extreme northwest of the cordon, and in the Don Territory, in the extreme southeast, there were, to be sure, conservative local governments which had created fairly effective armies. But in far the greater part of the cordon, in Ukraina, in Poland, in the Baltic States, the German occupation had suppressed any kind of independent political life and was itself the sole agency for maintaining public order. The sudden withdrawal of the occupation offered excellent opportunities for Bolshevik agitators, especially if they could be backed up by units of the Red Army. These regions were like a piece of butter, so soft, so disorganized by years of war and social upheaval that even a small armed force could cut through them like a knife.

The last German pre-revolutionary Cabinet, headed by Prince Max of Baden, broke off relations with the Soviet Government on November 5, stating as reasons for its action the carrying on of revolutionary propaganda in Germany by the Soviet Ambassador, Joffe, and the failure of the Soviet authorities to punish the assassins of Count Mirbach. A box brought by a Russian courier had conveniently broken open in the presence of the German police at one of the Berlin stations on November 4, and had been found to contain revolutionary appeals printed in the German language. It is quite possible that the police had a hand in this incident and in the "planting" of the incriminating material. But Joffe had unquestionably been engaged in revolutionary propaganda which was not consistent with conventional diplomatic usage; he subsequently boasted in Russia[14] that "in the preparation of the German Revolution the Russian Embassy worked all the time in close contact with the German Socialists." The Soviet Government retorted by declaring the Peace of Brest-Litovsk annulled "as a whole and in all its points" on November 13,—when it was already clear that no harmful results would follow such an action.[15] The Soviet statement repudiating the Peace asserted that the first act of the insurgent German workers and soldiers had been to greet the Soviet Embassy and exultantly declared: "So the Brest-Litovsk Peace of violence and robbery fell before the united efforts of German and Russian proletarian revolutionists."

Whatever may have been the case with the insurgent crowds of Berlin, the new German Government which was installed after the Revolution, composed of Majority and Independent Social Democrats, showed little cordiality in its relations with Moscow. When Chicherin and Radek got in touch with a member of the German Government, the Independent Social Democrat Haase, at the Foreign Office in Berlin, his replies to their proposals were so chilly that, as Radek subsequently wrote in describing the incident: "Our worst expectations were justified." To the Soviet proposal to send food to Germany, Haase coldly replied that it might better be used for the relief of hunger in Russia, and he showed little inclination to resume diplomatic relations or to discuss the evacuation of the Baltic Provinces by the German troops.

The new German Government was anxious to repudiate any suggestion of Bolshevik sympathy, which might compromise it in the eyes of the Allies. Shortlived Soviets sprang up in many German industrial towns and also among the German troops after the Revolution; and Russian representatives were invited to attend a Congress of Soviets in Berlin. A delegation consisting of Joffe, Rakovsky, Radek, Bukharin and Ignatov was sent, but was turned back by the German military authorities in the Baltic Provinces. Only Radek, travelling in the guise of a returning war prisoner, succeeded in making his way to Berlin, where he established contact with his old friends, the German revolutionary leaders, Karl Liebknecht and Rosa Luxemburg, and took an active part in framing the strategy of the young and inexperienced German Communist Party. But Trotzky's and Radek's dream of a triumph of Bolshevism in Germany and of a Red block of states which would stretch from the Rhine to the Pacific was not destined to be realized. The first outbreak of the more radical workers in Berlin in January, 1919, was suppressed, and Liebknecht and Rosa Luxemburg were killed. Radek stayed on secretly in Berlin, but was detected and arrested in February.[16] After being kept in prison for a time he was sent back to Russia in exchange for some Soviet prisoners whose liberation was desired by the German Government.

If it was impossible to kindle the flame of Bolshevik revolution in Germany itself, the situation was quite different in the former Russian territory which was under German occupation, especially in fertile Ukraina. The Germans and Austrians had moved into Ukraina during the spring and cleared it of the Red forces, suppressing the Soviets. They came as allies of the nationalist Ukrainian Rada. But the German Generals who were in command of the army of occupation and whose objectives were to restore and maintain order of the conservative Prussian type and to extract as much food from the country as possible regarded the Rada as too democratic and on April 28 promoted a *coup d'état,* as a result of which a Russian General, Skoropadsky, was proclaimed Hetman of Ukraina by a congress of *khleborobi,* or well-to-do peasants. The Rada was then promptly dissolved by the German troops.

Among all the figures in the anti-Bolshevik movement Skoropadsky is surely one of the palest and most colorless. Whereas most of the other White leaders attracted some kind of military following, Skoropadsky's *papier-mâché* dictatorship rested on nothing but the bayonets of the German troops. Although Skoropadsky was in no sense an Ukrainian nationalist he imparted to his regime a skin-deep Ukrainian coloring, using the Ukrainian language in official documents and reviving old Ukrainian names and titles, in order to please the Germans, who desired to detach Ukraina from Russia and dreamed of creating a long chain of vassal states, from Finland to the Caucasus, if they could win the War, or at least secure a draw on the Western front.

Skoropadsky's regime appealed only to those members of the richer classes in town and country who were willing to welcome anyone who would give them back their property. Russian nationalists looked askance at the Hetman for his play-acting in Ukrainian costume; Ukrainian nationalists disliked the puppet ruler who had been installed by the Germans after the dissolution of the Rada. With the poorer classes in the cities and with practically all the peasants (the congress of *khleborobi* which had proclaimed him Hetman was a decidedly handpicked body) Skoropadsky's Government was intensely unpopular because of the socially reactionary policies which it pursued.

The general labor policy of the Government was to restrict the rights of the labor organizations and to undermine the eight hour day; trade-unions were systematically harassed and persecuted, very much as in Tsarist times. The Union of Metal-Workers, for instance, according to its own report, was subjected to twelve searches and five smashings of its branch offices, while sixty-six of its employees were arrested during a period of six months.[17] Reductions in wages and long arrears in payment led to a spontaneous general strike of the Ukrainian railroad workers in the latter part of July; the strike failed partly because German and Austrian soldiers were brought in to operate the trains, partly because, in view of the disorganization of the country and the decline in production, a partial stoppage of transportation was not so keenly felt as it would have been in normal times. The German military authorities issued drastic orders against strikers, threatening them in some cases with death, and deported a number of labor leaders and agitators from Ukraina.

No open outbreaks of discontent in the towns were possible under the strict regime of military occupation. There were, however, a number of acts of terrorism and sabotage. On July 30 the Left Socialist Revolutionary, Boris Donskoy, threw a bomb at the Commander of the German forces, General Eichhorn, in Kiev and killed him. Donskoy was promptly hanged. On June 6 there was a huge explosion of military stores in Zverinitz, a suburb of Kiev; about eighty persons were killed. About the same time an ammunition warehouse in Odessa was burned down; a little later the newspapers reported a large explosion in the artillery park at Razdyelnaya, with numerous casualties.

In the country districts a fierce flame of discontent was fanned by the requisitions of the German troops and by the Hetman's policy of protecting the landlords and, in some cases, giving them back the land and property which the peasants had seized. The extensive forests in some parts of Ukraina were natural hiding-places for insurgent bands, recruited from local peasants, and the countryside was far more difficult to police than the towns. Despite the large number of foreign troops in the country, there was an intermittent guerrilla war, which sometimes assumed the form of local uprisings, and more often found expression in killings, robberies, burning of manor-houses. A single day's budget of news from the neighborhood of Ekaterinoslav in June, 1918, gives an idea of the violent social unrest which was seething in the country districts.[18]

The *zemstvo* office in Alexandrovsk County was attacked and robbed of 10,500 rubles. The landlords Kovalev and Mirgorodsky were assaulted and the latter was wounded. Seven persons were killed during an attack on the home of a certain Konko. The estate manager Ivakin was murdered. The landlord Budko was robbed of 20,000 rubles. The home of Prince Urusov, in Novo-Moskovsky County, was burned. There was an armed attack on the estate of a woman named Gersanova, in Pavlograd County; the home was blown up, two persons were killed and three injured. During an onslaught on the estate of Livtienko, in Bakhmut County, three were killed. A man named Peretyatko and all the members of his family were killed by robbers in Verkhne-Dnieprovsk County. The Nekazanov family were robbed and shot down in Slavianoserbsk County. A bomb was thrown into the home of Vartory; his wife was killed by the explosion. Robberies and assaults were also taking place in the town of Ekaterinoslav.

All this indicates that terrific upsurge of semi-political banditism and of sheer anarchy which came in the wake of the Revolution all over Russia, but which was especially marked in Ukraina. Once aroused and systematically incited to class hatred by the Bolshevik agitators and to race hatred, which often took the form of pogroms, or massacres of the Jews, by White and Ukrainian nationalist agitators, the turbulent Ukrainian peasants, many of whom had brought rifles and even machine-guns back with them from the front, were extremely difficult to tame. Years would pass and an inestimable amount of blood would flow before any semblance of peace and order would be restored in Ukraina.

The Ukrainian Communists were fully alive to the possibility of exciting disturbances in Ukraina, where the German regime of occupation, operating behind the transparent mask of the Hetman, was so extremely unpopular. Some of the bands which were systematically murdering landlords, richer peasants and police agents and occasionally cutting off small patrols of German and Austrian soldiers were under Communist leadership. More of them, however, seem to have been the followers of local chieftains or *batkos* (the Ukrainian word *batko* means father) or to have been under the leadership of Ukrainian nationalists.

After the Germans had crushed the first Ukrainian Soviet Republic most of its leaders took refuge in Soviet Russia. A sharp difference of opinion developed in the Central Committee of the Ukrainian Communist Party and came to the surface when a Party Congress was held in Moscow in July. A left-wing group in the Party, headed by Bubnov and Pyatakov, was in favor of immediate armed action in Ukraina, to be initiated by the launching of peasant uprisings. A more moderate group, headed by Kviring, held the view that reaction was firmly in the saddle in Ukraina and that the Communists, for the time being, should refrain from open revolt and concentrate on underground organization work among the industrial workers, virtually ignoring the peasants and postponing any armed movement until there was a revolution in Germany and aid could be openly given from Russia. The Russian Communist Party supported Kviring's viewpoint, because its leaders were very anxious to avoid a clash with Germany during the critical summer of 1918.

However, encouraged by reports of peasant disorders in various parts of the country and by the general railroad strike, the Ukrainian Party Central Committee, in which Bubnov's group had a slight majority, gave out the word for a general uprising early in August. Elaborate preparations for insurrection had been made in Chernigov Province, which bordered on Russia; an insurgent staff had its secret headquarters in the wooded, marshy region of Nezhin; and a systematic campaign of terrorization was carried on against the landlords and against government officials. However, the general uprising was a fiasco. A raid on the town of Nezhin was beaten off and the insurgents were obliged to flee into the woods and finally to quit the district altogether.[19] This failure had a sobering and discouraging effect on the Ukrainian Communists; for a time the Kviring group gained control, and it was even proposed to withdraw the Red partisans who were always hovering along the northern frontier of Ukraina and occasionally making furtive dashes across the uncertain demarcation line.

Later, when the German regime of occupation was clearly crumbling, the Central Committee of the Russian Communist Party decided to organize a "Provisional Revolutionary Government of Ukraina," headed by Pyatakov, its members largely recruited from the followers of Bubnov and Pyatakov.[20] This government acted cautiously, and only in December an infiltration first of Red partisans, then of regular Red Army troops into Ukraina began.

Meanwhile great changes had taken place there. As soon as they realized that the war was lost the German troops lost all stomach for fighting roving peasant bands in Ukraina. Soldiers' councils began to form in the German units. These were not Bolshevik organizations; they worked in close coöperation with the officers. But their appearance was a sign of the war-weariness of the Germans. The clause in the Armistice which prescribed that the German troops remain on Russian territory until the Allies saw fit to recall them (a clause which was doubtless inspired by the desire to check the spread of Bolshevism) remained a dead letter.

Deprived of German support, the Hetman was quite helpless. The few Ukrainian troops which were enrolled under his banner not infrequently proved highly unreliable in the political sense; the archives of the Hetman's regime are filled with complaints from local officials that the Ukrainian troops take the side of the peasants against the authorities and sometimes beat the police and encourage the peasants to keep what they have seized from the landlords. The small detachments of the Volunteer Army which existed in Kiev, recruited from Russians of the upper and middle classes, were barely sufficient to maintain order in the city; they could not hope to hold Ukraina.

The Hetman changed his political orientation with chameleonlike rapidity. He dropped the play with "independent Ukraina" and organized a Cabinet of conservative Russians, simultaneously entrusting the military government of Kiev to the leader of the Volunteer Army there, Count Keller, who was soon replaced by Prince Dolgorukov. He tried to get in touch with the Allied Governments and to secure their protection through the medium of the French consul in Kiev, Henaud.

But his brittle regime was collapsing like a house of cards. The first lead to the general mood of discontent was given by the Ukrainian Nationalists. Some of their leaders, who had already discussed for some time the desirability of initiating a rebellion, slipped away from Kiev in the middle of November and went to the provincial town of Belaya Tserkov, where they obtained the support of some Galician troops (a large part of the population of Eastern Galicia, the former northeastern province of Austria-Hungary, is very close to the Ukrainians in race and language) and proclaimed an Ukrainian People's Republic, to be headed by a Directory. Among the five original members of the Directory the chief figures were Simon Petlura, who had been War Minister in the Government of the Ukrainian Rada and who gave his name to the whole Ukrainian nationalist movement, and V. K. Vinnichenko, a well known Ukrainian writer and intellectual. The movement of revolt spread like wildfire from Belaya Tserkov throughout Ukraina, as it became evident that the Germans were no longer in a mood to support the Hetman. In the beginning it was largely a peasant uprising. The bands which had been operating in various parts of Ukraina swelled into small armies. Kiev held out for a time, because the Germans were unwilling to grant the Petlurists access to the capital. But in the rest of the country the power of the Hetman rapidly vanished; and Kiev was soon virtually blockaded by a cordon of insurgent troops.

An agreement signed by representatives of the Directory, the German Command and the German Soldiers' Council on December 2 established a temporary *modus vivendi,* under which the Ukrainian troops and the Germans were not to attack each other, Kiev was temporarily to be left unattacked and the Germans were assured uninterrupted transportation to their homes. The Petlurists gradually approached Kiev from the south, and on December 14 Skoropadsky fled from the city disguised as a wounded German officer after sending out a telegram announcing his resignation and declaring that God had not given him "strength to cope with the problem of leading the country out of its difficult condition." The Petlurists, most of them ragged, disorderly bands of hastily recruited peasants (only the Galician troops had some degree of stability and discipline) marched into Kiev, and a period of looting and disorderly requisitioning set in.

The Directory was a feeble improvisation of a Government. Its "army" was a disorderly horde, definitely inferior to the newly organized Red Army in discipline and in staffing with trained officers. Many of its troop units were Bolshevik in sympathy. The radical and socialist ideas of some members of the Directory clashed with the conservative militarist practise of some of the "atamans," or military chieftains, who showed a tendency to suppress trade-unions on the suspicion of Bolshevism. A roaring tide of peasant rebellion, all the fiercer because of the preceding period of repression, was spreading over the land; and the Directory was unable to check the drift of popular sentiment toward Bolshevism. The Ukrainian peasants so far knew the Bolsheviki only as the people who had given them the land, not as the people who would confiscate their grain. It was obvious that Petlura's regime could scarcely survive a serious aggressive push from the Bolshevik North.

The German collapse also adversely affected the fate of another regional South Russian Government, that of General P. N. Krasnov in the Don Cossack Territory. Krasnov, to be sure, was not a mere puppet, like Skoropadsky. He had come into power on the crest of a genuine popular insurrection of the Don Cossacks against the Soviets; and he was able to put into the field by the winter of 1918 an army of over 30,000 men, supported by a reserve of younger recruits numbering 20,000.

But from the beginning he had owed much to German aid. German troops had helped to drive the Soviets from Rostov, the chief city of the Don Territory. Krasnov's Cossack army was supplied with German arms; and the long western frontier of the Don Territory was guaranteed by the German occupation of Ukraina.

Although Krasnov, while he was still a General of the old Russian Army, had been inclined to denounce the Bolsheviki as traitors and agents of Kaiser Wilhelm, he himself, following the instinct of selfpreservation that is apt to be stronger than considerations of pure consistency in politics, on June 28, 1918, despatched a long and highly complimentary letter to the Kaiser. Krasnov addressed a number of requests to the Kaiser: to recognize the sovereignty of the Don Territory, to bring pressure on the Soviet Government to withdraw its troops from the Don, to settle a territorial dispute over the Taganrog Region which had arisen between Ukraina and the Don Territory in his favor, etc. He also appealed to the Kaiser to "help our young state with cannon, rifles, ammunition and supplies and, if you consider this advantageous, to set up in the Don Territory factories for the manufacture of cannon, firearms, shells and bullets."[21] Krasnov endeavored to make a sentimental plea for the Kaiser's favor by recalling the services of the Don Cossacks in the Russo-German campaigns against Napoleon and presented a more prosaic argument for German coöperation by recounting a list of foodstuffs and raw materials which the Don Territory was in a position to export.

During the summer months Krasnov was, in the main, successful in his military operations against the Bolsheviki and almost completely cleared the Don Territory of the Red forces. His main support was in the rich stanitsas of the Southern Don; in the poorer northern part of the large, but thinly populated Territory some Cossacks were on the side of the Reds, following a leader named Mironov. Krasnov's victories, however, were of a local character; he was not strong enough to undertake a march on Moscow, although he did push his lines beyond the Don frontier into Voronezh Province. He wanted to round out his territory by the occupation of Voronezh and of the Volga towns, Saratov and Tsaritsin; but these escaped his grasp. Tsaritsin, terminus of a railroad which runs through the North Caucasus to the port of Novorossisk, was a special thorn in Krasnov's side and a constant menace to his lines of communication. He made repeated attempts to capture this town; but it was stubbornly defended by Red partisan forces which had retreated eastward from Ukraina before the Germans and by cavalry recruited from the non-Cossack peasants of the Southeast. Stalin, sent to the Southeast to supervise the collection of grain, was a prominent figure in the defense of Tsaritsin (which was subsequently renamed Stalingrad); and K. E. Voroshilov, who was later to be Soviet War Commissar, was the commander of some Ukrainian partisan detachments, largely recruited among the miners of the Donetz Basin, which held the Tsaritsin front against all the attacks of Krasnov's Cossacks. Tsaritsin at this time acquired the name of "the Red Verdun." Its resistance possessed considerable strategic significance, because its fall in 1918 would have increased the possibility of linking up the anti-Bolshevik forces in the East and in the South. The "Red Verdun" finally fell before the onrush of the Volunteer Army in the summer of 1919. But by this time it had become strategically less important, because the Eastern White front of Admiral Kolchak had been pushed back so far that military coöperation between him and the Volunteer Army had become impracticable.

Krasnov's Don Cossacks were local patriots; they fought best when they were defending their own stanitsas against the attacks of the Reds. They had little desire to embark on a crusade against the Soviets in Russia outside the Don Territory. Despite this fact and despite his failure to capture the Red stronghold of Tsaritsin, which was a standing menace to his right wing, Krasnov during the summer and autumn fully held his own in the military struggle with the Reds and was even able to take a few towns north and northwest of the old frontier of the Don Territory.

His position sharply deteriorated in late November and early December, when the breakdown of the German military occupation forced him to divert troops for the occupation of the Donetz Basin, where, as he says, "many Bolsheviki remained among the workers." Moreover, his long left flank, hitherto adequately covered by the Germans, became completely denuded and exposed to attack by the Red forces which began to filter into Ukraina. At the same time symptoms of exhaustion and demoralization began to appear among the Cossacks; there was considerable desertion and some stanitsas refused to obey his orders.

So, while hopes of a Bolshevik Revolution in Germany were not realized, the defeat of Germany in the World War and the consequent collapse of the extensive regime of German occupation in Western and Southern Russia made possible a new, although short-lived, triumphant advance of Bolshevism to Russia's old natural boundaries, the Baltic and Black Seas.

NOTES

[1] L. D. Trotzky, "Mein Leben," p. 381.

[2] N. E. Kakurin, "How the Revolution Was Fought," Vol. I, p. 244.

[3] If the Czechs and the anti-Bolshevik Russian forces had been able to destroy

the Red Army at Sviazhsk there would have been no organized force to check their further advance on Nizhni Novgorod and Moscow.

[4] *Cf.* article by S. Gusev in *Proletarskaya Revolutsia* (Proletarian Revolution), Vol. II, for 1924.

[5] *Cf.* *Izvestia,* for September 14, 1918.

[6] *Cf.* Soviet military archive reports on this subject, cited by Kakurin, *op. cit.*, Vol. I, p. 245.

[7] I. Maisky, "The Democratic Counterrevolution," pp. 276, 277.

[8] V. I. Lenin, "Collected Works," Vol. XV, pp. 420–422.

[9] No food was actually sent to Germany. It would certainly have been difficult, in the conditions of 1918, for the Soviets to export any appreciable quantity; and the Germans declined the offer, probably fearing that acceptance would compromise them in the eyes of the Allies.

[10] Lenin's speech was delivered at a joint session of the All-Russian Soviet Central Executive Committee, the Moscow Soviet and the trade-unions. *Cf.* his "Collected Works," Vol. XV, pp. 430ff.

[11] L. D. Trotsky, "How the Revolution Armed Itself," Vol. I, p. 372.

[12] *Ibid.,* Vol. I, p. 394.

[13] "The World Crisis: The Aftermath," p. 167.

[14] *Cf.* Louis Fischer, "The Soviets in World Affairs," who cites a Russian journal, *Vestnik Zhizni,* No. 5, for 1919, as authority for Joffe's statement.

[15] The full text of the declaration of repudiation is to be found in "Recent International Policy in Treaties, Notes and Declarations," by Professor Yuri Kluchnikov and Andrei Sabanin, Part II, pp. 198–201.

[16] Radek describes his illegal trip to Germany in an article entitled "November" (a Page of Reminiscences), published in *Krasnava Nov* (Red Soil), No. 10, for 1926, pp. 139–175.

[17] B. Kolesnikov, "The Trade-Union Movement and Counterrevolution," p. 81.

[18] *Cf.* *Kievskaya Misl* (Kiev Thought), for June 21, 1918.

[19] *Cf.* "The History of One Partisan Staff," by A. Bubnov, in *Letopis Revolutsii* (Chronicle of the Revolution), No. 2 (17) for March–April, 1926.

[20] N. N. Popov, "Sketch of the History of the Communist Party of Ukraina," pp. 200, 201.

[21] *Cf.* the article, "The Great Don Military Territory," by General P. N. Krasnov, in *Arkhiv Russkoi Revolutsii* (Archive of the Russian Revolution), Vol. V, pp. 210–212.

CHAPTER XXVII

DENIKIN AND THE COSSACK VENDEE

THE main centre of popular resistance to the French Revolution was La Vendée, where the Breton peasants cherished sentiments of loyalty to King, Church and nobility and fought fiercely against the revolutionary armies. The Vendée of the Russian Revolution was the rich Cossack territory of the Southeast. It was here that opposition to the Soviet regime was most stubborn and most widespread. The fact that the Volunteer Army, with its experienced Generals and its high proportion of veteran officers, chose the Cossack Vendée as its field of operations made the Russian Southeast the base for the most formidable of the various efforts which were made to overthrow the Soviet Government by force of arms. The Volunteer Army and the Kuban Cossacks were mutually complementary. The Army supplied leadership and technical experience in the use of artillery and of modern weapons. The Cossacks furnished the rank-and-file soldiers which swelled the ranks of the Army and enabled it to develop into a force of All-Russian significance. Accustomed to riding horseback from childhood and trained for generations to serve in the cavalry the Cossacks were especially effective in this branch of the service, which played a very considerable rôle in the Russian civil war because of the level theatre of hostilities, the enormous distances of the fronts, which made trench warfare almost impossible, and the partisan character of many of the campaigns.

Unlike their historical predecessors in La Vendée the Cossacks do not seem to have been inspired to antipathy to the revolutionary order by sentimental feelings of attachment to Throne and Church. Monarchist sentiment was conspicuously absent among the rank-and-file Cossacks. General Denikin was certainly no doctrinaire republican; but he resisted the strong pressure of his predominantly monarchist officers to come out publicly for the restoration of the imperial regime on the ground that such a step would diminish and not increase the number of his Cossack supporters. No doubt the outrages which marauding Red Guards not infrequently committed against priests and churches had some effect in inflaming the sentiment of the Cossacks; but religion also seems to have been a distinctly secondary factor in setting them against the Soviet regime. The main causes of the Cossack counterrevolution were fear of losing their former privileges and a part of their land as a result of the levelling agrarian policy of the local Soviet regime and the numerous acts of robbery and violence which were perpetrated by undisciplined Red bands.

After the unsuccessful first invasion of the Kuban Territory the Volunteer Army entered on a period of rest and recuperation near the southern boundary of the Don Territory.[1] While it was not exposed to any immediate military threat, its position was difficult and unpleasant. It was largely dependent on the Don Government for supplies and munitions and the relations between the leaders of the Volunteer Army, Alekseev and Denikin, and the Don Ataman, General Krasnov, were at best chilly and often exceedingly strained. Krasnov openly asked for and accepted help from the Germans; Denikin and Alekseev preserved the Allied orientation and refused to have any open dealings with the Germans, although their dire shortage of munitions caused them sometimes to compromise their consciences to the point of accepting supplies from Krasnov which the latter had obtained from the Germans.[2] One of Krasnov's Generals superciliously referred to the Volunteers as "wandering entertainers."

A personal meeting of Krasnov and some of his aides with the leaders of the Volunteer Army in the stanitsa Manichskaya on May 15 did not improve relations. Krasnov was most anxious to obtain the coöperation of the Volunteer Army in his drive against Tsaritsin. He was lavish in promises of money, arms and ammunition. But Denikin's eyes were turned southward, to the Kuban, the scene of the Army's first offensive. He wanted a territorial base on which he could feel independent of Krasnov. Moreover, a considerable part of the Army already consisted of Kuban Cossacks; and the fugitive Government elected by the Kuban Rada was with him. An abandonment of any attempt to liberate the Kuban, a movement in the northeastern direction of Tsaritsin would alienate the sympathies of these Cossacks and would make probable an occupation of the Kuban by the Germans, who had already engaged in skirmishes with the North Caucasian Red troops near Bataisk, south of Rostov, and on the Taman peninsula.[3]

So the order was given for the second offensive into the Kuban

Territory; the advance began on the night of June 22. Like the first Kuban drive, it seemed a desperate adventure. The ranks of the Volunteer Army had been increased by the accession of Colonel Drozdovsky's detachment of officers, which had marched from Rumania to the Don, and by refugee Cossacks from the Kuban. Still its numbers at the beginning of the offensive amounted to only eight or nine thousand, with twenty-one cannon and a limited supply of ammunition. Against them were Red troops of an estimated strength of eighty or a hundred thousand, with an abundance of cannon and shells.[4] But the Volunteers were far stronger in discipline, morale and military experience; and a number of internal developments in the Kuban and other regions of the North Caucasus gave them good reason for hoping that their second drive would end more successfully than their first.

The most important of these developments was the change in the mood of the Kuban Cossacks. When Kornilov entered the Kuban in March even the Cossacks, to say nothing of those classes which were naturally more inclined to sympathize with the Soviets, the *inogorodni* (or non-Cossack peasants), and the town workers, had received him with indifference and distrust, sometimes with positive hostility. When Denikin moved southward on the second offensive his progress was made easier by continual flare-ups of revolt in the Cossack stanitsas behind the Red lines and so many Cossack recruits flowed into his ranks that his originally small force swelled rapidly, in spite of the losses in fighting.

The typical Kuban Cossack was a farmer with a better house, a more liberal land allotment and considerably larger possessions in the shape of livestock and machinery than the average Russian peasant. Even without the intervention of the Volunteer Army, therefore, Bolshevism in the Kuban would have faced a harder struggle than it encountered in the much poorer agricultural regions of Northern and Central Russia. The *kulak* of Moscow or Tver Province would have been only a *seredniak,* or middleclass farmer, in the fertile valley of the Kuban. The number of individuals who stood to lose as a result of a policy of wholesale requisitioning and smashing of old property rights was, therefore, very much greater in the Cossack territory; and most of these individuals were ex-soldiers with quick tempers and ability to use a rifle and a sabre.

Moreover, the civilian control of policy and administration by the Communist Party organization and by the central and local Soviets in the North Caucasus was much weaker than it was in

"Brothers," by P. Skala
(Red Soldier and White Guard)

A Red Army cart used in the civil war

Central Russia. There were few veteran Communists in this part of Russia; the industrial workers were a very small element in the population; the revolution in the Kuban had largely been made by partisan bands of self-demobilized soldiers, returning from the Caucasian Front. Actual power was in the hands of military chieftains and band leaders, who paid little attention to the orders of the Tsik, or Soviet Executive Committee in Ekaterinodar. Many of these chieftains were irresponsible adventurers, such as are apt to spring up like mushrooms in periods of social chaos and upheaval; some of them were ordinary criminals, whose cruelty and pillaging discredited the Soviet regime in the eyes of the Cossack masses. Matters became markedly worse in this respect after the German occupation of Ukraina, when demoralized fugitive Ukrainian "partisans," who were often scarcely distinguishable from bandits, flooded the North Caucasus. A Soviet historian, Borisenko, characterizes the situation on the eve of Denikin's advance in the following terms: [5]

> "Anarchy, taking root in the army, and especially in the completely demoralized Ukrainian detachments, became the scourge of cities, railroads and villages. Detachments with bandit sentiments had arms and anyone whom the bandit or robber wanted to expropriate was called a counter-revolutionary."

Some of the Ukrainians, especially ex-sailors, marched through the Cossack villages in drunken, marauding processions which acquired the popular name of "devil's weddings." Playing accordions and gramophones, dressed in weird costumes, accompanied by carts in which they took along prostitutes who sat on plundered rugs or on priests' robes, these hooligans moved about the country, plundering and shooting at will,—and creating many potential recruits for the approaching Volunteer Army. How far the irresponsible acts of local chiefs could go is shown by the act of a certain Molokanov, commander of the garrison in the town of Armivir, who casually shot thirty-eight Georgians who were perfectly good Bolsheviki, bound for their native country in order to carry on underground work, on the suspicion that they were counterrevolutionaries.[6] In the town of Stavropol, where the garrison consisted of a detachment of some 200 men under the command of a sailor named Yakshin there was a sanguinary orgy of killing and robbing after an unsuccessful uprising launched by an officers' organization in July, 1918, and the Stavropol Soviet Executive Committee found itself obliged to put out an order "to stop immediately shootings of arrested citizens, which are being carried out without trial and investigation and without the knowledge of the authorities" and to restore to their owners articles which had been seized without warrant or reason.

The North Caucasian Tsik was quite unable to combat these excesses; its authority was so little respected that a strike of the printers prevented the issue of the Soviet official newspaper in Ekaterinodar for several weeks during the heat of the campaign. And, if the Soviet rear in the North Caucasus was far from sound, the condition on the front was, if anything, still worse. True the numbers of Red troops, up to the final catastrophe in the winter of 1918–1919, considerably exceeded those of the Whites. With all its shortcomings, the Soviet regime was popular with the masses of the *inogorodni,* who feared, with good reason, that the return to power of the Cossack Rada would mean not only an end of their dreams of confiscating some of the more abundant possessions of the Cossacks, but also a period of very sanguinary revenge and repression. But the Red forces of the North Caucasus, although very numerous, measured by the standards of the Russian civil war (on the eve of the last crushing defeat they were estimated at about 150,000) represented, as Trotzky said on one occasion, "a swollen horde, rather than an army." They were a loose agglomeration of partisan detachments, which were sometimes hostile to each other and fought, advanced and retreated with little regard for the orders of any central command.

The North Caucasian Soviet authorities were singularly unsuccessful in controlling the amateur commanders of their motley partisan hosts. Indeed this was ultimately perhaps the most direct and decisive cause of the collapse of their regime. The first serious clash between the Tsik and the army command occurred in May, 1918, when Avtonomov, a junior Cossack officer who was in command of the Red armies, quarrelled violently with the Tsik and with the "Extraordinary Council of Defense" which the Tsik had appointed with the idea of controlling him. Avtonomov called the civilian Soviet authorities "German spies and provocators" and even gave orders for their arrest and despatched troops from the front to Ekaterinodar for this purpose. Avtonomov's mutiny did not succeed, but it added to the confusion and disorganization in the army just on the eve of Denikin's offensive.

The first important success which Denikin achieved in his second invasion of the Kuban was the capture of the railroad station Torgovaya on June 25. This broke the connection between Tsaritsin and Ekaterinodar and threw the North Caucasian Government on its own resources. The victory was dearly bought, however, by the death in battle of General Markov, Denikin's Chief of Staff in the World War, an old and inseparable friend, who was renowned even among the early leaders of the Volunteers for his dauntless courage. A more decisive victory was won on July 14, when the Red forces, now under the command of a Lettish officer named Kalnin, were driven from the important junction of Tikhoretzkaya, where the main line from Moscow to the Caucasus is intersected by the Tsaritsin-Novorossisk line. The official Soviet military history appraises the significance of this battle in the following terms: [7]

> "The capture of Tikhoretzkaya had important strategic results; the originally weak fighting capacity of Kalnin's force of 30,000 was finally undermined; an important railroad junction passed into the hands of the Volunteer Army and enabled it to develop its further operations in three directions; the communication of the Volunteer Army with its rear was strengthened; the separate groups of Soviet troops were finally disunited."

The Soviet newspapers, which had hitherto made the mistake of concentrating attention on the hypothetical threat represented by the Germans and ignoring or at least underestimating the menace of the Volunteer Army, now raised an outcry of alarm. Kalnin, who lost all selfconfidence after the defeat, was removed and supreme command passed into the hands of Sorokin, another obscure young Cossack officer who, like Avtonomov, had risen very quickly in the Red Army, which, in the North Caucasus, was almost completely lacking in trained officers. Sorokin was an adventurous figure, fond of drink and revelry, popular with his soldiers, headstrong and impatient of control by the Soviet civilian authorities. Denikin credits him with genuine natural military capacity.

The fortunes of partisan war are fickle. A month elapsed between the taking of Tikhoretzkaya and the achievement of the next goal of the Volunteer Army, the capture of Ekaterinodar; and at one time Sorokin, by moving large numbers of his troops into the rear of a comparatively small force of Volunteers which was advancing on Ekaterinodar placed the latter in a difficult position. But the temperamental instability of the Reds was too great for sustained defense; and in the middle of August, Ekaterinodar was evacuated so hastily that the Tsik almost fell into the hands of the Whites. The occupation of the Kuban capital occurred on August 16; it was followed by public prayers and services of thanksgiving in the churches, by parades of the Volunteers and Cossacks and by banquets and speeches of celebration.

In the first exultation of victory little attention was aroused by one or two incidents marking the rift, which would later become quite serious, between the Kuban Rada and the Volunteer Army. A Kuban General named Bukretov issued a proclamation referring to the Volunteer Army as "part of the *inogorodni*," a characterization at which Denikin took great offense. The Kuban Rada politicians, in their turn, were somewhat piqued because Denikin entered the capital ahead of the members of the Rada Government.

These were small pinpricks; but bigger disagreements would follow. The White movement in the North Caucasus was composed of a coalition of two different elements, the Volunteers, whose goal was the restoration of a "great, united, undivided Russia," to use one of their favorite phrases, and the Kuban Cossacks, whose political representatives in the Rada were primarily interested in driving the Bolsheviki out of the Kuban. As soon as this goal was achieved they were lukewarm about the struggle with Bolshevism in the whole of Russia and were inclined to resent any interference of the Generals of the Volunteer Army with the internal sovereignty of the Kuban Territory.

The continual disputes between Denikin's military and civilian officials and the advocates of Kuban autonomy in the Rada constituted a serious source of weakness in the White movement. From the standpoint of their own interests, both sides seem to have been at fault. The Kuban politicians did not adequately realize their own dependence on the Volunteer Army, which had supplied the trained leadership and technical military experience, without which the Soviet regime might not have been overthrown. They were naïve in believing that the Kuban, which had no natural frontier to divide it from the rest of Russia, would have been permitted by the Soviets to exist as an independent state. On the other hand the blunt and outspoken Denikin and his non-Cossack officers not infrequently failed to show reasonable consideration for the local patriotism of the Kuban Cossacks.[8] The Volunteer Army and the Kuban Cossacks were interdependent. The former could not win the civil war without the support of the Cossacks; the latter could not hope to lead their former free life and to lord it over the *inogorodni* if the Volunteer Army was defeated. But neither side seems to have realized this interdependence; and continual bickerings, culminating in the use of military force by Denikin against the Rada in November, 1919, weakened the strength of the common effort against the Reds.

In most respects the Kuban Rada was more liberal and democratic than the Volunteer Command, which consisted of veteran Generals, most of whom cherished decidedly conservative views. But in one point the Volunteers were less ruthless than the Cossacks, in their treatment of the *inogorodni.* At the moment of the capture of Ekaterinodar, Denikin had appealed to the Kuban Ataman, Filomonov, to show discrimination and moderation in the treatment meted out to the non-Cossack peasants. Actually, however, the Rada did little or nothing to mitigate the fierce excesses in the stanitsas, where the Cossacks often revenged on the whole non-Cossack population the excesses and brutalities which they had suffered during the Soviet regime. The property of *inogorodni* who had disappeared and who were suspected to be with the Bolsheviki was confiscated; their children were driven from the schools; many were shot and hanged by the sentences of "stanitsa courts." [9] The question of the complete expulsion of the *inogorodni* from the Kuban Territory was discussed in the Rada; some speakers substituted the word "extermination" for "expulsion."

The Volunteer Army gained an outlet to the sea when it captured the port of Novorossisk on August 26. Many of the leading Soviet officials of the Black Sea Province were captured and shot. Two months earlier, on June 18, the harbor of Novorossisk had witnessed a naval tragedy, the deliberate sinking of about half the vessels of the former Russian Black Sea Fleet.[10] The Fleet had sailed away from Sevastopol to Novorossisk in order to escape the Germans. The German Government insisted that the warships should be handed over and interned for the duration of the War, in conformity with the terms of the Brest-Litovsk Treaty. The Soviet Government, too weak to resist the German demand openly, despatched two telegrams to the Novorossisk authorities. One, sent for purposes of record, instructed them to hand over the ships; the other, a cipher message, ordered the sinking of the Fleet.

A considerable number of the sailors, instigated by the more conservative officers, opposed the decision to sink the Fleet, which soon became known, despite the effort to keep it secret, and a number of the ships sailed back to Sevastopol and surrendered to the Germans. The other vessels, displaying the slogan "I perish, but don't yield" were taken into the harbor and sunk. The vessels which went to Sevastopol later passed into the possession of the Whites and were taken over by the French Government after the defeat of Wrangel.

With the capture of Ekaterinodar and Novorossisk the West Kuban was definitely in possession of the Whites. Denikin, with an army which had grown to thirty-five or forty thousand as a result of the mobilizations which were carried out in the occupied territory (the term "volunteer" could be accurately applied to his army only during the first few months of its existence) decided to strike for the "natural boundaries" of the North Caucasus, the main range of the Caucasus Mountains in the South and the Caspian Sea in the East.

Sorokin blocked the way with an army that had taken up its stand around the town of Armavir, which changed hands repeatedly during the summer and autumn fighting. The Tsik for a short time dragged out a wretched existence there; it was literally "held up" and arrested on one occasion by a disorderly Ukrainian detachment, which took the last million rubles out of the Soviet treasury. After this incident the Tsik shifted its residence to Pyatigorsk, farther to the southeast, putting out a manifesto to the effect that "regular work for the creation of new units of the revolutionary army, for its supply, for the administration of the country is impossible on the line of the front, where Armavir is." [11]

The drooping spirits of the Red forces were somewhat raised in the middle of September, when the Taman Army, much the best disciplined and most effective Red force in the North Caucasus, arrived in Armavir, after executing a long circuitous march and fighting its way through a cordon of encircling White troops. The Taman Army originally grew up in the Taman peninsula, where it was fighting against insurgent Cossacks. As the field of insurrection grew with the victories of Denikin this force under its leaders, a former officer named Kovtyukh and a sailor, Matveev, decided to move southward along the coast of the Black Sea and then to strike overland through the hilly country south of the Kuban River. The march, difficult at best, was impeded because families of Red Army soldiers and other fugitives joined the Army, fearing the merciless revenge of the triumphant Cossacks.[12] However, the Taman Army held together and fought its way through. The entire North Caucasian Red Army was now estimated at 150,000, of which about 30,000 were enrolled in the Taman Army. The forces of the latter recaptured Armavir, which had been lost to the Whites, after hard street fighting on September 21.

The leaders of the Red Army now felt strong enough to undertake a large-scale offensive. But a sharp difference of opinion developed between the Commander-in-chief, Sorokin, and the leaders of the Taman Army. The latter wanted to strike along the line of the main railroad which connects Moscow with the Caucasus, aiming at the recapture of Tikhoretzkaya, the restoration of direct communication with Tsaritsin. Sorokin proposed to achieve the same objective in a different way, by choosing a more easterly route of advance, striking at the town of Stavropol.[13]

Sorokin's plan was accepted by the Military Revolutionary Council of the Front; and early in October the sailor, Matveev, a popular commander of the Taman Army, was shot for refusing to obey orders when he continued to protest against Sorokin's plan. Formally his execution was perhaps justified; but in the light of subsequent events Soviet historians are inclined to deplore it as an example of severity displayed in the wrong place. There was already bad feeling between Sorokin's troops and the Taman Army; and there was a considerable element of personal feud in Sorokin's insistence on the shooting of Matveev.

Despite the great indignation which the soldiers of the Taman Army felt in regard to the shooting of Matveev, they displayed qualities of discipline and restraint which were decidedly rare among the Red troops of the North Caucasus at that time, attacked Stravropol and carried it by storm, with their bands playing the *Marseillaise* on October 30. This military success, however, was rendered nugatory by a major political crisis which had broken out in Pyatigorsk, the temporary capital of the Soviet Government.

The long smoldering antipathy between Sorokin and the Tsik came to a sudden and violent head. The Tsik for some time had planned to curb and ultimately to depose the unruly Commander-in-chief, whom it suspected of dictatorial designs. The antagonism was sharpened because a number of the leading members of the Tsik and of the Military Revolutionary Council which it had created were Jews, whereas Sorokin, the adventurous young Cossack officer, like the members of his Staff, was an outspoken anti-Semite. "On every occasion Sorokin emphasized the Jewish nationality of the members of the Military Revolutionary Council," says a chronicler who was a participant in these events.[14]

Knowing that plans for his deposition were on foot, Sorokin decided to strike first. On October 21 his adjutant Grinenko seized the President of the Tsik, Rubin, together with Krainy, Rozhansky,

Dunaevsky and other prominent members of the Tsik and the Military Revolutionary Council, took them out of Pyatigorsk in an automobile and shot them.[15] Sorokin then published a fantastic story of a "plot," in which the men who had been executed were involved. He hoped in this way to win the confidence of the soldiers who were inclined to attribute their frequent defeats and retreats to betrayal from above.

But the members of the Tsik who escaped arrest and execution succeeded in rallying the army at the front against Sorokin, who had already alienated the Taman forces by the execution of Matveev. An "extraordinary army congress," which gathered in Nevinnomisskaya on October 28, under the protection of troops which were hostile to Sorokin, declared Sorokin "outlawed as a traitor to the Soviet Government and the Revolution." Finding his support among the troops slipping away from him, Sorokin, apparently without any definite plan, went to Stavropol, where he was arrested and killed with little formality by the commander of one of the Taman regiments. His brief *coup* had disastrous consequences for the "bourgeoisie" of Pyatigorsk; by order of the Cheka over a hundred people were taken out of the town on October 31 and their heads were struck off with swords.[16] Among the victims of this slaughter were two well known Generals of the World War, Ruzsky and the Bulgarian Radko-Dimitriev, who had refused all proposals to serve in the Red Army.

Although Sorokin's mutiny was quickly suppressed, it affected the future military fortunes of the Red Armies very adversely. In the midst of an important campaign the forces at the front were left without organized leadership or direction. Waiting for instructions and supplies, the Taman Army made no effort to advance beyond Stavropol. The cavalry of General Shkuro, one of the most daring of the White partisan raiders, taking advantage of the disorganization in the Red ranks, thrust itself across the line of communication between Pyatigorsk, the source of orders and supplies, and Stavropol. The latter town was soon surrounded by the Whites.

After a battle that lasted about three weeks and that may be considered decisive for the North Caucasian campaign, the Taman Army struggled through the enveloping cordon of the Whites (who occupied the much suffering town, which had experienced so many cases of capture and recapture, on November 20) and retreated in an eastward direction. About half of this army, the only unit of the North Caucasian Red forces which could compare in military quality with the Whites, had been destroyed during the fighting around Stavropol; and the physical and moral condition of the remainder was badly shattered.

A wet, cold autumn, combined with the lack of clothing and medicines, made for the prevalence of disease; scurvy and typhus ravaged the ranks.[17] Moreover the Red Army in general, and especially the Taman forces, had been pushed into a most unfavorable strategic position. Whereas Denikin had behind him the fertile regions of the Kuban Valley the Red armies had at their backs the vast desert which stretches along the Caspian Sea southwest from Astrakhan. The effort to guide the operations of the North Caucasian Red front from Astrakhan was inevitably ineffective; the distance was too great and communication was too uncertain.[18]

While the Reds were discouraged by repeated defeats, by the gradual loss of the main towns and the more fertile regions, by the explosion of internal strife which found expression in Sorokin's revolt, the Whites were buoyed up by the knowledge that Germany had collapsed and by the expectation that substantial Allied aid, in the form of supplies and munitions, if not of troops, would soon be on the way.

Under these circumstances the end could not be postponed much longer. The Red command in Astrakhan had little idea apparently of the weakness of the front and in December issued an ambitious order to the troops of the North Caucasian Army "to master the railroad line, Tsaritsin-Tikhoretzkaya-Novorossisk, on one side and the port Petrovsk on the other, as bases for further advance to the north and to the southeast." Before the 11th Army, the largest unit of the Soviet front, began to attempt to carry out this order the cavalry of General Baron Peter Wrangel, one of Denikin's chief lieutenants, hurled itself on the battered Taman Army, which occupied the right wing of the Soviet forces, and by December 27 Denikin's Staff could report that "the Taman Army has been completely disorganized."

On January 2, 1919, the Eleventh Army launched its offensive, which, in view of the low morale of the troops and the lack of munitions (the supplies sent from Astrakhan were greatly delayed in transit and finally fell into the hands of the Whites), had little chance of success. The Reds did advance as far as Batalpashinsk, but then fell back to their original position around the Caucasian mineral water resorts. The Whites then initiated a sweeping counter-offensive, broke through the centre of the demoralized Red forces and swept forward with irresistible force. General Wrangel, a born cavalry leader, an aristocrat who was well over six feet tall,[19] was the leading figure in this offensive until he was stricken with typhus, a widespread disease at this time; while he was recuperating the drive was carried on with undiminished energy by other White cavalry leaders, such as Pokrovsky and Shkuro. By January 21 the Red line was completely broken through and the Volunteers had entered the mineral water resorts. What followed was a disorderly rout and massacre, rather than a series of battles. On January 24 Ordzhonikidze, the chief commissar on the North Caucasian front, sent a despairing telegram to Lenin: [20]

> "The Eleventh Army has ceased to exist. It has finally gone to pieces. The enemy occupies cities and stanitsas almost without resistance. . . . There are no shells or bullets . . . We all perish in the unequal struggle, but we will not disgrace our honor by fleeing."

The ease and the speed of the White advance may be judged from the fact that the Kuban Cossack cavalry corps of General Pokrovsky covered a distance of over two hundred miles in two weeks. By February the North Caucasian Red Army had ceased to exist. In the hands of the Whites were 50,000 prisoners, without reckoning sick and wounded, together with 150 cannon, 350 machine-guns and considerable military stores. The majority of the Red troops who escaped death or capture made their way over the desert to Astrakhan, strewing the sands with their dead, victims of a typhus epidemic which was as deadly as the White cavalry. Bitter storms, extreme cold, lack of food and water made this retreat across the desert a protracted agony.[21] The Eleventh Army alone lost 25,000 men between Kizlyar, where the movement into the desert began, and Astrakhan.[22] Some of the Red soldiers fled southward across the Caucasian mountain passes into Georgia.

The tremendous epidemic of typhus and the failure to organize a regular flow of munitions from Astrakhan to the front were important immediate factors in leading to the crushing defeat of the North Caucasian Red Army. The basic causes of its defeat by a numerically weaker force were inferiority in leadership and technique and the fatal inability of the North Caucasian civilian Soviet authorities to maintain adequate control over the forces which were supposed to be fighting under their direction.

Trotzky subsequently held up the North Caucasian Red forces to opprobrium as an example of the bad results of partisan methods of warfare. Denikin, on the other hand, speaks more favorably

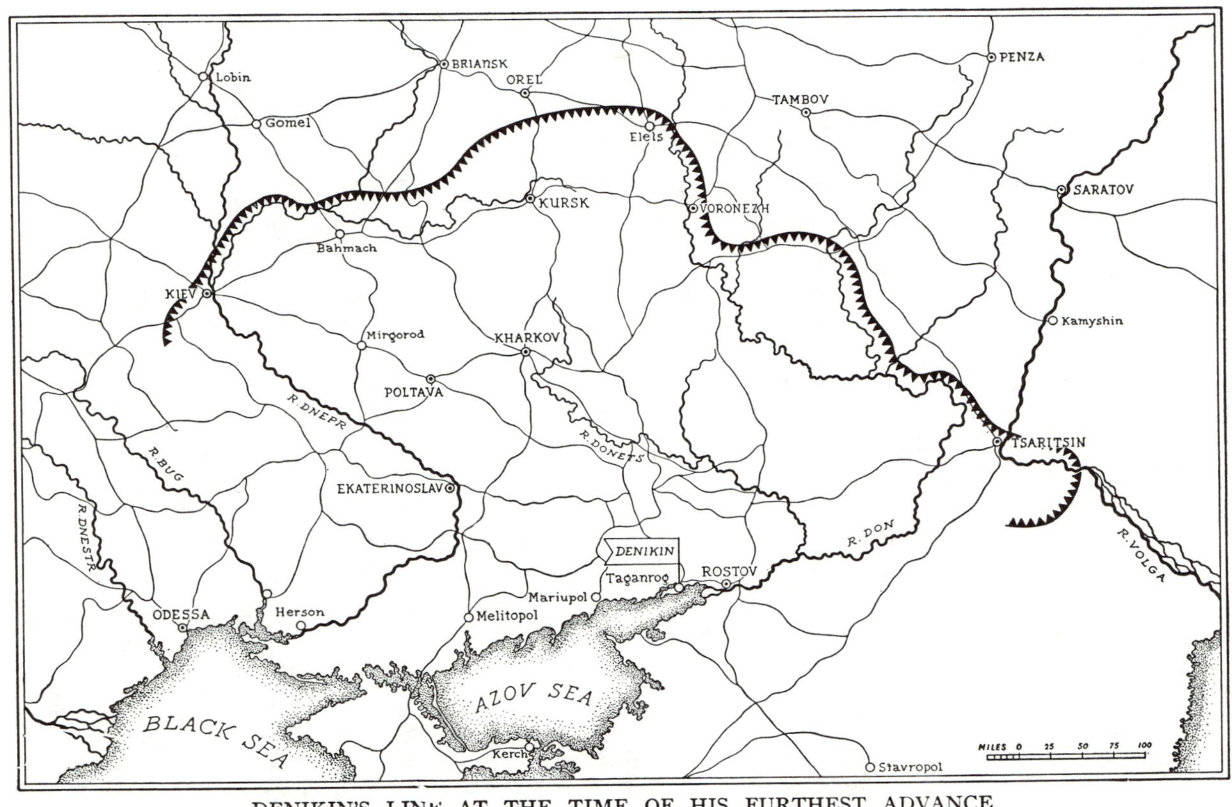

DENIKIN'S LINE AT THE TIME OF HIS FURTHEST ADVANCE

of his former opponents, saying that the fighting spirit of the North Caucasian Red Army was higher than that of many of the other Red Armies which he encountered during the civil war.[23] Trotzky did not, perhaps, take adequate account of the fact that the North Caucasian Red Army was compelled to fight much the strongest of the White armies in a territory where popular resistance to Bolshevism was greater than anywhere else in Russia. There were individual brilliant achievements of the Soviet troops, such as the march of the Taman Army; and the losses which the Volunteer Army sustained, both among its higher officers and among its men, were very heavy. Many of the most distinguished leaders of the Volunteer Army, Kornilov, Markov, Drozdovsky (the latter died of blood poisoning as a result of a wound which he received), perished on the battle-fields of the North Caucasian steppes. The founder of the Volunteer Army, General Alekseev, an elderly man in poor health when the civil war began, died in the autumn of 1918; and Denikin became the undisputed chief and leader of the Army and of the civil administration which developed as the Army's sphere of influence expanded beyond the Cossack territories.

Several times the Volunteers, who were always weaker in numbers than their opponents, were in difficult military situations, where a talented Red General, supported by a disciplined army, could perhaps have crushed them. But the conditions of civil war in the North Caucasus did not produce talented generals or disciplined armies (with the exception of the Taman force); and there seems no reason to dispute the general correctness of Trotzky's view that lack of regular military organization and adherence to partisan methods brought about the final collapse of the North Caucasian Red front.

The effect of this collapse on the general course of the civil war was very important. With a secure and untroubled rear, based on the massive range of the Caucasus Mountains, Denikin could turn northward in pursuit of his dream of creating with the bayonets of the Volunteer Army a "great united undivided Russia" and of achieving in Russia what he had achieved in the North Caucasus: the smashing of the Soviets. From a local he had become an All-Russian figure.

NOTES

[1] *Cf.* Chapter XVII.

[2] Krasnov once sarcastically remarked in this connection: "The Volunteer Army is pure and innocent. But I, the Don Ataman, with my dirty hands take the German shells and bullets, wash them in the waters of the Tranquil Don and hand them over

clean to the Volunteer Army." *Cf.* Krasnov's article, "The Great Don Military Territory," in *Arkhiv Russkoi Revolutsii* (Archive of the Russian Revolution), Vol. V, p. 205.

[3] *Cf.* General A. I. Denikin, "Sketches of Russian Turmoil," Vol. III, p. 154.

[4] *Ibid.*, Vol. III, p. 156.

[5] I. Borisenko, "The Soviet Republics in the North Caucasus in 1918," Vol. I, p. 167.

[6] *Ibid.*, Vol. I, p. 168.

[7] "The Civil War, 1918–1921," Vol. III, p. 99.

[8] How little susceptibility Denikin showed for the local patriotism of the Kuban is evident from an incident which occurred when he was speaking at a banquet given in the palace of the Kuban Ataman, Filomonov. Denikin ended his speech as follows: "Yesterday the Bolsheviki ruled in Ekaterinodar. Over this building floated a dirty red rag. Cursed yesterday. To-day it is the Kuban flag that floats over the building. Strange to-day. But I believe that to-morrow the tri-colored national Russian flag will fly, that here they will sing the Russian national hymn. Splendid to-morrow. We will drink to that happy, joyous to-morrow." *Cf.* Filomonov's article, "The Crushing of the Kuban Rada," in *Archive of the Russian Revolution,* Vol. V, p. 324.

[9] Denikin, *op. cit.*, Vol. III, pp. 205, 206.

[10] *Cf.* V. A. Kukel's article, "The Sinking of the Black Sea Fleet," in *Proletarskaya Revolutsia* (Proletarian Revolution), No. 6, for 1925, for the details of the sinking.

[11] Borisenko, *op. cit.*, Vol. II, pp. 169, 170.

[12] E. Kovtyukh, "From the Kuban to the Volga and Back," p. 24.

[13] N. E. Kakurin, "How the Revolution Was Fought," Vol. I, pp. 254, 255.

[14] Baturin, "The Red Taman Army," p. 33.

[15] The fullest and best account of the events connected with Sorokin's mutiny is to be found in I. Borisenko, *op. cit.*, Vol. II, pp. 186ff.

[16] Denikin, *op. cit.*, Vol. III, p. 229.

[17] Kovtyukh, *op. cit.*, p. 65.

[18] M. Svechnikov, "The Struggle of the Red Army in the North Caucasus," p. 45.

[19] Wrangel was an excellent representative of the die-hard upholder of the old regime, ready to fight and to risk his life for his convictions. The following brief note in his reminiscences ("Memoirs of General Wrangel," p. 18) throws revealing light on his personality. Referring to conditions in Petrograd in 1917, after the Revolution, when many officers put on red rosettes, Wrangel writes: "Throughout my stay in the capital I wore the badge of the Tsarevitch, the distinguishing mark of my old regiment, on my epaulettes; and, of course, I wore no red rag."

[20] *Cf.* Svechnikov, *op. cit.*, p. 221.

[21] A Soviet author, Serafimovitch, has taken the theme of his novel, "The Iron Flood," from the experiences of the Taman Army.

[22] *Cf.* Kochergin, "Sketches of the Civil War in the North Caucasus," pp. 53, 54.

[23] Denikin, *op. cit.*, Vol. IV, p. 113.

CHAPTER XXVIII

ALLIED INTERVENTION

THE military collapse of Germany brought the Allied powers face to face with revolutionary Russia. As has been pointed out, Allied military intervention had set in during the summer of 1918 and Allied military forces were in occupation of Vladivostok, Archangel, Murmansk and other Russian towns. But this early phase of intervention was represented, not very ingenuously in some cases, as a part of the general war effort against Germany. A justification for the Archangel and Siberian expeditions was sought in such arguments as the necessity for guarding military stores and for thwarting ostensible German designs to establish submarine bases on Russia's northern coast and to utilize armed German and Austro-Hungarian war prisoners in Siberia. The possibility of a German-Turkish thrust into the Middle East and ultimately toward India was cited as the reason for the activities of the British General Dunsterville, who with a small force temporarily occupied the great oil centre of Baku, on the Caspian Sea, in the summer of 1918, but was forced to evacuate it before the advance of superior Turkish forces; and of General Malleson, who extended military and financial aid to an anti-Bolshevik Government which had sprung up in the Trans-Caspian Territory after a revolt against the Soviet regime, which had its headquarters in Tashkent. It must be borne in mind that at that time there was a widespread belief, both in foreign countries and among anti-Bolshevik Russians, that the Bolsheviki were German agents and that a blow against the Soviets was, therefore, a blow against Germany.

With the elimination of Germany as a combatant force the situation, of course, radically changed. The little interventionist fronts in Russia could no longer be regarded as part of the general front against the Central Powers. The insistent question arose: Was it to be war or peace with Soviet Russia?

To this question the Allied statesmen, assembled at Versailles, could not find a clearcut answer. They could not bring themselves either to make outright war on the Soviets or to make peace with them. It is not surprising, therefore, that the course of Allied policy toward Russia excited almost an equal measure of denunciation from Soviet sympathizers, who pointed to the maintenance of a blockade of Soviet territory and to the extension of aid with supplies and munitions to the White Governments as acts which were inconsistent with the Allied professions of unwillingness to interfere in Russian internal affairs, and from anti-Bolshevik Russians, who complained that Allied help was tardy, irregular and insufficient.

One searches in vain in the records of the time not only for a consistent Allied policy, but even for a steadfast policy on the part of the individual Allied powers. Great Britain made far and away the largest contribution to the interventionist cause; its expenditures are officially estimated at approximately a hundred million pounds sterling.[1] Yet more than once Great Britain's mercurial Premier, Lloyd George, displayed a tendency to come to terms with the Soviet rulers. Moreover, it cannot be said that Great Britain's interventionist policy hewed to a single line. On the one hand it gave lavish aid to the champions of the restoration of a "great undivided Russia," Admiral Kolchak in Siberia, General Denikin in South Russia, General Yudenitch in the neighborhood of Petrograd. At the same time it actively protected and supported little independent states which had sprung up on foreign Russian territory in the Caucasus and in the Baltic Provinces, although Kolchak and Denikin would never, in the event of victory, have reconciled themselves to the independence of these states. War Minister Churchill, a steady advocate of the maximum degree of intervention, was often at cross-purposes with Premier Lloyd George; and British military representatives in Russia often wished to embark on more ambitious projects than Cabinet Ministers in London, keenly alive to the factor of expense and more responsive to critical public opinion, were willing to sanction.

From the diplomatic standpoint France was most implacable in its hostility to the Soviet regime, most firmly determined to engage in no dealings with it. But France gave far less practical aid to the Whites than did England; its sole independent venture in intervention, at Odessa, ended in a complete fiasco. The obvious waverings and inconsistencies of the Allied policy in relation to Russia are vividly summarized and satirized by Churchill in the following passage:[2]

"Were they [the Allies] at war with Soviet Russia? Certainly not; but they shot Soviet Russians at sight. They armed the enemies of the Soviet Government. They blockaded its ports and sunk its battleships. They earnestly desired and schemed its downfall. But war—shocking! Interference—shame! It was, they repeated, a matter of indifference to them how Russians settled their own internal affairs. They were impartial—Bang! And then at the same time: parley and try to trade."

The inability of the Allies either to make war effectively on Soviet Russia or to come to an amicable agreement with it can only be understood if one takes into account the political and social conditions which prevailed in Europe immediately after the end of the War. The statesmen in Paris were sitting on a thin crust of solid ground, beneath which volcanic forces of social upheaval were seething. Two of the most pronounced psychological characteristics of the time were immense war-weariness, in the victorious as well as in the defeated countries, and acute labor unrest. So there was one absolutely convincing reason why the Allied powers could not fulfill the hopes of the White Russians and intervene with large numbers of troops: no reliable troops were available. It was the general opinion of leading statesmen and soldiers alike that the attempt to send large numbers of soldiers to Russia would most probably end in mutiny.

At the same time there were strong factors which militated against the conclusion of peace with Soviet Russia and the cessation of aid to the Whites. The Bolshevik Revolution had been sanguinary enough; and its cruelties had been greatly magnified by the anti-Bolshevik émigrés who to some extent had the ear of the Allied statesmen. There was bitter resentment in France and England over the repudiation of the Russian pre-War debts, the confiscation of foreign property and what was regarded as a shameful desertion of the Allied cause during the War.

But probably the decisive factor in bringing about a continuation of the policy of limited intervention was the fear, by no means unreasonable or ungrounded in 1919, that Bolshevism in one form or another might spread to other European countries. The Bolshevik leaders had made no secret of their belief in the speedy coming of an international socialist revolution, as a sequel to the World War, or their intention and desire to promote it by every means in their power. East of the Rhine conditions were certainly not unfavorable to a collapse of the traditional social and economic order. So, consciously or unconsciously, the aid which was extended to

Kolchak, Denikin and other White leaders had a defensive as well as an offensive character. If it could not lead to the crushing of Bolshevism in Russia it might at least keep the Bolsheviki so fully occupied on the various fronts of the civil war that the spread of their militant doctrine beyond Russia's frontiers would become less probable.

The conclusion of the Armistice considerably increased the possibilities of direct contact between the Allied powers and Russia, since it opened the Black and Baltic Seas to Allied war vessels. On November 23 the French cruiser *Ernest Renan* and the British cruiser *Liverpool* arrived in the harbor of Novorossisk, accompanied by two torpedo-boats; early in December a British military mission, headed by General Poole, arrived in General Denikin's capital, Ekaterinodar, and received an enthusiastic welcome.[3] Poole declared he had come to find out how Great Britain could help its faithful ally, Russia. Denikin's hopes of large-scale Allied aid with troops as well as with munitions had been aroused still earlier when his representative in Rumania, General Sherbatchev, sent him an enthusiastic message to the effect that General Berthelot, commander of the Allied troops in Rumania, had decided to send twelve divisions of French and Greek troops to replace the Germans as a force of occupation in Ukraina. According to Sherbatchev, the French would first occupy the Black Sea ports, Odessa and Sevastopol, and then extend their occupation northward until it included Kiev and Kharkov. With this substantial aid it was expected that the White armies could launch a drive against Moscow. But the promised twelve divisions never appeared; the French intervention in Ukraina, when it did occur, was limited in scope and highly unsuccessful in execution.

In December a British fleet entered the Baltic Sea and on December 12 unloaded rifles and cannon at Reval for the use of the newly formed Esthonian army, which had more success than the neighboring Latvian army in holding back the new offensive of the Bolsheviki into the Baltic provinces.

A few weeks after the Bolshevik Revolution, on December 23, 1917, an Anglo-French convention had been concluded in Paris, regulating the future operations of British and French forces on Russian territory.[4] This convention defined as a British "zone of influence" the Cossack regions, the territory of the Caucasus, Armenia, Georgia and Kurdistan, while the French zone was to consist of Bessarabia, Ukraina and the Crimea. There was a certain economic background for this convention; British investment predominated in the Caucasian oil-fields, while the French were more interested in the coal and iron mines of Ukraina. So long as the Black Sea was closed the convention had no practical effect. But it was confirmed by the British War Cabinet on November 13, 1918, immediately after the Armistice; and both countries adhered to the spheres which had been marked out for them. The British promptly occupied Baku, on the Caspian, and Batum, on the Black Sea, thereby acquiring a firm grip on the Trans-Caucasus; they also assumed the main burden of supplying Denikin with munitions. The French intervention took place in Ukraina and the Crimea.

An urgent appeal for Allied military aid was voiced by a conference of prominent Russians, representing various schools of political thought, which was held at Jassy, in Rumania, from November 14 until November 23 at the suggestion of the French and British Ministers in Rumania. The participants in the conference ranged from monarchists to moderate Socialists; and the Allied representatives were somewhat disconcerted by the disagreements which manifested themselves about the future form of government. The majority of the delegates favored, as a temporary arrangement, a military dictatorship, headed by General Denikin; but a few monarchists upheld the claims of the Grand Duke Nicholas Nicholaevitch, while the right-wing Socialists felt that Denikin's power should be limited by a civilian Cabinet.[5]

On the need for military aid, however, the conference was unanimous; and it appointed a delegation of six members to go to Paris and present the case for intervention to the Western powers. This delegation had no success, however; and was even ordered to quit Paris, apparently because Clemenceau resented the fact that one of its members, Professor P. N. Milyukov, had adopted a German orientation for a short time in 1918.

One of the first Bolshevik reactions to the approaching victory of the Allies was a very curious note, signed by Chicherin and addressed to President Wilson, dated October 24, 1918.[6] The well-known publicist Karl Radek coöperated in framing it. The note is couched in terms of the bitterest scorn and abounds in flourishes of revolutionary rhetoric and thrusts of revolutionary sarcasm. So, referring to Wilson's insistence that governments participating in the peace negotiations must reflect the will of the peoples which they represent, the Soviet note observes that "we do not want to fight with America even though your government is still not replaced by a

Council of People's Commissars and your place is still not occupied by Eugene Debs,[7] whom you hold in prison," and that "in the name of humanity and peace we do not set as a condition of general peace negotiations that all peoples participating in them should be represented by Councils of People's Commissars, elected at Congresses of Soviets of Workers', Peasants' and Soldiers' Deputies." The note further remarks that "strangely we do not notice in your demands the liberation of Ireland, Egypt, India or even of the Philippines, and we should regret it very much if these peoples could not, along with us, take part in the organization of the League of Nations through their freely elected representatives." The note further suggested that "the expropriation of the capitalists of all countries" should be the foundation of the League of Nations, demanded the withdrawal of Allied troops from Russian territory and finally hinted, in extremely contemptuous tones, at the possibility of economic concessions from the Soviets to the Allies. This part of the note read in part as follows:

> "Will the governments in America, England, France cease to demand the blood of the Russian people and the lives of Russian citizens if the Russian people agree to pay them for this and to buy themselves off, as a man who has been subjected to a sudden attack buys himself off from the one who attacked him? And in this case what contributions do the governments of America, England and France demand from the Russian people? Do they demand concessions, the transfer to them on definite conditions of railroads, mines, gold resources, etc., or territorial concessions of some part of Siberia or the Caucasus or of the Murmansk coast?"

As a piece of revolutionary propaganda this note doubtless had its merits; but its phrasing was scarcely calculated to predispose President Wilson in favor of its authors; and the advisability of its despatch, in view of the Soviet interest in obtaining a cessation of intervention, is certainly open to doubt. It is noteworthy that the subsequent numerous communications with which the Soviet Commissariat for Foreign Affairs almost inundated the Allied powers are couched in more sober and realistic language and dispense with the rhetorical touches which distinguish the note of October 24.

Lenin had foreseen that the end of the World War would bring increased danger as well as increased revolutionary possibilities. "Now world capital will start an offensive against us," he said to Chicherin at this time.[8] And, in agreement with the other Bolshevik leaders, he seems to have decided that the proper Soviet policy, under the circumstances, was to play for time, to take every opportunity of offering peace, even on unfavorable conditions, to avoid provoking the Allied Governments. The Bolsheviki during this period might well consider that time was on their side. The breakdown of the German military power laid open wide regions of Southern and Western Russia for Bolsheviki penetration. The White Governments in Siberia, in the Don and Kuban were shaky and unstable.

If large-scale Allied military intervention could be staved off, still more, if Allied aid with munitions, on which the White Governments, located in unindustrialized parts of Russia, were extremely dependent, could be stopped, there was every prospect that the Soviet Government would come out victorious in the civil war. And beyond Russia's frontiers the Soviet leaders saw glittering revolutionary prospects in the war-weary European countries. The Peace of Brest-Litovsk had been annulled eight months after it had been signed. An unfavorable peace with the Allied powers might well be swept into oblivion by the onrush of social revolution.

So between the beginning of November and the beginning of February the Soviet Government addressed no fewer than seven peace proposals, couched in the most conciliatory language, to the Entente powers and to America.[9] One of these proposals took the form of a note addressed by Maxim Litvinov, then a member of the collegium of the Commissariat for Foreign Affairs, to President Wilson, despatched from Stockholm on December 24. Litvinov suggested that the Allied statesmen must choose between two alternatives: a continuation of intervention, which would lead to vastly more bloodshed and "to perhaps complete extermination of the Russian bourgeoisie by the desperate masses," and a cessation of intervention and blockade, accompanied by "help to Russia to regain access to its sources of supply and the giving of technical advice how most effectively to exploit its natural resources for the benefit of all the countries which are in acute need of food supplies and raw material." The note concluded with the assertion that "the dictatorship of the workers and producers is not an end in itself, but a means for the building up of a new social system, under which beneficial labor and equal rights will be granted to all citizens, regardless of the class to which they formerly belonged" and with an appeal to the President's "sense of justice and impartiality."[10]

This note apparently made an impression on Wilson, who sent W. H. Buckler, attaché to the United States Embassy in London, to confer with Litvinov in Stockholm. Buckler told Litvinov that his message had made a favorable impression on Wilson and on Lloyd George;[11] and Litvinov took advantage of this opportunity to make further proposals which were communicated to Wilson. On January 5 the British Government suggested that representatives of the Soviet Government and of the regimes which opposed it be invited to declare a truce and to send representatives to Paris.

This proposal foundered on uncompromising French opposition. The French Foreign Minister, Pichon, somewhat smugly announced that "the French Government will make no contract with crime." The French in general were strongly opposed to any negotiations with the Bolsheviki. Foch wanted to hurl against the Soviets an army composed of American troops "together with Polish forces and well disposed Russian prisoners of war."[12] But no American troops, apart from the small contingents stationed in Siberia and North Russia, were available for interventionist purposes; and Russian war prisoners did not furnish hopeful recruiting material. Premier Clemenceau dreamed of an Allied "defensive front," which would shut the Bolsheviki off from Ukraina, the Caucasus and Western Siberia.[13] Here again, however, the essential element, dependable troops, could not be found.

Despite their failure to bring Russian representatives to the Peace Conference, Wilson and Lloyd George did not abandon their efforts to find a pacific solution for the Russian problem. On January 21, at Wilson's suggestion, it was decided to invite representatives of the Soviet Government and of the anti-Bolshevik governments in Russia to a conference with representatives of the Allied powers and of America on Prinkipo Island, in the Sea of Marmora, near Constantinople. President Wilson was entrusted with the framing of the invitation; and he suggested as the purpose of the meeting a free and frank exchange of views, so that the desires of all groups of the Russian people might be made known and so that an agreement might be reached, by means of which Russia could define its own intentions and establish a basis of cooperation with other nations. The invitation proposed a general armistice between the contending forces in Russia and set February 15 as the date for the conference.

In the light of actual Russian conditions there is something naïve about this Prinkipo proposal. Russian Reds and Whites were engaged in a life-and-death struggle, in which there could be no compromise and no agreement. The French and Italian representatives had yielded very reluctantly to Wilson's insistence in this matter and doubtless foresaw, not without satisfaction, the collapse of the project.

The Russian Whites unanimously and indignantly rejected the proposal. Their attitude was summed up in the communication of the head of the North Russian Government, General Miller, who crisply observed: "Moral considerations do not permit us to confer on an equal basis with traitors, murderers and robbers."

The Soviet Government, on the other hand, accepted the proposal with some delay (its note of reply is dated February 4), which it attributed to the fact that it never received the original invitation and only learned of the proposal accidentally as a result of the picking up of a news message by the Moscow radio station. There is one noteworthy omission in the Soviet acceptance; there is no concrete promise to cease fighting on any given date.

On the other hand very considerable material and economic concessions are offered to the Allied powers. So the note states that "the Soviet Government does not refuse to recognize its financial obligations in regard to those creditors who are citizens of the Entente powers." This is followed by proposals to guaranty the payment of interest on the loans with raw materials and to grant "mining, forest and other concessions" to Entente citizens. Finally the note expresses willingness to consider territorial concessions to the Entente powers.[14]

This rather crude attempt to buy off the Allied powers did not make a favorable impression on Wilson and Lloyd George; and the Prinkipo project was allowed to die the death to which it was condemned by the refusal of the Whites to consider either an armistice or a conference and by the failure of the Soviet Government, despite its acceptance of the invitation, to make any specific pledges about stopping the advance of the Red Army, which at this time was proceeding very rapidly, both in Ukraina and in the Baltic Provinces.

The negative attitude of the White regimes toward the Prinkipo suggestion was doubtless stiffened by intimations which were received from their friends in the Allied Governments that refusal to go to Prinkipo would not involve any stoppage of the former flow of supplies. Proof of this is to be found in a telegram which Sazonov, the former Tsarist Foreign Minister, who was the authorized representative in Paris of all the White Governments, despatched to Admiral Kolchak, on February 5: [15]

"I learn that the proposal for a conference on Prinkipo Island is being regarded as doomed to failure. France intends to continue support with supplies and does not intend to withdraw the military units which are in Russia."

After the Prinkipo proposal had fallen to the ground Wilson and Lloyd George tried another method of substituting a peaceful settlement for armed struggle with the Soviet regime. They sent William C. Bullitt, an attaché of the American Peace Delegation, who almost fifteen years later became the first American Ambassador to the Soviet Union, to Moscow with the double mission of finding out what peace conditions the Soviet Government would accept and of making a report on the general situation in Russia. Bullitt made a flying trip to Russia and on March 14 received from Chicherin and Litvinov the "text of a projected peace proposal by the Allied and Associated Governments," which the Soviet Government declared itself bound to accept, provided that it should be made not later than April 10.[16] This project provided for a general cessation of hostilities on the various Russian fronts, with each government retaining the territory of which it was actually in control, for a general all-around amnesty to political offenders, both in Soviet and in non-Soviet territory, for lifting of the blockade, withdrawal of Allied troops from Russian territory and a general resumption of commercial relations. The Soviet Government, along with the other states which would presumably arise under this arrangement on Russian territory, was to be responsible for the payment of the pre-War Russian state debt.

The map of Russia, if these proposals (which closely coincided with the tentative suggestions which Colonel House and Philip Kerr, Lloyd George's secretary, had put forward as likely to commend themselves to American and British opinion) had been carried into effect would have been a curious sight. The Soviet Government would have been in control of the greater part of European Russia; Kolchak would have had for a realm Siberia and a considerable part of the Ural Territory; the Cossack territories and the Crimea would have been under Denikin; a North Russian Government would have existed in Archangel; while a number of mushroom states would have existed in the Caucasus and in Central Asia.

In their proposals to Bullitt the Soviet leaders again proceeded on the assumption that it was worth while to pay a high price for the cessation of intervention and direct military aid to the Whites. They doubtless reckoned on a speedy collapse of the White Governments from processes of internal disintegration, as soon as the Allied aid was withdrawn.

But when Bullitt returned to Paris with the proposals and a favorable report on general Soviet conditions in his pocket he found the atmosphere very unsympathetic. Wilson did not receive him; Lloyd George, hard pressed by a Conservative majority in the House of Commons which wanted to hear nothing of agreement with the Bolsheviki, made haste to repudiate him.

The emergence of a Soviet Government, headed by Bela Kun, in Hungary, and Kolchak's advance toward the Volga, which was most successful during March and April, were two reasons for the failure to grant serious consideration to the Soviet proposals. The Hungarian upheaval, which was soon followed by a more short-lived Soviet regime in Bavaria, was an unpleasant reminder to the statesmen in Paris how shaky was the ground on which they were trying to build up a new European edifice. It certainly did not predispose them to a slackening of hostility to the main source of Bolshevism in Russia. The significance and the prospects of Kolchak's advance were naturally exaggerated by his sympathizers in Paris; for a short time it was believed that his entrance into Moscow was only a matter of weeks.

Early in April, Wilson, Lloyd George, Clemenceau and Orlando, replying to an appeal for aid in relieving the widespread hunger and disease in Russia from Dr. Fridtjof Nansen, the well known Norwegian Arctic explorer and humanitarian, expressed willingness to support a scheme for installing a regime in Russia similar to that of the Belgian Relief Commission, provided that "cessation of all hostilities within definitive lines in the territory of Russia" could be achieved. But no practical steps to carry this proposal into execution were taken. During the period of civil war Allied relief was distributed exclusively in the new border states and in territory occupied by the Whites.

After abandoning any effort to reach an agreement with the Soviets the statesmen in Paris decided to give a more formal character to their relations with the Government of Admiral Kolchak in Omsk, which was acknowledged by the other outstanding White leaders (General Denikin in South Russia, General Miller in Archangel and General Yudenitch in the Northwest) as the all-Russian national Government. On May 27 Clemenceau, in the name of the Allied Supreme Council, addressed a note to Kolchak, proposing to continue supporting his Government by the despatch of munitions, supplies and food, provided that "the Allied Governments will have proofs that they are really helping the Russian people to achieve freedom, selfgovernment and peace."

The note[17] then proceeded to subject the Admiral to a sort of political catechism, laying down as conditions for support that he should convene a Constituent Assembly as soon as he captured Moscow, that free elections should be guarantied in the territory under his control, that he should make no attempt to grant special class privileges or to "restore the regime destroyed by the Revolution." The note also demanded a recognition of the independence of Finland and Poland and of the autonomy of Esthonia, Latvia, Lithuania and of the Caucasian and Trans-Caspian territories and of the right of the Peace Conference to determine the fate of "the Rumanian parts of Bessarabia." Finally it referred to a declaration by Kolchak acknowledging responsibility for Russia's state debt.

Kolchak was considerably irritated by this searching inquiry into his political views and plans, although it was dictated probably not so much by interest in the pure democracy of Kolchak's dictatorial regime as by a desire to have formally satisfactory replies, which could be cited as a reply to critics who objected to the extension of aid to a government with a reactionary reputation. However, with the continuance of Allied supplies and perhaps formal Allied diplomatic recognition hanging in the balance, the Omsk Government hastened to draw up a reply which would produce a satisfactory impression in Paris. Kolchak pledged himself to convene a Constituent Assembly and to hand over power to it as soon as the Bolsheviki were overthrown. He rejected the suggestion in the Allied note that the Constituent Assembly which had been elected in 1917 might be temporarily convened on the ground that "it had been elected under the violent regime of the Bolsheviki, and the majority of its members are now really in the Bolshevik ranks."[18] Kolchak recognized the independence of Poland, but declared that the final decision of the Finnish question must be reserved for the Constituent Assembly. He safeguarded himself against undue concessions by stating that this body must have the right of finally sanctioning all the decisions of his Government, professed willingness to let the League of Nations arbitrate any disputes which might arise with the non-Russian nationalities, and declared that there could be no return to the pre-revolutionary regime.

The Allied representatives on June 12 expressed willingness, as a result of this reply, to continue supporting Kolchak's Government. They did not, however, extend official diplomatic recognition to the Omsk regime. As Sazonov, Kolchak's Foreign Minister, in Paris, telegraphed to Vologodsky, his Premier, in Omsk on June 17: "Further steps toward official recognition are doubtless directly dependent upon the successes of the Siberian armies." But the Siberian armies after April had little but defeats to record; and the visibly increasing disintegration of Kolchak's regime during the summer and autumn of 1919 made official recognition unthinkable.

In July the American Ambassador in Tokyo, Roland Morris, went to Omsk to investigate the situation at first hand. This aroused some hope of American recognition; and Kolchak's officials, in traditional Russian manner, made a strenuous effort to create a favorable impression on the newly arrived visitor. "Reliable" delegations of zemstvo workers, members of coöperatives, etc., were paraded before him, in an effort to convince him that the regime enjoyed the support of the democratically minded part of the population.[19] Sukin, head of the Foreign Ministry in Omsk, told Morris that effective enforcement of the Siberian railway agreement, under which an inter-Allied Board was nominally in charge of the communication system, would require American recognition, a loan of two hundred million dollars and the sending of twenty-five thousand American troops to replace the Czechs, who were becoming steadily more hostile to the Kolchak regime.[20] There was, of course, not the slightest prospect of Congressional approval either for such a loan or for the despatch of troops; and Morris's visit remained without any practical result.

A popular Siberian song during the period of Kolchak contained the following words: "Uniform, British; boot, French; bayonet, Japanese; ruler, Omsk."

Indeed the international support accorded to the Omsk Government was of an extremely motley character. While the front was held exclusively by Russian troops (the Czechs ceased to take any active part in the civil war soon after Kolchak's *coup* of November 18) the guarding of long stretches of the Trans-Siberian Railroad, the sole artery of communication with Vladivostok, from which port Kolchak received munitions and supplies, was in the hands of Czechs, Japanese, British, Americans, French, Poles, Rumanians and Italians.

Where there were so many interventionists, clashes of national interest and viewpoint were almost inevitable. The British military and civilian representatives in Siberia seem to have pursued a consistent policy of supporting Kolchak's authority to the best of their ability. American policy in the Far East was somewhat confused because the commander of the American expeditionary force, General William S. Graves, as is very evident from his reminiscences, did not share the benevolent attitude of the American State Department toward the Kolchak Government. He came to regard it as an ineffective and sanguinary tyranny and, after the autumn of 1918, forbade American soldiers to engage in any military operations against the partisan bands which were beginning to harass Kolchak's lines of communication. The Americans, therefore, confined themselves to policing those sections of the railroad which were entrusted to their care. Relations between the Americans and the much more numerous Japanese, who were pursuing a policy of active occupation of Siberia east of Lake Baikal, were chronically strained; and this was even more true as regards the relations between the Americans and two Atamans, Semyenov in Chita and Kalmikov in Khabarovsk, local chieftains who governed the regions under their control with a good deal of brutality and were openly supported by Japan.

Toward the end of the occupation, on January 9, 1920, there was even an armed clash between an American detachment and one of Semyenov's armored cars at the station Posolskaya; this ended in the capture of the car and over fifty prisoners by the Americans.[21] The Americans sheltered deserters from Kalmikov's forces and helped the escape of some of the leaders of an uprising against the Kolchak authorities in Vladivostok in the autumn of 1919. The Kolchak authorities accused the Americans of supporting Bolshevik agitation and the Admiral himself, in an exasperated memorandum, called for their removal from Russia, writing: [22]

> "The American troops, consisting of the offscourings of the American Army, Jewish emigrants, with a corresponding commanding staff, are only a factor of disintegration and disorders. I consider their removal from Russian territory necessary, because their further presence will lead only to a final discrediting of America and to extremely serious consequences."

This demand of the Admiral was not carried out; Sazonov remarked that a withdrawal of the Americans from Siberia would create an unfavorable international impression. That American relations with the Kolchak regime remained far from cordial is evident from an entry in the diary of Pepelyaev, Kolchak's last Premier, for the month of September: "The behavior of America is disgusting. It has presented us with a demand to remove Semyenov and Kalmikov. General Graves has delayed the sending to us of arms, for which we paid in gold." [23]

Kolchak's relations with Japan were also unsatisfactory, although for quite different reasons. In contrast to the British and Americans, who pursued no territorial aims in Siberia, the Japanese were primarily interested in obtaining a permanent foothold in Russian territory east of Lake Baikal. Unlike the West European powers, Japan had no particular reason at this time to fear Bolshevism as a menace to its political and social order; it was only several years later that communism, as a political theory, began to exert a perceptible influence in the Far East.

But the sudden weakening of Russia seemed to the Japanese military leaders to present an admirable opportunity for rounding out the Japanese Empire by the addition of the northern half of Sakhalin Island, with its rich oil and coal deposits, the port of Vladivostok and an undefined slice of Siberia, perhaps as far as Lake Baikal. The Japanese steadfastly refused to send their troops west of Lake Baikal and took little interest in promoting Kolchak's military success. Their preferred Russian agents were Semyenov and Kalmikov, who could not hope to stand without Japanese support.

After the collapse of Kolchak's Government in the winter of 1919–1920 the other interventionist forces left Siberia. But the Japanese, who had been the first to arrive, were the last to leave. At first they endeavored to support Semyenov in Chita; then they decided to restrict themselves to a smaller zone of occupation, and Chita was taken by the Bolsheviki on October 21, 1920. The Japanese remained in Vladivostok and in the adjacent coastal region for two more years; their last troops left Siberia on October 25, 1922; and Vladivostok promptly passed into the possession of the Soviet Union. The so-called Far Eastern Republic, which had been set up by the Communists as a "democratic" buffer state, with its capital in Chita, during the period of the Japanese occupation, was then considered to have served its purpose, and promptly dissolved itself.

Several factors conduced to the abandonment of this venture in Japanese imperialism; the heavy expense of a prolonged military occupation, the inability to find any broad base of support for a puppet government among the Russian population; the severity of the climate; the uncompromising refusal of America to consider recognizing the legality of the Japanese occupation. The Soviet-Japanese Treaty of January 20, 1925, restored to the Soviet Union the last bit of occupied territory in the Russian Far East: the northern part of the Island of Sakhalin. The treaty also gave to Japanese companies long-term concession rights for the exploitation of Sakhalin oil and coal.

This, in brief outline, was the course of intervention in the East. In South Russia, Great Britain and France played the leading rôles. The most ambitious effort at direct military intervention, as distinguished from the sending of aid with munitions and supplies to the Whites, was made by the French in Odessa. The first descent in Odessa occurred on December 18. The city was in an extremely chaotic condition, with representatives of Denikin's Volunteer Army, of the Ukrainian Nationalists, of the local city council and of the Soviet, which was emerging from an underground existence, all claiming power.

The French regarded Denikin's representatives as the lawful authority and appointed General Grishin Almazov, who was subordinated to Denikin, military governor of the city. The interventionist forces in the beginning consisted of 6,000 French, 2,000 Greeks, and 4,000 Polish Legionaries. Later their strength was brought up to two French and two Greek divisions, reinforced by a small number of Rumanians; altogether the foreign troops in the Odessa region at the high point of the occupation numbered forty or forty-five thousand; there were also 7,500 French and Greeks in the neighboring Crimea.[24] General Borius, Commander of the 156th French Infantry Division, which was first to arrive in Odessa, announced in a proclamation that the Allies had arrived in Russia "in order to give the healthy and patriotic elements the possibility to restore order."[25] The intervention was generally greeted by the propertied and conservative classes; and General Denikin, whose own military strength was fully absorbed in wiping out the North Caucasian Red armies, hoped that the French would replace the Germans as an anti-Bolshevik force in Ukraina.

But a process of mutual disillusionment as between the French and the Russian Whites set in almost from the moment when Odessa was occupied. The French found in Odessa a great many disputing politicians, but very few organized Russian troops. They had come in the expectation that their mere presence would give the "healthy and patriotic elements" the upper hand; they found Ukraina in the throes of social upheaval, with no conservative military force of any consequence, and with the country passing rapidly from the "semi-Bolshevism" of the Ukrainian nationalist leader, Petlura, to real Bolshevism, which was being brought from the North by the advancing Red Army.

The White Russians, who always cherished an exaggerated idea of the willingness of other people to fight their battles for them, were correspondingly disappointed when they realized that the French had no intention of doing any serious fighting. The morale of the Allied troops, as was natural after the end of the World War, was extremely low. The soldiers wore red rosettes; discipline was loosely observed; there were several cases of refusal to obey military orders and even of desertion to the Reds. As Colonel Freydenberg, Chief of Staff to General D'Anselme, commander of the forces of occupation, remarked on one occasion: [26] "No French soldier who saved his life after the Marne and Verdun would want to lose it on the fields of Russia."

Social and economic conditions throughout the period of the occupation were extremely unfavorable. Most of the factories had ceased to operate; food was scarce and expensive; the local paper money lost ninety percent of its value between November and April. Odessa, as a cosmopolitan seaport, had always possessed a considerable number of professional criminals. As a result of the general breakdown of morale and authority armed banditism increased enormously; at the end of January the Society of South Russian Industrialists addressed a petition to the Allied and Volunteer Army command, pointing out "the great number of cases of bold robberies and extortions and the inactivity of the local authorities, who are completely terrorized by bandits."

At first the Allies gradually pushed out their lines in a northward direction; and in February they were occupying the towns of Tiraspol, Kherson and Nikolaev. But they had little stomach for fighting and they crumpled up before the first onslaught of Ataman Grigoriev, an Ukrainian partisan who at this time was fighting on the Soviet side. On March 10 Grigoriev drove the French and Greeks from Kherson; they lost about 400 killed and wounded; and this intensified the demoralization of the soldiers and sailors in Odessa. On the 14th Nikolaev, which was feebly defended by a German garrison which had remained there, was also taken and Grigoriev pressed on toward Odessa.

Meanwhile active Bolshevik propaganda was going on in Odessa and found receptive soil among the French soldiers and especially among the sailors. A regional Communist Party committee was formed and pursued three objectives: to disorganize the hostile troops by means of propaganda, to obstruct the movement of forces to the front and to prepare the workers for armed revolt. A so-called "foreign collegium," consisting of Communists with a knowledge of French, was formed and for a time regularly printed a newspaper, *Le Communiste* in an abandoned quarry outside the city. Propaganda was carried on by word of mouth in cafés and cabarets; the French were urged to remember their own revolution and not to interfere in other people's quarrels. The collegium held its last meeting on March 2, when it discussed plans for arousing mutiny on the ships and a revolt among the soldiers, to coincide with the approach of Grigoriev's partisan forces. The meeting was betrayed by an *agent provocateur;* and eleven arrested members of the collegium were shot. But the seeds of disaffection were already widespread. The French authorities in Paris doubtless received information about the flagging morale of their forces in Odessa and decided to wind up the entire unfortunate enterprise as rapidly as possible. Apparently as a result of a peremptory order from Paris, received on April 2, a hasty evacuation was decreed; and on April 6 the last French ship had steamed away and Grigoriev's forces entered the city. Increasingly bad feeling had grown up between the French commanders and Denikin's representatives; and shortly before the evacuation Denikin's Generals, Grishin Almazov and Sannikov, were practically ordered out of the city.

Events followed much the same course in the Crimea, where a well-meaning but helpless Government of Zemstvo Liberals, organized after the withdrawal of the Germans, found itself compromised by the cruelties and excesses of a small detachment of the Volunteer Army, which represented the sole armed force at its disposal. The Volunteers were too weak to make a stand at the natural defense of the Crimea, the Isthmus of Perekop; the French disgustedly expressed unwillingness to aid an "army which flees from the field of battle"; and by the end of April the Crimea was also evacuated and the Soviet troops were in full occupation, except in the region of Kertch, at the extreme eastern end of the Crimea.

This marked the end of the French direct intervention in South Russia; subsequent French activity assumed the form mainly of giving naval aid to the Whites.

British intervention in the South pursued two separate and sometimes clashing ends: to support General Denikin and to foster the new Republics which had sprung up, claiming independence, on the southern side of the main Caucasus range. The lively British interest in the security of Georgia, Azerbaidjan and Armenia can scarcely be attributed to abstract zeal for the rights of small nations. Some of the richest oil deposits in the world are in the neighborhood of Baku; and the possible implications of a British programme of expansion in the Caucasus were vividly outlined as follows by the chairman of four Caucasian oil companies at a meeting of the Bibi-Eibat Oil Company in London in December, 1918: [27]

"In the Caucasus from Batum on the Black Sea eastward to Baku on the Caspian and from Vladikavkaz southward to Tiflis, Asia Minor, Mesopotamia and Persia British forces have made their appearance, and have been welcomed by nearly every race and creed, who look to us to free them—some from the Turkish yoke and some from that of Bolshevism.

"Never before in the history of these islands was there such an opportunity for the peaceful penetration of British influence and British trade, for the creation of a second India or a second Eygpt, but the feeble voices of our politicians, under the heel of democracy, drown all such aspirations . . .

"The oil industry of Russia, liberally financed and properly organized under British auspices would, in itself, be a valuable asset to the Empire."

The British military authorities in the Near East laid down a demarcation line, running from the Black to the Caspian Sea and roughly coinciding with the northern frontiers of the new states, Georgia and Azerbaidjan. North of the line Denikin was to have a free hand; but he was not to undertake any military operations south of it.[28]

British interest in the Trans-Caucasian Republics was liveliest during the first months after the Armistice. By the summer of 1919 the British Government, faced with unrest in Ireland, India and Egypt, decided to clear out of Russia, abandoning dreams of political or economic expansion there. On July 1, 1919, the former Russian Ambassador in London reported to Omsk that Churchill had warned him of the necessity of gradually withdrawing British troops from all the Russian fronts. British forces left Baku and Tiflis in the summer of 1919; there were inconclusive negotiations about the replacement of the British by Italians in the Caucasus. Batum, the last British foothold in the Caucasus, to which Lord Curzon stubbornly clung for some time, was evacuated in July,

1920, when the civil war had virtually ended in favor of the Soviet regime and an attempt to remain on Caucasian territory with small forces was clearly likely to end in disastrous failure.

The "sideshows" in North Russia, where the British had furnished the main interventionist forces, were wound up in the autumn of 1919; Archangel was abandoned on September 27 and Murmansk on October 12. This North Russian intervention had never exercised any decisive strategic importance; the forces involved were too small and the places occupied were too remote from the main centres of the civil war. The inconsiderable British forces which had been sent to Siberia were withdrawn in September and in November, 1919, when Kolchak was clearly doomed. Another minor interventionist venture in the Trans-Caspian Territory came to an end in the summer of 1919. The British and Indian troops which, under the direction of General Malleson, had been coöperating with the anti-Bolshevik rebels in this desert region, were withdrawn from the front in June and from the town of Krasnovodsk, opposite Baku, on the other shore of the Caspian Sea, somewhat later.[29]

The British actively aided General Yudenitch, who recruited a White army in Northwestern Russia and made two dashes on Petrograd, one in the spring and one in the fall of 1919. The latter was almost successful. In September a flotilla of British motorboats broke into Kronstadt harbor and inflicted some damage. The British not only aided Yudenitch with munitions and supplies, but gave the Northwestern Government which was associated with him some very forceful advice. So the British General Marsh, weary of the endless arguments and disagreements of the civilian politicians, called a number of them together on August 11 and gave them forty minutes in which to form a "democratic government," simultaneously demanding the recognition of the independence of Esthonia. The stubborn unwillingness of the Whites, obsessed with the idea of "great undivided Russia," to recognize the independence of Finland and Esthonia, the coöperation of which would have been very desirable in the operations against Petrograd, was a not inconsiderable cause of their defeat.

When Denikin's army definitely collapsed, in March, 1920, British warships assisted and covered the evacuation of the troops from Novorossisk to the Crimea, thereby saving them from annihilation at the hands of the pursuing Reds. After Wrangel took over the command from Denikin and made a last stand for the

White cause in the Crimea British aid greatly diminished if it did not cease altogether. On June 3 the British Admiral Hope informed Wrangel that, if he should undertake an offensive, the British Government would be unable to concern itself with the fate of the army.[30] The offensive was undertaken; and from that time Wrangel became a French rather than a British *protégé*. On August 10 the French Government even extended *de facto* recognition to his regime; and when it fell before the onset of the Red Army in November Wrangel placed "my Army, my Navy and all those who have followed me under the protection of France," simultaneously making an agreement with the French representatives, Count de Martel and Admiral Dumesnil, that the Russian warships and commercial vessels in his possession would be security for funds which France had advanced or would advance.

Few soldiers of the Allied powers or of America lost their lives as a result of intervention. The total British losses in North Russia, where there was more direct fighting with the Soviet troops than in other theatres of intervention, are officially stated as 983, including 327 killed. On the other hand the material contribution to the White Governments was very considerable, and doubtless prolonged their existence far beyond the time to which they might have been expected to survive if they had been left to their own resources. Churchill declares that almost 100,000 tons of arms, ammunition, equipment and clothing were sent to Kolchak by Great Britain during 1919 and summarizes the British aid to Denikin as follows:[31]

> "A quarter million rifles, two hundred guns, thirty tanks and large masses of munitions and equipment were sent through the Dardanelles and the Black Sea to the port of Novorossisk; and several hundred British officers and non-commissioned officers, as advisers, instructors, storekeepers, and even a few aviators furthered the organization of his armies."

The French contribution was less than the British; but was also fairly large. America advanced no direct loans to the Whites; but the Ambassador of the Provisional Government, Bakhmetiev, was able to use considerable sums accruing from a credit which had been advanced to the Kerensky Government before its fall in sending supplies to the Whites.

Regarded as an aggressive enterprise Allied intervention in Russia was a complete and unmitigated failure. The Soviets smashed every one of the White Governments which opposed them; and considerable quantities of the Allied supplies finally fell into the hands of the Red Army. Intervention, in the long run, brought absolutely no territorial or economic advantage to any of its participants.

But intervention had also its defensive, negative aspect; and here it was perhaps more effective than might appear at first sight. There is an element of truth in the reflection with which Churchill, the sturdiest advocate of intervention, consoles himself in surveying its results:

> "The Bolsheviki were absorbed during the whole of 1919 in the conflicts with Kolchak and Denikin. Their energy was turned upon the internal struggle. A breathing-space of inestimable importance was afforded to the whole line of newly liberated countries which stood along the western borders of Russia. . . . Finland, Esthonia, Latvia, Lithuania and, above all, Poland were able during 1919 to establish the structure of civilized states and to organize the strength of patriotic armies."

Two things should not be forgotten in judging the events of 1919. First, a large part of Eastern and Central Europe was in varying degrees of political, social and economic disorganization and was correspondingly receptive to Bolshevik agitation. Second, the Bolshevik leaders at that time took their international revolutionary mission very seriously. It was lack of strength, not lack of will, that prevented them from supporting Bela Kun in Hungary and apostles of social revolution in other countries as energetically as Great Britain supported Kolchak and Denikin.

Had there been no intervention, had Allied aid to the Whites stopped after the end of the War, the Russian civil war would almost certainly have ended much more quickly in a decisive victory of the Soviets. Then a triumphant revolutionary Russia would have faced a Europe that was fairly quivering with social unrest and upheaval.

It is quite impossible, of course, to say with certainty what might have happened in such a case. But there were several episodes in the civil war when Bolshevik progress to the West was directly hampered by the temporary military successes of the Whites. When Kolchak made his thrust toward the Volga in the spring of 1919 he unconsciously sealed the doom of the Soviet Republics which had been set up in the Baltic States. When Denikin's Cossack cavalry pierced the Red lines in May and June, 1919, they put an end to revolutionary dreams of moving westward into Bessarabia, with a view to linking up with Soviet Hungary. The issue of the battle before Warsaw in August, 1920, might have been different if the large forces which were concentrated against Wrangel had been available on the Polish front.

So, while intervention did not overthrow the Soviet Government, it did, in all probability, push the frontier of Bolshevism considerably farther to the East.

NOTES

[1] Winston Churchill, "The World Crisis: The Aftermath," p. 256.

[2] *Ibid.*, p. 235.

[3] General A. I. Denikin, "Sketches of Russian Turmoil," Vol. IV, p. 36.

[4] *Cf.* Churchill, *op. cit.*, p. 166. The text of the agreement is printed in Louis Fischer's "The Soviets in World Affairs," Vol. II, p. 836.

[5] Further details of the Jassy Conference are contained in Professor P. N. Milyukov, "Russlands Zusammenbruch," Vol. II, pp. 72, 73, and in the excerpts from the work of M. S. Margulies, "A Year of Intervention," reprinted in S. A. Alekseev's compilation, "Civil War in Siberia and the Northern Territory," pp. 383–395. Both Milyukov and Margulies were participants in the Conference.

[6] For the complete text *cf.* Professor U. B. Kluchnikov and Andrei Sabanin, "Recent International Policy in Treaties, Notes and Declarations," Part II, pp. 181–188.

[7] Eugene Debs was an outstanding American Socialist leader, who had been sentenced to imprisonment under the terms of the Espionage Act.

[8] Fischer, *op. cit.*, Vol. I, p. 150.

[9] G. V. Chicherin, "Two Years of Foreign Policy of Soviet Russia," pp. 25–29.

[10] Kluchnikov and Sabanin, *op. cit.*, pp. 210–212.

[11] Fischer, *op. cit.*, Vol. I, p. 159.

[12] Churchill, *op. cit.*, p. 168.

[13] Milyukov, *op. cit.*, Vol. II, p. 75.

[14] Kluchnikov and Sabanin, *op. cit.*, Part II, pp. 221–223.

[15] I. Subbotovsky, "The Allies, the Russian Reactionaries and Intervention," p. 230.

[16] *Cf.* "The Bullitt Mission to Russia," p. 39.

[17] The substance of the Allied note and the full text of Kolchak's reply may be found in Professor S. P. Melgunov, "The Tragedy of Admiral Kolchak," Vol. III, Part I, pp. 320–325.

[18] This is doubtless a reference to the fact that some former Right Socialist Revolutionaries, after Kolchak's *coup,* regarded Bolshevism as a lesser evil than conservative military dictatorship and passed over to the Soviet side of the front. This incident is described in more detail in the following chapter.

[19] *Cf.* the telegram of Sukin to Sazonov, reproduced in Subbotovsky, *op. cit.*, p. 117.

[20] General William S. Graves, "America's Siberian Adventure," p. 240.

[21] *Ibid.*, p. 312.

[22] Subbotovsky, *op. cit.*, p. 102.

[23] Melgunov, *op. cit.*, Vol. III, Part I, p. 114.

[24] A. I. Gukovsky, "French Intervention in South Russia, 1918–1919," pp. 45ff.

[25] *Cf. Odessa Listok,* No. 275, for December 18, 1918.

[26] Gukovsky, *op. cit.*, p. 123.

[27] Cited by Professor E. A. Ross, "The Russian Soviet Republic," pp. 235, 236. Denikin also refers to this statement.

[28] There was disagreement as to whether the mountainous territory of Daghestan, along the coast of the Caspian Sea, lay north or south of the line. Taking advantage of a favorable opportunity, Denikin seized Daghestan in May, 1919; and the British finally agreed that it should lie within his sphere of influence. *Cf.* "Sketches of Russian Turmoil," Vol. IV, pp. 134ff.

[29] *Cf.* article of Z. I. Mirkin, "Intervention in Trans-Caspia," in the collection, "The Tenth Anniversary of Intervention," p. 197.

[30] "Memoirs of General Wrangel," pp. 209ff.

[31] *Cf.* "The World Crisis: The Aftermath," pp. 246, 250.

CHAPTER XXIX

THE RISE AND FALL OF KOLCHAK

Almost simultaneously with the end of the War which was supposed to make the world safe for democracy, the democratic anti-Bolshevik regime represented by the Directory at Omsk[1] was overthrown, with the willing acquiescence of the local representatives of the Allied powers. A military dictator, Admiral Kolchak, took supreme command of the forces which were fighting against the Soviets in Siberia and in European Russia.

The speedy end of the Directory could have been foreseen almost as soon as it was formed. It came into existence as a result of a compromise between the left wing and the right wing of anti-Bolshevik Russia; its five members were all men of moderate views. And compromises and moderation are never popular in a period of revolution and civil war. The mere fact that two members of the Socialist Revolutionary Party, Avksentiev and Zenzinov, belonged to the Directory made it violently disliked by the Siberian military leaders, conservative politicians and propertied classes. And the Directory found no compensating support among the industrial workers or among the poorer classes. For them it was not radical enough. The Central Committee of the Socialist Revolutionary Party, which was established in the Ural capital, Ekaterinburg, was profoundly dissatisfied with many of the concessions which Avksentiev and Zenzinov felt obliged to make to their more conservative colleagues. The two Socialist Revolutionaries in the Directory were continually at odds with their non-Socialist associates, Vologodsky and Vinogradov; and General Boldirev was not always an effective mediator.

From the moment when the Directory took up its residence in Omsk, on October 9, 1918, until its overthrow a few weeks later, it was enveloped in an atmosphere of hostility, plots and intrigues. The town was filled with reactionary officers who, especially after their frequent hearty drinking bouts, insisted on singing the old Russian hymn "God Save the Tsar," and made no secret of their intention to grant short shrift to all Socialists. The population was greatly swollen by the influx of refugees from European Russia; order was very badly maintained; robbery was common and murders, both political and criminal, were not infrequent.

General Boldirev's diary during the month of October vividly reflects the general feeling of nervous tension, of expectancy of some kind of *coup*.[2] On October 15 he notes that "in the city there is definite agitation against the Government, in which detachments of the type of Krasilnikov's [3] and other representatives of monarchism indirectly participate." On the 18th there are "rumors of revolutions in purely Mexican style." On the 19th an officer twice ran in to warn Boldirev that "we are in a network of intrigues and plots," proposed to strengthen the guard and plainly hinted that General Belov, the Chief of Staff, could not be trusted.

All the apprehension was not on one side. Although, as events showed, the most probable outburst of violence would be against the Directory, or rather against its left-wing members, Boldirev reports on October 23 that a special guard has been assigned to the home of a conservative member of the Directory, Vologodsky, as a result of the insistence of the Minister of Finance, Mikhailov, who is convinced that there is a plan to arrest Vologodsky. "This," Boldirev disgustedly comments, "is like a farce . . . Mexico amid snow and frosts." On October 26 a veteran Socialist Revolutionary, B. N. Moiseenko, disappeared; it was later found that he had been murdered. It is unclear whether Moiseenko was the victim of a political assassination or of an act of banditism; he was the treasurer of the Committee of Members of the Constituent Assembly.

An entry in Boldirev's diary for October 28 forecasts the future: "The idea of a dictatorship grows stronger and stronger in political and military circles. I have hints from different sides. Now this idea will probably be connected with Kolchak."

Admiral Kolchak, the future dictator, had arrived in Omsk from Vladivostok in October with the intention of making his way to South Russia. There was a distinct lack of men of firstrate military experience and reputation in Siberia; Kolchak was known as an innovator in the Naval Ministry in pre-War days and as a polar navigator; he had also become something of a hero in conservative circles because of his refusal to submit to the demands of the Soviets when he was commander of the Black Sea Fleet in 1917. So Boldirev invited him to assume the vacant post of War Minister in the Cabinet; the proposal aroused no objection on the part of Avksentiev and Zenzinov. Kolchak immediately began to play an active part in Omsk politics, vigorously taking the conservative side on several disputed question; and Boldirev undoubtedly regretted his invitation when it was too late to withdraw it.

In this general atmosphere of intrigue and violence Avksentiev and Zenzinov carried on a hopelessly uneven struggle with their political opponents, members of the Siberian Government, which, although it had formally ceded its claims to sovereignty to the Directory, actually retained full control of the administrative apparatus. Avksentiev and Zenzinov could not even get into direct telegraphic communication with their Party associates in European Russia without securing the consent of the Siberian Minister of Post and Telegraph.

The Cabinet of Ministers which was formed under the Directory was to a very large extent simply the old Siberian Ministry; even Mikhailov, who was especially objectionable to the radicals because of his active part in the suppression of the Siberian Regional Duma, was included in the Cabinet as Minister of Finance, despite the opposition of Avksentiev and Zenzinov. The latter did secure the appointment of one of their Party comrades, Rogovsky, as assistant Minister of the Interior; but this afforded the Directory no real protection. Another demand of the Siberian conservatives was fulfilled when Avksentiev persuaded the Siberian Regional Duma to vote for its own dissolution.

The impending outbreak in Omsk was certainly hastened by the publication and circulation of a proclamation which had been drawn up by the Central Committee of the Socialist Revolutionary Party on October 11, and which reflected the growing indignation and concern of the Party at the obvious swing to the Right in the Siberian political situation.[4] As proof of the growth of reactionary tendencies the proclamation cited "the repeal by the Siberian Government of the Land Law of the Constituent Assembly, the suppression in Siberia of the trade-union congress and of other workers' organizations and peasants' movements, a whole series of crying violations of liberty of speech, press and person, from which private individuals and entire organizations of Socialist parties suffer more and more frequently, the reëstablishment of epaulettes and army discipline of the old type, a whole series of personal appointments which hand over the army to reactionary generals and atamans." Perhaps the most militant phrase in the proclamation was that "all the forces of the Party at the present time must be mobilized, given military training and armed, so as to be ready at any moment to resist the blow of the counterrevolutionary organizers of civil war in the rear of the anti-Bolshevik front."

Under the political circumstances of the time it would have perhaps been more advisable for the Socialist Revolutionaries to do more and to talk less for publication. The subsequent course of events showed that their fear of impending reaction was fully justified. But the issue of their wordy proclamation raised no army for them and placed an excellent propaganda weapon in the hands of their conservative opponents, who were only too anxious to find a pretext for the military *coup* which they wished to bring about.

The phrasing of the proclamation aroused great indignation, especially in military circles. Even General Boldirev, who often sided with Avksentiev and Zenzinov in the continual disputes which occurred in the Directory, was in favor of starting judicial proceedings against the authors of the proclamation. Zenzinov tells us [4a] that it was just the conservative groups in Omsk which showed the greatest energy in distributing copies of the proclamation and bringing it to public attention.

The complexity of the situation in Omsk on the eve of the downfall of the Directory was intensified because foreign as well as domestic forces were at work. The Czech representatives at times displayed an almost proprietory interest in the Siberian Government, which they had helped so much to create; and their civilian representatives were generally inclined to side with the more left-wing members of the Directory. They made strong but ineffective representations against the appointment of Mikhailov as Minister of Finance; and one Czech representative is said to have told Avksentiev and Zenzinov that "within two days we can clear Omsk of all the reactionary scoundrels." [5] Avksentiev and Zenzinov did not accept this offer of intervening; they did not wish to assume the responsibility for precipitating a new civil war. Apart from the fact that the Czechs, who, in their majority, were democratically disposed, were naturally inclined to sympathize with the Socialist Revolutionaries rather than with the Russian conservatives, they had military grievances against the Siberian generals; they complained that they were obliged to remain on the front without rest, reinforcements or supplies, while Siberian forces were slowly being formed in the rear. In November, a few days before the *coup,* the impulsive and adventurous Czech General Gaida went so far as to threaten to send troops against Omsk if within forty-eight hours General Belov were not removed and reinforcements were not sent. Boldirev was very indignant at this crass breach of discipline; and the incident was adjusted without any resort to warlike activity on either side. But it showed how strained were the relations between the Czechs and the Siberian military authorities.

If the Czechs were inclined to cast such influence as they possessed on the side of the Directory, the British General Knox, who arrived in Omsk in October as chief British military representative in Siberia, made little secret of his preference for the method of dictatorship. A few days after his arrival he paid a visit to Boldirev, "drank tea and threatened to collect a band and overthrow us if we don't come to an agreement with the Siberians."[6] Knox said this, to be sure, as a joke; but against the Omsk background it was a joke with some significance. Knox expressed the strongest indignation at the proclamation of the Socialist Revolutionaries, declared that in England people would be shot for such conduct and threatened to stop the flow of British supplies if such agitation were not checked.

Avksentiev and Zenzinov were keenly aware of the precarious situation of the Directory. In a letter which they addressed to some of their Party comrades in Ekaterinburg on October 30 they wrote: "We live, as it were, on a volcano, which is ready to begin an eruption at any moment. Every evening we sit and expect that they will come to arrest us." Declaring that they understand the reproaches which have been directed against them because of their compromises with the Siberian conservatives, they protest, rather fatalistically, that they could not have acted otherwise, and ended on the note: "We desire one thing: that what must happen should happen quickly."[7]

The *coup,* which almost every political figure in Omsk anticipated, some with hope, some with fear, occurred on the night of November 17. A small group of prominent Socialist Revolutionaries, including Avksentiev and Zenzinov, three delegates who had just arrived from the Archangel Government and two other members of the Party Central Committee, Rakov and Gendelman, were in the apartment of the Assistant Minister of the Interior, Rogovsky. Here, if anywhere, they might have been considered safe, because a guard was posted outside the building. But a number of officers and Cossacks who belonged to the detachment of Krasilnikov, a well-known reactionary partisan chieftain, disarmed the guard, burst into the apartment and carried off Avksentiev, Zenzinov,

Rogovsky and Rakov to the Staff of Krasilnikov's detachment, on the outskirts of the town.

The Premier, Vologodsky, apparently learned of the arrests soon after they occurred and called a meeting of the Cabinet early in the morning of November 18. It is impossible to say with certainty how many of the Ministers had been initiated into the secret of the *coup* and how many were genuinely surprised by the new turn of events. No one seems to have suggested that steps should be taken to release Avksentiev and Zenzinov and to punish the persons responsible for their arrest. There was some half-hearted talk of carrying on the administration with a Directory of three, Vologodsky, Vinogradov and General Boldirev. (The latter at this time was absent at the front, a fact which was probably taken into account in the planning of the *coup*.) But this was soon dropped; and there was general agreement that a personal dictatorship offered the only solution for the political crisis. Only one Minister, Shumilovsky, expressed dissent.[8]

Then the question arose who should be the dictator. Kolchak, largely, one suspects, for form's sake, urged the claims of General Boldirev, as the actual Commander-in-chief of the Army. But the overwhelming majority of the Cabinet voted in favor of Kolchak; and he accepted the election, with the title of Supreme Ruler. He also assumed the office of "Commander-in-chief of all the land and naval forces of Russia," thereby combining supreme military and civil authority in his hands. In an appeal to the population he briefly summed up his programme of action as follows:[9]

"I shall not go either on the road of reaction or on the fatal road of Party partisanship. I set as my main objective the creation of an efficient army, victory over Bolshevism and the establishment of law and order, so that the people may choose the form of government which it desires without obstruction and realize the great ideas of liberty which are now proclaimed in the whole world.

"I summon you, citizens, to unity, to struggle with Bolshevism, to labor and to sacrifices."

Avksentiev and Zenzinov, with Argunov, an associate member of the Directory, and Rogovsky, were transferred from the headquarters of the Krasilnikov detachment to house arrest in Avksentiev's apartment, and were soon afterwards deported abroad. Knowing the occasional habit of Siberian military detachments of shooting prisoners, ostensibly while the latter were trying to escape,

Atamans Semyenov (*left*) and Kalmikov, two leaders of the White Cossacks in Eastern Siberia

A group of Ural Red partisans

they insisted on "international guaranties" of their safety while travelling through Russian territory; and Kolchak, in agreement with Colonel John Ward, who was in command of a small force of British soldiers in Omsk, made arrangements for them to have British as well as Russian guards during their trip through Siberia. Their trip was without incident and they finally reached Paris.

These are the main visible facts of the *coup* of November 18. There is still considerable room for doubt and dispute as to the precise organization of the movement. It is uncertain who gave the signal for Krasilnikov's men to act on the night of the 17th. Kolchak, on the eve of his execution, declared that he was not himself aware of the conspiracy before it was carried into effect, but asserted that he was later informed that among the participants were "almost the whole Staff, part of the officers of the garrison, the Staff of the Commander-in-chief and some members of the Government."[10] Kolchak had returned to Omsk from a trip of inspection to the front on November 16 and offers the following interesting testimony about conversations which he had at this time:[11]

> "After my arrival in Omsk many officers from the Staff and representatives of the Cossacks came to me and said quite definitely that the Directory had little longer to live and that the creation of a single-headed authority was necessary. When I asked about the form of this single-headed authority and whom they proposed to put forward, so that there would be a single-headed authority, they said to me directly: 'You must do this.'"

Kolchak asserts that he declined to assume this responsibility. But, while he most probably preserved himself from technical implication in a conspiracy directed against a regime with which, in his capacity as War Minister, he was associated, he can scarcely have been much surprised by the subsequent course of events and was evidently ready, after a little decent prompting, to assume the rôle of a dictator. The Omsk leaders of the Cadet Party, especially V. Pepelyaev, whom Kolchak subsequently appointed Minister of the Interior, seem to have played a prominent part in preparing the way for the *coup*. A Cadet Party conference which opened in Omsk on November 15 pronounced itself in favor of dictatorship. And in Pepelyaev's diary, under the date of November 17, one finds a mysterious entry, which seems to suggest close association with the impending *coup*. It reads as follows:[12]

"I went from the conference [presumably of the Cadet Party], *to the meeting. Meeting. All* participated. *Decided.* I went to P. Full agreement."

There was also some international influence in Kolchak's rise to power. The French General Janin, commander of the Allied forces in Siberia during Kolchak's regime, makes the definite statement that his British colleague, General Knox, knew of "Kolchak's conspiracy" and that one of Knox's Intelligence officers, Captain Steveni, had admitted being present at a secret meeting where the plans for the *coup* were decided on. This, of course, may be only hearsay. But we have Kolchak's own testimony to the effect that, when he intended to go to Mesopotamia for service with the British forces there, he found at Singapore a suggestion from the British Intelligence Service that he should return to the Far East and place himself at the disposal of the Russian Ambassador in Peking, who commissioned him to organize anti-Bolshevik forces in the region of the Chinese Eastern Railroad, in Manchuria. Moreover, before Kolchak arrived in Omsk, he had discussed with Knox in Japan means by which Great Britain could aid an anti-Bolshevik Russian army and the desirability of military dictatorship as a means of struggle against the Bolsheviki.[13] A more direct form of support to the new dictatorial regime, in case it should be threatened by the Czechs, is suggested by Colonel Ward, who writes: [14] "My machine-guns commanded every street leading to the building of the Russian headquarters."

However much the British representatives may have known about the *coup* before it took place, they certainly gave every sign of being satisfied with it after it had occurred. The French seem to have shared this satisfaction, if one may judge from Janin's instructions to the Czechs from Vladivostok to maintain strict neutrality (a line of action which, under the circumstances, could only be favorable to Kolchak), and from the following excerpt from Pepelyaev's diary for November 19:

"Ward told Kolchak that the British force in Omsk is at the disposition of the Admiral. The French are bringing favorable pressure on the Czechs for the purpose of neutralizing them."

The mood of the Omsk garrison was also an important factor in bringing Kolchak into power. It consisted largely of Siberian Cossack units which were extremely conservative in their political views. A leading officer in the garrison, Krasilnikov, had been involved in an incident at a banquet in honor of a newly arrived French mission on November 13; along with other officers, all rather far gone in their cups, he had insisted on singing "God Save the Tsar," despite the remonstrances of a representative of the Government. General Boldirev had given instructions to arrest the persons responsible for this affair; according to Zenzinov the Directory had given an order for the arrest of Krasilnikov and for the despatch of his unit to the front.[15] Krasilnikov himself testified before the court which tried him and two other officers prominently implicated in the overturn, Volkov and Katanaev, that he had arrested the members of the Directory because he had learned that his own arrest was under consideration. Under the circumstances, of course, the trial was a mere formality; the officers were not only acquitted, but promoted to higher ranks in the service.

So, while subsequent research may reveal that the events of November 17–18 were carefully planned in advance by a conspirative group, it is not impossible that the Cossack officers acted, to some extent, on their own initiative, knowing, of course, that powerful forces were in favor of a dictatorship, and that their act would bring them reward rather than punishment. Kolchak was certainly not the sole candidate for the part of dictator. Ivanov-Rinov, Belov and other Siberian military leaders doubtless had their own ambitions and were chagrined at his speedy success. But Kolchak was a man of all-Russian reputation, while his rivals were provincial Siberians; and the fact that he stood outside the petty factional strife and intrigue of Omsk doubtless was in his favor. Finally, he clearly enjoyed the preference of the British representatives in Omsk; and the Siberian Whites hoped for substantial aid from England in munitions and supplies, if not in soldiers.

The seizure of power in Omsk, which passed off quietly and without bloodshed, did not necessarily guaranty the success of the *coup* which had proclaimed Kolchak as dictator. Omsk was after all an accidental and artificial capital; there was no certainty that the territory under White control would follow its lead. There were several potential centres of opposition: the Czechs, General Boldirev, who was near the front, in Ufa, at the time of the overturn, the Socialist Revolutionaries, who were grouped around two centres: the Committee members of the Constituent Assembly, in Ekaterinburg, and the fugitive Samara Government, now established, with a very frail remnant of authority, in the town of Ufa, in the foothills on the western side of the Ural Mountains.

One by one, however, these sources of possible opposition melted away or proved ineffective. The representatives of the Czech National Council did place themselves on record as opposed to the *coup,* issuing a statement to the following effect on November 21: [16]

> "The overturn in Omsk on November 18 violated the principle of legality, which must be placed at the foundation of every state, including the Russian. We, as representatives of the Czecho-Slovak troops, on whom falls the main burden of struggle with the Bolsheviki at the present time, regret that violent *coups* are carried out in the rear of the operating army by forces which are needed on the front. It cannot continue thus any longer. The Russian Department of the Czecho-Slovak National Council hopes that the crisis of authority which has been created by the arrest of members of the All-Russian Provisional Government will be solved legally and therefore considers the crisis unfinished."

But no deeds followed these strong words. There were three causes for the sullen inaction of the Czechs. First, they were dependent on the Allies for transportation to their native country; and the representatives of Great Britain and France had given them clearly to understand that any hostile movement against the new regime in Omsk would not meet with favor. Second, while the civilian politicians and the majority of the Czech rank-and-file certainly disapproved of Kolchak's dictatorship, several of the Czech Generals, including the ambitious and adventurous Gaida, sympathized with him and hoped to make careers for themselves in the Russian service. Third, the Czech troops had no stomach for further fighting and desired only to return home, now that the World War was over. However much they might dislike the growth of militarist reaction, they were not inclined to take up arms in a new outburst of Russian civil strife. So the Czechs remained passive,—and were soon withdrawn altogether from the front and assigned to the task of guarding a long stretch of the Trans-Siberian Railroad.

General Boldirev keenly resented the *coup* which had been made behind his back. But, as he expressed it himself, "I thought too much, instead of acting." For a moderate democrat, such as Boldirev seems to have been, the position was intolerably complicated. To have sent troops from the front against Omsk, even if he could have found troops who were willing to go (almost all the commanders were in sympathy with the idea of a military dictatorship), would have played into the hands of the Bolsheviki, who were pressing hard toward the east. The only organized group to which Boldirev could have looked for support was the Socialist Revolutionary following of Chernov; and they were too "left" for the General's taste; moreover, he felt that they represented little real force. Boldirev relieved his feelings by telling Kolchak, "as a soldier and a citizen," that he regarded as necessary the restoration of the Directory, the release of its arrested members and Kolchak's own abdication. Then, after writing, and tearing up an order to the army and an appeal to the population, he went to Omsk, safeguarding himself against the possible employment of gangster methods against him by taking along a guard of fifty-two officers, armed with machine-guns. After a brief meeting with Kolchak he left the country.

The Socialist Revolutionaries in Ekaterinburg and Ufa came out with vigorous denunciations of the new regime. The Congress of Members of the Constituent Assembly elected a committee of seven members and commissioned it "to take all necessary measures for the liquidation of the conspiracy, the punishment of the guilty and the restoration of legal order and authority on all territory freed from the Bolsheviki." The Ministers of the Samara Government in Ufa talked self-confidently of sending "its volunteer units against the reactionary bands of Krasilnikov and Annenkov" and "furnishing the forces necessary for crushing the criminal mutiny." Kolchak replied with an order for the arrest of the members of the Constituent Assembly, whom he accused of "endeavoring to arouse an insurrection against the state authority."

All the effective physical force was on the side of the new dictator. On the night of November 19 officers and soldiers of a Siberian regiment stationed in Ekaterinburg carried out a violent raid on the hotel where Chernov and the members of the Constituent Assembly had their headquarters, arrested them and might very well have killed them if the Czech commandant of the town had not learned of the event and ordered their release. Gaida, who was in command of the Czech forces in Ekaterinburg, wanted to hand over Chernov, who was especially hated by the Russian conservatives, to the Kolchak authorities. A typically romantic Socialist Revolutionary named Chaikin went to Gaida and threatened to shoot himself and publish the circumstances to the whole world if Chernov were delivered up; [17] and Gaida agreed to let Chernov leave Ekaterinburg with the other members of the Constituent Assembly. These harassed Socialist Revolutionaries sought refuge with their friends in Ufa. But here also the clouds were thickening; on the night of December 2 the Siberian military authorities raided the headquarters of the Samara Ministers and arrested those Socialist Revolutionaries who had not been prudent enough to go into hiding in advance. A Socialist Revolutionary commentator sums up as follows the results of the struggle between the Omsk dictatorship and the Socialist Revolutionaries: [18]

"Kolchak and the officers' clique which supported him alone acted without losing time, while their opponents limited themselves to resolutions and did not have sufficient military forces to send immediately against Omsk."

The Socialist Revolutionaries in their hiding places in Ufa tried to work out a scheme for the capture of Ufa by means of a military uprising before the advancing Red troops should take the town. But the forces on which they counted were either non-existent or unavailable; and on December 31 the Red Army arrived.

A split now developed among the Socialist Revolutionaries. A minority of them, including Volsky, the former President of the Committee of Members of the Constituent Assembly, were so embittered by the triumph of militarist reaction that they were willing to discuss terms of agreement with the Bolsheviki. In return for an agreement to recognize the Soviet regime, to cease any form of armed struggle with it and to employ all their efforts for the overthrow of Kolchak and other White dictators, Volsky and his associates obtained a very temporary and precarious legalization of the Socialist Revolutionary Party in Soviet territory. Chernov and the majority of the Party members were not concerned in this agreement; they clung to the formula of the struggle on two fronts, against the Bolsheviki and against the Whites, although an underground Socialist Revolutionary Party conference in the spring of 1919 decided that, as a matter of tactics, the Party should cease employing armed force against the Soviets, while using all available resources, including terrorism, against the Whites. Chernov himself successfully played hide-and-seek with the Cheka until he escaped abroad and joined the ranks of the émigrés.

Kolchak could now feel that his title of Supreme Ruler was justified, so far as the territory of Siberia and Eastern Russia under White control was concerned. His authority east of Lake Baikal was very limited. Immediately after his accession to power he became involved in a sharp clash with the Japanese favorite, Ataman Semyenov, who had been on bad terms with him when both were endeavoring to organize anti-Bolshevik forces along the boundary of

Manchuria and Siberia, flatly refused to recognize Kolchak's authority. The impulsive Admiral dismissed Semyenov from his command and proposed to send military forces against him. But Semyenov enjoyed the powerful protection of Japan; the idea of employing drastic measures against him had to be abandoned. Ultimately a rather hollow and insincere compromise was reached; Semyenov acknowledged Kolchak's authority, and the latter withdrew his order dismissing Semyenov. Throughout the period of Kolchak's regime Semyenov, in Chita, like the neighboring Ataman Kalmikov, in Khabarovsk, assured of Japanese support, behaved like an independent ruler and paid little attention to orders from Omsk.

Professor S. P. Melgunov, the author of the most comprehensive work on Kolchak which has yet appeared, chose as his title: "The Tragedy of Admiral Kolchak." And in Kolchak's career there certainly are profound elements of tragedy, both for him personally and for the cause which he served.

In some respects he seemed the most suitable candidate for the rôle of dictator. He was a man with an established reputation as a naval commander and Arctic explorer, of unblemished personal integrity, of absolute devotion to the oldfashioned conceptions of patriotism and national duty which he cherished. His courage was distinguished; General Inostrantsev, who was closely associated with him, recalls the long automobile trips which the Admiral took, with complete disregard for personal danger, in regions near the front where hostile patrols might easily be encountered. Baron Budberg, a merciless critic of Kolchak's political and military policies and advisers, describes the Admiral as "a big child," a man who is quite devoid of selfishness and who "passionately desires everything good," but who is fatally handicapped by lack of knowledge, experience and criticism and spoiled by bad counsellors.[19]

But along with the strong features in Kolchak's character there were fatal weaknesses and defects. By general testimony he was extremely nervous, almost hysterical in temperament, quite lacking in the capacity for cool and balanced judgment. His past life as a naval officer, accustomed to giving orders and to having them automatically obeyed, wrapped up in a narrow specialized career, had not been calculated to cultivate in him the qualities of a popular leader, able to persuade and to inspire, as well as to command. And it was only as a popular leader that Kolchak had any chance of realizing his dream of crushing Bolshevism. The physical odds were heavily against him. Under his rule were some twelve million people, scattered over an enormous expanse of sparsely populated, undeveloped territory. Against him the Soviets were in control of a much more compact and industrialized territory, with a population at least five times as great. Kolchak's prospects of victory were slight at best and were non-existent unless he could win the definite sympathy of the population, in Soviet territory as well as in his own; and this he was quite unable to achieve.

The Admiral was not predisposed to reactionary views by considerations of aristocratic birth or great wealth. The son of an engineer, he had won promotion in the naval service by merit. But there was always a wall between him and the masses. Gins, a member of his Cabinet, tells us that he was even kept in ignorance of the details of debates in his Cabinet, which never possessed any real power. Absorbed in the purely military aspects of his struggle, Kolchak realized only too late, if he ever fully realized, that in civil war good administration in the rear is even more important than successful strategic operations on the front.

Moreover, Kolchak's knowledge and experience were confined to naval affairs. He was a complete amateur in directing operations on land, and in the first and decisive months of his operations against the Bolsheviki he was singularly unlucky in his choice of high military counsellors. This was not altogether his fault. Almost all the more distinguished White Generals were in South Russia, with Denikin. Kolchak had unpromising material from which to make a choice. Yet he does seem to have made a grave error of judgment in keeping an experienced General like M. K. Diederichs in the background until the military situation was already almost hopeless and entrusting the leadership of his forces to ambitious young men whose capacity was in inverse ratio to their selfassurance, such as the Chief of Staff, Lebedev, and the Czech adventurer, Gaida.

Kolchak was also handicapped by a romantic approach to the prosaic problems of everyday policy. Believing ardently in his mission as the restorer of a "great undivided Russia," he more than once adopted a stiff, uncompromising attitude in foreign policy which inflicted much damage on his own cause. Perhaps the most conspicuous illustration of this tendency was his stubborn refusal to recognize the independence of Finland, despite the fact that the success of Yudenitch's campaign against Petrograd was dependent on Finnish support and the commander of the Finnish army, General Mannerheim, had made it very clear that recognition of Finland's independence was an indispensable condition for any movement of Finnish troops against Petrograd. "History will never forgive me if I surrender what Peter the Great won," Kolchak melodramatically declared to General Inostrantsev, who had employed every argument to persuade the Supreme Ruler to yield to the Finnish demand. And Kolchak's stubbornness in this question persisted even after his armies were in full retreat and it was obvious that only favorable developments on other anti-Bolshevik fronts could save his regime from collapse.

So there were many threads in the pattern of the psychological tragedy of Admiral Kolchak. A "polar dreamer," as he has been called, a specialist wrapped up in naval affairs, he was almost predestined to be a very unsuccessful politician and commander of armies. A proud Russian patriot, he was compelled by force of circumstances to operate under conditions of humiliating dependence on the caprices of foreign interventionist powers. A man of passionate integrity, he was compromised at every turn by the corruption and arbitrariness of the subordinate officials of his regime. Devoted to the ideal of restoring respect for law and order, he was unable to check what has been appropriately described as "Bolshevism from the Right"—the wild and brutal excesses of the military chieftains who had helped to bring him into power and on whom he was dependent.

One of the most notorious and conspicuous of these excesses occurred soon after the *coup* of November 18. On the night of December 21 an uprising broke out in Omsk and in the neighboring railroad town of Kulomzino. It had been prepared by the secret Bolshevik organization which continued to function after the Soviets were overthrown; the main participants were the railroad workers of Kulomzino, a suburb of Omsk. It was mercilessly crushed; almost 300 people were killed during the suppression of the uprising; and 166 more were shot by courtmartial sentences.[20] The Government Intelligence Service knew of the preparation of the outbreak, and many of its organizers were arrested before it took place.

The sanguinary crushing of an uprising in time of civil war is common enough; one can imagine how the Cheka would have dealt with a secret organization of Whites which raised a rebellion in Moscow or Petrograd. But an incident that followed the suppression of the uprising aroused bitter indignation even among opponents of the Bolsheviki, and was subsequently described by Kolchak himself as designed to discredit his regime. In the course of the outbreak a number of political prisoners, Socialist Revolutionaries, Social Democrats and members of the Constituent Assembly, had been forcibly released by the insurgents. Most of them returned to prison and gave themselves up to the authorities. On the night of the 22nd a young lieutenant named Bartashevsky took from the prison a number of these prisoners and had fifteen of them shot on the bank of the river Irtish. Five of these had been condemned to death by a drumhead courtmartial; the others were killed by the arbitrary decision of Bartashevsky. One of the victims was N. V. Fomin, a leader of the Siberian coöperative movement and an active participant in the overthrow of the Soviets in the spring and summer. He had been quickly disillusioned by the militarist reaction which had emerged instead of the democratic government which he desired. The coöperative organization to which Fomin belonged issued a pathetic appeal, which doubtless fell on deaf ears amid the growing brutalization of civil war, but which seems worth quoting, in part, as an illustration of how the majority of the Russian radical and liberal intelligentsia felt about Red Terror and White Terror alike: [21]

> "And we ask and appeal to society, to the contending political groups and parties: when will our much-suffering Russia outlive the nightmare that is throttling it, when will deaths by violence cease? Doesn't horror seize you at the sight of the uninterrupted flow of human blood? Doesn't horror seize you at the consciousness that the deepest, most elementary bases of the existence of human society are perishing: the feeling of humanity, the consciousness of the value of life, of human personality, the feeling and consciousness of the necessity of legal order in the state? . . . Hear our cry and despair: we return to prehistoric times of the existence of the human race; we are on the verge of the death of civilization and culture; we destroy the great cause of human progress, for which many generations of our worthier ancestors labored."

Kolchak from the beginning of his regime always emphasized the importance of military victory over the Bolsheviki. And the fate of his system was to a large extent decided on a number of obscure battle-fields between the Ural Mountains and the Volga River during the spring and early summer of 1919.

At first the course of the struggle with the Soviet troops wavered indecisively. Toward the end of December the Siberian Army on the northern right wing of Kolchak's front [22] won a considerable success by capturing the town of Perm; this was offset when the Soviet armies farther to the south continued their victorious advance from the Volga and occupied Ufa and Orenburg, approaching the passes of the Ural Mountains.

Indirectly the capture of Perm may have had a harmful effect on the further course of Kolchak's military operations. It encouraged a concentration of forces on the northern wing, whereas sound strategy would rather have called for greater effort in a more southern direction, where the advance would have led into more populous regions and would have offered a prospect of ultimate union with the Volunteer Army of General Denikin. But Kolchak's military advisers were inclined to follow the will-o'-the-wisp of a junction with the British forces in Archangel, apparently overlooking the fact that such a union, even if it had been achieved, would have possessed little value, in view of the enormous expanse of thinly populated forest land in which it would have been necessary to operate. Jealousy of Denikin, desire to reach Moscow before he did, may have also played its part in the choice of the northern route of offensive.

Kolchak's armies enjoyed a brief period of substantial success during March and April. As often happened during the Russian civil war, the victories at this time are attributable not so much to the strength of the Siberian forces as to the weaknesses of their opponents. The central section of the eastern front of the Red Army, which covered the line of advance on Ufa and thence to Samara, was unduly weak; the Fifth Army, which held this sector of the Front, counted only 11,000 troops, as against 40,000 of Kolchak's Western Army.[23] Moreover, the rear communications of the Fifth Army were threatened and in some cases destroyed by a serious peasant uprising in the Syzran and Sengilei districts of the Middle Volga. The food situation in Soviet Russia, always difficult, regularly became seasonally worse in the spring; the pressure to extract the last reserves of grain from the peasants was correspondingly increased; and this, combined with the invariable and inevitable abuses of the local authorities, led to an uprising which was ultimately put down, but which facilitated the advance of the Whites.

Ufa, which had been lost to the Reds at the end of 1918, was retaken on March 13; and the forward movement of the Whites continued until the last week in April. At the high point of the offensive the important Volga towns, Kazan and Samara, were seriously threatened, while in the north the Siberian Army, under the command of Gaida, reached Glazov, midway between Perm and Vyatka.

Even during this period of success, however, Kolchak's Staff revealed serious shortcomings in its operative directions. There was little effort to coördinate the movements of the separate armies, which moved forward disconnectedly, each trying to gain as much territory as possible, without considering the general position or the practicability of holding the extended front. The Staff could not or at least did not put a stop to the open hostility and rivalry between the Siberian and the Western Armies, which led, among other things, to a continual struggle for supplies and to a complete lack of military coöperation. Baron Budberg, an official of the old school, who, from his post of vantage in the War Ministry, continually noted down acid but shrewd criticisms of the military and political conduct of affairs, makes the following entry in his diary for May: [24]

> "The whole trouble is that we have neither a real Commander-in-chief nor a real Staff nor any competent senior commanders. The Admiral understands nothing in land warfare and easily yields to advice and suggestions; Lebedev [the Chief of Staff] is incompetent in military affairs and an accidental upstart; in the whole Staff there is not one man with the least serious military and Staff experience."

As Kolchak's armies surged forward over the wide theatre of hostilities from the woods of the Northern Urals to the Orenburg steppes, they tried to fill up their ranks with mobilizations of the population. These were unsuccessful because of lack of equipment and instructors; the raw recruits who were obtained in this way usually dispersed to their homes at the first serious reverse.

The advance of the Whites on the Eastern Front called forth a vigorous mobilization of fresh forces behind the Soviet lines. The Communist Party and the trade-unions, which at this time were almost all under Communist control, decreed special levies of their members for the front. Reading through *Izvestia* for April, the most critical month on the Eastern Front, one finds the Penza Executive Committee forming a "Communist shock regiment," the Samara County Committee forming a "volunteer peasant regiment," the Novgorod Provincial Committee mobilizing half its members for the Eastern Front. Twenty-two provinces sent their representatives to the main points of concentration behind the lines: Samara, Simbirsk, Kazan and Vyatka.[25] The Orenburg workers themselves organized the defense of this town and prevented it from falling into the hands of the Whites, even at the height of their drive.

A definite turn in the tide on the Eastern Front occurred in the last days of April. A strong Red Army force which had been concentrated in the neighborhood of Buzuluk, on the Samara-Orenburg railroad, under the command of Mikhail Frunze, a veteran Communist who subsequently held the post of War Commissar, struck hard and successfully at the left flank of General Khanzhin's Western Army, which, in the course of the advance, had become spread out too thinly over too wide a front. The effectiveness of Frunze's drive was heightened because an Ukrainian national detachment in Kolchak's forces killed its officers and passed over to the Reds. Although the Staff in Omsk was informed of the threatening concentration of Frunze's forces it took no steps either to parry effectively the danger of a breach of the front or to repair its consequences after they had occurred. Throughout the month of May the White front steadily rolled back from the neighborhood of the Volga toward the Urals; and on June 9 the Red Army, which had forced the river Belaya, captured Ufa, the startingpoint of the offensive.

The Siberian Army, instead of coming to the rescue of its hard-pressed neighbor to the south, obstinately pressed on its own offensive, which reached its farthest point of advance, the town of Glazov, early in June. But it was also forced to begin a retreat which soon assumed the characteristics of a disorderly rout. At the southern extremity of the long front, in the territory of the Orenburg and Ural Cossacks, the Whites also met defeat after defeat; ultimately a considerable part of their forces in this region was caught in a wedge between the advancing Red Army from the West and the Turkestan Red forces, which were moving up from the south-east, and obliged to surrender. Some of the more resolute escaped by making a difficult long march over the waterless Kirghiz steppes.

After the capture of Ufa there was a sharp difference of opinion among the Soviet leaders as to the further course of operations on the Kolchak front. Lenin felt strongly that the Ural Territory should be conquered as soon as possible; one of his typically insistent, detailed, strongly phrased telegrams, addressed to the Revolutionary Military Council of the Eastern Front, on May 25, reads in part as follows: [26]

"If we don't conquer the Urals before winter I think the destruction of the Revolution is inevitable; strain all forces; look out carefully for reinforcements; mobilize the population in the front territory; take care of the political work; inform me every week by cipher telegram of the results; you are responsible for seeing to it that the units don't begin to disintegrate and that sentiment doesn't fall."

War Commissar Trotzky and Commander-in-chief Vatzetis, on the other hand, were primarily concerned with the advance of Denikin, which assumed very considerable proportions in May and June. They were in favor of stopping the advance on the line of Belaya and transferring a considerable number of troops to the Southern Front. They did not realize the extent of the demoralization which had set in among Kolchak's troops.

The advocates of a continuation of the drive against Kolchak prevailed; Vatzetis resigned and was replaced by S. S. Kamenev, the former Commander of the Eastern Front, a pre-War Colonel who served the Soviet regime loyally; Trotzky also wished to resign, but was persuaded to remain at his post. It soon became evident that the White armies were no longer capable of offering serious resistance. The natural barrier represented by the wooded range of the Ural Mountains was forced by the capture of Zlatoust on July 13; and on the following day the important railroad centre of Ekaterinburg, the capital of the Ural Territory, fell into the hands of the Reds. The White armies were displaying familiar signs of break-up: widespread desertion and voluntary surrender to the Reds.

Kolchak nervously made shift after shift in the leadership of his armies. After more than one stormy interchange of reproaches he dismissed his original favorite, the Czech General Gaida, who departed for Vladivostok with a special train which was rumored to be well provided with war booty, and placed General Diederichs in full command of his forces. Diederichs wanted to withdraw the shattered remnants of the White armies into Siberia, bring them into some kind of order and make a last stand on one of the rivers which form natural lines of defense in Western Siberia. But the young Chief of Staff, Lebedev, whose cocksure blunders had already exerted an unfavorable effect on the course of the campaign, obtained the consent of the impressionable Admiral for a complicated maneuver, designed to envelop and destroy the Reds at Cheliabinsk. For the sake of this attempt the last untrained reserves were thrown into action. Lebedev proposed to let the Reds occupy the town of Cheliabinsk and to outflank them from neighboring heights. The scheme would have required for successful execution a well-disciplined army with experienced leaders; it was foredoomed to failure when it was entrusted to forces which were already exhausted and demoralized by a prolonged retreat and numerous defeats. The fighting around Cheliabinsk in the last days of July and the first days of August ended in a rout; 15,000 prisoners were captured by the Reds. Diederichs had the ungrateful task of trying to organize the

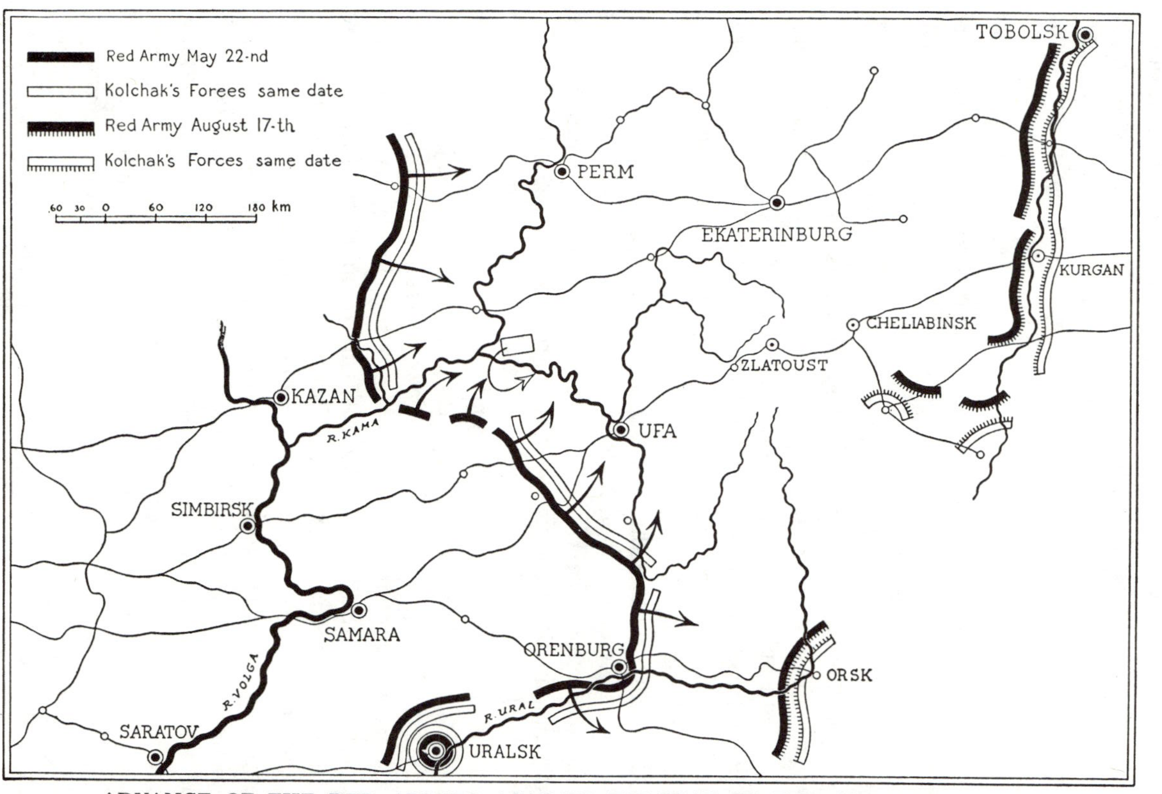

ADVANCE OF THE RED ARMIES AGAINST KOLCHAK IN THE SUMMER OF 1919

defense of Siberia with the shattered remnants of Kolchak's armies, which by this time scarcely numbered more than 50,000. Kolchak had now lost the whole Ural industrial region, with its mines and metallurgical factories, and was thrown back on the resources of Siberia alone.

In a civil war which is also an embittered class war the issue of campaigns depends upon conditions in the rear of the fighting army quite as much as upon the strategic dispositions of the army commanders. Kolchak's advance in March and April would probably not have gone so far if it had not coincided with a wave of peasant discontent behind the Red lines. And the failure of his armies, once they were driven back, to rally and make a stand at any natural barrier can only be understood if one takes into account the complete failure of the Omsk dictatorship in the field of civil administration,—a failure which led to a swelling tide of peasant insurrection within Siberia itself.

In trying to solve the problem of governing the territory under his control Kolchak found himself involved in a vicious circle, from which not one of the White leaders found a means of escape. He was quite sincerely convinced that his regime could not stand without a background of severe militarization. And in view of the fact that the enemy was not only beyond the Red lines, but in the towns and villages of Siberia, the dispensing with the ordinary safeguards of justice, the granting of sweeping powers to the military commanders was probably an inevitable, if regrettable, accompaniment of civil strife. But this dictatorial rule of military officers led to so much arbitrariness and brutality that it alienated large numbers of the people who in the beginning were indifferent, if not sympathetic, in their attitude toward the new regime. Postnikov, who for a time served as civil administrator of the Ural Territory and finally resigned his post in despair at accomplishing anything amid the general atmosphere of uncontrolled military excesses, speaks of the complete absence of genuine civilian authority and of such abuses as "condemnation without previous judicial investigation, beatings with rods, from which not even women were spared, killing of arrested persons 'while trying to escape.'" All this, taken together, in his opinion, made any orderly administration of the country impossible.[27]

The picture does not vary much in other parts of Kolchak's territory. In one of his frequent outbursts of sweeping condemnation Budberg in August, 1919, gives the following gloomy picture of the situation of the Omsk regime: [28]

"In the army, decay; in the Staff, ignorance and incompetence; in the Government, moral rot, disagreement and intrigues of ambitious egoists; in the country, uprising and anarchy; in public life, panic, selfishness, bribes and all sorts of scoundrelism."

Kolchak's Government was unable to find a satisfactory solution either for the land or for the labor problem. On April 8, when the advance into European Russia was proceeding satisfactorily, a declaration was issued on the land question, granting to those peasants who had sowed the land the right to collect the harvest, but warning against any new seizures of state or private land and declaring that the land problem would be solved in final form by the future national assembly. At no time did the Government show a genuine willingness to recognize the agrarian revolution which had taken place or to assure the masses of middleclass and poor peasants who had seized the large estates in 1917 that their right of permanent possession would be recognized. The Chief of Staff, General Lebedev, was even opposed to the noncommittal declaration of April 8, on the ground that many officers of the landlord class might resent it. As G. K. Gins, a member of Kolchak's Cabinet, remarks: "Lebedev didn't think of the sentiment of the masses of the soldiers, or of peasant Russia."

In Siberia landlordism was not an issue. There were practically no big estates in Siberia; social and economic lines of cleavage there were not between peasants and big landowners, but between peasants and Cossacks, with their special privileges; and also between the old, established and relatively prosperous peasant households and the poorer emigrant settlers who had come out to Siberia in the years before the War. But the chances of rallying peasant support in European Russia for the White armies during their drive toward the Volga were certainly compromised by the failure to issue an official slogan which could compete in clearcut finality with the Bolshevik "Land to the peasants."

The status of the labor movement under Kolchak is reflected in a note in the Siberian newspaper *Zarya,*[29] which, after describing the arrest and imprisonment of some trade-union leaders without the bringing of any definite charge against them, observes:

"The further activity of the trade-unions is very much crippled. Some die a natural death; others liquidate themselves in order to avoid unpleasantnesses."

That the Siberian industrial workers, many of whom cherished Bolshevik sympathies, should be in opposition to a conservative military dictator like Kolchak was inevitable. Much more serious, from the standpoint of the Omsk regime, was the rebellious sentiment which prevailed among the peasants and which found expression in the formation of partisan bands that in some cases grew into small armies and tore up the rear of Kolchak's forces at the same time that the Red Army was smashing their front. By March, 1919, the partisan movement was seriously hampering transportation over the main artery of communication, the Trans-Siberian Railroad; between Taishet and Kansk, where the wooded, hilly character of the country created favorable conditions for partisan warfare, it was found necessary to stop all movement of trains at night; and even so there were frequent wrecks. There were times when long stretches of the southern branch of the Trans-Siberian Railroad, between Barnaul and Semipalatinsk, were in the hands of insurgents for two and three weeks.[30] The main centres of the partisan movement were Kansk, Achinsk and Krasnoyarsk counties, in Yenisei Province; the Altai and Semipalatinsk regions in southern Siberia; and the lower course of the Amur River. While Kolchak's lieutenant, General Rozanov, with the aid of very ruthless measures, including the wholesale shooting of hostages and the burning of villages which sheltered insurgents, succeeded by June in driving the partisans back from the railroad in the neighborhood of Kansk and Achinsk, he did not destroy their forces, which moved into other provinces. When Kolchak's regime collapsed in the last months of the year the partisans occupied a huge expanse of territory on both sides of the railroad and occupied a number of provincial towns, where they dealt mercilessly with the classes which they suspected of sympathy with the dictator.

What were the causes of this farflung peasant revolt in a country where the issue of landlordism did not exist? They were many and varied. The Siberian village wanted, more than anything else, to be let alone. Kolchak's officials demanded recruits for the army and taxes and gave little or nothing in return. The Bolsheviki had been overthrown in Siberia before their policy had assumed its more extreme forms, such as ruthless food requisitioning and the organization of "committees of the poor." Consequently, while the peasants did not rise in defense of the Soviets, they remembered them with indifference rather than with hostility and were not inclined to go far away into European Russia to fight against them. When Gins, the voluminous chronicler of the Kolchak regime, talked with wounded White soldiers in a hospital he was surprised to find that the soldiers from European Russia were far more convinced of the necessity of going on with the struggle than the Siberians, who were for peace as soon as possible. Even before Kolchak came into power there had been revolts against mobilization, notably in the Slavgorod district, southeast of Omsk. These outbreaks tended to increase; and there were also mutinies of newly recruited peasant soldiers in Tyumen, Tomsk and other towns.

As a general rule the partisan movement showed its greatest strength in regions where new settlers had come after the unsuccessful Revolution of 1905. These new settlers were mostly poor peasants from Russia who had not reached the level of material prosperity which was general among the peasants who had lived longer in Siberia; their desire to enrich themselves at the expense of their more prosperous neighbors was a factor of no inconsiderable importance. Siberia had been used by the Tsars as a region for the forced settlement of criminals, as well as of political offenders; and ordinary banditism played some part in the growth of the partisan movement. When the Soviets were overthrown in the early summer of 1918 the Red military forces were not entirely destroyed; some of them retreated into the more inaccessible parts of the *taiga,* as the thick, often swampy forest country of Siberia is called, and waited for new opportunities. These units were natural rallying points for the discontented peasants. The wild, inaccessible character of many districts in Siberia away from the railroad also afforded excellent bases and places of refuge for guerrilla bands.

The Kolchak authorities made two very serious mistakes in dealing with the partisan movement in the first stages of its development. They sent too small forces against the insurgents, underestimating their numbers and military capacity, and they used for pacification undisciplined units which by their cruelties and outrages often made the population sympathize with the insurgents. Indiscriminate pillage, wholesale floggings, attacks on women were common. An official report to the Omsk War Ministry in the spring of 1919 reads as follows: [31]

> "Ataman Krasilnikov is completely inactive, devotes himself exclusively to drinking and disorderly conduct; his officers act in the same way; the soldiers carry out arbitrary searches with the purpose of robbery and violate women. The whole population is eager for Bolshevism. The situation is critical."

The outstanding partisan chieftains seem to have been mostly local peasants, with a little more education and experience of the outside world than their fellow-villagers. One of them, Kravchenko, was an agronomist of Socialist Revolutionary views. Another, Shetinkin, was a peasant who, starting as a private soldier, had been promoted to a captaincy during the War. Mamontov, a partisan leader in the Altai, was a peasant who had enlisted in the police during the early period of the Soviet regime. Two other Altai partisans, Rogov and Novoselov, carried out a veritable pogrom of the educated classes in the town of Kuznetzk when they occupied it; hundreds were slaughtered without distinction of age, sex or profession.[32]

This was an extreme instance of the hatred of the towns which characterized the psychology of the Siberian, as also of the Ukrainian peasant guerrillas. While the underground Communist organization which survived in Siberia, despite the betrayal of some of its leading members to the military authorities, who promptly shot them, tried to guide the partisan movement and while some of the partisan leaders became Communists, the movement as a whole could not be fairly described as Communist. It was rather a huge peasant outburst against what was considered the oppression of the town government and the educated classes, who were held responsible for the civil war, the levying of recruits, the lack of manufactured goods and all the other grievances of the peasants. The views of the partisans in some cases were very confused; one of their leaders, Shetinkin, according to some accounts, issued a proclamation in which he announced that he was fighting against "the destroyers of Russia, Kolchak and Denikin," in the name of—the Grand Duke Nicholas Nicholaevitch, who had appointed Lenin and Trotzky as his Ministers![33] Some of the partisans, however, had a more intelligent idea of their goals; a peasant congress which was held in April, with representatives from the districts of Achinsk, Kansk and Krasnoyarsk, which were under the control of the insurgent Peasant Army, adopted a long list of quite serious laws and regulations, abolishing the death penalty, except in the region of the front, prescribing that chronic drunkards should be set to public works, regulating the taxes and requisitions to which the population was liable, etc.[34] How far these regulations were carried out is difficult to say.

The struggle between the Government troops and the partisans was carried on with the utmost ruthlessness by both sides. "No quarter," was the general rule; and ferocious mutilations of prisoners were sometimes practised. The warfare was as savage as the primitive forests in which it was carried on. Very characteristic of the spirit of the time was an exchange of views between Kolchak and a member of the Irkutsk Revolutionary Committee which was soon to order his execution. The latter told the Admiral that, when he entered a village with partisans, he found there insurgents whose ears and noses had been cut off by the Government troops. As a reprisal he had the leg of a prisoner hacked off and tied to his body and sent him back in that condition to the Kolchak forces. The Admiral replied: "The next time it is very possible that people, seeing one of their men with a leg hacked off, will burn and cut up the village. That is the way of war."[35]

By the autumn of 1919 it was evident that the very existence of the Kolchak regime was closely bound up with the fate of its capital, Omsk. In the neighborhood of Omsk were the Siberian Cossacks, who had the best reasons to fear merciless reprisals at the hands of the Bolsheviki and the partisans and who might, therefore, be expected to fight. A retreat into the vast spaces of Siberia east of Omsk was highly unpromising; amid the ever swelling tide of peasant uprisings it was equivalent to a movement into a hostile country. Moreover, strong oppositionist sentiment, fanned by the defeats on the front and the obviously growing disintegration of the regime, was making itself felt in various towns along the line of the Trans-Siberian Railroad, especially in Irkutsk.

Kolchak struggled desperately for a way out of his hopeless position. He proposed to call a state conference of representatives of the peasants and the Cossacks. At the suggestion of General Diederichs, a religious fanatic, whose car was filled with ikons before which he prayed, an effort was made to raise a "holy war" against the Bolsheviki, to raise volunteers "of the Holy Cross and the Green Crescent." Kolchak appealed to "the propertied population of Siberia," warning them that "all the expanse of Siberia will not save you from pillage and a disgraceful death" and that "no one, except yourselves, will defend or save you."

But the response to these appeals was negligible. The tide was flowing too strongly in the other direction. Kolchak's armies did launch a feeble counteroffensive in the last days of September and pushed the advancing Reds behind the Tobol River, which they had previously crossed. But this was a halfhearted rally; and it was the last one. By mid-October the Red Army, reinforced by new levies (peasant recruits were found most easily in those regions which had suffered from Kolchak's punitive expeditions) was again on the march to Omsk and advanced practically without resistance.

Diederichs wanted to hasten the evacuation of Omsk. But Kolchak, with his weakness for listening to bad military advice, believed the self-assured statement of General Sakharov, a pompous reactionary, that Omsk could be held, and appointed Sakharov Commander-in-chief. Sakharov himself soon admitted the hopelessness of trying to defend the capital; the delay merely added to the confusion and disorganization of the retreat. The Red Army triumphantly entered Omsk on November 14.

From this date Kolchak's regime may be considered to have broken up. The Cabinet, headed by a new Premier, V. Pepelyaev, was in Irkutsk; Kolchak himself, with six special trains, one of which contained the remains of the part of the former Russian gold reserve which had been captured from the Bolsheviki in Kazan, moved very slowly along the Trans-Siberian Railroad, which was hopelessly choked with trainloads of refugees and almost blockaded because of the insistence of the Czechs, who were in control of the railroad, that they must be evacuated ahead of everyone else. The part of Kolchak's army which still held together, under the leadership of General Kappel, one of the few men of strong character whom the White movement in East Russia and Siberia produced, retreated along the main Siberian highroad. Kappel's forces could no longer resist the regular Red Army. But they retained enough discipline and cohesion to fight their way through the enveloping partisan bands and to reach Semyenov's territory, east of Lake Baikal, after enduring the terrific hardships of a march of thousands of miles in the Siberian winter and sustaining heavy losses, which included the death of their gallant leader.

Almost simultaneously with the fall of Omsk the representatives of the Czech National Council, Pavlu and Girsa, aimed a blow at the obviously collapsing regime, issuing a memorandum, the general tone of which is characterized by the following paragraph: [36]

> "Under the protection of Czecho-Slovak bayonets the local Russian military authorities permit themselves activities at which the whole civilized world is horrified. The burning of villages, the beating of peaceful Russian citizens by hundreds, the shooting without trial of representatives of democracy, on the mere suspicion of political unreliability, became habitual developments."

The memorandum appealed to the Allied Governments to permit the immediate return of the Czechs to their native country and also to give them "freedom to prevent crimes, by whichever side they may be committed."

The purpose of the memorandum was twofold: to hasten the evacuation (the Czechs feared that they might come into contact with the advancing Red Army) and to conciliate the Russian oppositionist elements which seemed likely to come into power in Eastern Siberia if Kolchak were overthrown. It is probably not accidental that the restless Gaida took an active part in an abortive attempt to oust General Rozanov, Kolchak's representative in the Far East, from power in Vladivostok on the night of November 17, almost simultaneously with the publication of the memorandum.

After the fall of Omsk the Red Army pushed on as rapidly as transportation facilities permitted. Many towns either were taken by partisan bands or overthrew the Kolchak authorities by means of local uprisings before the Red troops arrived. The most significant of these was in Irkutsk, where the efforts of Pepelyaev and his successor as Premier, Cherven-Vodali (Pepelyaev resigned when he could not persuade Kolchak to adopt what he considered a sufficiently democratic programme), to conciliate the local representatives of the radical opposition failed. An uprising broke out on the night of December 27; and after several days of desultory fighting and ineffective mediation by the local Allied representatives the commander of the garrison, Sichev, withdrew from the town; and on January 5 the so-called Political Centre, an organization which included the non-Bolshevik opponents of the dictatorial regime, was installed in power. The Political Centre proclaimed as points in its programme the convocation of a constituent assembly, peace with the Soviet Government, restoration of all civil liberties. The workers and soldiers who had taken an active part in the Irkutsk revolt were much more Bolshevik in sympathy than the leaders of the Political Centre, as subsequent events would show.

Meanwhile Kolchak had experienced one blow after another. When he gave the soldiers of his personal convoy the choice of remaining with him or going over to the Bolsheviki almost all of them deserted. Even one of the officers with whom he proposed to flee overland to Mongolia suggested that it would be better for the Admiral to place himself under the protection of the Allies, as the officers could escape more easily without him.[37] Oppressed by a heavy feeling of being generally deserted, Kolchak on January 4 announced his decision to abdicate in favor of General Denikin and appointed Semyenov commander of all the Russian armed forces in Irkutsk Province and east of Lake Baikal. (Semyenov had already made an unsuccessful attempt to intervene in the fighting in Irkutsk on the side of the Kolchak garrison.) At the same time Kolchak entered a secondclass car which displayed the flags of the Allied powers, formally placed himself under Allied protection and proceeded to Irkutsk under a guard of Czechs.

Immediately after his arrival in Irkutsk, on the morning of January 15, Kolchak and his former Premier, Pepelyaev, were handed over to the representatives of the Political Centre and placed in prison. A Soviet narrator is substantially correct when he writes: [38] "The head of Kolchak had to serve as the purchase price for free transit to the East."

The direct responsibility for the surrender of Kolchak rests with General Janin, commander of the Allied forces, and with the Czechs, although there were Japanese forces in Irkutsk which could have rescued the Admiral, had they been willing to assume the responsibility for doing so. The handing over of Kolchak was an understandable, but certainly not a chivalrous act, and it indicates that the general wolfish atmosphere of "everyone for himself," which prevailed during the Siberian collapse had not spared the foreigners.

Janin and the Czechs, to be sure, might have argued quite reasonably that they were under no moral obligation to risk bloodshed for the sake of an unsuccessful dictator, with whom they had been on decidedly bad terms. But they might have given Kolchak an opportunity to escape at his own risk when he appealed for their protection, instead of taking him to Irkutsk and handing him over to certain execution.

The Political Centre enjoyed a very short existence. On January 21, under pressure from the Irkutsk Communists, who possessed the support of the majority of the local workers and soldiers, it abdicated in favor of a revolutionary committee, which consisted of four Communists and one Left Socialist Revolutionary.

Kolchak was cross-examined by an investigating commission; and, had circumstances permitted, he would probably have been given a demonstrative trial before a revolutionary court. But, as in the case of the members of the Tsarist family, an emergency arose which expedited the inevitable execution. The remnants of the White armies, under the command of Voitzekhovsky, the successor of Kappel, who had died of pneumonia, appeared west of Irkutsk, while Semyenov was a constant threat from the East. Voitzekhovsky demanded the liberation of Kolchak; this only hastened his shooting. The Irkutsk Revolutionary Committee got in touch with the command of the Soviet Fifth Army and received authorization to execute the former Supreme Ruler at its discretion.

Kolchak had no illusion about the fate which awaited him and realized that the movement of his troops against Irkutsk was more likely to hasten his end than to avert it. By general testimony he bore himself with courage and dignity throughout the period of his imprisonment. He was permitted to have meetings in the prison with Mme. Temireva, with whom he had been living in Siberia.

On the cold early morning of February 7 Kolchak and Pepelyaev were led out and shot on a hill outside Irkutsk by a firing squad under the direction of the Chekist Chudnovsky. Kolchak's last message was a request to convey his blessing to his son, who was with his wife in Paris. An element of grisly mockery was added to the execution by the simultaneous hanging of a Chinese who had served as executioner in the Irkutsk prison. The bodies of the former Supreme Ruler and of the man who had assisted his rise to power, Pepelyaev, were cast into an icehole in the river Angara. The tragedy of Admiral Kolchak was finished.

Kolchak in his fall dragged down with him a considerable part of the Siberian educated and middle classes. The ranks of the hosts of refugees, Government officials, Army officers, their families, together with many people who had sought refuge from Bolshevism in Siberia and now saw themselves obliged to move on farther, were rapidly thinned by disease, hunger and cold.

Siberia witnessed terrible scenes during that winter of the collapse of the White movement. During the disorderly evacuation of Omsk, followed by the virtual blockade of the railroad by the Czechs, who were determined to get out first at any cost, about two hundred trains with refugees and with the families of the army officers were simply stranded and acquired the grim name, "trains of death."[39] Often left without food, fuel or medicine, these unfortunate people perished in enormous numbers; typhus, which had appeared in Siberia before the collapse, became a devastating epidemic; the bodies of the victims of these trains could scarcely be burned up fast enough to prevent the further spread of the infection.

The Orenburg Cossacks, with their wives and children, under their Ataman Dutov, marched thousands of miles over the wastes of Central Asia, willing to go anywhere if they could only escape the Bolsheviki. Of 150,000 who fled, about 30,000 survived long enough to cross the frontier into Chinese Turkestan. A tragedy on a smaller scale occurred with the Ural Cossacks, who struck southward over deserts toward Persia. "Every night halt was a cemetery," briefly reports General Akulinin.[40]

The strongest proof both of the depth and of the fierceness of the Bolshevik Revolution was the number of people who were willing to endure every deprivation, to risk death itself, rather than remain under Soviet rule. Of such victims of social upheaval and class war Siberia supplied its full quota.

NOTES

[1] *C.* Chapter XX, pp. 21ff.

[2] V. G. Boldirev, "Siberia, Kolchak, Interventionists," pp. 73–87.

[3] Krasilnikov was a well-known Cossack partisan leader.

[4] This proclamation is published in full in the Paris journal, *Sovremenni Zapiski* (Contemporary Notes), No. XLV, for 1931.

[4a] *Cf.* Zenzinov's letter in *Obstchee Dyelo* (The Common Cause), for April 22, 1919.

[5] N. Svyatitzky, "The Congress of Members of the Constituent Assembly," pp. 64ff.

[6] V. G. Boldirev, *op. cit.*, p. 84.

[7] Svyatitzky, *op. cit.*, p. 91.

[8] Three of the most detailed and authoritative descriptions of the *coup* of November 18, each written from a different standpoint, are those of Kolchak, in the published account of his cross-examination, of Avksentiev, in a collective work, "The *Coup d'état* of Admiral Kolchak in Omsk, November 18, 1918," and of G. K. Gins, in his work, "Siberia, the Allies and Kolchak."

[9] *Cf. Pravitelstvenni Vestnik* (The Government Messenger), No. 2, for November 18, 1918.

[10] "The Cross-Examination of Kolchak," pp. 174, 175.

[11] *Ibid.*, p. 167.

[12] "Chronicle of the Civil War in Siberia, 1917–1918," p. 98.

[13] "The Cross-Examination of Kolchak," pp. 140, 141.

[14] Cited in the work of Professor S. P. Melgunov, "The Tragedy of Admiral Kolchak," Part II, p. 165.

[15] "From the Life of a Revolutionary," p. 114.

[16] *Cf.* the newspaper *Armiya i Narod* (Army and People), of Ufa, for November 23, 1918.

[17] This incident was personally related to me by Chernov.

[18] N. I. Rakitnikov, "The Siberian Reaction and Kolchak," p. 30.

[19] *Cf.* the excerpts from the Diary of Baron Budberg, published in the collection, "Civil War in Siberia and in the Northern Territory," p. 145.

[20] *Cf.* the newspaper *Sibirskaya Ryetch,* for December 28, 1918.

[21] Melgunov, *op. cit.*, Part III, Vol. I, p. 57.

[22] At the time of the spring offensive Kolchak's forces were divided into three armies: the Siberian, under General Gaida, at the northern end of the front; the Western, under General Khanzhin, and the Southern, under General Belov, which was partly composed of Orenburg Cossacks.

[23] N. Kakurin, "How the Revolution Was Fought," Vol. II, p. 166.

[24] Budberg, *op. cit.*, p. 125.

[25] S. A. Piontkovsky, "The Civil War in Russia (1918–1921)," pp. 108–110.

[26] "The Civil War, 1918–1921," Vol. III, pp. 202, 203.

[27] Professor P. N. Milyukov, "Russlands Zusammenbruch," Vol. II, pp. 114, 115.

[28] Budberg, *op. cit.*, p. 170.

[29] *Cf.* the issue of March 1, 1919.

[30] *Cf.* E. Kolosov in *Biloe* (The Past), Vol. XX, p. 225.

[31] "The Partisan Movement in Siberia," p. 147.

[32] Kolosov, *op. cit.*, p. 242.

[33] Melgunov, *op. cit.*, Part III, Vol. I, p. 167.

[34] *Cf.* "The Partisan Movement in Siberia," pp. 128ff.

[35] "The Cross-Examination of Kolchak," p. 213.

[36] *Cf.* "The Last Days of the Kolchak Regime," pp. 112, 113, for the full text of the Czech memorandum.

[37] Melgunov, *op. cit.*, Part III, Vol. II, pp. 153ff.

[38] A. Shiryamov, in his article, "The Irkutsk Uprising and the Shooting of Kolchak," in the collective work, "The Struggle for the Urals and Siberia," p. 293.

[39] Melgunov, *op. cit.*, Part III, Vol. II, pp. 160, 161.

[40] Cited by Melgunov, *op. cit.*, Part III, Vol. II, p. 159.

CHAPTER XXX

THE NEW REVOLUTIONARY OFFENSIVE

THE new revolutionary offensive toward the West and the South which set in after the breakdown of the German military power[1] began under very favorable auspices for the Bolsheviki. No organized political or military anti-Bolshevik force existed between the frontiers to which Russia had been condemned by the Peace of Brest-Litovsk and the Black and Baltic Seas. The prevalent war-weariness and hunger, the collapse of old political and economic relations all contributed to the spread of Bolshevik ideas. Moreover, in their race with the Allies for the establishment of their supremacy in the wide stretches of southern and western Russia which were left undefended and unorganized when the German regime of occupation collapsed, the Bolsheviki possessed two distinct advantages. They had troops available for immediate use and they were much better acquainted with the local situation than were the Allied powers. So it is not surprising that the end of 1918 and the beginning of 1919 witnessed a second triumphal march of Bolshevism, somewhat similar to the one which had taken place after the seizure of power in Petrograd a year earlier, until it was checked by the hard barrier of German militarism. The second advance would also be checked, by other forces: the military strength of the White movements headed by General Denikin and Admiral Kolchak, the swelling tide of peasant disaffection, especially in Ukraina, the growing national consciousness of the peoples which inhabited Russia's former western provinces, Poles and Letts, Esthonians and Lithuanians. But in the beginning the field was clear for a sweeping advance of the Red forces; and a very considerable, although a transitory, gain of territory was achieved.

With a view to facilitating the conquest of Latvia and Esthonia, national armies, recruited from natives of these Baltic territories, were formed on Soviet territory.[2] There was a promising nucleus for a Latvian army in the form of nine Latvian regiments which had constituted one of the most reliable fighting units of the early Red

Army. In the latter part of December a self-styled Provisional Revolutionary Workers' Government of Lithuania issued a manifesto declaring the German occupation authorities and their puppet government overthrown and announcing the nationalization of all land, factories and buildings. On December 24 the All-Russian Soviet Executive Committee recognized the independence of the "Soviet Republics of Esthonia, Latvia and Lithuania" and promised to give all aid to the workers of these countries and of Ukraina in their struggle against the system of exploitation and in their defense against foreign aggression.[3]

This declaration was accompanied by military action; Russian as well as Latvian and Esthonian forces took part in the drive into these territories. The Red offensive was much more successful in Latvia than in Esthonia. Riga, the capital and main seaport of Latvia, was occupied on January 3, 1919; and by the end of March the whole of Latvia, with the exception of a little territory around Libau, was under Red occupation.

Esthonia possessed much more favorable conditions for defense than its southern neighbor, Latvia. Its eastern boundary was covered by large lakes; between these lakes on the south and the Gulf of Finland on the north there was a narrow strip of territory, which was relatively easy to defend. Moreover the Esthonian anti-Bolshevik forces received help from Finland and from a small Russian anti-Bolshevik force which had been formed in Northwestern Russia under German auspices. So the Esthonian capital, Reval, and most of the country's territory escaped conquest by the Reds; and by February Esthonian territory was cleared of the invaders. The Northwestern White Army, subsequently headed by General Yudenitch, who had served with distinction on the Caucasian front during the World War, was able to use Esthonia as a base for attacks on Soviet territory.

The Soviet occupation of Latvia was unstable because of the long front which had to be held to the north against hostile Esthonia. The Latvian Red Army, although large in numbers, had preserved the habit of electing its officers, and its discipline was loose and shaky. Moreover, a serious hostile force appeared in the Iron Division of Count von der Goltz, which consisted of volunteers from the German army of occupation and also included recruits from the German landed aristocracy, which had been a dominant force in the Baltic provinces before the Revolution. Von der Goltz and Latvian national forces began to push back the Reds, and on

May 22 Riga was captured. The town had lived through a severe period of Red Terror; and the Whites inflicted the usual ruthless reprisals. The loss of Riga was the signal for a general retreat and complete evacuation of Latvian territory. By spring the situation on both the Eastern and the Southern Front demanded the concentration there of all the Soviet available military resources; and efforts at expansion to the west, where the resistance to Bolshevism was enhanced by the nationalist spirit of the Baltic peoples, who desired to sever all connection with Russia, were abandoned.

Farther to the south, where the Red Army at first moved forward with little opposition, but then encountered the forces of the Polish Legionaries, under General Haller, the Red Front also rolled back during the spring. At their farthest point of advance the Soviet forces were well to the west of the present Soviet-Polish frontier and were in possession of Vilna, Lida and Baranovici. But the same cause that contributed to the evacuation of Latvia (preoccupation with more important fronts) brought about a steady retirement of the Soviet troops before the Poles, who occupied Vilna in April and pushed steadily forward during the summer until the line of the front was east of Minsk. The Soviet troops, until the outbreak of the Soviet-Polish War in 1920, confined themselves to passive defense and made no effort to take the initiative for a new offensive on the Western Front.

In May and June the Russian Northwestern Army, which at first had been simply a supplementary corps attached to the Esthonian forces, began to display more activity. It pushed out beyond the Esthonian border and, still coöperating with the Esthonians, occupied the towns of Yamburg and Gdov and the old Russian city, Pskov. The Commander-in-chief of this army was General Yudenitch, who organized a Political Council to assist him with the civil administration. One of its chief figures was a partisan leader named Bulak Balakhovitch, who acquired a grim reputation through his habit of publicly hanging real or suspected Bolsheviki.[4]

The forces of the Whites were increased by frequent desertions of officers, sometimes accompanied by their soldiers, from the Reds. Food conditions in Petrograd and its environs were desperately bad; and this doubtless had its effect on the morale of the Red troops. The former Semyenov Guard Regiment passed over to the Whites; and on June 12 the garrison of the fort of Krasnaya Gorka, on the Gulf of Finland, mutinied, expecting that help would come from the British Fleet in the Baltic and from the Northwestern Army. As often happened in the civil war, however, this outburst, which might have had grave strategic consequences for the Soviet forces if it had been coördinated with a land and naval attack on nearby Petrograd, was premature and isolated. After four days the rebellious garrison was obliged to quit the fort.

Both the desertion of the Semyenov Regiment and the mutiny in Krasnaya Gorka were apparently attributable, in part at least, to the work of a secret White military organization which succeeded in placing its agents in many responsible military posts in the Petrograd region.[5] After the recapture of Krasnaya Gorka the Petrograd front remained relatively quiet and unimportant until autumn, when Yudenitch launched a serious drive against the former Russian capital.

Simultaneously with the effort to take advantage of the disappearance of the iron German cordon and to extend the Soviet frontiers to the west, the Red Army massed very considerable forces against one of the main centres of the White movement: the Don Territory. Toward the end of the year the Red forces on this front numbered 100,000 infantry and 17,000 cavalry. Against them were 76,500 Don Cossacks under Ataman Krasnov.[6]

The Cossacks, the traditional cavalry of the old Russian Army, more than once during the civil war revealed caprices of temperament. Sometimes they fought like lions against greatly superior Bolshevik forces. Sometimes they lost heart and gave way with little resistance. In the winter of 1918–1919 the Don Cossack army experienced a severe crisis of morale, which greatly facilitated the advance of the numerous Red forces. Not only was the ground which had been gained outside the Don Territory quickly lost, but the northern Don regions were overrun with little serious fighting. Some Don stanitsas, such as Veshenskaya and Kazanskaya, repudiated Krasnov and accepted the Soviet regime. Some Cossacks surrendered; others deserted. During January and February the Reds pushed ahead steadily; and both Novo-Cherkassk, the Cossack capital, and Rostov, the largest city of the Territory, were seriously threatened.

The defeats on the front had a decisive effect on the political fortune of Krasnov. The British military representatives in South Russia had already forced him, very reluctantly and half-heartedly, to recognize Denikin as Commander-in-chief of the White forces in South Russia. In February the Don Krug, or Cossack Parliament, voted lack of confidence in Krasnov's leading military counsellors;

and the Ataman himself thereupon resigned and was succeeded by General Bogaevsky, who worked in close harmony with General Denikin. With the retirement of Krasnov from the political stage Denikin became the sole undisputed leader of the South Russian White movement.

Having made a clean sweep of the Red armies in the North Caucasus, Denikin began to send reinforcements to the hardpressed Don front. The arrival of fresh troops raised the drooping morale of the Don Cossacks; the spring flooding of the rivers delayed the advance of the Reds and made it possible to reorganize the Don Army. The threatened fall of Rostov and Novo-Cherkassk did not occur.

The strategic plan of the Red command in this campaign against the Don Territory seems to be open to criticism. There were two ways of approach to the centres of the Don Territory, Rostov and Novo-Cherkassk: through the Donetz Basin, the largest coal region of Russia, where there was a fairly extensive network of railroads; and through the Don steppes, inhabited largely by Cossacks, where the conditions both of railroad and of ordinary road transportation were much less favorable. In the beginning the Soviet military leaders seem to have overlooked the importance of the Donetz Basin and did not despatch sufficient forces into this region, where the predominantly workingclass population would have most probably sympathized with them. Instead they concentrated their efforts on conquering Cossack regions north and northeast of Rostov, which were hard to hold for political reasons (a very short Red occupation, with the excesses and outrages, the desecration of churches, the settling of old scores which it was apt to involve usually sufficed to turn a Cossack stanitsa into an angry hornets' nest of potential insurrection) and which lacked the economic significance of the Donetz Basin.

Denikin, on the other hand, appreciated fully the strategic and economic importance of the Donetz Basin and sent there a small but highly picked corps of veterans of the Volunteer Army under the command of General Mai-Maevsky. This corps held the southern part of the Donetz Basin, barring the approach to Rostov and the neighboring port of Taganrog, on the Sea of Azov, and resisted stubbornly and successfully the attacks of greatly superior Soviet forces. Mai-Maevsky made skillful use of the numerous railroad lines of the Donetz Basin, holding a considerable number of his troops in reserve and throwing them hastily to the points where they were most needed.[7] In this way he created the impression of having at his disposal a much larger number of troops than he actually possessed. Later in the year Mai-Maevsky acquired a bad reputation for chronic drunkenness and for not only tolerating, but encouraging his troops to rob indiscriminately. But his defense of the Donetz Basin was one of the notable military feats of the civil war.

While the right wing of the Soviet armies on the Don front was unable to break through Mai-Maevsky's resistance and the centre was checked by the Don Army on the line of the river Northern Donetz, a large-scale insurrection broke out in the rear of the Red Army in the very stanitsas of the upper Don, curiously enough, which had been the first to throw down their arms and to desert the banner of Krasnov. The causes of this outbreak are somewhat obscure. Denikin, who is naturally inclined to take a dark view of the Soviet regime, speaks of "burning and pillage, violations of women and children." Trotzky, in the course of an order demanding a "quick, ruthless, smashing blow" at the insurgents, admits that "it is very possible that in some cases the Cossacks suffered injustice at the hand of passing military units or individual representatives of the Soviet Government." [8]

However this Don uprising may have started, it stands out among many outbreaks which occurred behind Red and White lines alike by its unusual stubbornness and success. Forces which were sent against the insurgents were defeated; the Cossack forces grew into a small army of 30,000; White aviators flew over the Red lines and were enthusiastically received with the pealing of churchbells in the region of the insurrection. This uprising was not the least of the causes which account for the smashing defeat of the Red armies on the fronts of the Don and the Donetz Basin. While the early successful advance of the Reds into the Don Territory was thus being followed by a period of deadlock, in which superiority was gradually but definitely inclining to the side of the Whites, a spectacularly rapid second conquest of Ukraina by Soviet troops under the command of Antonov-Ovseenko was giving way to a period of violent peasant insurrections which were to exert an important influence on the course of the civil war in South Russia.

The second occupation of Ukraina by Soviet troops is attributable to political and social, rather than to military causes. The Commander-in-chief of the Red Army, Vatzetis, was inclined at first to discourage any ambitious operations in Ukraina, on the ground that too few troops were available for this new front. But, under the circumstances which prevailed after the fall of the Hetman and the disappearance of the German and Austrian forces of occupation, very few troops were required in order to set up a Soviet regime in Ukraina.

The Ukrainian peasants did not know from personal experience of such features of Communist policy as the institution of Committees of the Poor, the incitation of the poorest peasants to rob those who were less poor, the requisitions at the point of the bayonet. They remembered the Bolsheviki quite favorably as the people who had told them to seize the land and other property of the rich and who had then been driven out of Ukraina by the Germans, who had to some extent restored the hated landlords and had squeezed grain and other food products out of the peasants by ruthless measures. So the idea of a Soviet regime was popular not only with the town workers, but also with the peasants.

The nationalist Directory which had come into power after the fall of the Hetman was somewhat discredited because it was, after all, the successor of the Rada which had invited the intervention of the Germans. The political leaders of the Directory, especially the well known Ukrainian writer, V. Vinnechenko, tried to fall in line with the popular mood of radicalism and issued a declaration which in some of its phrases vied with the Communists in extremism and in denunciation of the bourgeoisie. So it was stated in this declaration: [9]

> "The right to govern the country belongs only to those classes which create material and spiritual values. . . . Power in the Ukrainian People's Republic must belong only to the workers and peasants, to those classes which achieved power at the cost of their blood. . . . The nonworking classes, which live at the expense of the workers, have no voice in the government of the country. The Directory hands over its power only to the working people."

This declaration was followed by the convocation of a so-called Workers' Congress, from which the propertied classes were excluded, just as they were excluded from membership in Soviets. The make-up of the Workers' Congress, however, was quite different from that of a Soviet Congress under Bolshevism. Far more representation was accorded to the peasants and to the "toiling intelligentsia," among whom were the village teachers, doctors, agronomist, coöperative store employees, who were among the most loyal supporters of Ukrainian nationalism.[10] Soviets were to be tolerated, but only on condition that they did not attempt to seize power.[11]

With all its radical professions, however, the Directory was unable to build up a firm basis of popular support. The actions of the "atamans," or military leaders of the Ukrainian troops, who were usually inclined to shoot or at least to imprison Communists as a matter of course and to raid the premises of suspected trade-unions, did not agree with the words of the civilian leaders. The numerous and active Jewish Socialist groups in the Ukrainian cities were alienated by the attacks on individual Jews and the little pogroms which were already being carried out in some places by the Petlurist troops. Rumors were circulated by the Communists that the Directory had concluded a secret treaty with the Allied military authorities in Odessa. Most probably these rumors were false or at least greatly exaggerated. The French Generals, after they had become convinced of the weakness in Odessa of Denikin's representatives, did carry on discussions with representatives of the Directory. But there is no evidence that these discussions led to any final or binding agreement. However, the mere suggestion that the Directory might be responsible for a new form of intervention was calculated to lower its prestige still further. Only the relatively small city middle class and the larger landowners remembered the German occupation with regret; the peasants and workers, with a keen recollection of the requisitions, the low wages and long hours which had been enforced during the period of occupation, and the stern activity of the German court-martial and the Hetman's police, were at least agreed on one point: uncompromising opposition to a new foreign military occupation.

Over and above all these factors of weakness, it must be borne in mind that the military forces of the Directory were extremely weak, consisting largely of peasant levies, which obeyed only their local atamans and were equally deficient in discipline, trained officers and munitions for large-scale warfare. Almost all witnesses of the Petlurist troops speak of their weakness for heavy drinking and pillaging,—the typical characteristics of a peasant partisan force. The Galicians, who were Ukrainian in language and who made common cause with Petlura, seem to have been an exception and to have maintained fairly good discipline. But they were also inferior as a fighting force both to the Red Army and to Denikin's troops.

So it is not surprising that the Red advance into Ukraina swept forward with little effective opposition. Kharkov passed under Soviet control as a result of a local workers' uprising on January 3. By February 5 the Red troops were able to occupy Kiev, the Directory fleeing to the neighboring town of Vinnitza.

The Soviet forces then moved against the Allies in the South. Ataman Grigoriev, a very typical leader of insurgent peasants, with a keen eye for the prevalent mood among his followers, had readily passed over, like many other similar chieftains, from the Petlurist to the Soviet camp. He led a spirited and successful drive against the French and Greek units which were taking part in the occupation, occupying Kherson on the 10th of March and Nikolaev on the 12th.[12] After this he despatched an ultimatum to the military governor of Odessa, General Grishin-Almazov, demanding the prompt surrender of the city and threatening that, if his demand were refused, he would flay Grishin-Almazov and make a drum out of his skin.[13] Grigoriev had no opportunity to carry out this threat (very typical of the spirit of Ukrainian civil war); but the French hurriedly evacuated Odessa early in April; and the Soviet troops swept on and occupied the Crimean peninsula.

In this month of April, which was the period of the greatest Soviet military success in Ukraina, the Red troops drove the fugitive forces of Petlura from several towns west of the Dnieper, Zhitomir, Kamenetz-Podolsk and Tiraspol, and forced him to take refuge in a sort of No Man's Land which existed between the eastern extremity of the Polish front and the western extremity of the Soviet front, in Eastern Galicia and in Rovno. The Soviet regime was now at least nominally installed all over Ukraina, with the exception of the portion of the Donetz Basin which was held by Denikin.

A Soviet Republic was established in Hungary on March 21; and Soviet strategy in Ukraina during the next few weeks was definitely shaped with a view to establishing contact with Hungary and affording it as much military aid and coöperation as possible. An order of Commander-in-chief Vatzetis to the commander of the Ukrainian Red Army, Antonov-Ovseenko, dated March 26, mentions "direct, close connection with the Soviet troops of Hungary" as one of the objectives of the movements of the Ukrainian Red troops.[14] And Antonov-Ovseenko himself, referring to the period when practically all Ukraina was occupied by Soviet troops, writes: [15]

> "Considerable forces were freed and we prepared to send them to the aid of Red Hungary. We prepared for this on the basis of the direct instructions of the Centre [the high Party and military authorities in Moscow], because the Centre had never countermanded for us the order to break through and unite with Hungary,—a project which was confirmed by the Commander-in-chief in his directions of May 5."

As early as January outbreaks against the Rumanian rule in newly annexed Bessarabia (the former Russian province which lay between the Dniester and the Pruth) had aroused hopes of a westward extension of Bolshevism in this direction. These outbreaks were suppressed; but military units were formed out of Bessarabian fugitives who had taken refuge in Soviet territory. On May 1 the Soviet Government sent an ultimatum to Rumania, demanding the evacuation of Bessarabia and Bukovina. Rumania was at war with Soviet Hungary and a message had been received from a Hungarian Communist in Budapest: [16]

> "If you can make even a little conquest, a little demonstration on the Rumanian front, if you can cross the Dniester for even three days, and then return, the panic will be tremendous."

Actually during the month of May there were little raids across the Dniester; the town of Benderi was occupied for a short time; Kishenev was threatened. But the large-scale offensive against Rumania of which the more ardent Russian Communists dreamed, as a means of breaking through to Europe and making the Revolution international, never took place. It was thwarted first by the mutiny of Ataman Grigoriev, then by the sweeping advance of Denikin, which placed the Bolsheviki on the Southern Front very definitely on the defensive for several months.

In order to understand the underlying causes of Grigoriev's mutiny, which was only the largest and most serious of a number of such revolts, one must take into account the rapid change which had taken place in the mood of the Ukrainian village since the establishment of the Soviet regime. In the beginning, as has been pointed out, the peasants reacted favorably or at least without hostility to the establishment of the Soviet regime. By April the sentiment had changed so much that numerous anti-Soviet bands, recruited mainly from peasants, were roaming about, attacking small Red patrols, wrecking trains, harassing lines of communication. On April 10 some of these guerrillas dashed into Kiev, the capital. The troops there were few and unreliable; and it required the personal presence of some of the members of the Government with military experience, such as Pyatakov, Bubnov and Voroshilov, together with the mobilization of all Communist Party members capable of bearing arms to beat off the raid.

What were the causes of this sharp change of sentiment? A good witness on this point is the Commander of the Soviet forces in Ukraina, Antonov-Ovseenko. In a memorandum which he drew up and submitted to the Party Central Committee he listed the following eleven reasons for the disturbances which were continually breaking out in the rear of the Red troops: [17]

1. Local governmental authority is completely unorganized and to a certain degree is imposed on the majority of the population.
2. Food officials who are not appointed from among local people, acting without knowledge of the situation, have aroused the village very much against the central Soviet Government.
3. The Chekas, which have become a state within a state, are almost universally hated and almost everywhere create complications for the Soviet regime.
4. Local Party work is completely neglected.
5. The population after the arrival of the Soviet regime received almost nothing except an increase in the cost of living and a lack of products. The villages, as formerly, do not see manufactured goods; the railroad workers are begging.
6. The bureaucratic machine is scarcely in working order, especially in the war department; the Government has extraordinarily little contact with the working masses.
7. The supply of our army is in an extremely difficult condition.
8. Complete disregard of the prejudices of the population,—in the matter of its attitude toward the Jews.
9. Tactless attitude of the central authorities toward the national feelings of Ukraina (for instance, the despatching of food directly addressed to Moscow, including such rare things as tea and coffee).
10. The land programme of the Government up to this time remains unclear and some of its statements are only calculated to disquiet the peasant,—for instance, the placing in the foreground of the idea of communes.
11. Representatives of the middleclass peasantry are remote from the central Government and the Party.

This list covers fairly adequately the main causes of dissatisfaction and rebellion. The Ukrainian village experienced the same disillusionment with Soviet agrarian policy that the Russian village had experienced in 1918. And the Ukrainian peasants were able to make their discontent felt much more vigorously than their Russian brothers because the Soviet regime was newly established and weakly organized and because it proved much harder in Ukraina than in Russia to break the united peasant front and to set the poor peasants to plundering the so-called kulaks.

Ataman Grigoriev's troops were mainly peasants from the southern part of Ukraina. After their successful operations in capturing Odessa and in overrunning the Crimea they were given a rest in the villages around Kherson, Nikolaev and Elizavetgrad. By the latter part of April their behavior was already becoming suspicious; there were continual reports of attacks on Jews, robberies and clashes with the local Communist authorities. Antonov-Ovseenko hoped to the last that it would be possible to use these troops against Rumania. Grigoriev played at loyalty to the Soviet regime as long as possible. But on May 7, after he had received definite orders to march on Rumania, he raised an open revolt, seizing the town of Elizavetgrad and issuing a manifesto, or "Universal," in which he called on the peasants to march on Kiev and Kharkov, with arms, if possible, with pitchforks, if they had no other weapons, and to overthrow the Government of the "adventurer Rakovsky." [18] The "Universal" quite skillfully appealed to the peasants' grievances in the following phrases:

> "Instead of land and liberty they violently impose on you the commune, the Cheka and Moscow commissars. You work day and night; you have a torch for light; you go about in bark shoes and sacking trousers. Instead of tea you drink hot water without sugar, but those who promise you a bright future exploit you, fight with you, take away your grain with arms in their hands, requisition your cattle and impudently tell you that this is for the good of the people."

The manifesto proposed to call a freely elected Congress of Soviets, in which eighty percent of the places would be reserved for Ukrainians, five percent for Jews and fifteen percent for other nationalities, and contained some high-sounding phrases, such as the following:

> "Long live freedom of speech, press, assembly, unions, strikes, labor and professions, security of person, thought, convictions. God's People! Love one another, don't shed your brothers' blood. Forget party hostility and bow before the power of honest labor." [19]

Decidedly more realistic, concise and original was a message which Grigoriev sent to Tkachenko, a Red Army commander whom he wished to win over to his side. The message, couched in picturesque Ukrainian dialect, may be freely rendered as follows: [20]

> "Why do you stand up for the hooknosed commissars? Stop being a fool. Let's take Odessa again and rob so that the place will be pulled to pieces. Warm greetings.
>
> "Your brother,
> "GRIGORIEV."

Grigoriev was confident at the beginning of his mutiny that he could smash the Communist regime throughout Ukraina. At his disposal were 16,000 troops, sixty cannon and a number of armored trains. The Red garrison of the town of Cherkassy passed over to his side. He sent troops in various directions, northeast toward Kharkov, northwest toward Kiev, southward toward Odessa and Ekaterinoslav, evidently hoping to gain peasant recruits in the course of his offensives. His troops made ferocious pogroms in the towns which they occupied, especially in Elizavetgrad. The Soviet Government, which promptly declared Grigoriev an outlaw and urged any citizen to shoot him on sight, had enough reliable troops to crush the revolt after some hard fighting. Grigoriev's own troops were demoralized by drink and loot. By the end of May he had been driven from the large towns and railroads and had taken to the roving life of the many little "atamans" who wandered through the villages with their bands, evading the troops which pursued them. But the mutiny was by no means without consequences. It shook up the rear of the Red armies which were fighting against Denikin and considerably reduced the number of troops which were available for the defense of Ukraina. It vividly revealed the unreliability of Ukrainian peasants as recruits for the Red Army.

It was not only in Ukraina that outbursts against the Soviet regime from within occurred in the spring of 1919. The month of March was marked by rebellions and mutinies in widely separated parts of the country. The Don Cossack rebellion has already been mentioned. Approximately at the same time there was a considerable revolt of peasants on the Volga, in the Syzran and Stavropol districts, which indirectly aided Kolchak's advance by disrupting the rear bases and communications of the Red armies on the Eastern Front. A diminution of the bread ration led to an uprising of part of the garrison of Astrakhan, at the mouth of the Volga, on March 10; many Astrakhan workers showed their sympathy with the movement by striking at the same time.[21] There was an outbreak in the garrison at Briansk in the early part of March; and on March 24 Gomel was seized and held for several days by insurgent soldiers, who killed a number of Communists. About the same time there were strikes in some factories in Petrograd and in Tula. The slogans of the insurgents were varied; the Don Cossacks welcomed the arrival of Denikin; the Gomel insurgents called for a Constituent Assembly; the Volga rebels proclaimed themselves "for the Bolsheviki, but against the Communists and Jews." Grigoriev, as we have seen, professed to be for freely elected Soviets.[22] One thing that is noticeable and significant is the absence, in all these anti-Bolshevik outbreaks, of monarchist appeals or suggestions that the pre-War order should be restored.

Increasing shortage of food and more intense pressure to squeeze the last reserves of grain out of the peasants seem to have been the main causes of the wave of unrest which swept over Soviet territory in the spring of 1919. Such uprisings, which could be crushed in territory which was firmly under Soviet control, had much more destructive consequences, of course, in newly occupied Ukraina.

Trotzky's dream of a "free" (*i.e.*, Communist) Poland, Finland, Latvia and Lithuania, which would serve as a bridge between Soviet Russia and "the future Soviet Germany and Austria-Hungary,"[23] was not realized. The resisting power of the new Baltic states and of Poland was too strong; in Europe outside of Russia the Soviet idea triumphed only, and very temporarily, in Hungary and in Bavaria. The Russian and Ukrainian peasants and peasant-soldiers who weakened the Soviet regime by their uprisings and mutinies were, quite unconsciously, combating the spread of Bolshevism in Europe much more effectively than the war-weary Allied troops who were sent on interventionist expeditions. It is one of the ironies of history that just at the time when Bolshevism made its most seductive appeal to the embittered masses of the war-torn countries of Europe, it was leading to desperate explosions of revolt among the people who were actually experiencing its rule.

NOTES

[1] The events which immediately preceded this offensive and its general background are described in Chapter XXVI.

[2] "The Civil War, 1918–1921," Vol. III, p. 152.

[3] *Cf. Izvestia* for December 19 and December 24, 1918.

[4] A detailed account of the activities of Balakhovitch is to be found in Vassily Gorn's book, "Civil War in Northwestern Russia."

[5] An account of this organization is given in an official Soviet Government communiqué, published in *Izvestia* for June 18, 1919.

[6] N. E. Kakurin, "How the Revolution Was Fought," Vol. II, p. 51.

[7] General A. I. Denikin, "Sketches of Russian Turmoil," Vol. V, p. 76.

[8] L. D. Trotzky, "How the Revolution Armed Itself," Vol. II, Book I, p. 174. Elsewhere Trotzky speaks more definitely of the abuses and excesses which sometimes accompanied the establishment of the Soviet authority in a new place. So (*cf. op. cit.*, Vol. II, p. 164), he speaks of "the storm of contributions and of senseless and unjust shootings" which occurred in Valuiki County after the Red troops had occupied it.

[9] *Cf.* M. Rafes, "Two Years of Revolution in Ukraina," pp. 117ff.

[10] On one of my first trips in Russia I met a teacher in an Ukrainian village who, in a private talk, described with growing enthusiasm the guerrilla activity of the peasants against the Soviet regime during the period of civil war. He finally said: "The Communists said we were bandits. But I think we were like Garibaldi."

[11] S. A. Piontkovsky, "The Civil War in Russia (1918–1921): Documents," p. 381.

[12] *Cf.* Chapter XXVIII, pp. 165ff.

[13] *Cf.* the article of F. Anulov, "The Allied Descent in Ukraina," published in the collection, "The Black Book," p. 167.

[14] Kakurin, *op. cit.,* Vol. II, p. 90.

[15] V. Antonov-Ovseenko, "Reminiscences of the Civil War," Vol. IV, p. 330.

[16] *Ibid.,* Vol. IV, p. 275.

[17] *Ibid.,* Vol. IV, pp. 153, 154.

[18] Christian Rakovsky, a Rumanian by origin and a physician by profession, a veteran participant of the revolutionary movement in the Balkans, was the Premier of Soviet Ukraina.

[19] The complete text of Grigoriev's "Universal" is reproduced by Antonov-Ovseenko, *op. cit.,* Vol. IV, pp. 203ff. Grigoriev communicated it to Antonov-Ovseenko in the course of a telegraphic conversation; and a rather amusing argument between the Soviet Commander-in-chief and the Ataman about the proper method of carrying out a Soviet election followed. Neither succeeded in convincing the other by means of arguments.

[20] *Cf.* "The Civil War, 1918–1921," p. 83.

[21] The mutiny in Astrakhan is described by M. Svechnikov in "The Struggle of the Red Army in the North Caucasus," pp. 160ff. G. Lelevitch has written a short brochure, "Strekopitovstchina," about the Gomel outbreak. The newspaper *Dyelo Naroda* of March 27, 1919, contains interesting details of the Volga uprising. An official statement by the Cheka, published in *Izvestia,* of March 18, 1919, throws additional light on the wave of internal unrest which swept over Soviet Russia at this time.

[22] It is significant that Grigoriev, in his "Universal," gave himself out as a loyal supporter of the Soviet form of government. He knew very well that any suggestion of a return to pre-War conditions or of a restoration of conventional "law and order" would not appeal to his wild partisans.

[23] *Cf.* "How the Revolution Armed Itself," Vol. I, p. 394.

CHAPTER XXXI

UKRAINA, WHIRLPOOL OF PEASANT ANARCHISM

A POWERFUL strain of peasant anarchism runs through the whole course of the Russian Revolution. The Bolsheviki, in their effort to create a new social and economic order, and the Whites, in their desire to restore an old one, both found their active supporters mainly in the cities. Neither had real roots in the peasant villages.

And the desires of the peasants, so far as they were intelligent enough to have conscious desires, were equally far removed from communism and from restorationism. They were determined to keep the land they had seized and were quick to rebel as soon as the Whites showed a tendency to bring back the landlords. At the same time they hated the state farms and communes which the Bolsheviki desired to substitute for individual farming. And they were resentful of demands for food and army recruits, whether they proceeded from the Reds or from the Whites. What the Russian village most wanted during these years of civil war was to be let alone.

But this, under the circumstances, was an unattainable ideal. Straining every nerve for victory, Red and White leaders alike mobilized, to the best of their ability, the peasant population of the regions which they occupied. In Red and White Russia alike industrial production was almost at a standstill; it was quite impossible to give the peasants a fair equivalent for their food products in manufactured goods. The Reds outlawed free trade and collected food by forcible requisitions. The Whites permitted freedom of trade, but, in view of the shortage of manufactured goods, this led to an enormous amount of speculation and to a continual rise in prices. The needs of the White armies were covered to a considerable extent by forced levies and sometimes by outright robbery.

So, among the innumerable hatreds which came to the surface during the Revolution, there grew up among the peasants a bitter hatred of the towns, in which they saw the source of oppression and exploitation. Nowhere was this peasant hatred of the towns so great as in Ukraina, nowhere did it assume such sanguinary forms, nowhere was peasant anarchism during 1919 and 1920 so much in the ascendant.

Many factors marked out Ukraina for a regime of anarchy such as no European country had experienced for centuries. In the first place, Ukraina, much more than any other part of Russia, witnessed a continual rapid shifting of governments. Immediately after the Bolshevik Revolution the nationalist Rada established itself as the state authority in Ukraina. Then there was a shortlived period of Bolshevik rule, followed by the German occupation and the puppet regime of Hetman Skoropadsky. After the fall of Skoropadsky the Ukrainian Nationalists again stepped in for a short time, only to be pushed out again by the Bolsheviki, who, in turn, were driven out of Ukraina by Denikin during the summer of 1919, returning and reëstablishing their rule in the winter. The Ukrainian Nationalists continued to struggle in the western part of the country; and in 1920 two new claimants for power appeared in the Poles, who occupied Kiev for a short time, and Denikin's successor, General Baron Wrangel, who occupied part of southern Ukraina.

Each change of regime brought with it new slogans, new decrees, a new brand of worthless paper money and, as a general rule, an opening of the prisons and a release of their inmates. Small wonder if all conception of respect for state authority tended to disappear.

The Ukrainian peasantry showed itself far more conscious of its interests, far more ready to fight for them effectively than did the peasants in Russia. There was perhaps something of nationalist temperament here; it was in Ukraina that the anarchical Zaporozhian Cossack Republic, which for many decades acknowledged no authority except that of its roughly elected ataman, had existed; serfdom did not have such a long tradition behind it in Ukraina as in European Russia. Moreover, the average standard of living among the peasants was higher in Ukraina than in Northern and Central Russia. There was, consequently, a larger class of peasants with a sense of property, who were ready to form guerrilla bands and fight the Soviet requisitioning detachments to a finish.

Questions of race and nationality also played a great rôle in stimulating the Ukrainian peasant anarchism. The village population of the northern and western provinces was almost solidly Ukrainian.

In the towns, on the other hand, there were a great many Russians and Jews. Native Ukrainians were a minority in the Communist Party of Ukraina,[1] which recruited its members very largely from the towns. Consequently, when Soviet measures were unpopular, it was easy to arouse agitation against them on racial lines, to stir up the peasants against the *katzapi* and the *zhidi,* to use two derogatory Ukrainian words for Great Russians and Jews. Savage pogroms, far exceeding in the number of their victims anything that had been known under the Tsars, were a feature of the struggle of the Ukrainian peasantry against the Bolsheviki. "All Jews are Communists" and "Kill the Jews and Communists" were two popular catchwords of the time. Nationalist feeling also strengthened the antipathy of the Ukrainians toward the regime of General Denikin, who was unwilling to recognize the claims of the Ukrainian intellectuals to a separate, non-Russian language and culture, to say nothing of conceding Ukraina's right to political independence.

Of the three governments that fought for power in Ukraina in 1919, the Soviets, Denikin's regime, and Petlura's, the last was apparently the least objectionable to the peasants. This is the judgment of a Communist named Popov, who went on a mission to Petlura's temporary headquarters in Kamenetz-Podolsk in the autumn of 1919 and stated in his report that, while the peasants were opposed to all governments, since they all took without giving anything in return, the least of the three evils, in the eyes of the peasants, was Petlura.[2]

Petlura, however, was quite unable to make military headway against either Reds or Whites, if only because his army lacked any adequate source of supply with munitions. Consequently the Ukrainian nationalist movement took the form of guerrilla band activity, headed by a host of big and little "atamans," each of whom was a temporary sovereign on the territory where he operated. The atamans worked sometimes in loose contact, sometimes in hostility with one another and with Petlura. And in view of the inability of Petlura to create a disciplined and well equipped army this guerrilla warfare was much more dangerous and annoying to Reds and Whites alike than the regular military operations of the Petlurist troops. Ten thousand Petlurists in the open field could usually be put to rout by an equal or smaller number of Reds or Whites. The same ten thousand Petlurists, broken up into a score of bands, operating in territory with which they were well acquainted, could inflict far more damage and were much harder to suppress. A typical Red Army military report, indicating the difficulty of coping with these insurgent bands, reads as follows: [3]

> "It is extremely difficult to catch the former teacher, the Petlurist agent, Ataman Volinetz, first, because he has a mass of adherents among the peasants in the villages where his bands operate, second, because, avoiding battle with regular forces, he hides in forests where he knows every path."

Volinetz was not the only former teacher who could be found heading a detachment of peasant partisans. Struk, whose band was very active in the Chernobil district, north of Kiev, was a former teacher who wore a sailor's uniform; Sokolovsky, who operated in the Radomisl region, west of Kiev, had completed the course in a teachers' seminary. Zeleny, another well known ataman in the neighborhood of Kiev, is variously described as a former student and as a carpenter. Angel, who terrorized Bakhmach, was an ex-officer of the Hetman's army. Farther to the south, in the region of Bar, an imaginative teacher named Bozhko proclaimed the restoration of the Zaporozhian Cossack Republic and went about with a golden rod of office, the traditional ataman's *bulava;* his lieutenants bore silver rods. Bozhko, who in August occupied the territory from Bar to Moghilev-Podolsk, announced that Ukraina would be reborn when his *bulava* was in Kiev.

Although the atamans sometimes quarrelled with and killed one another they employed very similar methods of propaganda in their appeals, which reflect quite accurately the mood of the majority of the Ukrainian peasants at that time. The peasants are called on to rise against the requisitions and against the cruelties of the military detachments which carry them out; there is much denunciation of *zhidi* and *katzapi,* of Chinese and Letts who formed part of the Red Army of occupation; religious feeling is sometimes invoked. So Struk, who, like most of the atamans, carried out many pogroms and made a special practise of drowning in the rivers Jews who fell into his hands, issued a proclamation in which he called for the socialization of factories and land but simultaneously accused the Bolsheviki of closing churches, turning them into brothels, selling priests' robes for women's hats, etc. Zeleny's followers fought under a red flag, calling themselves at the same time enemies of "the commune, the Chinese, the *zhidi,* the *katzapi.*" A Petlurist propaganda poster showed two Russian peasants driving with whips two Ukrainian peasants hitched to a plough; it bore the sarcastic caption: "The brotherly life of the *katzapi* with the Ukrainians."[4] An appeal of another ataman, Tiutiunuk, speaks of "our age-long enemies, the Great Russians, and their agents, the Jews." Grigoriev, in his "Universal," denounced commissars from "ever-greedy Moscow and from the country where they crucified Christ." Sokolovsky referred to the communes which the Soviets wished to establish as "Jewish slavery, which has replaced the landlords' yoke." A characteristic manifesto of the Kiev "Ukrainian Military Revolutionary Committee," issued in June, 1919, addressed to the Red Army soldiers, ends as follows: [5]

> "Join us and clear Ukraina of all these Trotzkys, Rakovskys and other speculators of the Revolution. Don't obey them when they will send you to the Petrograd or Volga front, because instead of you they will bring Chinese and Letts against your fathers and brothers. *Your front is in Ukraina, your front is in Kiev.* All the scoundrels who are sitting in the Commissariats and the Soviets must be destroyed; you must immediately reëstablish the genuine rule of the Soviets. So don't go anywhere from here and don't give up your arms to anyone. Rise quickly and help your brothers, who rebelled with pitchforks and rakes, and fight for land and liberty, for the genuine power of the working people. Down with the age-long enemies and bloodsuckers of the people. Rise up, time does not wait. Down with the Communists, Chekas, commissar-tyrants. Long live the Ukrainian independent Soviet Republic."

Such appeals often found a ready response in the ranks of the Ukrainian Red troops. Rakovsky, at that time Premier of Ukraina, gives a gloomy picture of the condition of the Ukrainian units of the Red Army, from the standpoint of reliability and discipline.[6] So a battalion of the Kherson Regiment killed twenty-two Communists. The second Tarashansk Regiment organized a Jewish pogrom in Chudnov. The Red Army units of the Galyatch garrison took part in a counterrevolutionary outbreak on June 2. "The Sixth Regiment carries on agitation against the civil authorities and the Chekas. The Ninth Regiment robs. The Tenth Regiment also robs. On May 25th Red Army soldiers, stirred up by agitators, left the front and appeared in Kamenetz-Podolsk, 'to beat the Jews.' "

On May 21st half of the thousand Soviet troops who were stationed in Chernobil passed over to Struk; the others surrendered to him. The Eighth Regiment of the Red Army, after driving Ataman Volinetz from the town of Uman, proceeded to emulate him by robbing and attacking Jews in the town. Early in May sailors in Nikolaev went on a debauch, arrested and shot the President of the local Cheka, Abaridze. In August the Fifty-eighth Division, which was in Nikolaev, became demoralized and set fire to military property around the station. All these facts indicate that the wild, anarchistic spirit of Ukraina did not spare the Ukrainian Red Army.

Interesting testimony as to the mood and condition of the Ukrainian villages is furnished by a Red Army military-agitation commission which investigated Kiev and part of Chernigov Province. Some of the excerpts from this report read as follows:

> "Makarov—Almost all the population is armed; there is continuous shooting; no sort of governmental authority is recognized; pogrom agitation is carried on. Glivakhni—A negative attitude toward the Soviet regime and its orders. The agitation of Petlurist agents is noticed; anti-Semitism is strongly developed; the literature which was distributed produced a good impression.* Barishevka — The majority of the Executive Committee consists of kulaks, who ignore orders from the centre. The poor are powerless. Borispol — The Soviet consists of local traders. Motizhino — The village is a nest of uprisings; the population is completely armed."

This "complete arming" of the rural population, of course, explains the persistence and effectiveness of the guerrilla band movement. As a result of the utterly chaotic and disorderly "selfdemobilization" of the Russian Army, peasants often carried home with them not only rifles, but even machine-guns. The rapid shifting of regimes and continual disorder prevented the peasants, especially the younger ones who had returned from the front, from settling down to peaceful work; and almost every village of any size was an arsenal for the ataman who gained control of it.

The upsurge of militant peasant anarchism was bound to inflict terrible suffering on the considerable Jewish population of the former Pale of Settlement[7] in western and southwestern Ukraina. The disappearance of any kind of effective authority in the country districts, the brutalization wrought by war and civil strife, the feeling, widespread among the masses, that the Revolution meant freedom to indulge in any kind of pillage or violence, directed against the *"boorzhui,"*—all created the background for wave after wave of pogroms, far exceeding in the number of their victims and

* One is tempted to doubt the reality, or at least the permanent validity, of this last statement.—The Author.

Nestor Makhno, anarchist guerrilla leader of the Ukrainian peasants, with members of his staff at his headquarters in Gulai-Polye. Makhno is wearing a white sheepskin cap

Peasants greeting a White general, according to the old Russian custom, with bread and salt

in the wholesale destruction which accompanied them, anything of the kind that had taken place under the Tsarist regime.

Ukraina was historically a country of pogroms. When the Zaporozhian Cossacks under Bogdan Khmelnitzky rose against the Polish rule in the seventeenth century they systematically massacred Jews, some of whom acted as stewards on the landlords' estates and as tax-collectors, along with the landlords and the Polish officials. The so-called *haidamak* disturbances in the following century were also characterized by the killing of many Jews.

The policy of the Tsarist Government was unconcealedly anti-Semitic; Jews, unless they were converted to Christianity, were generally excluded from the state service, were forbidden to acquire land and were subjected to a quota system of admission to the universities and higher schools. Apart from these legal discriminations, the Jews from time to time had to fear pogroms, or outbursts of mob violence, accompanied by murder, outrage and looting. Such outbreaks were not, as a rule, repressed very severely by the Tsarist authorities; sometimes, especially during the 1905 Revolution, pogroms were even encouraged as a means of diverting the rage of the masses away from the Government against the Jews.

The unprecedented scope and ferocity of the pogroms in 1919 cannot be attributed simply to the old heritage of Tsarist anti-Semitism. New factors paved the way for the killings which took place in hundreds of places, ranging in size from large towns, like Elizavetgrad, to obscure *mestechki,* or Jewish hamlets, and which probably resulted in tens of thousands of deaths.[8] One such factor was the prevalent anarchy, the certainty that the pogrom would go on unchecked and unpunished. Another was the wellnigh continuous fighting of regular and irregular troops, which naturally stimulated every kind of violence. The abnormal economic condition of the country also promoted pogroms. The ordinary interchange of goods between city and village had broken down. The peasants saw that when the Soviet authorities in the towns wanted grain they took it by force. What was more natural than that the peasant bands, when they had the power to do so, should swoop down on the towns and carry out their own primitive "requisitions" for manufactured goods, looting indiscriminately warehouses and private homes? Inasmuch as a considerable part of the middle class and especially of the traders in Ukraina consisted of Jews, such peasant raiding expeditions were very apt to turn into pogroms. To the traditional peasant belief that the modern Jews were responsible for the crucifixion of Christ there was added a new cause of race antagonism: the feeling that the Jews, so many of whom were traders, were *"boorzhui,"* who deserved extermination on this ground.

A very important cause of the pogroms was the identification, in the popular mind, of the Soviet regime, or at least of the Communist Party, with the Jews. The latter consequently became scapegoats for all the unpopular acts of the Soviet regime, for the brutalities of the Cheka, for the suppression of private trade and the requisitions which were carried out at the expense of the peasants. The troops or the bands which made the pogroms, inspired by lust for blood and loot, did not, of course, make any effort to discriminate between those Jews who were active Communists and those who had nothing to do with the Revolution.

That Jews played a prominent part both in the Communist Party and in the Russian revolutionary movement generally is obvious and understandable. The systematic racial discrimination to which the Jews were subjected under Tsarism was admirably calculated to make the more educated of them revolutionaries of one kind or another. A considerable number of outstanding Bolshevik leaders of that time, such as Trotzky, Zinoviev, Kamenev, Sverdlov and Sokolnikov, were of Jewish origin; and as soon as the Soviet regime was established in Ukraina a considerable number of Jewish minor officials made their appearance. It is a matter of common testimony that the prominence of Jews, especially of the younger generation, in the Soviet administration, often had the most fatal consequences for their co-racialists as soon as an anti-Soviet force, whether represented by the regular troops of Denikin or Petlura or by the band of some roving ataman, occupied a town which the Red troops were compelled to evacuate.[9]

The main perpetrators of pogroms were the Ukrainian troops of Petlura, the various atamans and the forces of General Denikin. There was some killing and more robbing of Jews by undisciplined units of the Ukrainian Red Army. But the Soviet authorities prescribed the death penalty for pogroms and strictly forbade the circulation of anti-Semitic literature; and the Jews were safer from murder and outrage under the Red regime than under any other. The number of pogroms showed a tendency to rise and fall, depending upon the military fortunes of the Red troops.

There is a story that at the time of the first retreat of the Ukrainian nationalists from Kiev before the advancing Bolsheviki in 1918 one member of the Rada spoke pessimistically to another about the weakness of the Ukrainian troops before the Bolshevik offensive. His companion replied:

"Wait, we haven't yet played our main trump. Before anti-Semitism no Bolshevism will stand." [10]

Whatever may be the truth of this, the beginning of large-scale anti-Jewish excesses coincided with the period of the second retreat of the Ukrainian nationalists before the Bolsheviki early in 1919. The first of these excesses seems to have occurred in January in the town of Ovruch in Volhynia, where a Petlurist Ataman, Kozyr-Zyrka, abused the local Jews in various ways, flogging them, extorting money from them and killing a number. About the same time there were attacks on Jews at some railroad stations. When a Jewish delegation visited Vinnichenko, the head of the Directory, to ask for protection, the latter promised to take all the measures in his power, but made some critical remarks about the sympathy of some Jews with Bolshevism and let slip the phrase: "Don't compromise me with the army." [11] Vinnichenko, a radical Socialist who soon resigned from the Directory because he regarded it as too conservative, was certainly not an anti-Semite.[12] But his rather indiscreet reply to the Jewish delegation showed the difficulties which the Ukrainian nationalist leaders experienced in controlling the pogrom tendencies of their armed forces.

And there were some cases when the participation of Jewish workers in Bolshevik outbreaks on Petlurist territory furnished a convenient excuse for an outburst of mass killing. This was the prelude to one of the most sanguinary of the Petlurist pogroms, which took place in Proskurov on February 15 under the direction of Ataman Semesenko; the Galician troops vowed that they would kill without robbing; and great numbers of people were slaughtered, mainly by thrusts of the bayonet. Semesenko issued the following proclamation to the Jews: [13]

> "You are a people hated by all nations. And yet you bring such confusion among the baptized. Do you really not want to live? Are you not sorry for your own people?"

Officially Petlura's regime was not anti-Semitic; it organized a Ministry of Jewish Affairs, headed by a Jew; and in July, 1919, Petlura issued an order forbidding any pogrom agitation.[14] But the Petlurist Government exercised little effective control over its regular troops and no control whatever over the atamans who vied with one another in organizing pogroms in the Jewish towns and villages in their territory.

Grigoriev's rebellion in May brought about a big increase in the number of pogroms, of which perhaps the fiercest was in the town of Elizavetgrad and lasted for three days, from the 15th until the 17th. Grigoriev's soldiers began the killing; they were soon joined by a mob of townspeople, and on the second and third days peasants poured in from surrounding villages to take part in the slaughter and, still more, to carry off the loot in their carts. July was another very bad month for pogroms; Kiev Province registered 27, Volhynia 12 and Podolia 14.[15] This upsurge is largely attributable to the fact that in this month the Soviet regime in Western Ukraina was definitely losing ground before the insurgent bands. Some places experienced repeated pogroms; some of the smaller Jewish communities were virtually wiped out.

The movement of General Denikin's forces into Western Ukraina in August and September, 1919, was marked by a new series of pogroms, of which the most ferocious was in the town of Fastov in the latter part of September. The customary revolting features of a pogrom, murder, robbery, torture, violations of women, went on day after day, without any check from the military authorities. In larger cities order was somewhat better preserved; but there also, especially in Kiev, so-called "quiet pogroms," characterized by individual murders, beatings, attacks on women, kidnapping of Jews for the purpose of extorting money, robberies, etc., were carried on. It became especially dangerous for the Jews in Kiev after the Red troops made a brief raid into the city and were pushed out again by the Whites. As usual the Jews were accused of firing from ambush at the Whites and displaying sympathy with the Reds; and the "quiet" pogrom was intensified. A hostile observer, the conservative anti-Semitic publicist, V. V. Shulgin, in an article entitled "Torture with Fear," published in Kiev at this time, gives the following vivid picture of the agony of terror in which the Jewish population lived: [16]

> "A dreadful medieval spirit moves in the streets of Kiev at night. In the general stillness and emptiness of the streets a heartrending cry suddenly breaks out. It is the cry of the Jews, a cry of fear. In the darkness of the street appears a group of 'men with bayonets.' At this sight large five- and six-story houses begin to shriek from top to bottom. Whole streets, seized with mortal anguish, scream with inhuman voices . . ."

Shulgin then raised the question what the Jews would do after this "torture with fear."

"Will the Jews beat their breasts, cover their heads with ashes and repent before the whole world because the sons of Israel took such an active part in the Bolshevik madness? Will they found a league to combat socialism? Or will everything remain as before after these dreadful nights, full of anguish, and will they, as before, form a league to combat anti-Semitism, senselessly denying well-known facts and thus inflaming anti-Jewish feelings still more? The Jews have two ways before them. One is to confess and repent. The other is to accuse everyone but themselves. Their fate will depend upon the way they follow. Is it really possible that the torture with fear will not show them the right way?"

A Jewish investigator of the pogroms carried out by Denikin's troops [17] finds four distinguishing features: their purely military character, the mass violations of women, the special cruelty and tortures and the rooting out of whole communities. It is questionable whether any of these features except the first are peculiar to the pogroms of the Denikin period. Struk, who made a practise of drowning Jews in the Dnieper, or the mob leaders in Trostyanetz, who butchered some hundreds of Jews who were confined in a public building, had little to learn in inhumanity from Denikin's officers.

Denikin himself vigorously denies that he desired or encouraged pogroms by his armies,[18] observing: "With the sentiments that prevailed at that time, the fate of the Jews of South Russia would have been incomparably more tragic, if the troops had had the least reason to suppose that the supreme command looked on pogroms with favor." Bluntly telling a Jewish delegation that "he had no reason to regard the Jewish people with special sympathy," Denikin undoubtedly recognized that the pogroms, apart from any humanitarian considerations, demoralized his forces, undermined their discipline and accustomed them to robbery and violence against the civilian population.

But Denikin's hands were bound, to a considerable degree, by the mood which prevailed in his army. He could no more make his conservative officers, whose traditional anti-Semitism had in many cases reached a pitch of veritable fanaticism as a result of the Revolution, take drastic measures against pogroms than he could induce the landlords, who constituted a considerable part of his following, to agree to a liberal agrarian policy.

The pogroms committed by Denikin's forces may be set down to the account of militarist reaction; the more numerous massacres which took place before Denikin occupied Western Ukraina were a result of unbridled popular passion, let loose by the revolution. The peasant who had been encouraged by Bolshevik agitation to kill the neighboring country squire and loot his property saw no reason why he should deal any differently with the Jewish trader in the nearby town.

The Jews were not, of course, the only sufferers in Ukraina during the chaotic year 1919. Bands of Red partisans often committed outrages against the families of the propertied classes which were as revoltingly inhuman as the atrocities which characterized the pogroms.[19] The Chekas carried on a sanguinary activity; according to a Soviet official report the number of their victims in Ukraina in the single year 1920 was about 4,000.[20] Among the people slaughtered by the Chekas in Ukraina were three elderly professors, well beyond the age of sixty, P. Y. Armashevsky, P. Y. Doroshenko and V. P. Naumenko.[21] As wave after wave of killing and plundering swept over the unhappy country its few educated inhabitants must have felt that they were living through a modern repetition of the Troubled Times, or of the *jacqueries* of Stenka Razin and Emilian Pugachev.

Indeed this floodtide of peasant anarchy brought to the surface one man who might reasonably be regarded as the spiritual successor of Razin and Pugachev, whose personality was the veritable incarnation of the primitive village anarchism of the time. This was Nestor Makhno, who for long periods of time was more of a power in the steppes of southern Ukraina than either Trotzky or Denikin. His base was his native village, Gulai Polye; his sphere of activity was the wide stretch of open country between Ekaterinoslav and the Sea of Azov.

Several traits distinguish Makhno from the Ukrainian nationalist atamans who operated in the western and northern provinces of Ukraina. First, he was a theoretical anarchist, an absolute opponent of any kind of state. Then he was not an Ukrainian nationalist and not an advocate of pogroms. Jewish anarchists came to his ever shifting partisan headquarters, wrote his appeals, helped to edit the newspaper *The Road to Freedom,* which he published when his military fortunes were favorable. A Jew, Zinkovsky, who had spent many years in prison (whether for political or for criminal causes is not clear) was head of Makhno's private cheka, which quickly disposed of anyone who was suspected of plotting against his life. Among his lieutenants, who seem to have included all types, from sincere anarchists and peasant revolutionaries to abandoned criminals, one found people of various classes and nationalities: Russians, Greeks and Jews, as well as Ukrainians; ex-workers and sailors, with here and there an educated anarchist from the towns, who perhaps felt out of place among the wild, semi-bandit peasant partisans.

Makhno, who was born in 1889, came of a poor peasant family and lost his father as a child. As a boy he worked as a shepherd and farm laborer and also learned something of the carpenter's trade. His revolutionary career began early. He took part as a mere lad in the killing of a local official; and in 1908 received a long sentence of imprisonment, which he served in the Butirki Prison, of Moscow. Along with many other unruly spirits, he was released under the amnesty which was declared by the Provisional Government after the downfall of Tsarism in March, 1917.

While he was in prison Makhno came in contact with an older anarchist, Arshinov, who won him over to the ideas of anarchism and later became the editor of his newspaper and the author of a semi-official history of his movement. Makhno first became locally prominent in 1918, when he displayed great daring in leading a detachment of armed peasants to attack a force of German soldiers which had threatened to burn a village for some act of insubordination. The Germans were driven away and Makhno's fame as a "*batko*" (the Ukrainian word literally means "little father"), or partisan chieftain, rapidly attracted recruits. In the beginning, despite his anarchist views, Makhno worked in close coöperation with the Bolsheviki. He participated with them in an effort to wrest control of the town of Ekaterinoslav from the Petlurists in the last days of 1918;[22] he sent some carloads of grain and other foodstuffs to the hungry workers of Petrograd; his partisan force, which had grown into a small army, was included among the Red troops which fought against the Whites in the southeastern corner of Ukraina.

But difficulties between Makhno and the Red Command soon began to develop. Makhno encouraged and protected congresses of the insurgent peasants of the Gulai-Polye and adjacent regions, where criticism of Soviet policy was free and outspoken. Holding a part of the railroad line near the town of Mariupol, Makhno's troops demanded manufactured goods in exchange for the grain and coal which the Soviet leaders wanted to send into Central Russia. When Grigoriev raised his revolt early in May he made overtures to Makhno for coöperation. Makhno refused; but in messages to the Bolshevik leader, Leo Kamenev, who was then in Ukraina and who had asked Makhno to denounce Grigoriev's action, the anarchist chieftain made it clear that he was remaining on the front "to fight for the freedom of the people, but not in any case for governmental power or for the baseness of political charlatans," simultaneously denouncing "institutions of violence, such as your Commissariats and Chekas, which commit arbitrary violence against the working masses." [23]

Trotzky, always an advocate of extreme centralized discipline, soon came to the conclusion that Makhno's army, in its existing form, was more of a menace than a help and on June 2 published an article [24] declaring that it was time to finish once for all with this "anarchist kulak abuse" and acidly observing: "Scratch a Makhno follower and you find a Grigoriev follower." Makhno was dismissed from his post as Commander of his army. He accepted his dismissal without resistance and left the front with a few of his more devoted followers. Instead of going into the rear of the Whites for partisan activity he moved in the opposite direction and engaged in brushes with Red detachments in the neighborhood of Elizavetgrad. Meanwhile Denikin's Cossack cavalry had broken through the Red front and swept over Makhno's former field of activity, occupying Gulai Polye. During the summer of 1919, when Denikin's successes were most pronounced and the White regime was being established all over Ukraina (at least in the large towns and along the railroad lines), Makhno remained in comparative obscurity, leading the familiar hunted roving life of an insurgent ataman. Late in July he met Grigoriev, who was in much the same situation. A conference of the two chieftains and their partisans was arranged in the village Sentovo on July 27. Makhno denounced Grigoriev for his pogroms and his readiness to go with the Whites; and one of Makhno's aides, Simon Karetnik, shot Grigoriev before the latter realized what was being planned. Several of his lieutenants were also killed; his followers, impressed by this display of gangster technique, mostly joined Makhno.

It was in the autumn of 1919 that Makhno's movement reached its zenith. Breaking through the cordon of White troops which had encircled him near Uman, in western Ukraina, the anarchist insurgent chieftain made straight for his native southern steppes, calling on the peasants to rise against the *zolotopogonniki* ("gold-epaulettes"; a familiar term of abuse for the White officers), and against the former ruling classes generally. The situation was extremely favorable for him. The reappearance in territory which Denikin occupied of pre-War landlords, police chiefs and other decidedly unpopular figures, the threat of losing the land which they had seized, the predatory violence of the Cossacks and Caucasians who formed the bulk of Denikin's forces, all helped to inflame the village against the new rulers. Moreover, Denikin, in his desperate drive for Moscow, had thrown almost all his reliable troops on the front. The rear was almost bare; there were only small garrisons even in many large towns.

With an army that rapidly swelled with insurgent peasants and that amounted to forty or fifty thousand men at the high point of its successes,[25] Makhno was able to play a most devastating rôle in Denikin's rear. By October 11 the port of Berdiansk, on the Sea of Azov, was taken; the insurgents seized sixteen cannon, 2,000 shells, thirty trucks, a considerable quantity of bullets: Alexandrovsk, Nikopol, Mariupol and other towns in the same region were seized and held for varying lengths of time; and Makhno, by seizing the important railroad junctions, Lozovaya and Sinelnikovo, temporarily cut off the Whites from their bases of supply. His mobile partisans, moving very rapidly on horseback, or on peasant carts, on which machine-guns were mounted, even threatened Taganrog, where Denikin and his Staff had their headquarters. And late in October Makhno's forces marched into Ekaterinoslav, one of the largest towns of south central Ukraina, and announced the inauguration of a regime of anarchy.

Makhno's "governmental" acts were in close harmony with his anarchist philosophy, which itself harmonized admirably with the mood of his peasant partisans, who from personal experience were inclined to regard the state, whether Tsarist or Soviet, as an unmitigated evil. Wherever he went he opened the prisons and destroyed them. He issued money, on which it was printed that no one would be prosecuted for forging it. When railroad workers in Ekaterinoslav asked for arrears of pay Makhno replied that the state could not help them, that they must help themselves; and recommended that they should organize transportation on the railroads and charge what seemed to them a fair price for their services. On November 5 he issued a manifesto of the following content: [26]

> "Granting all political parties and organizations complete freedom in spreading their ideas, the army of the Makhno insurgents at the same time warns all parties that the revolutionary insurgents will in no case permit them to prepare, organize and impose political power upon the toiling people."

In another declaration the anarchist conception of how life should be organized is stated in the following terms:

"For the organized carrying on of the new economic and social life free peasants and workers naturally create everywhere their social-economic organizations: village committees or Soviets, all kinds of trade-unions, coöperatives, factory and mine committees, railroad, post and telegraph and other organizations. For the purpose of broad union and mutual connection these organizations naturally create, from the bottom upward, institutions which unite them, in the form of economic Soviets, which fulfill the technical problem of regulating social-economic life on a broad scale. These Soviets may represent townships, cities, regions, etc. They are organized as they are needed on a free basis. In no case may they be political institutions, guided by politicians or parties, dictating their will and realizing their political power under the mask of 'Soviet power'; they are only consultative executive organizations, which regulate economic activity on the spot . . . Such a Soviet system will really be an organization of free workers and peasants."

Profound hatred and distrust of the state, as an organ of power, and of political parties characterize all Makhno's public proclamations. These were often written by anarchists of the *"Nabat"* ("Tocsin") group, who had assumed a sort of intellectual sponsorship of Makhno's movement.

About the behavior of Makhno's followers there is contradictory evidence. The system of elected commanders prevailed; and no old officers or military specialists were tolerated. It is amusingly suggestive to read of one meeting of Makhno's partisans,[27] in which it was unanimously resolved "to obey the orders of the commanders if the commanders are sober when they give them." There was a strong bandit streak in the whole movement. Yet it is the testimony of some witnesses that Makhno's partisans committed less looting in Ekaterinoslav than the Whites who had preceded them; and no large pogroms are associated with the name of Makhno.

Makhno himself had a peasant fondness for heavy drinking, as may be seen from the following typical entry in the diary of his wife for March 13, 1920:

"March 13, 1920—Batko also to-day got drunk. Talked very much. Wandered drunk along the street with an accordion and danced. Exchanged curses with everyone. Fell asleep after talking and dancing."

But, however much Makhno may have enjoyed drinking, dancing to the tune of the beloved Ukrainian instrument, the accordion, and bandying full-throated peasant curses with passers-by in his moments of relaxation, he was a partisan chieftain of rare daring, shrewdness and resourcefulness, who was never captured during three years of uninterrupted campaigning. He was a master not of formal strategy, but of the tricks which are effective in a time of general turmoil and guerrilla warfare. Innumerable legends grew up among the peasants about his marvellous escapes; three authenticated cases may be mentioned as typical.[28] In 1918 he clothed his troops in the uniforms of the Hetman's police and moved about launching sudden attacks on unsuspecting German and Austrian detachments. In 1919 he transferred his detachment through the line of the front as a Red Army unit. Temporarily bottled up in the Crimean peninsula in 1921, he slipped through the Red forces by learning and giving the Bolshevik password.

Makhno's spectacular victories in the autumn of 1919, like most guerrilla triumphs, were shortlived. He was obliged to quit Ekaterinoslav under the pressure of the retreating forces of Denikin, who in turn, quickly abandoned the town to the advancing Red Army. His army melted away; some of the peasants dispersed to their homes and its ranks were greatly thinned by an epidemic of typhus. With the "gold-epaulettes" of Denikin driven from Ukraina, Makhno soon turned on the other enemies of the insurgent peasants whom he led: the Communist food collectors and local officials, the Chekas which were installed with the reëstablishment of the Soviet regime in Ukraina. Refusing to go to the Polish front and fight along with the Red Army, he was declared an outlaw, and throughout the greater part of 1920 he moved about Ukraina, making long raids, but usually returning in the end to his native Gulai Polye. Typical excerpts from the diary of his wife for this period are: [29]

February 23, 1920—Our men seized Bolshevik agents, who were shot.

February 25, 1920—Moved over to Maiorovo. Caught three agents for the collection of grain there. Shot them.

March 14, 1920—To-day we moved into Velikaya Mikhailovka, killed here one Communist.

Further details of Makhno's harassing guerrilla activity are to be found in the reports of the Soviet Ukrainian Front for the same year 1920:

June 8—At the station Vasilevka Makhno blew up the railroad bridge.

July 18—Makhno carried out a raid on the station Grishino, held out there three hours, shot fourteen captured officials of Soviet and workers' organizations, destroyed the telegraph communication and robbed the food warehouse of the railroad workers.

July 26—Bursting into Konstantinograd County, Makhno in the course of two days cut down 84 Red Army soldiers.

August 16—Having seized Mirgorod for a day and a half Makhno's followers robbed all the warehouses of the county food committee, destroyed the buildings of Soviet and workers' organizations, smashed fifteen telegraph machines, killed twenty-one workers and Red soldiers.

In these dry reports there is a decided hint of a fierce hatred of Makhno's partisans for everything connected with the city: railroads, telegraph lines, everything that seemed to give the town an advantage over the village. There can be little doubt that Makhno was popular with a considerable part of the peasants; and their sympathy probably explains his continual success in evading pursuit. His followers seized what they could in the towns, but largely spared the villages; and Makhno often gave part of his plunder to the peasants.

In October and November, 1920, there was a brief period of co-operation between Makhno and the Red Army. General Wrangel, the last of the White leaders, had pushed into Makhno's territory, captured Alexandrovsk and Sinelnikovo and was threatening Ekaterinoslav. Makhno had already given an emphatic reply to Wrangel's proposal for common action against the Soviets by hanging the unfortunate envoy who brought the proposal. Makhno would fight the Communists as an anarchist peasant insurgent, but not in alliance with a White Baron.

Wrangel's advance in September made it almost necessary for the Makhno forces to take one side or the other in the struggle. Overtures were made to the commanders of the Soviet Southern Front, and in October a military-political agreement was signed, under which Makhno's partisans agreed to obey the operative orders of the Red Army, retaining, however, their internal organization and independence. At the same time the Soviet authorities agreed to release imprisoned anarchists and to grant anarchists full freedom of propaganda, provided that they did not appeal for the violent overthrow of the Soviet Government.[30]

Makhno's insurgents then took the field against Wrangel and played a contributory, although not a decisive part in his final defeat in November. The Soviet leaders had never regarded their agreement with the anarchist guerrilla as more than a scrap of paper; Makhno himself could scarcely have been so naïve as to believe that the Communists would tolerate his anarchist community in Gulai Polye in the midst of their tightly regimented, ironclad dictatorial system. Pretexts were found for alleging that Makhno had broken the agreement; and in the last week of November the Red troops simultaneously launched an offensive against the Batko in Gulai Polye and against his cavalry units in the Crimea. Makhno himself escaped; but a considerable number of his followers in the Crimea were killed, including one of his chief lieutenants, Simon Karetnik. At the same time three members of the anarchist delegation which had gone on Makhno's behalf to Kharkov to discuss the application of the agreement were arrested and subsequently shot by the Cheka. One of its members was Popov, the Left Socialist Revolutionary who had led the uprising in Moscow in July, 1918.

A last phase of guerrilla activity now set in. On December 12 Makhno made a successful raid on Berdiansk, killing 83 Communists. Then he wandered all over Ukraina, appearing also in the Don Territory and in Kursk Province, in Central Russia, trying to arouse the peasants to fight for "free Soviets." But this last phase of Makhno's partisan campaigning was foredoomed to failure. With no more White fronts to occupy their main attention, the Red Army authorities were able to concentrate their efforts on the liquidation of peasant insurgents like Makhno and Antonov, in Tambov Province. The peasants themselves were tired of the endless round of killing, raiding and punitive expeditions; even Ukrainian peasants could not live in a state of permanent revolution.

The number of Makhno's followers diminished in numerous obscure clashes; about 250 cavalry remained when he gave up the struggle as hopeless and crossed the Dniester River into Rumania in August, 1921. He had carried out in practise, in primitive, effective fashion, what the Socialist Revolutionary intellectuals had advocated in theory; he had fought on two fronts, against Reds and Whites alike, in the name of what he and the peasants who followed him believed was freedom. Like almost all peasant partisan leaders, Makhno was something of a marauder; but he cannot be dismissed, as some Soviet and White authors are inclined to dismiss him, as simply a bandit. He saw in the landlords and "gold-epaulettes" the standardbearers of an old servitude; in the Communist commissars and food collectors the heralds of a new slavery for the peasants with whom he was connected by the closest ties of blood and race; and he fought both in wild, merciless, truly peasant guerrilla fashion, with all the stormy energy of his nature. He wrote his name large in the grim chronicle of Ukraina's blood-stained chaos.

NOTES

[1] According to a Party census in 1922 native Ukrainians constituted only 23.3 percent of the membership of the Communist Party of Ukraina: 53.6 percent of the Party members reported themselves as Great Russians, 13.6 percent as Jews. As a general rule the percentage of Jews in the educated upper layer of the Communist Party was considerably higher than in the mass of Party members. Details of the Party census are to be found in "History of the Communist Party of Ukraina," by M. Ravitch-Cherkassky, pp. 239ff.

[2] *Cf. Letopis Revolutsii* (Chronicle of the Revolution), No. 2, for 1926, pp. 43–49.

[3] *Cf.* Christian Rakovsky, "The Struggle for the Liberation of the Village," pp. 19ff. The report is dated June 11, 1919.

[4] *Ibid.*, pp. 27ff.

[5] This proclamation is preserved in the Kiev historical archives.

[6] Rakovsky, *op. cit.*, pp. 49ff.

[7] Under the Tsarist regime Jews, except for certain special exceptions, were confined, as regards the right of residence, to the so-called Pale of Settlement, in Western and Southern Russia.

[8] It is obviously impossible to determine with any exactitude the number of pogrom victims during such a period of chaotic upheaval. S. Gusev-Orenburgsky, in his "Book about Jewish Pogroms in Ukraina in 1919" (p. 14), expresses the view that no fewer than 100,000 people perished as a result of pogroms. He asserts that detailed figures show 35,000 deaths and cites estimated numbers of victims in about thirty of the largest pogroms, totalling more than 10,000. E. Heifetz, chairman of the All-Ukrainian Relief Committee for Victims of Pogroms, in his book, "Material Gathered by the All-Ukrainian Committee for the Relief of Victims of Pogroms" (pp. 176ff.), first estimates that 15,000 were killed by Petlurist regular troops, an equal number by the leaders of guerrilla bands and 500 by Red troops, then characterizes this figure as an underestimate and suggests that the grand total of victims would show 70,000 killed by the Ukrainian nationalists and 50,000 by Denikin's forces. Quite probably these vague estimates of 100,000 or more victims are exaggerated. But it is scarcely open to doubt that the Jews, because they were so often singled out for massacre, suffered proportionately more than other nationalities in the town population of Ukraina.

[9] In this connection it is interesting to cite the testimony of a Jewish student, B. Z. Rabinovitch, about the background for the pogrom in Uman (*cf.* Heifetz, *op. cit.*, p. 312):

"The young Jews of Uman took an active part in the Communist movement in general and in the establishment of the organizations of the Soviet regime in particular. At the head of the executive organs was the Jew Buhl; Jews occupied a decided majority of the Commissariats and other higher offices. . . . From the very beginning of the establishment of the Soviet regime in Uman the preponderance of Jews everywhere struck one forcibly. And from various quarters began to spread criticism and expressions of extreme disapproval of the 'Jewish oppression.' . . . The peasants in the neighborhood became violently dissatisfied and antagonists of the Soviet rule. This secret dissatisfaction soon began to appear on the surface, and they gradually poured into the rebel detachments with the object of moving on Uman and overthrowing the Soviet regime." Not infrequently a pogrom was preceded by some acts of terrorism by the local Cheka which were rightly or wrongly attributed to Jewish Communists and which irritated the population without really cowing it.

[10] M. Rafes, "Two Years of Revolution in Ukraina," p. 132.

[11] Arnold Margolin, "Ukraina and the Policy of the Entente," p. 325.

[12] V. Vinnichenko, in the third volume of his work, "Vidrozhenye Natsii" (The Resurrection of a Nation), attributes the pogroms to the influence of traditionally anti-Semitic Russian officers in the Petlurist army, and also to the conduct of some of the purely Ukrainian atamans, "sons of shopkeepers, kulaks, priests and simple peasants, poisoned from childhood with the spirit of anti-Semitism."

[13] Heifetz, *op. cit.*, pp. 40ff.

[14] Margolin, *op. cit.*, p. 334.

[15] Gusev-Orenburgsky, *op. cit.*, p. 11.

[16] Heifetz, *op. cit.*, pp. 113, 114.

[17] *Cf.* the excerpts from the book of N. I. Stif, "Pogroms in Ukraina," published in the collection, "Denikin, Yudenitch, Wrangel," p. 150. Stif cites many details of sex outrages against Jewish girls and women committed by the White troops.

[18] *Cf.* his "Sketches of Russian Turmoil," Vol. V, pp. 146ff.

[19] Many years ago, in the Ukrainian town of Bogodukhov, I accidentally met a young man who belonged to the former well-to-do classes. He told me how a band of Red partisans burst into his home during the civil war, assaulted his mother and smashed his ribs when he attempted to defend her.

[20] A Report of the Central Administration of the Extraordinary Commissions of Ukraina for 1920, which is preserved in the Foreign Archive of the Russian Revolution, in Prague, states that 3,879 people were shot by the Chekas in Ukraina during 1920. The Odessa Cheka seems to have been especially homicidal and put to death 1,418 persons. Kiev reported 538 executions.

[21] *Cf.* A. Tsarinni, "The Ukrainian Movement," pp. 157ff.

[22] *Cf.* G. Igrenev's article, "Ekaterinoslav Reminiscences," in *Arkhiv Russkoi Revolutsii* (Archive of the Russian Revolution), Vol. III, pp. 234–247, for a vivid description of the painfully exciting experiences of a university professor in Ekaterinoslav who suddenly found a group of Makhno partisans quartered on him.

[23] P. Arshinov, "History of the Makhno Movement," pp. 107ff.

[24] L. D. Trotzky, "How the Revolution Armed Itself," Vol. II, Book I, pp. 189–191.

[25] The numbers of Makhno's army at its high point of success, in October and November, 1919, were estimated at 40,000 infantry and 15,000 cavalry by Makhno's Chief of Staff. A Communist underground Party worker in Ekaterinoslav at this time estimates Makhno's forces at 25,000, including 14,000 infantry, 6,000 cavalry and 5,000 in other branches of service. Perhaps the actual figure is between these estimates.

[26] Arshinov, *op. cit.*, pp. 151ff.

[27] M. Kubanin, "The Makhno Movement," p. 184, citing the archives of the Red Army.

[28] Lebed, "Results and Lessons of Three Years of Anarcho Makhnovism," pp. 31ff.

[29] Y. Yakovlev, "Russian Anarchism in the Great Russian Revolution," p. 30.

[30] The full text of these agreements is reproduced by I. Teper (Gordeev), "Makhno," pp. 117ff.

CHAPTER XXXII

"RUSSIA SHALL BE GREAT, UNITED, UNDIVIDED"

DECISIVE victories over four Red armies in the last days of May and the first days of June transformed General Anton Ivanovitch Denikin, head of the Volunteer Army, now renamed as the Armed Forces of South Russia, from a local into an all-Russian standard-bearer of anti-Bolshevism. The long deadlock on the Southern Front was broken; the offensive launched by Denikin on three sectors almost simultaneously was successful everywhere.

At the western end of the front the Cossack cavalry of the Whites broke through the Red defense in the Donetz Basin. The Thirteenth and Eighth Red armies, which were operating in this region, were badly smashed and the former was obliged to retreat almost two hundred miles before it could be brought into order. At the same time the Don Cossack forces north and east of Rostov crossed the Donetz and hurled back the Ninth Red Army, which was already seriously embarrassed by the large-scale uprising of the Don Cossacks in its rear. The general victory of the Whites was made complete when the dashing General Baron Wrangel routed the Tenth Red Army, which had forced its way to the river Manich and was threatening Rostov from the southeast, and forced it to retreat toward Tsaritsin.

There were several reasons for this abrupt turn of the military tide, which created a new and ultimately much more formidable White menace from the South just at the time when the threat from the East, in the form of Kolchak's armies, was disappearing. The numerical relation of the forces on the Southern Front had changed to the disadvantage of the Reds;[1] the appearance of the first British tanks on the front raised the morale of the Whites as it depressed that of their opponents; the Red troops in the Donetz Basin consisted to a considerable extent of former partisan detachments, among which the infectious example of Makhno's bands, with their elected officers and their contempt for regular discipline, was quick to spread.[2] The effect of the Don Cossack uprising in the rear and of Grigoriev's mutiny, which absorbed all the forces of the

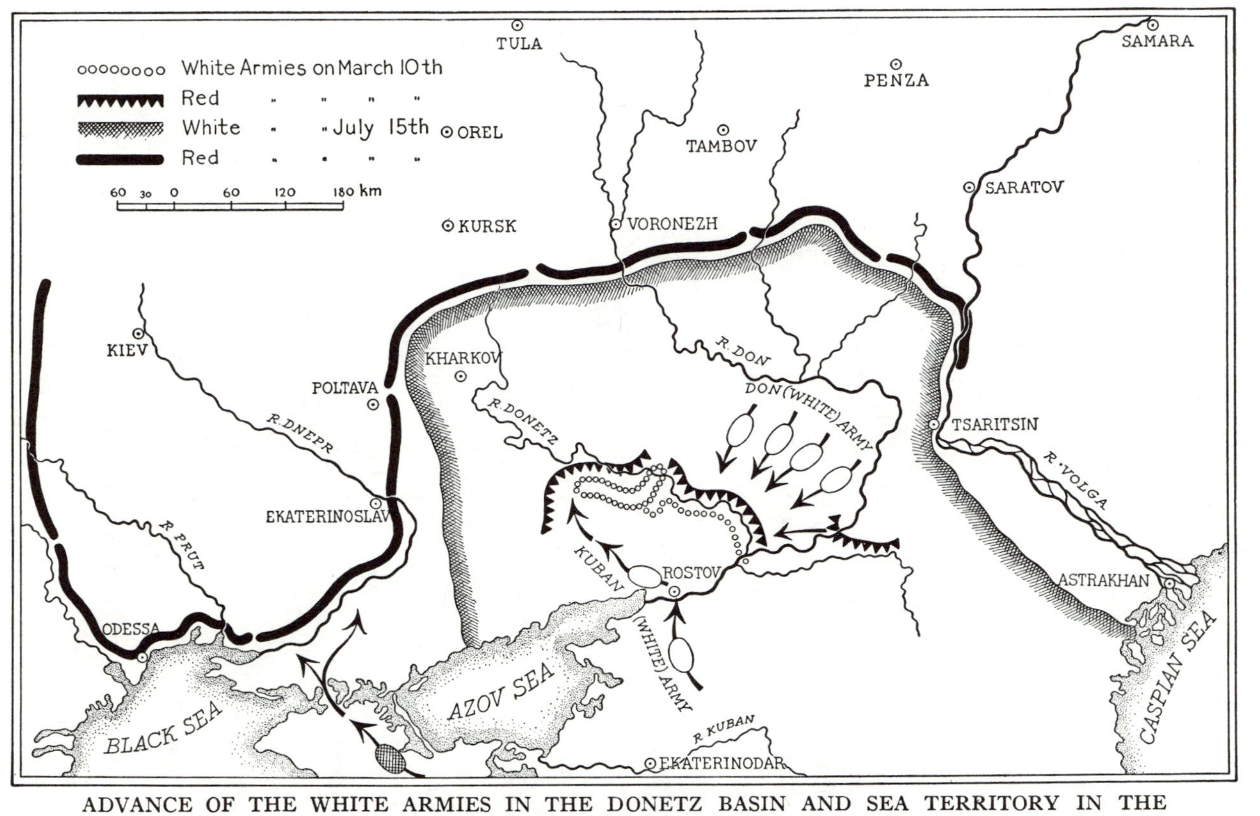

ADVANCE OF THE WHITE ARMIES IN THE DONETZ BASIN AND SEA TERRITORY IN THE SUMMER OF 1919

Ukrainian Red Army during the greater part of May, was also considerable. The Commander of the Soviet Ninth Army, Vsevolodov, passed over to the Whites; it is uncertain whether he deliberately gave blundering orders in order to bring about the defeat of the Army or whether he was simply an incompetent commander who fled to escape possible punishment; but, however this may have been, his desertion still further demoralized the Red troops and aroused suspicion of all the pre-War officers who were serving in the Red Army.

During the month of June the Whites reaped the fruits of their victories in a sweeping addition to the territory under their control. In vain Trotzky gave orders to create a fortified region around Kharkov, the largest city of Eastern Ukraina and an important railroad junction; in vain he called for general arming of the proletariat. The Kharkov workers were to a considerable extent under the influence of the Mensheviki, who predominated in the local trade-union leadership; and their response to the call to arms was sluggish and indifferent. The Whites entered Kharkov, after encircling it from the north, on June 25; a few days later, on the 30th, the "Red Verdun," Tsaritsin, was captured by Wrangel. By the end of June the Don Territory was freed from the Bolsheviki; a large slice of Eastern Ukraina, including the economically valuable Donetz Basin, was firmly occupied; Shkuro's wild horsemen from the Kuban, who displayed on their banners a wolf's head with bared fangs, had overrun Makhno's "anarchist republic" in Gulai Polye and had captured the important town of Ekaterinoslav, on the Lower Dnieper.

There were differences of opinion among the White military leaders as to how the sweeping victories should be developed. General Wrangel, commander of the Caucasian Army, which now constituted the right wing of Denikin's forces, resting on the Volga, advocated a concentration of effort on a drive up the Volga, pursuing the goal of union with the forces of Kolchak. General Sidorin, commander of the Don Cossack Army, was in favor of a more cautious policy, organizing and pacifying the regions which had already been occupied before reaching out for new conquests.[3]

Denikin adopted a much more expansive plan of advance, embodied in his so-called "Moscow order" of July 3.[4] This order proclaimed as the final goal "the seizure of the heart of Russia, Moscow." The drive on Moscow was to proceed in three directions. Wrangel was to advance up the Volga; Sidorin was to strike northward from the Don Territory; Mai-Maevsky, Commander of the Volunteer Army (this name was now reserved for a special part of Denikin's forces, the nucleus of which was provided by the original units of the Volunteer Army), was to move northward from Kharkov along the main railroad line to Moscow. At the same time Mai-Maevsky was to strike westward, aiming at the occupation of Kiev; and operations looking to the occupation of Kherson and Nikolaev, in South Ukraina, were to be undertaken.

This order is open to criticism on the ground of too great optimism and too great dispersion of inadequate forces over extremely wide territory. This criticism derives still more weight from the fact that the actual military operations undertaken by Denikin's forces brought about an even greater extension of a thinly held front than was contemplated in the original order. The campaigns of the Armed Forces of South Russia took them far into Western Ukraina; at the time of the decisive battles in October and November they were spread out on a front that stretched for seven hundred miles from the Volga to the Dniester. Better military results might well have been achieved if a shorter front, resting with its left flank on the Dnieper, had been established and greater forces had been concentrated for a direct drive on Moscow on the main railroad line through Kursk, Orel and Tula. The innumerable guerrilla bands whose activities were described in the last chapter made Western Ukraina a military liability rather than an asset and could have been relied on to keep the Bolshevik forces in that part of the country fully occupied.

On the other hand Denikin seems to have been correct in rejecting the schemes of Wrangel and Sidorin. Kolchak was already in full retreat; the idea of linking up with his forces, which would have been highly desirable in April, was already outdated by July, when the Whites, after the capture of Tsaritsin, were in a position to advance up the Volga. And the logic and psychology of a class civil war demanded a continuous offensive; to have stood still, in all probability, would have been fatal to either Reds or Whites. That Denikin, like Kolchak, conspicuously failed to organize an effective and popular administration of the territories which he conquered and that this contributed very much to his defeat are obvious. But this failure was political and social, rather than strategic.[5]

Throughout the summer and early autumn of 1919 the general balance of military success on the Southern Front was in favor of the Whites and fully justified Trotzky's statement that "Denikin is an incomparably more serious enemy than Kolchak."[6] The eastern flank of Denikin's forces, under Wrangel, remained relatively stationary. After occupying Kamishin, a town on the Volga, midway between Tsaritsin and Saratov, Wrangel's Caucasian Army was obliged to evacuate it under the pressure of superior Red forces, but held Tsaritsin firmly. Meanwhile, profiting by the difficult position in which the Soviet forces in Western Ukraina were placed by the wave of guerrilla peasant insurrections in their rear, the Whites, making good use of their superior cavalry, added substantially to the territory under their control. A combined attack from land and sea, coördinated with an uprising of an officers' organization inside the city, placed Odessa in the hands of Denikin on August 23. Kherson and Nikolaev were taken still earlier, on the 18th. A westward thrust from Kharkov, combined with the sudden disappearance from the Red front of some units headed by an anarchical "ataman" named Bogunsky, led to the occupation of Poltava by the Whites on July 31. General Bredov, one of Denikin's lieutenants, occupied Kiev, "mother city of Russia," on August 31st, pushing out the Petlurist troops which had entered the city the day before.

The Soviet leaders fully realized the critical situation which was arising on the Southern Front and made every effort to reinforce their armies there and to take the initiative again into their own hands. By July 29 Trotzky announced that "we are already considerably stronger than Denikin on the Southern Front." By the middle of July, according to a Soviet estimate, there were 171,600 Red troops on the Southern Front, against 151,900 Whites.[7]

The Red Army took the offensive on two sectors of the front in August. One force, under the command of Selivachev, threatened the security of Kharkov and Belgorod by striking southward somewhat east of these towns and occupying Volchansk and Kupiansk; farther to the east a number of units, selected from the Ninth and Tenth Soviet Armies, under the command of Shorin, moved into the Northern Don and also launched a drive against Tsaritsin. Neither of these offensives, however, led to any permanent or significant success. Selivachev was turned back by a successful flanking movement on the part of the Whites. Shorin's advance was first delayed and then stopped without reaching any important objective as a result partly of the skilful maneuvering of the White forces which opposed him, partly of the resolute courage which the Don Cossacks displayed in defending their native stanitsas, which lay in the region through which the Reds were advancing. The selection of the Don Territory as the region against which the Red offensive should be aimed, while it may have been strategically sound, was politically unwise, as Trotzky pointed out in a memorandum which he drew up after the operation had failed.[8] By striking directly at the Cossacks the Red forces were taking the line of greatest resistance. They were operating in a hostile country, whereas a blow farther to the west, aimed at Kharkov and the Donetz Basin, would have brought them into territory where the peasants were certainly dissatisfied with Denikin and many of the workers were sympathetic with Bolshevism. To some extent, no doubt, the concentration of the Soviet troops at the eastern end of the Southern Front was inspired by an old fear: that Denikin, advancing up the Volga, might unite with Kolchak. But this fear was now unfounded; Kolchak had already been driven beyond the Urals. The result of a strategic plan that left out of account the political and moral factors, so important in civil war, and that was based on an antiquated conception of the possible moves of the Whites, was, in Trotzky's vigorous words, "a pitiful standstill on the eastern half of the Southern Front and a serious retreat, destruction of units, break-up of organization in the western half."

Another circumstance that helped to thwart the August offensive of the Red Army was the sweeping raid carried out far in the rear of the Soviet line by the Don Cossack General Mamontov. The latter, with a picked force of seven or eight thousand cavalry, recruited in part from stanitsas which had suffered especially from the Reds during the civil war, broke through the Soviet front in the neighborhood of Novokhopersk on August 10 (the lightly held and shifting fronts of the Russian civil war were rather easy to "break through") and rapidly moved northward, destroying railroad and telegraph communication, dispersing newly recruited Red soldiers, plundering and burning military stores as he went. On August 18th Mamontov seized Tambov, where he remained three days; then he moved westward, seizing Kozlov, Eletz, Ranenburg and other towns and continuing his work of devastation, not stopping long enough anywhere to permit the Red troops to catch up with him. The poor condition of railroad transportation, of course, facilitated the success of such a cavalry raid.

As the numbers of Red troops sent in pursuit of him increased Mamontov turned southward again, carried on a battle of several days with the garrison of the town of Voronezh and finally, after forty days of wild raiding, in the course of which he covered a distance of about five hundred miles, slipped through the circle of his pursuers and joined the Kuban cavalry corps of General Shkuro on September 19. Mamontov's spectacular expedition aroused vast enthusiasm on the side of the Whites and corresponding exasperation in the camp of the Reds. At first Trotzky, in his published orders, treated the raid contemptuously, as a desperate enterprise which was certain to end in failure. On August 24 he called on the "deluded Cossacks" to "arrest their criminal officers" and surrender. By September 4, finding that this appeal had no success and visibly chagrined by the long continuance of the raid, he published a bitterly worded order, declaring that Mamontov's cavalry had carried on its raid almost with impunity and threatening that members of local Soviet detachments in the sphere of Mamontov's movement which failed to oppose him energetically would be shot.[9]

From the military standpoint the results of the raid were somewhat mixed.[10] Mamontov unquestionably created havoc and confusion in the rear of the Red front and some units which might have taken part in the offensive were devoted to pursuing him. The effect of the raid was heightened by an accidental circumstance; it coincided with the mutiny of a Red Cossack leader, Mironov, who started to move toward the front with a force of five thousand troops which he commanded behind the lines, announcing as his programme simultaneous struggle against the Bolsheviki and against Denikin. Mironov's rebellion was suppressed without bloodshed, but it diverted the valuable cavalry corps of Budenny for a time from the front.

On the other hand Mamontov was so far away from the front that he did not coöperate closely with the main forces of the Whites. And his unwillingness or inability to check the predatory tendencies of his Cossacks had a double bad effect, from the White standpoint. It disorganized his corps even more than the hardships of the many forced marches; the temptation to many of his horsemen to slip away to their homes with their booty was irresistible. Moreover, the plundering tendencies of the Cossacks, which were not confined to state property, alienated the local population and made it impossible for Mamontov to kindle any widespread revolt in the Soviet rear. The peasants of Tambov Province could certainly not be regarded as enthusiastic upholders of the Soviet regime; their large-scale rebellion under their local leader, Antonov, in 1920 and 1921 offered convincing evidence on this point. But a White General could not arouse them against the Soviets.

Stalin and Voroshilov

General Denikin reviewing his troops before the Cathedral in Tsaritsin in the summer of 1919

The Whites responded to the unsuccessful August offensive of the Reds on the eastern end of the Southern Front with new drives, which led to further territorial gains in Ukraina and in the central section of the front, north of Kharkov. On September 20 picked units of the Volunteer Army, after stubborn fighting, captured Kursk; Voronezh, farther to the east, a town which had been repeatedly fought over, passed into the hands of the Whites on October 6. The climax of Denikin's successes occurred in the second week of October, when the Whites on the 12th occupied Chernigov, near the northern frontier of Ukraina, and on the following day took Orel, on the direct road to Moscow. With the capture of Orel Denikin's forces were within two hundred and fifty miles of Moscow.

Only one large town, Tula, an important munitions centre, was between him and the Red capital. No doubt the more optimistic officers of his army, after the taking of Orel, already heard in imagination the pealing of the bells of Moscow's traditional "forty times forty" churches and envisaged the triumphal procession through the streets of Russia's historic city.

But at this high point of the advance of the Armed Forces of South Russia there were circumstances that made the more sober and thoughtful of Denikin's military and civilian counsellors gravely doubtful about the prospects of final victory. The long line of the White front from the Volga to the Rumanian frontier was thinly held; the final victories, culminating in the occupation of Orel, were achieved by shifting of units from other parts of the front, because there were no more free reserves.[11] It was ominously significant that just at the time when the front reached its farthest point of advance, beyond Orel, one town after another in southern Ukraina was falling into the hands of the partisan bands of Makhno, and Taganrog, Denikin's military headquarters, was seriously threatened. Troops had to be diverted from the front to combat Makhno and other insurgents in the rear; a fierce insurrection against the White rule which flamed up in wild, mountainous Daghestan, swallowed up more forces which were sorely needed for the drive on Moscow. The capture of Moscow became not so much a serious military objective as a romantic dream, a means of escaping from the social and economic problems which Denikin's regime was unable to solve. As a prominent member of the Special Conference, which functioned as a sort of civilian Cabinet, writes, in referring to the autumn of 1919: [12]

"By autumn we were hearing more and more frequently such phrases as 'We must be in Moscow at any cost by winter'; or 'If we are not in Moscow by November our position will be bad.' One obtained the impression that the military activities had assumed a forced, adventurous character."

Political, economic and social causes were of primary importance in compassing Denikin's ultimate extraordinarily rapid military collapse. In some respects, to be sure, his position was more favorable than that of Kolchak, and this explains why he was a much more serious enemy of the Soviet regime than his fellow-dictator in Siberia. In character he possessed a quality of phlegmatic selfcontrol in which Kolchak was conspicuously lacking; only at the very end, when the whole edifice which he had reared had crumbled like a house of cards, Denikin seems to have suffered something in the nature of a psychological breakdown. Moreover Denikin, in contrast to Kolchak, was a capable, if not a great general, able to direct the operations of his armies with capacity and discrimination.

The Cossack Southeast was a far better base for an anti-Bolshevik movement than peasant Siberia. With several Black Sea ports and a network of railroads in his possession, Denikin could utilize foreign aid in the form of munitions and supplies much more effectively than could Kolchak, who was obliged to depend on long hauls over the single Trans-Siberian Railroad. The South had attracted far more officers than the East as a place of refuge. Consequently Denikin had at his disposal a much larger staff of experienced generals, officers and military specialists of all kinds.

But all these advantages did not make Denikin's regime successful or stable. There were incurable weaknesses, which military success, in some cases, accentuated, instead of curing, and which ultimately made all military successes quite nugatory.

Denikin did not possess the attributes of a popular leader. He was emphatically not a Mussolini or a Hitler, not a man who could talk to the masses in their own language and substitute a positive programme of wide appeal for the Bolshevik programme which he was combating. Like Kolchak, he would have resented the epithet of "reactionary." He was of quite humble origin; when he was imprisoned and threatened with lynching by his soldiers at Berditchev after his open participation in the Kornilov revolt, he recalled with honest bitterness how his father, born a serf, had gradually advanced to the post of a minor officer, how he himself had gained promotion in the military service through merit and not through the influence of birth or wealth, and how little this accorded with the hostile outcries of the soldiers, who, under the influence of revolutionary agitators, were inclined to regard every officer as a landlord or a capitalist.

It is noteworthy that Denikin never authorized the use of monarchist slogans, despite the pressure of many of his higher officers. But, if he could not fairly be called a reactionary or a monarchist, he was also certainly not a liberal, with clearcut ideas of reform to offer as an alternative to the Bolshevik ideas of sweeping revolution. He was first of all a soldier, a man of no previous political experience; and one often feels, in reviewing his career, that he was simply not at home in politics, much less in economics. The most definite idea for which he stood was nationalism, devotion to the frequently expressed ideal:

"Russia shall be great, united, undivided."

Now this slogan could elicit roars of sympathetic applause at gatherings of officers, former officials, landlords, businessmen, to whom a restoration of the old Russia meant the return of a pleasant and comfortable existence. But it had little or no appeal to the masses of the peasantry, the industrial workers and the poorer classes generally, whose recollections of Tsarist Russia were far from enthusiastic and who more or less consciously felt that, whatever might be the mistakes of the Bolsheviki in ideas and methods, great changes in pre-War conditions were desirable.

Denikin did not proclaim, perhaps did not believe in, the ideal of restoring Russia, much as it was in 1913, with or without a Tsar. But the majority of his intimate advisers, both military and civilian, were definitely more to the Right than he was; and the trend of administrative activity, in the territory occupied by his troops, was unmistakably restorationist. As soon as his troops occupied new territory old officials, old landlords, old policemen were apt to follow in their wake; the Cossack whip was sometimes used to teach the peasants respect for the property of the landlords. The practise of Denikin's military officers and civil administrators was almost invariably much more restorationist than the vague generalized official declarations about the aims of the movement. A shrewd observer on the White side of the civil war front points out that the White propaganda was exclusively negative in character, that it was concentrated on denunciation of the Bolshevik regime without giving any concrete indication of what the Whites wished to put in its place and adds: [13]

"The declarations of the leaders of the struggle with the Bolsheviki, especially regarding the land problem and the political structure of reviving Russia, were ambiguous and conditional and often, perhaps against the will of General Denikin, served as a screen for the desires of the landlords and big industrialists, who played a big rôle, behind the scenes, in the Staff."

One cannot read the reminiscences of General Denikin, which contain many passages of eloquent selfrevelation, without a feeling of sympathy and respect for the personality of the author. Quiet fortitude, crystal integrity, willingness to fight in the face of overwhelming odds, unselfish devotion to his ideal of patriotism are reflected there. One understands the sentiment of admiration that led one of the members of his Government, Professor Sokolov, to refer to him, in somewhat flowery language, as "the gallant knight of the beautiful lady, Great, United Russia." But at the same time, as one considers Denikin's own often frank record of his own mistakes, one thinks of another gallant knight who travelled about the world tilting at windmills.

There was not a little of Don Quixote in Anton Ivanovitch Denikin; no matter how staunchly he might fight, he was foredoomed to failure and disillusionment. And, like Don Quixote, he operated in an unreal world of fantasy. Absorbed in the contemplation of high abstract ideals, duty, honor, motherland, he tended to lose sight of the practical problems to which the masses insistently demanded answers. And these ideals, in which Denikin himself doubtless sincerely believed, were continually mocked by the conduct of many of his supporters, who proved unable to rise above narrow, shortsighted, class selfishness and class vengeance and profiteering of the crudest kind. Indeed it was the tragedy of the genuine patriots in Denikin's ranks that the old Russia which they were consciously or unconsciously fighting to restore proved itself in practise both incapable and unworthy of restoration.

The form of government which evolved in South Russia was a military dictatorship, with Denikin concentrating in his hands all military and civilian authority. The Cossack territories, the Don, Kuban and Terek, enjoyed some administrative autonomy; in other territory occupied by the Volunteer Army Denikin's authority was absolute. The Special Conference, which had been created for the purpose of attending to matters of civil administration in 1918, before the death of General Alekseev, and which exercised the functions of a Cabinet, was a body with purely consultative functions.

Among the twenty-four members of the Special Conference there were three main groups. One consisted of Generals and one Admiral; the political views of its members, with the exception of Denikin's Chief of Staff, General I. P. Romanovsky, were strongly conservative. Romanovsky, like Denikin himself, seems to have been slightly more liberal in outlook than the average Tsarist General; he occasionally expressed misgivings about the reactionary trend of agrarian policy. The civilian members of the Special Conference were divided into conservative and liberal groups. The former were grouped around an organization known as the Council of State Union and represented, in the main, the landowners and the higher bureaucracy of pre-War Russia. The latter consisted largely of Cadets and mostly belonged to an organization known as the National Centre. No Socialists, even of the most moderate type, found a place in Denikin's Government, although the Union of Regeneration, which included in its membership right-wing Socialists and liberal intellectuals, supported his regime while criticizing some of its measures, especially in the field of agrarian legislation and local administration.

When the territory under Denikin's control had greatly expanded it was considered advisable to reorganize the Special Conference and to create a sort of state council, in which representatives of various groups and classes would have seats, along with elected representatives of the Cossack territories. At the same time it was proposed to bring these Cossack territories into a federal union. But the negotiations which began early in the autumn between Denikin's representatives and the Cossack delegations led to no result and by the end of the year the military situation had become so catastrophic that there was little reason to continue them. The Special Conference had become very unpopular; it was a convenient scapegoat for the disastrous turn of affairs; and on December 29 Denikin abolished it and replaced it with a nominated Cabinet.

The liberals in the Conference were at a distinct disadvantage. They were very much outnumbered; against them on almost all disputed points was a bloc of the Generals and the conservative political leaders. Moreover, even when a compromise decision was reached as a result of their influence it was often not carried out in practise, because conservative predominance in the executive apparatus was even greater than in the Conference itself.

On a small scale the Special Conference reproduced the debates of the pre-War Russian Duma,—without any spokesmen for views more radical than those of the Cadets. And what Denikin writes of the groups represented in the Special Conference might be equally well applied to the Duma: [14]

> "They included only a thin layer of the Russian intelligentsia, without roots in the people. Their significance was based not on the support of the masses, but only on the participation of people who had acquired a reputation in state, political or social activity.
>
> "Therefore these organizations could give and gave only advice, but not support. Neither I nor they were able to find support."

Among Denikin's military and political counsellors there was not one who, by past experience or activity, was qualified to speak for the peasants, not one who could express the viewpoint of the industrial workers. It is not surprising, therefore, that the efforts of his regime to solve the agrarian and labor problems were completely unsuccessful, so far as winning the support of the masses was concerned.

Denikin issued two declarations, one on land, one on labor policy, on April 5, 1919. Shortly after this, at the insistent prompting of the British military representative attached to his headquarters, General Briggs, he published a statement of the aims for which his army was fighting.[15] As the bases of his agrarian policy he mentioned "the safeguarding of the interests of the working population, the creation and solidification of small and medium-sized farms at the expense of state and privately owned land." Transfers of land might be carried out by voluntary agreement or by forced alienation, but the principle of payment must be observed. The main points in his declaration on the labor problem were "the restoration of the legal rights of the factory owners and, along with this, defense of the trade-union interests of the working class; establishment of state control over industry in the interests of national economy; raising of productivity of labor by all means; establishment of an eight-hour working day in factories." The general programme for which he professed to be fighting, read as follows:

1. Destruction of Bolshevik anarchy and introduction in the country of law and order.
2. Restoration of a powerful, united, undivided Russia.
3. Convocation of a National Assembly on the basis of universal suffrage.
4. Decentralization of authority through establishment of regional autonomy and broad local selfgovernment.
5. Guaranty of full civil liberty and freedom of conscience.

6. Immediate approach to land reform for the elimination of the land needs of the working population.

7. Immediate carrying out of labor legislation, guarantying the working classes against being exploited by the state and by capital.

Of these seven points only the first two, in all probability, would have commanded the sincere adhesion of the majority of Denikin's associates. Certainly the administrative practise of his officials suggested little sympathy for democratic liberties, agrarian reform or labor protective legislation.

Among all the social and economic questions which confronted Denikin the land problem called most insistently for a popular solution.[16] The peasants constituted the majority of the Russian population. There could be no triumphal entry into Moscow unless the majority of the peasants could be convinced that Denikin was at least a lesser evil than the Soviets. A relatively small force of embittered and resolute ex-officers could overthrow the Soviet regime in Cossack territories where the psychology of the population was different from that of the peasants, where the standard of living was higher and large estates were exceptional. This same force, swelled by the addition of mobilized and volunteer Cossacks, could make spectacular temporary territorial gains by taking advantage of the bitter resentment which the Ukrainian peasantry felt against the Bolsheviki. But to go further, to break the Soviet rule in its industrial workingclass strongholds in Northern Russia was only possible if the turbulent Ukrainian peasants could be convinced that Denikin's system was more compatible with their interests than was the Soviet regime. This political and social test Denikin signally failed to pass.

The general declaration of April 5 did not, of course, represent a definite solution of the agrarian problem. A commission under the presidency of Kolokoltzev, who had been a Minister in the Cabinet of Skoropadsky, worked out a project of a new agrarian law, which Denikin rejected as too conservative. Kolokoltzev proposed to restore to their original possessors the land belonging to the Church, to monasteries, to banks and towns and, in some cases, also the land of private owners. Admitting very grudgingly the principle that the state might compulsorily purchase land for subsequent resale to the peasants from large proprietors, Kolokoltzev's project established very high quotas (from 800 to 1,350 acres) for land which should not be subject to alienation and furthermore contained the provision that there should be no compulsory alienation for three years after the end of the civil war. A second effort to draw up an agrarian law was made by Professor Bilimovitch. His project was less openly restorationist than Kolokoltzev's; in Tsarist Russia it might have been regarded as progressive. But Bilimovitch's project failed to recognize that the transfer of the landlords' estates to the peasants was an accomplished fact, which could not be undone; it was not a piece of legislation which would have satisfied Makhno's partisans, or the other insurgent bands which were operating in the Ukrainian steppes and forests. Moreover, by the time it was drawn up and submitted by Denikin for informal discussion by the press and by various public groups the White armies of South Russia were in full retreat; and new decrees had no practical significance.

Denikin himself had, as he tells us, "tormenting doubts" about some of his own agrarian measures; but the pressure of the landlord interests on his regime (many of the Generals and officers of his army were themselves owners or sons of owners of large estates) was too strong to permit any radical land reform. Other measures which excited much dissatisfaction among the peasants and provided recruits for the guerrilla bands were the demand that the peasant who had seized land should pay a third of the grain harvest to the former owner in the form of rent (this levy was later reduced to one fifth) and a tax in kind which was taken for the needs of the Volunteer Army. That restorationism of a cruder kind, installing of the old proprietors with the aid of troops, was not uncommon is evident from the following order, which Denikin issued in June: [17]

> "According to reports which have come to me, immediately after the troops enter places which have been cleared of the Bolsheviki, appear proprietors, who by force regain, often with the direct support of the military units, their property rights, which have been violated at different times. In this connection they resort to activities which are characterized by the settling of personal scores and the taking of revenge. I order that such actions be severely repressed and that those who are guilty of them be held to strict responsibility."

This order, like many others which condemned pogroms, robbery and drunkenness, failed to produce the desired effect; the spirit of restorationism was too strong. Denikin's forces came to be looked on more and more as a landlords' army; and this alone was sufficient to spell defeat in a civil war where the issue depended so much on the attitude of the peasants.

The industrial workers, who for decades had been under almost exclusively Socialist influence, were even less accessible than the peasants to the conservative nationalist agitation of Denikin's regime. The promised eight-hour day never received legal sanction in Denikin's territory, and the trade-unions and the Menshevik Party organization led a persecuted, semi-legal existence, not unlike that which they experienced under Tsarism. The workers were invited to elect delegates for participation in the work of a commission for the consideration of labor legislation which had been set up by the Special Conference. The representative of the workers' delegation began by reading a declaration which contained sharp denunciation of the anti-democratism of the Denikin regime. The president of the commission, the Cadet Fedorov, warned him not to indulge in political criticism; and when the workers' representative, disregarding the warning, continued to read the declaration and pronounced the words, "The death sentence has become a familiar occurrence," Fedorov ordered him to stop, whereupon the workers' delegation left the commission and refused to take any further part in its work. The grievances of the industrial workers against Denikin's authorities are summarized in the following resolution, adopted at a conference of the trade-unions of South Russia, held in August, 1919: [18]

> "Elementary civil liberties are violated all over the territory occupied by the Volunteer Army. Among the occurrences which take place are: murders and arrests of trade-union workers; militarization of all workers, as in Taganrog; confiscation of union funds, as in Armavir, Maikop and Alexandrovsk; prohibition of the labor press (the Don Territory), closing of labor newspapers, which may be seen everywhere; forbidding of strikes."

The workers of Ukraina, like the peasants, had been disillusioned by the period of Soviet rule, with its food shortage and executions. A minority of active Communists and sympathizers withdrew to the north or remained behind for the difficult and dangerous "underground work" of endeavoring to sow disorganization in the rear of the Whites. But the majority of the workers received the incoming White troops passively, if not enthusiastically. They would probably have welcomed a regime that brought about an improvement in the standard of living and granted freedom of speech and organization, even if this had been accompanied by the return of the factories to private ownership. But Denikin's system did neither. Industry remained largely paralyzed and unemployment was very great. Trade-union organizers, even if they belonged to parties which were opposed to Bolshevism, led a harassed and insecure life. The class sympathy of the typical White General or civil administrator was with the employer against the worker, just as it was with the landlord against the peasant. In view of these circumstances the action of the workers in an Odessa factory who greeted Denikin with the traditional Russian "bread and salt," the occasional resolutions passed by factory workers in Tsaritsin and other towns, praising the Volunteer Army and denouncing the Bolsheviki were of little significance. The general sentiment of the industrial workers remained actively or passively hostile.

After the occupation of Kiev an engineer named Kirsta endeavored to organize the workers in unions on a definite programme of sympathy with the Volunteer Army and to recruit a workers' regiment for service with Denikin's forces. Kiev had always been a city with strong conservative and anti-Semitic influences; and at first Kirsta met with some success and naturally evoked the enthusiastic praise of Denikin's local representative, General Dragomirov, who ceremonially conferred the Cross of St. George, the highest Russian military decoration, upon a worker who had distinguished himself in fighting against the Bolsheviki, when they made a raid into Kiev. But, despite this and despite the lavish subsidies which were granted to Kirsta, the workers soon drifted away from his organization. Equally unsuccessful were his efforts at propaganda and agitation in Odessa.

Another stumblingblock in the path of Denikin's success was the strongly nationalistic psychology which animated his movement. "Great, united, undivided Russia" naturally appealed to the old General or Colonel of the Tsarist Army, to the pre-War governor or court official. But it aroused very different feelings in the minds of the representatives of the non-Russian nationalities which were asserting their claim to an independent existence. It was Denikin's misfortune that much of the population in the territory under his control was non-Russian and that his prospects of military victory depended very much on his ability to conciliate Ukrainians and Poles, Georgians and Caucasian tribesmen: a task for which he was completely unfitted by his blunt, direct, soldierly mentality and his strong Russian nationalism.

Denikin's relations with the new Caucasian Republics, Georgia and Azerbaidjan, were chronically strained and only British mediation helped to avert out-and-out clashes on some occasions. Daghestan, a very warlike part of the Caucasus, inhabited by a medley of Mohammedan tribes, flared up in open revolt in August; Cossack garrisons which had been posted there were massacred and forces had to be withheld from the front in order to cope with the insurgent mountaineers.

Denikin's Russianizing policy had still more serious consequences in Ukraina. Teaching in Ukrainian was forbidden in state-supported schools after Denikin's troops had occupied the country; there were frequent suppressions of Ukrainian newspapers and raids on Ukrainian bookstores; Denikin himself and his lieutenants habitually referred to Ukraina as "Little Russia,"—a traditional term which the Ukrainian nationalists resented. Instead of establishing some temporary form of coöperation with the Ukrainian nationalist leader, Petlura, until the main enemy, the Bolsheviki, were crushed, Denikin's Generals in Western Ukraina carried on hostilities with Petlura's troops, thereby diverting still more troops from the all-important front immediately south of Moscow.

When Denikin ordered the offensive against Kiev, which involved a dangerous lengthening of his front, he counted on the establishment of military contact and coöperation with the Poles, who, taking advantage of the confused state of civil war, were already penetrating into Western Ukraina.[19] He hoped that the Poles would advance as far as the Dnieper and guaranty his western flank, thereby freeing a good many of his own troops for the drive on Moscow. Such a movement on the part of the Poles, accompanied by a hard blow against the Soviet armies from the west at the moment when Denikin's armies were fighting around Orel, might conceivably have changed the issue of the civil war and brought Denikin's armies victoriously to Moscow.

But the Polish aid did not materialize. During the decisive autumn months of the campaign on the Southern Front the Polish armies remained notably inactive, observing a *de facto* armistice. A Polish Communist, Julian Markhlevsky, was admitted to Poland in October. Ostensibly Markhlevsky was a representative of the Russian Red Cross who had come to discuss the repatriation of Russians in Poland and Poles in Russia. Actually he was an authorized representative of the Commissariat for Foreign Affairs; and his talks with a confidential agent of Marshal Pilsudsky covered much broader political questions.[20] Markhlevsky's arguments apparently strengthened Pilsudsky's conviction that a victory of the Russian Whites would not be in accordance with Polish national interests. Denikin, as a victorious all-Russian dictator in Moscow, might recognize Poland's independence, but certainly would be unlikely to concede the extremely generous eastern frontier, including territory inhabited by millions of White Russians, Ukrainians and Lithuanians, which Pilsudsky was anxious to achieve. So the Polish mission which arrived at Denikin's headquarters in Taganrog in September came to no political agreement with him; and the Polish army remained an inactive spectator of his defeat and collapse.

Denikin was also on bad terms with the local government of his original base, the Kuban Cossack Territory. Here again the nationalist element played some rôle. The members of the Rada, the Kuban Cossack parliament, were divided into two main groups, the representatives of the Black Sea districts, who spoke Ukrainian and were extreme in their demands for Kuban autonomy, and the *"lineitsi,"* who inhabited the inland districts and were less hostile to Denikin's regime. When the Black Sea group gained the upper hand in the Rada, coöperation with the Volunteer Army became almost impossible. There were disagreements over a number of subjects. The Rada desired a separate Kuban army, which Denikin, for considerations of military efficiency, was unwilling to establish. Economic disputes reached such a pitch that in September General Lukomsky, one of Denikin's chief assistants and the head of the Special Conference, laid a blockade on the Kuban as a reprisal for the action of the Kuban authorities in restricting exports from their territory.[21]

Later in the autumn Denikin decided to take strong measures against the refractory Rada. A Kuban delegation in Paris at the time of the Peace Conference, breathing the intoxicating air of nationalist selfdetermination, had signed a project for a "treaty of friendship" with the delegates of a government which professed to represent the mountaineers of the Eastern Caucasus. Denikin interpreted this as an act of state treason and on November 7 issued an order for the arrest and trial, by court-martial, of the members of the Kuban delegation.

Military preparations were made in the event that the Rada should offer resistance; General Pokrovsky, who possessed a reputation for ordering summary wholesale hangings, concentrated troops in the neighborhood of Ekaterinodar, where the Rada was in session; the Kuban Territory was placed under the military authority of General Wrangel, who authorized Pokrovsky to act as his deputy. The orators in the Rada foamed with rage; even the members of the body who disapproved of the projected treaty resented Denikin's rough military method of dealing with the situation. But, as usually happened when democratic theory clashed with armed force during the Russian civil war armed force won an easy victory. Pokrovsky surrounded the assembly hall of the Rada with his troops and arrested a number of the deputies who were known as opponents of Denikin's regime. One of these, Kalabukhov, who had signed the projected treaty, was tried by court-martial and promptly hanged on the night of November 19. The lives of a number of other prisoners were saved when the Rada, cowed into complete submission, agreed to change its constitution in conformity with Denikin's demands and to adopt a declaration of complete loyalty and determination to fight on in coöperation with the Volunteer Army. The other prisoners were then deported abroad.[22]

How far Kalabukhov's execution and the brusque treatment of the Rada conduced to disaffection among the Kuban Cossack units at the front is hard to say. Some observers believe that the Kuban Cossack military units knew little and cared less about the speeches and resolutions of the Rada. But a breakdown of morale among the Kuban Cossacks was certainly observable in the last period of Denikin's struggle; and the execution of Kalabukhov may have furnished a convenient pretext for inaction to many Cossacks who were simply tired of the war and cherished the illusion that if they ceased to fight side by side with Denikin's troops the Soviet regime would respect their Cossack autonomy and leave them alone.[23]

Denikin's experiments in the field of local administration were notably unsuccessful. He characterizes his own governors in the following terms: [24]

> "In psychology, world outlook and habits they were so alien to the upheaval that had taken place that they could neither understand it nor deal with it. For them everything was in the past and they attempted to resurrect this past in form and in spirit. After them followed the minor agents of the old regime, some of them terrified by the Revolution, others embittered and revengeful."

The right and left wings in the Special Conference carried on protracted arguments as to how the zemstvo, or organ of rural administration, should be constituted; in actual practise, especially in Ukraina, Denikin's regime failed to establish any kind of effective administration in the rural districts; anarchy was the rule rather than the exception.

Preparations for elections to the town councils dragged on for a long time; when the first elections were held in September only about fifteen percent of the qualified voters went to the polls in

Kharkov[25]; and this was a characteristic manifestation of apathy and indifference.

Formally Denikin acknowledged the supreme military and civil authority of Admiral Kolchak. It was typical of his unselfish devotion to what he regarded as the cause of Russia's national regeneration that he announced his subordination on June 12, at a time when his armies were in the midst of a victorious offensive, while Kolchak was already in full retreat. Denikin's act, however, remained little more than a generous gesture. Practically there was little possibility of political or military coördination. The sole means of direct communication by courier was a long and hazardous trip across the Caspian Sea and through the steppes of Central Asia; messages were sometimes exchanged through Paris. Kolchak granted Denikin full authority to legislate on the territory under his control and on one occasion sent him a letter warning him against adopting agrarian legislation which would favor the landlord against the peasant. In the main the two White dictators had a very similar political outlook, and apparently there were no serious differences of opinion between them on matters of policy.

Denikin and Kolchak nominated the same Foreign Minister, Sazonov, who had occupied this post in the Tsarist Government at the outbreak of the War. Sazonov made his headquarters in Paris and endeavored to promote the interests of the White cause through informal contacts with the Allied statesmen. A Russian Political Conference, consisting of Sazonov, Maklakov, the former Russian Ambassador in Paris, Prince Lvov, the head of the first Provisional Government, and Nicholas Chaikovsky, a veteran revolutionary who was a bitter and consistent anti-Bolshevik, functioned in Paris as a representative body for the various White Governments. Denikin's relations with the Political Conference were considerably chilled in the spring of 1919, when he delivered a tart answer to what he regarded as uncalled-for advice from Lvov, on behalf of the Conference. Lvov had suggested:

"Every rumor about disputes of the military authorities with local governments and elected governmental organizations, the bringing of political considerations into military affairs and, still more, the revelation of reactionary sympathies, of aspirations for political restorationism, for the taking away of the land from the peasants on the part of individuals who are associated with the Volunteer Army destroys sympathy and faith in the national movement. . . . It is not enough to avoid such mistakes, it is necessary to establish clearly friendly relations with the local governments, to have popular names in the personnel of the Government, to reestablish and maintain a broad political front, so that the Bolsheviki should be isolated from all Russia in their struggle."

This message reached Denikin when he was involved in one of his frequent acrimonious disputes with the Kuban Rada, and he sharply replied to the effect that he considered it "completely useless for persons who are torn off from Russia and who do not know and understand the circumstances in which the difficult task of state upbuilding is being carried out, to attempt to guide the activities of the Ekaterinodar Government." [26]

If one looks through the newspapers published in South Russia during the period of Denikin's rule or reads the reminiscences of participants in his movement one cannot escape the impression that the towns in the rear of the advancing White armies represented a veritable bacchanalia of drunkenness, corruption and speculation. The following order, issued by General Fetisov, commandant of the town of Rostov, on October 11, 1919, is typical of many others and reflects the loose discipline of the Whites: [27]

"Recently cases have been very often noticed when officers and soldiers appear in an intoxicated condition on the streets, in clubs and at charitable entertainments. Some get into such a state of drunkenness that they are completely irresponsible for what they do: they quarrel among themselves, curse publicly, demand identification papers without being authorized to do so, draw their arms, shoot from revolvers."

Some of the highest Generals set a bad example for their subordinates; General Mai-Maevsky, military governor of Kharkov, and commander of the Volunteer Army, was often intoxicated for days at a stretch. Along with the debauchery went a wave of bribetaking and speculation, which Denikin, himself a man of incorruptible integrity, vainly endeavored to combat by means of threatening orders. Everything was an object of speculation and profiteering: grain and sugar, army stores and manufactured goods; it was impossible to obtain a truck or a freightcar without bribery. A British journalist who was in South Russia during the period of Denikin's rule gives the following concrete illustrations of waste and corruption in connection with the British supplies which were sent to this part of Russia: [28]

"About the middle of 1919 the British sent out a complete two-hundred-bed equipment for a hospital at Ekaterinodar. Not a single bed ever reached its destination. Beds, blankets, sheets, mattresses, and pillows disappeared as if by magic. They found their way to the houses of staff officers and members of the Kuban Government. . . . In 1919 we sent Denikin 1,500 complete nurses' costume outfits. I did not, during the whole of my service with the Army in Russia, ever see a nurse in a British uniform; but I have seen girls, who were emphatically not nurses, walking the streets of Novorossisk wearing regulation British hospital skirts and stockings. Britain sent Denikin enough soldiers' clothing to equip an army twice the size of her own peace establishment. He never claimed to have had more than 300,000 men at his disposal; but neither at the Tsaritsin nor the Don front did I ever see as many as 25 percent of the fighting men in British kit. . . . I saw and talked to young ladies of good social standing at Taganrog who were wearing costumes made of British officers' serge, and I can name Russian officers attached to the British Mission who deliberately 'wangled' a double issue of clothing from our Ordnance and at once sold the surplus set at a fabulous price."

Many factors contributed to this orgy of speculation and corruption, which demoralized the rear of the White armies and gravely interfered with the supply of the fronts. Salaries in the state service were pitifully low and were paid in constantly depreciating paper money; the temptation to eke them out by illegal means was irresistibly great.[29] All Russia at this time was starved for manufactured goods; and when some stocks filtered in through the channels of British military aid a certain amount of leakage was almost inevitable. The various kinds of money in circulation and the customs restrictions which were imposed by the Cossack Territorial Governments invited speculation.

Moreover, the faults and weaknesses of the pre-War Russian ruling classes avenged themselves on this movement, which aimed at their restoration. The pre-War Russian officer was not infrequently inclined to hard drinking and loose living. The Tsarist bureaucracy did not possess a high reputation for integrity.

But the corruption and debauchery which swept over South Russia under the regime of the Whites and which thwarted all the efforts of the courageous officer at the front, of the conscientious official who was willing to work faithfully for his small salary were more than a mere outcropping of the faults and weaknesses of the pre-War Russian ruling classes. Five years of the most sanguinary war and the most far-reaching social upheaval in world history had left the average Russian in a psychological condition akin to acute shellshock. Normal standards of duty, obligation, selfsacrifice were obliterated. Extreme selfishness, sometimes of the most shortsighted kind, governed the conduct of individuals and classes. As Denikin himself writes:[30]

"Especially strange was the attitude of the majority of the bourgeoisie toward that regime which was establishing the bourgeois order and private property. The material help which the propertied classes gave to the Army and the Government was negligible. And the demands of these classes were very great."

So Denikin's position at the moment when his decisive battle with the Reds began around Orel in October was far less favorable than a glance at the map and a record of purely military operations up to that time would suggest. True, he had driven the Bolsheviki from an extensive and fertile territory; he was in nominal control of regions with a population of 42,000,000. But, outside the Cossack Territories, he could count on the active sympathy of only a small minority of the population, represented by the Russian propertied and middle classes, along with some radical and liberal intellectuals who considered him a lesser evil than the Soviets. Even in the Don and Kuban there were signs of demoralization; the military authorities in Rostov were continually publishing lists of deserting Cossacks, along with the number of lashes which were to be inflicted on them; in the forests, swamps and hills of the Kuban bands of so-called "greens," consisting largely of deserters, were beginning to operate. So bitter was the antagonism aroused by many features of Denikin's policy and by many acts of his local administrators that efforts to carry out mobilizations in Ukraina were more apt to produce rebellions and new "internal fronts" than reliable recruits. The wholesale economic speculation in the White South was a reflection of the hazardous political speculation represented by Denikin's whole movement. In it there was a strong element of feeling: "After us, the deluge."

However difficult the strategic problems involved, it was an absolute political necessity for Denikin to capture Moscow in the autumn of 1919. His system could not stand the shock of a serious reverse on the front.

NOTES

[1] There is sometimes wide divergence between the figures given by Red and White historical sources. The Soviet official military history, "The Civil War, 1918–1921," states (p. 242) that at the time of the decisive operations on the Southern Front in May the Reds had 73,000 troops, as against 100,000 Whites. Denikin, on the other hand ("Sketches of Russian Turmoil," Vol. V), asserts that at this time he had 50,500 troops, as against 95,000 to 105,000 Reds.

[2] Trotzky ("How the Revolution Armed Itself," Vol. II, Book I, p. 222) compares the "infection" of partisanism which spread from Makhno's units with typhus or cholera.

[3] G. Rakovsky, "In the Camp of the Whites," pp. 1, 2.

[4] General A. I. Denikin, "Sketches of Russian Turmoil," Vol. V, pp. 108, 109.

[5] Trotzky declared on June 27 that "behind Denikin there is nothing but a rear that is hostile to him." At this time the statement was perhaps premature, but it was fully borne out by the circumstances of Denikin's retreat in the autumn and winter.

[6] Trotzky, *op. cit.,* Vol. II, Book I, p. 302.

[7] "The Civil War, 1918–1921," Vol. III, p. 248.

[8] Trotzky, *op. cit.,* Vol. II, Book I, pp. 301–303.

[9] *Ibid.,* Vol. II, Book I, pp. 280, 281.

[10] Denikin (*op. cit.,* Vol. V, p. 122) and the Soviet military historian, N. E. Kakurin ("How the Revolution Was Fought," Vol. II, pp. 301, 302) gave very similar appraisals of the significance of Mamontov's raid.

[11] "The Civil War, 1918–1921," Vol. III, p. 267.

[12] K. Sokolov, "The Government of General Denikin," p. 191.

[13] G. Rakovsky, *op. cit.,* pp. 3, 4.

[14] "Sketches of Russian Turmoil," Vol. V, p. 157.

[15] *Ibid.,* Vol. IV, pp. 212–216.

[16] Kolchak early in November despatched a secret telegram to Denikin, suggesting that the peasants' lack of land was a main cause of the Revolution and that only a policy of leaving the land in the hands of the peasants could guaranty their sympathy for the White movement and avert uprisings and "demoralizing anti-governmental propaganda among the troops and the population."

[17] This order was published in the newspaper *Donski Vedomosti,* for June 20–July 3. (The Whites, as a general rule, employed the pre-revolutionary Russian calendar.)

[18] B. Kolesnikov, "The Trade-Union Movement and Counterrevolution," p. 207.

[19] "Sketches of Russian Turmoil," Vol. V, p. 175.

[20] Interesting details of Markhlevsky's mission are communicated by Louis Fischer ("The Soviets in World Affairs," Vol. I, pp. 239ff.).

[21] A serious cause of economic disorganization in Denikin's territory was the creation of quite artificial "frontiers" with customs barriers between the various Cossack Territories.

[22] Full details of this military *coup* against the Rada may be found in I. Kalinin, "The Russian Vendée," pp. 264ff., in G. Pokrovsky, "The Denikin System," pp. 181ff., and in D. Skobtsov's article, "The Drama of the Kuban," published in the magazine, *Golos Minuvstchevo na chuzhoi storone,* No. I/XIV, for 1926.

[23] The Bolsheviki were lavish in making promises to respect the special customs of the Cossacks, to permit them to trade freely and to employ hired labor. (An example of this propaganda is an appeal to the Cossacks, signed by Lenin and Kalinin, published in *Pravda,* for August 17, 1919.) These pledges were broken as soon as they had fulfilled their purpose of sapping the Cossack morale and thus promoting the defeat of the White armies.

[24] "Sketches of Russian Turmoil," Vol. IV, p. 218.

[25] D. Kin, "The Denikin System," p. 77.

[26] "Sketches of Russian Turmoil," Vol. IV, p. 241.

[27] N. E. Kakurin, "How the Revolution Was Fought," Vol. II, p. 180.

[28] J. E. Hodgson, "With Denikin's Armies," pp. 180ff.

[29] K. Sokolov ("The Government of General Denikin," p. 184) expresses the view that "if bribery and embezzlement were so developed in South Russia one of the causes was our system of 'starvation' salaries." Of course the low salaries were primarily attributable to the economic prostration of the country and the lack of normal industrial and agricultural productivity.

[30] "Sketches of Russian Turmoil," Vol. V, p. 273.

CHAPTER XXXIII

THE DECISIVE CAMPAIGNS OF THE CIVIL WAR

THE first major crisis of the Soviet regime occurred in the summer of 1918, when the Czechs were in Kazan, the provinces around Moscow were swept with a wave of local peasant uprisings and the Red Army was just in the process of being transformed from a group of loosely disciplined partisan units into an effective fighting force. It was faced by a second crisis in the middle of October, 1919, when Denikin's foremost regiments were in Orel, less than two hundred and fifty miles from Moscow, and the Northwestern Army of General Yudenitch, after an unexpectedly successful surprise offensive, had fought its way into the suburbs of Petrograd.

The circumstances of 1919 were different from those of 1918. The Red Army was vastly stronger in numbers, discipline and military experience. But there had been a corresponding gain in organized strength on the side of the Whites. The campaign against Yudenitch was of secondary importance, compared with the main operations on the Southern Front against Denikin. Yet Yudenitch possessed a more formidable force than the Czechs and the troops of the Constituent Assembly which represented the main threat to the Soviet Government in 1918. The military challenge to the Revolution was genuine enough; the course of Russian history would have been profoundly changed if Denikin had taken Moscow and Yudenitch, Petrograd. The battles which raged around the obscure Russian provincial towns, Orel and Voronezh, and on the outskirts of the former capital, Petrograd, were the decisive struggles of the civil war.

The Communist leaders were under no illusions as to the seriousness of the situation which confronted them. On October 14, the day after Denikin's picked Volunteer units took Orel, the Communist Party newspaper, *Pravda,* wrote:

"Now even the blind see that the decisive days of the Revolution have come. . . . The fate of the whole movement is now being decided on the Southern Front."

And the Commander of the Red Southern Front at this time, Egorov, discussing the circumstances which led him to launch a counter-attack against the Whites in October, before the concentration of all his reserves had been completed, says: [1]

> "Further retreat could not be permitted, because it threatened the complete disintegration of the armies, unloosed the counterrevolutionary forces within the country and strengthened the position of the White armies."

Retreat under the conditions of the Russian civil war, when the general morale of the soldiers on both sides was not very high, was always a dangerous operation and not infrequently turned into complete rout. But the retreat of the Red armies from Ukraina had compensating advantages. It brought them closer to the workingclass centres of Northern Russia, where at least an active minority of the industrial workers was still ready to fight and die for the Soviet cause.

Moreover, the Russian peasant districts between Moscow and the front were not in the state of chronic turbulent revolt that was so characteristic of Ukraina in 1919. The Russian, like the Ukrainian, peasants were certainly bitterly resentful of many features of the Soviet regime, notably of the requisitions and the prohibition of free trade. But their resistance had been pretty effectively broken in the suppression of the numerous revolts of the preceding year. Here and there the forests sheltered bands of deserters; but there was no guerrilla leader of the type of Makhno, with an insurgent army, to tear up the rear communications of the Red Southern Front. Moreover, as the experience with the Mamontov raid had shown, the peasants were not inclined to rally to the banner of an army which robbed indiscriminately and was reported to be bringing back the landlords. It was Denikin who now faced the disadvantage of having in his rear ever rebellious Ukraina, with its many bands of well-armed peasant partisans.

The Red rear was indeed disturbed by two developments in September, the Schepkin plot and the bombing of the headquarters of the Moscow Committee of the Communist Party. But neither of these exerted great influence on the course of military developments. It was announced on September 23 that sixty-seven persons had been shot by the Cheka for participation in political and military organizations which were working on behalf of Denikin.[2]

The list of persons executed was headed by N. N. Schepkin, an engineer and member of the Cadet Party, who was an active member of two anti-Bolshevik political organizations, the National Centre and the more left-wing Union of Regeneration. Schepkin described himself as follows: [3]

"I belonged to the Union of Regeneration as a lover of liberty, hating oppression, from whatever source it might come. My grandfather, the famous actor, M. S. Schepkin, was a serf and bequeathed to us the idea of struggle with all forms of serfdom, regardless of what fine slogans they might cover themselves with."

What Schepkin especially disliked about the Soviet regime was

"the taking away of property under the form of requisition and confiscation, sometimes indistinguishable from raids and robberies, the complete absence of any guaranty of personal safety and of any assurance that the fruits of one's labor will not be taken away."

Schepkin was as sincere in his conception of what constituted liberty as Lenin was in his; and he paid for it with his life. He kept up a clandestine correspondence with fellow-members of the National Centre (which was closely identified with the Cadet Party) in Denikin's territory and in one of his letters suggested that, in view of the sentiment of the masses, it would be advisable, in propaganda, to be silent about the Soviets, while advocating such slogans as: "Free trade and security of private property," "Down with the civil war," "Down with the Communists." Among his papers were found plans of the Red Army dispositions around Saratov, a description of one fortified region, with its batteries and base warehouses, details about the numbers of the Red Army divisions, shifts in their staffs, etc. Associated with Schepkin were some former officers in the service of the Red Army, who were also arrested and shot.

Two days after the announcement of the executions of Schepkin and his companions a powerful bomb was hurled into the meeting-place of the Moscow Committee of the Communist Party, on Leontiev Street; twelve persons, including the Secretary of the Committee, Zagorsky, were killed and twenty-eight were injured. At first it was assumed that this was an act of terrorism carried out by the Whites in revenge for Schepkin. Actually a group of Anarchists and Left Socialist Revolutionaries planned and executed the bombing of the headquarters of the Moscow Committee.[4]

Holding almost daily sessions, the Central Committee of the Communist Party, in this critical period, made every effort to bring about first a turn in the tide and then final victory. Just as at the time of Kolchak's advance in the spring, there was an intensive mobilization of Communists for the front. Petrograd first despatched a number of mobilized Party members to the Southern Front; the example was soon followed by Moscow, Vladimir and other towns throughout the country.

A new experiment, calculated to test the loyalty of the working class, was made. In mid-October, when the military crisis was at its height, a special "Party Week," when new members were accepted without the usual requirements of recommendations and a period of probation, was declared. It was assumed that anyone who joined at such a moment was devoted to the Communist cause, because a victory of the Whites would almost certainly be followed by a hunting down and slaughter of all known Communists. The response to the Party Week was surprisingly vigorous, if one considers the hunger and privations which the workers, along with all other classes, suffered under the Soviet regime. Moscow alone furnished about 14,000 new Party members.[5] The propaganda apparatus at the disposal of the Communist Party functioned vigorously; the workers were told that the victory of Denikin meant "capitalist slavery"; vivid descriptions of the revenge of the returning landlords and of the plundering and outrages which characterized the conduct of Denikin's troops in the regions which they occupied were given for the benefit of the peasants. Daily cartoons showed the Whites crushing the peasants with their fists, stepping on their bound bodies, hanging them to gibbets.

One of the most effective agitators among the peasants was the President of the Soviet Central Executive Committee, M. I. Kalinin, who, as a peasant himself by origin, was an admirable apostle of the Bolshevik gospel of class hate, of setting the poor and uneducated majority of the Russian population against the well-to-do educated minority. Kalinin was almost as indefatigable a traveller as Trotzky; while the fiery War Commissar rushed from front to front to bolster up the morale of the troops, the peasant President addressed countless peasant meetings, answering questions, redressing grievances to the best of his ability, and always trying to turn the current of peasant discontent into the channel of hatred for the former privileged classes. A typical specimen of Kalinin's propagandist methods is the following excerpt from one of his speeches in the summer of 1919: [6]

"Formerly the elect of the Lord were in the seats of government. Now Kalinin is at the head of the government; the grey, uncouth *muzhik,* with

Stalin reviewing the first cavalry army in 1919

The Soviet President, M. I. Kalinin, seated with military cap, listening to the representations of peasants in a Ukrainian village in 1920

his dirty feet, has climbed up on the throne of the elect. The nobles will not pardon us for this. . . . Of course we make many mistakes, because we did not learn to rule before. But we cannot place at the head of the government a wise man of other classes, because he will betray us. Perhaps Kalinin is stupid, but the masses of workers and peasants pushed him to the fore."

Just at the time when all the military resources of the Soviet Union were being concentrated on the preparation of a counter-blow against the advancing forces of the most formidable enemy, Denikin, the Northwestern Army of General Yudenitch[7] launched a sudden and unexpected drive against Petrograd. Yudenitch's offensive against Petrograd was in some respects an even more desperate venture than Denikin's against Moscow. The Northwestern Army mustered only 18,500, against 25,500 troops of the Seventh Red Army, which blocked its direct road of approach to Petrograd.[8]

Its communications, in the event of an advance on Petrograd, could be threatened in flank and rear by another Red Army, the Fifteenth, which was stationed farther to the south. Petrograd itself was a city with a population of almost a million, even after the wholesale exodus which was caused by the desperately bad food situation; there were tens of thousands of Communists and Soviet sympathizers in the former capital; the revolutionary spirit of such workingclass districts as the Viborg Section was proverbial. Yudenitch certainly had far less chance than his opponents of winning reinforcements in the course of his campaign. Another White force in the Baltic region, operating in Latvia under the command of Colonel Bermont, instead of coöperating with Yudenitch, turned against Riga at this time, in an effort to overthrow the existing Latvian Government. This diverted the Esthonian army and British warships, which were cruising in the Gulf of Finland, to Riga, in order to check the ambitious designs of Bermont and also increased the suspicions of the Esthonian Government regarding the intentions of the Northwestern Army, if it should succeed in taking Petrograd.

However, desire to break up the peace negotiations which were proceeding between Soviet Russia and Esthonia and to aid the progress of Denikin induced the leaders of the Northwestern Army to risk the offensive. There was the further consideration that their army might break up if it remained inactive; the British military representatives encouraged the enterprise and held out hopes, which were not realized, of extensive coöperation on the part of the British warships.[9]

While the basic factors in the situation were unfavorable to Yudenitch, several circumstances helped to make the first stages of his drive very successful. The Seventh Army, although superior in numbers to the Whites, was spread out over a longer front, and its military vigilance was relaxed because of the peace negotiations with Esthonia. The quality of its troops was not high; and its Chief of Staff, Colonel Lundquist, was in communication with the North-western Army and conveyed valuable information about the disposition of the Red troops and the weak points in the line of defense. The offensive started auspiciously when Yamburg was taken by a surprise attack on October 11. It is less than a hundred miles from Yamburg to Petrograd, and within a week Yudenitch was almost at the gates of "Red Peter," as the Communists called the city. The Seventh Army rolled back in disorderly retreat; the appearance of a few British tanks had a very demoralizing effect on the raw Red Army recruits. On October 13 the commander of the Seventh Army characterized the condition of his forces as follows: [10] "Our units are in a panicky mood and retreat at the mere appearance of a cavalry patrol of the enemy."

It was part of Yudenitch's plan to isolate Petrograd from reinforcements by cutting the railroad lines which radiate from the city toward the southeast and the southwest. Two of these lines were cut off by the Whites; but the most important of them, connecting Petrograd with Moscow, remained in the hands of the Reds. After Gatchina, thirty miles southwest of Petrograd, had been captured on October 16 the commander of the Third Infantry Division of the Whites received orders to proceed to Tosno, a station on the Petrograd-Moscow Railroad, and occupy it. Confident that Petrograd itself would soon be taken and eager to be one of the first to enter it, he disregarded the order; and when the attempt to break the railroad connection between Petrograd and Moscow was renewed by the Whites a few days later, sufficient forces had been concentrated around the railroad to defend it. The failure to interrupt communication with Moscow was a costly strategic mistake; "kursanti," or Red officers in training, and other forces were brought up from Moscow to strengthen the defense.

Yudenitch's dash for Petrograd created a difficult problem for the Soviet leaders. Under ordinary conditions troops would have been hastily despatched to the threatened city from other fronts. But the Southern Front was of such primary and decisive importance that any weakening of it was out of the question. Lenin was in favor

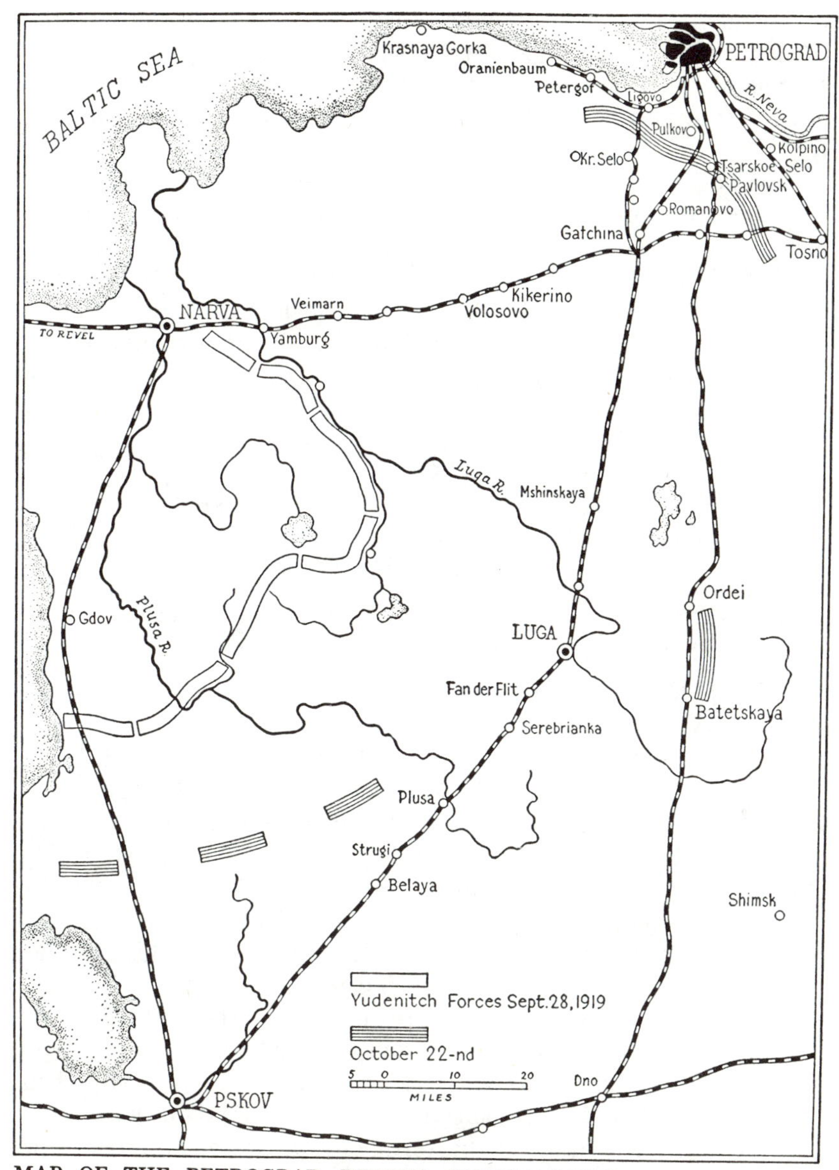

MAP OF THE PETROGRAD REGION, ILLUSTRATING THE CAMPAIGN OF YUDENITCH

of abandoning Petrograd, rather than weakening by one iota the concentration of forces against Denikin. But Trotzky insisted that Petrograd could be saved without diverting troops from the Southern Front and rushed to Petrograd himself to take charge of the defense.[11]

He worked out a double scheme of resistance. Every effort was to be made to improve the morale and increase the numbers of the Seventh Army, so that a successful stand could be made outside the city. If Yudenitch's troops broke through and entered Petrograd elaborate plans were made to destroy them in desperate, merciless street fighting. On October 16, as Trotzky was approaching Petrograd, he formulated his scheme for defending Petrograd from within as follows: [12]

> "Bursting into this gigantic city the Whites will come into a stone labyrinth, where every house will be for them either a riddle, or a threat or a mortal danger. Whence can they expect a blow? From the window? From the attic? From the cellar? From around the corner? Everywhere. At our disposition are rifles, machine-guns, hand-grenades. We can cover some streets with barbed-wire entanglements, leave others open and turn them into traps. It is only necessary that some thousands of men should firmly decide not to give up Petrograd."

Trotzky's theory that it would be possible to destroy the Whites, even if they forced their way into the city, was not put to the test. On October 20 the Reds were pushed back to the Pulkovo heights, the last line of defense on the outskirts of Petrograd. There is a story that one of the White Generals, Rodzianko, at this time, declined an offer to look at Petrograd through field-glasses, saying that on the next day he would be walking on the familiar Nevsky Prospect (the main boulevard of Petrograd). But the Red lines held on the Pulkovo position. On the 21st Trotzky, in one of his glowing, feverish orders, was already announcing a turn in the tide, the repulse of all new attacks, the capture of prisoners. By the evening of the 23d the Whites had been pushed from the nearer suburbs of Petrograd, Pavlovsk and Tsarskoe Syelo. Yudenitch's troops, with their high contingent of former officers, fought, in the main, with stubborn courage, according to the testimony of Soviet observers and historians. But the issue of the drive against Petrograd was no longer in doubt. If the city could not be carried in the sweep of the first sudden onset it could not be taken at all. Yudenitch did not possess sufficient troops to carry out a siege or to sustain a long struggle of attrition.

Conscious, probably, that defeat and retreat meant the collapse of his whole movement, Yudenitch continued to hold out at Gatchina during the last days of October, and occasionally launched counter-attacks, apparently hoping that an outburst of revolt within the city might bring him final victory. But now the Fifteenth Red Army, swinging into action from the south and occupying Luga, began to threaten very directly his line of retreat. He evacuated Gatchina on November 3, Gdov on November 7 and Yamburg, the startingpoint of his offensive, on the 14th. Driven from its last foothold on Russian territory, his army crossed the frontier into Esthonia, where it was disarmed, interned and soon disbanded. The Northwestern White Front, insignificant as regards territory and population, but annoying because of its constant potential threat to the security of Petrograd, had ceased to exist.

The defense of Petrograd was a very striking episode in the civil war. It was a noteworthy personal triumph for Trotzky, who was ceremonially awarded the Order of the Red Banner, the highest Soviet military decoration, for his conspicuous services on this occasion. It was also a demonstration of the ability of the Communists to rally around them a considerable part of the industrial workers. All the descriptions of Petrograd during the critical days of the second half of October mention the activity of the workingclass quarters: the hasty throwing up of barricades and barbed-wire entanglements in the southern sections of the city, which would have first been exposed to attack; the creation of partisan detachments for the defense of the city from within; the sending of workingclass recruits and agitators to the front. The workers of the large Putilov Factory gave valuable aid to the Red Army by producing a few hastily improvised tanks. These were useful not so much for actual military efficiency as for familiarizing the Red Army soldiers with the actual character of a tank; in the beginning Yudenitch's tanks had produced the terrifying effect of mythical monsters.

But the really decisive battles of the civil war were being fought on the Southern Front, simultaneously with the defense of Petrograd. And the favorable news from the Southern Front exerted a stimulating influence on the defenders of Petrograd.

The physical odds, expressed in terms both of men and of guns, were heavily against Denikin when the campaign on the Southern Front reached its decisive phase. On the seven-hundred-mile front from Kiev to Tsaritsin 186,000 Reds faced 112,600 Whites. The Red Armies possessed over a thousand cannon and 4,500 machine-guns, as against 542 cannon and 2,326 machine-guns of the Whites.[13] The Reds possessed another advantage which was of considerable importance in a closely contested campaign; west of Orel they had formed a fresh shock group, consisting of a Lettish infantry division, the brigade of Pavlov and a brigade of Ukrainian cavalry under the command of Primakov. This shock group, consisting of 10,000 infantry and 1,500 cavalry and reinforced by an Esthonian division, played an important part in forcing the Whites to evacuate Orel on October 20 by striking hard at them from the southwest and threatening to cut the railroad communications in their rear. As has already been pointed out, the Whites had brought all their reserves into action and were even compelled to detach some units from the front, in order to combat Makhno's growingly dangerous insurgent movement in South Ukraina. So they were under the great disadvantage of being obliged to fight without being able to strengthen the weak spots in their line with timely reinforcements. Around Orel were some of the best divisions of the Volunteer Army, named after the heroes of the early period of the Volunteer movement, General Kornilov and Colonel Drozdovsky. Composed largely of officers, filled with burning hatred of the Bolsheviki, accustomed neither to giving nor to taking quarter, they fought resolutely even after the loss of Orel, the capture of which had marked the high point of their advance. But the throwing on the front of a fresh Esthonian division, the growing pressure on the left flank of the Whites of the Fourteenth Red Army, which was stationed west of Orel and which had been neglected in the calculations of the White commanders, and a series of successful raids on railroad stations in the rear of the Whites by Primakov's cavalry all helped to turn the scale definitely against the Volunteers on this sector of the front. Fighting steadfastly, but losing ground steadily, they fell back on Kursk.

Meanwhile there had been equally significant developments around Voronezh, east of Kursk. The Red cavalry corps of Budenny, a veteran sergeant of the Tsar's army and a non-Cossack peasant of the Don Territory by origin, had beaten the best cavalry of the Whites, under the command of the Don Cossack General, Mamontov, and the noted Kuban White partisan leader, Shkuro, and occupied Voronezh on October 24. Budenny's victory was doubly encouraging to the Reds because up to this time the Whites had owed their victories, in very large degree, to the superiority of their horsemen. But Mamontov's corps had been demoralized by the hard riding and intensive looting of its famous raid; Shkuro's forces were also not disinclined to pillage and had been weakened on the eve of the clash with Budenny by the diversion of some of their units for action against Makhno. It was characteristic of the haphazard methods of the civil war that Budenny had come into the region of Voronezh at his own initiative and, indeed, in defiance of specific orders to proceed in a southeastern direction for activities in the Don Territory. Having heard that the famous Mamontov was making a new raid, he moved northward; and, as subsequent developments showed, his disobedience of orders turned out favorably for the Red cause.[14] Up to the middle of October the Red command showed a tendency to adhere stubbornly to the mistaken plan of hammering away at the secondary Don front, overlooking the danger of a White advance through Orel and Voronezh.

The recapture of Orel and Voronezh marked the turning point of the campaign on the Southern Front, the passing of the initiative into the hands of the Reds. Three weeks of hard fighting followed, with the advantage inclining more and more definitely to the side of the Reds. And the victories at Kastornaya on November 15 and at Kursk on November 17 marked a new stage in the campaign; these were followed by a swift and visible collapse of the morale of the Whites and by an easy, unbroken forward sweep of the Red armies which was not checked until a large part of Ukraina and almost the whole Don Territory, including its main centres, Rostov and Novo-Cherkassk, had passed into their hands.

Kastornaya was an important junction on the Kursk-Voronezh railroad; and its capture enabled Budenny to drive a deep wedge between the Don Cossack Army to the east and the Volunteer Army to the west. The White Cossack cavalry, so formidable during the spring and summer campaigns, was now completely demoralized; and Budenny, along with minor Red cavalry chieftains, such as Doumenko and Zhloba, tore up the rear communications of the enemy and helped to transform the retreat of Denikin's forces into a disorderly rout. If Kastornaya was a fatal blow to the Cossack cavalry of Mamontov and Shkuro, Kursk seems to have had an equally bad effect on the spirit of the Volunteer infantry units. Between Orel and Kursk they had fought stubbornly, if unsuccessfully. After Kursk there was scarcely any serious fighting until the front had been pushed back as far as Rostov.

The defeat of Denikin's forces in October and November was natural enough, in view of the superiority of the Soviet forces in men and munitions. Their absolute collapse and inability to make a stand during December is only explicable in view of the condition of the rear. Ukraina bristled with insurgent partisan detachments, which naturally increased the boldness and scope of their raids as the defeat of the Whites on the front became more evident. The troops themselves were demoralized by pillage; some units had whole trainloads of booty, which obstructed the retreat.

When the Bolsheviki were driven out of Ukraina they did not by any means abandon the struggle there. In every large town they left an underground organization; and a so-called "Trans-Front Bureau" of the Communist Party of Ukraina, established in Russia, kept up communication with centres of peasant revolt, issued directions to those partisan leaders who were Soviet sympathizers, despatched organizers, military specialists and funds to regions which were hopeful centres of insurrection against Denikin.

The Ukrainian partisan movement was by no means entirely or even chiefly Bolshevik in character. In the southeastern steppe country Makhno was the most potent figure; in Western Ukraina Petlurist influence was strong. But the Communists welcomed the activities of those guerrillas whom they would shoot as soon as they were in power themselves, because anything that contributed to the disorganization of Denikin's rear was an aid to the Red Army. They endeavored to place their agents in the ranks of Makhno's detachments and of the Petlurist bands, with a view to winning over as many of their followers as possible. "Revkoms" (military revolutionary committees) were set up in all the districts where there was an active insurgent movement; these regularly organized five departments, operative, espionage, communications, formations and supplies. An interesting and detailed picture of the Bolshevik methods of upsetting Denikin's civil administration and of coördinating the activities of the partisan bands in the rear with the offensive of the Red Army on the front is conveyed in the following instructions to county Part Committees and revkoms, issued by the Trans-Front Bureau of November 9: [15]

"At the present moment the basic problem of the revkoms is to help the Red Army in its struggle with Denikin.

"1. Mass partisan activities, aiming at the destruction of railroad lines, the wrecking of trains, the systematic interruption of telegraph and telephone communication, must be organized as soon as possible. The Red partisans must strike organized blows at the most important railroad junctions, in order completely to deprive the enemy of the possibility of transporting freight and troops and of keeping up telegraph and telephone communication. We must quickly send tens, hundreds of our agents, experienced Communist insurgents, into the forests and rebellious villages, where many partisan detachments are hidden, awaiting the signal and guidance of our Party. It is extremely important, under slogans which are popular among the peasants now, to organize the food blockade of the cities, the extermination of the landlords and police who appear, supported by the kulaks. It is necessary cleverly to sharpen and deepen the class antagonisms in the village.

"2. The utmost energy and organization must be shown in the cause of disorganizing Denikin's Army and destroying the political, economic and technical resources of the White state order. In order to disorganize the White Army it is necessary to shape and organize every expression of discontent in the workingclass and peasant masses in connection with mobilization, lowering of wages, taking back of land, requisitioning of bread, cattle and horses into an armed protest, into a destructive revolutionary uprising, even of local significance.

"Forces will be drawn away from the front in order to suppress these uprisings. And experience has already shown that an army, mobilized from among workers and peasants, disintegrates and becomes revolutionized most quickly in the suppression of workers' and peasants' uprisings. This method has already been proved by experience more than once during our civil war.

"The Tsarist-nationalist and bourgeois-landlord character of the Denikin regime must be exposed and revealed at every step by means of revolutionary activity.

"3. Revkoms are bound to show the greatest energy in exploiting all possibilities of disorganizing the forces of the enemy within the shortest period of time, with a consciousness of the highest responsibility before the Revolution and the Party.

"Immediately give the order for partisan outbreaks to the detachments at your disposition, without waiting for a general uprising. The road to general uprising lies through systematic partisan activities with little detachments."

The effect of this and similar orders and, still more, of the elemental dissatisfaction of the peasants with the White regime, quickly made itself felt. The peasant bands raided stations, cut off stragglers, mercilessly harassed the retreating columns of the Volunteer Army.

Denikin was slow to recognize the full measure of his defeat. A soldier by instinct and training, he probably did not realize, until it was all over, how brittle, how full of internal decay was his administrative structure. From a technical military standpoint the situation was still not hopeless. Denikin planned to form a powerful cavalry force east of Kharkov which would, as he hoped, not only check but drive back the advancing horsemen of Budenny. At the same time the commander of the Volunteer Army, General Mai-

Maevsky, whose chronic alcoholism and tendency to loot himself and to permit his subordinates to do likewise had become a public scandal, was dismissed; General Wrangel was transferred from the Caucasian Army, on the Tsaritsin Front, and placed in command of the Volunteer Army. Wrangel had displayed conspicuous ability in handling large masses of cavalry; and this fact probably induced Denikin to appoint him to a responsible command, although the previous relations between Denikin and the temperamental and self-willed Baron Wrangel had been generally cool and often strained.

Wrangel's appointment, however, had no effect on the military situation, which was rapidly going from bad to worse. The effort to form a cavalry corps capable of resisting Budenny was a total fiasco. Wrangel was convinced that stern disciplinary measures were a primary necessity. "An army taught by the example of its leaders to loot and drink," as he said in a subsequent bitter letter to Denikin, "such an army could not restore Russia." One of the first objects of Wrangel's reforming zeal was the Don Cossack General Mamontov, whom he dismissed from his command, replacing him by a Kuban General, Ulagai. Mamontov was bitterly offended and indifferently left his corps before Ulagai had arrived to take over the command. The regional pride of the Don Cossacks was hurt by this slight to their best known general; and the disintegration of the White cavalry went on, if possible, faster than ever after Ulagai's appointment. The latter on December 21 sent Wrangel two messages; the following excerpts from them illustrate the hopeless state of the White cavalry at that time: [16]

> "The cavalry group has become completely incapable of fighting. Small by comparison with the cavalry army of the enemy, it has completely lost heart and disintegrates more and more every day. Enriched with stolen property, especially with the rich booty after the raid [of Mamontov], shaken by repeated defeats, the cavalry simply doesn't want to fight and often a whole division runs away from a few squadrons. It is completely impossible to strike any kind of blow or to beat off the offensive of the enemy against the flank.
>
> "I have already reported repeatedly that the cavalry group cannot fight. The Don units, although they are numerous, do not want to fight and cannot resist the slightest pressure of the enemy. There are no Kuban and Terek units. The pitiful remnants, assembled in one regiment, are good for nothing. There is almost no artillery, there are almost no machine-guns."

Under these circumstances the third conquest of Ukraina by the Red Army was little more than a parade. Kharkov was taken on December 12; Kiev on December 16. Denikin's troops in Ukraina broke up into several discontented groups. Wrangel conducted the retreat of the main body in a southeastern direction; the Donetz Basin, which had been the scene of such fierce fighting in the spring, was surrendered almost without a struggle. General Bredov's troops in Kiev made their way into Polish territory and were interned. The corps of General Slaschev, which had been fighting Makhno in the neighborhood of Ekaterinoslav, retreated to the Isthmus of Perekop, the narrow strip of land which connects the Crimean peninsula with the mainland, and here made a successful stand. Had the Red Army Command thrown considerable forces against the Crimea at this time the Whites would probably have been driven into the sea and the whole subsequent struggle with Wrangel would have been avoided. But the possibilities of the Crimea as a future base of the White movement were overlooked; the main attention of the Soviet leaders was directed to the traditional "Cossack Vendée," the Don and the Kuban; and Slaschev, who was a resolute and courageous commander, despite the fact that he had a weakness for drink and drugs, maneuvering with his small force, warded off the feeble Red attacks.

Wrangel seems to have desired to fall back on the Crimea with the greatly shrunken Volunteer Army under his command. (It was soon reduced to the status of a corps and placed under the command of General Kutepov, one of the most steadfast of the original leaders of the movement.) Such a line of retreat would have led to a complete military and political breach with the Cossack Territories; and Denikin, who cherished suspicions, which were apparently not altogether unfounded, of Wrangel's political loyalty, insisted that the Volunteer forces should unite with the Don Cossack Army, which had fallen back almost to Rostov. By means of a difficult march, harassed by peasant guerrillas and by Red cavalry, Wrangel carried out this order, thereupon leaving the Army at the front, with Denikin's permission and going to the Kuban, where he hoped to raise reinforcements.

Denikin's prestige as leader of the White movement in South Russia was naturally severely shaken by the overwhelming defeats which he had sustained. His Chief of Staff, General Romanovsky, one of the few men who enjoyed his entire trust, was the target of especially bitter criticism; the Staff was considered responsible both for the collapse at the front and for the break-up in the rear. Wrangel became the favored candidate of those elements in the

White movement, military and civilian, which considered a change of leadership necessary. If we are to believe Denikin, who cites the testimony of the Kuban General Shkuro and of the Terek Ataman, General Vdovenko, Wrangel, in the course of his trip to the Kuban, sounded out the sentiment of Shkuro, Vdovenko and others as to the desirability of deposing Denikin and creating an all-Cossack Government and an all-Cossack Army, with Wrangel at the head of it.[17] However this may be, Wrangel had no success in arousing the Kuban Cossacks to fight for the White cause and soon departed for Novorossisk, for the purpose of supervising the fortification of this port. Later he went to the Crimea, where Denikin's representative, General Schilling, was a weak and unpopular figure. When a certain Captain Orlov raised a rebellion in the Crimea with no very clearly defined objective (Orlov's movement was to some extent an expression of the feeling of resentment which had grown up among the junior officers of the White Army against the higher Generals) a number of prominent military and civilian leaders petitioned Denikin to appoint Wrangel governor of the Crimea instead of Schilling. Denikin, who cherished increasingly strong suspicions of Wrangel's loyalty, sharply refused to do this; and the head of the British Military Mission, General Holman, a loyal friend of Denikin, conveyed to Wrangel a politely but firmly worded suggestion that it would be advisable for him to leave the Crimea. Wrangel complied with this request very unwillingly and despatched a bitter letter to Denikin which provoked an equally bitter reply. He then went to Constantinople, where he waited until a new turn of events gave him the opportunity to become the head of the South Russian White movement.

There were both personal and political causes for the bad feeling between Denikin and Wrangel. Wrangel was an aristocrat, while Denikin was of humble origin. The more conservative politicians who were associated with the White movement, especially the former landowners and high Tsarist officials, regarded Wrangel as a more desirable dictator than Denikin; Wrangel also enjoyed the favor of some of the more politically minded high ecclesiastics of the Orthodox Church. There could be no doubt that Wrangel at heart was a thorough monarchist; Denikin's position was more indefinite and General Krasnov with some justice observes that republicans were inclined to consider Denikin a monarchist and monarchists looked on him as a republican.

In his memoirs and in communications which he sent to Denikin during 1919 Wrangel is a bitter critic of the administrative and military activities of his Commander-in-chief. Some of his criticisms, especially in regard to the loose discipline of the Army, are based on fact. But it is certainly questionable whether he would have been more successful as a leader of the White movement than was Denikin. He might have been a better disciplinarian; there was a streak of softness in Denikin's character that made him slow to take drastic action against his own subordinates, even when their incompetence or misconduct called for severe punishment. But Wrangel, as a Baron of well-known conservative views, would have been even less likely than Denikin to win the popular support, the absence of which was the fundamental cause of the defeat of the Whites.

The first phase of the retreat of Denikin's forces from the farthest points of their advance, Orel and Voronezh, ended with an irregular three-day battle outside Rostov and Novo-Cherkassk on January 6–8, 1920. Denikin hoped that his Cossacks would display more fighting spirit when they were defending their chief towns. But this battle ended unfavorably for the Whites; the resistance of the Volunteer Corps before Rostov was offset by the speedy loss of Novo-Cherkassk, which made possible an encircling movement of the Red cavalry, and by a failure of the temperamental Mamontov, who was now reinstated as commander of a cavalry unit in the Don Cossack Army, to carry out an order to attack. The White Army crossed over to the left bank of the Don, which became a difficult obstacle to the Reds because of a thaw in the ice, and entrenched itself on the heights around Bataisk, immediately south of Rostov.

The last months of the White regime in Rostov were characterized by ever increasing speculation, disorder and general economic chaos, aggravated by a fearful epidemic of typhus which swept over South Russia at this time and which affected troops and civil population alike.[18] Typical of the atmosphere of the time are two orders published by the Don Cossack Ataman, General Bogaevsky, on November 4.[19] One states that now, when the front is under fire, many people desert and try to hide in rear institutions and factories. The other speaks of the terrible speculation and upsurge in prices, which no increases in wages and salaries could match, and declares that "speculation has become a national calamity."

As the situation became more threatening one emergency order after another was issued. Lists of petty officers and soldiers who were to be given fifty strokes of the lash for drunkenness, desertion and other offenses were published. On December 6 Bogaevsky imitated a familiar Soviet practise, issuing an order to requisition warm clothes for the front, in order "to unclothe the rear and clothe the front." On December 17 there was an order for the mobilization of all students above the age of seventeen. On January 3, when it was already too late to achieve any noteworthy results, Bogaevsky ordered a labor mobilization of the whole population between the ages of seventeen and sixty for the purpose of strengthening the fortifications. Employees of the "Osvag" (the Denikin propaganda department) and of other institutions were given compulsory military training.[20] All these measures proved to be only feeble gestures, which could not avert the impending catastrophe.

There was some revival of the morale and fighting capacity of the Whites after the evacuation of Rostov. The veteran officers of the Volunteer Corps fought with the courage of despair; they knew that for them there would be no quarter, no prospect of life in Soviet Russia. The much more numerous Don Cossacks, who had been almost completely demoralized for some weeks, began to fight more energetically in the hope of winning back their native stanitsas, now in the hands of the Reds. During the first weeks of 1920 the attempts of the Reds to force the passage of the Don around Bataisk were repulsed with considerable losses. Even Budenny's formidable cavalry suffered defeat in some engagements.

So, even after the loss of Rostov, Denikin's military position was far from hopeless. His front was covered by the Don and Manitch Rivers; the Kuban Territory, in his rear, had a fairly good network of railroad lines, which made it possible for him to transfer troops from one part of the front to another. The numbers on the two sides were more even than in most of the battles of the civil war; indeed Denikin estimates that both his forces and those of the Reds numbered slightly more than 50,000.[21] Had the Kuban Cossacks responded to Denikin's appeals for a determined resistance to the advancing Reds as vigorously as the Moscow and Petrograd workers responded to the appeals of the Communists when the offensives of Denikin and Yudenitch were at their height, Denikin might quite conceivably have not only held the territory which he occupied, but undertaken a counter-drive and recovered the Don Territory, where the arrival of the Bolsheviki was certainly not greeted with enthusiasm. But the all-important element of morale was lacking among the Kuban Cossacks. The Kuban units in the White Army had simply melted away during the retreat. The stanitsas were full of Cossacks of military age, whom neither threats nor appeals could induce to go to the front. In the mountainous and wooded districts "green" bands of deserters and insurgents were becoming more and more active. The spirit of the Kuban had completely changed since the summer and autumn of 1918, when the majority of the Cossacks regarded the Volunteers as deliverers from the tyranny and marauding of the Reds and fought shoulder to shoulder with them.

The political atmosphere in Ekaterinodar was unfavorable to Denikin. The Kuban Rada had been quick to take advantage of his weakened position by restoring the old constitution, which had been so sumarily changed under the pressure of Generals Wrangel and Pokrovsky, and had elected as Ataman General Bukretov, a weak-willed and incompetent man, whose primary qualification for office was his antipathy to Denikin. A new Cossack parliamentary body, the Supreme Krug, consisting of fifty representatives of each of the Cossack Territories, the Don, the Kuban and the Terek, had come into existence and showed a disposition to create a Cossack state, with a separate army, and to dissociate itself from Denikin's effort to fight for a non-Bolshevik Russia.

Denikin addressed the Krug on January 29. Pointing out that victory was still possible if the Cossacks and the Volunteers fought in coöperation with each other, he warned his auditors that "the Volunteer Army and its Commander-in-chief serve Russia and not the Supreme Krug" and that there was no place for the Volunteer Army in the Kuban if the Krug insisted on creating an independent Cossack state and renounced the struggle with the Bolsheviki on an all-Russian scale. In such a case it would be necessary "to seek other means for the liberation of Russia." Denikin also asked whether it was not strange that at this hour of gravest danger only 8,500 Kuban Cossacks were at the front. Early in February Denikin reached a political agreement with the Krug under which a new South Russian Government was formed, with the head of the Don Government, Melnikov, as Premier. The list of ministers included one striking name, that of Nicholas Chaikovsky, the veteran revolutionary, who detested the Bolsheviki so much that he was willing to assume the post of Minister for Propaganda in Denikin's Government. Denikin retained in his hands supreme military authority; the new Government was supposed to be responsible before a future elected legislative assembly.

The South Russian Government was a shadowy and short-lived creation. Inasmuch as it did not include the more radical Kuban autonomists it did not pacify the opposition among the Cossack politicians. Indeed the Kuban Rada refused to recognize its authority on Kuban territory. The basic problem, that of persuading or compelling the Kuban Cossacks to fight, proved quite insoluble. The appeals of the Rada in this connection were as fruitless as Denikin's own orders or the efforts of the British General Holman who flew over some stanitsas in an airplane, dropping proclamations which he signed in his capacity as an "honorary Cossack" and urging the Cossacks to rally for the defense of their homes. Punitive detachments of Don Cossacks, sent into the Kuban villages to force their brothers to take up arms, were also quite ineffective. The Kuban at this decisive moment simply would not fight.

In view of this circumstance the issue of the campaign could not be long in doubt. Finding themselves balked in frontal attacks on the Bataisk position of the Whites, the Red command shifted Budenny's cavalry and some of their other forces to the east and undertook a large-scale flanking operation. Taking advantage of the weakening of the front opposite them Denikin's troops seized Rostov on February 20. But this was a hollow and brief triumph. For almost at the same time a disastrous accident destroyed the last opportunity of offering successful resistance to the flanking movement of the Soviet troops from the east. The commander of Denikin's best cavalry corps, General Pavlov, who was not acquainted with local physical and climatic conditions, brought his corps into almost uninhabited steppe regions during a severe snowstorm, with the result that about half the men and horses were frozen and the fighting capacity of the corps was completely undermined. When Pavlov on February 25 met Budenny's cavalry and the infantry of the Soviet Tenth Army near Belaya Glina he was completely routed.[22]

The Whites held Rostov only three days. Threatened with encirclement from the flank and rear, they abandoned Bataisk on March 2; by March 9 Budenny had occupied the important railroad junction of Tikhoretzkaya. There was now no serious thought of resistance; the Volunters and Don Cossacks confined themselves to fighting feeble rearguard actions in an effort to safeguard their movement to the sea at Novorossisk. This port was the thin bottleneck through which the "armed forces of South Russia" had to

General Sergei Budenny

pass, if they were to escape. A peasant uprising, headed by Socialist Revolutionaries and aided from neighboring Georgia had already overthrown the power of the Denikin regime in the Black Sea Province, a long narrow strip of territory bounded by the mountains and the sea southeast of Novorossisk.[23] Still farther to the south was Georgia, which had never been friendly to the Volunteer Army.

In the raw early spring days of 1920 a host of tens of thousands of fugitives poured along the roads to Novorossisk. The troops still retained some elements of discipline, although they had lost all stomach for fighting. Mixed in with them were masses of civilian fugitives, especially families of the Don Cossacks. Calmucks from the neighborhood of Astrakhan, with their camels and mullahs in bright robes, added a touch of oriental color to this drab and gloomy picture of masses of uprooted people, fleeing to unknown destinations, ready to go anywhere if they could only escape from the oncoming tide of Bolshevism. If the Russian fugitives were mainly people of the propertied and educated classes, families of army officers, etc., the Don Cossacks and Calmucks fled in whole communities, dragging along with them the few household goods they could transport.

The Crimea was the one bit of Russian soil which remained under White rule, and it was there that Denikin decided to bring his routed forces. Denikin had hoped to utilize the Taman peninsula, which at its farthest western extremity is very close to Kertch, at the eastern extremity of the Crimea, as a road of retreat for part of his forces, transshipping the remainder from Novorossisk. But the listlessness and apathy which were now affecting the Volunteers, as well as the Don Cossacks, made it impossible to forestall the Red occupation of the Taman region. After the evacuation of Ekaterinodar on March 15 the whole mass of soldiers and refugees poured on to Novorossisk, where there were not enough ships to transport even the soldiers.

The evacuation of Novorossisk, which was completed on the evening of March 26,[24] took place in an atmosphere of chaotic disorder. There was an ugly spirit of "everyone for himself," and Denikin by this time seems to have lost the will and ability to control fully his own troops. General Sidorin, commander of the Don Cossack Army, bitterly denounced Denikin for favoring the Volunteers, as against the Cossacks, in carrying out the shipments. There were tragic scenes in the last hours of the evacuation, when members of families lost each other, sometimes forever. Those Cossacks who embarked were obliged to leave their horses behind; and the faithful animals often dashed up to the water's edge neighing for their departing masters.

Twenty-two thousand prisoners and a vast quantity of military stores, which were neither carried off nor destroyed, fell into the hands of the Red Army when it moved into Novorossisk. In the general mood of panic and utter depression the British preserved composure; they brought some measure of order into the evacuation and carried off a number of the White troops in their warships.

The Kuban Army, which had broken off all political and military connection with Denikin, retreated over the mountains to a region on the Black Sea coast north of Gagri, and was joined here by some Don units which had not been able to get away from Novorossisk. Hungry, exhausted and war-weary, hemmed in between the advancing Reds and the Georgians, who were determined not to permit any organized armed force to cross their frontier, these troops finally capitulated to the Red Army. Some Don Cossacks and a few Kuban detachments were taken off by sea before the surrender and transported to the Crimea.

After his arrival in the Crimea Denikin still had thirty-five or forty thousand troops. The Volunteers had arrived with full arms and equipment; the Don Cossacks were without their horses and mostly disarmed. Denikin soon felt that it was impossible for him to remain as leader of the South Russian White movement. There was a strong sentiment in favor of Wrangel among the military leaders and the politicians; the erratic General Slaschev, who had commanded the defense of the peninsula, treated the head of the South Russian Government, Melnikov, with such public contempt that Denikin felt obliged to dismiss his shadowy government, in order to protect its members against possible acts of violence. He had already sacrificed his Chief of Staff, Romanovsky, a highly valued friend, to the general clamor against him, replacing him with General Makhrov. Sick at heart, feeling that even his veteran Volunteer troops were no longer unquestioningly devoted to him,[25] Denikin decided that the time had come for him to withdraw from the struggle. He summoned a conference of his senior officers and proposed that it elect a successor. This aroused objection, on the ground that such procedure would set an undesirable precedent for the election of officers. It was decided to make the change in the form of a command; and Denikin's brief farewell order read as follows: [26]

"1. Lieutenant-General Baron Wrangel is appointed Commander-in-chief of the Armed Forces of South Russia.

"2. To all who loyally went with me in the difficult struggle,—a deep bow.

"Lord, grant victory to the Army and save Russia.

GENERAL DENIKIN"

One last heavy blow remained for Denikin; his closest friend, Romanovsky, was assassinated immediately after his arrival in Constantinople. So ended the unsuccessful crusade of Denikin for "great, united, undivided Russia,"—an enterprise which proved as quixotic in the end as it must have seemed in the heroic early period of the movement, when a few thousand devoted Volunteers stood against the whole of Bolshevik Russia. Perhaps, as Denikin passed into the life of emigration which must have been especially painful for one who felt himself so completely Russian in every fibre, he envied those gallant companions of his first campaigns, Kornilov, Markov, Drozdovsky and many others, who had fallen on the obscure battlefields of the North Caucasus when there was still hope that their cause might prevail.

NOTES

1 A. I. Egorov, "The Smashing of Denikin in 1919," p. 146.

2 *Cf. Izvestia,* for that date.

3 *Cf.* M. N. Pokrovsky, "The October Revolution," pp. 397–412.

4 M. Kubanin, "The Makhno Movement," p. 216.

5 *Pravda,* for October 23, 1919.

6 *Bednota,* for August 8, 1919.

7 *Cf.* Chapter XXX, pp. 208ff.

8 N. E. Kakurin, "How the Revolution Was Fought," Vol. II, p. 330.

9 One finds a good description of the background of the drive on Petrograd in A. P. Rodzianko's "Reminiscences of the Northwestern Army," pp. 92–99.

10 "The Struggle for Petrograd," p. 30.

11 *Cf.* L. Trotzky, "Mein Leben," p. 408.

12 Trotzky, "How the Revolution Armed Itself," Vol. II, Book I, pp. 383ff.

13 *Cf.* Egorov, *op. cit.,* pp. 139, 144. Denikin gives lower estimates, 98,000 of his own troops against 140,000 to 160,000 Reds. *Cf.* "Sketches of Russian Turmoil," Vol. V, p. 230.

14 *Cf.* Egorov, *op. cit.,* p. 179. The Mamontov raid had brought home to the Soviet leaders the need for creating cavalry units which could combat the White Cossacks on equal terms; and Trotzky issued one of his familiar colorful appeals: "Proletarians, to horse." Actually it seems doubtful whether many proletarians became expert cavalry soldiers; the Red horsemen were mainly recruited from the non-Cossack peasantry of the South and Southeast and from the minority of Cossacks (mainly those of the poorer regions of the Northern Don), who took the Soviet side in the civil war.

15 *Cf.* the *Archive of the Trans-Front Bureau,* No. 169.

[16] *Cf.* Wrangel's Memoirs, published in the magazine *Byeloe Dyelo,* Vol. V, pp. 255, 256.

[17] "Sketches of Russian Turmoil," Vol. V, pp. 288ff.

[18] Both the well known Don Cossack General Mamontov and the Kuban Ataman, General Uspensky, died of typhus contracted during this winter.

[19] *Cf.* the newspaper *Priazovskoe Krai,* for November 8, 1919.

[20] *Cf.* K. Sokolov, *op. cit.,* pp. 216, 217.

[21] "Sketches of Russian Turmoil," pp. 268, 269. The Soviet official military history ("The Civil War, 1918–1921," Vol. III, pp. 294–297), on the other hand, gives a lower estimate of Denikin's forces and considers that the Reds had a considerable advantage in men and guns along the whole Don-Manitch front.

[22] "The Civil War, 1918–1921," Vol. III, p. 301.

[23] An interesting and detailed sketch of the peasant uprising in the Black Sea Province, written by one of its prominent leaders and organizers, is to be found in N. V. Voronovitch's article, "Between Two Fires," published in *Arkhiv Russkoi Revolutsii,* Vol. VII.

[24] *Cf.* G. Rakovsky, "In the Camp of the Whites," pp. 223–257, for a vivid description of the circumstances of the Novorossisk evacuation.

[25] Denikin says that he decided to resign his command before the evacuation of Novorossisk, as a result of an insistent memorandum which was conveyed to him by the commander of the First Volunteer Corps, General Kutepov, demanding preference for the Volunteers in connection with the evacuation. Denikin considered the tone and substance of this memorandum inconsistent with the requirements of military discipline.

[26] "Sketches of Russian Turmoil," Vol. V, p. 358.

CHAPTER XXXIV

MASS LABOR CONSCRIPTION; WAR WITH POLAND

By the end of 1919 the Bolsheviki could feel that they had emerged as victors from the civil war. Kolchak and Denikin were beaten. Poland and Wrangel, the main enemies of 1920, had not yet appeared on the scene as active foes. But this moment of military triumph was also a moment of profound economic crisis and of almost indescribable misery for all classes of the population. The situation early in 1920 was tersely and vividly summed up in the following sentences, taken from a Soviet official appeal: [1]

> "The workers of the towns and of some of the villages choke in the throes of hunger. The railroads barely crawl. The houses are crumbling. The towns are full of refuse. Epidemics spread and death strikes to the right and to the left. Industry is ruined."

The Russian passion for minute statistics did not die out even in those cold and hungry years; one writer calculated that there were seventeen cartloads of filth and refuse for every house in Moscow, inasmuch as city cleaning had virtually stopped since 1916.[2] The railroad shops were cemeteries of damaged locomotives and cars, laid up for repairs which were not carried out by the hungry and indifferent workers. Typhus was rampant; syphilis was widespread in villages which had suffered especially from the ravages of civil war. The realm which the Bolsheviki had conquered bore strong resemblance to a desert.

Faced with this catastrophic breakdown of all the elements of civilized life, confronted with difficulties which Trotzky several times characterized as graver than the worst difficulties of the dark days of the civil war, the Communist leaders sought a way out not in relaxing the system of war communism, but in expanding it. They proposed to apply military methods in the economic field, to make out of the Russian population one vast army of labor, where everyone would be assigned to an allotted task and severely punished as a "deserter from the working front" if he shirked or evaded his task.

The moving spirit in this drive to militarize and regiment the labor power of the country was Leon Trotzky. Flushed with his victories over Tsarist Generals, he believed that he could overcome the economic difficulties of the country partly by utilizing some of the armies themselves for labor tasks, partly by imposing on workers and employees in the towns and on peasants in the villages a system of universal liability to service, accompanied by trumpet blasts of propaganda to the effect that achievements on the labor front were as necessary and as glorious as victories on the military fronts.

These projects for universal regimentation and militarization of labor excited some misgivings, even among prominent Communists. Trade-unionists in some cases felt that the independent existence of their organizations was threatened, and feared that this method of applying the "dictatorship of the proletariat" might arouse a good deal of discontent among the workers. Economic administrators, such as Rykov, were sceptical about the practicability of managing factories on the model of commanding army divisions.

But Trotzky won the support of Lenin for his schemes; and they were sanctioned by the Party Central Committee. This effort to reconstruct the ruined Russian national economy by methods of military mobilization and extreme compulsion was bound to fail. It ran too definitely against the grain of human nature. The analogy which Trotzky hopefully drew between the successes of the Red Army and the possible successes of his labor armies and regimented workers and peasants was misleading. It was one thing to recruit an army and, half by compulsion, half by propaganda, lead it to victory over the weaker armies of the Whites. It was a very different thing to make every Soviet citizen perform an assigned task in the economic life of the country. With all its resources of espionage and terrorism the Soviet Government could not effectively control or direct its forces on the "economic front." Moreover, all the operations of economic reconstruction, the bringing into cultivation of waste fields, the opening up of closed and flooded mines, the repairs of locomotives and freightcars, the restarting of factories, the provision of adequate reserves of raw materials, were much more complicated than the problems of military strategy and required different methods of approach.

But the experiment had to be made. Given the economic system known as war communism, it had a certain logic. The sole alternative method of reconstruction, and the one which was actually employed in 1921, was an appreciable loosening of the bonds of war communism, a reintroduction of freedom of trade, a restoration of money as an important factor in economic life, an appeal to the motive of private initiative as a means of improving the material condition of the country. But the opinion of the Communist leaders was not prepared for such a step. They were not yet ready to admit that war communism, however necessary some of its features may have been during the temporary emergency of the civil war, was not capable of bringing the country back to normal productivity of industry and agriculture and to tolerable living conditions.

The ideas which dominated Soviet policy during the first months of 1920 are admirably summed up in a series of theses which the Communist Party Central Committee adopted on the themes, "mobilization of the industrial proletariat, liability to labor service, militarization of economic life and the use of military units for economic needs." [3]

Starting out from the proposition that the organization and distribution of labor power represent the basic stimulus for the economic revival of the country, the theses propose to collect the scattered skilled workers of the country, taking them "from the Army, from the food detachments, from the Soviet institutions in the rear, from the village, and, first of all, from the ranks of the speculators." [4] Declaring that "socialist economy rejects in principle the liberal-capitalist principle of 'freedom of labor,'" the Central Committee proposes to recruit unskilled peasant labor on a much larger scale than formerly and to give every Soviet citizen a "labor book," for purposes of registration and control.[5] The theses also call for the formal militarization of some undertakings and some branches of industry and for the employment of military units and of whole armies for the simpler forms of labor and, first of all, for the collection and storing of food stocks. The reliance which was placed at that time on military methods in economic life is emphasized in the following passage:

> "The methods of the army (with all necessary changes), must be applied in the field of labor organization, with the direct utilization of the experience of those Party workers who will be transferred from military to economic work."

The theses contain a plain intimation that stern measures will be taken against slackers.

"The transition to planned organized social labor is unthinkable without measures of compulsion both for the parasitic elements and for the backward elements of the peasantry and of the working class itself. The weapon of state compulsion is military strength. Consequently the element of militarization of labor within some limits, in some form, is inevitably characteristic of a transitional economic system, based on universal liability to labor service. . . . All forms of labor desertion must be removed within the shortest possible time, even if this requires the most severe measures."

The programme of militarization and labor conscription was carried out with special vigor on the railroads, which were under Trotzky's personal direction. In the course of a speech on April 18, 1920, he proposed to combat "desertion" and absence from work with a variety of means.[6] Theatres and moving-picture performances were to be utilized for propaganda against absence from work; the labor deserter was to be confronted on every side by accusing and condemning posters; for the benefit of peasant recruits on the railroads gramophone records were to be employed. Those obstinate workers who remained unmoved by this deluge of propaganda were threatened with various punishments; they were to be assigned to the roughest and most difficult work in punishment squads; deductions were to be made from their scanty rations. What was taken from them was to be given to other workers, who were to be induced in this way to spy on their comrades and to report their delinquencies.

One of Trotzky's pet ideas was the utilization of armies which were no longer needed in military operations for such forms of mass physical labor as woodcutting, grain collection, peat digging, carrying out repairs on the railroad lines. A pioneer in this field was the Third Army, which was stationed in the Ural Territory and found its military services no longer required after the collapse of Kolchak. Two of the leaders of the Third Army on January 10, 1920, addressed a telegram to Lenin and Trotzky asking that the Army be renamed "the first Revolutionary Army of Labor" and be assigned to transportation and other work in the Ural Territory. The request was promptly granted; and for a time this "labor army" became the supreme economic power in the Urals, superseding the ordinary Soviet economic administrators. Other labor armies were quickly formed; the Reserve Army in Kazan

The military Revolutionary War Council and the commanding officers of the First Cavalry Army. Behind the table, left to right, are K. E. Voroshilov, the present Soviet War Commissar, and the cavalry general, S. Budenny

Lenin addressing troops departing for the Polish front

became the "second Revolutionary Army of Labor" and was set to work on the Moscow-Kazan Railroad. The Seventh Army, which had fought against Yudenitch, turned to digging peat in the neighborhood of Petrograd. An Ukrainian Labor Army was organized, with headquarters in the Donetz Basin, where an enormous amount of reconstruction work in damaged mines and factories was required.

The commanders of the labor armies presented reports about the amount of work done in regular military style. Every effort was made to give the work of these armies an attractive and romantic appeal; glowingly worded orders were issued; bands of music sometimes played during the marches to and from work. But the results which were achieved by the labor armies did not justify the hopes which had been placed in them. The army organization proved unsuitable even for simple unskilled labor tasks. The soldiers, who had more or less willingly fought against the Whites, chafed at the idea of being held together far away from their homes under military discipline when no enemy was in sight. A critical observer who saw something of the functioning of the labor army system in the Ural Territory does not seem to have exaggerated its defects when he writes: [7]

> "From the very beginning the productivity of the labor armies was negligible and the cost of their maintenance enormous. Peasants from remote provinces, driven as members of the labor armies to the Urals, could not understand why, when the war with Kolchak was finished, they had to cut wood, mow grass, etc. here, in a foreign district, under military command and could not do this freely in their own homes. Therefore they ran away in masses and the local peasants, in their turn, angry that outsiders should have been ruling in their home districts, burned up the heaps of timber and hay which the labor army soldiers had piled up. The whole plan of the labor armies proved an empty bureaucratic fantasy."

Another practise which was much in vogue at this time was that of the *"subbotnik,"* or voluntary work on holidays. It was the obligation of every Communist to take part in these subbotniki, which were usually organized with the idea of completing some necessary and limited task, such as cleaning up a section of the city or unloading freightcars. Lenin greeted the idea as a symbol of the new Communist spirit and often took part in the subbotniki himself. Although they were supposed to be voluntary, some moral and perhaps other pressure was placed on nonparty workers and employees to participate in them. In 1920 it was decided to make the traditional workingclass holiday, May First, an "All-Russian Subbotnik." On the following day Lenin published an article,[8] in which he said that the old Russian motto "Everyone for himself and only God for everyone" would be replaced with the slogans "One for all and all for one" and "From each according to his ability, to each according to his needs." He declared that the idea of labor as a duty to be paid for would be abolished; in its place would come Communist subbotniki and Communist labor.

No doubt the subbotniki, when they were well organized, by their very novelty, evoked some enthusiasm among the participants and led to higher productivity than was customary in those hungry years. But, like the labor armies, they were quite inadequate as a means of bringing about a genuine revival of production. The number of sincere Communists, willing to work hard and conscientiously without regard for the immediate reward, was far too small to leaven the whole mass of the workers or to break the vicious circle under which the worker was too hungry to produce sufficient goods for the consumption of the peasants, while the peasant, seeing no reward for his labor, more or less deliberately cut down his cultivation of foodstuffs to the level of his own minimum requirements, thereby making the food situation in the towns still worse.

In reading the records and the impressions of personal observers of this period one is constantly impressed by the strong element of bureaucratic unreality in this closing epoch of military communism. Elaborate plans for new hospitals were drawn up, when everyone knew that there were neither building materials, nor medicines, nor hospital equipment. A conspicuous illustration of this unreality was the framing of a so-called unified economic plan, under which the process of Russian reconstruction was divided into four successive stages, as follows: [9]

(*a*) Improvement of the condition of transportation, shipment and storage of the most necessary reserves of grain, fuel and raw material.
(*b*) Machine building for transportation and for the output of fuel, raw material and grain.
(*c*) Intensified development of machine building for the production of objects of mass consumption.
(*d*) Intensified production of objects of mass consumption.

The framers of this highly theoretical plan apparently overlooked the fact that, by postponing to the final stage the production of "objects of mass consumption," they were making very improbable the successful extraction of any large quantity of grain and raw material from the peasantry. When recovery did set in, during 1921 and, still more, in 1922, it proceeded along lines which were diametrically opposed to those of the "unified economic plan." It was the industries that ministered to daily consumption that were the first to revive; the recovery of the metallurgical and machine-building industries came about later.

While the Soviet leaders could always count on a nucleus of active Communists in every factory and labor organization, the mood of many of the workers seems to have been listless and apathetic, if not definitely hostile. On January 2, 1920, a strike, led by Left Socialist Revolutionaries, broke out in the large railroad shops of the Moscow-Kursk line. As usual the cause of the strike was the extremely difficult food situation. Somewhat later the Moscow Printers' Union earned the denunciation of the Communists as "a yellow organization, which is demoralizing the workers, blaming the Communists for the lack of food and demanding that food be obtained, no matter from where." [10]

It would be an exaggeration to say that the tremendous concentration of effort on economic reconstruction, especially in the vitally important field of transportation, yielded no results. Daily freightcar loadings, which had sunk to 5,900 in February, 1920, had risen to 12,000 by November.[11] The progressive increase in the number of disabled locomotives, which reached its culminating point in the winter of 1919–1920, was checked during 1920. But the dream of turning the curve of Russian economic life decisively upward by a mixture of Communist exhortation and ruthless military compulsion remained a dream. The labor armies were no more effective, in the long run, than the military colonies of peasants established by Trotzky's unconscious predecessor, the Tsarist Minister, Arakcheev.[12] And the drive for reconstruction along war communist lines, futile in any case, was interrupted in the spring by a new outbreak of large-scale hostilities with Poland. The resources in men and material which had been devoted to economic restoration were again demanded for the front. The reports from the labor armies paled in interest before the new reports from the front.

Throughout the winter and early spring the outlook for peace with Poland had been growing steadily less promising. The Soviet Government was sincerely anxious at this time to conclude peace with Poland and with the other new states on its western border, in order to be able to concentrate all its energies on crushing the remains of the counterrevolutionary forces in Russia and on the economic reconstruction of the country. On December 22, 1919, the Soviet Government invited the Polish Government to begin peace negotiations. This invitation was repeated in a special appeal of the Council of People's Commissars to the Polish Government on January 28, 1920; this latter appeal contained a specific pledge that, during the course of the negotiations, the Soviet armies on the Western Front would not transgress the military line held by the Polish armies, a line which ran well to the east of the territory where the Poles constituted the majority of the population.[13] On February 4 the All-Russian Soviet Executive Committee addressed a message to the Polish people which emphasized Russia's need for peace, its willingness to make far-reaching concessions and in the following terms repudiated any intention of spreading communism in Poland by means of force: [14]

> "The Communists of Russia now attempt only to defend their own land, their peaceful constructive work. They do not and cannot attempt to bring about a forcible penetration of communism into foreign countries. The reorganization of Poland in the interests of the working masses must be the work of those masses themselves."

There is no reason to doubt the sincerity of the Soviet desire for peace at this time. Circumstances had changed since the disappearance of the German military occupation had made a wide area in Eastern Europe almost defenseless against a revolutionary offensive. Poland and the smaller Baltic States were now definitely organized political units, capable of defending themselves. Russia's desperate economic condition imperatively demanded a cessation of hostilities. The Soviet leaders doubtless realized that an aggressive westward movement of their armies would strengthen the position of the advocates of armed intervention against the Soviets in the Allied countries, just at a moment when this policy was losing ground, as a result of the defeat of the Whites.

Poland, like Russia, was urgently in need of peace. While it had escaped the ravages of civil war, it had been one of the main battlefields of the World War and had sustained devastation at the hands of retreating Russians and advancing Germans and Austrians. Compounded of territory which had belonged to three pre-War states (Russia, Germany and Austria-Hungary), inhabited by considerable national minorities (Germans, Jews, White Rus-

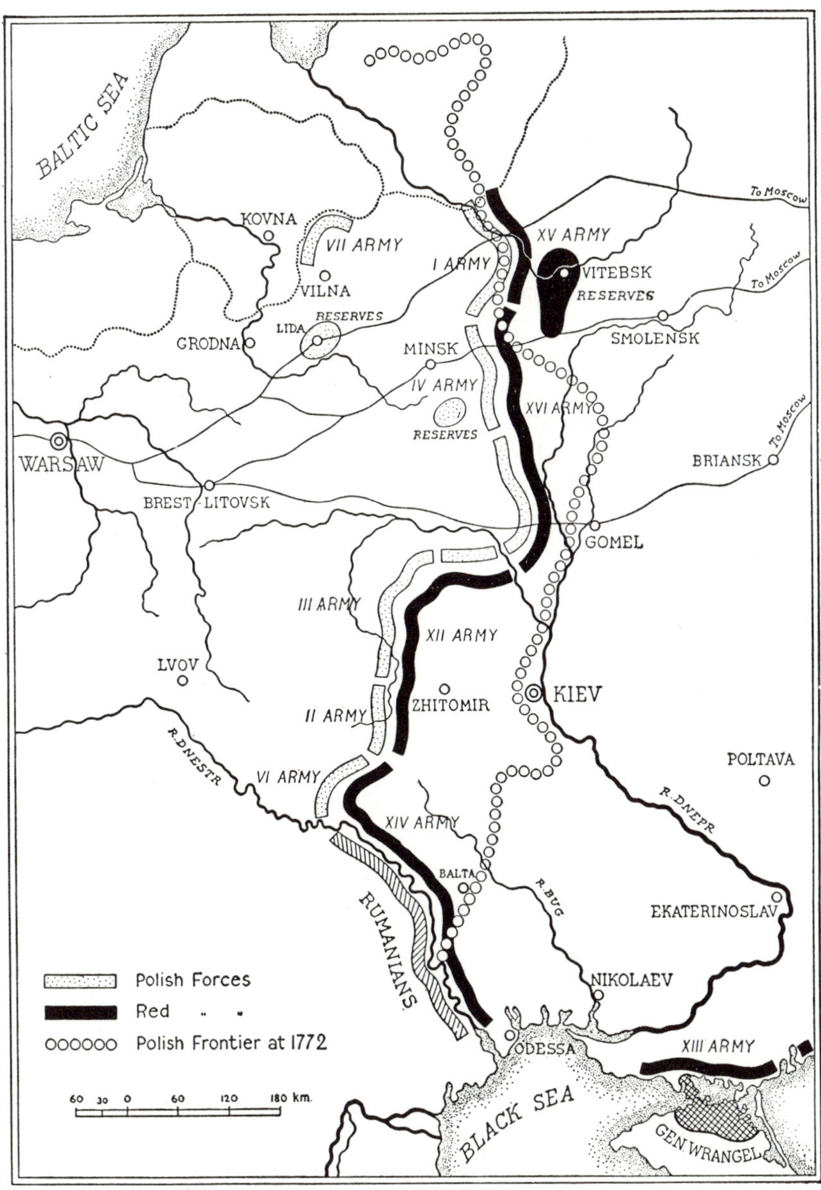

LINE OF THE FRONT BEFORE THE BEGINNING OF THE SOVIET–POLISH CAMPAIGN

sians, Ukrainians), Poland has still to prove its political stability. While its internal condition, as regards hunger and epidemics, was not as appallingly bad as that of Soviet Russia, Poland was also experiencing a grave economic crisis, with many of its factories closed, many of its fields untilled, part of its population dependent on foreign relief organizations for feeding.

But, despite these considerations, despite the likelihood that the Soviet Government would make extensive territorial concessions as the price of peace, Marshal Pilsudsky, the virtual dictator of Poland, was indisposed to conclude peace. The Soviet proposals at first were left unanswered; Polish forces here and there undertook small but ominous operations along the line of the front. When the Polish Foreign Minister, Patek, finally replied to the Soviet peace proposals on March 27 he suggested that peace negotiations should take place in the town of Borisov, immediately behind the Polish line and added the rather singular suggestion that the negotiations should not be accompanied by a general armistice, but only by a local cessation of hostilities in the region of Borisov. The Soviet Government suggested that any town in a neutral country would be preferable to Borisov; the Poles declined to consider this suggestion; and there was no further discussion of peace negotiations.

On April 25 the Poles struck suddenly and hard at weak Soviet forces which were stationed west of Zhitomir, in Western Ukraina, covering the approach to Kiev. The Polish offensive was quickly and entirely successful. The Soviet troops, hopelessly outnumbered in any case, were further handicapped by the mutiny of some Galician troops (which had successively passed over from Petlura to Denikin and from Denikin to the Red Army and now, finding the Red Army little to their liking, deserted to the Poles), and by the familiar flare-up of political banditism and guerrilla warfare in the Ukrainian villages in their rear. So serious was this problem of repressing internal revolt in Ukraina that the head of the Cheka, Dzerzhinsky, was sent to Ukraina and took over the newly established post of chief of military administration in the rear of the Red Army. Meeting little effective resistance, the Poles swept on and occupied Kiev on May 6. The Soviet Government was confronted with a serious new war.

It may seem surprising that Pilsudsky, who had refused to launch an offensive against the Bolsheviki in coöperation with Denikin, when the military situation would have been far more favorable to the Poles, should have decided to act alone, with only a very weak ally in the Ukrainian nationalist leader, Petlura. The key to an understanding of Pilsudsky's policy, however, lies in an understanding of the fact that, as an old nationalist revolutionary and a passionate Polish patriot, he cherished a deep suspicion and dislike of a strong Russia, whether that Russia was conservative or Bolshevik in political coloration. He listened readily to Markhlevsky's overtures[15] and remained passive in the autumn of 1919, when a well-directed blow of the Polish armies might have brought Denikin to Moscow, because he believed, not without reason, that a government like Denikin's, in which chauvinistic Russian officers played such a leading rôle, would scarcely be a friendly neighbor to an ambitious young Poland, anxious to establish boundaries which were more justified by historical and sentimental traditions than by ethnographical considerations.

In refusing to consider the Soviet proposals to open peace negotiations, in deciding to launch a drive against the Soviets after Kolchak and Denikin had been smashed Pilsudsky was pursuing a lifelong dream: the permanent weakening of Russia through the detachment of the non-Russian territories of the former Tsarist Empire. The creation of a chain of new states, Finland, Latvia, Esthonia, Lithuania, to the north of Poland had already undone the work of Peter the Great and shut Russia off from access to the Baltic Sea. Far away, in the semi-oriental Caucasus, were now national Republics, Georgia, Armenia, Azerbaidjan. Pilsudsky's drive into Ukraina was designed to bridge the gap between these groups of little states by creating an independent Ukraina, which would be dependent on Poland, and, perhaps, independent Cossack states in the Don and Kuban. Reduced to its frontiers of the sixteenth century, cut off from the Black and Baltic Seas, deprived of the agricultural and mineral wealth of the South and the Southeast, Russia might easily sink to the status of a second-class power, incapable of seriously threatening the newly gained independence of Poland. And Poland, as the largest and strongest of the new states, might easily establish a sphere of influence which would range from Finland to the Caucasus Mountains.[16]

Such grandiose dreams were encouraged by the attitude of the Ukrainian nationalist leader, Petlura, who, losing hope of obtaining help anywhere else, turned to Poland for aid. An agreement between Petlura and Pilsudsky was reached before the launching of the offensive of April 25. Its precise terms have not been published. But apparently Petlura renounced in favor of Poland Eastern Galicia, with its largely Ukrainian population,[17] and he may have also given assurance that Polish landlords would not be harshly treated in the Ukrainian national state.

Despite the ease with which the occupation of Kiev was carried out, Pilsudsky's invasion of Ukraina proved to be both a political and a strategic blunder. There were Petlurist sympathizers in the villages; but Petlura, now as always, was unable to organize either a strong regular army or an efficient civil administration. His agreement with Poland was not popular with his own followers. The majority of the Ukrainian peasants certainly disliked the rule of the Bolsheviki. But they also hated the Polish "pans," or landed aristocracy, just as they hated the Russian landlords who returned in the wake of Denikin's Volunteer Army. The Polish advance into Ukraina, therefore, brought no appreciable influx of new recruits; it lengthened the line which the Polish forces were required to hold very considerably and exposed them to a severe counterstroke as soon as reinforcements, and especially cavalry, could be brought up. The capture of Kiev and the occupation of a little territory on the left bank of the Dnieper marked the end of the Polish offensive; the Polish troops after this took up defensive positions.

The Soviet Government was quick to take up the challenge of the Polish attack. The labor armies were again placed on a military footing. There was the usual mobilization of Communists for the threatened Western Front. The fact that a foreign country was attacking Russia imparted to the war a nationalist character in the eyes of those former army officers and members of the middle classes who were not irreconcilable enemies of the Soviet regime and won support for the latter in unexpected quarters. A number of old generals who had hitherto stood aside offered their services to the Red Army; and on May 2 a special military council, under the chairmanship of a distinguished General in the World War, A. A. Brussilov, was organized and attached in an advisory capacity to the headquarters of the Commander-in-chief. This council did not assume any operative functions; it offered advice on technical problems and doubtless influenced a number of former officers who had evaded service in the civil war, or who had fought on the side of the Whites and were in concentration camps, to volunteer for the Red Army.

While the Soviet leaders were glad to exploit this upsurge of

Russian national feeling, in so far as it increased the numbers and strengthened the morale of the Red Army officers, they made every effort, in their propaganda, to give the war a class, not a national character. The slogan was always "Against the Polish Pans," never "Down with Poland." Every Soviet appeal emphasized respect for Poland's independence and sympathy with the Polish "toiling masses." Trotzky on one occasion severely disciplined the editor of a Red Army newspaper who had made some attacks on the Poles as a people.

From the beginning the Communist leaders professed the utmost confidence in the successful outcome of the new war. After referring to Pilsudsky as "a third-rate Bonaparte" Trotzky, on May 2, made the following forecast of the course of hostilities in the course of a press interview: [18]

> "There can be no doubt that the war of the Polish bourgeoisie against the Ukrainian and Russian workers and peasants will end with a workers' revolution in Poland. . . . It would be pitiful lack of spirit to be frightened at the first successes of Pilsudsky. They were unavoidable. They were foreseen. They were a result of the earlier development of our relations with Poland. The deeper the right wing of the Polish troops penetrates into Ukraina, turning against itself Ukrainian insurgents of all kinds, the more fatal for the Polish troops will be the concentrated blow which the Red troops will give them."

And indeed, after the easy dash on Kiev, the Poles lost the initiative; and for some time it seemed that the result of the war might be not the overthrow of the Soviets in Ukraina, but the establishment of Soviets in Poland. The front on which the Russo-Polish campaign of 1920 was fought out was divided into two main sectors, the White Russian to the north and the Ukrainian to the south. These two sectors were separated by the wellnigh impassable swamps of Polesia. The heaviest concentration of Soviet troops was on the White Russian sector, where the road which Napoleon had followed to Moscow lay through Smolensk.

Soon after the Polish occupation of Kiev the twenty-seven-year-old commander of the Soviet Western Front, Tukhachevsky, on May 14, initiated a drive near the northern end of the White Russian sector, aiming at the important railroad junction of Molodechno. The Poles resisted, in the main, stubbornly; and the drive failed to reach its major objectives. It shook up the Polish forces, however, and caused a withdrawal of some units from the

Ukrainian front, where the Reds were rapidly gaining the upper hand.

The main instrument in bringing about a turn of the tide in the region of Kiev was Budenny's famous Cavalry Army. This formidable force, consisting of 16,700 mounted men, equipped with forty-eight cannon, five armored trains, eight armored automobiles and twelve airplanes,[19] was in the neighborhood of Rostov when the Poles launched their offensive. Galloping across restless Ukraina, Budenny's horsemen were in Elizavetgrad on May 18. In co-operation with several infantry units they were thrown against the Polish lines south and southwest of Kiev; and on June 5 the Cavalry Army broke through the Polish lines in the neighborhood of Kazatin and raided far to the west of Kiev, sweeping into the towns of Berditchev and Zhitomir. On June 12 the Poles, menaced in flank and rear, evacuated Kiev and retreated to the line which they had held on the eve of their advance. The Soviet plan of cutting off and destroying the Poles was not realized; the latter fought their way through the enveloping cordon of Red troops. But the enemy had been quickly maneuvered out of Kiev; the whole trend of military fortune was now clearly on the side of the Reds. Not content with driving the Poles back to their original line, Budenny's cavalry rapidly moved westward, reducing the triangle of fortified towns which figured in the operations of the World War, Rovno, Lutzk and Dubno, and driving into Eastern Galacia, where it pushed forward to the suburbs of Lvov.

On the more important northern sector of the front July witnessed a sweeping advance of the Red Armies. The prelude to this advance was a three-day battle on the line of the river Berezina from July 4 until July 7. This ended in a defeat of the Poles; their First Army, on their left flank, was badly shattered, although the ambitious plan of the Soviet Command of driving the Poles southward into the Polesian swamps and annihilating them was not realized. The Polish retreat was a hasty one, but it did not assume the proportions of an utter rout; their armies did not lose discipline and fighting capacity. One important town and one natural barrier after another fell before the advance of the Reds, who moved forward at the rate of about thirteen miles a day and continually outflanked the weak First Polish Army, which regularly fell back, pulling the neighboring Fourth Army with it. Minsk was occupied on July 11 and Vilna on the 14th. The appearance of the Soviet troops and the capture of Vilna, which had been an object of dispute between Poland and Lithuania, brought about the intervention of the small Lithuanian army on the side of the Reds; and this still further intensified the demoralization of the retreating Poles. A temporary demarcation line was arranged between the Soviet and Lithuanian troops and Vilna remained in the possession of the Reds. The old line of the German trenches and the natural barrier represented by the river Niemen were quickly forced by the energetic pursuit of the Soviet troops. The Poles fell back on the Bug and the Narew, the last rivers which covered the approach to Warsaw from the east and northeast.

A spirit of fierce crusading enthusiasm prevailed among the Communists; they could already see the Polish workers raising the red flag over Warsaw; Soviet Poland serving as a bridge to a future Soviet Germany; the whole structure of the Versailles Peace crumbling before the blows of the Red Army.[20] The nonparty masses of soldiers and officers seem to have been caught up by the mood of triumphant advance; the general slogan of the Red Army during July and August was: "Give us Warsaw." There was corresponding depression on the side of the Poles. According to Pilsudsky, the uninterrupted forward march of the Reds produced the impression of "a terrible kaleidoscope, of something irresistible, like a heavy, miraculous cloud, for which there is no barrier." [21]

Pilsudsky planned to check Budenny's roving cavalry, which he regarded as far more formidable than the Soviet infantry, in Galicia and at the same time to concentrate considerable forces around Brest-Litovsk, a fortress-town on the Bug, with a view to striking back at the rapidly advancing forces of Tukhachevsky, on the northern sector of the front. But the Red armies, which during the last week of July had entered Bialystok, Pinsk and Volkovisk, pressed hard on their retreating enemies, and on August 1 captured Brest-Litovsk. The line of the Bug was lost; and it became evident that Warsaw could be saved only if a decisive stand was made on its very outskirts. The northern armies of the Soviet front and the cavalry corps of Gai, which had contributed a good deal to the rapid advance, began to move into the territory north of Warsaw, occupying some regions which Poland had recently acquired from Germany and cutting off communication between Warsaw and the port of Danzig.

When the Red forces had reached the line of the Bug they were on the ethnographic frontier of Poland. East of Brest-Litovsk the population is of mixed national origin, with the White Russians and

Ukrainians outnumbering the Poles as one travels farther to the east. The July victories placed before the Soviet Government the problem whether it was to regard its war with Poland as defensive or as aggressive in a revolutionary sense. It definitely chose the second alternative and decided to strike for Warsaw, not as a means of Russian territorial aggrandizement, but with the objective of spreading communism with the aid of the Red Army. Lenin is said to have used the phrase: "We shall break the crust of Polish bourgeois resistance with the bayonets of the Red Army."

In the fanatical atmosphere of Moscow in the summer of 1920, when revolutionary speeches and the strains of the "Internationale" were resounding in the hall where revolutionists from all over the world had gathered for the Congress of the Third International, it was not easy soberly to appraise the thickness and resisting power of this Polish "crust." Both the Communist leaders and the Red Army military authorities seem to have been at fault in this case. The former, remembering that Warsaw, Lodz, Bialystok and other Polish towns had taken an active part in revolutionary demonstrations and outbreaks under Tsarism, easily convinced themselves that Poland was seething with revolutionary ferment and that only a little pressure from the Red Army was needed in order to make possible the emergence of a Polish Soviet Republic. This belief was strengthened by news which came from a number of countries of refusal of workingclass organizations to ship munitions to Poland. In England, where the trade-unions at that time, although far from Communist in domestic practise, were very pro-Bolshevik so far as Russia was concerned, Councils of Action were created for the purpose of obstructing the sending of aid to Wrangel or to Poland. In Danzig longshoremen, who may have been influenced by German nationalist as well as by proletarian sentiment, struck and refused to unload munitions which were bound for Poland. However, events showed that Poland possessed unsuspected reserves of resistance to Bolshevism. There was a strong nationalist feeling among all classes of the people, not excluding the workers. The peasants, the majority of the Polish population, generally followed the leadership of the priests and of the middleclass intellectuals. And when the Red Army troops were actually within sight of the suburbs of Warsaw they were profoundly discouraged to find Polish workers coming out, not with red flags to greet them, but with rifles to fight them.[22]

The responsible Soviet military authorities displayed a tendency to underestimate the Polish capacity for resistance. On July 16 the Commander-in-chief, Sergei Kamenev, presented a report to Trotzky, in which he declared that, while the Western Front, as a result of the shortage of supplies, could reckon on only two more months of intensive struggle, Polish resistance would be broken within that period, if no other states intervened in the struggle.[23] The Field Staff of the Red Army, in a report of July 21, suggested that, even if one of the four armies of the Western Front were withdrawn from the fighting line and used as a reserve force, the remaining three armies could "finally crush Poland." [24]

By July the victories of the Red armies on the Polish front were arousing serious concern in London and in Paris. On July 12 Lord Curzon, the British Foreign Minister, addressed a note to the Soviet Government, proposing that a truce should be concluded on the Soviet-Polish front, that the line of the river Bug should be accepted as a provisional frontier between Russia and Poland, and that final peace conditions should be worked out at a conference in London. Curzon also suggested that an armistice should be concluded with General Wrangel in the Crimea and that he should participate in the proposed London Conference. The note contained the threat that Great Britain and France would aid Poland with all the means at their disposal if the Red troops crossed the Bug and entered indisputably Polish territory.

Chicherin, in his reply of July 17, rejected Curzon's proposed London conference, but expressed the willingness of the Soviet Government to discuss peace terms directly with Poland. By August 1st the Red Army had transgressed Curzon's imaginary frontier. The situation as regards peace negotiations in the summer was the precise reverse of what it had been in the preceding winter and spring. Then the Soviet Government was eager to conclude peace and Poland returned evasive or negative answers. Now the Poles were desperately anxious to avert the threat to the independent existence of their state; but the Soviet Government, with its eyes fixed on Warsaw and its conviction that the emergence of Soviet Poland was only a matter of weeks, showed little interest in peace discussion, while pressing on the advance of its armies as rapidly as possible. On July 22 the Polish Government addressed a direct appeal for an armistice and peace negotiations to the Soviet Government. The latter agreed to give this proposal favorable consideration; but when a Polish delegation arrived in the town of Baranovici on August 1 the Soviet military authorities sent it back, on the ground that it was authorized only to discuss an armistice on behalf of the Polish military authorities and lacked credentials for peace negotiations. The Polish delegates who set out for a second conference in Minsk were found by the Soviet troops after the latter occupied the town of Sedletz, near Warsaw, and were sent on to Minsk. Finally, on August 10, when the fate of Warsaw hung in the balance, the Polish Government asked the Soviet Government for a statement of its peace terms. Some of these were highly propagandist in character; the first, and most important, was almost equivalent to a demand for the establishment of a Soviet Government in Poland. It called for the limitation of the Polish army to 50,000 men and for the additional creation of armed militia, to consist entirely of urban industrial workers "under the control of the labor organizations of Russia, Poland and Norway.[25] Other suggested peace terms called for the demobilization of the rest of the Polish army and of the Polish war industry, for the handing over of surplus munitions to Soviet Russia and Ukraina, for the participation in the peace negotiations of organizations of factory workers and farmhands, for the granting of land to Polish citizens who had been killed and disabled in the war. The frontier between the two states was to be more favorable to Poland than the Curzon Line; the Soviet Government was quite willing to be territorially generous to a prospective Soviet neighbor state. Captured Polish officers were to be hostages for Polish Communists. For the Polish Government to have accepted these conditions would have been little short of outright capitulation. Ten days after they had been proclaimed a dramatic and decisive change in the military situation at the very gates of Warsaw made them meaningless and unreal.

The clearest evidence that the main objective of the Soviet Government in the war was the creation of a Soviet regime in Poland was furnished by the organization of a "Revolutionary Committee" as the supreme authority in Poland immediately after the occupation of the first large Polish town, Bialystok, at the end of July. The head of this Committee was the veteran Polish Communist, Julian Markhlevsky; two of his chief associates were the formidable Dzerzhinsky and an old Jewish revolutionary named Felix Kon. This Committee issued a lengthy appeal to "the Polish working people of city and village"; the main points in its programme were stated as follows: [26]

"We must tear the factories and the coal mines out of the hands of the capitalists and robber-speculators. They shall pass into the possession of the people and under the administration of workers' committees.

"Estates and forests also pass into the possession and under the administration of the people. Landowners are to be driven away; the management of the estates is to be entrusted to committees of farm laborers.

"The land of working peasants is not to be touched.

"Power in the towns is transferred to workers' deputies; communal Soviets are created in the villages."

Subordinate revolutionary committees were created in all the larger towns which were occupied by the Red troops; it was attempted, but with little success, to extend these institutions to the villages. The Red Army itself took the initiative in establishing revolutionary committees as organs of administration in occupied territory. An order issued on the Western Front on May 19, 1920, provides for the establishment of provincial, county and village "revkoms," under the supervision of the Front department of revkoms. Their functions were to confiscate the arms of the population, to furnish supplies for the Red Army, to organize those classes of the population which sympathized with the Soviet regime around Communist cells and to maintain "firm revolutionary order." The Chief of the Political Department of the Twelfth Army, Degterev, on July 1 issued instructions for the formation of "peasant commissions," to consist of three Communists in each regiment with a good knowledge of peasant conditions. These commissions were to combat "criminal activities, robberies, illegal requisitions from the working peasants by irresponsible elements of the Red Army and local authorities." [27]

In general the Soviet military authorities made strong efforts to repress pillage and outrage on the part of the troops; this, of course, was a first prerequisite for winning the confidence of the population. In the main the discipline of the Red troops seems to have been fairly good; there were occasional lapses, however, especially on the part of Budenny's cavalry. These wild sons of the steppes were not unlike the men who rode with Mamontov and Shkuro. Excellent fighters, they included a very small percentage of Communists and listened suspiciously and coldly to the moral lectures of the political workers who were sent into their ranks for purposes of agitation. For many of them booty was a more desirable objective than the triumph of the world revolution. An order issued to the Sixth Division of the Cavalry Army at a time when it seemed that Lvov, the chief town of Eastern Galicia, might be taken, provides that twenty or twenty-five reliable soldiers from each regiment shall be held in readiness to guard the city and "stop on the spot any attempts at banditism." A conference of the political workers attached to the Cavalry Army on June 29 discussed means of combating "anti-Semitism, banditism, and inhuman treatment of prisoners."

In general Markhlevsky's Communist Revolutionary Committee in Bialystok exerted little influence on the course of hostilities. The Bialystok factories were nationalized; there were meetings with speeches, red flags and singing of the "Internationale." But the industrial regions of Poland, where some of the workers might have responded to the Communist propaganda, did not lie in the region of advance of the Red Army. The coal mines of Dombrovo, the textile factories of Lodz, the industrial plants of Warsaw itself remained on the Polish side of the line.

So there were few industrial workers in the territory under the temporary control of the Revolutionary Committee. It signally failed to win the support of the peasants, especially in Poland proper. The Red Army gained no Polish peasant recruits; and during its retreat was severely harassed, especially in the Sedletz region, by insurgent bands, consisting of straggling Polish soldiers, who had been left behind during the retreat, and by peasants, armed with hunting rifles. The failure to win appreciable sympathy, even among the poorer peasants, may have been partly attributable to the agrarian policy of the Polish Communists, who desired to retain the landlord estates as units, to be supervised by committees of farmhands, instead of breaking them up and giving the land outright to the peasants. The very short period during which the Revolutionary Committee could exercise effective authority was another handicap. But probably the main reason for the failure of the invading Soviet troops to gain support, even among the poorest classes, by installing a Polish Soviet regime was the profound difference of national psychology between Poland and Russia, which, in turn, was caused in some degree by the differing social and economic conditions in the two countries. Poland was, in the main, a richer country than Russia before the War; this meant that it possessed a stronger middle class and a larger number of peasants who felt that they possessed a stake in the maintenance of private property rights. The newly triumphant Polish nationalism was also a strong factor against Bolshevism. To the average Pole of all classes a Russian Army, no matter what glowing proclamations it might issue, was an army of hereditary enemies and oppressors.

The battle which decided the issue whether Poland should or should not be drawn into the current of Russian development as a Soviet state, was fought in the vicinity of Warsaw in the middle of August. For the Poles the holding of the capital was even more important from the moral than from the military standpoint. The fall of Warsaw, coming as the climax to a series of defeats and a long retreat, might well mean the break-up of their state. Therefore the Commander-in-chief of the Polish armies, Marshal Pilsudsky, and his French military adviser, General Weygand, Foch's Chief of Staff, who had arrived in Warsaw for the purpose of assisting the Polish defense, decided not only to hold Warsaw, but also to organize a strong counter-offensive, with a view to driving the Red forces far back from the Vistula. Covering Warsaw with about three fourths of his troops from the north and east (the directions from which the Red offensive was proceeding), Pilsudsky organized a special shock force of five divisions fifty miles southeast of Warsaw in the neighborhood of Demblin, or, to give the town its Russian name, Ivangorod. With this force he proposed to strike at the flank and rear of the Red troops which were moving on Warsaw from the east.

The execution of this Polish counter-offensive was made unexpectedly easy by a grave defect in the grouping of the Red troops. The commander of the Western Front, Tukhachevsky, had massed three of his four armies, the Third, the Fourth and the Fifteenth, in the region north of Warsaw. Consciously or unconsciously he was imitating the strategy of the Tsarist General Paskevitch, who had crushed the Polish rebellion of 1830 by encircling Warsaw from the north. The Sixteenth Army was advancing on the Polish capital directly from the east. Between the Sixteenth Army and the next large Soviet unit, the Twelfth Army, which was in the neighborhood of Kovel, there was an ominous gap, thinly held by the small and exhausted "Mozir Group," consisting of only 6,600 men. Against this Mozir Group was concentrated the full weight of Pilsudsky's shock force around Demblin, which amounted to about 30,000.[28]

Who was responsible for this fatal gap on the left wing of the Sixteenth Army, which was the most important and obvious cause of the crushing defeat of the Red forces? Soviet military literature is full of controversy on this point, in which one may sometimes detect notes of the old jealousy between the Western and the Southwestern Fronts. So far as an impartial non-military observer may judge, the main share of direct responsibility would seem to fall on

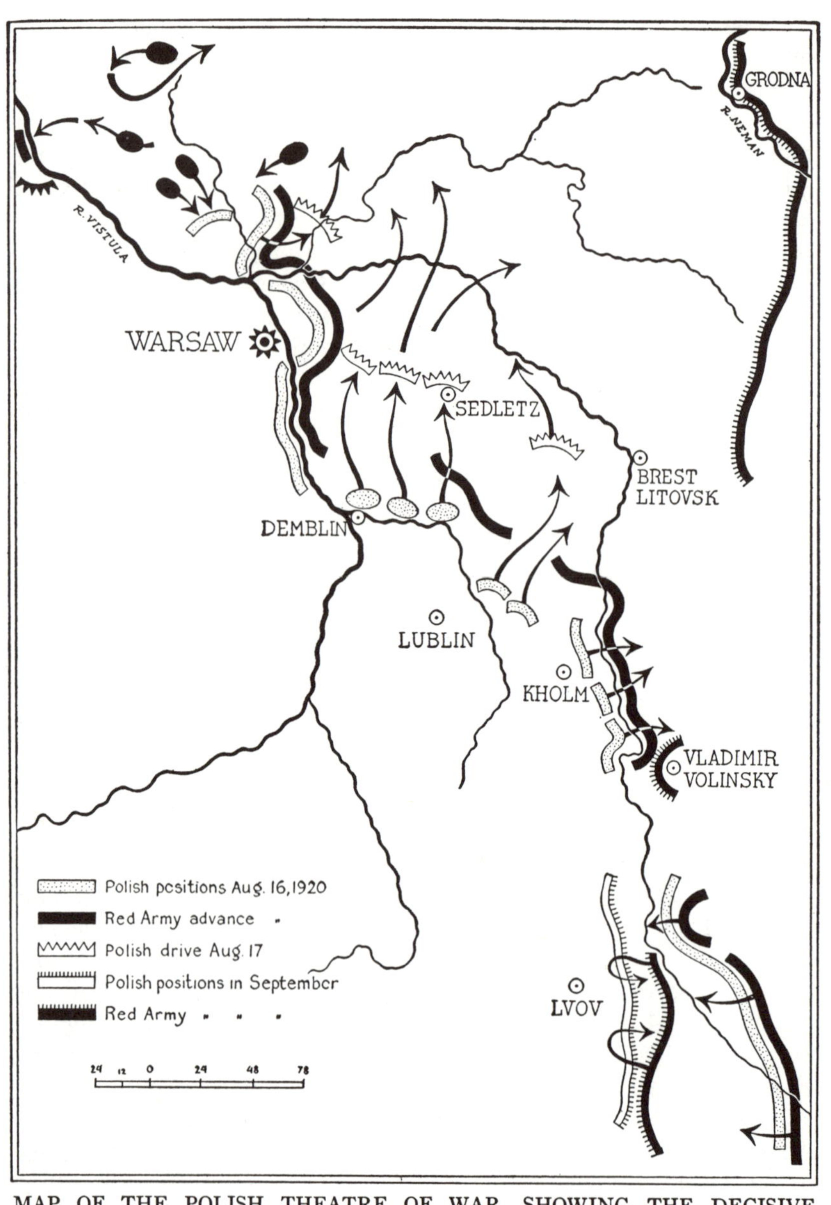

MAP OF THE POLISH THEATRE OF WAR, SHOWING THE DECISIVE BATTLE AROUND WARSAW

the commander of the Southwestern Front, Egorov, and the commander of the Cavalry Army, Budenny, who displayed a tendency to sabotage, if not to direct insubordination, when they were ordered to break off their operations around Lvov, in Eastern Galicia, and to move to the northwest with a view to assisting the decisive drive against Warsaw. At the same time the Commander-in-chief, Kamenev, was unmistakably slow in ordering this shift; and Tukhachevsky's youth and inexperience in handling large masses of troops were revealed in several unwise dispositions of his forces around Warsaw and in a failure to appreciate and to react promptly to the grave menace of Pilsudsky's counter-attack. A typically Russian case of carelessness in attention to detail also played a disastrous rôle in the development of the Soviet plan of campaign. Kamenev on the night of August 10 gave a very important order for the transfer of Budenny's cavalry to the west. The order was inaccurately put into cipher, with the result that three precious days were lost before it finally, in corrected form, reached the commander of the Southwestern Front. When the order reached Egorov on the 13th, instead of promptly obeying it, he began to argue about its advisability, with the result that more time passed; and the decisive battle before Warsaw was lost before Budenny made any movement to come to the aid of the hardpressed armies of Tukhachevsky.[29]

Without the aid of the Cavalry Army and of the Twelfth Army Tukhachevsky, in his operations against Warsaw, had fewer than 60,000 troops at his disposal, as against almost 90,000 Poles. The fortifications of Warsaw were strengthened by a heavy concentration of artillery. The Red troops were tired out from their long marches and in most cases had left their baggage-trains and their supply bases far behind. But fighting spirit, determination to take Warsaw at any cost, still remained. On August 13 two front-line Soviet divisions broke through the first line of the Polish defense and captured Radimin, only fifteen miles from Warsaw. The immediate suburbs of the Polish capital, Praga and Yablonno, were threatened. But the fresh reinforcements which might have turned the breach of the Polish line at Radimin into a decisive victory were lacking. After hard fighting, in which the town changed hands more than once, the Red forces were pushed out. The Polish line on the river Vkra, north of Warsaw, held. The Soviet Fourth Army and the Cavalry Corps of Gai were so far away, in the Danzig corridor, that they did not exert an important influence on the outcome of the struggle. The location of these forces was one of Tukhachevsky's mistakes in the conduct of the battle; another, and graver, blunder was his failure to take effective steps to parry Pilsudsky's counteroffensive, although a captured Polish order had given the Red Army leaders information of the basic plan and direction of the impending Polish drive. The 16th of August may be regarded as the turningpoint of the struggle for Warsaw. On this day Pilsudsky launched his drive and, to his own great surprise, encountered no serious opposition.[30] The Reds also began to lose ground in other sections of the front. By the evening of the 17th the left wing of the Sixteenth Army had been badly smashed (one probably exaggerated estimate places its losses at 10,000 prisoners and forty cannon[31]) and the Poles were already in the rear of those Red troops which were fighting near Warsaw and Brest-Litovsk. The defeat soon became little short of catastrophic; the Red armies north of Warsaw fell back rapidly; the Fourth Army and Gai's cavalry corps were pinned against the East Prussian frontier and forced to cross it into German territory, where they were interned. The rapidity of the Polish advance may be measured by the fact that Brest-Litovsk was again in their hands on August 19 and Bialystok on August 23. Budenny, after making a belated effort to improve the situation by moving westward with his cavalry, was defeated at Zamoste on August 27. The Soviet effort to capture Lvov also ended unsuccessfully and a Polish offensive along the whole line brought about the evacuation of Eastern Galicia and a speedy withdrawal of the Soviet armies beyond the line of the old German trenches.

The character of the peace negotiations which had begun in Minsk was naturally radically changed by the spectacular breakdown of the Red offensive at Warsaw. The place of the negotiations was shifted to neutral Riga; there was no more talk of imposing on Poland an armed proletarian militia or of limiting its army to 50,000 soldiers.

The last phases of the Soviet-Polish War in September and early October are of minor military and political interest. Both sides had abandoned their more ambitious dreams of conquest; the Poles were interested in occupying as much territory as they could, in order to insure an advantageous permanent frontier; the defensive operations of the Reds were rather listless. Once the dream of a Soviet Poland had vanished, the Soviet leaders were not interested in fighting for a few thousand square miles, more or less, of extra White Russian swamp and forest land. They wanted peace as quickly as possible, in order to be able to concentrate their forces against the last of the Whites, Baron Wrangel. So the terms of the preliminary peace treaty and armistice concluded at Riga on October 12 were quite favorable to Poland. The Soviet-Polish frontier was well to the east of the Curzon Line and assigned to Poland considerable regions with a predominantly White Russian and Ukrainian population. Russia was shut off from direct contact with Lithuania and, through Lithuania, with Germany (Russo-German coöperation was a nightmare of Polish and French statesmen at that time), by the allotment to Poland of a long narrow corridor, which included the disputed town of Vilna and gave Poland a common frontier with Latvia. At the same time the peace terms were less favorable than Poland could have obtained in the winter of 1919–1920, before Pilsudsky launched his ill-starred Ukrainian drive. By comparison with the line which the Poles held in January, 1920, the new frontier assigned to the Soviet Union an area of about 60,000 square kilometres, inhabited by about four and a half million people.

Immediately after the armistice the partisan bands of Petlura dashed into the northwestern corner of Soviet Ukraina and a similar force, under the command of Bulak-Balakhovitch, struck into Soviet White Russia, temporarily seizing the town of Mozir. These raids were crushed by the Red Army before the end of November; the remnants of Petlura's and Balakhovitch's forces were driven back into Polish territory, where they were disarmed.

In looking back at the military aspect of the drive for Warsaw one is struck by the curious inability of the Red Army Supreme Command, despite its enormous paper military establishment, to put as many as 60,000 troops in the front line for the decisive operation of a most important campaign. Nominally the Red Army in 1920 amounted to more than five million soldiers and officers. On the fighting fronts against Wrangel and against Poland, however, were only a few more than 200,000 men; the enormous majority of the Red troops were in the interior of the country.

When one makes every allowance for such negative factors as the breakdown of the transportation system, the lack of clothing and munitions (complaints of lack of shells, bullets and weapons are frequent in the Red Army reports of 1920), the difficulty of giving recruits proper military training, it must still be regarded as a signal, disastrous and almost inexplicable failure of Soviet military organization that only one out of every hundred Red Army soldiers was on the actual firing line when the issue of the Soviet-Polish campaign was being decided on the outskirts of Warsaw. This was an equally important cause of defeat with the blunders of some Red commanders, the insubordination of others and the conspicuous absence of smooth coöperation between the Western and the Southwestern Fronts.

On the political side the Soviet-Polish War of 1920 was a lesson to fanatical Polish chauvinists and to fanatical Communist world revolutionaries alike. It showed the former that Poland was overtaxing its strength and inviting disaster when it went far beyond its ethnographic boundaries and endeavored to detach Ukraina from Russia. It showed the latter the folly and futility of trying to force communism on an unwilling country by using the Red Army for crusading purposes outside the Soviet frontier.

NOTES

[1] This appeal was issued by the Main Committee for Labor Conscription and was published in *Pravda* for February 26, 1920.

[2] *Cf. Pravda* for February 25, 1920.

[3] *Cf.* Leon Trotzky, "The Economic Upbuilding of the Soviet Republic, pp. 107–114.

[4] This transformation of many industrial workers, members of the class on which the Communists wished to base their state, into small speculators was only one of several paradoxes of the period of war communism. Developments which were equally incongruous, from the Communist standpoint, were the drift away from the towns to the villages and the fact that small handicrafts survived better than large factories.

[5] The labor book was a document which every Soviet citizen had to carry, indicating, among other things, his place of employment. It was designed to prevent evasion of the compulsory labor system.

[6] Trotzky, *op. cit.*, pp. 374, 375.

[7] F. Dan, "Two Years of Wanderings," p. 46.

[8] *Cf. Pravda* for May 2, 1920.

[9] Trotzky, *op. cit.*, p. 115.

[10] *Cf. Pravda* for February 25, 1920.

[11] Trotzky, *op. cit.*, p. 465.

[12] Count Arakcheev was War Minister during the reign of Alexander I. He introduced a system under which the members of military units were used as agricultural colonists, the former soldiers performing compulsory labor under the direction of the officers. This experiment proved economically unprofitable and was abandoned in 1854, after a trial of over forty years.

[13] The Poles before they started their spring offensive held a military line somewhat east of the present Soviet-Polish frontier. The line followed the Berezina River, including the towns of Borisov and Bobruisk; farther south, in northwestern Ukraina, it ran east of Proskurov and west of Zhitomir.

[14] The full text of this appeal is published in *Izvestia* for February 5, 1920.

[15] *Cf.* Chapter XXXII, p. 259.

[16] It is difficult to establish with absolute certainty the relative weight of the various factors which induced Poland to take the offensive in the spring of 1920. But it seems probable that Pilsudsky's agreement with Petlura, and his hope of fostering the development of a chain of new republics in the non-Russian regions of the former Tsarist Empire, were of dominant significance. The Polish offensive is sometimes attributed to French influence; and France probably made no effort to restrain it. But if Pilsudsky had been a mere puppet in the hands of France, French prompting, in all probability, would have caused him to launch his drive in the autumn of

1919, when Denikin's military success was at its height and the Polish action might much more easily have brought about the overthrow of the Soviet regime.

[17] Arnold Margolin, "Ukraina and the Policy of the Entente," p. 193.

[18] Trotzky, "How the Revolution Armed Itself," Vol. II, Book 2, pp. 102ff.

[19] "The Civil War, 1918–1921," Vol. III, p. 392.

[20] Lenin attached great importance to the drive on Warsaw as a means of stimulating revolutionary sentiment in other European countries, besides Poland. He declared on one occasion that "all Germany boiled up when our troops approached Warsaw," and traced a connection between the march on Warsaw and the seizure of factories by Italian workers in the autumn of 1920. (*Cf.* his "Collected Works," Vol. XVII, pp. 308 and 337.)

[21] *Cf.* his "1920" (Russian translation), p. 100.

[22] V. Putna, in his work, "To the Vistula and Back" (pp. 137ff.), speaks of the discouraging effect on the Red soldiers who had almost reached the outskirts of Warsaw when it was learned that there were some workers among the volunteers who were increasing the numbers of the Polish forces against them.

[23] N. E. Kakurin and V. A. Melikov, "The War with the White Poles," p. 206.

[24] "The Civil War, 1918–1921," Vol. III, p. 392.

[25] *Ibid.*, Vol. III, p. 390. Louis Fischer, in "The Soviets in World Affairs" (p. 267), states 60,000 as the proposed figure of the Polish army. According to Fischer, Leo Kamenev, who, with Krassin, was at that time carrying on informal discussions in London with Lloyd George, deliberately concealed from the British Premier the most unacceptable feature of the Soviet peace terms: the demand for the creation of an armed exclusively proletarian militia. Consequently Lloyd George advised the Polish Government to accept the terms offered to them.

[26] The entire text of this document is printed in I. Stepanov's "With the Red Army Against Noblemen's Poland," pp. 92–95.

[27] *Cf.* P. V. Suslov, "Political Measures in the Soviet-Polish Campaign of 1920," pp. 164ff. Suslov's work is based on Red Army archive material.

[28] "The Civil War, 1918–1921," Vol. III, p. 437.

[29] Egorov, in his book, "Lvov-Warsaw," contends that the Cavalry Army, even if it had started on August 11, could not have reached the region of concentration of Pilsudsky's shock force near Demblin, which was 160 miles away, before August 21 or 23, too late to influence the course of the Polish counter-offensive. Budenny considers that it was a mistake to have broken off the struggle for Lvov just at the moment when, as he thinks, it was nearing success. However, the Soviet official military history ("The Civil War, 1918-1921"), points out, in opposition to Egorov, that the Cavalry Army would have exerted a disturbing effect on the Polish movements long before it reached the neighborhood of Demblin; and the Polish General Sikorsky, who may be regarded as an impartial witness in a dispute among Soviet military leaders, says that the intervention of the Twelfth Army and the Cavalry Army in the operation on the Vistula was possible and would have played a very great rôle. (*Cf.* his book, "On the Vistula and the Vkra," p. 245.)

[30] *Cf.* his "1920," pp. 130ff.

[31] *Cf.* E. N. Sergeev, "From the Dvina to the Vistula," pp. 92ff. Sergeev was the commander of the extreme right-wing Soviet military force during the advance on Warsaw.

CHAPTER XXXV

THE LAST STAND OF THE WHITES

WHITE RUSSIA made its last stand on the picturesque Crimean peninsula, the favored pleasure ground of Tsars and Grand Dukes, who had built many palaces and villas along the southern coast, where the combined beauty of surging sea and blue sky, of palms and cypresses and vineyards against a background of mountains, suggests the French Riviera. Here was the last bit of Russian land that had not been occupied by the Reds. Here were the remains of the Volunteer Army. And here was a vast host of refugees, mainly of the former upper and middle classes: bishops and priests who had fled from the persecution of religion, former governors without provinces, former industrialists without factories, former aristocrats without estates, former state officials without appointments. Mingled with the predominantly conservative refugees was a group of pre-War liberals and radicals, lawyers, writers, publicists, politicians, who had been frowned on by the Tsar's police as too advanced, but who felt themselves safer and more at home on the White side of the civil war front.

At the head of the forlorn cause represented by this last stand of the Whites was Baron Peter Wrangel, an impressive figure of a man, in the Cossack uniform which he liked to wear, with his stature of more than six feet and his resonant booming voice. Wrangel was a typical soldierly aristocrat; he might make democratic-sounding declarations for the benefit of public opinion in France and America, but at heart, as a shrewd observer remarks,[1] he was always "an officer of the cavalry regiment of His Imperial Majesty." He was devoutly attached to the Orthodox Church and made a practise of having priests bless his troops with holy water and of presenting his Generals with ikons. He had long been a favored candidate of those conservatives and clerical circles which regarded Denikin as too liberal, too much under the influence of the Cadets.

Yet, paradoxical as it may seem, Wrangel's policy was, on the whole, both more progressive and much more flexible than that of Denikin. As a younger man, he was more ready to experiment, less attached to romantic formulas than his predecessor. Moreover, he had taken to heart the political lessons of the collapse of the White movement in the winter of 1919–1920. He realized that the pre-War Russian ruling class, of which he very definitely felt himself a member, was far too weak to conquer power on a programme of open or thinly disguised restorationism. It had to win popular support, especially among the peasantry, even if this meant the renunciation of its old large estates. He was also willing to seek allies where Denikin had seen enemies, in Ukrainian nationalists, in peasant insurgents, like Makhno. Wrangel's policy has been sometimes summed up in the phrase: "Even with the devil, but against the Bolsheviki." Another phrase which describes the spirit and practise of his Crimean regime was: "To make a Left policy with Right hands."

At the moment when Wrangel took over power, early in April, the situation of the Whites seemed absolutely hopeless. The thirty or forty thousand troops which had been transported from Novorossisk to the Crimea were almost completely demoralized by the long succession of defeats, culminating in the panicky and chaotic evacuation of Novorossisk. Moreover, the British Government, the main source of military supplies for the Volunteer Army, had just served notice that it did not favor a continuance of the armed struggle by the Whites, that it would intercede with the Soviet Government for the purpose of safeguarding the lives of the officers, soldiers and civilians who had taken part in Denikin's movement, but that it would repudiate all responsibility for their fate if they should renew hostilities.

Wrangel himself seems to have been doubtful at first of his ability to do more than to arrange an evacuation of those members of the Volunteer Army and of the civilian population who were unwilling to live under Soviet rule. He communicated the new intentions of the British Government to the participants in the military council which selected him as Denikin's successor and insisted that every participant should sign a document to the effect that Wrangel, as the new Commander-in-chief, should assume responsibility only for rescuing the Army from its difficult situation, not for continuing an active struggle.[2]

Wrangel refused to enter into direct negotiations with the Bolsheviki. He waited to see what terms the British Government would arrange in its capacity as mediator. But as time passed without any definite results from the British suggestion of mediation and also without any new Red drive against the Crimea, the Whites began to gain new hope. There was always the faint chance that the Soviet regime might blow up from within, that a new turn in the international sphere might make a renewal of the apparently hopelessly uneven struggle possible. Wrangel himself brought a new infusion of energy into the White camp; working night and day, he completely reorganized the military and civil administration of the small area which he controlled and transformed the troops from the listless mob of refugees into which they had deteriorated into an efficient fighting force. Some of the measures which his lieutenants took in this connection were extremely brutal; General Kutepov publicly hanged officers and soldiers who were caught in drunken orgies on the streets of Simferopol.[3] But they achieved their effect; the fighting spirit which had almost evaporated during the long dreary retreat from Orel to Novorossisk was restored. A Soviet writer pays the following tribute to Wrangel's army as it was in the spring and summer of 1920: [4] "Qualitatively it was the best fighting force of which the Russian and international counterrevolution ever disposed in armed struggle against the Soviet Republics."

This estimate is confirmed by the course of military operations. Wrangel's troops not only held at bay but drove back considerably superior Soviet forces and only succumbed when they were overwhelmingly outnumbered after the conclusion of the war with Poland. Around Wrangel naturally rallied the most desperate, the most uncompromising enemies of the Soviets, men who felt they had no quarter to expect. Among them, of course, was a high percentage of former officers. Wrangel's forces, which he called the Russian Army, resembled the original Volunteer Army of 1918, before it had become diluted by forced mobilizations and corrupted by drink and pillage. Its striking power was out of proportion to its numbers.

The outbreak of the Soviet-Polish war at the end of April was of the greatest benefit to Wrangel. It made his front secondary, in the eyes of the Soviet Government. Throughout the period of the Polish campaign military units of inferior quality and training were used against Wrangel, the best armies, including Budenny's famous cavalry, being engaged on the Polish Front. While the British military representative in South Russia, General Percy, acting on instructions from his Government, warned Wrangel that "he must not expect any change in British policy as a result of the Polish offensive," the French military representative, General Mangin, suggested that Wrangel coördinate his activities with those of the Polish and Petlurist forces. Wrangel gladly accepted this proposal, ex-

General Baron Peter Wrangel, head of the last White government, established in the Crimea. On Wrangel's right is one of his chief ministers, A. V. Krivoshein; on his left is General Shatilov

Sculpture by Manannikov

Civil war in Crimea in 1920

pressing the desire that his coöperation with the Poles should be purely military and should not touch any "delicate political questions" until the end of the struggle against the Bolsheviki.[5] However, the rapid retreat of the Poles from Kiev and from Western Ukraina eliminated the possibility of any close coördination of the Polish and White fronts. Wrangel aided the Poles very substantially by holding large Soviet forces both in South Ukraina and in the Cossack Territories, where the Bolsheviki feared a widespread outburst of rebellion. The Poles, on their part, permitted some thousands of Denikin's troops who had fled into Poland and were interned there to return to the Crimea and to enlist in Wrangel's Army. France, as the ally of Poland, looked favorably on Wrangel. On May 8 the French assistant Minister of Foreign Affairs, Paléologue, confidentially promised that, until Wrangel received guaranties safeguarding his troops, France would endeavor to supply him with provisions and with materials for defense against the Bolsheviki. Moreover, the French fleet would protect the Crimean coast against any Bolshevik descents and, if necessary, France would coöperate in the evacuation of the peninsula.[6] On August 10, when the Red drive on Warsaw was at its height, the French Government emphasized its anti-Soviet position by formally recognizing Wrangel's regime as the *de facto* government of South Russia.

Great Britain, on the other hand, showed a tendency to dissociate itself with the White movement in South Russia. On June 3 Wrangel received a peremptory warning from the British High Commissioner in Constantinople to the effect that, if he took the offensive, the British Government would be unable to concern itself further with the fate of his army. After Wrangel did assume the offensive the British Government withdrew its official representatives from his territory, leaving only a few officers for informative purposes. The somewhat fitful negotiations which had been carried on between Lord Curzon and Chicherin during April and May regarding the conditions for a cessation of hostilities on the part of Wrangel's forces broke down, of course, after Wrangel resumed active hostilities.[7]

Several causes induced Wrangel to take the field, in spite of the British warning. The Crimea was a poor base for his movement, from the standpoint of supply; with its mountains and arid steppe lands it could not feed its own population, to say nothing of the large influx of refugees. The Army had required a period of rest, recuperation and reorganization; but too long inactivity might lead to disintegration. Moreover, a successful offensive would be the best aid to the efforts of Wrangel's Foreign Minister, the ex-Marxist, P. B. Struve,[8] to convince influential statesmen in Paris and London that the Baron's Government should be regarded as a serious factor in the Russian situation.

The offensive began on June 6 and was brilliantly successful. While Wrangel's best troops, the veteran Volunteers, smashed through the Red lines north of the Isthmus of Perekop, which unites the Crimea with the mainland, a force under the command of the eccentric but talented General Slaschev[9] made a descent on the shore of the Sea of Azov and, taking advantage of the unpreparedness of the Reds, pushed forward and captured Melitopol, the capital of the Northern Tauride Province, which adjoins the Crimea. Within a period of little over two weeks Wrangel had occupied the entire Northern Tauride, doubling the territory under his rule and acquiring a rich grain region.

Here, for the time being, he stopped. His Army was too small to hold extensive territorial gains, and Wrangel himself had more than once sharply criticized Denikin's policy of rushing on to Moscow without taking steps for the consolidation of his rear. His own viewpoint, expressed in a press interview in April, was that "Russia cannot be freed by a triumphant march on Moscow, but by the creation even on a small bit of Russian soil of such order and such living conditions as would attract the people, who are suffering under the Red yoke."[10]

On the eve of his drive into the North Tauride he issued two orders, one a statement of the ideals for which his Army was fighting, the other a new declaration on the land problem. The former was couched in the rather highflown oldfashioned style which Wrangel not infrequently used in official proclamations, and read as follows:

"Hear, Russian people, for what we are fighting:
"For outraged faith and its desecrated shrines.
"For the liberation of the Russian people from the yoke of the Communists, tramps and criminals who have completely ruined Holy Russia.
"For the stoppage of civil war.
"For the right of the peasant, after acquiring the land which he cultivates as his property, to engage in peaceful labor.
"For the rule of real freedom and right in Russia.
"For the right of the Russian people to choose for itself a MASTER (*KHOZYAEN*).
"Help me, Russian people, to save the Motherland."

The phrase about choosing a "master" ("*khozyaen*") caused Wrangel some political embarrassment; it was widely interpreted in a monarchical sense; and his explanation that he meant only the right of the people to choose its own form of government did not ring very convincingly. The most important point in Wrangel's programme was his land policy, which was soon embodied in a formal law. The outstanding feature of this law was that the peasants should retain a large, although not precisely specified portion of the land which they had seized as their own hereditary property. Over a period of twenty-five years they were to pay the state one fifth of the harvest reaped on such land; out of this payment the state was to compensate the original owners. Wrangel's land law, which was worked out with the agreement of his Premier and main adviser on questions of civil administration, the former Tsarist Minister of Agriculture, Krivoshein, might be described as Stolypinism modified by revolution. Stolypin, who was Premier during the years immediately after the 1905 Revolution, had endeavored to meet the constant threat of agrarian disorder by smashing the communal system of land ownership and creating a new class of well-to-do peasant proprietors, whose stake in the private property system would, as Stolypin believed, cause them to uphold the Tsarist regime.

Faced with the accomplished fact of a huge agrarian revolution, Wrangel and Krivoshein decided to go farther than Stolypin; retaining his theory that individual ownership of the land should be the basis of Russian agrarian development, they were willing to legalize retrospectively, in consideration of the payment of compensation, a part of the wholesale peasant land seizures. Wrangel's land law was an advance by comparison with the indefinite promises and incomplete projects of Denikin. But it did not bring him the political advantages which he had expected. The majority of the peasants were firmly convinced that all the land of the estate-owners should pass to them without compensation. Wrangel's advance into Southern Ukraina brought him into a relatively rich agricultural region, where the Soviet grain requisitions were certainly unpopular. But this peasant discontent with the Bolsheviki, which found expression in chronic guerrilla warfare, was only of indirect benefit to Wrangel. When he tried to win the direct coöperation of the insurgent peasants he suffered a complete fiasco. Makhno hanged the envoy who proposed common action with Wrangel against the Communists. Wrangel's efforts to get in touch with peasant insurgent leaders brought into his ranks only a few disreputable bandits, who were of no military advantage to him.

So Ukraina was not a politically promising field for the extension of the territory held by the Whites. After solidifying his position in the North Tauride (a Red counter-offensive which began in the last days of June was decisively defeated and the cavalry corps of the well known Red partisan Zhloba was cut to pieces) Wrangel decided to direct his next offensive into the Cossack territories, especially into the Kuban. This had been the original base of the White movement; and it seemed reasonable to expect that a few months of Red rule and reprisals would have kindled the spirit of revolt in the Kuban Cossacks and stirred them out of the lethargic defeatism which had contributed so much to the collapse of Denikin. A guerrilla anti-Soviet movement was in progress in the Kuban; the Staff of the Soviet Ninth Army, which occupied this territory, estimated on August 3 that about fifteen thousand insurgents were operating in various parts of the country.[11] The strongest individual force was the so-called Army of the Regeneration of Russia, headed by General Fostikov, which was active in the foothills of the Caucasus south of Maikop and Batalpashinsk.

With its Cossack population and its rich agricultural reserves of grain and cattle, which had not been entirely destroyed even by the ravages of civil war, the Kuban was a far more promising base than the Crimea. The Don and Kuban Cossacks who had been transported to the Crimea along with the Volunteer units were eager to return to their homes; and it seemed probable that they would fight better on their native soil.

With all these considerations in view, Wrangel decided in the summer to suspend any attempt to penetrate farther into Ukraina and to concentrate all his spare forces on operations in the Kuban and the Don. If these operations were successful, if the Kuban, on which the main attempt was to be made, could be reconquered, Wrangel proposed to evacuate the North Tauride, to hold the approach to the Crimea through the Isthmus of Perekop and to make the Kuban his main base.[12]

Wrangel determined to safeguard himself in advance against any excessive Cossack demands for autonomy. The Atamans of the Cossack Territories had fled to the Crimea and were in a position of helpless dependence on the Commander-in-chief. Their sole prospect of regaining the regions over which they claimed authority was a successful campaign of Wrangel's forces. The latter took advantage of his position and drove a hard bargain with the Cossack Atamans, embodied in a treaty which he signed with them on August 4.[13] While the treaty guarantied "full independence of internal administration to the Don, Kuban and Terek" it provided that Wrangel alone should command the armed forces of these Territories, that the railroads and telegraph lines should be under his control, that there should be no customs frontiers between the Territories and that the conclusion of political and commercial treaties should be the prerogative of the Commander-in-chief. The more oppositionist members of the Kuban Rada had taken refuge not in the Crimea, but in the more congenial Tiflis, capital of democratic Georgia, and they denounced and repudiated this agreement.

As commander of the main expeditionary force to the Kuban Wrangel selected a Kuban Cossack General, Ulagai, who possessed a reputation for personal courage and also for the quality, less common among the White leaders, of unblemished integrity. Ulagai issued a very stern order against plundering, pointing out that this had been a main cause of the unpopularity of Denikin's troops and threatening to shoot anyone who stole even a chicken.

Overburdened with other work, Wrangel, as he recognizes himself, did not devote sufficient attention to the preparation of the descent. There was too much talk about the proposed expedition; and the vessels, which should have carried only soldiers, were crowded with noncombatants, including members of the families of the officers and Cossacks. Victory was taken for granted; and there was a general desire among the Kuban natives to return home. Wrangel also seems to have made a mistake in assigning to Ulagai as Chief of Staff General Dratzenko, who continually quarrelled with Ulagai during the expedition and subsequently proved himself an incompetent commander in an important battle.

Ulagai's main force of about 7,000 infantry and cavalry disembarked successfully at Primorsko-Akhtarskaya, on the Kuban coast of the Sea of Azov, on August 13. Small subsidiary descents were made about the same time near Novorossisk and on the Taman peninsula; and Colonel Nazarov made a landing west of Taganrog and pushed into the Don Territory, hoping to arouse the Cossacks there to revolt. The Soviet leaders had anticipated Wrangel's move; Trotzky had mentioned it as a probability in a speech early in August.

At first Ulagai was quite successful. He moved over fifty miles inland from the coast and by August 18 had occupied the important

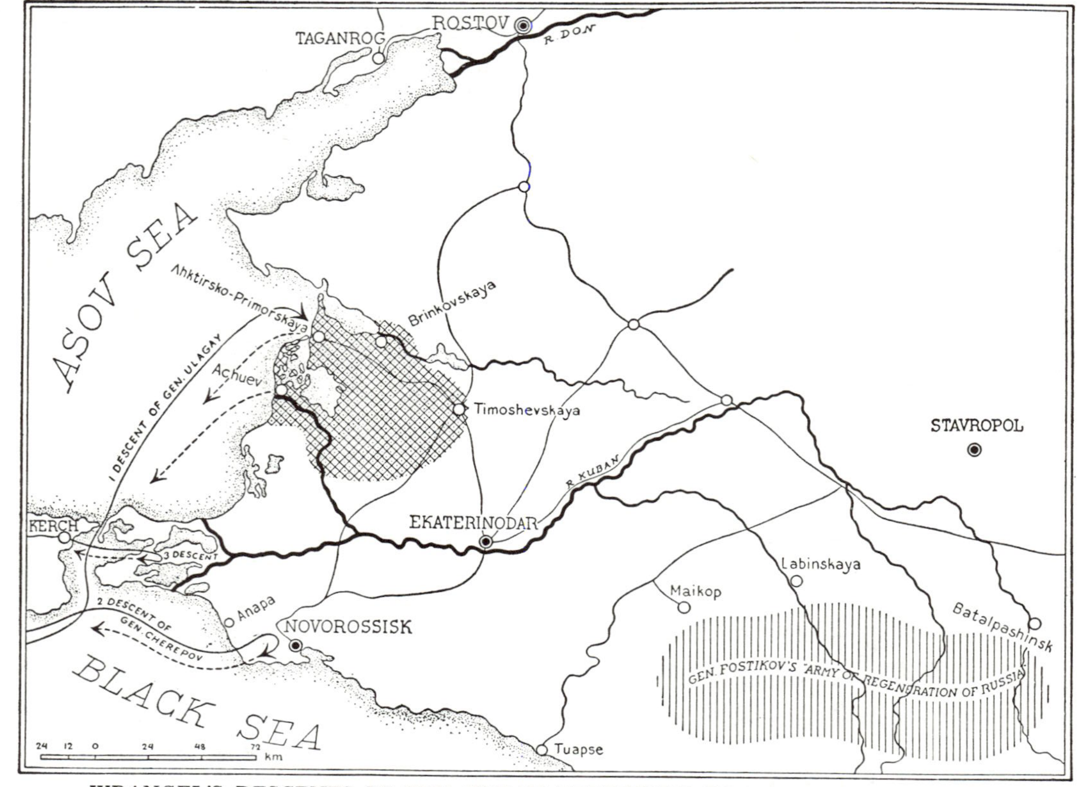

WRANGEL'S DESCENTS IN THE KUBAN TERRITORY IN THE SUMMER OF 1920

railroad junction of Timoshevskaya, about thirty-five miles north of the Kuban capital, Ekaterinodar. There was a panic in the latter town and Soviet military and civilian institutions were hastily evacuated from it. Had Ulagai pressed on from Timoshevskaya he might have taken Ekaterinodar. This would have had great moral effect and might have opened up the possibility of a union with Fostikov's "Army of the Regeneration of Russia" in the Caucasian foothills south of the Kuban River. But Ulagai hesitated for two or three days, looked anxiously back at the base of his expedition in Primorsko-Akhtarskaya and tried to carry out local mobilizations. Hesitation, under the circumstances, was fatal. For the Bolsheviki, knowing that the Kuban was potentially hostile territory, maintained there, despite the demands of the Polish and Wrangel Fronts, an army of about 30,000 men.[14] The only chance of overcoming such a superiority in numbers was to move rapidly, striking at the Red units separately and raising local insurrections wherever possible. Recovering from the first surprise, the Red troops began to close in on Ulagai and soon forced him to abandon Timoshevskaya. At the same time movements against the rear communications of the Whites forced them to transfer their base on the sea to Achuev. After a number of clashes with varying results Ulagai's forces by September 7 had been completely forced out of the Kuban. The minor descents were still more unfortunate. Ulagai, curiously enough, brought back to the Crimea more men than he had taken with him, deserters and new recruits more than compensating for his losses in battle. But Nazarov's small force in the Don was practically annihilated in a battle at the stanitsa Konstantinovka; Nazarov made his way alone back to the Crimea. The small forces which landed near Novorissisk and on the Taman peninsula were also largely wiped out.

A disillusioned White author[15] attributes the failure of the Kuban descent in part to the rough and tactless conduct of some of the officers attached to the expeditionary force, who are alleged to have behaved in the occupied villages as if they were in a conquered country. Individual cases of this kind may have occurred; but it seems that the main reason for the failure of the expedition, apart from Ulagai's hesitation after his first successes, was the unwillingness of the majority of the Cossacks to risk their lives and their property by supporting what was evidently a desperate adventure, in view of the pronounced numerical superiority of the Red troops in the Kuban.

Wrangel's incursion into Cossack regions aroused considerable anxiety in Moscow. Trotzky rushed to Taganrog, on the Sea of Azov, to supervise operations against the Whites and published a number of typically vitriolic orders about the "German Baron who is a protégé of the French Bourse," and who was trying to poke his head out of the "bottle," the Crimean peninsula, in which he had been confined.[16]

The failure to expand his territorial base eastward by regaining the Cossack Territories may be considered the turningpoint in Wrangel's military career. He now decided to make another effort to break through the cordon of Red troops in a different direction, to the west and north. During the latter part of August and September there had been a complete reversal of the situation on the Polish Front; the Red armies had been repulsed and the Poles were again approaching the frontier of Ukraina. Wrangel proposed to cross the river Dnieper, the lower course of which had hitherto marked the northwestern boundary of the territory under his control, and to push ahead into Western Ukraina, hoping to establish contact with the Poles, or, at least, with a Russian White force which he was trying to form on Polish territory. Before undertaking this "trans-Dnieper operation" he aimed blows at the Red forces to the north and east of his lines and made appreciable territorial gains. His cavalry patrols at one time were in the vicinity of Ekaterinoslav, in the northern direction, and of Taganrog, to the east; he occupied the port of Mariupol, on the Sea of Azov, and raided the important railroad junction, Sinelnikovo, east of Ekaterinoslav.

But these were local and transitory successes and were more than counterbalanced by the complete failure of the drive across the Dnieper. This operation began auspiciously; Wrangel's troops crossed the river and the dashing Kuban Cossack cavalry General, Babiev, seized the town of Nikopol. But the incompetent handling of the main body of troops by General Dratzenko and the death of the gallant Babiev in battle on October 13 led to disastrous defeat; the Whites were driven back across the Dnieper with heavy losses. The Reds retained an important strategic foothold on the left bank of the Dnieper at Kakhovka, from which they could easily strike at the approach to the Crimea through the Isthmus of Perekop and gravely endanger the position of Wrangel's forces in the North Tauride. Even more depressing than the defeat was the news, which arrived at about the same time, that Poland had signed an armistice and a preliminary peace treaty. This meant that the Soviet Government could throw overwhelming forces against the sole organized anti-Bolshevik army which remained on Russian soil, that of Wrangel. The importance of liquidating Wrangel as soon as possible was fully recognized in Moscow. The Southern Front was heavily reinforced, Budenny's Cavalry Army being one of the units which were transferred there. The veteran Communist military leader, Frunze, who had played a large part in the defeat of Kolchak, was placed in command of this Front. A stream of propaganda was directed against the "black Baron," who, with his White Army, was represented as wishing to restore the Tsarist throne and to trample on the workers and peasants. There was the usual mobilization of Communists and of *"kursanti,"* Red officers in training, who usually constituted a reliable shock force, for service against Wrangel.

The latter now had to decide whether to meet the blow which was being prepared against him in the North Tauride or to retreat behind the fortified lines of the Isthmus of Perekop. After a conference with his chief lieutenants, General Shatilov and General Kutepov, he decided to make his stand in the North Tauride. A retreat into the Crimea, as he felt, would expose the army and population to hunger and would eliminate any prospect of the future military aid from France with which he hoped to continue the struggle.[17] He knew very well that he faced desperately uneven odds. Against his army of approximately 35,000 the Reds could place in the field about 137,000.[18] They also possessed a substantial advantage in cannon and in machine-guns. Moreover, there had been a gradual but unmistakable deterioration in the quality of the White troops. Their numbers had remained fairly constant, between 30,000 and 40,000, throughout several months of hard campaigning. But the personnel had altered, mainly for the worse. As the ranks of the veteran Volunteer units were thinned in battle they were filled up with recruits of less reliable calibre, with refugees from the Cossack territories, with locally mobilized peasants, even with captured Red Army soldiers. Wrangel himself notes more than once that the spirit of his troops had declined in the last battles in the North Tauride and at the Isthmus of Perekop.

In the light of all these circumstances the issue of the battle which began on the North Tauride Front on October 28 and lasted for several days was pretty well determined in advance. Wrangel's forces were smashed and driven back into the Crimea. Frunze had hoped, by setting the Cavalry Army in motion from Kakhovka, to reach the narrow bottleneck entrance to the Crimea before the main body of the Whites had completed their retreat there and not only to defeat, but to annihilate Wrangel's army on the steppes of the North Tauride. This plan was not carried out; the picked Volunteer Kornilov, Markov and Drozdovsky divisions fought their way through to the comparative safety of the fortified Isthmus of Perekop. But Wrangel's already small army had been reduced in numbers and shaken in morale by this engagement in the North Tauride; the chances of holding out for a long period of time at the entrance to the Crimea were not great. Wrangel began to make hasty plans for evacuation, simultaneously encouraging the publication of reassuring statements about the impregnable character of the Perekop defenses, with a view to preventing a general outburst of panic.

On the Isthmus of Perekop, a strip of land varying in width from five to ten miles which constitutes the sole land connection between the Crimea and the mainland, there were three lines of White defenses. The first was north of the town of Perekop and consisted largely of barbed-wire entanglements. The second utilized an old Turkish or Tartar barrier known as the Turkish Wall and was well equipped with machine-gun emplacements, some of which were proof against bombardment by heavy artillery. The last, so-called Ushun, line of defense was at the southern end of the peninsula and utilized several small lakes. Another way of approach to the Crimea, farther to the east, is from the Chongar peninsula, which juts out from the mainland and is connected with the northern coast of the Crimea by two narrow bridges.

The storm on the last stronghold of the Whites began on November 7, the third anniversary of the Bolshevik Revolution. Wrangel placed his best Volunteer troops on the direct defenses of Perekop. Protected by trenches and machine-gun nests they stubbornly resisted the frontal attacks of the Reds. But on the night of November 7th a picked force from the Soviet Army took the first two lines of Perekop defenses in flank and rear by crossing the Gulf of Sivash, attacking and driving back a weak Kuban Cossack division under the command of General Fostikov, which was guarding the small Lithuanian peninsula, southeast of Perekop. The efforts of the Whites to regain the peninsula by means of counter-attacks were unsuccessful. Fearing that they would be cut off and attacked from the rear, the Volunteer units on the night of November 8 abandoned the Turkish Wall and fell back to the Ushun position. Here the struggle went on for two days without a definite result.

The 11th was the decisive day. At first the results were rather

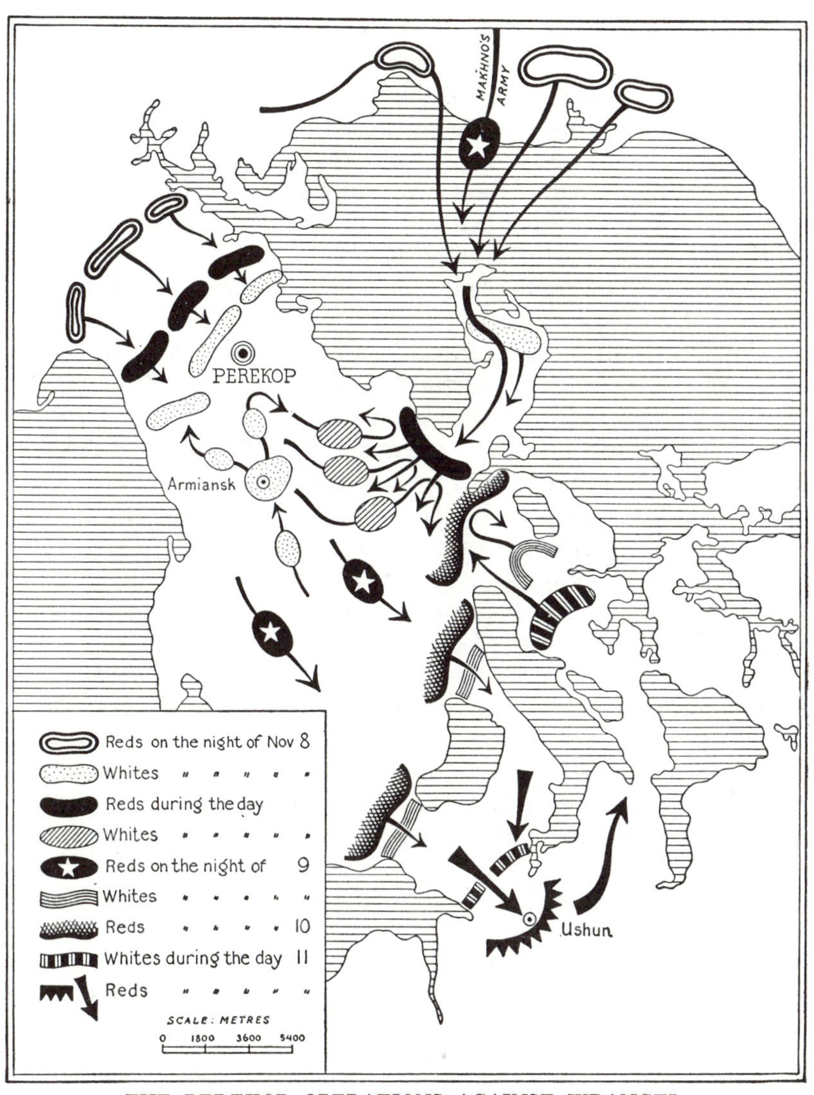

THE PEREKOP OPERATIONS AGAINST WRANGEL

contradictory. In a last desperate effort a specially picked group of the Whites threw back the Soviet troops and almost drove them to the end of the Lithuanian peninsula. But meanwhile the Red forces on another sector broke through the Ushun line of defense. Each side was in a position to threaten the rear of the other. The uncertain issue was decided when the Thirtieth Division of the Red Army, crossing over an improvised bridge from the Chongar peninsula, in the face of heavy artillery and machine-gun fire, scattered the Whites on the northern coast of the Crimea and began to move forward into the Crimean plain, threatening the headquarters of the Whites at Dzhankoi.

The successful crossing from the Chongar peninsula, in which, as in the storming of the fortified positions around Perekop, the Red troops displayed conspicuous gallantry and pushed forward, regardless of heavy losses, was the final blow. Wrangel realized that his cause was lost and gave orders for the immediate retreat of his troops to the various ports of the Crimea, the infantry being transported on carts, while the cavalry covered the retreat. Every bit of available shipping was pressed into service; French warships and transports assisted the evacuation. Utilizing the several ports at his disposal Wrangel carried out his evacuation very smoothly and successfully. While there was a "green" insurgent movement in the mountainous districts of the Crimea it was not strong enough to harass seriously the last stages of the retreat or to interfere with the transportation of the White troops abroad. According to Wrangel's own figures,[19] 145,693 people, including, besides his troops, great numbers of members of their families and of civilian refugees, quit the Crimea with him. The fugitives went first to Constantinople and gradually dispersed from there among the various centres of Russian émigré life.

The speedy fall of the supposedly strong Perekop defenses surprised not only civilians, but also some military experts among the Whites. As a matter of fact the defenses were not as invulnerable as they were popularly supposed to be; their fortification during the summer had been neglected.[20] More important, however, than the defects of the defense system was the lack of a sufficient number of reliable troops to man the trenches. Wrangel did not possess enough firstrate units to guard adequately every possible avenue of penetration.

Wrangel was the last leader of the organized White movement in Russia. Faced with very unfavorable odds from the beginning, his defeat was almost a foregone conclusion. Few prominent anti-Bolshevik statesmen wished to accept office in his government. He performed no miracles; he could not, with a small army and an inadequate base, cope indefinitely with the huge Red Army, which had almost all Russia as a recruiting ground. With his background as an aristocratic officer, he could not bridge over the wide gulf of suspicion and hostility which always existed between the White movement and the peasant masses of the people, and which was the fundamental cause of its defeat.

But within his inevitable limitations Wrangel put up a good fight. He inherited a wreck of an army; he refashioned it into a fighting force which gave the Reds more than one hard blow. Wrangel could not save the old Russia whose champion and representative he was. But his military activity, which kept large numbers of Red troops occupied both in Ukraina and in the Kuban, was certainly not the least of the reasons why the Red armies before Warsaw lacked the ultimate bit of reserve strength that might have created a Soviet Poland and have extended Bolshevism far beyond Russia's frontiers. Viewed from this standpoint the White epilogue represented by Wrangel was as helpful to Poland and perhaps to other new national states of Eastern Europe as it was harmful to the Soviet Government and the Communist International.[21]

NOTES

[1] *Cf.* Prince V. Obolensky, "The Crimea Under Wrangel," p. 36.

[2] General A. I. Denikin, "Sketches of Russian Turmoil," Vol. V, pp. 362, 363.

[3] *Cf.* A. A. Valentinov's article, "The Crimean Epilogue," published in the symposium of White reminiscences entitled "Denikin, Yudenitch, Wrangel," p. 356.

[4] *Cf.* the article of A. Golubev in the book, "The Defeat of Wrangel," p. 62.

[5] *Cf.* "The Memoirs of General P. N. Wrangel," published in Vol. VI of the journal *Byeloe Dyelo,* pp. 83–85.

[6] *Ibid.,* Vol. VI, p. 89.

[7] For the details of the Anglo-Soviet negotiations in connection with the terms of Wrangel's prospective capitulation, *cf.* Boris Stein's article in "The Defeat of Wrangel," pp. 14, 15. One stumblingblock was that Chicherin wished to make an amnesty to the Whites dependent on the release of some imprisoned commissars of the Hungarian Soviet Republic,—a question which the British Government was unwilling to take up.

[8] Struve composed the first manifesto issued by the Russian Social Democratic Party at the time of its establishment in 1897.

[9] Slaschev was a decidedly unbalanced character, largely as a result of his addiction to drink and drugs. He lived with a whole menagerie of birds. Wrangel ultimately felt obliged to dismiss him from his command, soothing his vanity by simultaneously conferring on him the title "Slaschev the Crimean," in view of his services in preventing the peninsula from being overrun by the Reds early in the year. Slaschev went into emigration, but subsequently returned to Russia and accepted service in the Red Army. He was ultimately assassinated, allegedly by the relative of one of the victims of his numerous executions in South Russia and the Crimea.

[10] Obolensky, *op. cit.,* p. 25.

[11] *Cf.* A. Golubev, "Wrangel's Descents in the Kuban," p. 27.

[12] *Byeloe Dyelo,* Vol. VI, p. 121.

[13] *Cf.* G. Rakovsky, "The End of the Whites," p. 109.

[14] Golubev, *op. cit.,* p. 33.

[15] Rakovsky, *op. cit.,* pp. 123ff.

[16] *Cf.* Leon Trotzky, "How the Revolution Armed Itself," Vol. II, Book 2, pp. 193ff. Wrangel belonged to an aristocratic German family in the Baltic Provinces, where the landed nobility largely consisted of Germans.

[17] *Byeloe Dyelo,* Vol. VI, pp. 206, 207.

[18] Golubev, *op. cit.,* pp. 87, 88.

[19] *Byeloe Dyelo,* Vol. VI, p. 242.

[20] Details of the shortcomings in the fortifications of the Perekop Isthmus and the neighboring regions are to be found in A. Valentinov, *op. cit.,* pp. 379, 380.

[21] The Crimean last stand of the Whites was only made possible by a careless oversight in the organization of the pursuit of Denikin's armies in the winter of 1919–1920. The approaches to the peninsula were defended only by the small corps of General Slaschev and could easily have been captured if a sufficient force had been despatched against them. In this case the transportation of the remnants of Denikin's army to the Crimea would have been impossible and the Wrangel Front could not have come into existence. Lenin was quick to recognize the mistake which had been made in not hastening to occupy the Crimea and on March 19, 1920, sent a message to Sklyansky, a prominent member of the Revolutionary Military Council, speaking of the "clear mistake which had been committed" in not directing sufficient forces against the Crimea. (*Cf.* A. Golubev's article in "The Defeat of Wrangel," p. 59.)

CHAPTER XXXVI

THE REVOLUTION AND DAILY LIFE

THE Abbé Sieyès, when asked what he did during the French Revolution, briefly and eloquently replied: "I lived." And great numbers of Russians who had never heard of Sieyès doubtless felt with him that the mere preservation of existence under the conditions of revolution and civil war, when hunger, cold, disease and terror stalked through the country like the Four Horsemen of the Apocalypse, was a noteworthy achievement.

Human life was very cheap in those years. The fanaticism of the leaders, the growing brutalization of the rank-and-file on both sides of the fighting line, the fact that so much of the fighting was of an irregular, guerrilla character—all these factors helped to make the Russian civil war one of the most cruel in history. The casualties in outright fighting, to be sure, were far fewer than those of the World War; but the crushing of uprisings behind the lines, the hunting down of suspected enemies among the general population after the occupation of a town or region, the ceaseless and merciless activity of the Red Cheka and the White *kontra-razvedka* all took a very large number of victims.

Quite apart from the casualties of warfare or of governmental terrorism, the ordinary mortality swelled enormously and inevitably as a result of the appalling deprivations to which the country was subjected as a result of prolonged civil warfare, economic and social upheaval and virtually complete isolation from the outside world, all coming after Russia's resources had already been gravely taxed by the World War. People who were delicate, who required special diet, died almost automatically as a result of chronic malnutrition, exposure to cold and the epidemic diseases, cholera, typhus, typhoid, influenza which raged with sporadic degrees of intensity but without interruption during these "bare years," to borrow the title which a Soviet novelist, Pilniak, bestowed on a novel which he wrote about this period. People fell off the roofs of the few crowded railroad cars which were running, contracted typhus from the lice which crawled everywhere when they were driven by gnawing hunger to undertake the perilous adventure of a railroad trip in order to forage for bread in the villages.

Some concrete illustrations may help to re-create the general atmosphere of bleak misery. A British journalist, Arthur Ransome, visiting Moscow early in 1919, saw a flock of famished crows pursuing a cart loaded with horseflesh, quite indifferent to the blows which the driver aimed at them with his whip.[1] The Anarchist Alexander Berkman, visiting Moscow in the following year, when he could not stomach soup made with bad fish as an ingredient, found an engineer at his elbow, eager to gulp down the liquid.[2] Bread and kasha, a Russian cereal made out of grits, were the staple articles of diet for the masses of the population; the bread was often of extremely bad quality and was sometimes given out irregularly, depending on the condition of the railroad transportation. Fish, which was sometimes used in the soup, was apt to be rotten, and potatoes were usually frozen. What little meat was available came largely from horses which had died of exhaustion.

Some foreign observers who visited Moscow at this time express the view that the inhabitants of the Soviet capital looked no more underfed than the poorer classes of Vienna after the end of the War. Blockade certainly played havoc in Germany and Austria; and perhaps the Muscovites, with the aid of the illegal food supplies which continually trickled through by the agency of speculators, had as much to eat as the Viennese in their worst months. But the breakdown in other fields of life was unmistakably greater in Russia.

Cold was as deadly an enemy as hunger during the long and severe Russian winters. Pipes burst in the underheated houses and were left unmended for lack of metal and skilled labor. Sanitation broke down almost completely. When the winter of 1919–1920 was just beginning the Commissar for Health, Semashko, declared that from the hospitals there was a general cry that the patients were freezing to death. Therefore these institutions had the first claim on the wood as it arrived.[3]

The ambitious desire of the Soviet Government to abolish illiteracy and to place all the Russian children in school was thwarted by the hard material circumstances of the situation. New school buildings could not be built, and there was no fuel to heat those which already existed. Employees went to almost unheated offices in heavy coats and gloves. Pavlovitch, a high Soviet official, told Ransome that two of his assistants had to be taken home "in a condition something like that of a fit, the result of prolonged sedentary work in unheated rooms." Pavlovitch had temporarily lost the use of his right hand for the same reason.[4] So desperate was the fuel situation that houses were knocked to pieces for the sake of the wood, while families which were total strangers sometimes voluntarily moved into common quarters during the winter months, in order to keep each other warm with heat generated from their bodies.

The spread of typhus was enormously facilitated by the huge movements of troops and refugees all over Russia, by the acute shortage of soap, by the undernourishment which made people especially susceptible to the disease. A well known Soviet writer, Serafimovitch, tells in *Pravda*[5] how hosts of fugitives from the advance of Yudenitch's Army in the autumn of 1919 fled into the forests near Lake Peipus and died in great numbers of typhus because there was no one to care for them; how, when the clothes of Bashkir soldiers[6] of the Red Army were disinfected, a pile of what looked like grey sand two inches high remained on the floor of the disinfecting room. On closer examination the "sand" was found to consist of lice.

A kind of deathlike pall hung over Moscow and Petrograd in those years; many normal features of the life of a large city had disappeared or had become rare and infrequent. The great majority of the former private shops were closed; here and there one could find a state shop, with its shelves usually empty, or a public dining-room, where the meagre and unappetizing fare of the time was served out. There were periods when the streetcars ceased to run altogether; at other times they functioned very irregularly and were invariably jammed with passengers. A few of the individualist izvoschiks, or cabmen, of whom there were so many in pre-war Russia, survived all the rigors of war communism and demanded enormous prices in paper rubles for their services. The Anarchist Berkman once asked a Communist acquaintance why the izvoschiks had not been nationalized, along with practically everything else, and received the following sarcastic reply:[7]

"We found that if you don't feed human beings they continue to live somehow. But if you don't feed horses, the stupid beasts die. That's why we don't nationalize the cabmen."

One extraordinary exception to the drab, regimented life of Moscow under war communism, a place where every Soviet decree and every communist principle was openly, flagrantly and impudently violated every day, was the Sukharevka Market. Here Red Army soldiers came to sell the shoes which they had surreptitiously taken from commissary stores. Here the numerous workmen who joined the ranks of the speculators offered for sale tools which were stolen from state factories. Here were all the things which could not be had, or could be obtained only with great difficulty and with an enormous outlay of time and patience in the state shops: linen, blankets, rugs, underwear, household utensils. In the Sukharevka, for speculative prices, one could buy the things which somehow did not find their way into the channels of state distribution: butter, eggs, fresh meat, sugar. To many of the former wealthy classes the selling and barter possibilities of the Sukharevka represented the sole means of escape from virtual starvation. Things which must have seemed incongruous at the time—precious oriental rugs, old furniture, ball gowns, cosmetics, toilet articles, porcelain pieces and sets—could be found in abundance on this market.[8]

The Soviet policy toward the Sukharevka and toward the lesser markets which existed in Moscow was wavering and uncertain. Communists of the stricter persuasion looked on them with utter aversion; it was no secret that a large part of the manufactured goods on the markets represented property which had been stolen from the state in one way or another, and the speculators who flourished against the background of the Sukharevka constituted a new class of capitalists, cruder and more primitive in their methods than the industrialists, bankers and merchants who had been swept out by what Communists liked to call "the iron broom of the Revolution." But the regular provision for the needs of the Moscow population was so scanty and unsatisfactory that the Soviet authorities could not bring themselves to suppress all private trade. The police made frequent raids on the Sukharevka and other markets and confiscated some of the produce which was offered for sale, dragging off some of the traders for compulsory labor. But the need to buy and the impulse to sell were so strong that soon after a raid trading would begin much as before.

Public order was well maintained in Soviet towns. There was a good deal of petty stealing at markets and railroad stations; but crimes of violence were relatively infrequent and the streets were fairly safe, even at night.

Some phases of cultural life proceeded with surprisingly little change, in spite of the tremendous social upheaval and the difficult material conditions. Moscow remained one of the best theatrical centres in the world. On the occasion of his visit to Russia in February, 1919, Ransome found the opera-houses and theatres of Moscow playing to crowded audiences of spectators who shivered in their overcoats and fur coats, but gave every evidence of enjoying the performance as much as ever.[9] There were almost no new plays at this time; the classical authors whose works were given included such Russians as Gorky, Ostrovsky, and Saltykov-Schedrin and such foreigners as Shakespeare, Molière, Maeterlinck and Dickens.

The same situation prevailed in Petrograd; Russia's world-famous actor-singer, Chaliapin, continued to hold audiences fascinated with his impersonations of Faust and Boris Godunov; the Menshevik Dan, correctly anticipating his own arrest in February, 1921, counts himself fortunate that he was able to hear Chaliapin before he received the expected visit at his apartment from the agents of the Cheka.[10] Chaliapin, incidentally, carried out a successful form of individual resistance to the application of Communist principles. It had been proposed to pay the singers equally with the scene-shifters and other stage-hands. Chaliapin, a man of powerful physique, who had started life as a manual laborer, thereupon declared that, in this case, he would not sing; he would prefer to take his place with the stage-hands. Reckoning with the singer's enormous popularity, the Soviet authorities gave in and paid him regularly for his appearances in allotments of flour, sugar and other scarce and highly prized commodities.

There was a hectic flush of activity on the part of painters and sculptors immediately after the Revolution, and for a time futurists and cubists held the centre of the scene and decorated blank walls, pavements and other available places with their creations. Statues of well known revolutionaries were set up in various parts of the city. In the main, however, artistic, like literary and scientific, activity was largely paralyzed during the years from 1917 until 1921. Physical conditions were too difficult to permit creative work on any large scale. The artist lacked painting materials; the author lacked paper for the publication of his work; the scientist lacked new instruments and materials and contact with scientific thought and discoveries in other countries. Such significant works as A. Blok's poem "The Twelve," with its amazingly gripping and lyrical picture of the cold, windswept streets of Petrograd, through which twelve Red Guards are marching, and its strange, mystical end, when the figure of Christ appears at the head of the twelve, were exceptions. First consideration was given to the production of artistic efforts with a definitely propagandist content, such as the poems of Demyan Byedny, who wrote jingling verses of a type comprehensible to the most scantily literate worker or peasant, and to the numerous posters which were placed in workers' clubs, *agitpunkti* (agitation points), a feature of every large station, and in other places where large masses of people could be reached.

The Revolution from the beginning had aroused a demand for education among the masses; and the Soviet Government did what it could, in the face of very unfavorable conditions, to satisfy this demand. New libraries were established; a large cheap edition of the works of the leading Russian classical authors in all fields was initiated; there was an effort to expand the primary school system, which had been decidedly inadequate under Tsarism; one exuberant decree opened the doors of the universities to anyone who desired a higher education, whether he had passed through preliminary training or not. This last decree was of little practical benefit and hampered rather than helped the work of the universities by bringing into them a considerable number of raw and untrained students.

The civil war and the extreme impoverishment of the country, which made it impossible for many years to support teachers adequately or to provide a sufficient number of buildings and equipment, thwarted for a long time the desire of the Soviet Government to introduce universal primary education. Lunacharsky asserted in the autumn of 1920 that the number of elementary schools had increased by 12,000 since pre-War times, and that the number of pupils had grown by 1,500,000.[10a] But it would be difficult to say with certainty how many of the schools, new and old, actually functioned and how many existed only on paper; there were frequent unavailing complaints about the occupation of school buildings for military purposes. When the Soviet Government, with the introduction of the New Economic Policy, adopted more realistic methods of economic calculation and restored the money system, there was a sharp decline in the number both of schools and of teachers; and several years passed before the pre-War figures of attendance at school were reached and exceeded. The Red Army proved a good means of reducing adult illiteracy. Courses in reading and writing were instituted during the soldiers' free time; and many quite illiterate peasant lads who had been conscripted for service returned to their homes with at least a smattering of literacy. Children's homes were created in considerable numbers during this period. They were in harmony with a theory held by many Communist educationalists, that children should be brought up in collective groups, free from the individualist influence of home and family. They were also an emergency necessity; war and revolution had created a very large number of orphans and also of children whose parents had somehow become separated from them and lost trace of them. (The continually shifting line of the civil war front not infrequently led to the break-up of families, some of whose members would remain in Red territory, others in White.) There were not nearly enough children's homes to care for all the homeless and neglected children; and juvenile criminality became a serious social problem.

The Revolution tore to pieces the conventional patterns of family life. The accidents of flight and evacuation disrupted many families. In some cases fathers and sons fought on different sides of the front; one of the most vivid literary works on the civil war depicts a Cossack father on the side of the Whites having one of his sons, a captured Red Army soldier, killed, and then being killed himself by another son.[11] Such extreme cases were no doubt infrequent. But it often happened that boys and girls in Russian families were caught up by the revolutionary movement which left their fathers and mothers sceptical or bitterly hostile. This led to many family schisms, especially among the intelligentsia.

The general chaotic breakdown of everything that had seemed stable before the Revolution naturally had its effect on sex relations. There seems to have been much more promiscuous living together during the time of the civil war than in earlier or later periods. At the same time visible organized prostitution largely disappeared, to the great edification of sympathetic British Labor visitors with firm convictions on domestic morality. Anything in the nature of luxurious night life, of course, disappeared under war communism, and, beginning early in 1920, every man and woman was liable for labor service. Former prostitutes were rounded up, sent to concentration camps and taught trades. But a new form of irregular sex relations, generated by new social conditions, grew up. The numerous girl employees in the Soviet offices, the *sovietski barishni,* or "Soviet young ladies," as they were half derisively called, received semi-starvation wages, like almost everyone else. Many of them were willing to enter into *liaisons* with speculators or with high Soviet officials who were able to offer such luxuries as flour and sugar, or even cosmetics and silk stockings.

The Communists advocated the theory of absolute equality of

the sexes in political and social life and swept away all the Tsarist legislation which placed the wife in a subordinate position in regard to her husband. Some veteran women Bolsheviki held prominent posts in the administration at various times. The most prominent of these was Alexandra Kollontai, who for a time was Commissar for Social Welfare. Some simple working women also joined the Communist ranks and served the Revolution devotedly, sometimes at the front, with the Red Army, and sometimes as propagandists and Soviet officials. But women did not participate in the Revolution to the same extent as men. The influence of the pre-War inequality of the sexes as regards educational and other opportunities was too strong.

A hostile critic once observed that the only equality the Communists succeeded in creating was the equality of universal misery. This is not strictly accurate. It is probably true that no European country within recent centuries has endured such widespread and acute physical distress of various kinds as Russia experienced during the years from 1918 until 1921. But this distress was by no means equally distributed. If to the masses of the people who knew and cared little about politics and social theories the years of civil war seemed a nightmare of unparallelled hardship there were individuals, if not whole classes, to whom the social upheaval brought an intoxicating sense of liberation, of newly found power.

More than one foreign pilgrim who believed that the Communists had created a system under which everyone shared alike was sadly disillusioned after going to Moscow and finding that there were appreciable differences in the standard of living between a high Party or Soviet official and the typical workman in a factory. True, the fare served to prominent Soviet leaders in their office diningrooms was scarcely calculated to excite envy. Ransome describes a meal of which he partook with Zinoviev and other high Petrograd Communists as follows: [12]

> "The meal was extremely simple, soup with shreds of horseflesh in it, very good indeed, followed by a little kasha, together with small slabs of some sort of white stuff of no particular consistency or taste. Then tea and a lump of sugar."

On another occasion, when Ransome was visiting the town of Yaroslavl, he found that the local officials made a practise of going to the local prison for their midday meal, because the organizer of the prison diningroom was much more competent than the person in charge of the regular Soviet diningroom.[13] But opportunities for "wangling" an undue share of the very limited supply of foodstuffs and commodities were numerous, and were not neglected by the less scrupulous and less idealistic Communists. Berkman, an Anarchist with a sharp eye and a sharp tongue, gives us a series of pen pictures of men who seemed to have done rather well out of the Revolution: Assistant Foreign Commissar Karakhan, "tall, good-looking, well groomed, sitting in a sumptuous office, his feet resting on a fine tigerskin"; Melnichansky, head of the Moscow trade-unions, whose "prosperous appearance, well fitting clothes and ruddy face" caused him to be taken for a foreigner by the hungry Russian workers; or the well known Communist military leader, Lashevitch, looking "fat, greasy and offensively sensuous," as he denounced the halfstarved Petrograd workers who had come out on strike for higher food rations, as "leeches, who were practising extortion." [14]

The very conditions of life under war communism tended to give those Communists who occupied the higher posts of military and civil administration, perhaps unconsciously, some of the attributes and characteristics of a new ruling caste. They monopolized the country's few automobiles. They alone could ride on the railroads with comfort. Their living quarters in the Kremlin in Moscow, in the former leading hotels in other cities may have been simple enough, but they were luxurious by comparison with the unheated, crumbling houses in which the majority of the population lived throughout the bare years. Bertrand Russell, the British mathematician and philosopher, who came to Russia with a British Labor Delegation in May, 1920, thinking himself a Communist and left it certain that he was not, saw in the Communists the virtues and faults of a young aristocracy: willingness to fight and die, to work hard for their system, combined with aloofness from the population and a hard indifference as to how many lives might have to be sacrificed before their cause would prevail.

In general, life reverted to very primitive and brutalized forms during those years. The sincerely humanitarian efforts which the Soviet regime made in many fields, in caring for children, in providing education and recreation for workers, etc., were of small account in a society where the lives of human beings were of less account than the lives of animals in softer countries and at softer times. In war and frontier zones the mere denunciation of a man as a White agent or a foreign spy was often sufficient to bring about his summary execution by the Cheka. A saying grew up in those years that "every Soviet citizen is, has been or will be in prison"; and the prisons in Moscow and other cities were always crowded, sometimes under such unsanitary conditions that a high mortality rate was almost inevitable, especially when pregnant women were not infrequently thrown in among the other prisoners. The Cheka proceeded on the theory that it was better that a hundred innocent people should be arrested than that one guilty person should escape; and a remarkably varied assortment of victims was swept in by its farflung net. Along with real or suspected members of anti-Bolshevik political parties and groupings, ranging from Monarchists to Anarchists, it rounded up more or less sporadically and indiscriminately "speculators" and "labor deserters," categories in which a large part of the Soviet population almost inevitably fell. Desired witnesses were arrested and held in prison along with persons charged with offenses; and the mills of Soviet justice at this time ground exceedingly slowly. As was inevitable under the arbitrary regime which prevailed, large numbers of quite innocent people were placed in prison. The Cheka had an extremely highly developed imagination with regard to plots. Persons were often caught and detained if they were visiting the apartment of a man who had been placed under arrest, or if their names were found, no matter in what connection, when the quarters of arrested persons were searched. In Moscow, where the presence of the central Government made, on the whole, for greater moderation, beating and torturing of prisoners seem to have been uncommon, at least in 1920,[15] although a serious case of maltreatment of political prisoners in the Butirki Prison occurred in the spring of 1921. The food of the prisoners, bad as it certainly was, was regularly given and was not much worse than the rations of the general population; and there was some, although inadequate, provision for medical attendance. In provincial towns, on the other hand, extremely bad conditions, including beatings of prisoners, were not uncommon.

The typical pre-War Russian of the common people, although he could be very brutal in a drunken brawl or in a pogrom, was normally rather kindhearted and hospitable. These qualities seem to have dried up to a considerable degree during the years of war communism. General privation developed a general wolfish psychology of every man for himself. The law of the survival of the fittest found its crudest, most naked application in the continual struggle for food. The weaker failed to get on the trains to the country districts, or fell off the roofs, or were pushed off the platforms, or caught typhus and died, or had the precious fruits of their foraging taken away by the *zagraditelni otryadi,* the hated guards who boarded trains as they approached cities and confiscated surplus food from the passengers. The physically strongest and most cunning evaded these guards or bribed their way past them and returned laden with food which they could barter for rugs and jewels or sell at enormous prices in paper rubles. A hardy class of primitive capitalists was born in these years of war communism; out of the *meshochniki,* or bagmen, who dodged past the cordon of guards with which the towns were surrounded, out of the professional despoilers of state warehouses, out of the cunning "black bourse" traders who somehow contrived to carry on an illicit trade in gold, jewels and foreign currency developed the Nepmen, or new private traders, who sprang up with such amazing rapidity when the long struggle against private trade was abandoned in 1921.

Another cause of the heartlessness, the indifference to human suffering which impressed many visitors to Russia at that time was the almost incredible growth of bureaucracy. The immediate instinct of anyone in the state service (and almost everyone was in the state service) was to send the unfortunate petitioner for any kind of service to some other department for a paper and a stamp. Emma Goldman, as an Anarchist who was profoundly disillusioned by the Soviet system, is a harsh and sometimes unfair critic of the Communists; but her sharp characterization of Soviet bureaucracy is borne out by other witnesses: [16]

> "Everywhere the numerous employees deliberately wasted their time, while thousands of applicants spent days and weeks in the corridors and offices without receiving the least attention. The greater part of Russia did nothing else but stand in line, waiting for the bureaucrats, big and little, to admit them to their sanctums."

There are several explanations for the colossal growth of futile red tape in Russia at this time. The practise of nationalizing everything, from public baths to metal factories and from medical sanatoria to bakeries, made the state responsible for the carrying on of innumerable institutions which it had no means of administering effectively. Then, while bureaucracy had always been a curse in Russia, the pre-War officials were at least literate. In the upheaval many of them ran away or were removed from office; their places were taken by Soviet nominees who were often semi-literate and sometimes actually illiterate. Finally, the universal undernourishment stimulated everywhere a mood of subconscious sabotage. A diet of substitute tea, black bread with many dubious ingredients, bad fish and frozen potatoes did not cultivate an ardent will to work on the part of the average Soviet employee or clerk.

The characteristic feature of Soviet industrial administration might be described as paralyzing bureaucracy, alleviated to some extent by the almost universal practise of bribery. An official who worked in the Soviet Chief Timber Committee in 1919 and 1920 gives the following picture of the corruption which prevailed here: [17]

> "In the preparation and transportation of timber and wood material, where private initiative was permitted, although in distorted and predatory form, through the letting of contracts, bribes were taken for the signing of contracts, for the allotment of timber tracts, for the granting of advances, for the giving out of provisions and tools, for the acceptance of the timber, for false documents in connection with the measurement of the wood and the statement regarding the distance over which it was transported. . . . Not only private persons but organizations give bribes. The Food Commissariat does not give the Chief Timber Committee food, the Leather Trust does not give it leather until the necessary people have been 'squared'; in its turn the Chief Timber Committee does not distribute its products among other organizations without bribes."

Despite the theoretically complete nationalization of industry the "Glavki," or heads of the various industries, usually had only the vaguest idea of the condition of the plants which were nominally under their control. Early in 1920 the Chief Timber Committee received an urgent governmental request for a report on the number of factories and sawmills, the number of workers and employees, the financial expenditures and other data regarding the Russian timber industry. The report was to be presented within two days; and everyone who coöperated in its preparation was to receive a tempting bonus in the form of two pounds of sugar and a quarter of a pound of tea. When the employees of the Main Timber Committee set about preparing the report they discovered that only five out of some two thousand undertakings in the timber industry had turned in somewhat fragmentary reports on their activity. However, two pounds of sugar represented a strong inducement in those days; and a highly imaginary report was prepared by guessing roughly at the number of plants and the number of machines in operation and multiplying the number of machines by twenty-five in order to arrive at the number of workers.[18] One suspects that not a few of the statistics of that troubled period were arrived at by similar methods.

In reading the dreary chronicles of life under war communism even in the Soviet newspapers (putting aside the reminiscences of émigrés and anti-Soviet observers) one is sometimes led to wonder: How could such a system survive under the pressure of civil war and blockade? Why did it not simply topple over from its own inherent elements of futility and decay? The Cheka supplies part of the answer to these questions; the devoted fanaticism of the sincere Communists is another explanation. Moreover, one must always bear in mind that conditions on the White side of the front were only a little better as regards food supply and were even more provocative of discontent among the masses, because of the open and uncontrolled speculation and the much sharper visible contrasts of wealth and poverty. Bribetaking and speculation flourished even more under Denikin and Kolchak than under the Soviets, because the Cheka sometimes shot and often imprisoned the more flagrant offenders, while the Whites made no serious effort to stop the wild speculation that was so characteristic of their regimes. In White, as in Red, Russia the minority of honest state employees who tried to live on their salaries almost literally starved; bribetaking and speculation were the sole means of eking out a passable existence. White Russia also had its terror, its all-pervading espionage, its frequent executions, its crowded prisons. The chief difference was in the types of people whom one would have found in the prisons of Moscow and Petrograd, on one side, and of Omsk and Rostov, on the other. The Cheka directed its raids mainly against the former wealthy and middle classes. The White police rounded up more workers and people of the poorer classes.

An important psychological key to understanding of the grip which the Soviet regime had on the masses and of its ability to hold out against armed attack from without and economic breakdown from within was the bitter hatred and envy which the poor, illiterate or semi-literate majority of the Russian people felt for the well-to-do educated minority. This feeling was blind and elemental and had little to do with individual justice. It might and often did direct itself just as strongly against a radical lawyer or publicist who had always been an enemy of the autocracy as against a landlord who was notorious for squeezing his peasant laborers and tenants or an employer who had been hardfisted in dealing with his workers. It was as undiscriminating as the *jacqueries* of Pugachev and Stenka

Razin. But there it was, an enormous and apparently inexhaustible reserve of class hatred, on which the Bolsheviki could always draw with conspicuous success.

Macaulay once observed that the English Puritans objected to bearbaiting not because it gave pain to the bear, but because it gave pleasure to the spectators. With a psychology that was not altogether dissimilar the Bolsheviki during the years of war communism based their popular appeal not on the improvements which they had brought about in the lot of the poor, but on the misery, humiliation, social annihilation which they brought to the pre-War well-to-do classes. A typical expression of the Communist spirit of fierce delight in the thoroughgoing destruction of the old Russian life is to be found in a New Year leading article in *Pravda.*[19]

"Where are the wealthy, the fashionable ladies, the rich restaurants and private mansions, the beautiful entrances, the lying newspapers, all the corrupted 'golden life'? All swept away. You cannot meet on the street a rich *barin* [gentleman] in a fur coat reading the *Russki Vedomosti.*[20] There is no *Russki Vedomosti,* no fur coat for the *barin;* he is living in Ukraina or in the Kuban or is exhausted, emaciated from living on a ration of the third class; he has lost the appearance of a *barin.*"

The article, which was published on January 1, 1919, goes on to predict that within a year capitalism in Germany and France, in England and Italy would be nothing but picturesque ruins. Throughout these bare and hungry years the Russian Communists were buoyed up by an almost Messianic faith in the imminent coming of world revolution, which could miraculously solve all their problems. Lenin, who was often more moderate, less inclined to self-delusion in his judgments than other prominent Communists, declared on July 12, 1919, at a meeting of the Moscow Committee of the Communist Party: [21]

"This is the last difficult summer, the last difficult July. If we hold out through it, and we certainly shall hold out, the victory of the world revolution is assured."

One of Chicherin's first questions to Berkman, who saw him early in 1920, was how soon the revolution might be expected in the United States.[22] If Lenin and Chicherin cherished such exaggerated optimism it is easy to imagine how high were the hopes of the rank-and-file Communist, who was profoundly ignorant of conditions in foreign countries and firmly convinced that Russia had set an example which would be followed in all other countries.

The Revolution was a most prodigious experience not only for Russia, but for each individual among its hundred and fifty million inhabitants. Perhaps a brief imaginative sketch of a few of the people who might have been living in a Moscow apartment house in 1919 and 1920 may convey some suggestion of how the upheaval affected the personal lives and the psychology of people of various classes.

In two rooms of a formerly luxurious large apartment lives old Colonel Ivanov with his wife and a daughter, who has a post in a Soviet institution. Two sons have disappeared; perhaps they have been shot by the Cheka; perhaps they are fighting in the army of Denikin or Kolchak. The colonel's age has saved him from arrest or mobilization in the Red Army. He lives as quietly and inconspicuously as possible. But his sword and his commission and his resplendent uniform are hidden away; if the day ever comes when the Whites make their triumphal entry into Moscow he will be on the Red Square to receive them.

New neighbors of the Colonel are the Morozovs, a workingclass family, who were given a part of the Ivanov apartment when the Moscow Soviet decided to transplant as many workers as possible into the quarters of the bourgeoisie. Morozov is an old textile worker in one of the Moscow mills, not a Communist, but he thinks of putting in an application for membership in the Party. He knows that times are bad, but he remembers the cruel repression of the 1905 uprising, when he was out on the barricades shooting at the police and the Cossacks; and he feels that worse things might happen to him and his fellows in the mill if the "barins" came back in power again. His wife, Lisa, is far from what the Communists would call class-conscious; she still prays before her ikons, curses the Communists and the Jews when she has to stand in line on a freezing day for a small allotment of frozen potatoes. But his son Vasya, in the Red Army, is an ardent Young Communist; he once heard Trotzky deliver one of his fiery speeches and was carried away with enthusiasm for the international workingclass revolution; he got the highest new military decoration, the Order of the Red Banner, for leading his company in a charge against one of Yudenitch's tanks and taking it in hand-to-hand fighting.

On the floor below the Ivanovs and the Morozovs are two Jews, Lev Moiseevitch Dvorkin, of Gomel, and Joe Goldfarb, recently of Brooklyn, New York. They are quite different in views, character and background. Dvorkin is of a trading family. Coming to Moscow after the Revolution, he finds trading difficult, to be sure, but not impossible to a man of the requisite suppleness and cunning. He is one of the main pillars of the Sukharevka, and has never yet been caught in a raid. Officially he is a "responsible worker" in a Soviet economic institution where there are numerous opportunities for quiet pilfering of the state stocks. He holds the profits of his surreptitious transactions not in worthless paper money, but in gold and jewels and foreign currency. He will be a flourishing Nepman some day, if the Cheka doesn't cut his career short.

Joe Goldfarb emigrated to America after the unsuccessful Revolution of 1905 and took his full share of hard knocks in the labor movement. Returning to Russia as soon as the Tsar was overthrown, he joined the Bolshevik Party and worked up to the post of member of the Moscow Committee. He is a fanatic of his cause and looks askance at any comrade who seems to be taking more than the meagre ration which is officially doled out. Mobilized once for the Kolchak front, he did his best, as a political commissar, to raise the morale of a regiment of peasant recruits and to give them a course in the elements of Marxism. Now he is working twelve hours and more a day, trying to bring some order out of the chaos of the city electrical system.

Perhaps the unhappiest man in the whole house, not even excepting Colonel Ivanov, is Professor Michael Dukelsky, formerly of the Voronezh Agricultural Institute, now employed in the Soviet leather industry. Dukelsky's experience is that of a great many pre-War Russian radical intellectuals. Eager for the downfall of the Tsarist regime, harassed and persecuted as a student and professor because of his known anti-monarchist views, he finds in the Revolution, when it actually comes, the greatest disillusionment of his life. Not only have physical conditions changed immeasurably for the worse; but Dukelsky feels that all the things to which he objected most violently in Tsarism, administrative brutality and espionage, utter intolerance of free speech and political opposition, have survived in intensified form. Dukelsky finds his sense of values drastically changed by the Revolution. Before the War he would have instinctively disliked Colonel Ivanov, as an upholder of the autocracy; now he feels only sympathy for the harassed and broken old man. Before the War he was delighted when some of his students joined the workers and held a demonstration with red flags on the First of May, in defiance of the police. Now the organized mass demonstrations on May First and November Seventh fill him with a sense of weary disgust. When he is in a circle of intimate friends he is fond of repeating Chernishevsky's characterization of Russia: "A pitiful nation, a nation of slaves." His indignation passed all bounds when he read in the Soviet newspapers that Lenin had suggested the winning over of "bourgeois specialists" to the Soviet cause by paying them high salaries. Regardless of the possible consequences he wrote an "Open Letter to Lenin" and despatched it to the *Pravda.* Instead of receiving a midnight call from agents of the Cheka, as he expected, he saw his letter printed and discussed. It read in part as follows: [23]

"Having read your report on specialists in *Izvestia* I cannot suppress within me a cry of revolt. Is it possible that you do not understand that not one honest specialist, if he has preserved a shred of selfrespect, can go to work for the creature comforts which you are about to assure him? Is it possible that you are so shut up in your Kremlin isolation that you do not see the life around you and do not know how many of the Russian specialists obtained their knowledge by straining their strength to the utmost, not from the hands of capitalists and not for the purposes of capital, but by a stubborn struggle with the deadly conditions of student and academic life under the former regime? . . . It is difficult to describe the horror of the humiliation and suffering through which these specialists have passed under the Soviet regime. Continuous espionage and empty accusations, searches which give no results, but which are very humiliating, threats of shooting, requisitions, confiscations, interference in the most intimate details of personal life. (The head of the regiment which was stationed in the school building where I taught demanded that I sleep with my wife in one bed.) These are the conditions under which many university specialists had to work until very recently. And still these 'petty bourgeoisie' did not leave their posts and faithfully carried out their moral obligation to preserve, at any sacrifice, culture and knowledge for those who humiliated them. . . . If you want to utilize specialists, learn to respect them as men and do not regard them as livestock which you need for the time being."

The schism between the ruling Communists and the great majority of the members of the professional classes, of which Dukelsky's letter is such a vivid piece of evidence, persisted throughout the period of civil war. The tendency of the more ignorant rank-and-file Communists to lump the entire intelligentsia with the "boorzhui" and to treat them accordingly, despite occasional reproofs from the higher authorities, kept open the wounds. As time passed and as the futility of the White efforts became evident, more and more of the intelligentsia came over to the view that it was necessary to give up any idea of sabotage or non-coöperation and to adapt themselves to Soviet conditions as well as possible. But cases of genuine conversion to the Communist faith among the pre-War intellectuals were not numerous.

The churches were open and were well attended during the revolutionary years. The Communists, of course, were avowed dogmatic atheists and those workers, soldiers and sailors who were under their influence, generally became hostile or indifferent to religious faith. But many individuals of the former wealthy and middle classes who had suffered greatly as a result of the Revolution were drawn closer to the traditional Orthodox faith; and there were considerable numbers of the simple people who were scarcely touched by the revolutionary agitation and who continued to go to church as before.

The Cheka was merciless with ecclesiastics who were suspected of fomenting counterrevolution. The Patriarch Tikhon, interviewed by the enterprising Mrs. Marguerite Harrison while he was under house arrest in 1920, declared that, so far as he was able to compile a list, which was difficult because of poor facilities for communication, three hundred and twenty-two bishops and priests had been executed since the beginning of the Revolution.[24] But the mere going to church was too common to be particularly dangerous. It was the safest form of passive protest against the Soviet regime.

That the relations between the extremist revolutionary Government and the Orthodox Church, which was so intimately bound up by historical associations with the autocracy, should have been chronically strained and hostile was quite inevitable. At the time when the Bolshevik Revolution took place a *Sobor,* or Orthodox Church Council, was in session at Moscow. The *Sobor* decided to revive the office of Patriarch of the Church, which had been abolished by that masterful autocrat, Peter the Great. This decision was in some measure a reaction to the Revolution. It was felt that the people might ultimately rally around a strong Church leader when all secular authority seemed to be crumbling away. The choice of the Patriarch was in the nature of a surprise. The names of the three candidates who had received the highest number of votes, the Metropolitan of Kharkov, Antony Khrapovitzky, an outstanding conservative clerical leader, the Archbishop Arsenius of Novgorod and the Moscow Metropolitan, Tikhon, were placed in wax rolls of equal size and placed in an urn before the ikon of the Virgin of Vladimir; Tikhon's name was drawn, although he had been third in the number of votes which he received.[25] The new

Patriarch was a man of rather mild and passive character, not especially well fitted for the rôle of a militant leader, such as the conservatives of the *Sobor* wished to see at the head of the Church.

From the very beginning Soviet legislation had run decidedly counter to the wishes of the predominantly conservative ecclesiastical leaders of the Orthodox Church. The laws which abolished private property in land and buildings destroyed a large part of the wealth of the Church. On December 24 all educational institutions, including even theological seminaries, were taken away from the Church and handed over to the Commissariat for Education. A decree of December 31 recognized as valid only civil marriages.

The heaviest blow of all fell on the Church with the promulgation, on February 5, of a decree on the separation of Church and State. This decree not only eliminated any form of connection between Church and State, but forbade all religious organizations to own property or to exercise the rights of a juridical person and declared all the possessions of religious societies to be people's property. It forbade the teaching of religion in any schools.[26]

The *Sobor* promptly characterized this decree as "a hostile attack on the life of the Orthodox Church and an act of open persecution" and issued a strongly worded appeal, which read in part as follows: [27]

> "Even the Tartars had more reverence for our holy faith than our present lawgivers. Up to this time Russia was called holy, but now they want to make it pagan. Who has ever heard that Church affairs should be decided by atheists who are not even Russians or Orthodox? . . . Rally, Orthodox people, around your churches and pastors; unite yourselves, men and women, old and young, and form associations for the defense of our inherited sanctuaries. . . . Guard and defend God's churches, handed down through many centuries, the most beautiful ornaments of the Russian land. . . . It is better to shed one's blood, to become worthy of the martyr's crown than to permit the Orthodox faith to be insulted by its enemies."

Tikhon still earlier had anathematized the Bolsheviki, referring to the murder of Shingarev and Kokoshkin and, in vaguer terms, to other excesses of the first months of the Revolution and pronouncing his anathema in the following terms: [28]

> "Come to your senses, ye madmen, and stop your bloody actions. For what you are doing is not only a cruel deed; it is in truth a Satanic act, for which you shall suffer the fire of hell in the life to come, beyond the grave, and the terrible curses of posterity in this present, earthly life.

"By the authority given us by God we forbid you to present yourselves for the sacraments of Christ and anathematize you, if you still bear the name of Christians."

There were no immediate reprisals either against Tikhon or against the *Sobor* on account of their fierce denunciations of the Soviet Government and its policies. Somewhat later the Patriarch protested against the conclusion of the Peace of Brest-Litovsk, again with impunity. But the new laws regarding the nationalization of Church property and the separation of Church and State were carried out inflexibly. Here and there clashes with bloodshed occurred in the provinces. Thirteen people were killed when Red troops fired on an ecclesiastical procession in Tula. A commissar who tried to take over a monastery near Voronezh was murdered. But there was no sweeping large-scale rebellion against the anticlerical measures of the Soviet regime. These measures gradually went more and more into practical effect. On August 24, 1918, the Commissariat for Justice issued explanatory instructions in regard to the enforcement of the decree of separation of Church and State, some points of which had been rather unclear in the original phrasing.

Under these instructions churches and ritual objects were to be handed over to groups of believers (the minimum number necessary for the formation of such a group was twenty) which were responsible for maintenance and upkeep, for the payment of taxes and for seeing to it that the edifices were not used for other purposes than those of worship. Religious processions and public ceremonies were permitted only with the special approval of the authorities. No religious instruction was permitted in state, public or private educational institutions. There was a suggestion that the buildings of former theological seminaries might be leased to groups of theological students; but this was not carried out; and two of the chief handicaps of the Church in its struggle against the aggressively anti-religious policies of the Soviet Government were that it was deprived of means of training new recruits for the priesthood and was unable, as a result of the censorship and of inability to acquire paper, to publish religious literature as an offset to the anti-religious literature which was issued in large quantities by the state publishing-houses.

When an inventory of property was being taken in the monastery of St. Alexander Svirsky, in Olonetz Province, on October 22, 1918, it was discovered that the vessel which was supposed to contain the miraculously preserved remains of the saint actually contained a wax doll. This inspired a widespread movement on the part of the Soviet authorities to open and investigate all such supposedly miraculous relics. The frequent discovery of all sorts of undignified substitutes for the imaginary miraculously preserved bones of saints and martyrs exerted a considerable effect on the ignorant and superstitious masses and was a successful form of anti-religious propaganda.

A number of churches were closed or used for other purposes, often in connection with the needs of the front. Not wishing to aggravate the situation by giving the believers a sense of persecution, the Soviet Commissariat for the Interior issued instructions to the effect that churches should not be closed without the approval of the majority of their congregations and should not be used for non-religious purposes if other buildings were available.[29]

There was a pretty clean sweep of the monasteries and nunneries which had been such a prominent and characteristic feature of Russian religious life. In some cases monks and nuns were permitted to retain part of the monastery land and to cultivate it as an agricultural commune. Such communes were closely watched and broken up at the first suspicion of secretly retaining the old form of religious organization. In 1920 the new uses of the monasteries were officially listed as follows: 349 hospitals and first-aid stations, 287 Soviet institutions, 188 military barracks, 168 social welfare establishments, 197 schools, 48 sanatoria, 14 prisons, 2 maternity homes.[30]

The course of events during and after the Revolution would seem to suggest that the devotion of the masses to the Orthodox Church was considerably exaggerated in pre-War years by some Russian and foreign observers. That the Soviet Government not infrequently employed methods of brutal persecution, including wholesale arrests and banishments and even executions of bishops and priests, in its effort to exterminate religion, which it regarded as "opium for the people," is undeniable. But the efforts of the Whites to impart a kind of religious fervor to their cause by arousing the fanaticism of the masses against the unconcealedly atheistic Soviet regime met scanty success. Denikin admits [31] that "the preachings of the Church showed little influence on the masses; the sowers were unskillful or the soil was too thickly overgrown with weeds."

During the years of revolution and civil war and during the subsequent period of Soviet domination the Russian Orthodox Church paid dearly for the stultification which had been its fate during centuries when it was little more than an agency of the Tsarist state. In its drive against religion, as in many other activities, the Soviet Government was favored by specific Russian conditions. It would have been faced with more difficult problems if it had confronted in Russia as the prevalent faith either Roman Catholicism or Protestantism.

As one surveys the broad panorama of Russian life during the period of social upheaval and civil strife three circumstances stand out with special vividness. First, is the probably unparallelled physical suffering of all classes of the population, caused partly by the unloosing of the fiercest passions, partly by the merciless ravages of cold, hunger and epidemic disease. Second, is the prodigious uprooting of innumerable human existences. Never before in history, perhaps, did so many people suddenly feel conscious of having what they regarded as the solid ground suddenly crumble and disappear from beneath their feet. The peasants were less affected than the city people in their daily life. Yet they also must have often felt that the world had gone completely topsy turvy. For the first time they were given the idea that the Government regarded wealth as a crime and poverty as a virtue. Instead of the scanty savings of pre-War rubles, which had extensive purchasing power, they found themselves in the possession of enormous sums of paper money, which they were mostly too illiterate to count, but which bought them little or nothing. They saw a new type of ruler; the city worker who was sent out to govern a county might be good or bad as an administrator; but he was certainly different in many of his habits and background from the pre-War Marshal of the Nobility.[32]

Finally, the Russian Revolution was one of the greatest explosions of hatred, or rather hatreds, old and new, organized and instinctive, some of them causes, some of them results of the Revolution, ever witnessed in human history. There was hatred of man against man, of class against class, of race against race.

First of all there was the overwhelming hatred of the majority of the Russian people, who formerly lived in poverty, ignorance and filth, for anyone who possessed property, education or breeding. It was by exploiting and fanning this sentiment that the Communists could hold a certain part of the poorer classes even when material conditions under their rule were most desperate. The peasant hated the city, which, as he felt, robbed him of his products and gave him nothing in return. The halfstarved town worker, if his sympathies were with the Communists, hated the "kulak," the well-to-do peasant who was holding back his bread. The non-politically minded worker hated the armed guards who were apt to take away the bread which he tried to bring from the village.

The ruined and miserable "bourgeoisie" cherished bitter hatred for the masses and more especially for Communists and Jews. The traditional Russian anti-Semitism flared up in this age of famine and hatred in ferocious pogroms in many places where the Soviet regime was overthrown and in continual bitter gibes in regions where the Soviets were still in power.[33] Traditional racial feuds in the Caucasus and in Central Asia found expression in outbursts of pillage and murder.

Amid all this welter of wild passion the Communist leaders, sustained by fanatical faith in the ultimate victory of their cause, not only in Russia, but in the whole world, moved steadily and remorselessly toward their goals. Amid all the chaos of those wild years a discerning eye could see the features of the new dictatorship that was establishing itself in the place of the old, could piece out the dim outlines of new ruling classes, new economic forms, new ways of life.

NOTES

[1] *Cf.* A. Ransome, "Russia in 1919," p. 42.

[2] *Cf.* "The Bolshevik Myth," p. 57.

[3] *Cf. Pravda* for November 26, 1919.

[4] Ransome, *op. cit.*, p. 102.

[5] *Cf.* the issue for March 14, 1920.

[6] The Bashkirs are a primitive Asiatic people who live in the territory around Ufa, west of the Ural Mountains.

[7] *Cf.* "The Bolshevik Myth," p. 248.

[8] *Cf.* Marguerite Harrison, "Marooned in Moscow," pp. 151ff., for a lively and detailed description of the Sukharevka.

[9] Ransome, *op. cit.*, pp. 89ff.

[10] "Two Years of Wanderings," p. 115.

[10a] *Cf. Izvestia* for November 6, 1920.

[11] This incident occurs in I. Babel's series of sketches of the life of Budenny's Cavalry Army, translated into English under the title, "Red Cavalry."

[12] "Russia in 1919," p. 19.

[13] A. Ransome, "The Crisis in Russia," p. 73.

[14] *Cf.* "The Bolshevik Myth," pp. 52, 134, 292.

[15] A vivid and apparently fair account of Soviet prison life is to be found in Mrs. Harrison's "Marooned in Moscow." Mrs. Harrison writes with the benefit of extensive personal experience, as she spent many months in prisons in Moscow in 1920 and 1921, being suspected of espionage.

[16] *Cf.* her book, "My Further Disillusionment in Russia," p. 5.

[17] *Cf.* the article by I. Rappoport, "A Year and a Half in a Soviet Glavka," in *Arkhiv Russkoi Revolutsii,* Vol. II, pp. 104, 105.

[18] *Ibid.*, p. 99.

[19] *Cf.* its issue for January 1, 1919.

[20] A pre-War Moscow liberal newspaper.

[21] *Cf. Izvestia* for July 13, 1919.

[22] "The Bolshevik Myth," p. 50.

[23] Dukelsky's letter is a matter of historical record; it was printed in *Pravda* for March 29, 1919. Everything else in the foregoing sketch of the apartment house and its inmates is purely imaginary.

[24] "Marooned in Moscow," p. 132. A considerable number of ecclesiastics were executed later, mainly on charges of stirring up the people to resist the confiscation of the treasures of the Church, which was decreed as a measure of famine relief in 1921.

[25] M. Spinka, "The Church and the Russian Revolution," pp. 89, 90.

[26] Its full text is published in "Collection of Decrees, 1917–1918," p. 9.

[27] Reprinted in A. Vedensky, "Church and State," pp. 192–193.

[28] *Ibid.*, pp. 114–116.

[29] Two dispassionate narratives of the main events in the struggle between the Soviet regime and the Orthodox Church are Spinka's "The Church and the Russian Revolution" and Professor B. V. Titlinov's "The Church in the Time of Revolution." The latter book, to be sure, is somewhat inhibited because of the fact that it was published in the Soviet Union.

[30] *Revolutsia i Tserkov* ("The Revolution and the Church"), No. 9–12 for 1920, pp. 83, 84.

[31] "Sketches of Russian Turmoil," Vol. IV, p. 236.

[32] Baron Budberg, a shrewd commentator on conditions in Siberia under Kolchak, mentions a report that the peasants preferred Reds to Whites on the ground that the former were "the same kind of scoundrels as ourselves." There may well have been some psychological basis for this alleged reason for preference. A peasant might easily become a commissar; he could never become an aristocrat.

[33] The Soviet newspapers for that period often contain appeals and arguments against anti-Semitism, sometimes specifically addressed to workers and Red Army soldiers. The usual arguments put forward are that class, not race, is the dividing line between exploiters and exploited, that the Jews themselves, like all other races, are divided into a bourgeoisie and a proletariat, that the Soviet Government combats wealthy Jews as capitalists, not as Jews and welcomes the participation of working-class Jews in the building up of a socialist order.

CHAPTER XXXVII

THE COMMUNIST PARTY: ORGANIZER OF VICTORY

SHORTLY after the end of the civil war a young Communist writer, Yury Libidinsky, published a short novel, describing an episode of fierce struggle in the Russian provinces, under the title, "The Week." There is growing discontent among the peasants, cleverly fostered by the local Whites and by the people who have lost their property as a result of the Revolution. Finally a revolt breaks out; many of the leading Communists are killed. But in the end the uprising is put down; the Communist Party organization remains intact; new leaders are chosen in the places of those who have fallen; the revolutionary regime goes on.

"The Week" was one of the first Soviet novels of any literary merit and it brings home quite vividly one most important source of Communist strength: the existence of that powerful, impersonal force known as "the Party." Individual Communist leaders might die, like Sverdlov, or be assassinated, like Uritzky and Volodarsky. Whole groups of Communists might be wiped out in revolts of a vengeful population or tracked down, arrested, shot and hanged when the Whites gained control of some piece of territory. Individuals and whole groups might be expelled from the Party for failure to comply with its stern disciplinary requirements or might leave it in disgust and disillusionment. But in the poorer classes, especially in the industrial workers, Lenin and his associates had an inexhaustible reservoir of new recruits for their cause. The losses from battle, from expulsions, from defection could always be made good. The structure of authority and discipline which developed side by side with the numerical growth of the Party creaked badly at times, but never broke down altogether.

In the uprooted Russia of revolution and civil war, when so many of the bases of ordinary life had crumbled away and disappeared, it is difficult to overestimate the psychological strength represented by this tightly organized body of half a million Communists, bound together by common hopes, common ideals, common hates and further cemented by an instinctive feeling that, if they did not hang together, they would, in all probability, hang separately.

The Communist Party possessed a strong and gifted group of leaders. Foremost among them, of course, was Lenin, who almost literally burned up his vast reserve of mental and physical vitality in those years, when no problem was too complicated and no detail too small to claim his personal attention. Lenin's voice was usually the decisive one in the highest Communist councils, whether it was a question of deciding where to strike in the civil war or of prescribing the formulas to which foreign Communist parties must subscribe. Trotzky's rôle as organizer of the Red Army and later as an industrial administrator was also very great. Stout, curly-headed Zinoviev fulfilled a number of important functions as the local "boss" of Petrograd, the original stronghold of the Revolution, and later as head of the newly organized Third International. The ruthless, idealistic fanatic, Dzerzhinsky, was irreplaceable and invaluable as the head of the Cheka. Sverdlov, until his death, was an extraordinarily capable Party organizer. Stalin, little known outside the higher Party ranks at that time, was assigned to several important fronts as a commissar. Leonid Krassin, an unusual type of engineer and successful businessman who had retained many of the radical ideas of his student days, placed at the disposal of the Soviet regime a badly needed element of industrial and commercial experience. Leo Kamenev, who shared with Zinoviev the distinction of being one of Lenin's oldest disciples, occupied the same post in Moscow that Zinoviev filled in Petrograd, and was frequently employed as a plenipotentiary of the Party Central Committee, authorized to communicate its decisions to subordinate bodies. Foreign Commissar Chicherin was a striking figure in the early Bolshevik hierarchy. A descendant of an old aristocratic family[1] which had supplied more than one diplomat to the Tsar's service, he soon acquired an international reputation through his qualities and eccentricities: his enormous erudition and rare gift for foreign languages, his acid sarcasm, his conspicuous inability to organize his department or to delegate minor details to others, with the result that he was always extremely overworked; his habit of working and giving audiences late at night. Rykov and Bukharin were two other important figures in the Bolshevik leading group of that period, the former as a director of the nationalized industries, the latter as a fiery popular orator and a leading theoretician.

But no one of these individuals, not even Lenin, seems to have contributed so much to the issue of the civil war as that collective entity, the Communist Party. Although scarcely one Russian in two hundred was a member of the Party, it was by far the largest organized body of the time. Again and again one feels that the disciplined strength of the Communists supplied the decisive ounce of superior force and willpower that determined the uncertain issue of many a struggle on the front and behind the lines.

Long before he became heir to the power of the Tsars, Lenin had seen a highly organized and disciplined, unified party as the indispensable instrument for the success of the workingclass revolution. Among a number of significant passages in such of his works as "What Is to Be Done" and "One Step Forward, Two Steps Backward" one may quote the following clearcut statement of the idea that organization alone can overcome the handicaps which the proletariat faces in its struggle for power:

> "The proletariat has no weapon in the struggle for power except organization. . . . Constantly pushed down to the depths of complete poverty the proletariat can and will inevitably become an unconquerable force only as a result of this: that its ideological union by means of the principles of Marxism is strengthened by the material union of an organization, holding together millions of toilers in the army of the working class."[2]

An authoritative official definition of the character of the Communist Party and of the functions which it is supposed to perform is contained in a resolution adopted by the Second Congress of the Communist International, which met in Moscow in the summer of 1920. It reads as follows:[3]

> "The Communist Party is part of the working class: its most progressive, most classconscious and therefore most revolutionary part. The Communist Party is created by means of selection of the best, most class-conscious, most self-sacrificing and farsighted workers. The Communist Party has no interests which are different from those of the working class. The Communist Party is distinguished from the whole mass of the workers because it surveys the historical road of the working class as a whole and attempts at all the turningpoints of this road to defend the interests of the working class as a whole, not of separate groups and trades. The Communist Party is the lever of political organization, with the help of which the more progressive part of the working class directs on the right path the whole mass of the proletariat and the semi-proletariat."

Here one has, in the typical phraseology of Russian communism, a statement of the theory on which the Bolshevik Revolution was based, the theory that power should be in the hands not of the whole people, not even of the working class as a whole, but of an *élite*, selected minority, recruited predominantly from the working class and organized in the form of the Communist Party. Whatever one may think of the abstract desirability of this theory, it was successfully put into practise in Russia; and the essential technique of Bolshevism, dictatorship by a single party which tolerates no political opposition or criticism and which constantly carries on intensive propaganda among the masses, has been consciously or unconsciously imitated, with equal success, although with somewhat different social and economic objectives, in Germany and in Italy.

There is an extremely wide discrepancy, in many respects, between Soviet constitutional theory and practise. One finds in the Soviet Constitution no mention of perhaps the most important fact of Russian political life after the Revolution: that the Communist Party held a monopoly of administrative and political power. After the crushing of the uprising of the Left Socialist Revolutionaries in the summer of 1918 only the faintest traces of non-Communist political activity were tolerated. The Mensheviki and Socialist Revolutionaries were sometimes permitted to hold conferences, the participants in which, however, were apt to find themselves in the prisons of the Cheka soon afterwards. For extremely short periods of time early in 1919 Menshevik and Socialist Revolutionary newspapers were tolerated; but these were soon suppressed. The Mensheviki and the Socialist Revolutionaries usually contrived to elect a handful of delegates to Soviet Congresses, where they delivered critical speeches. The Mensheviki also offered some opposition within the trade-unions. But all executive power was firmly retained in the hands of the Communist Party. The Soviets lost any independent character; they became obedient agencies for carrying out the policies which the Party prescribed. The Bolsheviki had captured the Soviets from the Mensheviki and Socialist Revolutionaries under a regime when freedom of speech and press prevailed. By speedily abolishing freedom of speech and press they insured themselves against any adverse new swing of the pendulum away from them.

The Communists established their political control not only over the Soviets, but also over other mass organizations, such as the trade-unions and the coöperatives. The official Party policy in this respect was laid down in the following terms at the Eighth Party Congress, which was held in March, 1919: [4]

"The Communist Party sets as its goal the achievement of decisive influence and complete leadership in all organizations of the workers: in trade-unions, coöperatives, agricultural communes, etc. The Communist Party especially tries to carry out its programme and its complete domination in the state organizations of the present time, the Soviets. . . . The Party attempts to guide the activity of the Soviets, but not to replace them."

The Communist Party naturally changed very greatly in numbers, in character, in psychology as a result of its extraordinary transformation from a small band of hunted revolutionaries into the ruling power in the land. First of all, there was a steady growth in the number of Party members. It was estimated that there were about 80,000 Bolsheviki at the time of the Party Conference in April, 1917. When the Sixth Party Congress was held at the end of July and the beginning of August, 1917, this figure had increased to about 200,000. No reliable count of members seems to have been taken at the Seventh Party Congress, which was hastily called for the purpose of discussing the issues raised by the conclusion of the Peace of Brest-Litovsk. 313,766 members were registered at the time of the Eighth Party Congress, in March, 1919. This figure increased to 611,978 in the spring of 1920 and to 705,245 at the time of the Tenth Party Congress, in March, 1921.

The character of the Party recruits varied from time to time. The Party "old guard," the backbone of the organization, consisted of the members who had joined before 1917. Practically all the higher Party leaders belonged to this category of pre-revolutionary Communists, who had been tested and hardened by persecution. During 1917 there was a big inflow of industrial workers into the Party. After the Soviet regime had been established a difficult moral problem arose in connection with the number of careerists and place-seekers who sought admission to the Party purely for reasons of personal advantage. The Tsarist police had been the best kind of automatic purge for the Party before 1917. In those years no one who thought primarily of his personal comfort and selfish interests was likely to embark on the dangerous and persecuted career of a revolutionary.

The situation altered very considerably when the Communists became the supreme power in the land. So long as the civil war lasted, to be sure, there were risks connected with membership in the Communist Party, especially in regions which were hotbeds of insurrection or which were near the line of the front and likely to pass into the possession of the Whites. But these risks were not sufficient to deter a hoard of seekers after the loaves and fishes of power from seeking and sometimes gaining admission to the Communist ranks. These new recruits, especially when they succeeded in gaining responsible posts in the Soviets, the Chekas, the organs of economic administration, not infrequently disgraced and discredited the Party and the Soviet regime. They seized the best houses for their own use, divided up clothes, furniture and other fruits of requisitions and generally acted like the least reputable Carpetbaggers of American Reconstruction days. The people found a special name for these dubious converts to Communism; they were called "radishes," red outside, but white underneath.

The problems of careerism in the Party ranks and of abuses in office by Communists who were vested with sweeping powers aroused a good deal of discussion at the Eighth Party Congress. Zinoviev frankly said: [5]

> "It is impossible to conceal the fact that in places the word commissar has become a curse, a hated word. The man in the leather jacket [the leather jacket was often a distinguishing mark of a Communist commissar], as they said in Perm, has become hateful among the people."

Zinoviev mentioned concrete facts which illustrated the abuses that often sprang up in places which were far away from Moscow. So in Lodeinopolye County, in Northwestern Russia, some of the local "bourgeoisie" had been summarily killed, as an act of vengeance for the assassination of Karl Liebknecht in Germany. In the Ukrainian town of Elizavetgrad, after the Petlurists had been driven out and a Soviet regime had been established, seventeen speakers in the local Soviet debated for four and a half hours whether or not to "beat the Jews," finally deciding in the negative. At the same Congress a resolution was passed warning commissars at the front to see to it that "unstable elements shouldn't enter the Communist groups of soldiers in a chase after expected rights and privileges." [6] The Congress resolved that "the increase in the numbers of the Party organizations must not in any case be purchased by a deterioration in their quality" and that persons who were not of workingclass or peasant origin should be admitted to the Party with great discrimination. It was also decided to carry out a new general registration of members of the Party and to apply "special measures of control" to those who had joined after the Bolshevik Revolution.

A year later, at the Ninth Party Congress, Lenin spoke of the danger of careerism, in view of the rapid growth of the Party.[7] In the past "Party Weeks," when admission was open to everyone, were declared in moments of crises, as when Denikin was in Orel; now the time of such tests was over and Lenin therefore saw as the immediate problem not so much the expansion of the Party as the working over and development of the members who already belonged to it.

This problem of careerism had its cruder and its subtler sides. If a Communist at the head of some provincial Soviet was an outright and obvious drunkard and grafter, who extorted money from terrorized citizens and carried on debauches with "requisitioned" wines and liquors the case was quite simple; once detected, he was likely to be shot, or at least to be placed in a concentration camp. It was more difficult to deal with the Communist who was not guilty of any outright corruption but whose head had been turned by elevation to high office, who, in a common phrase of the time, "had become torn off from the masses."

Strained relations developed between the so-called *"verkhi"* and *"nizi"* in the Party, between "those at the top" and "those at the bottom," between the men in the Kremlin or in the provincial seats of authority who gave orders and the Party rank-and-file members who were supposed to carry them out. A good deal of attention was devoted to this question at a Party conference in September, 1920.[8] The spirit of strained bitterness, of jealousy of the better living conditions and other privileges of the more highly placed Communists was aggravated by the desperately difficult conditions under which the masses of the Party members, along with all other Soviet citizens, were living. Even a very modest degree of comfort at that time seemed intolerable luxury. The Party Conference of 1920 adopted a number of measures which were calculated to avert the danger that the hatred and envy of the Russian masses for any classes which were better off, their primitive desire for absolute equality, might, in the long run, turn against the new ruling class: the higher Communist bureaucracy. It was decided to hold more frequent meetings where the Party leaders would come into contact with the rank-and-file members; to reduce the material inequality among Communists (although it was recognized that this could not be altogether abolished), to establish

Control Commissions, recruited from old Party members of tested irreproachable character. These Commissions were entrusted with the function of supervising the conduct of individual Communists and calling to account those who brought discredit on the Party by extravagant and excessively loose living and also those who transgressed the strict rules of Party discipline.

This discipline, which was of almost military severity, was a very distinctive and important characteristic of the Communist Party. Whereas other Russian revolutionary parties, even before they were ruthlessly suppressed by the Cheka, tended to divide into groups which disagreed among themselves, the Bolsheviki both before and after the Revolution demanded from their members absolute obedience to the decisions of the Party leadership and absolute unity of action. Lenin saw in this disciplined unity of the Party the explanation of the victory in the civil war. As he said on one occasion: [9]

> "Only because the Party was most strictly disciplined and because the authority of the Party united all departments and institutions and because tens, hundreds, thousands and, in the last account, millions marched as one man when the Central Committee gave the order and only because unprecedented sacrifices were made, only for these reasons the miracle which occurred could occur. Only for these reasons we were in a position to conquer, despite the onset of the imperialists of the Entente and of the whole world."

Ransome, during a visit to Russia in 1920, encountered a characteristic illustration of how this discipline compelled Communists to subordinate their individual beliefs and feelings to the will of the Party leadership.

> "For example," he writes,[10] "I heard Communist Trades Unionists fiercely arguing against certain clauses in the theses on industrial conscription at a Communist Congress at the Kremlin; less than a week afterwards I heard these same men defending precisely these clauses at a Trades Union Congress over the way, they loyally abiding by the collective opinion of their fellow Communists and subject to particularly uncomfortable heckling from people who vociferously reminded them (since the Communist debates had been published) that they were now defending what, a few days before, they had vehemently attacked."

The constitution of the Communist Party was theoretically based on "democratic centralism." In actual practise the centralism was far more evident than the democracy. The basic Party unit was the *yacheika* (the word literally means cell) or local branch, consisting of all the Communists employed in a factory, office or other institution. Between the *yacheika* and the highest directing body of the Party, the Central Committee, was a network of committees, representing towns, counties, provinces, sections and national subdivisions of the country. Under the Communist Party constitution the supreme authority in determining Party programmes and tactics belonged to the annual Party Congress. Between Congresses this authority was vested in the Central Committee, which consisted of nineteen members. Inside this Central Committee were two smaller groups of still greater influence and power. One was the Political Bureau, originally consisting of five members, two of whom were always Lenin and Trotzky. This body was supposed to decide questions which demanded immediate action.[11] In actual practise the authority of the Political Bureau was so great that its decisions were rarely questioned or reversed by the Central Committee. It was the inmost and strongest lever which set in motion the whole Party mechanism. Another group of five members of the Central Committee constituted the Organization Bureau. This body possessed the very important function of selecting Party members for definite tasks. It was one of the first obligations of Party discipline that no Communist could refuse any work which was assigned to him, no matter how difficult, dangerous or personally distasteful it might be.

In theory the various Communist Party committees were elected by corresponding congresses of Party members, the Party Congress electing the Central Committee. This was supposed to represent the democratic side of the system of "democratic centralism." But in practise the initiative almost invariably came from above, rather than from below. Both the past traditions of the Party and the conditions under which it functioned during the civil war tended to make its methods of internal administration authoritarian, rather than democratic. The severe police repression of the Tsar's regime in pre-revolutionary days made any kind of free and open discussion and election impracticable for a revolutionary party. The first condition of safety and success in distributing illegal literature and carrying on surreptitious propaganda was unhesitating obedience to the orders of the Party members who had been chosen to direct this work by the Central Committee of the Party abroad. During the civil war, when the Party was carrying on a life-and-death struggle for its very existence, democratic methods were naturally at a discount. The Party itself was organized on a semi-military basis; its psychology was that of an army, rather than that of a political organization in a parliamentary country.

Still another factor that militated against any genuine democratism in the inner life of the Party was the very wide intellectual gulf between the small group of educated, sometimes very highly cultured leaders at the top and the simple workers, peasants and Red Army soldiers who made up the rank-and-file. Typical of the mentality of this rank-and-file was a soldier whom Ransome heard at a Communist Party Provincial Conference at Yaroslavl, which was discussing the new proposals for compulsory labor in 1920.[12] The substance of the soldier's remarks was that "Comrades Lenin and Trotzky had often before pointed out difficult roads, and that whenever they had been followed they had shown the way to victory, and that therefore, although there was much in the Central Committee's theses that was hard to digest, he was for giving them complete support, confident that, as Comrades Lenin and Trotzky were in favor of them, they were likely to be right this time, as so often heretofore."

The requirements of the Party constitution were often set aside in the stress of the struggle. When a local Party committee, even if it represented quite a large territorial unit, fell out of step with the desires of the Central Committee in Moscow it was apt to be summarily dissolved.[13] Nomination often replaced election as a means of selecting Party secretaries in responsible posts. At the Eighth Party Congress, V. Ossinsky, a well known Communist publicist and theoretician, declared that recently the Central Committee had ceased to function as a collective body. The most important questions of policy were settled by means of informal talks between Lenin and Sverdlov, then President of the Soviet Central Executive Committee, and those individual Communists who were at the head of various branches of Soviet work.[14]

One of the delegates at the Ninth Party Congress, Yurenev, protested against "one of the Central Committee's methods of administration, the method of exile, of sending people away under various pretexts." So the Communist trade-union leader, Shlyapnikov, who had become identified with a dissident movement known as the "Workers' Opposition," had been conveniently sent as a delegate to a labor conference in Norway just on the eve of the Party Congress, where his presence was not desired.[15]

Like many other leaders of new causes Lenin combined unquestionable fanatical devotion to his ideals with a very large share of practical political shrewdness, not to say cunning. He realized and exploited from time to time the possibilities of getting rid of opponents within the Party by imposing on them as a Party obligation missions which would take them to remote places. Yet, if one surveys the records of the Party Congresses between 1917 and 1921, during the years of greatest strain and crisis, one is struck by the fact that there was far more freedom of speech within the Party than one could observe in the Party Congresses between 1927 and 1934. Decisions in this earlier period were by no means always taken unanimously. Spokesmen for varying shades of thought within the Party possessed a fair degree of opportunity to state their cases. To criticize Lenin publicly and sharply was far easier than to criticize Stalin during the more recent period of Soviet development. He held his Party together not only by measures of disciplinary repression (although he was quite ready to employ these when they seemed necessary), but by persuasion, adroit political maneuvering and, above all, by the tremendous weight of personal authority which he enjoyed. It speaks highly for his gift of leadership that during this strenuous and critical period, when nerves were constantly on edge and disputes even over minor questions tended to become acrimonious, Lenin, although he differed sharply with almost all his associates in the Central Committee at various times and on various issues, never found it necessary to break politically and to drive out of the Party any man of firstrate ability.

Each of the four Party Congresses which took place between 1918 and 1921 revealed new problems and new differences of opinion, although certain factions which formed within the Party, such as the Workers' Opposition and the Group of Democratic Centralism, put forward similar criticisms and proposals from year to year. At the Seventh Party Congress, in March, 1918, Lenin was faced with a strong opposition on the issue of the signing of the Peace of Brest-Litovsk. His opponents on this issue, the so-called Left Communists, were also against his policy of relative moderation in the economic field, against such measures as the payment of high salaries to "bourgeois" engineers and specialists.

This Left Communist opposition lost its main issue, the Peace of Brest-Litovsk, after the breakdown of Germany and the formal annulment of the Treaty in the autumn of 1918. The most controversial issue at the Eighth Party Congress, in March, 1919, was whether pre-War officers should be used in the Red Army. Lenin and Trotzky were agreed that the widespread utilization of these officers was necessary. A number of former Left Communists, V. Smirnov, Pyatakov, Bubnov and Yaroslavsky, adopted a different viewpoint. Without proposing to exclude pre-War officers altogether, they emphasized the disadvantages of employing them, the possibilities of treachery, the likelihood that peasant soldiers would be alienated if the oldfashioned disciplinary rules, including the compulsory giving of the salute, were reintroduced. They suggested that the political commissars should be given the right to countermand operative orders and that the officers should not be permitted to have orderlies. Smirnov's opposition theses received 37 votes out of 57 in the military section of the Congress; there was still a strong distrust of the old officers among the Communists. But the viewpoint sponsored by Lenin and Trotzky prevailed in the vote taken at the whole Congress.

At this same Congress, Lenin disagreed with Bukharin and Pyatakov as to the proper formulation of the Communist theory on the nationality question. Bukharin proposed to replace the slogan "Selfdetermination of every nation" with the formula "Selfdetermination for the working classes of every nation." "We respect the will of the Polish proletariat, if it does not wish to be in the same state with us; but we do not respect the will of the Polish bourgeoisie." [16]

Lenin replied that it would be definitely incorrect to substitute "Selfdetermination of the workers" for "Selfdetermination of the nations," because any ignoring of nationalist sensibilities would make it easier to arouse prejudice against communism as a foreign, Russian importation.

"The slogan, 'Selfdetermination of the workers,'" declared Lenin, "will not help the situation when the German bourgeoisie and the Social Democrats try to frighten the masses with the idea that Russia wishes to impose its system by means of violence and military force. . . . Surveying all the stages of development in other countries, we must decree nothing from Moscow."

In practise the Bolsheviki paid only lip service to the ideal of national selfdetermination. The Red Army, predominantly recruited from Russia, was employed to Sovietize Ukraina and Georgia, Azerbaidjan and Turkestan, non-Russian parts of the former Tsarist Empire where the masses of the population certainly gave little evidence of regarding the Soviet regime with favor. As we have seen, Lenin forgot his own wise counsels of moderation and respect for the nationalist sensibilities of other countries when there seemed to be a chance of making Poland Soviet with the aid of the Red Army. The Soviet Government, so loud in its denunciation of the imperialism of other countries, had no scruple about using the Red Army in order to set up a puppet government, completely dependent on Moscow, in Outer Mongolia. But from a standpoint of practical politics Lenin was undoubtedly wiser than Bukharin in choosing to retain the old slogan, "Selfdetermination of nations."

The Eighth Party Congress made some conciliatory gestures in the direction of the middleclass peasants. The Party programme adopted at this Congress contains the following passage:

> "The Party aims to separate the middleclass peasantry from the kulaks, to attract it to the side of the working class by an attentive attitude toward its needs, combating its backwardness by means of persuasion, not by methods of repression."

More concretely the Congress decided [17] that measures directed against the kulaks should not touch the middleclass peasants, that no compulsion should be tolerated in inducing the peasants to join communes and collective farms, that arbitrary requisitions should be severely punished and that Soviet and Party representatives in the villages should base their tactics on the assumption that there would be a long period of coöperation with the middleclass peasantry. The Communist leaders realized that the issue of their struggle with the Whites would largely depend on which side was more attractive, or rather, perhaps, less objectionable, to the middleclass peasants who furnished the bulk of the recruits for Red and White armies alike. Commenting on this turn of Party policy a Communist historian writes: [18]

> "The whole Congress was marked by a turn toward the middleclass peasant. This turn was marked by help which was given to individual holdings from the scanty state resources of the time, by the decision not to transform individual into collective farms by violence and by the beginning of a merciless struggle against abuses which were committed against the middleclass peasantry. This was the little that the Party at that time could give to the middleclass peasantry. But that little was sufficient to determine finally the position of the peasantry, to incline its sympathy to the side of the Red Army."

The Ninth Party Congress, which was held at the end of March and the beginning of April, 1920, concentrated its attention mainly on the new schemes for militarization and regimentation of labor which were especially sponsored by Trotzky as affording the sole means of escape from the crisis. These schemes received official Party sanction, despite the clear misgivings of economic administrators, like Rykov, and of some Communists who were engaged in trade-union work.

At the same time sharp differences of opinion about the functions of the trade-unions in the Soviet state, which reached their full development almost a year later, began to manifest themselves. Trotzky wished to take away from the trade-unions the last shreds of independent initiative and to fit them into his projected framework of a vast bureaucratized, militarized, rigidly controlled national economic structure. He made a beginning in this direction by installing on the railroads a political organization called the Glav-Polit-Put, which was accused of supplanting both the Party and the trade-unions. At the other extreme from Trotzky and some of the military Communists who wished to transform very radically the character of the trade-unions and to make them state organizations was a group of Communist trade-unionists, among whom Shlyapnikov and Lutovinov were the most prominent, who wished to increase very much the power of the trade-unions and to transfer to them many, if not all the functions of managing the state industries. This latter tendency crystallized into the programme of the so-called Workers' Opposition, which was one of the most significant and persistent heresies of the latter period of the civil war.

The proposals of the Workers' Opposition reflected a very widespread mood among those industrial workers who considered themselves Communists, but who had not been drawn into the new Soviet bureaucracy. Its leaders were mainly men like Shlyapnikov, Lutovinov, and Medvedev, workers by origin themselves, who had remained closer to the factory workers than those Party members who were swallowed up in high administrative posts in the Soviet institutions, in the Red Army and in the Party organization. The Workers' Opposition demanded greater democracy within the Party, freedom of local Party organizations and of the trade-unions from the domination of the Party Central Committee and its appointed nominees, greater infusion of workers into the higher Soviet posts and stricter limitation on the admission of nonproletarians into the Party. The members of the Workers' Opposition regarded with distrust the granting of authority and privileges to non-Communist specialists in the factories and were jealous of any trend in Soviet policy which seemed to favor the peasants at the expense of the workers.[19]

Along with a number of ex-workers the Workers' Opposition numbered among its leading members Alexandra Kollontai, a woman of aristocratic origin, whose warm, impulsive nature more than once caused her to break the bonds of Party discipline. She published a pamphlet on the aims and programme of the movement; this pamphlet contains the following basic economic thesis, which Lenin seized on to denounce the Workers' Opposition as anarcho-syndicalist in character: [20]

> "The organization of the administration of national economic life belongs to an All-Russian Congress of Producers, united in trade-unions and producers' unions, which elect a central organ, to administer national economic life."

The Workers' Opposition retained a good deal of the original spirit of 1917, when many revolutionary workers certainly thought that they were taking away the factories from the capitalists to operate them directly themselves, through their factory committees or trade-unions, and when the elaborate bureaucratic system of state management of nationalized industry was not generally anticipated. Lenin set his face sternly against what he regarded as the bad syndicalist economics of the Workers' Opposition. But he recognized the moral and political dangers which would threaten the Party if a part of its workingclass members would split off from it; and he endeavored to give the Workers' Opposition some satisfaction in such matters as bringing more workers into responsible posts and combating the tendency of some highly placed Communists to lose all social and personal contact with the workers.

A milder critical tendency within the Party was represented by the Group of Democratic Centralism, the principal spokesmen of which were Ossinsky and Sapronov. This Group did not go as far as the Workers' Opposition in the direction of syndicalism. But it concentrated its fire on bureaucratism and stifling of free criticism within the Party; it wished to see democratism as well as centralism exemplified in practise.

Such were the main trends and the main problems of the Communist Party during the epoch of civil war. Despite its victories on all the internal fronts of the civil war, the Party toward the end of 1920 was faced with a grave crisis, which was part of the general crisis of the social-economic system of war communism. This will be described in a subsequent chapter.

No account of the activity of the Communist Party would be complete without some description of its underground work behind the White lines. Whenever the Soviet regime was temporarily overthrown in some region a number of Communists remained behind for the purpose of stirring up disaffection and revolt as soon as the population became disillusioned with the Whites. In Siberia the Communist Party held an illegal conference and elected a secret Regional Committee in August, 1918, soon after the Soviets were overthrown. This Committee proclaimed as its objectives: [21]

> "Simultaneously with the organized preparation of an armed uprising of the workers and soldiers all over Siberia, disorganization of the enemy by breaking up railroad and telegraph communication, destruction of military supplies, wrecking of trains, blowing up of bridges, sabotage of the railroad workers and miners and, finally, sowing panic in the ranks of the enemy by other means."

After Kolchak had established his dictatorship in Siberia the Communist Regional Committee shifted its headquarters to the Siberian capital, Omsk, and took an active part in the preparation of the unsuccessful Omsk uprising in December. Despite several betrayals and the shooting of a number of the Communist underground workers, the Regional Committee maintained a thread of existence throughout the period of Kolchak's rule. New members stepped into the places of those who were shot; communication was sometimes established with Moscow and with the Red Army; some work was carried out among the peasant partisan detachments which were playing such havoc with Kolchak's rear.

Much the same development occurred in South Russia, when it was occupied by the Whites. The underground experience of the veteran Bolsheviki who had passed through the school of the Tsarist police, spies and prisons was valuable, although it was far more dangerous to be a revolutionary agitator under the Whites than under the old regime. The treatment which was usually meted out to captured Red agents on White territory, as to captured White agents on Soviet territory, was summary execution.

One may accept as fairly typical the account of Bolshevik underground work in Ekaterinoslav under Denikin.[22] The town was evacuated on June 12; a group of five was left behind for underground work. This secret committee organized a printing-press and a Red Cross department, which did what it could to aid arrested

Communists and captured Red Army soldiers. Gradually connections were established with the Communists who remained in the town; these were organized in groups of five, each with a leader who alone maintained direct contact with the committee. The Communists, under instructions from the committee, worked in the trade-unions and the coöperatives and sometimes succeeded in securing the adoption of Communist proposals by the trade-unions. An underground newspaper, *Molot* (The Hammer), was published from time to time; it reported victories of the Red Army and outrages of the Cossacks against the peasants. These underground Communist organizations became much more active when an insurgent peasant movement broke out in the neighborhood or when the line of the front came closer.

In contemporary Soviet newspapers and books one frequently finds the expression: *zakalenni Bolshevik* (a hardened Bolshevik). The whole Party indeed went through a series of hardening processes that placed an indelible stamp on the more devoted of its members. First was the merciless harrying of the Tsarist police. Then came the greater test of the civil war, when isolated groups of Communists were sometimes cut down to the last man and when every Party member must have lived in the grim consciousness that defeat would mean something very close to physical extermination.

Finally, there was the hardening effect of the Party machine which was built up and which constantly drilled into the individual Communist the idea that disobedience to the Party orders was the sole unforgivable sin. The Party *apparat,* or directing bureaucracy, worked with the merciless impersonality of a juggernaut. It cleared out of the ranks with equal pitilessness corrupt careerists and honest idealists who felt stifled in the atmosphere of close control over every spoken and written word which gradually developed within the Party, who felt that the Revolution was not bringing to the workers or to the whole population what they had dreamed of. Bit by bit this system tended to produce a type of rank-and-file Communist who did what he was told, without questioning, who was content to leave all critical thinking to the Central Committee.

The stern discipline of the Russian Communists probably saved them from the fate of their historical predecessors, the French Jacobins, who tore themselves to pieces in internal feuds. Like the early Mohammedans, the Order of Jesuits and the British Puritans of the seventeenth century (with all of whom the Russian Communists have some traits of psychological kinship) the Communists proved that a relatively small disciplined body of human beings, welded together by fanatical faith in an idea, can achieve results that seem out of all proportion to their numerical strength, can overcome obstacles that seem insuperable. In the ordeal by battle which was represented by the Russian civil war the Whites possessed some advantages that were naturally connected with their former privileged social and economic position: advantages of education, of administrative experience, of technical military knowledge. Not the least of the counterbalancing factors which more than offset these advantages was the hard closeknit Party organization which Lenin had foreseen many years ago as an essential condition of the success of a proletarian revolution.

The ardent belief of the Communists, from Lenin down, that they had kindled a revolutionary flame which would soon spread from Russia to other countries was not realized. They underestimated the significance of certain specifically Russian conditions, political and economic, social and psychological, which favored their success but which were not paralleled either in the more highly industrialized countries of Europe or in the more primitive peasant lands of Asia. But their method of government, the establishment of the absolute dictatorship of a single Party, responsive and submissive to the orders of its supreme leadership, had already been taken over, for other social and economic purposes and goals, by two large European countries, Germany and Italy, and has definitely influenced the development both of China and of Turkey. While many of the economic and social institutions of the Soviet regime have remained restricted to Russia, its political technique has spread far beyond Russia's borders and seems bound to exert a powerful influence on world development during the present century.

NOTES

[1] Chicherin took offense at what he regarded as Lord Curzon's brusque personal attitude toward him at the Lausanne Conference in 1923 and remarked to a friendly journalist: "I think my family is at least as old as Curzon's."

[2] Cited by E. Tamarkin and S. Posse, "Lenin's Teaching About the Party," p. 48. The passage is taken from Lenin's pamphlet, "One Step Forward, Two Steps Backward," which appeared in 1904.

[3] *Ibid.*, p. 144.

[4] "The All-Union Communist Party in the Resolutions of Its Congresses and Conferences (1898–1926)," p. 244.

[5] "The Eighth Congress of the Russian Communist Party: Stenographic Report," pp. 188ff.

[6] "The All-Union Communist Party in the Resolutions of Its Congresses and Conferences (1898–1926)," p. 237.

[7] "The Ninth Congress of the Russian Communist Party: Stenographic Report," pp. 362ff.

[8] "History of the All-Union Communist Party (Bolsheviki)" (under the editorship of E. Yaroslavsky), Vol. IV, p. 430.

[9] V. Lenin, "Collected Works," Vol. XVII, p. 64.

[10] A. Ransome, "The Crisis in Russia," pp. 63, 64.

[11] "The All-Union Communist Party in the Resolutions of Its Congresses and Conferences," p. 242.

[12] Ransome, *op. cit.*, p. 78.

[13] In the spring of 1919 the Party Central Committee dissolved an elected Central Committee of the Communist Party of Ukraina, which was out of line with the policies of the Moscow central organization and appointed a new Central Committee for Ukraina. *Cf.* M. Ravitch-Cherkassky, "History of the Communist Party of Ukraina," pp. 156, 157.

[14] "The Eighth Congress of the Russian Communist Party: Stenographic Report," pp. 141ff.

[15] "The Ninth Congress of the Russian Communist Party: Stenographic Report," pp. 38–40.

[16] "The Eighth Congress of the Russian Communist Party: Stenographic Report," pp. 40ff.

[17] "The All-Union Communist Party in the Resolutions of Its Congresses and Conferences (1898–1926)," p. 245.

[18] N. N. Popov, "Sketch of the History of the All-Union Communist Party," p. 277.

[19] At the Fifth Ukrainian Party Conference a member of the Workers' Opposition named Antonov accused the Party leadership of selling out the workers for the benefit of the peasants. Certainly Communist policy toward the peasants in the years of civil war could scarcely be regarded as unduly favorable. But the hungry workers were jealous of even the slightest gesture of favor toward the village, just as they envied the better rations enjoyed by the higher Party officials and by the "bourgeois specialists." *Cf.* "The Workers' Opposition: Material and Documents, 1920–1926," pp. 88, 89.

[20] A. Kollontai, "The Workers' Opposition," p. 25.

[21] *Cf.* the article by Gerasim Shpilev, "Party Work in Siberia Under Kolchak," in *Preletarskaya Revolutsia,* No. 72, p. 72.

[22] *Cf.* the article by Konovetz, "1919 in Ekaterinoslav and Alexandrovsk," in *Letopis Revolutsii,* No. 4, for 1925.

CHAPTER XXXVIII

THE DRIVE FOR WORLD REVOLUTION

THE dream of a world, or at least of a European, Revolution was the bright mirage that helped to sustain the morale of the Communists in the most difficult times of struggle with the Whites and with those still more formidable enemies, cold, hunger, general disorganization. How high their hopes rose in this connection is evident from some utterances of Gregory Zinoviev, President of the newly formed Third, or Communist, International, in the spring of 1919: [1] "The movement advances at such dizzy speed that it may be said with confidence: Within a year we will already begin to forget that there was a struggle for communism in Europe, because within a year all Europe will be Communist."

In looking through Lenin's collected writings and speeches for 1919 and 1920 one is surprised to find how much time and attention he devoted to the smallest details of the revolutionary movement in other countries, despite the fact that, as head of the Soviet state, he was continually faced with the gravest and most urgent internal political, economic and military problems. He listened eagerly to Indian nationalist revolutionaries, radical British trade-unionists, German syndicalists and Independent Socialists. He followed closely the fierce arguments over programme and tactics which not infrequently broke out among the newly formed Communist groups outside of Russia. He despatched practical counsels to the Hungarian Communists after they had set up a Soviet Republic. On the basis of his hard, dogmatic theories and of his understanding of conditions in European countries, combined with the experience of the Russian Revolution, he endeavored to work out a general scheme of revolutionary strategy which would make possible the overthrow of capitalism in at least some of the more important European countries.

Lenin believed that the Russian Revolution, in its main essentials, pointed the way to similar upheavals in other countries. Convinced that the World War had shaken the capitalist system so severely that a potentially revolutionary situation had been created in almost all European countries, he laid the greatest stress on the creation everywhere of militant Communist parties, which would be able to guide, organize and direct into revolutionary channels the formless, elemental discontent of the masses. Soviets, organized very much on the Russian model, were to be the instruments of upsetting the established order. Once a "bourgeois" government was overthrown a merciless "dictatorship of the proletariat" must safeguard the new regime against open or passive resistance on the part of the dispossessed classes.

In working out his strategy Lenin was continually pointing out and denouncing two tendencies which threatened the success of the revolutionary cause. "The main enemy," as he said on more than one occasion, "is opportunism."[2] He concentrated his heaviest verbal artillery on moderate Socialists of the type of Ramsay MacDonald in England and the more orthodox Marxian, Karl Kautsky, who were unwilling to subscribe to all the implications of his fundamental dogma: the dictatorship of the proletariat. He saw, not by any means inaccurately, in the moderate interpretation of Marxism which had become so general in the West European parties and, still more, in the trade-unions before the War, the principal obstacle to transforming the very general mood of post-War unrest among the working classes into concrete, violent revolutionary action. Lenin was, therefore, most concerned to stamp out in the new Communist parties any remnants of pre-War faith in parliamentarism, democracy, class coöperation, possibility of a peaceful improvement of the condition of the working class.

At the same time he was quite conscious of the existence of a peril of quite a different character in the shape of pseudo-extremism which he once called "the infantile disease of communism." He regarded as typical manifestations of this pseudo-extremism refusal of Communists to take part in elections and in political life generally or to participate in trade-unions which were under reformist leadership, and also the raising of armed uprisings under circumstances when there was no prospect of victory. For Lenin, although he was certainly one of the greatest fanatics in all history, was no revolutionary romanticist, like Bakunin or like some of the Socialist Revolutionaries of the terrorist type. He was a shrewd political strategist and he had little patience with Communists whose emotional enthusiasm made them shut their eyes to reality. He was never in favor of "putschism,"[3] of throwing the vanguard represented by the Communists into battle when the majority of the workers were not prepared to support it. Hence he argued that Communists must work within the trade-unions, taking every opportunity to expound their views and to denounce the moderate leaders. In the same way they must participate in national and municipal elections, not with any idea of coöperating with the other political parties, but because an election campaign afforded an excellent means of propaganda. He even favored the adhesion of the British Communists to the Labor Party, on the ground that the latter was not an ordinary Social Democratic party, with strict internal discipline, but rather a loose federation of political and industrial organizations, with a predominantly trade-union membership. To work within the Labor Party, therefore, was not unlike working within the trade-unions.[4]

Bolshevik efforts to promote internal unrest and upheaval in other countries began almost from the moment when they seized power in November, 1917. Naturally agitation of this kind was carried on as secretly as possible; but the Soviet Government on December 24, 1917, rather naïvely called attention to it by publishing a decree which appropriated two million rubles "for aid to the left internationalist wing of the labor movement of all countries." A press bureau for international propaganda was organized; according to John Reed, a radical American journalist who was one of the pioneers of the Communist movement in the United States, literature was published in German, Hungarian, Rumanian, Bohemian and Turkish.

"By September, 1918," declares Reed, "the [Soviet] Ministry of Foreign Affairs had on its payroll sixty-eight agents in Austria-Hungary and more than that in Germany, as well as others in France, Switzerland and Italy." [5]

Until December, 1918, when he set out on his secret mission to Berlin, where he worked in the closest contact with the German Communist Party, Karl Radek was head of the foreign propaganda work of the Bolsheviki. A Galician Jew by origin, Radek was a man of considerable erudition, a brilliant controversial polemicist and a thoroughgoing cosmopolitan, who felt equally at home in any European centre. He had always belonged to the left wing of the pre-War Socialist International. Radek tells us [6] that the Communist Party gave modest material support to comrades from France, Austria, Germany and other countries who were in Russia, in many cases as war prisoners, and who were sent abroad "for revolutionary work." Radek warned German, Hungarian, Czech and Yugoslav

Communists with whom he talked in the autumn of 1918, before their departure for work in their respective countries, against a mere copying of Russian models in the first stage of the expected revolution in Austria-Hungary.

The first Soviet Ambassador in Berlin, A. A. Joffe, later boasted that he aided the German Independent Socialists, the largest organized group which was definitely in favor of the overthrow of the Imperial regime. Two Soviet representatives who for a time had been permitted to remain without receiving official recognition, Berzin in Switzerland and Vorovsky in Sweden, were requested to leave by the Swiss and Swedish Governments, Berzin in November, 1918, and Vorovsky in January, 1919. It is difficult to say with certainty, on the basis of the available evidence, whether Berzin and Vorovsky had invited expulsion by engaging in subversive propaganda or whether they were driven out merely because of the general fear and hatred of Bolshevism which were prevalent in government circles at that time.

The Russian Communist leaders regarded the creation of a new International, which would embrace the Communist Parties of all countries, as a most important and indispensable step in the preparation of a general revolution. From the beginning of the War Lenin had bitterly denounced not only those Socialists who supported their national governments, but also those who opposed the World War, but were unwilling to accept his slogan: "Turn the imperialist war into civil war." At the conferences attended by radical Socialists at Zimmerwald and at Kienthal he had organized a group of uncompromising delegates from various countries who shared his view that the pre-War Second International of Socialist Parties had proved itself hopelessly bankrupt in facing the issue represented by the World War and that a new, genuinely revolutionary International must be created.

The Bolshevik Revolution in Russia naturally gave a strong impetus to this movement for the creation of a new International. The All-Russian Soviet Executive Committee on January 4, 1918, passed a resolution to the effect that a delegation, consisting of Bolsheviki and Left Socialist Revolutionaries, should be sent abroad, with a view to preparing "a conference of representatives of the left wing of the International, who stand for the Soviet regime and for the necessity of struggling against the imperialist governments in each of the belligerent countries." Shortly afterwards a conference of representatives of British, American, Swedish, Norwegian, Polish,

Rumanian and Yugoslav parties and groups which sympathized with Lenin's ideas took place in Petrograd. It proposed as conditions for the participation of parties in a future international Socialist conference "agreement of the Parties to carry on a revolutionary struggle against their own Governments for immediate peace and support of the Russian Bolshevik Revolution and the Soviet regime."[7] So from the beginning a strongly Russian stamp was placed on the new organization.

Communication between Soviet Russia and the outside world was extremely difficult; and the formation of the Third International (which assumed the name of Communist International) was delayed until March, 1919, when its first Congress was held in Moscow. Representatives of nineteen Parties and groups were admitted to full participation in the Congress; delegates of fifteen others were given consultative votes. No large organized body, with the exception of the Russian Communist Party, was represented at this Congress; many of the delegates belonged to tiny groups, like the Socialist Labor Party of America, which were scarcely known in their own countries. The main act of the Congress was the adoption of a long set of theses, drawn up by Lenin, upholding the necessity of proletarian dictatorship and denouncing "bourgeois democracy" as a device of the capitalists, designed to mask their class rule over the masses of the population. The international Socialist Conference which had been held in Berne in February, 1919, and which represented an attempt to recreate the pre-War Second International was, of course, denounced and repudiated. Lenin greeted the Congress with the following confident words:[8]

"Let the bourgeoisie rage; let them still kill thousands of workers. The victory will be ours. The victory of the world Communist revolution is assured."

This belief in the spread of Bolshevism beyond Russia's frontiers was less fantastic, at that time, than it might seem to the reader who does not take into account the widespread unrest which prevailed among the masses in Europe after the War. Even in the victorious countries, where material conditions were naturally much better than in Germany or in Austria-Hungary, there was a pronounced swing to the Left in the labor movements. The British Labor Party grew in numbers very considerably and developed a much more definite Socialist philosophy. In France it was decidedly unpopular to say anything critical about the Bolsheviki, even at moderate Socialist meetings. Italy seemed to be quivering on the brink of revolution; many leaders of its powerful Socialist Party, which had maintained an anti-war attitude and had not split into "patriotic" and "pacifist" factions, were outspoken in their expressions of solidarity with the Russian Bolsheviki. There were a number of psychological factors in this post-War extremism: resentment against the system of government which was held responsible for the War, the frequent labor disputes which were inevitable in a period of depreciated currencies and rising prices, the habit of thinking in terms of violence which was a natural accompaniment of the War.

And if this extremism was perceptible in the victorious countries it was naturally much stronger in the nations which had been defeated and which, in addition to all the other causes of unrest, felt the burden of harsh peace treaties, which mutilated them territorially and saddled them with an almost endless prospect of reparation tribute payments. All the serious armed uprisings of the post-War period occurred within the territory of the Central Powers; the highest expression of Italian workingclass radicalism, the seizure of a number of factories by the workers in the autumn of 1920, was virtually bloodless.

Germany was the pivotal force in deciding whether Lenin's great dream of liquidating the World War by means of a World Revolution could be realized. Should Germany, with its highly developed industry and its capacity for organization, undergo a social revolution and cast in its lot with Soviet Russia the effects might well be tremendous. A huge block of Red territory would then, in all probability, stretch from the Rhine to the Pacific, because the stability of the newly created buffer states between Russia and Germany, dubious at best, could scarcely withstand the shock of double pressure from Soviet Russia to the east and Soviet Germany to the west. On the other hand, if the old social and economic order, with minor reforms and modifications, persisted in Germany, there was little prospect that Communist revolutions in the smaller states of Central and Eastern Europe would survive.

Some developments in Germany after the Revolution of November 9 suggested comparisons with Russia in 1917. Workers' and soldiers' councils, German Soviets, came into existence. The prestige and authority of the traditional German ruling classes were shattered by the military defeat. The Government consisted of Socialists, half of them members of the more radical, Independent wing of the Party. There was a strong mood among the workers to come out on the streets and demonstrate with red flags on the slightest provocation. Such developments were well calculated to inspire in the Russian Communists the hope and the belief that it was only a question of months, perhaps of weeks, before the German moderate Social Democrats, Scheidemann and Ebert, went the way of Kerensky.

But there were differences between the Russian and German situations which, in the end, proved considerably more significant than the similarities. There was no peasant insurgent movement of any consequence in Germany; the radicalism of the town workers had no ally on the countryside. The German Social Democrats were considerably more ruthless and realistic than the Russian Mensheviki and Socialist Revolutionaries; they were much readier to use the services of pre-War officers in putting down the outbreaks of their more radical former comrades. Many of the German workers, accustomed to a much higher standard of living than the Russian workers, displayed what the Communists bitterly called a "petty bourgeois" psychology and showed no eagerness to plunge into an orgy of expropriation and destruction.[9]

Moreover, Germany had no organization comparable in revolutionary efficiency and steadfastness with the Russian Communist Party. The German Social Democratic Party was soft as a result of decades of peaceful legal existence. During the War there had been a movement to the Left, which found expression in the formation of the Independent Social Democratic Party; but this organization, in ideas and psychology, would have been closer to the left-wing Mensheviki than to the Bolsheviki in Russia. On the extreme Left in Germany stood the Spartakusbund, whose chief leaders, Karl Liebknecht and Rosa Luxemburg, were in prison during the War. But numerically the Spartakusbund was a very small organization. When Rosa Luxemburg and Karl Liebknecht, released from prison, began to rally their sympathizers around their newspaper, *Die Rote Fahne* (The Red Flag), they could count on only a few dozen active associates in Berlin. There was not even a special Communist group in the Berlin Soviet of Workers' and Soldiers' Deputies. In Hamburg, a large workingclass centre, there were only seventy members of the Spartakusbund.[10] Only toward the end of December the Spartakusbund decided to reorganize itself as the Communist Party of Germany. And in January this young, inexperienced Party was pulled into street fighting and insurrection, against the judgment of one of its ablest leaders, Rosa Luxemburg. The dismissal of a radical Social Democrat, Eichhorn, from the post of Chief of Police in Berlin was the startingpoint of this January outbreak, which lasted for a week, from the 6th to the 13th of January, and ended in the suppression of the insurrection and the killing of the outstanding Communist leaders, Karl Liebknecht and Rosa Luxemburg. A second unsuccessful insurrection occurred in March; it was marked by the death of Leo Yogisches, a Jew from Vilna, who, along with Liebknecht and Rosa Luxemburg, had constituted the leading triumvirate in the Communist Party.

There were a number of sporadic outbursts of rebellion in workingclass centres in various parts of Germany; but these were mostly uncoördinated and the Government troops had little difficulty in crushing them one after another. A Soviet Republic was proclaimed in Munich, the capital of Bavaria, on April 7 and lasted until the end of the month. It never dominated the whole of Bavaria, its power being restricted to the towns of Munich and Augsburg, with some uncertain control of the territory south of the Danube River. This Munich Soviet regime was loosely organized and rather indefinite as to its goals, although the nationalization of the banks and state control of industry were proclaimed. Power shifted between a semi-anarchist pacifist group, in which the student Ernst Toller, who subsequently acquired international reputation as an author, was the most prominent figure, and a more extreme Communist group, headed by Eugene Levine, who was killed after the troops supporting the Social Democratic government which had been ousted by the Soviet forced their way into Munich. A Communist judgment on the basic cause of the failure of the Munich Soviet experiment, which might easily find a wider application to the breakdown of all efforts to bring about Bolshevism in Germany, reads as follows: [11] "The pronounced petty-bourgeois character of the Munich proletariat and the factory committees led to the breakdown of the proletarian regime, causing it to disintegrate from within."

A more serious and longlived Soviet state was established in Hungary. After the military defeat of the Central Powers Hungary had passed under the rule of a radical pacifist regime, headed by Count Karolyi. The hope of the Hungarians that such a change of internal administration would obtain milder peace terms was not fulfilled; the Allied military authorities prescribed a line of demarcation which clearly foreshadowed an intention to lop off from Hungary large slices of territory for the benefit of Rumania, Yugoslavia, and Czecho-Slovakia. There was great unemployment, aggravated by the return of the demobilized soldiers, and general unrest throughout the country.

Karolyi, who seems to have been a Kerensky of a more left-wing cast of thought, finally decided that he was incapable of coping with the situation and felt it would be best for him to step aside and give the extremist parties an opportunity to show what they could do. On March 20, 1919, the Hungarian Social Democratic leaders went to the prison where some of the more prominent Hungarian Communists were confined and invited the latter to participate in the formation of a Soviet Government. An agreement was worked out under which the Social Democrats and Communists were to fuse into the Socialist Party of Hungary. This Party was to assume all power, set up a Soviet form of government and conclude an alliance with Soviet Russia. The Communist Bela Kun was head of the new Government, which was established without any resistance. Not only were the wealthy and middle classes cowed and disorganized, but the idea of an alliance with Russia, which might make possible resistance to the Entente, appealed to the nationalist spirit of the country.

The social and economic policies of the new regime in many respects followed Russian models. All industries which employed more than twenty workers were nationalized on March 27; the banks were nationalized on March 28. The Hungarian Soviet Land Law differed from the Russian; it permitted holders of farms which did not exceed 138 acres to retain possession of their holdings; the alienation of these holdings was forbidden. The big estates were nationalized and turned over for operation to farm laborers' cooperatives. This policy, incidentally, was subsequently recognized by some of the Hungarian Communists as a political mistake; the outright division of the land among the peasants would have enlisted more support. Children's homes were established in the castles and mansions of the rich; workers' families were shifted to the quarters of the rich; there were the familiar Russian requisitions of furniture and clothing. A Red Army was created, with political commissars to watch out for the behavior of the officers.

The news of the establishment of the Hungarian Soviet Republic was announced at the Eighth Congress of the Russian Communist Party and let loose a scene of wildest jubilation. It brought new courage and enthusiasm to the Russian Communists, who felt themselves in a besieged fortress. It seemed that the Messianic dream of world revolution was becoming a reality. The Russian Soviet

Government was naturally eager to give all possible aid to its new ally. Soviet military strategy in Ukraina was immediately shaped with a view to bringing pressure on Rumania, which threatened Hungary from the East.[12] The more enthusiastic Communists dreamed of cutting across Rumania and directly linking up with Hungary, throwing out sparks of revolution wherever possible in the process.

Lenin yielded to no one in his sympathy and enthusiasm for the new Soviet Republic. But his keen eye detected two weaknesses in Bela Kun's regime: its more vulnerable position, in relation to the hostile outside world, and the element of instability represented by the inclusion of Social Democrats in the Government. "The difficulties of the Hungarian Revolution," he said, after the news of the setting up of the Soviet regime had arrived, "are enormous. This country, small by comparison with Russia, can much more easily be throttled by the imperialists."

After the Hungarian Soviet Republic had existed for more than two months Lenin on May 27 sent the Hungarian Communists the following crisp piece of advice as to how to deal with wavering moderates:[13]

> "Be firm. If there are waverings among the Socialists who came over to you yesterday, or among the petty bourgeoisie, in regard to the dictatorship of the proletariat, suppress the waverings mercilessly. Shooting is the proper fate of a coward in war."

The Hungarian Communists, however, could not carry out this stern recommendation in regard to the Social Democratic leaders, because the latter enjoyed the support and confidence of a good many of the workers and also occupied a number of important posts in the administration. The War Commissar, Bem, was a Social Democrat.

The existence of Soviet Hungary was a threat and a challenge to the claim of the Allied statesmen in Paris to be the arbiters of the new Europe. From the beginning the Allied attitude toward Bela Kun's regime was definitely hostile. Hungary was blockaded. But, although there was a fairly large and well-equipped French army in the Balkans, the French Government, warned by the fiasco of intervention in Odessa, did not choose to take the risk of sending its own troops against Red Hungary. The Rumanians and the Czechs, traditional national enemies of the Hungarians, were encouraged to carry on hostilities against the Soviet Republic. The military fortunes of the Hungarian Red Army followed a checkered course. Soon after the establishment of the new regime the Rumanians invaded Hungary from the east and reached a point a little over fifty miles east of Budapest. On the other hand the Hungarian Red Army, animated by a peculiar mixture of nationalist and social revolutionary spirit, won some victories over the Czechs and occupied part of Slovakia.

The position of the Hungarian Soviet regime, however, was undermined from within. The internal difficulties of Russia were reproduced in Hungary on a smaller theatre. Normal exchange between town and countryside completely broke down. The peasants rebelled when there were efforts to take their foodstuffs by force. The workers, especially the railroad workers and metal workers, cooled noticeably in their attitude toward the Soviets when they began to feel the pinch of hunger. Tibor Samueli, head of Bela Kun's Political Police, acquired a reputation for ferocity comparable with that of Latzis, Peters, Boki and some other figures in the Russian Cheka. But shootings and punitive expeditions against the peasants could only delay the inevitable end. The Social Democrats became less and less reliable allies of the Communists and looked longingly to the Allied missions in Budapest, which promised food if the Soviet dictatorship were overthrown. The Social Democratic War Commissar Bem and his Chief of Staff resigned.

The last blow to the crumbling Soviet edifice in Hungary was the launching of an ill judged and worse executed offensive against the Rumanians. The latter repulsed the attack and took the offensive themselves. On July 30 the Rumanians crossed the river Theiss and advanced on Budapest. On August 1 Bela Kun and his Cabinet abdicated in favor of a moderate Socialist Ministry, headed by Julius Peidl, and fled for their lives. Many of the Hungarian Commissars made their way to Russia and settled there as political refugees. Samueli, who was particularly hated because of his cruelties, was shot on the Austrian border. The moderate Socialist Government of Peidl lasted only a few days; Hungary witnessed the working out of the familiar law of historical development under which a violent swing of the pendulum in one direction is apt to be followed by an equally pronounced swing in the other. The conservative dictatorship of Admiral Horthy was installed in Hungary; and a period of White Terror set in as the sequel to the Red Terror of Bela Kun and Samueli. As in Russia, the Hungarian White Terror was markedly anti-Semitic, and for much the same reason:

the very high proportion of Jews among the Hungarian Soviet Commissars.

Ataman Grigoriev, who responded to an order to move against Rumania early in May, 1919, by inciting his Ukrainian peasant soldiers to fall on the Jews and Communists, and General Denikin, who shortly afterwards launched his northward drive for "great, united, undivided Russia," unconsciously sealed the doom of the Red Republic in Hungary. It had only two chances of long survival: a military union with Soviet Russia, and a spread of the revolutionary flame to neighboring countries. Neither chance materialized.[14] Bela Kun, surveying the later phases of his regime in retrospect, writes: [15]

> "The depressed sentiment in the country was intensified by the news that the Red Army was evacuating Ukraina, so that hope of establishing connection between the Hungarian and Russian Red Armies in the nearest future was lost."

Despite the collapse of the Soviet Governments in Hungary and Bavaria, the Second Congress of the Communist International, which held its sessions in Moscow from July 21 until August 6, 1920, after a preliminary meeting in Petrograd on July 19, was filled with a spirit of exalted and, as events proved, greatly exaggerated revolutionary optimism. The spirit of the Congress is reflected in the following excerpt from one of its resolutions: [16]

> "The world proletariat is on the eve of decisive battles. The epoch in which we live is the epoch of direct civil war. The decisive hour approaches. In almost all the countries in which there is a significant labor movement the working class is on the eve of a series of embittered struggles, weapons in hand."

There were several reasons for this mood. The military situation in the Soviet Union had improved. The Congress was held just at the time when the Red Army was pushing victoriously into Poland. The appearance of the Red Army in the Caucasus and of the Red Fleet on the Caspian Sea opened up prospects of revolutionary contact with the countries of the Near and Middle East, where there was much inflammable material at that time. Communism seemed to be gaining ground in some of the most important labor parties of the Continent. The Italian Socialists were outspoken sympathizers with Moscow. There was a strong trend in favor of affiliation with the Communist International in the German Independent Social Democratic Party and in the French Socialist Party. Even in Great

Britain, traditional stronghold of compromise and moderation, the Independent Labor Party was seriously considering the advisability of joining the Communist International. The Communist leaders in Moscow did not realize that, side by side with this growth of organized Communist strength, there had been a perceptible decline in the spontaneous ferment of the months immediately after the War, in the willingness of the majority of the workers to come out on the streets and fight the troops and police. They did not appraise the process of consolidation of old political, economic and social relations which had already made appreciable progress.

Over two hundred delegates, apostles of world upheaval from thirty-nine countries and five continents, gathered in the ornate throne-room of the Kremlin palace of the Tsars for the deliberations of "the general staff of the world revolution," as the Communist International was sometimes called. It was a motley and varied gathering, in which genuine revolutionists and radical labor leaders rubbed shoulders with cranks, simpletons and charlatans. There was a Babel of European and Asiatic tongues; and the backgrounds of the delegates were as varied as their races and nationalities. Fugitive Hungarian Commissars, high-caste Brahmins, devoted to the ideal of Indian national liberation, British ex-suffragists who had gone socially revolutionary, American Negroes, basking in the consciousness that in Moscow they were the honored representatives of an "oppressed nationality": these were only a few of the varied human types represented at the Congress.

If there was great variety among the individual participants, there was stern uniformity in the system of thought which found expression in the decisions and resolutions of the Congress. Here Lenin's influence was all-powerful. His hand is visible not only in the general construction, but even in the phrasing of the two most important resolutions adopted at the Congress: the twenty-one conditions of admission to the International and the theses on national and colonial questions, which pointed to Asia and, to a lesser extent, to Africa, as new fields of Communist activity.

The twenty-one conditions of admission were framed with a view to making it easier for a camel to pass through the eye of a needle than for a moderate Socialist to enter the ranks of the Communist International. They were also designed to introduce, on an international scale, the centralized discipline which was so characteristic of the Russian Communist Party.[17] So the twelfth condition calls for "iron discipline, with a Party central committee which will be a powerful, authoritative organ, with wide powers"; the thirteenth demands "systematic purges to clear the Party of petty-bourgeois elements"; the sixteenth states that "the Communist International must be much more centralized than the Second International."

With a view to banishing the spectre of "opportunism" the Communist International demanded that "every organization which desires to belong to the Communist International must systematically remove from all responsible posts reformists and centrists,[18] even if it proves necessary to replace experienced people with simple workers." Parties which desired to join the International, but had not radically changed their theoretical position had to choose not less than two thirds of the holders of their most important offices from among those comrades who were in favor of entering the Communist International before the Second Congress was held. A number of reformist Socialists, such as Hilferding and Kautsky in Central Europe, Turati and Modigliani in Italy, MacDonald in England, Hillquit in America and Longuet in France, were singled out by name as debarred from admission to the Communist International.

Some of the twenty-one conditions seemed to be almost deliberately framed with a view to making the legal existence of Communist parties impossible. So the fourth condition calls for "illegal agitation among the troops"; the eighth condition repeats this demand, with special reference to colonial countries. Communists everywhere were required to create an illegal organization, which was to function secretly alongside the legal Party.

Besides thus endeavoring to prescribe for the whole world the Russian receipt for revolutionmaking the Congress laid stress on the necessity of stirring up rebellion in the Eastern colonies and dependencies of the European states. Lenin's theory that imperialism represented the final stage of capitalist development naturally turned his attention to the black- and brown- and yellow-skinned races, to the "seventy percent of the inhabitants of the earth," as he calculated, who were the objects of imperialism, the inhabitants of the countries which were politically and economically dependent on the colonial empire states of the West. If the fortress of capitalism could not be taken by direct frontal attack, by means of workers' uprisings in the European countries, perhaps it could be reduced by a sapping process, by tearing off the colonies which supplied profits and raw materials.

"The imperialist War," Lenin declared at the Second Congress of the Communist International, "drew the dependent peoples into world history. It taught them how to use arms. This is very useful knowledge, and we can thank the bourgeoisie very deeply for this, in the name of all the Russian workers and peasants, and especially in the name of the whole Russian Red Army." [19]

The Congress instructed all Communist Parties to give practical aid to the revolutionary liberating movements in colonial lands. A special obligation was placed on the parties of "imperialist" countries to aid the insurgent movements in the colonies and dependencies of their own country. It was declared necessary "to combat the reactionary, medieval influence of clergy, missionaries and other such elements." [20] Pan-Islamic and Pan-Asiatic movements were denounced as strengthening Turkish and Japanese imperialism. The Congress called for "the closest possible union of the West European Communist proletariat with the revolutionary movement of the peasants in the East."

A delicate point of strategy was the attitude which Communist parties should adopt toward "bourgeois democratic nationalist movements" in colonial countries. It was decided that the Communists should support such movements, in so far as they were genuinely directed against foreign imperialist domination. But the Communists should never fuse their organization with such movements; they should "unconditionally preserve the independence of the proletarian movement, even in its most embryonic form." [21]

This new stress on the potential revolutionary significance of the East had a picturesque aftermath when almost two thousand Easterners, including 235 Turks, 192 Persians, 157 Armenians, 14 Hindus, 8 Chinese, and representatives of almost all the numerous Asiatic nationalities of Soviet Russia gathered in the old Tartar city of Baku, on the Caspian Sea, for the "First Congress of Peoples of the East," which was held during the first week of September, 1920. Three experienced revolutionary agitators, Zinoviev, Radek and Bela Kun, were the general stage-managers of the Congress; and Zinoviev and Radek indulged in vivid flights of rhetoric. After announcing that "a new page in the history of humanity has opened; the sun of communism will shine not only on the proletarians of Europe, but on the working peasantry of the whole world," Zinoviev brought a long speech to a passionate oratorical climax with the following outburst:

"The real revolution will blaze up only when the 800,000,000 people who live in Asia unite with us, when the African continent unites, when we see that hundreds of millions of people are in movement. Now we must kindle a real holy war against the British and French capitalists . . . We must say that the hour has struck when the workers of the whole world are able to arouse tens and hundreds of millions of peasants, to create a Red Army in the East, to arm and organize uprisings in the rear of the British, to poison the existence of every impudent British officer who lords it over Turkey, Persia, India, China."

At this moment the audience, mostly clad in colorful oriental costumes, sprang up. Swords, sabres and revolvers were flourished in the air, while the vow of a *jehad,* or holy war, was pronounced. Radek endeavored to conjure up the spirit of Tamerlane and Genghiz Khan. After saying that the East, under capitalist oppression, created a philosophy of patience he added: [22]

"We appeal, comrades, to the spirit of struggle which once animated the peoples of the East when they marched against Europe under the leadership of their great conquerors. And when the capitalists of Europe say that there is the menace of a new wave of barbarism, a new wave of Huns, we reply: Long live the Red East, which, together with the workers of Europe, will create a new culture under the banner of communism."

The American, John Reed, had harsh words to say about the "imperialism" of his native country in the Philippines, Cuba, Haiti, Santo Domingo, etc., and declared that "American Negroes who are burned alive with impunity, begin to see that their sole hope is in armed resistance to the white bandits." He also painted a vivid, if not particularly accurate, picture of sinister American designs in the Near East, declaring, according to the stenographic report of the Congress:

"American capitalists want to exploit Armenian mineral wealth. America promises to feed Armenia because it fears a revolution in the Near East. But Uncle Sam gives nothing free of charge. Uncle Sam has a sack of hay in one hand and a whip in the other; and whoever believes his promises will pay in blood."

This gathering of oriental revolutionaries on the shores of the Caspian had its romantic and colorful aspects and doubtless caused annoyance and some apprehension to British Political Officers in such explosive regions as the Indian Northwest Frontier Province. But the practical results of the Congress, and of the whole policy of "uniting the workers of the West with the peasants of the East in a struggle against imperialism" were negligible. Even at the

Congress certain discordant notes were audible. A Turkish nationalist expressed opposition to the idea of diverting the nationalist insurgent movement of the Eastern peoples into socially revolutionary channels. A delegate from Russian Central Asia protested vigorously against the cruelties, abuses and oppression which had characterized the first stages of Soviet rule in that part of the world.

The whole idea of arousing hundreds of millions of Asiatics to remember the deeds of Tamerlane and Genghiz Khan and to march under the red banner of the Communist International was nothing but a fantasy of professional revolutionaries. There was no effective means of reaching these largely illiterate masses; there were no Communist parties of any significance in Eastern countries at that time; there was only a handful of individual Asiatic Communists. Moreover, the policy of casting insurrectionary sparks indiscriminately into all Eastern countries had distinct drawbacks, from the standpoint of the interests of Soviet foreign policy. Not only did it threaten to make the breach with Great Britain permanent and irremediable; it was also calculated to alienate the leaders of the non-Communist nationalist movements in such countries as Persia and Turkey.

In the spring of 1920 the Red Volga flotilla, pursuing Denikin's warships on the Caspian, occupied the town of Enzeli, on the northern coast of Persia, and the occupation was extended to include the neighboring province of Ghilan. Communist agitators were rushed over from Baku; and a form of Soviet Government was established in Ghilan and lasted until October, 1921. This act of intervention in Persia was naturally resented by the Persian Government in Teheran and offset the favorable impression which had been created in June, 1919, when the Soviet Government renounced all concessions and debts claims in Persia, together with the preferential status which Russians had enjoyed in Persia before the War. After Georgia had been forcibly Sovietized in 1921 some of the hotheads among the Caucasian Communists were proposing to march on Teheran and set up a Soviet regime there; and it required strenuous representations to Moscow on the part of Theodore Rothstein, first Soviet Ambassador in Persia, to thwart this adventurous scheme.[23] Eventually the Communists very greatly curtailed the policy of indiscriminate fomenting of rebellion in Asiatic countries. The Soviet Government concentrated its attention on a more realistic goal: the resumption of the traditional struggle for influence with

England in the buffer states of the Near and Middle East, Turkey, Persia and Afghanistan.[24]

The hope of promoting revolution in Western Europe also rapidly dimmed. The promulgation of the twenty-one conditions of admission to the Communist International drove a deep wedge into most of the European parties which were inclined to consider affiliating themselves with that organization. The German Independent Social Democrats and the French Socialists decided to affiliate, and promptly created a split within their own ranks, a considerable minority refusing to stomach the stern Moscow discipline. In the case of the Italian Socialist Party, which had originally been very sympathetic with Bolshevism, it was the minority that accepted the conditions and constituted itself as the Communist Party of Italy. The majority, headed by Serrati, refused to comply with Moscow's ultimative demand for the expulsion of the reformist wing of the Party. But this considerable numerical adhesion to the world forces of organized communism was more than counterbalanced by the rapid ebbing of the post-War wave of violent extremism, of readiness for direct militant action among the European masses.

The Third Congress of the Communist International, which met in Moscow in July, 1921, gathered in a decidedly chastened mood. Its psychology was affected both by the failure of the long expected revolutions in European countries and by the recent declaration of the New Economic Policy and the scrapping of the system of war communism in Russia. There was no more confident talk of an impending general outburst of civil war. The Congress recognized in its resolutions that "neither European capitalism nor world capitalism had been swept away," that "the selfconfidence of the bourgeoisie as a class and the external firmness of its state organization has doubtless strengthened" and that "the panic fear of communism, if it has not altogether vanished, is diminished."[25] It was indicated that Communists must resign themselves to a period of slow preparatory work, of effort to win the support of the masses by supporting prosaic everyday demands.

In some respects the Communist drive for world revolution is comparable with the Allied intervention in Soviet Russia. Both efforts ended in complete defeat, so far as their more ambitious objectives were concerned. The Soviet regime survived in Russia. No enduring Soviet regime came into existence anywhere else. But just as Allied intervention had a retarding, defensive value against the very real threat of widespread social upheaval in 1919, so the Communist movements outside of Russia indirectly benefited the Soviet Government. The continual agitation against intervention in Russia in labor circles, backed up from time to time by refusal of workers to load munitions for use against the Red Army had a limiting, paralyzing effect on the plans of ardent interventionists like Foch and Churchill. The menacing gesture of the Baku Congress of Eastern Peoples doubtless had some influence in hastening the decision of the British Government to seek some political and economic *modus vivendi* with the Soviets.

NOTES

[1] *Cf.* "Twenty-five Years of the Russian Communist Party," p. 286.

[2] *Cf.* Lenin, "Collected Works," Vol. XVII, p. 267.

[3] *Putsch* was a German word which came into general use after the War, suggesting an adventurous and unsuccessful stroke for power.

[4] Lenin's viewpoint that the British Communists should remain within the Labor Party prevailed against the objections of some British Communists. Ultimately this issue was settled when the Labor Party refused to tolerate Communists among its members.

[5] *Cf.* Professor E. A. Ross, "The Russian Soviet Republic," p. 96.

[6] *Cf.* his book, "Five Years of the Communist International," p. 179.

[7] "The History of the All-Union Communist Party," Vol. IV, pp. 252, 253.

[8] Lenin, "Collected Works," Vol. XVI, p. 36.

[9] Something of the contrast between Russian and German national psychology is reflected in Lenin's indignation at the suggestion of the German Independent Social Democrat, Crispien, that revolution should only be made, if it did not "too much" worsen the situation of the workers. Lenin regarded Crispien's viewpoint as counterrevolutionary, declaring: "The victory of the workers cannot be achieved without sacrifices, without a temporary worsening of their position." (*Cf.* his "Collected Works," Vol. XVII, p. 294.)

[10] *Cf.* the introduction to Vol. II of K. Radek's "The German Revolution."

[11] *Cf.* Large Soviet Encyclopedia, Vol. IV, pp. 95–99, for a brief description of the Bavarian Soviet regime.

[12] *Cf.* Chapter XXX, pp. 214, 215.

[13] Lenin, "Collected Works," Vol. XVI, p. 229.

[14] An irresponsible young Communist from Hungary named Bettelheim made an opéra-bouffe attempt to "proclaim" a Soviet Republic in Austria on June 15, 1919. *Cf.* Radek, "Five Years of the Communist International," pp. 178ff.

[15] *Cf.* his article on the Hungarian Soviet Republic in the Large Soviet Encyclopedia, Vol. X, p. 80.

[16] Cited by A. Rosenberg, "Geschichte des Bolschevismus," p. 161.

[17] Bela Kun, "The Communist International in Resolutions," pp. 53–58.

[18] "Centrist" was a familiar derogatory Communist term for those Socialists who took up a theoretical position somewhere between Bolshevism and right-wing Socialism.

[19] Lenin, "Collected Works," Vol. XVII, p. 268.

[20] *Cf.* Bela Kun, *op. cit.*, pp. 89–99, for the complete text of the resolutions on the national and colonial question.

[21] This problem of how far it was feasible to coöperate with "bourgeois nationalists" assumed considerable practical importance for the Chinese Communists in 1926 and 1927.

[22] *Cf.* "The First Congress of the Peoples of the East: Stenographic Report," pp. 53–72, for a complete description of Radek's speech.

[23] Interesting details of the Soviet policy in Persia are to be found in Louis Fischer, "The Soviets in World Affairs," Vol. I, pp. 288, 289.

[24] The Soviet Government later became involved in the intricacies of maneuvering for an oriental social revolution in China, when a Chinese Communist Party grew up as the left wing of the Kuomintang, the Chinese nationalist organization, and Michael Borodin, a Russian agent of undefined status and wide powers, played a guiding rôle in the direction of the Chinese revolutionary movement until the breach between the Kuomintang and the Communists in 1927. But this episode lies outside the scope of the present work.

[25] Rosenberg, *op. cit.*, p. 160.

CHAPTER XXXIX

MINOR THEATRES OF REVOLUTION AND CIVIL WAR

THE Russian Revolution and the civil war which followed it had a number of minor theatres, which were so remote from the main centres of action and from the decisive fronts that their influence on the final issue of the struggle was indirect and secondary. The physical and social backgrounds of these minor fronts varied very greatly. In the frozen, marshy forest country of North Russia, around Archangel and Murmansk, the drama of Eastern Russia and Siberia was played out on a smaller stage. A weak Soviet regime was overthrown with the aid of foreign intervention; the anti-Bolshevik groups which came into power failed to attract any large measure of popular support; in the end the intervention was abandoned and the White Government collapsed. In the hot deserts of Central Asia and the picturesque mountains of the Caucasus old racial antipathies mingled in a confusing blend with the new elements of social antagonism which were let loose by the Revolution.

The Allied intervention in North Russia, which ultimately led to the creation of a secondary civil war front in this bleak and remote region, began, curiously enough, in agreement and in coöperation with the Soviets. A small force of British marines landed at Murmansk on March 5 with a view to protecting this northernmost Russian port against possible attacks from Finland, where German influence was then predominant. This landing was secretly welcomed by the Soviet Government, which then regarded Germany as its chief enemy and was on bad terms with White Finland. On March 21 Colonel Raymond Robins, the American Red Cross representative in Moscow, telegraphed as follows to the American Ambassador, David Francis, then resident in Vologda:[1]

"Wire from Murmansk states that English and French are cooperating with the Soviet Government in the protection of port and railroad, under express instructions from Moscow."

The Soviet attitude toward this intervention began to change after the Czecho-Slovak uprising. On June 8 a member of the

Murmansk Soviet said that telegraphic instructions had been received from Lenin to the effect that the Allies should be requested to quit the country.[2] On July 6 the British military authorities signed an agreement with the local Murmansk Soviet, under which the latter agreed to coöperate with the Allies if the latter sent food and money. This agreement was regarded as treasonable in Moscow; the head of the Soviet was declared an outlaw. Shortly after this the motley interventionist force in the Murmansk region, which was under British command, but which included, besides British troops, small detachments of Poles, Serbs, French, Finns and Russians, pushed southward, suppressing the Soviets and disarming the Bolsheviki in Kem and Kandalaksha. Anti-Soviet intervention had become a reality.

Murmansk always represented a minor sector of the northern interventionist front. At the high point of the military advance in this region, in the summer of 1919, the anti-Soviet forces reached the northern end of Lake Onega and threatened Petrozavodsk, the capital of Soviet Karelia. The withdrawal of the British and the abandonment of intervention in the autumn of 1919 put an end to any further aggressive plans on the Karelian front; it became merely a question of how long Murmansk, like its neighbor port, Archangel, could hold out.

The main centre of Allied intervention and the capital of the White Government in North Russia was Archangel, Russia's largest port on the White Sea. In some respects conditions in Archangel and in the surrounding territory were quite favorable for an attempt to overthrow the Soviet regime. As not infrequently happened in remote parts of Russia, the Soviet regime had been established almost mechanically, after the victory of the Bolsheviki in Petrograd and Moscow, without any very great struggle and also without any particular enthusiasm. Communist agitation and organization work was carried on weakly in the town of Archangel and was almost non-existent in the country districts.[3] The peasants gained very little as a result of the Revolution. There were no big landlord estates to be confiscated in this part of Russia; the amount of church and monastery land which could be handed over to the peasants was very limited. On the other hand the Revolution cut off the foreign trade on which this northern region relied for a considerable part of its livelihood. Amid the general disorganization of the country the normal interchange of furs and timber for grain and other food products broke down;[4] and the food situation in Archangel became very difficult. The town swarmed with Allied and Russian officers, the latter often living with assumed names and false passports.

In view of all these circumstances it is not surprising that when an Allied fleet, bringing a force of about six thousand British and Canadians, five thousand Americans and two thousand French, Italians and Serbs, appeared off Mudyug Island, near the Archangel harbor, on August 1, the attempts to organize the defense of the town proved feeble and ineffective. Several of the higher Soviet military and naval commanders were themselves in communication with the Allies; the execution of an order to block up the entrance to the harbor by sinking some icebreakers was systematically sabotaged. A detachment of Caucasian horsemen which had appeared in Archangel rather mysteriously shortly before the arrival of the Allies turned against the Soviet at the decisive moment and hastened the chaotic flight of the Communists and Soviet leaders from the town.

A new Government was quickly formed under the leadership of the veteran revolutionary, Nicholas Chaikovsky. Except Chaikovsky himself, who was a People's Socialist,[5] all the original members of the Government were Socialist Revolutionaries, members of the Constituent Assembly who had been elected from Archangel and other northern provinces. So it was very similar in character to the government of members of the Constituent Assembly which had been formed in Samara in June. It soon revealed the fatal weakness that haunted every government which was constituted by men of democratic convictions during the civil war.

On September 6 a group of irresponsible conspirators, headed by a naval officer named Chaplin, abducted several members of the Government, including the venerable Chaikovsky, and deported them to the nearby Solovetzky Islands. The American Ambassador, Francis, who, along with a number of other diplomats, had transferred his headquarters from Vologda to Archangel shortly before the Allied occupation took place, protested vigorously against Chaplin's highhanded action,[6] which was apparently less distasteful to the commander of the British troops, General Poole. A strike of protest broke out in Archangel; and detachments of peasant sympathizers with the arrested Ministers began to move against the town. The Ministers were soon brought back and restored to office; but the prestige of the Government had suffered a considerable blow. With the passing of time its composition was altered

Painting by P. S. Kala

Intervention in the North in 1918

The presidium of the Congress of Peoples of the East, held in Baku in the summer of 1920, where an effort was made to organize a revolutionary movement among the peoples of the Near and Middle East

by the inclusion of non-Socialists; some of the Socialist Revolutionaries who were most objectionable to the conservative and middleclass part of the population left the Northern Territory. Chaikovsky himself, whose age and temperament did not mark him out as a successful administrator of a region which was engaged in civil war, left Archangel in January, 1919, and devoted himself to anti-Bolshevik political agitation and activity in Paris. Supreme power gradually was concentrated in the hands of General Eugene Miller, who arrived in Archangel about the time of Chaikovsky's departure. Miller on April 30, 1919, acknowledged the supreme authority of Admiral Kolchak; the latter delegated to Miller full powers of military and civilian administration in the Northern Territory. In August, Miller took over operative command of the Russian army in the Territory, which had hitherto been under General Marushevsky. While Miller was a virtual dictator, democratic sentiment found expression in the local *zemstvo,* which occasionally came out with sharp criticisms of some of the harsher measures of the Government against real or suspected Bolsheviki. The *zemstvo,* however, represented a loyal opposition to Miller, inasmuch as it stood for the defense of the Territory against the Reds by all possible means.

Several considerations had dictated the choice of Archangel as a place of intervention. First of all, it was easily accessible by sea. Then large stocks of munitions and war material of all kinds had accumulated there during the World War, and the Allies hoped to salvage these. However, the Bolsheviki succeeded in removing most of the stocks before the intervention took place. Finally, there was the ambitious plan of striking southward and joining forces with the Czecho-Slovaks on the Volga. Against the realization of this plan, however, were strong considerations of space and of the physical condition of the country through which the advance would have to be made. South of Archangel are hundreds of miles of dense forests and treacherous swamps. Between Archangel and Vologda, the first town of any size on the Moscow-Archangel railroad is a distance of over four hundred miles. If an Allied army in Archangel was to be of any practical benefit to the Czechs and the anti-Bolshevik Russians who were fighting at this time a thousand miles away on the Volga it would have to be a force of very considerable size.

In view of the extreme weakness of the Red Army in the summer of 1918 it seems probable that a hundred thousand well equipped

Allied troops would have experienced little difficulty in advancing along the railroad and the river lines, seizing Vologda and Vyatka and perhaps seriously threatening Moscow and Petrograd. But the Allies assigned for service in North Russia fewer than fifteen thousand troops. This limited force could and did pursue only limited objectives. It pushed forward up the Northern Dvina and the other rivers and southward along the Moscow-Archangel railroad line, bringing under the control of the Northern Government a vast but very sparsely populated hinterland. Columns were pushed forward along a few of the main rivers and along the railroad and established themselves in stout blockhouses, with barbed-wire defenses. The southernmost point of the interventionist advance was the town of Shenkursk, about two hundred miles south of Archangel; it was held for a time by American troops, but was retaken by the Reds on February 25, 1919. In the main the Northern Front was inactive; the opposing sides confined themselves to small raids and skirmishes. The interventionist forces were unable to undertake large-scale offensive operations; the Soviet military leaders soon correctly appraised the secondary strategic significance of this military theatre and sent there troops of indifferent quality.

General Poole, the first commander of the expeditionary force, and his successor, General Ironsides, hoped that the North Russian Government could take advantage of the Allied military aid and create an effective Russian army. This hope was not realized. Apart from some of the officers and from some volunteer detachments of peasant partisans from Shenkursk and Kholmogorsk, who cordially disliked the Bolsheviki and fought hard and mercilessly against them (the officers of these detachments were largely themselves local peasants) the morale of the North Russian troops was extremely low; and mutinies of large bodies of troops, accompanied by killing of officers and wholesale desertion to the Reds, were not uncommon. The North Russian Whites had too many old generals in the rear and too few reliable soldiers at the front.

The British General Ironsides was convinced that the Russian soldier represented good fighting material and that the reason for the poor showing of the North Russian troops was to be found in the poor qualities of the officers.[7] With a view to proving his theory he recruited a force, known as the Dyer Regiment, because a Captain Dyer had initiated the enterprise, in which he enrolled recruits indiscriminately, taking even political and criminal prisoners and captured Red Army soldiers, and placed it under British officers. For a time this experiment worked out successfully; but in July, 1919, in the midst of an offensive on the Northern Dvina, the Dyer Regiment rebelled, killing several British and Russian officers. Some of the mutineers were shot down by British troops; others escaped and joined the Reds. About the same time the town of Onega was lost as a result of a rebellion; the peasants were exasperated by the decision of the Northern Government to withdraw from circulation a large quantity of old paper money.

The British officers were disgusted by the repeated proofs of the low morale and fighting capacity of the North Russian troops and welcomed the decision of the British Government to abandon North Russia. General Ironsides expressed himself in strong terms in a conversation with Boris Sokolov, a Socialist Revolutionary who took an active part in the defense of the Northern Territory, about the end of July: [8]

"It will soon be a year since the Allies arrived, and the Russian army, as a fighting unit, doesn't exist. Those few regiments that were formed with our help are simply good for nothing. The officers don't behave correctly and the soldiers are Bolsheviki who raise rebellions. Recently there were mutinies and plots in the Third, First, Sixth and Fifth Regiments, in almost all the existing regiments. The main Russian staff is badly organized and doesn't command the respect of its own troops. The situation is hopeless. . . . These mutinies in the regiments, and especially the sentiment of the population of Archangel and of the villages have convinced me that the majority of the population is in sympathy with the Bolsheviki."

The disillusioned British General may have been guilty of some exaggeration when he expressed the view that the majority of the population was in sympathy with the Bolsheviki. But he was quite correct in regarding the political and military position of the Northern Government as hopelessly weak. So far as public sentiment was concerned the middle classes and the majority of the educated and professional classes regarded the possibility of a Bolshevik victory with fear and aversion, but were not numerous enough to offer any effective resistance. Sokolov, an eyewitness and a keen observer, considers that the dominant sentiment among the peasants, with the exception of the partisans, was passivity. They had little reason to look forward to Bolshevism with enthusiasm, but they hoped it would at least bring peace. As for the workers, according to Sokolov, they lived through the same process that was to be observed among the workers in all the White regions. "At first they greeted the new regime; then their oppositionist sentiment increased, and in the end they desired just one thing: the coming of the Bolsheviki." [9]

This "oppositionist sentiment" of the workers was intensified by the severe repressive measures of the Government; a non-Bolshevik trade-union leader named Bechin received a sentence of fifteen years at hard labor for protesting against the intervention and praising the Soviets in a speech; executions of persons suspected of disaffection were fairly frequent; bleak and desolate places, such as Mudyug Island and the Yokhanga peninsula were crowded with political deportees, who were kept in very bad conditions.

The British urged General Miller to evacuate Archangel with them, taking along all those persons who had hopelessly compromised themselves in the eyes of the Soviet regime. Miller himself had no great confidence in his ability to hold out after the departure of the Allies. He telegraphed to Kolchak on August 4 that he could not hope to prolong the defence of Archangel for more than a month after the departure of the Allies and suggested that it might be advisable to evacuate the Northern Territory.[10]

However, on August 12 Miller announced his decision not to leave the Territory. Kolchak had instructed him to hold out to the end; and there seemed to be a possibility that Denikin and Yudenitch might save White Archangel by winning decisive victories on the Moscow and Petrograd fronts. Miller's officers generally accepted his decision without much enthusiasm.

Although the efforts of the North Russian Government to replace the departing Allies with soldiers of fortune, recruited in other countries, were not successful, the Northern Territory, left to its own resources when the last British ships sailed away on September 27, held out longer than Miller had considered possible. The British, before their departure, coöperated with the Russians in directing a few last blows at the Reds, both on the Archangel and on the Murmansk sectors of the front. Absorbed in the decisive struggles around Orel and Voronezh and on the outskirts of Petrograd, the Bolsheviki made no effort to take immediate advantage of the departure of the Allies by hastening the liquidation of the relatively unimportant Northern Front.

The spirit of the Whites was cheered by a few victories on the front, the most important of which was the recapture of Onega, which occurred simultaneously with the departure of the British. Miller took strong measures against possible explosions of internal discontent. About 1,200 suspected malcontents were banished to remote Yokhanga and the officers in Archangel were ordered to live together in a special, well lighted quarter of the town, and were organized in a special military unit, plentifully supplied with machine-guns, and prepared to suppress any outbreak of revolt.[11]

But all this could only delay the inevitable end. The collapse of Kolchak, Denikin and Yudenitch predetermined the fate of the isolated Northern Territory. The army of some 25,000 which held the enormously long front from Murman to the Northern Urals crumpled up in February as a result partly of new outbursts of internal disaffection, partly of pressure from the Sixth Red Army. General Miller fled on an icebreaker from Archangel on February 19, leaving his army pretty much to its fate. His general order to retreat to Murmansk and make a further stand there was not and could not be carried out, partly because a revolt, followed by the proclamation of the Soviet regime, broke out in Murmansk itself on February 21, partly because the moral condition of the army did not make possible a long retreat in winter over snowy wastes. The peasant soldiers of the White Army mostly dispersed to their homes, sometimes handing their officers over to the Reds, sometimes helping them to escape, depending on whether they regarded the officers as enemies or as friends. The Red Army entered Archangel on February 21; one of the last White detachments surrendered in the Karelian town of Soroka on February 27. The White Northern Front had ceased to exist.

During its existence of more than eighteen months this minor anti-Bolshevik regime in North Russia reflected, as if in a small mirror, all the defects, failings and mistakes which condemned the chief leaders of the White movement, Kolchak and Denikin, to defeat. Making allowance for lesser differences in time and place, one is struck by the amazing fidelity with which the Government in Archangel followed the course which history seemed to have marked out for all the White regimes. Even such little details as the sharp antagonism between front and rear and the reckless, desperate drinking are as characteristic of Archangel as of Omsk, Ekaterinodar and Rostov.

One feature peculiar to the North Russian Government was the predominant rôle which foreign military authorities played up to the time of the withdrawal of the Allied troops. Relations between the British and the Russians of all classes were far from cordial. Even those Russians who knew that their cause could be considered lost if the foreign troops departed sometimes resented the overbearing manner of some of their allies; the military prosecutor Dobrovolsky tells how, after the British had gone, a Captain of the White Army came up to him and said: [12]

"I congratulate you; we are again in Russia; how do you like the Russian town Archangel?"

As for the attitude of the more proletarian part of the Russian population toward the occupation, one may cite the outspoken testimony of General Maynard, who was in command of the British and other interventionist forces in Murmansk and Karelia: [13]

> "I was under the continued necessity of guarding against insurrection and riot within the limits of occupation. There existed still a strong undercurrent of Bolshevism, evidenced by agitation and strikes, and by persistent efforts to create trouble between the Allies and the local population. This culminated at times in demonstrations of active hostility, such as the destruction of railway-bridges and attempts to derail trains. . . .

Referring to Murmansk in March and April, 1919:

> "We lived practically in a state of siege. The more important buildings were surrounded by wire and miniature fortifications and stored with reserves of food and water; windows were loopholed and made bullet-proof by piling firewood logs against them; every officer and man slept with a loaded rifle at his side, with bayonet ready fixed; and individual movement after dark was always fraught with risk."

The struggle in North Russia was a struggle of Russians against Russians. In the picturesque Caucasus, at the other end of European Russia, the zigzag course of social upheaval and civil strife, culminating in ultimate Sovietization, was profoundly modified by the mixed and non-Russian racial character of the majority of the population. Three peoples, the Georgians, the Armenians and the Azerbaidjan Tartars, constituted the majority of the mixed population which dwelt between the southern slope of the main Caucasus range and the frontiers of Turkey and Persia. There were also a number of Russians in the Trans-Caucasus; many of the officials, businessmen and professional men of the Trans-Caucasus were of Russian origin; and here and there, as in the Mugan steppe, in Azerbaidjan, Russian peasants had settled as colonists. Racial frontiers in the Trans-Caucasus were confused and were calculated to arouse quarrels as soon as the question of setting up independent states there arose. The Armenians and Tartars, who were traditional enemies (the pogroms which were carried out against the Armenians in Baku during the 1905 Revolution rivalled the similar anti-Jewish excesses in many towns of Southern and Western Russia), were inextricably intertwined; Tartar enclaves existed in Armenia, while predominantly Armenian districts, such as Karabakh, existed in the midst of Mohammedan Azerbaidjan. Broadly speaking, the Azerbaidjan Tartars inhabited the more level and low-lying eastern part of the Trans-Caucasus, while the Georgians, along with a number of smaller peoples of somewhat different racial stock, dwelt in the more mountainous western part, with a stretch of Black Sea coast. The Armenians lived farther to the south, on a broad table-land which was overlooked by historic Mount Ararat. The oil centre of Baku, on the Caspian Sea, was the largest city in Azerbaidjan and in the whole Trans-Caucasus. With its cosmopolitan population, which included many Russians and Armenians, and its tradition of strikes and underground agitation (Stalin, Ordzhonikidze, Krassin and other prominent Bolsheviki had served a revolutionary apprenticeship there) Baku stood out in striking contrast to its hinterland, where the great mass of the peasant population consisted of devoutly Mohammedan and illiterate Tartars, very much under the influence of khans, beys and other semi-feudal dignitaries and of the mullahs, or Mohammedan priests.

As the authority and prestige of the Provisional Government steadily declined during 1917 nationalist stirrings were more and more evident in the Trans-Caucasus. Power drifted more and more into the hands of the leaders of the nationalist parties which existed in each of the three main territorial subdivisions of the region, Georgia, Armenia and Azerbaidjan; and these parties controlled the destinies of the countries until they were ultimately Sovietized and reunited with Russia.

The dominant party in Georgia was the Mensheviki, who for many years had been closely associated with the Russian Mensheviki. It will be remembered that Georgian Mensheviki, Chkheidze and Tseretelli, played an important part in Russian political life after the downfall of Tsarism. After the Georgian Mensheviki came into power they tended, after the fashion of parties which pass from the position of opposition critics to posts of responsibility, to turn to the Right. Their nationalism became more pronounced; their socialism, in practise, amounted to little more than moderate progressivism, although they continued to employ Marxian phraseology and endeavored to enlist the moral support of moderate Socialists in Western Europe for Georgia's independent national existence. Of the three Trans-Caucasian nationalist parties the Georgian Mensheviki possessed the greatest vitality and the largest measure of popular support; Georgia proved harder than either Azerbaidjan or Armenia for Soviet Russia to conquer and assimilate.

The Dashnak Party in Armenia played the same rôle as the Mensheviki in Georgia. Before the War the Dashnaki existed as a revolutionary group which desired to free Armenia both from Russia and from Turkey. They were loosely affiliated with the Russian Socialist Revolutionaries. Armenia had practically no industrial proletariat; and the Communist movement there was weaker than in Georgia or in Azerbaidjan. But the position of the Dashnaki as rulers of an independent Armenia was difficult from the beginning and ultimately became impossible because Armenia was almost surrounded by hostile and more powerful Mohammedan neighbors, Turkey, Persia and Azerbaidjan. It was almost an instinct of selfpreservation for Armenia to seek union with Russia, whether that Russia was Tsarist or Bolshevik.

The Musavat Party in Azerbaidjan consisted of representatives of the not very numerous Tartar educated and business classes. The Tartar peasants followed its leadership from a sense of racial loyalty.

Russia's political control over the Trans-Caucasus, which had become increasingly shadowy during 1917, ceased altogether after the Bolshevik Revolution. Two rival and contrasted centres of authority grew up in the Trans-Caucasus. The citadel of Bolshevism was Baku, where the Soviet, supported by the presence of a considerable workingclass population and led by a Bolshevik of unusual force of personality, the Armenian, Stepan Shaumyan, who was sometimes called the Lenin of the Caucasus,[14] was assuming more and more of the functions of state authority. On the other hand Tiflis, the capital of Georgia, was the rallying point of the moderate and anti-Bolshevik forces. On November 28 representatives of the nationalist and of the moderate Socialist parties of Trans-Caucasia organized the Trans-Caucasian Commissariat, "in view of the absence of a generally recognized central power and of the ever growing anarchy in the country, which may extend to Trans-Caucasia." [15]

The Menshevik leader, Noah Jordania, a man with a gift for pungent and outspoken expression (he once declared, in explaining why Georgia refused a Bolshevik offer of a military alliance: "We prefer the imperialists of the West to the fanatics of the East"), had said in the summer, when symptoms of disintegration and breakdown of discipline were becoming visible on the Caucasian Front: "If we don't want the rule of the mob, we must have an armed force and carry out a firm policy." [16] And it was attributable to the efforts of Jordania and his associates in the Trans-Caucasian Commissariat that Trans-Caucasia was not swamped by Bolshevism when the Caucasian Army began to return from the Turkish front. The soldiers, who were in the mutinous and socially revolutionary mood which characterized almost all Russian soldiers after the World War, were halted and disarmed with the aid of the national troop units which were formed in all three new Trans-Caucasian states. Sometimes this led to sanguinary clashes, notably at the station Shamkhor, on the Baku-Tiflis railroad line in January, 1918, where a number of returning soldiers were attacked and massacred by Tartar bands.

Although there were serious agrarian disorders in the Elizavetpol region of western Azerbaidjan and in various parts of Georgia, the authority of the new national government was strong enough to repress the more extreme excesses of social upheaval. On the other hand, the Trans-Caucasus witnessed savage outbursts of national hatred. At the end of December, 1917, Tartar bands attacked and destroyed a number of flourishing Russian villages in the northern part of the Mugan steppe; the Russians in other parts of this territory took revenge on any Tartar settlements which were within reach.[17] Tartars and Armenians commenced to cut each other to pieces with dismal regularity.

The Trans-Caucasian Commissariat endeavored to organize a federation of the three main peoples of the territory. A Seym, or Parliament, representing Trans-Caucasia was convened. But the fragile structure of the projected federation crumbled quickly under the impact of racial and religious hatreds. When the Turks, taking advantage of the disappearance of the Russian troops from the Caucasian Front, not only reoccupied the territory which the Russians had conquered during the War, but pushed on into former Russian Armenia, occupying Kars, Ardaghan and other towns, the

Azerbaidjan Tartars openly welcomed their co-religionists, instead of coming to the help of their nominal allies, the Armenians. On May 26 the Seym regretfully announced its own dissolution in the following terms: [18]

"In view of the fact that on the question of war and peace basic differences of opinion were revealed among the peoples which created the Trans-Caucasian independent republic, so that the functioning of a single authoritative Government, authorized to speak for the whole of Trans-Caucasia, became impossible, the Seym records the fact of the dissolution of Trans-Caucasia and surrenders its powers."

Georgia declared itself an independent state on May 26; Azerbaidjan and Armenia did likewise on May 28. Georgia welcomed the arrival of a small German expeditionary force, under General Kress von Kressenstein, seeing in the Germans protectors against the havoc which would accompany a Turkish invasion. A Turkish army under Nuri Pasha struck across hapless Armenia in the summer of 1918 and moved on the tempting rich oil centre of Baku.

That city had meanwhile gone its own way and was living under the sole Soviet regime which existed in Trans-Caucasia. For several months after the Bolshevik Revolution there was no firmly established and generally recognized local authority in Baku. The Soviet exercised considerable power, but the pre-revolutionary city council continued to exist and the confusion was intensified because Armenian and Tartar National Councils possessed a good deal of authority in the eyes of members of these two races. On April 6, 1918, a clash broke out between the Soviet and the Tartars because the former was determined to disarm some Tartar troops which it regarded as counterrevolutionary. After several days of street fighting the Tartars were defeated and driven out of the city. A racial element entered into the struggle, because the Armenians, who had first maintained neutrality, began to fight on the Soviet side when it seemed that the Tartars were being defeated and took this opportunity to settle old scores with the Tartars. The warships of the Caspian Fleet, lying in the harbor of Baku, also took the side of the Soviet and bombarded the Tartar positions with artillery.

The immediate result of this armed conflict was the establishment of the Soviet as the sole organ of authority in Baku. The local banks were nationalized in April; the turn of the oil industry followed in May. This first Communist experiment in a predominantly Asiatic city was attended from the beginning by immense difficulties. The food situation was desperate. The inflow of provisions from the Tartar villages in the neighborhood stopped. Black bread was available only for the army; the ordinary citizens had to get along as well as they could with the nuts and sunflower seeds which were given out on ration cards.[19] Even in normal times Baku depended on bread which was brought from outside Azerbaidjan; and the ordinary mechanism of exchange was now paralyzed.

The Baku Commune attempted to take the offensive and despatched its armed forces in a western direction, along the Baku-Tiflis railroad. It issued an appeal to the peasants to rise up and cast off the yoke of the khans and beys and hoped that energetic military action would extend the sphere of its revolutionary influence and ease the food situation. The campaign failed to justify these hopes. It was unfortunate, from the standpoint of the Communist ideal of internationalism, that most of the troops at the disposal of the Commune were Armenians, whose behavior in captured Tartar villages was far from irreproachable and quickly aroused in the Mohammedan masses the idea that the Soviet was merely a screen for Armenian rule. The fugitive Musavat leaders were busily organizing an army in the vicinity of Elizavetpol. When Nuri Pasha's Turkish troops arrived the balance of military strength was definitely against the Soviet forces; and these began to retreat toward Baku.

Foreseeing what would happen to their co-racialists if the Turks, together with the enraged Tartars, captured Baku, the Dashnak leaders began to urge that the British be called in to save Baku. The British General Dunsterville, with a force of about a thousand men, was in Enzeli, in North Persia. (At this time the British were seriously concerned over the possibility that the Germans and the Turks might not only seize the valuable oil stocks at Baku, but also push on toward India, and were using every means at their disposal to check this threatened penetration of the enemy into the Near and Middle East.) The Bolshevik leaders were strongly opposed to this invitation to "foreign imperialists"; in the stormy debates which raged in the Soviet on the question they displayed telegrams from Sverdlov, Stalin and other representatives of the central Soviet Government, forbidding coöperation with the British. But their hold on the masses had been shaken by the hunger and by the critical situation on the front. The Baku Soviet, in its session of July 25, decided, by a vote of 259 to 236, to invite the British to come to the aid of Baku against the Turkish advance and to create a new government, in which all parties which recognized the authority of the Soviet would be represented. The efforts of Shaumyan and his associates to arouse the masses against this decision failed. The resolutions which were passed at factory meetings usually expressed confidence in the Bolsheviki, but simultaneously called for the invitation of the British. The warships in the Caspian Sea, which, with their guns, represented an important part of the armed forces defending Baku, turned definitely against the Bolsheviki. After resigning their power the Bolshevik Commissars prepared to leave Baku, issuing the following farewell message to the workers of the city: [20]

> "With bitterness in our hearts, with curses on our lips we, who came here to fight and die for the Soviet regime along with the Baku workers, are compelled to quit Baku. But, as we leave this city, the loss of which may have fatal consequences for the whole of Soviet Russia, we do not lose hope that the Baku workers and the sailors of the Caspian Fleet will understand the treachery into which they have been led by the right-wing parties. We hope that workers' and peasants' Russia will again come to Baku. The Baku proletariat will again be connected with Russia."

Baku would indeed be ultimately reabsorbed into the Soviet Union. But the twenty-six Bolshevik Commissars who had governed the first Baku Commune would not live to see this day. After leaving Baku on a ship for Astrakhan they were pursued, brought back and placed in prison by order of the new government in Baku, in which representatives of the Caspian Fleet and of the moderate Socialist parties played a leading part. The arrival of General Dunsterville and his small British force on August 14 delayed, but could not avert the fall of Baku. The numerical superiority of the Turkish forces was too great. On September 13 the British abandoned the city and sailed off to Enzeli; the Turks and Tartars marched in on the next day and carried out a merciless slaughter of the Armenians in the city, with the usual oriental accompaniment of pillage, burning and wholesale outraging of women.[21]

The imprisoned commissars had been released on the very eve of the Turkish occupation. They boarded a vessel and again wanted to escape to Astrakhan. But the crew insisted that there was not enough fuel for this voyage and demanded that they make for a nearer port. The nearer ports were all in the hands of enemies; the British were in Enzeli; a Tsarist officer named Bicherakov was in control of Petrovsk, farther to the north; an anti-Bolshevik government was in possession of Krasnovodsk, on the eastern side of the Caspian Sea. Krasnovodsk was selected as the least dangerous of the possible destinations. As soon as they arrived there they were placed in prison. On September 19 they were sent with a guard on a train bound for Askhabad, the capital of the Trans-Caspian Government. Thence they were supposed, according to the statements of the Trans-Caspian authorities, to be sent to Meshed, the headquarters of the British General Malleson, in North Persia, for further transportation to India and internment there. But on the morning of September 20 they were taken from the train by their guards at a desolate place in the desert, about a hundred and forty miles from Krasnovodsk, and shot down to the last man.[22]

Whether and how far the British military authorities who were actively coöperating with the Trans-Caspian Government were responsible for the slaughter of the Commissars has been a matter of sharp debate.[23] The British commander, General Malleson, was far away in Meshed; and there seems to be no reason to doubt his statement that he would have preferred to hold the Commissars as hostages and had no desire to have them killed. On the other hand, the original head of the Trans-Caspian Government, Fyodor Funtikov, is said to have testified several months after the shooting that Captain Teague-Jones, the representative of the British Military Mission in Askhabad, "spoke to me personally before the shooting of the Commissars about the necessity of the shooting and afterwards expressed satisfaction that it had been carried out in accordance with the views of the British Mission."[24]

Subsequently Teague-Jones, who had formerly been a police officer in India, left the British service and disappeared. Funtikov was captured by the Soviet authorities and executed some years later. So the precise degree to which Teague-Jones may have been implicated in the killing of the Commissars remains obscure. Civil war in the Trans-Caspian Territory had been carried on with barbarous cruelty on both sides; and it is not surprising that the first impulse of the Trans-Caspian authorities, when they had captured a number of well known Bolsheviki, was to put them to death with scant formality. The Twenty-six Commissars naturally acquired a distinguished place in the list of Communist martyrs.

When the Turks captured Baku they brought with them and installed in power the Musavat Government. The period of Turkish domination was very short; it ended, of course, after the military collapse of the Central Powers in November. The Musavat Government, however, remained; the British for a time replaced the

Germans and the Turks as the dominant foreign influence in the Caucasus. When the British decided to leave the Caucasus, retaining only a temporary foothold in Batum, in the summer of 1919 the three little states, Menshevik Georgia, Musavat Azerbaidjan and Dashnak Armenia, were left largely to their own resources. They suffered a good deal economically because of the cessation of the normal commercial interchange with Russia and because of the customs walls which they insisted on building up against one another. The Governments of Georgia and Azerbaidjan were on very cool terms with Denikin, apprehending with good reason that their independence would not long survive his victory over the Soviets. Insurgents against the White regime in Daghestan received some surreptitious help from Azerbaidjan; Georgia gave shelter and probably more material aid to fugitives from Denikin's territory; and the revolt which overthrew the power of the Volunteer Army in the Black Sea Province was organized on Georgian soil.[25]

When Denikin collapsed in the first months of 1920 and the Red Army approached the frontiers of Trans-Caucasia the independence of the new little states was threatened from another quarter. The Allied Governments on January 11, 1920, granted *de facto* recognition to Georgia and Azerbaidjan; but no country was willing to assume the risk and responsibility of defending these remote lands against the advancing Reds.

Azerbaidjan was the first of the Trans-Caucasian Republics to undergo the process of forcible Sovietization; the Soviet industries were desperately in need of the Baku oil, of which a considerable quantity had accumulated for lack of a market during the years when Russia was cut off from the Trans-Caucasus. With strange blindness to the threat from the north the Musavat Government in the spring of 1920 plunged into war with Armenia, taking away many of its troops from its northern frontier. The Azerbaidjan Foreign Minister, Khan-Khoisky, on April 15 addressed a message to Chicherin, referring to the heavy concentration of Soviet troops on the northern border of Azerbaidjan and requesting that a time and place be suggested for negotiations looking to "the establishment of neighborly relations between the peoples of Russia and Azerbaidjan."[26] No reply to this overture was ever received; but on April 27 the Red Army crossed the frontier and simultaneously the Central Committee of the Communist Party of Azerbaidjan served on the Musavat Government an ultimative demand for abdication. Resistance in Baku, with its large workingclass population, was impossible; the Government simply ran away, and on April 28 the Red troops were in Baku. An effort to rebel against the newly imposed Soviet regime in Elizavetpol was mercilessly smashed.

The Sovietization of Armenia took place early in December.[27] It was the result not of any revolutionary initiative of the very weak Armenian Communist Party, but of the desperate plight into which Armenia had fallen as a result of a new very unequal war with Turkey. The Turks had pushed into Armenia, occupying Kars and Alexandropol, devastating the country with their usual ferocity. The Russian Red Army represented the only means of staying the hand of the Turks; and formal acceptance of a Soviet regime was the price of Russian military aid.

Georgia was the last of the Trans-Caucasian Republics to succumb. In the spring of 1920 the Soviet Government had recognized the independence of Georgia, the Georgian Government agreeing at the same time to legalize the activity of the Georgian Communist Party. By February, 1921, the Soviet leaders decided that the time had come to make an end of independent Georgia, which represented an embarrassing wedge in the Soviet Trans-Caucasus. The occasion for invading Georgia was a peasant rebellion in Borchalinsk County which had, in all probability, been fomented by the Georgian Communists themselves.[28] While the Red Army moved into Georgia from the east and the north the Turks advanced from the south, endeavoring to realize their old dream of annexing Batum. Under this double pressure the Georgian resistance was crushed. A new demonstration of the somewhat peculiar Soviet application of the principle of selfdetermination of peoples had been given. Among all the parts of the Trans-Caucasus, Georgia displayed the greatest dissatisfaction with the forcibly imposed Soviet regime. As late as 1924 an uprising, quickly suppressed with a good deal of bloodshed, broke out in the Chiatouri mining region and in some of the more remote parts of Georgia.

Such, in brief outline, was the course of revolution and civil war in the Trans-Caucasian theatre. A very turbulent bit of local revolutionary history was also made in Daghestan, the large, sparsely populated country which embraces the narrow coastal plain along the Caspian Sea and the jagged, forbidding mountainous regions behind it. Daghestan represents an extraordinary patchwork of races and tongues. People who live in one of its rocky valleys sometimes do not understand the language of the tribesmen in the neighboring valley. The inhabitants of Daghestan, divided by race and language, were united by their fanatical Mohammedanism. Under their great leader, Shamil, they offered stubborn resistance to the Russian conquerors in the nineteenth century.

In such a country the stream of social revolution was bound to run in strange channels. There were Communists among the few Daghestan intellectuals and they could reckon on some support among the Russian workers of such port towns as Petrovsk. But their influence was negligible in the wild mountain *auls,* or native villages, often perched on inaccessible mountain crags, where the majority of the Daghestan tribesmen dwelt. Daghestan was also a very unfavorable base for the White movement. Denikin had a small class of supporters among Russian officers and officials and among some of the richer Daghestan sheep-owners who had received a Russian education. But in its main mass the Daghestan mountain population, poor, illiterate, traditionally courageous in battle, imbued with fanatical hatred for the *giaour,* or infidel, as the Russian was considered, was hostile to Reds and Whites alike. Daghestan was destined to be a second Ukraina, on a smaller scale, a country without a settled government and with continual outbursts of partisan warfare.

After the Bolshevik Revolution shadowy governments rose and fell with kaleidoscopic rapidity in ever restless Daghestan. In the spring of 1918 a "National Committee," supported by some of the officers and soldiers of the former Savage Division of the Russian Army, established itself as the ruling power in Daghestan. A prominent figure in this Committee was Nazhmudin Gotzinsky, an influential feudal magnate whom some of the mullahs wished to proclaim as an imam, or Mohammedan spiritual and temporal ruler. Along with clericals and conservatives the Committee included Daghestan intellectuals, one of whom, at least, Haidar Bammatov, considered himself a Socialist. The National Committee soon gave way to a Military Revolutionary Committee when Soviet forces from Astrakhan overran the more accessible lowland stretches of Daghestan and seized control of the main towns, Petrovsk, Derbent and Temir-Khan-Shura. The Military Revolutionary Committee, however, never gained effective control over the mountain fastnesses.

In the summer of 1918 there was a turn in the tide, when the Russian officer, Bicherakov, with a detachment of Cossacks which had formerly served in Northern Persia, turned up in Daghestan, pushed the Bolsheviki out of Petrovsk and Derbent and paved the way for a restoration of the power of the Daghestan nationalists, who were soon reinforced by the Turks. Daghestan, like Azerbaidjan, was a Mohammedan country and had always maintained a sentimental attachment to Turkey, as the land of Islam. The Turks drove Bicherakov, who, as a Russian, was regarded with suspicion by the Daghestan nationalists, from the coast towns, Derbent and Petrovsk.

In the spring of 1919 Denikin occupied Petrovsk and gradually extended his power over the whole of Daghestan without encountering resistance from the feeble Daghestan nationalist government, which had no effective army at its disposal. The Daghestan former officers and feudal landlords were not unwilling to see a prospect of firm order with the coming of Denikin. On the other hand an influential mullah, Ali Khadji Akushinsky, pronounced the following picturesque anathema on any sons of Daghestan who would submit to Denikin's Cossacks: [29]

> "If you submit to your leaders in the event that they invite the Cossacks and give up your arms to the Cossacks you will answer for this before Allah. All who live in heaven and earth will curse you and this curse will fall on your children and on your property. All the peoples living on the earth will curse you, sacred Mecca and Medina will curse you."

Despite these execrations the Volunteer Army established itself in Daghestan and for a time seemed to have stamped out the last remains of Bolshevism in the country. But an upsurge of revolt swept the country in August, 1919, when General Khalilov, the military governor of Daghestan, endeavored to mobilize the mountain tribesmen for service in Denikin's Army. The natives of the mountain villages soon showed that they were as fierce and resolute fighters as their ancestors, who followed the green banner of the famous national and religious leader, Shamil. There was a strange mixture of Marx and Mohammed in the uprising; a Communist committee which guided the movement from the *aul* Levashi worked in coöperation with fanatical mullahs who simply wished to wipe out all traces of the hated Russian rule. This uprising in Daghestan, which soon cleared the mountainous part of the country of Denikin's garrisons and forced him to send troops which were badly needed on the front for its suppression was one of the most destructive of the many insurgent movements that tore up and disorganized the White rear.

When the Red Army entered Daghestan in the spring of 1920 it was at first cordially greeted by the victorious insurgents. But disillusionment soon set in as a result of the requisitions, which extended even to chickens and eggs, of the disorderly behavior of some military units and of the contempt which some Russian Party and Soviet officials displayed for the religion and customs of the Daghestan mountaineers. In August, 1920, a new formidable insurrection broke out, this time against the Soviets; and all mountain Daghestan was soon aflame. A moving spirit in the uprising was Imam Gotzinsky; and not a few recruits were won to the movement by the knowledge that Said Bey, a grandson of Shamil, who had been living in Turkey, was in the ranks of the insurgents.

Up to the end of 1920 military success inclined to the side of the insurgents, who exploited to the utmost their superior knowledge of the difficult mountainous craggy country in which operations were carried out. On several occasions whole detachments of Red soldiers were enveloped and annihilated in the grim ravines of the country; one such place has ever since been called "the valley of death." While the insurrection did not affect the strip of coastal plain or the larger towns it swept almost the whole of mountain Daghestan; only old fortresses, such as Gunib and Khunzakh, were able to stand off the attacks of the insurgents and to resist long sieges. The insurgents began to lose ground from the beginning of 1921; a contributing factor to the final crushing of the movement in the spring was the occupation of Georgia. In the beginning the insurgents had been able to obtain help through the mountain passes which lead from Daghestan into Georgia; after the latter country had been overrun by Soviet troops they were cut off from any outside aid.

The uprising cost the lives of over five thousand soldiers of the Red Army.[30] It was marked by repeated demonstrations of the desperate, fanatical courage which was characteristic of these Mohammedan tribesmen of the mountains. So, when the Red Army, in overwhelming force, stormed one of the insurgent strongholds, the *aul* Gergibl, house after house had to be taken by individual hand-to-hand fighting; and many of the defenders chose to perish in the burning mosque, rather than surrender.[31]

East of the Caspian Sea, in the vast stretches of Russian Central Asia, the attempt to introduce Bolshevism in the ancient lands that had once echoed to the tramplings of the hosts of Tamerlane and other Asiatic conquerors led to a sequence of strange and sanguinary events. From the time of the Czecho-Slovak offensive in the spring of 1918 until Kolchak's front collapsed almost eighteen months later a Soviet regime existed in Turkestan in a state of complete isolation from Moscow, except for one brief interval in the winter of 1918–1919. The Orenburg and Ural Cossacks stood astride the railroad line which runs from Moscow through Samara and Orenburg to Tashkent, the largest city of Russian Central Asia, which was the capital of the Soviet regime. Red Turkestan was encircled by a hostile ring. To the north were the anti-Bolshevik Cossacks. To the south and east, off the main railroad lines and outside the large towns, were considerable bands of native insurgents, who hated the Soviet regime because of its requisitioning policies and also because it was predominantly Russian in character. To the west were two oriental vassal states of Tsarist Russia, the Emirate of Bokhara and the Khanate of Khiva. Still farther to the west, beyond the Oxus River, was the rebel regime which had been created by the railroad workers of the Trans-Caspian Territory, who received support from the British General Malleson in Persia. To the northeast was Semirechye, scene of an obscure, complicated, fierce triangular war between Cossacks, peasants who had migrated there as colonists before the War and Kirghiz nomads. Besides carrying on irregular military operations on half a dozen fronts the Soviet Government in Tashkent was faced with a chronic acute food and fuel crisis. In normal times treeless Turkestan exchanged its cotton for grain and timber from Russia. Cut off and blockaded by the ring of enemies, the country lived through very hungry years; and it was sometimes found necessary to burn ties, cottonseed oil and dried fish in order to keep a few trains running.

Tashkent was one of the remote towns of Russia where the workers, under Bolshevik leadership, had seized power before the Revolution of November 7 in Petrograd. The Tashkent Soviet asserted the right to control the local military forces; a dispute over the disarming of one regiment led to an outbreak of street fighting which lasted from October 28 until October 31; after this date the Soviet remained as the sole authority. A Red Guard was created and was supposed to include all workers between the ages of eighteen and forty-five; it was recruited largely from among the Tashkent railroad workers. A number of Austrian and Magyar war prisoners also joined it.

The first challenge to Soviet rule in Turkestan was the formation in Kokand of a so-called autonomous government which consisted largely of representatives of the Central Asian native Uzbek population. This was smashed after a battle in Kokand on February 19; the Red troops carried out wholesale looting in the city. In general the first period of the Soviet regime in Turkestan, as in the North Caucasus and in some other places which were far away from Moscow, was characterized by the emergence of a good many marauders and adventurers in the guise of Soviet "commissars." Frunze, who later took over command of the Soviet armed forces in Turkestan, stated in an Army order: [32]

> "The local Soviet authorities in the first period of their rule did everything possible to alienate the working population. Power was seized by groups of adventurers who wished to fish in muddy waters. Instead of nationalization of production there was open robbery not only of the bourgeoisie but of the middleclass part of the population."

Shortly after the suppression of the Kokand Autonomous Government a commissar named Kolesov attempted to set up "the dictatorship of the proletariat" in a stronghold of medieval Islamic faith, the ancient walled city of Bokhara. In Bokhara there was a small Young Bokharan, or Jadid, Party which desired to bring about some democratic modification of the traditional despotic power of the Emir. Soon after the March Revolution in Russia the Emir issued a manifesto promising some reforms in administration; but this manifesto remained on paper; and, when the Jadids organized a demonstration demanding reforms, their leaders were seized by the Emir's order and soundly beaten with sticks. Some of the Jadid leaders appealed to Kolesov to help them overthrow the Emir; and on March 1, 1918, Kolesov's Russian Red Guards made a threatening demonstration outside the walls of Bokhara. The Emir gained time by pretending to yield to the demands of the insurgents, brought up considerable numbers of badly armed and badly trained troops and with the aid of the mullahs stirred up the fanatical rage of his subjects against the infidel invaders. Kolesov was ultimately beaten off; the Emir celebrated his victory by tearing up the railroad tracks which made his capital easily accessible from Russian territory and by killing considerable numbers of his subjects whom he suspected of cherishing subversive ideas. From this time the Emir was an implacable enemy of the Soviet regime and gave as much help as possible to the Basmachi, as the native insurgents who were continually active in Central Asia, especially in the more mountainous regions, were called.

A peculiar companion of conservative, fanatical Bokhara in the struggle against Red Tashkent was an eminently proletarian Government, headed by a locomotive driver named Funtikov, which came into existence at Askhabad, in the Trans-Caspian Territory, in the summer of 1918. Trans-Caspia, like Izhevsk, is one of the few places in Russia during the civil war where manual workers fought with arms in their hands against the Bolshevik Soviets and tried to create an alternative form of government. The immediate cause of the uprising was apparently the extreme brutality of a drunken commissar named Frolov, who, according to the euphemistic expression of a Soviet writer,[33] "arrived in Askhabad with Red Guards on June 24 and began to take drastic measures against counterrevolution." According to the British General Malleson, who may be as prone to exaggeration as the Soviet writer is to understatement, these "drastic measures" took the following form: [34]

> "Many prominent local people, and hundreds of lesser note, were shot down without trial and there was much looting. Frolov used to drive round the streets of Askhabad with a rifle in his hands, and shot at anyone he saw."

When Frolov went to the town of Kizil Arvat to continue his "drastic measures" a rebellion broke out on July 13 among the local railroad workers, headed by the locomotive driver Funtikov, who was a Socialist Revolutionary. Frolov and all his companions were killed. Askhabad was occupied by the insurgent railwaymen on July 16 and a Trans-Caspian Government, headed by Funtikov, was organized and soon controlled the vast territory from the Caspian Sea almost to the Oxus River. Most of its members were proletarians of the purest type; almost the only Minister who possessed a regular education was the Foreign Minister, a schoolteacher named Zimin. Fearing a revengeful new invasion of Red Guards from Tashkent, the Trans-Caspian regime appealed for help to the British General Malleson, who was stationed in Meshed, in Northern Persia, anxiously watching out for a possible German-Turkish thrust in the direction of the Near and Middle East. Malleson sent a few Indian troops and machine-gunners who were at his disposition; and with this aid the Trans-Caspian forces were able to hold their own for some time on a front near the town of

Chardzhui, where the Trans-Caspian railroad line crosses the Oxus River. In return Malleson obtained the right to mine the harbor of Krasnovodsk, where Turkish troops might appear after the capture of Baku, and to take engineering measures which would make the Trans-Caspian Railroad impassable for invading troops from the Caucasus. The British, under the circumstances, naturally dominated very much the policies of the Trans-Caspian Government. This was the background for the killing of the Twenty-six Commissars, which has been described earlier in the chapter.

In the spring of 1919 the Red Army took the offensive on the Trans-Caspian front and captured Merv, famous for its ancient ruins, on May 23. Advancing through the desert along the line of the Trans-Caspian Railroad the Reds captured Askhabad on July 11. The British had left the Trans-Caspian front in June, in line with their general policy of withdrawing from active intervention in Russia at this time, and the morale and fighting capacity of the Trans-Caspian insurgents were correspondingly depressed. A stand was made at Kizil Arvat; Denikin sent some reinforcements to the aid of the Trans-Caspian regime, which, after the fashion of anti-Bolshevik governments, had become steadily more conservative in its social makeup. But in October, Kizil Arvat was taken by a flanking maneuver; and the capture by storm of Krasnovodsk in February, 1920, completed the liquidation of the Trans-Caspian Front.

The Turkestan Soviet Government narrowly escaped destruction from within in January, 1919. The War Commissar, Osipov, who was supported by some of the troops, captured fourteen of the most prominent Communists in the Government, including the President of the local Council of People's Commissars, Figelsky, the President of the Soviet Executive Committee, Voitintsev, and the President of the Tashkent Soviet, Shumilov, and shot them all.[35] He seized the Tashkent fortress and proclaimed, as the ideal of the new regime which he proposed to introduce, the convocation of a Constituent Assembly. At the same time he promised to give the people bread and fuel, as a result of the opening up of the Askhabad front. Despite the loss of so many of the leaders, the local Communists who survived succeeded in rallying enough workers and Red Guards to drive Osipov from the city. The suppression of Osipov's rebellion was followed by an extremely ruthless campaign of terror against suspected counterrevolutionaries in Tashkent; revolutionary methods of government in Central Asia were far from mild at best, and the rage of the masses was naturally inflamed by the killing of so many of the Soviet leaders.

On the northern front of the Turkestan Soviet Republic the Orenburg Cossack leader Dutov at one time pushed the Red forces as far south as the Aral Sea, where they made a successful stand. The collapse of Kolchak and the disorderly retreat of his armies brought automatic relief to this sector of the front; on September 13, 1919, the long interrupted connection with Soviet Russia was restored when Red troops which were pursuing the left wing of Kolchak's forces joined the Turkestan Red Army at the little station Ber-Chogur. Hostilities were more prolonged in Semirechye, where the town of Sergiopol remained in the hands of the Whites and the White partisan leader, Annenkov, rallied the local Cossacks for the struggle against the Bolsheviki. After a good deal of guerrilla fighting in these distant eastern marches of Asiatic Russia Annenkov with some of his followers fled across the frontier into Chinese Turkestan.

The Turkestan Soviet regime was still faced with a generally hostile native population, and civil war in Central Asia went on for a much longer period than in other parts of Russia. Not only was the majority of the native population, consisting of Uzbeks, Tadjiks, Turcomans and other primitive peoples of Central Asia, opposed to the new regime for reasons which were partly racial and religious and partly economic,[36] but the Russian peasants who were scattered here and there in colonies which had been established on Central Asian soil before the War chafed impatiently under the regime of requisitions.

An order to move to a new section of the front, in Ferghana, aroused a serious mutiny in the Red Army units which were stationed in the frontier outpost of Verny; [37] the mutineers put forward the following demands: that the state grain monopoly be abolished, that no Mohammedan troop units be formed; that the Army Cheka and Revolutionary Tribunals be abolished, that arrested toilers be released and that the order to move into Ferghana to fight against the Basmachi be rescinded.[38] The mutiny was put down, but it reflected a fairly general mood among the Russian peasants in Central Asia. A common sense of economic grievance on at least one occasion bridged over the sharp racial antagonism between the Russians and the natives. A Russian "Peasant Army" under a leader named Monstrov in August, 1919, reached an agreement with a leading Basmach insurgent chieftain, Madamin Bek, on the basis of a platform which included such points as "freedom of labor, trade, education, speech and press," "abolition of Chekas and political commissars," "removal of the grain monopoly." [39] This effort at Russian-native coöperation on an anti-Bolshevik platform failed when the Peasant Army was decisively defeated near Andijan in September and subsequently dispersed. The Basmach movement, however, continued, especially in the territory which was near the border of Afghanistan. The latter country was a convenient refuge for insurgents when they were too hotly pursued and was a source of arms and other supplies. Although the King of Afghanistan, Amanullah Khan, exchanged complimentary messages with Lenin and welcomed the prospect of possible Russian aid against Great Britain, the general attitude of the Afghan officials and chieftains in the northern provinces of the country was distinctly sympathetic with their insurgent co-religionists in Ferghana and Bokhara.

The year 1920 witnessed the disappearance of two historic states of Central Asia, the Emirate of Bokhara and the still more remote Khanate of Khiva, on the southern shores of the Aral Sea. Khiva had experienced an oriental social revolution in 1918 and 1919. Formerly the town dwellers had lorded it over the roving Turcomans of the desert. Now the tables were turned as a result of the activities of an energetic Turcoman leader named Junaid Khan. The Turcomans raided the towns, looted the bazaars, carried off many women. Junaid had the last Khan of Khiva killed and declared himself Khan. Early in 1920 a "Young Khivan" party, with the aid of a rebel Turcoman chief and with support from the Red Army, pushed Junaid out of Khiva and established a so-called People's Republic of Khiva, which, like the similar Republic which was set up later in Bokhara, was simply a Bolshevik brand of protected native state.

Since the first unsuccessful attempt to overthrow the Emir of Bokhara in March, 1918, a number of Bokharan revolutionaries had been living in Turkestan, where they organized themselves as the Communist Party of Bokhara. By the summer of 1920 the commander of the Turkestan Red Armies, Frunze, decided that it was time to make an end of hostile and conservative Bokhara and on August 25 issued his Order Number 3667, instructing the Red Army to coöperate with the Bokharan revolutionaries. The purpose of this military activity was described as "revolutionary fraternal help to the Bokharan people in its struggle with the despotism of the

Bokharan autocrat."[40] Almost simultaneously the émigré Bokharan revolutionaries hastily organized a "Government of the Bokharan People's Republic" and all the printing-shops of the native city of Tashkent were mobilized to turn out revolutionary proclamations in the Uzbek and other Bokharan languages.[41]

The Bokharan revolutionary forces were negligible as regards numbers and quality; and the Russian Red Army carried out the capture of Bokhara, the old stronghold of Islamic faith, with its high thick wall and its numerous mosques and theological schools, almost singlehanded. The movement against Bokhara from the neighboring railroad station, Kagan, began on August 29. The Bokharans were rather soft and effeminate and not very sturdy fighters; moreover the artillery which the Emir possessed was hopelessly oldfashioned. But three thousand Afghans who were among his guards fought with stubborn courage. Heavy artillery had to be brought into action before the massive Karshi gates could be battered down. The city was finally taken by storm on September 1st; the Emir himself made good his escape and sought a refuge in the mountainous eastern regions of his realm.

The Red Army pushed on into Eastern Bokhara and occupied its chief town, Dushambe, on February 21, 1921. The Emir then fled into Afghanistan, where he found a permanent refuge and became a trader in karakul, a valuable kind of sheep's fleece. But the civil war in Central Asia was not ended. In the spring of 1921 there was a new upsurge of insurrection in Eastern Bokhara. Basmach bands were active and made raids into such towns as Andijan. The situation was further complicated in November, 1921, when the adventurous Young Turk leader, Enver Pasha, disgruntled by the refusal of the Bolsheviki to sponsor his schemes for overthrowing Mustapha Kemal in Turkey and dreaming of becoming the head of a vast Mohammedan Empire in Central Asia, the land of Tamerlane, slipped away from his Bolshevik hosts on the pretext of a hunting party and passed over to the insurgents. Enver was a well known name in the Mohammedan world; he proclaimed himself "Commander-in-chief of all the armed forces of Islam" and became the recognized leader of the anti-Soviet movement. In March, 1922, the Bokharan War Commissar, a former Turkish officer named Ali Riza, passed over to the insurgents.

But Enver, in his dreams of Asiatic empire, overlooked the immense advantage which modern weapons give to the forces of a European power against colonial rebels. He had plenty of fanatical

Mohammedan followers, but no artillery, a few machine-guns in bad repair and a motley assortment of rifles of various types and makes.[42] The Soviet military authorities organized a special army to crush Enver under the command of a former officer of the Russian General Staff named Kakurin. Enver was decisively defeated near Baisun in June, 1922, and driven back into Eastern Bokhara. Dushambe, which had fallen into the hands of the insurgents, was reoccupied by the Reds on July 14, and on August 4 Enver himself was killed in a brush with a Red cavalry patrol not far from the Afghan border.

The death of Enver may be regarded as marking the end of regular civil war in Central Asia, although guerrilla activity on the part of the Basmachi in mountainous and desert regions persisted for many years and proved very hard to eradicate. In surveying the stormy career of the Soviet regime in Central Asia one is struck by many similarities with the course of developments in the North Caucasus. Both these regions were cut off from Moscow; in both the prestige of the Soviet regime was compromised by the presence of many adventurers who committed all kinds of outrages; Osipov's action in executing the leading Tashkent Communists recalls the action of the unruly commander of the North Caucasian Red Army, Sorokin, in shooting out of hand several leading members of the North Caucasian Government. If the Tashkent Soviet regime survived, while the North Caucasian Soviets went down to temporary extinction, the explanation is to be found in the fact that there was no anti-Bolshevik force in Central Asia comparable in fighting efficiency with Denikin's Volunteer Army.

The Northern Territory, Trans-Caucasia and Central Asia were the main secondary theatres of revolution and civil war. One may dismiss in a few words a few still lesser episodes in the struggle. An officer in Kolchak's Army, Baron Ungern-Sternberg, who traced his descent from Genghiz Khan, believed in Buddhism and cherished an implacable hatred for revolutions and revolutionaries, embarked on an adventurous career that led him to the seizure of Urga, capital of Outer Mongolia, on February 3, 1921. He then invaded Russia, marching on Verkhne-Udinsk, but was beaten back. The pursuing Red troops entered Urga on July 7 and laid the foundation of another Asiatic protected native state, included in fact, if not in name, within the Soviet Union and embracing the vast, although scantily populated, deserts and steppes of Outer Mongolia. Ungern-Sternberg made a second raid into Russia, was captured and executed.

Apart from peasant uprisings in different parts of the country, a number of outbreaks and raids occurred in unsettled border districts of Russia during 1921. A miniature but fierce guerrilla struggle under polar conditions was fought out in Yakutia, where refugee officers from Kolchak's army stirred up the natives, especially those who occupied a more privileged economic and social position, to resist the Soviet regime in this remote part of northern Siberia. An uprising took place in the districts of Karelia which border on Finland in the autumn of 1921; about the same time one of Petlura's lieutenants, Tiutiunik, made a raid into northwestern Ukraina across the border from Poland. These were all very minor local disturbances, which did not in any way threaten the stability of the Soviet regime or require the employment of large forces for suppression.

So far as the chief secondary fronts of the civil war, the Northern Territory, Trans-Caucasia and Central Asia, were concerned, the issue was determined by the outcome of the struggle on the main fronts, against Kolchak and Denikin. The defeat of the Whites and the failure and abandonment of intervention made it certain that the Northern Territory, Trans-Caucasia and Central Asia would sooner or later be reabsorbed into the main body of Soviet Russia.

NOTES

[1] Cited by Professor E. A. Ross, "The Russian Soviet Republic," p. 187.

[2] General Sir C. Maynard, "The Murmansk Venture," pp. 26ff.

[3] *Cf.* article by A. Metelev, "The Fall of Archangel," in *Proletarskaya Revolutsia,* Vol. II, for 1926.

[4] I. Mintz, "British Intervention and the Northern Counterrevolution," p. 61.

[5] The People's Socialists were a moderately radical party, which stood somewhat to the left of the Cadets and somewhat to the right of the Mensheviki and Socialist Revolutionaries. Its socialism was not of the Marxian stamp.

[6] Francis's account of the little Archangel *coup d'état* reads as follows (*cf.* his "Russia from the American Embassy," p. 270): "General Poole turned to me and said: 'There was a revolution here last night.' I said: 'The hell you say. Who pulled it off?' He replied: 'Chaplin.' I said: 'There is Chaplin over there now.' I motioned for him to come over and join us. General Poole remarked: 'Chaplin is going to issue a proclamation at 11 o'clock.' It was then 10.15. I said: 'Chaplin, who pulled off this revolution here last night?' He said: 'I did. . . . The Ministers were in General Poole's way and were hampering Colonel Donop (the French Provost-Marshal). I see no use for any government here anyway.' I replied: 'I think this is the most flagrant usurpation of power I ever knew, and don't you circulate that proclamation that General Poole tells me you have written until I can see it, and show it to my colleagues.' "

[7] V. Marushevsky, "The Whites in Archangel," p. 194.

[8] *Cf.* Boris Sokolov's article, "The Fall of the Northern Territory" in *Arkhiv Russkoi Revolutsii,* Vol. IX.

[9] *Ibid.*

[10] Mintz, *op. cit.,* pp. 219, 220.

[11] *Cf.* S. Dobrovolsky's article, "The Struggle for the Rebirth of Russia in the Northern Territory" in *Arkhiv Russkoi Revolutsii,* Vol. III, p. 66.

[12] *Ibid.*, p. 68.

[13] Maynard, *op. cit.*, p. 214.

[14] Shaumyan's popularity among the Baku workers may be judged from the fact that he was elected President of the first Baku Soviet, despite the fact that he was a well known Bolshevik and the Bolsheviki were a small minority in the early period of the existence of the Soviet.

[15] Y. Shafir, "Sketches of the Georgian Gironde," pp. 39ff.

[16] S. Sef. "The Truth About Shamkhor," p. 6.

[17] B. Baikov, "Reminiscences of the Revolution in Trans-Caucasia," in *Arkhiv Russkoi Revolutsii,* Vol. IX, p. 115.

[18] B. A. Boryan, "Armenia, International Diplomacy and the Soviet Union," Vol. II, p. 54.

[19] S. Shaumyan, "The Baku Commune," p. 40.

[20] *Ibid.*, p. 54. A copy of the appeal is preserved in the Azerbaidjan Museum of the Revolution.

[21] Baikov (*op. cit.*) points out that no Russians were killed during the slaughter which followed the Turkish occupation of Baku; the Armenians were singled out for massacre.

[22] V. Chaikin, "The Execution of the Twenty-six Baku Commissars," pp. 79–81.

[23] Chaikin (*op. cit.*) considers that the British military authorities were responsible for the execution of the Commissars, while General Malleson, in an article, "The Twenty-six Commissars," which he contributed to *The Fortnightly Review* for March, 1933, attributes the entire initiative for this deed to the Trans-Caspian authorities, and declares that he endeavored to save the lives of the Commissars, but intervened too late.

[24] Chaikin, *op. cit.*, pp. 54, 55.

[25] *Cf.* in this connection the testimony of N. Voronovitch, one of the organizers of the rebellion, in his article, "Between Two Fires," in *Arkhiv Russkoi Revolutsii,* Vol. VII.

[26] A. Raevsky, "British Intervention and the Musavat Government," pp. 189, 190.

[27] B. Boryan, "Armenia, International Diplomacy and the Soviet Union," Vol. II, pp. 120ff., describes in some detail the process of Sovietization in Armenia.

[28] E. Drabkina, a Soviet historian, who gives an extremely one-sided account of developments in Georgia in her book, "The Georgian Counterrevolution," says (p. 167): "Those uninterrupted peasant uprisings, with which the whole history of Menshevik Georgia is filled, took place with the direct participation and under the leadership of the Bolsheviki." Communist writers, seeking to justify in retrospect the armed conquest of Georgia by the Red Army, always lay great stress on these uprisings as signs of popular discontent with the Menshevik Government. There were peasant uprisings in Georgia, and the Menshevik Government of that country was not very successful in its dealings with the national minorities. However, there were also "uninterrupted peasant uprisings" in Soviet Russia from 1918 until 1921, so that the similar disturbances in Georgia seem to represent a rather double-edged pretext for foreign intervention. The causes of the uprisings were different. The peasants in Soviet Russia repeatedly rebelled against arbitrary and excessive requisitions of their food products. In Georgia the poorer peasants were dissatisfied because the land holdings of the larger owners were limited, not confiscated altogether, and because the more well-to-do peasants acquired the lion's share of the land which was alienated from the big estates.

[29] A. Takho-Godi, "Revolution and Counterrevolution in Daghestan," p. 110.

[30] A. Todorsky, "The Red Army in the Mountains," p. 159.

[31] The rebellion was suppressed with great cruelty. N. Samursky, a Daghestan Communist who took an active part in the struggle, writes: "We applied the most ruthless measures against persistent insurgents." (*Cf.* his article, "The October Revolution and the Further Stages of Its Development in Daghestan," in *Proletarskaya Revolutsia* for October, 1924, p. 101.)

[32] E. Kozlovsky, "For Red Turkestan," p. 50.

[33] F. Bozhko, "Civil War in Central Asia," pp. 30ff.

[34] *Cf.* Major-General Sir W. Malleson's article, "The Twenty-six Commissars," in *Fortnightly Review,* for March, 1933.

[35] *Cf.* "The January Uprising," a brief pamphlet on Osipov's mutiny published by the Istpart (Communist Party Historical Commission) of Central Asia.

[36] E. Kozlovsky, *op. cit.*, repeatedly refers to the sympathy of the native population for the Basmachi.

[37] Verny was subsequently renamed Alma Ata and is the capital of Soviet Kazakstan.

[38] A Communist novelist, Dmitry Furmanov, has described the Verny mutiny in a novel entitled "Mutiny," which has been dramatized in Russia.

[39] Kozlovsky, *op. cit.*, pp. 43ff.

[40] "The Civil War, 1918–1921," Vol. III, p. 554.

[41] "Collection of Articles on the Tenth Anniversary of the Bokharan and Khivan Revolutions," p. 54.

[42] Kozlovsky, *op. cit.*, p. 79.

CHAPTER XL

THE CRISIS OF WAR COMMUNISM: KRONSTADT AND NEP

THE Soviet regime experienced the third major crisis of its existence during the winter and early spring of 1920–1921. The vital question at the time of the first crisis, in the summer of 1918, was whether the Red Army could be whipped into fighting shape in time to check the advance of the Czechs and their anti-Bolshevik Russian allies. The second crisis, in the autumn of 1919, was also predominantly military; it passed when Denikin was driven back from Orel and Voronezh, and Yudenitch from Petrograd.

In the crisis of 1920–1921, which was a crisis of the whole economic and social system of war communism, no military problem was involved. Active foreign intervention in European Russia had ceased. The last White Army had been driven into the sea. The blockade was rapidly crumbling; a trade agreement with Great Britain was in prospect. Blood was flowing, to be sure, in various parts of the country, in the mountains of Daghestan, in the faraway marches of Central Asia. The elusive Makhno was still carrying out his raids in Ukraina; the peasants of Western Siberia were up in arms; in the Province of Tambov a peasant leader named Antonov, who was second only to Makhno in capacity for guerrilla warfare, had raised a serious insurrection. But these and lesser peasant outbreaks, while they were ominously symptomatic from the political standpoint, represented no direct military menace. The superiority of the Red Army over these insurgent bands in trained officers, artillery, machine-guns and other modern implements of slaughter was too great.

The spectre that haunted the Kremlin at the end of 1920 and the beginning of 1921 was not that of forcible overthrow by foreign armies or by organized Russian Whites. It was rather that of sheer collapse from within, as a result of the profound mood of disillusionment and dissatisfaction among the masses, which reached its height just on the eve of the declaration of the Nep, or New Economic

Policy. The country as a whole was cold, hungry, disease-ridden, exhausted and embittered; and this was true as regards the majority of the industrial workers and a good many of the rank-and-file Communists.

In some respects the conclusion of peace with Poland and the elimination of Wrangel were psychologically disadvantageous, from the standpoint of the Communists. So long as these active enemies were in the field it was possible to bolster up the morale of wavering peasant soldiers by telling them that, however much they and their families might suffer from requisitions, things would be still worse if Polish pans and Russian landlords were allowed to conquer the country. It was possible to appeal to the class hate of the workers for the pre-War ruling and wealthy classes and to put forward the war as an excuse for all the country's sufferings.

But in November, 1920, regular civil war came to an end. The masses began to demand more and more insistently an improvement in living conditions which were intolerably bad. The peasants, whose stocks of surplus grain were much smaller because of the poor harvest of 1920, became increasingly resentful of requisitions. Distrust and antagonism grew between the nonparty workers and the Communists and between the rank-and-file Communists and those who were in higher posts.

When victory over Kolchak and Denikin early in 1920 had seemed to mark the end of the civil war and placed the problems of economic reconstruction in the foreground the Communist leaders had tried the experiment of intensifying the rigorous regime of war communism, establishing universal compulsory labor, militarizing labor discipline, turning superfluous military units into "labor armies." This experiment, in the main, had proved a complete failure; and there was little faith in the success of its continued application. But what was to be put in its place? How could the peasant be conciliated, how could an upward impetus be given to the shattered economic life of the country? These were the questions that baffled everyone, from Lenin and Trotzky to the humblest worker-Communist or Red Army soldier, during the four hard, bleak months which passed between the defeat of Wrangel, which removed the last military justification for some features of war communism, and the proclamation of the New Economic Policy. As a Communist writer says: [1]

"We could not pass over to the Nep in time of war, but we could have done this in January, 1921. But great is the force of inertia!

We could not quickly free ourselves from the traditions of war communism."

Instead of improving after the defeat of Wrangel, living conditions took a turn for the worse: a new proof that, quite apart from civil war and intervention, the system of war communism itself was hopelessly defective. On January 22, 1921, a cut of one third was announced in the meagre bread ration for Moscow, Petrograd and other large towns; what had formerly sufficed for two days must now last for three.[2] On February 6 a "terrible fuel crisis" was officially announced. Food trains from Siberia and the North Caucasus were stalled for days because of snowdrifts and lack of fuel. Several railroads in Siberia and Ukraina had fuel reserves for less than a single day. About the same time a number of paper factories stopped for lack of fuel; the State Publishing Company issued an appeal to institutions not to insist on "printing long books about their activities," since it was impossible to print the most necessary schoolbooks. On February 12 *Pravda* acknowledged a "severe defeat on the labor front"; sixty-four of the largest factories in Petrograd, including the well known Putilov metal works, had to close for lack of fuel.[3] This midwinter economic crisis was all the more severe because the Soviet authorities, very badly informed about the country's actual resources in food and fuel, had adopted a too ambitious programme of restarting factories, without reckoning with their ability to keep them open.

Echoes of workers' discontent at this time made themselves heard even in the carefully controlled Communist press. So at a factory *Postavshik* a Communist woman named Smit endeavored to solace the workers with the familiar long tables of statistics; she was angrily interrupted by her auditors, who told her that they were cold and hungry and asked her to stop giving figures. When a conference of Moscow metal workers met in February the mood of the nonparty delegates was one of extreme bitterness; on the first day Communist sympathizers were shouted down when they tried to speak. One of the delegates delivered a speech against the numerous Jews in the *Glavki,* or departments of economic administration. The *Pravda* correspondent who described this meeting wrote: [4] "A complete breach between the Party and these masses, between the masses and the trade-union, was felt."

The mood of bitterness and disillusionment was strong in the ranks of the Party itself. Cases when Communists tore up or turned back their Party tickets on the ground that the Revolution had not developed as they thought it should were not uncommon. Aaron Soltz, a veteran Communist with strict ideas about how Communists should behave, put his finger on a number of weak spots in the Party morale in a series of articles which he contributed to *Pravda* at this time.[5]

Soltz sensed a general tendency to rebel against the extremely centralized discipline which had been accepted as inevitable during the civil war. "The civil war," wrote Soltz, "made some Communists most devoted and heroic. But some, being in power under a dictatorship, lost the feeling of comradeship and became indistinguishable from former rulers." Many careerists had entered the Party, while many old Party workers, according to Soltz, became demoralized by power. There was a trend toward bureaucracy, toward supercilious treatment of rank-and-file comrades. Some Communists in lower positions endeavored to please their superiors by supplying them with all kinds of luxuries: extra food, special trains, automobiles, etc. Soltz quoted from the letter of a Communist who had recently resigned from the Party, with the explanation:

"I do not believe in the realization of communism, in view of all the privileges which are enjoyed by those Communists who occupy responsible posts."

Other letters were characterized by the same tone. Soltz declared that facts which had come to the knowledge of the Party Control Commission proved that "most comrades in responsible posts are carried away with the idea of supplying themselves first and do this with criminal lightmindedness."

Another contributor to *Pravda* at this time, a certain Speransky, declared that the hostility of some workers and rank-and-file Party members toward those Party officials who enjoyed a much higher standard of living, as regards food, clothing and housing, was so great that it sometimes turned into "class hatred." Every hostile reference to the way in which commissars lived was applauded at meetings.

While the lower ranks of the Party were seething with discontent and jealousy the Communist leaders became involved in a prolonged and acrimonious dispute about the proper functions of the trade-unions. For the first time since the discussion about the Brest-Litovsk Peace, Lenin and Trotzky openly sponsored opposing views. As Lenin said at this time, the Party was feverish; when the Central Committee decided on December 24, 1920, to open up a free discussion during the period preceding the convocation of the

Tenth Party Congress in March, 1921, no fewer than eight platforms were put forward by various individuals and groups. Only three of these platforms attracted any large measure of support: that of Lenin and of the nine members of the Party Central Committee who supported him; that of Trotzky, who had a smaller group of adherents in the Central Committee; and that of the Workers' Opposition, headed by Shlyapnikov and Kollontai.

Trotzky was convinced that the Soviet trade-unions were experiencing a grave crisis and needed a vigorous "shaking up," to cite an expression which he employed and which gave considerable offense to Tomsky, the head of the trade-unions. He attributed this crisis to the fact that the old functions of the trade-unions, their traditional task of defending the interests of the workers against the employers, had become superfluous, since the private employer had been virtually abolished. "In a workers' state the trade-unions cannot carry on class economic struggle," Trotzky declared at this time.[6] He saw new functions for the unions in training and disciplining the workers and in participating in the administration of industry. He believed that they would fulfill these new functions more effectively if they were fused with the general state administrative apparatus. At the same time he pronounced himself in favor of more democracy within the Party, more latitude for criticism, more application of the elective method, more meetings and discussions of controversial questions.[7]

Lenin felt that Trotzky approached the trade-union question too much from the administrative standpoint. He saw in the trade-unions in the Soviet state institutions for organizing and reëducating the workers—"schools of communism," to use his own phrase. He disagreed with Trotzky's idea that the workers needed no special organizations to protect them in the Soviet state. As he wrote during the discussion: [8]

> "Our present-day state is of such a character that the organized proletariat must defend itself and we must exploit these workers' organizations for the protection of the workers against their state and for the defense by the workers of our state."

The Workers' Opposition put forward a semi-syndicalist platform which was equally objectionable both to Lenin, who believed that the trade-unions should have educational and propagandist, rather than administrative, powers, and to Trotzky, who wanted, indeed, to bring the unions into closer contact with the problems of economic management, but desired to achieve this end by strictly controlling them from above. The Workers' Opposition proposed that the trade-unions should concentrate in their hands "the entire management of economic life." No one was to be appointed to an economic adminstrative post without the consent of the trade-union for the industry concerned; candidates who were nominated for such posts by the trade-unions must be automatically accepted. The Workers' Opposition wished to institute a system under which every factory would be managed by an elected factory committee, each member of which should attend to some particular branch of the administration.[9]

The Workers' Opposition was far from the seats of power in the Communist Party; its platform stood no chance of acceptance. The bitterness of the debate between Lenin and Zinoviev, his most active lieutenant in this controversy, on one side and Trotzky on the other was aggravated by two circumstances. Back of the relatively minor problem of how the trade-unions should be organized was the larger problem of the whole future course of Communist economic policy, now that the civil war was ended. Trotzky's idea of transforming the trade-unions into governmental administrative bodies was in line with the strict disciplined regimentation which had become characteristic of the system of war communism, especially during 1920. Lenin had apparently not yet decided to adopt the sweeping changes which were later lumped together under the name of the New Economic Policy. But there is reason to believe that he had already lost faith in the feasibility of war communism, that he was already feeling about in an experimental way for new methods of bringing about economic recovery. It was natural, therefore, that he should desire to preserve a freer and more elastic status for the trade-unions. Moreover, almost any controversy, even over some quite minor point, tended to become sharper because of the general consciousness that the Soviet regime was faced with a crisis from which the way of escape had not yet been shown. Many stalwart simpleminded rank-and-file Communists were doubtless concerned not so much by the substance of the argument between Lenin and Trotzky as by the fact that these two leaders should openly differ as to what should be done.

One of the chief episodes in the trade-union discussion was a Communist meeting in the Moscow State Opera-house on December 30, 1920, where Lenin, Trotzky and Zinoviev delivered speeches.[10] Trotzky pointed out that the trade-unions had already fulfilled some administrative functions; they had mobilized their members for the fronts, for food collection, for officers' training courses. This was natural in a workers' state. Now, Trotzky declared, the trade-unions must take charge of production and fuse with the organizations which were responsible for the management of industry. Until the trade-unions took greater hold of production the state would have to interfere clumsily in emergencies, as it had already done in regard to the transportation system and in regard to the Donetz coalmines. What Trotzky apparently regarded as especially desirable was an end of the dualism, which sometimes led to opposition between the Communists engaged in the management of industry and the Communists in the trade-unions.

Lenin set forth as his view that the trade-unions should not be state organizations or organizations for compulsion. He also took issue with Trotzky on the question of whether the workers needed special organizations to defend their interests in a "workers' state."

"Our state," said Lenin, "is not entirely a 'workers state'; we also have peasants. Then our state is bureaucratic. The trade-unions must defend the workers against the state bureaucracy."

Zinoviev suggested that the trade-unions are "schools of communism" and that in schools one must teach and not command. He characterized a phrase of which Trotzky was very fond, "productive democracy," as empty of content and declared that the transformation of the trade-unions into state organizations would merely play into the hands of the Socialist Revolutionaries, who wanted to form illegal unions.

While the Communist leaders were engaged in this controversy, while the mood among the workers and among some of the Communist rank-and-file grew steadily more sullen and menacing, the peasants in many parts of Russia were subjecting the policies of war communism to the most effective kind of criticism: the criticism of armed rebellion. Makhno was still active in Ukraina; the acute food difficulties of Moscow and the other towns of Central Russia were further aggravated by a peasant uprising in Western Siberia in the winter of 1920–1921 which was sufficiently serious to cause a temporary interruption of communication on the Trans-Siberian Railroad. But the chief peasant uprising of this period occurred in the Province of Tambov and was associated with the name of Antonov.

It not infrequently happened that just the regions which rebelled most violently against the landlords in 1905 and 1917 were later main centres of uprising against the Communist agrarian regime, with its wholesale requisitions, state farms and communes. This was certainly the case in Ekaterinoslav, Alexandrovsk and other Ukrainian districts where Makhno found his main following. It was also the case in Tambov, which acquired a reputation as the stormiest province in the course of the agrarian revolution of 1917. It was in the forefront of the peasant movement against the Communists in 1920 and 1921.

The past life and the personality of Antonov suggest several traits of similarity with Makhno, although the Tambov insurgent seems to have had fewer political ideas than the Ukrainian peasant-anarchist. Antonov had spent many years in exile for some act of violence which he committed during the 1905 Revolution. Set at liberty after the downfall of the Tsar, he returned to his native Tambov Province, where he called himself a Socialist Revolutionary and became head of the police in the town of Kirsanov, a post which he continued to hold for some time after the Bolshevik Revolution.

When and why he began to fight actively against the Communists is not altogether clear; there are conflicting versions. But by the autumn of 1919 Antonov was already head of a terrorist band, recruited largely from deserters from the Red Army and from peasants who resisted requisitions. In the beginning he confined himself to small activities, such as assassinations of particularly unpopular local Soviet officials and raids on state farms. His movement gained in strength during 1920; it is estimated that his bands killed about 200 food collectors in Kirsanov County alone up to October.

A widespread uprising broke out in the southeast corner of Tambov County in August, 1920; and from this time until the spring of 1921 the whole Province, along with some districts of the neighboring Saratov and Penza Provinces, was the scene of fierce partisan warfare. A Chekist who took part in the operations against Antonov estimates [11] that at the height of his movement, between January and April, 1921, about 20,000 insurgents had taken up arms. All such estimates are necessarily uncertain, because some of Antonov's followers were "bandits," as the Communists liked to call peasant rebels against their requisitions, one day and peaceful farmers the next. The main causes of the insurrection were requisitions (the same Chekist says that the Food Commissar of the Province, Goldin, "didn't spare frequent and sometimes fierce punishments" in carrying out food collection) and the desire to avoid service in the Red Army. This is reflected in the primitive songs of the insurgents. One of them may be literally translated as follows:

"Oh, sorrow, oh, sorrow, the soldier tortures the peasant and still takes, oh, sorrow, three poods [12] from each eater."

Another was popular among the deserters and ran as follows:

"Deserter I was born, deserter I shall die. Shoot me on the spot; I don't go into the Red Army. To us came a commissar and two Red Army soldiers. All the same we won't go. Don't hope for us."

Other songs promise to feed the Communists to the fishes and greet the coming of the partisans. The sympathy of the majority of the peasants was definitely with Antonov. Another participant in the suppression of the movement writes: [13]

"The peasants met the bandits like good guests, bringing them cups of milk on the street and even voluntarily gave them their horses, while they hid what they could from us and looked forward to our coming as to the plague."

One reason for this attitude was that Antonov's forces lived largely off the proceeds of plundered state farms and sugar factories, whereas the Red troops lived directly off the peasants.

As was usually the case with peasant insurgent movements, the political programme of the rebels was vague and confused. Although Antonov called himself a Socialist Revolutionary and although there was a traditionally strong Socialist Revolutionary organization in Tambov Province there does not seem to have been very close contact between the guerrilla chieftain and the Socialist Revolutionaries, who were inclined to look on him as an undisciplined adventurer.[14] The Socialist Revolutionaries had established in various parts of the province "Committees of the Toiling Peasantry"; and in some cases these Committees functioned as political staffs of the insurgent movement, giving the illiterate and semi-literate peasants some idea of slogans and demands, such as the calling of a Constituent Assembly and the establishment of free trade. Here and there proclamations appeared with the familiar motto of the Socialist Revolutionary Party: "In struggle you will gain your rights." But in the main "Antonovism," as the Tambov movement was sometimes called, like all the peasant insurrections of the Russian civil war, was elemental and destructive. It was the spontaneous outburst of a tormented population that knew that Soviet conditions were intolerable, but had little constructive idea of what to set up instead.

In suppressing the widespread peasant uprising the Communists imitated the most ruthless methods which had been employed by Kolchak's lieutenants against insurgent peasants in Siberia, notably the destruction of the homes of the peasants and the shooting of hostages who were taken for the good behavior of their relatives. Anyone who harbored an insurgent was liable to be shot.

> "In some villages," a Soviet description of the Antonov movement tells us,[15] "the families of the bandits began to leave their homes. . . . Then the plenipotentiary commission decided to demolish or burn the homes of bandits whose families were in hiding, to treat those who concealed bandits' families as harborers of bandits, to shoot the oldest in such families."

Antonov's success was greatest during the first months of 1921. While he was not sufficiently provided with artillery to hold any large towns, he reduced Soviet administration in most of the rural districts of the province to impotence; Communists and Soviet officials took refuge in Tambov and in the larger towns. The uprising began to wane in April and May, when large forces of especially reliable cavalry and *kursanti* were brought into the province. At the same time the announcement that the hated requisitions were abolished took the edge off the peasants' bitter resistance. By the autumn of 1921 the struggle had practically ceased; only little bands were still being hunted down in the swamps and forests. Antonov himself escaped capture for some time longer. But, like most peasant leaders, he could not stay away permanently from his native region. The Chekists reckoned with this; and on June 24, 1922, they surrounded a house in the village Nizhni Shibrai, in Borisoglebsk County, where Antonov and his brother had taken refuge. The house was set on fire and the Antonovs were shot down as they fled from it.

By 1921 the Soviet rulers had become accustomed to workers' grumblings and occasional strikes, to peasant riots, to a general atmosphere of cold, hunger and misery. Sooner or later, no doubt, war communism would have been discarded as an unworkable system. But its crisis might have dragged on much longer if it had not been for the sudden and unexpected mutiny of the sailors and the garrison in the island naval fortress of Kronstadt, near Petrograd. This uprising, in a place which had been a stronghold of

Bolshevism in 1917, sounded a warning too plain and imminent to be ignored and was the immediate prelude to the introduction of the New Economic Policy.

Some of the same factors that tended to make Kronstadt a centre of revolutionary agitation against the feeble Provisional Government of 1917 tended to make it the scene of one of the largest popular rebellions against the very strong dictatorship of the Communist Party in 1921. A hatred of privilege and authority was ingrained in the spirit of the place, where the population consisted almost exclusively of workers and sailors. Anarchism, as well as Bolshevism, had many adherents in Kronstadt in 1917; and it was natural that this sailors' fortress should be especially restive under the new yoke of the Communist commissars. A number of young peasants from Ukraina had been recently enlisted as sailors; and they brought with them the general mood of peasant discontent with requisitions, forced labor and other features of Communist agrarian policy. The Communist local branch in Kronstadt was badly "demoralized," in the sense that many of its members shared the mood of the sailors and were by no means disposed to uphold the dictatorship of the Party leaders.[16]

The Kronstadt sailors naturally responded readily to movements in nearby Petrograd. In the last days of February there had been a wave of strikes in Petrograd factories, excited, as usual, by the difficult food situation. The Mensheviki and Socialist Revolutionaries issued appeals, the former calling for freely elected factory committees and Soviets, the latter for the calling of a Constituent Assembly. Petrograd was declared under martial law; movement on the streets after eleven at night was forbidden; a special staff was formed to combat the "counterrevolutionary" movement of the workers. Patrols of *kursanti,* the most reliable military forces at the disposal of the Soviet authorities, appeared in the streets. After several days of tense excitement the strike movement declined. Hunger made the workers apathetic; moreover, there was no leadership, no clearcut programme.

The Petrograd strikes, however, represented the spark that set off the powder-magazine in Kronstadt. The sailors were greatly excited by rumors that the striking workers had been fired on. The Kronstadt rebellion began on March 1, when a mass meeting of fifteen thousand sailors and workers on Anchor Square, in Kronstadt, despite admonitory speeches which were delivered by the President of the Soviet Executive Committee, Kalinin, and by the

Communist Commissar of the Baltic Fleet, N. Kuzmin, passed a long resolution with a series of demands that were completely inconsistent with the theory and practise of the ruling Communist Party. The more important of these demands may be briefly summarized as follows:

Reëlections of the Soviets by secret voting, with free preliminary agitation among workers and peasants. Freedom of speech and press for workers and peasants, Anarchists and Left Socialist parties. Freedom of meetings, trade-unions and peasant associations. Liberation of Socialist political prisoners and of all workers, peasants, soldiers and sailors imprisoned for association with working-class and peasant movements. Abolition of political departments and of the requisitioning detachments which search passengers on trains for food; equalization of all rations, except for workers in harmful trades; the right of the peasant to possess land and to use cattle, provided that he does not employ hired labor. (This last demand was rather clumsily phrased, but was obviously directed against requisitions and against the forcible installation of communes and state farms.)

The mere publication of the programme of the Kronstadt insurgents is a sufficient refutation of the absurd propagandist falsehoods which were immediately put into circulation by the Moscow radio station, which broadcast the following message to "all, all, all": [17]

"Just at this moment, when in America a new Republican regime is assuming the reins of government and showing inclination to take up business relations with Soviet Russia, the spreading of lying rumors and the organization of disturbances in Kronstadt have the sole purpose of influencing the American President and changing his policy toward Russia. . . . The rebellion of the *Petropavlovsk* crew is undoubtedly part of a great conspiracy to create trouble within Soviet Russia and to injure our international position. . . . This plan is being carried out within Russia by a Tsarist General and former officers, and their activities are supported by the Mensheviki and Social Revolutionists."

Actually the Kronstadt outbreak had not the slightest connection with American policy toward Russia or with any imaginary "great conspiracy" to injure the international position of the Soviet Government or with Tsarist Generals. Its programme was of a decidedly left-wing character. It did not demand a Constituent Assembly or liberty for all. Its slogans were honestly elected Soviets and freedom only for workers, peasants and "Left Socialist" parties.

The demand for greater economic freedom for the peasant was qualified by the condition that he must not employ hired labor.

What the hastily chosen leaders of the Kronstadt sailors put forward as demands expressed pretty faithfully the more or less conscious desires of the great majority of the Russian workingclass and peasant masses. They emphatically did not desire a return to the old regime; they had proved this on many battlefronts of the civil war. But at the same time they felt that the dictatorship of the Communists had perverted the original ideals of the Revolution and had taken away its fruits from the workers and peasants in whose name it had been made.

The Kronstadt rebellion made further progress on March 2. A conference of delegates of the workers and sailors elected a temporary revolutionary committee of fourteen members. The most active figure in this committee was an Ukrainian sailor named Petrichenko, who occupied the post of a senior clerk on the warship *Petropavlovsk*. The revolutionary committee took up its headquarters on the *Petropavlovsk* and began to issue a daily newspaper. No opposition was encountered from the Kronstadt Communists, some of whom joined the insurgents. The more prominent Communist officials, such as Commissar Kuzmin and the President of the Soviet, Vasiliev, were arrested; but there were no killings and no cases of maltreatment of prisoners. Among many extremely sanguinary episodes of the Russian civil war Kronstadt is surprising because of its humanity. It had no executions, no lynchings even of the most unpopular local Communist and Soviet officials.

A conciliatory policy on the part of the Soviet authorities might have averted the subsequent bloodshed. The Kronstadt revolutionary committee took no aggressive steps. It rejected the proposals of the military experts of the fortress to move on the neighboring town of Oranienbaum and seize the stocks of food and munitions there. But the Communist leaders were in a nervously exasperated frame of mind that is understandable, in view of the general state of the country at that time. They felt that willingness to negotiate would be interpreted as a sign of weakness and would hear of nothing but unconditional surrender. On March 2 the Council of Labor and Defense declared "General Kozlovsky and his accomplices"[18] outlaws and instructed the Petrograd Committee of Defense to liquidate the uprising as quickly as possible. On the night of March 4 the Petrograd Soviet, which was, of course, packed with Communists, passed a resolution characterizing the Kronstadt movement as counterrevolutionary and demanding immediate surrender. On the following day Trotzky published the following imperious manifesto: [19]

"Last warning to the garrison of Kronstadt and the insurgent forts. The Workers' and Peasants' Government decided:

"To bring Kronstadt and the mutinous ships into the possession of the Soviet Republic.

"All who have lifted up hands against the socialist fatherland, lay down arms immediately. Disarm and hand over to the Soviet authorities those who are obstinate. Set free immediately the arrested commissars and other representatives of the Soviet regime.

"Only those who surrender unconditionally can count on the mercy of the Soviet Republic. At the same time orders are being given to make all preparations for the smashing of the mutiny and the mutineers by force of arms.

"All the responsibility for the sufferings which in this case will fall on the peaceful population lies on the White Guard mutineers.

"The present warning is the last."

Kronstadt refused to submit, and on the evening of March 7 military activities commenced with an artillery duel between the Soviet guns on the northern and southern shores of the river Neva and the guns of the Kronstadt forts and warships. The capture of Kronstadt was far from an easy task. The fortress was defended by a garrison of some fifteen thousand soldiers and sailors; attacking forces had to cross several miles of ice (the Neva was still frozen) exposed to artillery and machine-gun fire from Kronstadt and to cross-fire from the forts. The Seventh Red Army, which was located in the Petrograd region, was in a "demobilization mood" and Trotzky and his military advisers placed more reliance on the *kursanti,* on the special troops of the Cheka and on picked Communist units. The Tenth Communist Party Congress was in session in Moscow when the news of the Kronstadt revolt arrived; over three hundred delegates were promptly despatched to take part in the suppression of the revolt and to raise the morale of the Government troops by their presence.

The first direct attack on Kronstadt on March 8 was beaten off. The besieged insurgents, who regarded themselves as more genuine revolutionists than the troops which were attacking them, broadcast a message on the occasion of international working women's day, on March 8: [20]

"We Kronstadters, amid the thunder of cannon, amid the bursting of shells, hurled against us by the enemies of the working people, the Communists, send our brotherly greeting to you, working women of the world. We send you a greeting from insurgent Red Kronstadt, from the realm of liberty. . . . Long live the free revolutionary working women. Long live the World Social Revolution."

The Kronstadt newspaper denounced:

"sanguinary Field-Marshal Trotzky, who stands up to his waist in the blood of the workers and opened fire on revolutionary Kronstadt, which rose up against the Government of the Communists to restore the real power of the Soviets."

It further declared that:

"here in Kronstadt is laid the cornerstone of the Third Revolution, which will strike the last chains from the working masses and will open a new broad road for socialist creation."

Two more attacks on the rebel fortress, on the 10th and the 12th, were repulsed. But on the night of the 16th the assailants resorted to a successful stratagem. The *kursanti* and other shock units which were brought up to storm Kronstadt were clothed in white robes and moved over the ice unperceived until they had almost reached the outer lines of defense. Then there was an outburst of firing and fierce hand-to-hand fighting. Even taken by surprise Kronstadt did not yield without a struggle, which lasted throughout the 17th. By the early morning of the 18th the town and the warships were in the hands of the Soviet forces. Some of the more prominent leaders of the insurrection escaped over the ice to Finland. The Cheka did not emulate the humanity of the Kronstadt insurgents, who spared all their Communist prisoners. Alexander Berkman, an Anarchist whose stay in Russia led to his complete disillusionment with the Soviet regime, noted down two bitter entries in his diary for those days: [21]

"March 17. Kronstadt has fallen to-day. Thousands of sailors and workers lie dead in its streets. Summary execution of prisoners and hostages continues.

"March 18. The victors are celebrating the anniversary of the Commune of 1871. Trotzky and Zinoviev denounce Thiers and Galliffet for the slaughter of the Paris rebels."

Kronstadt fell. Isolated as it was, it could have scarcely escaped this fate, although the subsequent melting of the ice would have made its reduction more difficult and more costly. The workers' unrest in Petrograd had died down before Kronstadt raised its banner of "the Third Revolution"; the peasant uprisings in Tambov and other parts of Russia were too remote to be of any direct aid to the besieged sailors.

But, although the Kronstadt rebellion was crushed, it had an important effect in hastening the long overdue scrapping of the whole system of war communism. Armed mutiny in an important fortress, in a former stronghold of Bolshevism, was too significant a warning to be left unheeded. And, although the political aspirations of the Kronstadt sailors for free Soviets and the like remained "empty dreams" (to borrow a phrase which Tsar Nicholas II once employed in dismissing the suggestion of a liberal *zemstvo* that he might introduce a constitutional regime), the demands for greater economic freedom for the peasant and for the abolition of those oppressive features of war communism which bore heavily on every citizen were largely satisfied by the enunciation of the New Economic Policy at the Tenth Party Congress, in March, 1921.

The cornerstone of this New Economic Policy was the abandonment of the policy of requisitioning all the peasants' surplus produce and the substitution of a fixed tax in kind. Once this tax was paid the peasant was permitted to do what he liked with the remainder of his produce: to consume it himself, to sell it to the state, if the state could offer him any goods in exchange, or to sell it on the private market, which was definitely legalized. This basic change brought in its train a series of other changes, until the economic features of war communism became quite unrecognizable. To trace in detail the rise and subsequent fall of the Nep lies outside the province of this work. One may briefly summarize its more important characteristics as follows: abolition of labor armies and compulsory labor; restoration of a regular currency and taxation system (the tax in kind on the peasantry eventually became a money tax); a rapid spread of private retail trade and a much more limited toleration of private initiative in other fields, such as small industry and housing construction.

It is impossible to determine the precise moment when Lenin decided that freedom of private trade, even if it meant a temporary restoration of capitalist relations that had been abolished or at least driven underground, was part of the necessary price of economic recovery. On December 25, 1920, *Pravda* was still thundering in quite uncompromising fashion against any toleration of free trade. Shortly before this the famous Sukharevka Market in Moscow had been abolished. The Eighth Congress of Soviets, which met in December,

1920, took no steps which would foreshadow the relaxation of the prohibition of private trade; on the contrary, it adopted a law which contemplated forcing the peasants to plant their fields by the creation of a new huge bureaucratic apparatus in the form of "sowing committees."

The first sign of a changing attitude is to be found in *Pravda* of February 11, where a Siberian peasant named Chernov is permitted to express the viewpoint that it would be to the benefit of the state to get grain by means of a fixed tax, leaving the peasant free to dispose of his surplus. Chernov wrote: "In this way the Government will obtain a good deal more [so far it got only uprisings] and the peasants will be content and will produce more."

Two Moscow Communists, Sorokin and Rogov, on February 17 contributed to *Pravda* an article repeating Chernov's suggestion and declaring that efforts to force the peasants to cultivate their fields would scarcely yield any results. And on March 2 Lenin, addressing the Moscow Soviet, said that there was a "good deal of commonsense" in the advocacy of taxation as a substitute for requisitions.

The Party Congress, which opened on March 8, was strongly under the influence of the thunder of artillery at Kronstadt and of the fainter echoes of peasant hunting rifles on the fields of Tambov. The intensely disputatious mood which had characterized the period of the discussion about the trade-unions was gone; there was a feeling that Party unity was a matter of selfpreservation, and a general disposition to accept Lenin's leadership with a minimum of criticism. The proposal which Lenin broached on the first day of the Congress to substitute a tax in kind for requisitions was adopted virtually without opposition.

In his speeches at the Congress Lenin emphasized the exhaustion, misery and poverty of the country ("For a long time we are condemned simply to heal wounds," he said on one occasion), the vital importance of coming to an agreement with the peasantry, the necessity for reshaping policies in view of the transition from war to peace, the difficulties connected with the demobilization of the swollen Red Army at a time of general economic breakdown, the necessity for close unity and firm discipline in the ranks of the Party. He characterized the recent discussion as a "luxury," the wisdom of which he doubted. Reminding his audience that Russia was a country where small peasant holders constituted the enormous majority of the population, Lenin declared: [22]

"In such a country social revolution can be finally victorious only on two conditions: first, that it be supported in good time by social revolution in one of several advanced countries. The other condition is an agreement between the proletariat, which carries out its dictatorship or holds state power in its hands, and the majority of the peasant population."

Lenin was quite willing to face the fact that legalization of private trade would mean, to some extent, a return to capitalism. But he considered that the conciliation of the peasantry was such a vital necessity that he was willing to take this risk. He was also willing to permit capitalist relations of a different type by granting concessions to foreign firms. Here he repeated the argument which he had used against the "Left Communists" in 1918: that State capitalism would really be a step forward for a country like Russia, where a great part of the population was living under very primitive economic relations and where the devastation and destruction of seven years of foreign and domestic warfare had been so great.

As a revolutionary strategist Lenin knew that it was sometimes necessary to retreat. The signing of the Brest-Litovsk Peace was one such occasion; the declaration of the New Economic Policy was another. But, like every good general, Lenin was determined that retreat should not turn into disorderly rout. As he said somewhat later: [23]

"Of course freedom of trade means the growth of capitalism. If there are small enterprises, if there is freedom of exchange,—capitalism will appear. But is this capitalism dangerous to us, if we keep in our hands the factories, the transportation system and foreign trade? I believe that this capitalism is not dangerous to us. . . . (After characterizing as state capitalism the policy of granting concessions to foreign capital be continued) . . . Is state capitalism dangerous to us? No, because we will decide in what measure we shall grant concessions."

So there were to be economic guaranties against a full-blooded restoration of capitalism: the retention in the hands of the state of the big industries, the transportation system, the monopoly of foreign trade. There was also to be a political guaranty: the maintenance of the absolute concentration of power in the hands of the Communist Party. Lenin rejected any idea of granting freedom of speech, press and political activity to non-Communist parties. Even the very scanty facilities for agitation and participation in Soviet elections which were intermittently granted and denied to Mensheviki, Socialist Revolutionaries and other opposition Socialist parties during the period of civil war were soon definitely and completely withdrawn; the members of these parties were obliged to choose between going to prison, going abroad and abstaining from political activity. Lenin recognized publicly more than once that careerism, bureaucratism and other abuses tended to develop in the Communist Party after it had been transformed from a group of persecuted revolutionaries into the sole ruling party in Russia. But he was unwilling to grant the contention of some Communists that a free press would reveal and eliminate many of these abuses. He saw in a press uncontrolled by the Communist Party the cloven hoof of reviving capitalism, and insisted that abuses could and should be combated within the Party itself, with the aid of the Control Commissions.[24]

Lenin's announcement of the New Economic Policy was soon followed by the promulgation of a decree by the All-Russian Soviet Executive Committee.[25] Its main points were that the new tax should take less from the peasants than the former system of requisitions; that it should be progressive, bearing more heavily on the richer peasants and, in some cases, sparing the poorest altogether; that the responsibility for its payment should be individual and not collective (formerly the whole village had been held responsible for the delivery of the prescribed amounts of requisitioned produce); that those peasants who endeavored to improve their farms, to increase the planted area and the number of cattle should receive special privileges in paying the tax. Along with the decree appeared an appeal to the peasants, in which some especially important passages were emphasized by heavy type:

> "From now on, by decision of the All-Russian Soviet Executive Committee and the Council of People's Commissars, requisitioning is abolished and a tax in kind on agricultural products is introduced instead. . . . After the tax has been paid what remains with the peasant is left at his full disposal. . . . Every peasant must now know and remember that the more land he plants the greater will be the surplus of grain which remains in his complete possession."

The countless peasant uprisings, the warning of which had been driven home with special vigor when the predominantly peasant sailors of Kronstadt rose up in arms with the slogan of "a third revolution," had finally had their effect. The hopeless attempt to feed the towns by systematically inciting the poorest peasants against their neighbors who were a little less poor and by commandeering by force the foodstuffs of the village was abandoned; the Communists struck a new, very unfamiliar note of appeal to the self-interest of the small peasant proprietor.

Lenin's experiment was successful, despite the fact that the first year of its application, 1921, was characterized by an appalling famine, the result partly of an unusual drought, partly of the devastation and the requisitioning policies of the preceding years. Freedom of internal trade provided the stimulus that was necessary to stir Russian economic life from the state of lethargy and almost complete collapse which it had reached during the years of war communism.

The introduction of the New Economic Policy marked the sharp dividing line between two epochs of Russian historical development. "The heroic period of the Revolution," as Communists like to call the years of civil war, was ended. And indeed the struggle between the Communists, fanatically intent upon creating a new Russia in the image of Marx and Lenin, and their opponents, who either wished to restore Old Russia or envisaged New Russia differently from the Communists, was marked by no little heroism on both sides of the front, mingled with dark episodes of ferocious cruelty,—all against a background of almost indescribable human suffering.

NOTES

[1] A. Slepkov, "The Kronstadt Rebellion," p. 15.

[2] *Pravda,* for January 22, 1921.

[3] *Ibid.,* for February 12, 1921.

[4] *Ibid.,* for February 8, 1921.

[5] *Cf.* the issues for January 21, February 6 and February 12, 1921.

[6] "History of the All-Union Communist Party," Vol. IV, p. 434.

[7] *Cf.* his article in *Pravda* for December 19, 1920, entitled: "A New Period: New Problems."

[8] V. Lenin, "Collected Works," Vol. XVIII, Part I, p. 12.

[9] The theses of the Workers' Opposition were published in full in *Pravda* for January 25, 1921.

[10] *Cf. Izvestia,* for January 1, 1921.

[11] *Cf.* article by M. Pokolukhin in the collection, "Antonovism," edited by S. Evgenov and O. Litovsky, pp. 65–91.

[12] A pood is equal to thirty-six English pounds.

[13] *Cf.* article by Bogomolkin in "Antonovism," pp. 92–96.

[14] *Cf.* the account of Antonov's movement, written by a Russian correspondent of the Socialist Revolutionary journal *Revolutsionnaya Rossia,* No. 6, pp. 23–28.

[15] S. Evgenov and O. Litovsky, "Antonovism," p. 46.

[16] Typical of the spirit of some of the Kronstadt Communists was the letter of resignation from the Party written by Hermann Kanaev, a Red commander and son of a political exile who had been implicated in the well known "case of the 193," published in *Izvestia Vremmenogo Revkoma,* the organ of the Kronstadt Revolutionary Committee, of March 5, 1934. Kanaev expressed the view that the "Communist Party policy had led the country into a hopeless blind alley, because the Party became bureaucratized, learned nothing and did not want to learn anything or to listen to the voice of the masses upon whom it wished to impose its will."

[17] A. Berkman, "The Bolshevik Myth," p. 295. Especially amusing is the sug-

gestion that the entirely spontaneous revolt of the Kronstadt sailors was designed to achieve the Macchiavellian purpose of unfavorably influencing American policy toward Russia. Many years were still to elapse before the American Government was willing to consider seriously the advisability of according diplomatic recognition to the Soviet regime. A Soviet collection of historical articles and reminiscences, published under the title "The Kronstadt Mutiny" and edited by N. Kornatovsky, admits that there is no proof either that the movement was inspired from outside or that the participants received any aid from abroad.

[18] A good deal was made in the contemporary Soviet manifestos about Kronstadt of the supposed leading rôle of a pre-War General named Kozlovsky. The latter had been appointed to a command in Kronstadt by Trotzky as an artillery specialist. When the rebellion broke out Kozlovsky, along with most of the other professional officers, placed his services at the disposal of the insurgents. He had no share, however, so far as the available evidence shows, in framing the political platform and slogans of the insurgents, confining himself to his rôle as a military specialist.

[19] Trotzky's manifesto, dated March 6, is published in *Pravda,* of March 8, 1921.

[20] "The Truth About Kronstadt," p. 20.

[21] Berkman, *op. cit.,* p. 303. Thiers and Galliffet were respectively Premier of France and General commanding the troops at the time of the suppression of the Paris Commune in the spring of 1871.

[22] V. Lenin, "Collected Works," Vol. XVIII, Part I, p. 126.

[23] *Ibid.,* Vol. XVIII, Part I, pp. 182, 183.

[24] *Cf.* Lenin's letter to a dissident Communist named Myasnikov (who was subsequently arrested and finally escaped abroad), in his "Collected Works," Vol. XVIII, Part I, pp. 312–315.

[25] The decree is published in *Pravda* for March 23, 1921.

CHAPTER XLI

THE REVOLUTION IN RETROSPECT

THE Bolsheviki conquered all their enemies, from the conservative General Krasnov, who was proud of the fact that his laws were an almost exact copy of those of the former Tsarist Empire, to the peasant anarchist, Makhno, who, amid his pillage and debauchery, cherished dreams of a society without a state, where the peasant would be equally free from oppressive landlord and grasping commissar. They diverted the main stream of Russian historical development into a definitely new channel. They tore up the bases of pre-War Russian political, social and cultural life, root and branch. They destroyed with equal ruthlessness the traditional ruling Russia of the Tsar and the Orthodox Church, of the aristocrat and the gold-epauletted army officer and the radical and liberal Russia which stood in opposition to the Tsarist regime. Some of their bitterest enemies were men and women like Nicholas Chaikovsky and Katerina Breshkovskaya, who had given their whole lives to the struggle against the autocracy.

How was it possible for Lenin, with his relatively small band of followers (it is doubtful if there were more than twenty-five thousand Bolsheviki in and outside of Russia at the time of the overthrow of Tsarism) to conquer and hold power against the fierce resistance of the former ruling classes, supported by the Allied Governments? The Bolshevik leaders themselves must have been surprised on some mornings to wake up and find themselves still in Moscow's historic Kremlin; the majority of their opponents were at first firmly convinced that their rule would not last more than a few weeks and regarded its continuance as a kind of baleful miracle. But in history, as in natural science, there are no miracles. There is only the working out of the law of cause and effect.

There were two basic causes of the Bolshevik Revolution, without which Lenin's genius of leadership, Trotzky's fire and audacity, Dzerzhinsky's fanatical devotion and Stalin's cool resolution would have been in vain. One was the Tsarist system, with all its political, economic and social implications. The second, and more immediate, was the World War.

Tsarism paved the way for Bolshevism in several ways. It laid a heavy hand of repression on the young Russian middle class, denied it the opportunity to develop administrative experience and responsibility, imparted to the political life of pre-War Russia the unreality of a debating club. Its sudden fall, therefore, left a huge vacuum, which the liberal forces of Russian society were far too weak to fill effectively.

The social and economic policies of Tsarism, notably the failure adequately to satisfy the land need of the peasantry and the frequent employment of the police power of the state in repressing the trade-union organizing efforts of the workers, tended to create a constant ferment of embitterment among the more active-minded members of the poorer classes which constituted the vast majority of the population. In ordinary times this ferment could be repressed with the aid of spies and provocators, police and Cossacks. But when the whole system crumbled under the shock of the War this ferment was bound to carry the upheaval much farther than liberals or even moderate Socialists desired.

Russia had a relatively small class of "proletarians," in the sense of industrial wage-workers, at the time of the Revolution. On this account the outlook might have seemed unfavorable for revolutionaries who considered themselves disciples of Marx. But Russia had an immense class of poverty-stricken people, without firm roots either in town or in village; by comparison with Great Britain or Germany, France or America, Russia had far more inhabitants who lived perpetually on the narrow line between extreme poverty and actual hunger, who would have conformed to Marx's qualification of having nothing to lose but their chains.

The course of the War immensely increased the number of uprooted, disinherited, embittered people, who felt that they had nothing to lose and perhaps something to gain from the most extreme kind of social upheaval. It took from many a peasant family the main breadwinner and the last horse; it increased the poverty in the towns. Moreover, the Russian military authorities, in carrying out the retreat before the advancing Germans, deliberately devastated wide areas of Poland and the Baltic Provinces and threw the hapless inhabitants as miserable refugees into the interior of Russia. This added still another element of misery and unrest.

Bolshevism, with its terrifically violent and swift change of habits of life and work, could never have appealed to a population which was going about its normal activities. It found its staunchest and readiest supporters among people who felt themselves torn away from their homes, from their ordinary occupations. It was no accident that sometimes the most reliable and stubborn Red Army soldiers fell into this category: one thinks of the Letts and Esthonians, who had been cut off for years from their native countries, of the Chinese laborers and Magyar war prisoners whom the caprices of the World War had cast into Russia, of "dry land" sailors who had lost their ships.

Uprooted and declassified individuals were also prominent on the side of the Whites. Here were landlords without estates, governors without provinces, generals and colonels who had narrowly escaped lynching at the hands of mutinous mobs of soldiers. But of course the widespread destitution, the wiping out of normal opportunities for earning a living which were the result, first, of Tsarist social conditions, second, of the havoc wrought by the War, third, of the chaos which accompanied the revolutionary upheaval, were calculated to win more recruits for Bolshevism than for restorationism.

The steady swing to the Left which set in immediately after the breakdown of the Imperial regime and reached its culmination in the seizure of power by the Bolsheviki seems, in retrospect, logical and inevitable, incredible and outrageous as it must have seemed to the wealthy and middle classes while it was going on. The Provisional Government, in which was embodied the irresolute softness and mildness which were characteristic of many pre-War Russian liberals and radicals, was quite helpless in the face of the elemental popular demand for land, peace and socialism, which, to the average uneducated peasant or worker, meant plundering the rich for the benefit of the poor. It could neither make war nor make peace. It could neither place itself boldly at the head of the huge peasant movement and decree a radical expropriation of the big estates, nor enforce respect for the property rights of the landlords. Under these circumstances it is scarcely surprising that, when Lenin decided that the moment had come to strike for power in November, 1917, the Provisional Government collapsed with little bloodshed for sheer lack of defenders.

The holding of power by the Bolsheviki was a far greater achievement than the taking of it. In 1917 they had only to swim with the popular tide, to tell the peasants to take the land, the soldiers to cease fighting, the workers to organize Red Guard detachments and establish control over the factories. The bleak years from 1918 until 1921 brought an abundance of disillusionment to the masses who had accepted the Bolshevik teachings so enthusiastically and so uncritically in 1917. The workers found that, although they had driven away the capitalists, they had much less to eat than under the Tsar. The peasants learned that the new regime, while it had given them the broad acres of the former country squires, was determined, at the point of the bayonet, if necessary, to take away a large share of what they raised, giving them very little in return. The soldier who had cheered for the Bolsheviki because they were against the War found himself drafted for a new civil war, which in some ways was more inhuman and terrible for its participants than was the World War.

The question naturally arises: Why did the Soviet regime survive and triumph, in spite of the terrific hardships which accompanied the early years of its career, in spite of the disillusionment which found eloquent expression not only in the White movements, headed as they were by members of the former ruling classes, but in many peasant uprisings, workers' strikes, mutinies of Red Army soldiers? To this question there is no single simple answer. A number of factors, psychological, political, economic and geographical, must be taken into consideration.

There can be little doubt that if all the hatreds which the activities of the Soviet Government generated in various classes of the Russian people had ever found concentrated expression at one time under a single leadership the Bolsheviki would have been swept out of existence. Their salvation lay in the fact that, while they operated as a strongly disciplined, unified force, their opponents were hopelessly divided among themselves. One could point out innumerable concrete illustrations of this point.

Soviet rule in Petrograd was seriously threatened twice, once in the autumn of 1919 by the military drive of General Yudenitch, the other time by the uprising of the Kronstadt sailors, with their demands for free Soviets and an end of special privileges for Communists, in the spring of 1921. But it is safe to say that nine tenths of these Kronstadt sailors, had they been called on to make the decision, would have fought against the White General, Yudenitch, and not for him.

The three most redoubtable enemies of the Soviet regime in South Russia were Denikin, his successor, Wrangel, and Makhno. But Makhno fought against Denikin and Wrangel even more energetically than he fought against the Communists. Between the conservative Generals and the peasant anarchist there could be no basis of coöperation.

So anti-Bolshevik Russia was never able to create a united front under a leader who could win support in all classes of the population. In retrospect it is easy to recognize that only a man with a gift for popular oratory, with a capacity to put forward a positive programme as an alternative to the Bolshevik programme, would have stood a chance of opposing the Bolshevik regime successfully. But the White movement produced no Mussolini, no Hitler. It brought to the fore pre-War military and naval officers, accustomed to commanding and not to persuading or agitating and quite incapable of appealing to the masses as Lenin and Trotzky could appeal to them.

An absolutely impassable gulf separated the White Governments of Siberia and South Russia from the peasant majority of the population, on whose relative measure of sympathy the issue of the struggle depended. One year of Kolchak's rule was sufficient to turn Siberia into a hornets' nest of rebellious peasant partisans, who did half the Red Army's work for it. A still shorter period of occupation of Ukraina by Denikin created for his forces a number of internal "fronts," organized by Makhno and other peasant guerrilla leaders, which contributed greatly to the total rout of his armies in the winter of 1919–1920.

The Communists also had their hands full in endeavoring to clamp down a new kind of state authority on the aroused peasantry. From 1918 until 1921 the chronicles of Soviet Russia are full of sanguinary peasant outbreaks against the Soviet rules, mostly caused by the food requisitioning policy of the Soviet Government, supplemented by such causes as mobilization for the Red Army or resentment at the anti-religious activities of the Communists and the supposed predominance of Jews in their ranks. But what was important in determining the course of the civil war was not the fact of peasant discontent, but the degree of it. And the Soviets passed this test more successfully than the Whites. Kolchak and Denikin saw their rears simply crumple up in the last stages of their campaigns as a result of the peasant uprisings. Insurgent peasants more than once helped to cause serious defeats to the Red Army. But at the moments when a widespread flare-up of rebellion in the villages would have spelled disaster, when Kolchak was approaching the Volga, when Denikin was in Orel and Voronezh, when Yudenitch was hammering away at the heights of Pulkovo, the Red rear remained firm.

Elements of time and space also distinctly favored the Reds in the civil war. Their regime dated from November 7, 1917. Kolchak only came into power a year later; and still more time elapsed before Denikin emerged from his original position as a local figure in the North Caucasus and challenged Bolshevism on an all-Russian scale. This meant that the Soviet Government had a substantial advantage in time in the organization of its civil and military administration.

Moreover, the Bolsheviki possessed a desirable central position. Their adversaries, Kolchak in the East, Denikin in the South, Yudenitch in the West, Miller in the North, were separated from each other by wide stretches of land and sea and were unable to coördinate their military efforts, to send reinforcements to one another. The Reds, on the other hand, operating on interior lines, could strengthen the front that seemed most critical at any given moment at the expense of the others. Furthermore, by far the larger part of the munitions and other war material which had been accumulated for use in the World War was in Bolshevik territory; this was a very great advantage and more than offset the aid in munitions and supplies which the Whites received from abroad.

After Kolchak had ousted the Directory and assumed power as a dictator a group of Socialist Revolutionaries acquired the neckname of "Ninisti," because they proclaimed the slogan: "Ni Lenin ni Kolchak" ("Neither Lenin nor Kolchak"). In view of the fact that Communists and active Soviet sympathizers, on one side, and militant Whites, on the other, certainly constituted small fractions of the Russian population, since the peasants, who constituted the majority of the people, were certainly inclined, in the main, to call a plague on Red and White houses alike, it might have seemed that a democratic political movement, equally far removed from Bolshevism and from restorationism, would have stood a good chance of emerging victorious from the turmoil of revolution and civil war. Actually those regimes and political bodies which were relatively democratic in their aims and methods, the Government established by members of the Constituent Assembly in Samara, the subsequent Directory in Siberia, the Kuban Rada, the Ukrainian nationalist Government (in so far as it could be differentiated from the semi-bandit "atamans" who were its chief supporters) were pitifully weak and were brushed aside by Reds and Whites with little difficulty. It is a general law of revolutionary periods that extremists are always victorious; historical experience would have indicated that Russia's destiny was to be "either Lenin or Kolchak," not "neither Lenin nor Kolchak."

Apart from the rule that moderates get scant hearing in epochs of social upheaval and class war, there were several specifically Russian circumstances that doomed to impotence all attempts to create a democratic substitute for the Soviet regime and that created a sense of deepest tragedy for many radical and liberal intellectuals who saw in Kolchak and Denikin a return to a well known and hateful form of tyranny and in the Soviet regime a perpetuation of some of the worst features of the traditional Russian despotism in new forms and under new names. First of all, of course, Russia was completely lacking in the practise and tradition which are indispensable for the strengthening of democratic institutions. A constituent assembly, to be followed by a parliament, was the ideal only of the liberal and radical wing of Russia's small educated class. Pre-War conservatives, even some pre-War liberals, saw in the stormy excesses of the Revolution definite proof that Russia needed a monarchy or some form of authoritarian dictatorship.

The Cadet Party, the middleclass liberal political organization of pre-War days, had begun to move to the Right immediately after the March Revolution, as a natural reaction to the tremendous swing to the Left among the masses which clearly portended a major destructive social revolution, which the Cadet lawyer, university professor or progressive businessman emphatically did not desire. During the civil war the Cadets ranged themselves under the banners of Kolchak and Denikin. They were, therefore, definitely identified with the Whites; they did not aim at the creation of a democratic movement, equally opposed to Soviet and to White dictatorship.

The Socialist Revolutionaries adhered more faithfully to democratic slogans. But this very typical Party of the radical Russian intelligentsia proved itself again and again totally incapable of creative practical leadership. Its leaders could never agree among themselves; the Party was perpetually dividing up into "left" and "right" wings, with a "centre" vainly attempting to mediate between them. Prolific in wordy and melodramatic manifestos, capable of individual acts of rare daring and self-sacrificing heroism, the Socialist Revolutionaries were pathetically helpless when it was a question of organized mass action, whether to defend the Constituent Assembly against the Kronstadt sailors, or to defend the Directory against the reactionary Siberian officers.

Back of this helplessness was, of course, a lack of genuine mass support. Like the Girondists of the French Revolution, the Socialist Revolutionaries fell between two stools. They were not radical enough for the "classconscious workers"; they were too radical for the "classconscious bourgeoisie." There still remained the vast grey mass of the peasantry. The Socialist Revolutionaries always considered themselves a peasant party. They polled the great majority of the peasant votes in Russia's sole relatively free general election,—to the Constituent Assembly. The Bolshevik decree on land, in almost all its main features, was a Socialist Revolutionary project. Why then didn't the peasants rally around the leadership of the Socialist Revolutionaries, who wished to give them land and liberty without requisitions, state farms and more or less compulsory communes,—three features of Bolshevik agrarian policy which were cordially detested in the villages?

Part of the answer to this question is to be found in the peasants' frequent characterization of themselves as "a dark people." A large proportion of them were illiterate; very few had the slightest conception of national politics or had any idea that nationwide coöperative action could improve their lot. Consequently the rôle of the peasantry during the civil war, while very important, was almost exclusively negative. When the abuses and exactions of either Red or White local authorities became quite intolerable the peasants of a given district would not infrequently rebel, killing all the officers or Communists on whom they could lay their hands. The rebellion, in due course, would be put down by the sending of a Red or White punitive detachment. To combine with the peasants of other regions, to organize a regular army, to march on Moscow and install a central legislative body in which peasants would predominate as they predominated in the general population: such a programme of coherent activity would have been as incomprehensible to the average Russian *muzhik* as a page of Homer or Vergil.

There was a wide gulf between the Socialist Revolutionary intellectuals in the towns and the peasants in the villages, and the Socialist Revolutionary Party, as an organization, seems to have exerted little influence on the elemental course of the many peasant outbreaks, big and small, which occurred during the civil war. The peasants usually followed the leadership of some local chieftain, a man whom they knew, usually a man of their own class. Some of these guerrilla leaders, such as Makhno in South Ukraina and Antonov in Tambov, were quite successful in their operations; their bands, at times, swelled into small armies. But the Makhnos,

Antonovs and their hosts of lesser imitators could express only the blind rage of Russia's backward peasantry, conscious that it was being oppressed and defrauded, but quite unable to offer any constructive substitute for the regime against which it was rebelling. In basing their hopes on the Russian peasantry, a class that was still too primitive, too ignorant to be capable of conscious independent political action, the Socialist Revolutionaries had built on sand.

Nothing would so certainly have altered the course of the Russian Revolution as a higher level of education and material wellbeing among the peasantry; and here again the Tsarist system, with its consistent policy of preferring the interests of the landlords to those of the peasants, was unconsciously paving the way for a social upheaval of the most violent and extreme kind. If one should examine on a map the regions where the popular resistance to Bolshevism was strongest it would be found that those regions, with few exceptions, coincided with the districts where the peasants, on the whole, were relatively better off, where they had an opportunity to build up prosperous homesteads, to send their children to school, where, in short, they stood to lose in a process of wholesale levelling and confiscation and ruthless smashing of all property rights.

The Don and Kuban Cossacks, with their comfortably liberal land allotments, their herds of cattle and horses and flocks of sheep, were the backbone of the southern White Armies, the most formidable military force that took the field against the Soviets. The peasants of the fertile black-soil sections of Ukraina furnished the recruits for the innumerable insurgent bands, some of which fought the Soviets under the blue and yellow colors of Ukrainian nationalism, others under the black flag of Makhno's rural anarchism. Siberia might seem an exception to the rule, because here even well-to-do peasant districts participated in the partisan war against Kolchak. But the lead in this war was taken by the poorer migrants from European Russia; and, after the Soviet regime was established in Siberia, the peasants in some of the more prosperous districts of Western Siberia rose up against it. However, the well-to-do peasants who represented a natural barrier against the triumph of Bolshevism were not numerous enough to play a decisive part in Russia's decisive years of turmoil. They were outnumbered by their poorer neighbors, among whom the Bolsheviki were able to win supporters by holding out the alluring prospect of an equal sharing up of land, cattle and machinery.

Military and economic considerations alone do not explain the victory of the Bolsheviki. Important psychological factors must also be taken into account. First of all, the *Zeitgeist*, the characteristic spirit of the period of civil strife, was favorable to the Reds and unfavorable to the Whites. 1917, "the crazy year," as Russian conservatives sometimes call it, had unloosed among the masses a fierce desire to break up everything that belonged to the pre-War era. No matter how great the disappointment might be with many features of Soviet policy, any attempt at restorationism was certain to elicit a quick upflare of revolt. It is noteworthy in this connection that the Cadet Schepkin, writing from Moscow in 1919, advised his colleagues on the other side of the front "to be silent about the Soviets." Even such an embittered enemy of the Communist rule as Schepkin apparently realized that the Soviet idea still had deep roots in the masses.

Nowhere in the world, perhaps, was there so much class hatred and class envy as in Russia. The overthrow of Tsarism gave full rein to these long suppressed sentiments; and the Bolsheviki were adept in fanning the flames of class antagonism, in keeping alive and making articulate the sullen dislike which a large part of the poor and uneducated majority of the Russian people had always felt for the well-to-do and educated minority. It may have been because of the late persistence of serfdom; it may have been because contrasts of wealth and poverty were very sharp in pre-War Russia; but the course of the Revolution certainly indicated that the poorer classes derived a good deal of satisfaction from the mere process of destroying and despoiling the rich, quite irrespective of whether this brought about any improvement in their own lot.

Every great revolution affords a concrete illustration of Schiller's phrase: *"Die Weltgeschichte ist das Weltgericht."* ("The history of the world is the judgment of the world.") Revolutions accelerate by years or by decades the normally slow and gradual process of the vanishing of old classes of society and the emergence of new ones. The Russian Revolution and the civil war which followed it may be regarded as a kind of gigantic ordeal by battle as between those who were vitally interested in destroying the old social order and those who were interested in preserving it, in more or less modified form.

In this ordeal the Reds proved superior to the Whites. With all their faults of ignorance and inexperience, the former revealed the crude strength of a fresh young ruling class. The Whites, with all their natural advantages of education and military and administrative experience, displayed the decadence and weakness of a group on which history had already passed its sentence of condemnation. The typical figures of the new Soviet ruling class, the Petrograd metal worker, suddenly promoted to the post of governor of a province or commander of a regiment, the Jew from Gomel or Berditchev, emerging from the squalor and oppression of the Tsarist Ghetto to the intoxicating eminence of a commissar or an industrial administrator, the sullen Lettish ex-soldier, whose ancestors had felt on their backs the lash of the German baron's overseer and who wreaked vengeance on all the "boorzhooi" who might fall into his hands in the Cheka, the poor peasant who found himself head of a Soviet or chief of a Red partisan detachment displayed, in the main, more steadfastness, more devotion to their cause, more selfdiscipline than the officers and civil officials of aristocratic or middleclass origin who came to the fore in the White Governments. This fact is especially noticeable if one compares the atmosphere behind the Red and White lines.

When the issue of the civil war was being decided on the front the bars and cafés in the towns in Kolchak's and Denikin's territory were filled with drunken officers who somehow almost invariably escaped punishment. One officer who, at the risk of his life, deserted the Red Army and passed over to Kolchak was so disgusted by the prevalent indiscipline and debauchery that he drew an indignant contrast with conditions on the Soviet side, where, as he said, an intoxicated officer would have been shot by the first commissar who met him. Not all the Communists, certainly, were saints or puritans. But their general behavior and morale seem to have been better than those of their opponents. Their will to power, their determination to hold the seats of power which they had gained were stronger than the efforts of the former privileged classes to regain their old position.

The Bolsheviki always regarded their revolution as international in character and significance. In the darkest hours of military adversity and economic breakdown they were buoyed up by the belief that the European working class would come to their aid by carrying out revolutions in other countries. This, of course, did not occur. The Russian Revolution stopped at Russia's somewhat contracted frontiers.

It would lead one far afield to examine in detail the reasons why the formulas of revolutionary overturn which triumphed in Russia failed in all European countries, even in those which had sustained military defeat and very great economic hardship. A few of the main general reasons may, however, be briefly indicated.

In no European country was there a revolutionary group so hardened, experienced and fanaticized by governmental persecution as were the Russian Bolsheviki. And in no European country were the social and economic conditions so favorable to a large-scale upheaval, which would annihilate all property rights. With the possible exception of Spain no European country possessed an agrarian problem comparable in acuteness with Russia's. The new states which seceded from Russia or which emerged in new or enlarged form as a result of the peace treaties hastened to take the edge off peasant discontent by enacting measures of agrarian reform of varying degrees of radicalism. In the West European countries the majority of the peasants would have been regarded in Russia as "kulaks" and were naturally opposed to any revolution which would put forward a programme of wholesale general expropriation.

In Western and Central Europe, moreover, the middle class was much stronger and more numerous, in proportion to the general population, than in Russia and showed no disposition to let itself be crowded to the wall by a proletarian dictatorship. True, such countries as Great Britain and Germany possessed a much larger, better educated and better organized industrial working class than existed in Russia. But the hopes which Lenin and Trotzky based on this fact proved misleading. For the West European workers, with their higher material standard of living, responded feebly and ineffectively to the Communist international apostles of armed revolt. The Russian Revolution disproved most convincingly a very general belief among Socialists before the War: that socialism would first come about, peacefully or by violence, in highly developed capitalist countries when the capitalist system had outlived its progressive functions. The success of a Marxian revolution which, with all its zigzags of political and economic policy, has adhered steadfastly to the principle of eliminating private ownership of the means of production in Russia, taken together with the failure of all attempts to bring about such revolutions elsewhere, indicates that it is easier to overthrow private capitalism where it is fragile and slightly developed, as it was in pre-War Russia, than in countries where it has had a long cycle of development and has become firmly imbedded as part of the natural order of things.

Every revolution has its inevitable combination of tragedy and of triumph as it destroys, displaces, uproots individuals and whole classes and simultaneously pushes up others which were previously submerged. Whether measured by the misery which it caused to some or by the opportunity which it created for others or by the fundamental character of the social reorganization which it brought about, the Russian Revolution is the greatest event of its kind in history, just as the World War, which very directly generated it, was the greatest of all human conflicts. The victims of the guillotine in revolutionary France were far fewer than the numbers who perished in the notorious cellars of the Cheka; the predominantly aristocratic French émigrés are enormously outnumbered by the people of all classes, from Princes and Generals to humble, barely literate Cossack farmers, who were hurled out of Russia by the impact of the revolutionary storm. And there has perhaps never been so great and spectacular an inflow of fresh people, mainly recruited from classes which were formerly largely excluded from the governing group, into posts of authority. Out of the endless turmoil and bloodshed of the terrible years from 1917 until 1921 there emerged a new state order, a new economic system, a new world outlook, a new conception of life and ethics, in short, all the elements of a distinctive new epoch of Russian national development, which has yet to run its full course.

APPENDIX

DOCUMENTS OF THE REVOLUTION

June 9, 1918—March 23, 1921

Decree of the All-Russian Soviet Central Executive Committee on Mobilization for the Red Army, of June 9, 1918

The All-Russian Soviet Central Executive Committee considers that the transition from a voluntary army to a general mobilization of the workers and poorest peasants is imperatively dictated by the whole position of the country, both in order to carry on the struggle for bread and in order to beat back the counterrevolution, both internal and external, which is becoming more impudent as a result of hunger.

It is necessary without delay to proceed to a compulsory mobilization of one or of several categories of recruits. In view of the complicated character of the matter and of the difficulty of carrying it out simultaneously all over the country, it seems necessary to make a beginning, on one side, with the most threatened regions, on the other side, with the main centres of the workers' movement.

Proceeding from these assumptions, the All-Russian Soviet Central Executive Committee decides: to instruct the People's Commissariat for War within a week to work out for Moscow, Petrograd, the Don and Kuban Territories a plan of compulsory mobilization within such limits and forms as will least upset the productive and social life of the above mentioned Territories and cities.

The appropriate Soviet institutions are instructed to take the most energetic and active part in the work of the War Commissariat in carrying out the functions with which it has been entrusted.

President of the All-Russian Soviet Central Executive Committee, Y. Sverdlov,

Secretary, V. Avanesov.

(*Cf. Izvestia* for June 9, 1918.)

Decree of the All-Russian Soviet Central Executive Committee on Organization of the Village Poor and Supplying Them with Bread, Objects of First Necessity and Agricultural Implements, of June 11, 1918

I. Township and village Committees of the Poor, organized by the local Soviets with the obligatory participation of the food organizations and under the general guidance of the Food Commissariat and the All-Russian Soviet Executive Committee, are to be established everywhere. All the Soviets are requested to begin the execution of this decree immediately. The provincial and county Soviets must take a most active part in the organization of the village Committees of the Poor. The provincial and county Soviets are responsible, equally with the township and village Soviets, for the precise carrying out of this decree.

II. Both native and newly arrived inhabitants of the villages may elect and be elected into the township and village Committees of the Poor without limitation, with the exception of notorious kulaks and rich people, proprietors who have a surplus of grain and other food products, who possess commercial and industrial enterprises which use hired labor, etc.

Note. Peasants who employ hired labor to carry on their farms, if these do not exceed the average size, may elect and be elected into the village Committees of the Poor.

III. The township and village Committees of the Poor exercise the following functions:

(*a*) Distribution of bread, objects of first necessity and agricultural implements.

(*b*) Aiding the local food organizations in taking away surplus grain from the kulaks and the rich.

IV. The township and village Committees themselves decide which people they are to supply with bread, objects of first necessity and agricultural implements. Decisions which are taken by the township and village Committees of the Poor in agreement with the county food organizations may be repealed by higher food organizations if they are inconsistent with the basic purposes of the organization of the village poor.

V. The special stocks of bread, objects of first necessity and agricultural implements which are formed by the local food organizations, depending on the present reserves and the measure of the need of the population, pass under the control of the township Committees of the Poor.

VI. Distribution of grain, objects of first necessity and agricultural implements among the village poor on the privileged conditions which are outlined below is carried out by the village Committees of the Poor according to lists made up by them and approved by the township Committees of the Poor.

Note. Distribution lists made up by the village and confirmed by the township Committees of the Poor may be questioned by the county and provincial Soviets and by the corresponding food organizations.

VII. The distribution of bread, objects of first necessity and agricultural implements is carried out according to scales worked out by the provincial food organizations in strict accordance with the general plans of supply of the Food Commissariat and the scales established by the provincial food organizations.

Note. The amount of the bread ration distributed to the poor may vary in different periods of distribution among the provincial and food organizations, depending on the need for bread in the consuming regions and the success in taking bread away from the kulaks and the rich.

VIII. The following rules of bread distribution are laid down temporarily, pending the issue of a special order by the Food Commissariat:

(*a*) Out of the surplus grain taken away from the kulaks and the rich according to the decision of the provincial and county Soviets and the corresponding food organizations and delivered to the state grain storehouses before July 15 of this year grain is distributed to the village poor free of charge at the established scales at the expense of the state.

(*b*) From the surplus grain taken from the kulaks and the rich after July 15 but not later than August 15 of this year distribution of grain to the village poor is made according to the established scales for payment with a reduction of fifty percent from the fixed price.

(*c*) From the surplus grain taken from the kulaks and the rich during the second half of August of this year grain is distributed to the village poor at the established scales for payment, with a reduction of twenty percent from the fixed price.

IX. The following basic rules for the distribution of objects of first necessity and the simplest agricultural implements to the township Committees of the Poor are laid down temporarily, pending a special order of the Food Commissariat:

(*a*) In townships where by July 15 of this year, according to the provincial and county Soviets and the corresponding food organizations, the surplus grain has been completely taken away from the kulaks and the rich, objects of first necessity and the simplest agricultural implements are given to the village poor at a reduction of fifty percent from the established prices.

(*b*) In townships where the surplus grain will have been taken from the kulaks and the rich by August 15 of this year objects of first necessity and simplest agricultural implements will be given to the village poor at a reduction of twenty-five percent from the established prices.

(*c*) In townships where the surplus grain will have been taken from the kulaks and the rich during the second half of August of this year objects of first necessity and the simplest agricultural implements will be given to the village poor at a reduction of fifteen percent from the established prices.

X. The township Committees of the Poor take charge of more complicated agricultural machines in order to organize public tilling of the fields and harvesting for the village poor. For the use of this machinery payment must not be collected in regions where the township and village Committees of the Poor give energetic aid to the food organizations in taking away the surplus from the rich and the kulaks.

XI. For the realization of this decree the Food Commissariat receives money and resources in the necessary amount and according to need by decision of the Council of People's Commissars.

President of the All-Russian Soviet Central Executive Committee, Y. Sverdlov,

President of the Council of People's Commissars, V. Ulianov (Lenin),

Secretary of the All-Russian Soviet Executive Committee, Avanesov.

(*Cf. Izvestia* for June 12, 1918.)

Decree of the Council of People's Commissars on the Nationalization of the Largest Enterprises of the Metal, Metal-Manufacturing, Textile, Electrotechnical, Timber, Tobacco, Glass and Pottery, Leather, Cement and Other Branches of Industry, of Steam-Driven Mills, Enterprises of Local Benefit and Undertakings Connected with Railroad Transportation, of June 28, 1918

In order to combat decisively the breakdown in economic life and food supply and in order to strengthen the dictatorship of the working class and of the village poor the Council of People's Commissars decided:

I. To declare as the property of the RSFSR the industrial and commercial-industrial enterprises which are enumerated below, located in the Soviet Republic, with all their capital and property, whatever it may consist of.

IN THE MINING INDUSTRY

1. All enterprises belonging to stock companies and share societies which produce mineral fuel (coal, lignite, anthracite, shale, etc.).

2. All enterprises for mining iron and copper ore which belong to stock companies and share societies.

3–8. All undertakings producing platinum, silver, asbestos, gold, and salt.

IN THE METAL-MINING AND MANUFACTURING INDUSTRY

9. All undertakings with a capital of one million rubles and more and all big enterprises, the value of which is about one million rubles or more.

10. Irrespective of their capital, all metal-producing enterprises which are the only ones of their kind in the RSFSR.

IN TEXTILES

II. All enterprises which belong to stock companies and share societies, which work over cotton and have a basic capital of not less than a million rubles.

All enterprises with a capital of not less than half a million rubles which work over wool, flax, silk and jute.

All enterprises working over hemp with a capital of not less than 200,000 rubles.

ELECTROTECHNICAL INDUSTRY

All enterprises which produce electrical current and electrical machines.

TIMBER INDUSTRY

All enterprises belonging to stock companies and share societies with a capital of not less than a million rubles are nationalized.

III. Until a special order of the Supreme Economic Council is issued for each separate enterprise the enterprises which, according to the present decree, are declared the property of the RSFSR are regarded as being in the uncompensated leasehold use of their former owners; the managing boards of the former owners finance them on the previous basis and also receive income from them on the previous basis.

IV. From the moment when this decree is promulgated the members of the administration, the directors and other responsible managers of the nationalized undertakings are responsible to the Soviet Republic both for the integrity and upkeep of the enterprise and for its proper functioning.

In the event that anyone leaves his post of service without the consent of the proper organizations of the Supreme Economic Council or in the event of unjustifiable neglect in the management of the enterprise those who are guilty not only are responsible to the Republic with all their property, but also bear grave criminal responsibility before the courts of the Republic.

V. The entire employee, technical and working personnel of the enterprise, without exceptions, the directors, members of the board of management and responsible administrators, are declared as being in the service of the RSFSR and receive supplies according to the scales which prevailed before the nationalization of the undertaking, from the income and turnover capital of the enterprise.

VI. In cases when members of the technical and administrative personnel of the nationalized undertaking leave their posts they are liable to prosecution before the courts of the Revolutionary Tribunal.

VII. The sums which belong personally to members of the boards of management, to stockholders and owners of nationalized enterprises are enjoined until the relation between these sums and the turnover capital and resources of the enterprise is cleared up.

VIII. The Supreme Economic Council must quickly work out and send to all nationalized enterprises detailed instructions about organization there, about management and problems of labor organization, in connection with the execution of this decree.

IX. Undertakings which belong to consumers' coöperatives are not nationalized.

X. The present decree comes into force from the day of its signature.

PRESIDENT OF THE COUNCIL OF PEOPLE'S COMMISSARS, V. ULIANOV (LENIN),

PEOPLE'S COMMISSARS: TSURUPA, NOGIN, RYKOV,

ADMINISTRATOR OF THE COUNCIL OF PEOPLE'S COMMISSARS, VLAD. BONCH-BRUEVITCH.

(*Cf. Izvestia* for June 30, 1918.)

PROGRAMME OF THE COMMITTEE OF MEMBERS OF THE CONSTITUENT ASSEMBLY, WHICH FORMED AN ANTI-BOLSHEVIK GOVERNMENT IN SAMARA IN 1918, AS SET FORTH IN ITS DECLARATION, OF JULY 25, 1918

The Soviet regime is overthrown and Bolshevism suffered complete defeat on all the territory which is now subordinated to the Committee of Members of the All-Russian Constituent Assembly. Nevertheless there are still not a few people who dream of a return of the Soviet regime. These persons, together with the dregs of the population, energetically stir up the workers and peasants against the new Government, exploiting their inadequate knowledge and capacity for organization. These agitators suggest to them that the workers will again be under the power of capital and that the peasants will be deprived of the land and subjected to the landlords.

The Committee, regarding such agitation as clearly provocative, states that there is absolutely no basis for it and, in order to put an end to such malicious inventions, makes the following general declaration:

1. The land has once for all passed into the possession of the people and the Committee will not permit any attempts to return it to the landlords. The purchase, sale and mortgaging of agricultural land and of forests are forbidden, and secret and fictitious deals are declared invalid. Those who are guilty of violating this rule will be liable to the strictest responsibility.

2. The existing laws and decisions about the protection of labor preserve their force until they are revised in legislative order.

3. The Department of Labor, which has now replaced the Commissariat for Labor, is strictly instructed to watch out vigilantly for the execution of these laws and decisions and the judicial and examining authorities are instructed immediately to investigate and settle cases of the violation of labor laws.

4. Workers and peasants are requested to defend their interests only by legal means, in order to avoid anarchy and chaos.

5. Dismissal of workers and stoppage of the work of undertakings, if not justified by the conditions of production, or if undertaken by the employers in concert as a means of struggle with the workers or with the Government, are forbidden under pain of severest liability to punishment.

6. Enterprises may only be shut down with the permission of the state organizations which are supervising economic life (Councils of National Economy or Economic Councils).

7. The Department of Labor is commissioned to create appropriate organizations for the protection of labor in provincial and in county-seat towns.

8. The rights of trade-unions, as defined by law, preserve their force until the legal provisions are revised. Representatives of the workers and of the employers must be invited to participate in the preparation for a reëxamination of the laws about the protection of labor.

9. Collective agreements must preserve their validity until they are set aside by an agreement of the parties or until the laws affecting these agreements are revised.

Having in mind, at the same time, the interests of industry and of the economic life of the country, which has been completely shattered by the Bolsheviki, and desiring to coöperate with those better representatives of the commercial and industrial classes who honestly desire the recovery of the Motherland and who wish to promote the reëstablishment of normal economic life, the Committee of Members of the Constituent Assembly also considers it a duty to declare, for general knowledge:

1. The employers possess the right to demand from the workers intensive and efficient labor during all the working time which is prescribed by law and contract and to dismiss those workers who do not submit to these demands, observing the appropriate legal rules.

2. The employers possess the right to dismiss superfluous workers, observing the laws and rulings which have been established in this connection.

President of the Committee, Volsky,

Members of the Committee: N. Shmelev, I. Nesterov, P. Belozerov, I. Brushvit, P. Klimushin and V. Abramov.

(*Cf.* Samara newspaper, *Vechernaya Zarya,* for July 25, 1918.)

Resolution Declaring the Socialist Fatherland in Danger Adopted at Joint Session of the All-Russian Soviet Central Executive Committee, the Moscow Soviet, the Trade-Unions and Factory Committees, of July 29, 1918

The joint session of the All-Russian Soviet Central Executive Committee, the Moscow Soviet of Workers' Deputies, the Trade-Unions and the Factory Committees, after hearing the reports of the representatives of the central Soviet Government, decided:

1. To proclaim the Socialist Fatherland in danger.

2. To make the work of all Soviet and other workers' organizations subordinate to the fundamental tasks of the present moment: repulse of the attack of the Czecho-Slovaks and successful activity in collecting grain and transporting it to the regions which need it.

3. To carry on the broadest agitation among the working masses of Moscow and other places in explaining the critical period which the Soviet Republic is living through and the necessity, both for military reasons and for reasons of food supply, of clearing the Volga, the Urals and Siberia of all counterrevolutionaries.

4. To intensify vigilance in regard to the bourgeoisie, which everywhere takes the side of the counterrevolutionaries. The Soviet regime must safeguard its rear, placing the bourgeoisie under close watch and carrying out mass terror against it in practise.

5. For these purposes the Joint Session considers it necessary to transfer a number of responsible Soviet and trade-union officials to military and food supply activity.

6. Every session of any Soviet institution, of any organ of the workers' trade-union movement, or of any other workers' organization will henceforward place on its order of the day the problem of carrying out in practise the most decisive measures for explaining the situation which has arisen to the proletarian masses and for carrying out the military mobilization of the proletariat.

7. A mass drive for bread, mass military training, mass arming of the workers and straining of all effort for the military drive against the counterrevolutionary bourgeoisie, with the slogan:

"Death or Victory."

Such is our general slogan.

(*Cf.* S. A. Piontkovsky, "The Civil War in Russia: Documents," p. 96.)

The Question of the Death Sentence (September 13, 1918)

Many reproaches are directed against the workingclass and peasant regime in connection with the death penalty. They emanate mostly from the former great people of the world and their servitors, the officials and sabotaging intellectuals. It is really surprising how philanthropic they have become.

But with your words we remember something, humane gentleman! Weren't you the people who hurled the country into the dance of death, into that terrible whirlpool of World War, in which Europe has been choking for five years? And can the Russian worker and peasant forget that gradual sucking out of blood by means of the capitalist system of production, which you practised and they suffered on their own skins for whole centuries? All this was in the order of things, was considered proper, justified by the ruling morality: it was nothing criminal! But for this we know you, gentlemen, not by your words, but by your deeds.

Listen to the groans of our brothers in Ukraina, the Baltic States and Finland—in all the places where the heirs of Kerensky, the Krasnovs and Skoropadskys, have conquered. What bloody deeds are committed there! Remember, finally, the treacherous shot at Comrade Lenin, our beloved glorious leader. And let us put aside all these long fruitless, idle speeches about Red Terror, the necessity for which has long been confusedly felt and guessed by the working masses. It is time, before it is too late, to carry out the most pitiless, strictly organized mass terror, not in words but in deeds. Bringing death to thousands of idle white-hands, uncompromising enemies of socialist Russia, we save millions of workers, we save the socialist revolution.

The wheel of history has turned, historical truth has changed. And, instead of class murder in war, with its many millions of victims, instead of the slow, systematic sucking out of the blood of the working people through the cobweb network of capitalism, in the interests of the ruling minority, instead of all this we have gone over to merciless war, not excluding even the death penalty, against all irreconcilable enemies of Workers' and Peasants' Russia, who are digging its grave before it has become strong, before it has become unconquerable. And this is because we prize and love life so much—that sacred gift of nature—that we cannot be silent witnesses of mass murder in war and of gradual systematic murder, the sucking out of all the life juice of the toilers, through the capitalist system of production. We have raised the sword and we shall not lay it down until "the sun will begin to shed the blaze of its rays over us." We will conquer the sun for all the many millions of the working people. And let the cannon thunder, let them bring death, let them wipe from the face of the earth all that black plague that shuts off the source of life and happiness, the holy sun of the future: socialism!

Tremble, hangman of Workers' and Peasants' Russia. The hand does not shake. Wait. Your turn will come.

Y.

(*Cf. Bulletin of the Cheka,* No. 1, pp. 5, 6.)

Documents Illustrating the Extraordinary Commission's Attitude Toward the Use of Torture: a Letter Sent by Nolinsk Communists to the All-Russian Extraordinary Commission and the Reply of the Latter

WHY ARE YOU SOFT?

"The exposed British diplomatic representative [Lockhart] in great confusion left the building of the Cheka."—*Izvestia* of the All-Russian Soviet Executive Committee for September 3.

Revolution is a teacher. It showed us that in times of fierce civil war you cannot be soft. We felt on our backs what it means to release the Krasnovs, Kolchaks, Alekseevs, Denikins and Co. We also saw from the example of the murder of Volodarsky what it means to be merciful with the "domestic" counterrevolution. And we declared mass terror against our enemies and, after the murder of Comrade Uritzky and the wounding of our dear leader, Comrade Lenin, we decided to make this mass terror not a paper thing, but a reality. Mass shootings of hostages took place in many cities after this. And this was good. In such a business half measures are the worst of all; they exasperate the enemy without weakening him.

But here we read about one action of the Cheka which grossly contravenes all our tactics.

Lockhart, the very man who did everything in order to blow up the Soviet regime, in order to destroy our leaders, who scattered British millions on bribes, who unquestionably knew very much that it is important for us to know,—is released, and in *Izvestia* we read the following mild lines: "Lockhart [after his rôle had been exposed] left the Cheka in great confusion."

What a victory of the revolution! What frightful terror! Now we can be confident that the scoundrels from the British and French Missions will cease to organize plots. For Lockhart left the Cheka "in great confusion."

We say this outright: the Cheka, screening itself with "terrible words" about mass terror has still not got away from petty-bourgeois ideology, the cursed inheritance from the pre-revolutionary past.

Tell us, why didn't you subject this Lockhart to the most refined tortures, in order to get information and addresses, of which such a bird must have had very many? So you could easily have revealed a number of counterrevolutionary organizations, perhaps you could have even destroyed the possibility of financing them in the future, which would unquestionably have been equivalent to their destruction. Tell us why, instead of subjecting him to tortures, the mere description of which would have instilled cold terror into the counterrevolutionists, tell us why, instead of this, you permitted him to "leave" the Cheka in great confusion? Or do you suppose that to inflict terrible tortures upon a man is more inhuman that to blow up bridges and food stores in order to find in the pangs of hunger an ally for the overthrow of the Soviet regime? Or, perhaps, it was necessary to permit him "to leave the Cheka in great confusion" in order not to provoke the rage of the British Government.

But this last assumption would imply a complete renunciation of the Marxist viewpoint in foreign policy. It must be clear to every one of us that the British pressure on us depends *only* on the free forces at the disposal of the British imperialists and on the internal condition of that country. The British press on us as much as they can, and this pressure cannot be increased as a result of the tortures of Lockhart.

So far as the internal situation is concerned, it is to our interest to direct the eyes of the working masses of England to the disgusting conduct of their "representative." Let every British worker know that the official representative of his country was engaged in such affairs that it was necessary to put him to the torture. And it may confidently be said that the workers will not approve of the system of explosions and bribery, carried out by this scoundrel, who was directed by a scoundrel of higher rank.

Enough of being soft; put aside this unworthy play at "diplomacy" and "representation."

A dangerous scoundrel has been caught. Get out of him what you can and send him to the other world.

Signed by the President of the Nolinsk Committee of the Russian Communist Party, the President of the Nolinsk Extraordinary Staff for Struggle Against Counterrevolution, the Secretary of the Staff, the Nolinsk Military Commissar and Member of the Staff.

Nolinsk, Vyatka Province. September, 1918.

Comment: Not at all objecting in substance to this letter, we should only like to point out to the comrades who sent it and reproached us with mildness that the "despatching to the other world of base intriguers" representing "foreign peoples" is not at all in our interest.

(*Cf. Bulletin of the Cheka,* No. 3, p. 7 ff.)

Order for Intensified Red Terror, Issued by the Commissar for Internal Affairs, of September 4, 1918

The murder of Volodarsky, the murder of Uritzky, the attempt to murder and the wounding of the President of the Council of People's Commissars, Vladimir Ilyitch Lenin, the mass shooting of tens of thousands of our comrades in Finland, in Ukraina and, finally on the Don, and in Czecho-Slavia [*sic*] the constant discovery of plots in the rear of our army, the open implication of Right Socialist Revolutionaries and other counterrevolutionary scoundrels in these plots, and at the same time the extremely negligible number of serious repressions and mass shootings of the White Guards and the bourgeoisie by the Soviets, all this shows that, notwithstanding constant words about mass terror against the Socialist Revolutionaries, the White Guards and the bourgeoisie, this terror really does not exist.

There must emphatically be an end of such a situation. There must be an immediate end of looseness and tenderness. All Right Socialist Revolutionaries who are known to local Soviets must be arrested immediately. Considerable numbers of hostages must be taken from among the bourgeoisie and the officers. At the least attempt at resistance or the least movement among the White Guards mass shooting must be inflicted without hesitation. The local Provincial Executive Committees must display special initiative in this direction.

The departments of administration, through the militia, and the Extraordinary Commissions must take all measures to detect and arrest all persons who are hiding under assumed names and must shoot without fail all who are implicated in White Guard activity.

All the above mentioned measures must be carried out immediately.

The heads of the departments of administration are bound to report immediately to the People's Commissariat for Internal Affairs any actions in this connection of organs of the local Soviets which are indecisive.

The rear of our armies must, at last, be finally cleared of all White Guard activity and of all vile plotters against the power of the working class and of the poorest peasantry. Not the least wavering, not the least indecision in the application of mass terror.

Confirm the receipt of this telegram.

Communicate it to the county Soviets.

People's Commissar for Internal Affairs, Petrovsky.

(*Cf. Pravda,* for September 4, 1918.)

Decree of the All-Russian Soviet Central Executive Committee on the Extraordinary Revolutionary Tax of Ten Billion Rubles, of November 2, 1918

The international situation which has developed in connection with the latest events in the theatre of the world imperialist War and which has been created by the united international front of the proletarian army compels us to bend all our energies to the struggle for the defense not only of the Russian but of the World Revolution, and the Russian Socialist Federative Soviet Republic is creating a powerful Red Army.

Immense money resources are needed for the organization, equipment and maintenance of this army, and the ordinary state revenues cannot yield these resources.

At the same time the city bourgeoisie and the village kulaks during the years of imperialist war were able to acquire and still continue to acquire vast sums of money, mainly by means of predatory speculation with the first necessities of life and especially with bread.

This wealth must be immediately and completely taken away from the parasitic and counterrevolutionary elements of the population and used to meet the urgent needs of revolutionary upbuilding and struggle.

Therefore the All-Russian Soviet Central Executive Committee decides: to impose on the propertied classes of town and village everywhere a simultaneous tax to the amount of ten billion rubles, exacted on the following basis:

1. The simultaneous extraordinary tax is collected from persons who belong to the propertied classes of town and village.

2. Persons whose sole source of maintenance is wages, salaries or pensions of not more than 1500 rubles a month and who do not possess reserves of money are not subject to the simultaneous extraordinary tax.

3. The simultaneous extraordinary tax cannot be exacted from nationalized and municipalized undertakings, from consumers' coöperatives and from agricultural communes.

4. The general sum of the simultaneous extraordinary tax is distributed among the provinces of the Republic according to a list which is appended to the present decree.

Note. The general amount of the simultaneous extraordinary tax assessed on any given province may be changed by the People's Commissariat for Finance, in agreement with the People's Commissariat for Internal Affairs, after representations, based on precise data, have been submitted by the Provincial Soviet Executive Committees concerned.

5. The amount of the simultaneous extraordinary tax assessed on a province on the basis of Paragraph 4 is apportioned by the Provincial Soviet Executive Committee among the counties and among the towns which participate in the Provincial Soviet Congresses. (Constitution of the RSFSR, Article 53-b.)

The County Soviet Executive Committee apportions the amount of the simultaneous tax which has been fixed by the Provincial Soviet Executive Committee among the townships of the County, and the Township Soviets among the villages and hamlets. (Constitution, Article 57-b.)

6. Committees of the Poor, village, township and city Soviets of Deputies make up lists of persons who are liable to the payment of the simultaneous tax and apportion the amount of the tax which is assessed on the villages or the towns among the taxpayers according to the general position, as regards property and income, of each person. This apportionment is to be carried out in such a manner that the city and village poor shall be completely exempted from the simultaneous extraordinary tax, that the middle classes shall be lightly taxed, and that the whole burden of the tax shall fall on the rich part of the city population and on the rich peasants.

7. The introduction of the simultaneous tax does not cancel previous taxes.

8. Personal and property responsibility is established for the nonpayment of the simultaneous tax.

9. The simultaneous extraordinary tax is assigned to the general state resources according to the accounts of the Department of Income Collection of the People's Commissariat for Finance.

10. The present decree is put into effect immediately, so that the apportionment may be completed by December 1 and the collection not later than December 15 of this year.

11. The People's Commissariat for Finance is to give general instructions to the local Soviets of Deputies about the execution of the present decree and about supervision over the undeviating observance of the time limits mentioned in Paragraph 10.

President of the All-Russian Soviet Central Executive Committee, Y. Sverdlov,

President of the Council of People's Commissars, V. Ulianov (Lenin),

Secretary of the All-Russian Soviet Central Executive Committee, A. Yenukidze.

(*Cf. Izvestia*, for November 2, 1918.)

Kolchak's Order to the Population of Russia after the Assumption of Power, of November 18, 1918

The All-Russian Government has collapsed. The Council of Ministers assumed all power and transferred it to me, Admiral of the Russian Fleet, A. Kolchak.

Taking up the cross of this power in the exceptionally difficult conditions of civil war and complete breakdown of state life I declare: I will not go either on the road of reaction or on the fatal road of party politics. I set as my chief aim the creation of an efficient army, victory over the Bolsheviki and the establishment of law and order, so that the people can choose for itself, without obstruction, the form of government which it desires and realize the great ideals of liberty which are now proclaimed all over the world. I summon you, citizens, to union and to struggle with Bolshevism, to labor and to sacrifices.

Supreme Ruler, Admiral Kolchak.

Omsk, November 18, 1918.

(*Cf. Pravitelstvenni Vestnik*, for November 19, 1918.)

Resolution of the Eighth Congress of the Russian Communist Party on the Attitude Toward the Middleclass Peasantry,* of March, 1919

As regards the problem of work in the village, the Eighth Congress stands on the basis of the Party programme, which was adopted on March 22, 1919, and supports in its entirety the law which the Soviet Government has already passed about socialist land arrangement and transitional measures to socialist agriculture. The Congress recognizes that at the present moment a more correct execution of the Party policy in regard to the middleclass peasantry, in the sense of a more attentive attitude toward its needs, an elimination of arbitrariness on the part of the local

* "Middleclass" seems to be the best rendition for the Russian adjective *seredni,* as applied to the peasantry. It is meant to refer to those peasants who belonged neither to the poorest classes nor to the richer, so-called "kulaks."

authorities and an attempt to come to an agreement with the middleclass peasantry, possess special significance.

1. To confuse the middleclass peasants with the kulaks, to apply to the former in some degree measures which are directed against the kulaks, means the crudest violation not only of all the decrees of the Soviet Government and of its entire policy, but also of all the basic principles of communism, which point to the agreement of the proletariat with the middleclass peasantry during the period of the decisive struggle of the proletariat for the overthrow of the bourgeoisie as to one of the conditions of a painless transition to the elimination of any exploitation.

2. The middleclass peasantry, which has comparatively strong economic roots, because agricultural technique is more backward than industrial even in the leading capitalist countries, to say nothing of Russia, will hold out quite a long time after the beginning of the proletarian revolution. Therefore the policy of Soviet officials and Party representatives in the village must reckon with a long period of coöperation with the middleclass peasantry.

3. The Party must at any cost make Soviet officials in the village clearly recognize the truth which has been established by scientific socialism, that the middleclass peasantry does not belong to the exploiters, because it does not extract profit from the labor of others. Such a class of small producers cannot suffer from socialism, but, on the contrary, will gain very much from the overthrow of the yoke of capital, which, even in the most democratic republic, exploits it by thousands of means.

A quite correct policy of the Soviet regime in the village will thus guaranty the union and agreement of the victorious proletariat with the middleclass peasantry.

4. Encouraging coöperatives of every kind, including agricultural communes of the middleclass peasantry, the representatives of the Soviet Government must not permit the least compulsion in creating these communes. Only those coöperatives are valuable which the peasants have created at their own free initiative and which have yielded advantages that have been tested in practise. Extreme haste in this matter is harmful, because it can only strengthen the prejudices of the middleclass peasantry against novelties.

Those representatives of the Soviet Government who permit themselves to employ either direct or indirect compulsion in order to bring peasants into communes must be held to the strictest responsibility and removed from work in the village.

5. Any arbitrary requisitions, which are not based on the precise instructions of the laws of the central government, must be mercilessly repressed. The Congress insists on a strengthening of the control of the People's Commissariat for Agriculture, the People's Commissariat for Internal Affairs and the All-Russian Soviet Central Executive Committee in this connection.

6. At the present moment the extreme economic breakdown, caused in all the countries of the world by four years of imperialist war for the predatory interests of capitalists and especially intensified in Russia, places the middleclass peasants in a difficult position.

Taking this into consideration, the law of the Soviet Government about the Extraordinary Tax, in contrast to all the laws of all the bourgeois governments in the world, insists that the burden of the tax should rest entirely on the kulaks, on the few representatives of the exploiting peasantry who heaped up special riches for themselves during the War. The middleclass peasantry must be taxed extremely moderately, to a degree that is quite bearable and not burdensome for them.

The Party demands that, as regards the middleclass peasantry, the collection of the extraordinary tax shall be moderated in any case, even if this involves a reduction of the general sum of the tax.

7. The socialist state must give the most extensive aid to the peasantry, mainly by supplying the middleclass peasants with products of city industry and especially with improved agricultural tools, seeds and all kinds of material for improving agriculture and guarantying the labor and the life of the peasants.

If the present breakdown does not make it possible to carry out these measures immediately and fully, still it is the duty of the local Soviet authorities to seek all possible means of giving to the poorest and middleclass peasantry all kinds of real aid, which would support it at the present difficult moment. The Party considers it necessary to assign a large state fund for this purpose.

8. It is especially necessary to carry out in practise immediately and fully the law of the Soviet Government which demands that state farms, agricultural communes and all such organizations should give immediate, all-around aid to the neighboring middleclass peasants. Agreement with the middleclass peasants can only be achieved on the basis of actually giving such help. Its confidence can and must be conquered only in this way.

The Congress directs the attention of all Party workers to the necessity of immediate actual realization of all the demands which are mentioned in the agrarian party of the Party programme, as follows:

(*a*) Regulation of peasant use of the land (abolition of scattered holdings, long strips of land, etc.), (*b*) Supply of the peasants with improved seeds and artificial fertilizers, (*c*) Improvement of the breed of peasant stock, (*d*) Extension of agricultural knowledge, (*e*) Agricultural help to the peasants, (*f*) Repairing in Soviet workshops of the peasants' agricultural tools, (*g*) Organization of sales points, experimental stations, model fields, etc., (*h*) Improvement of the peasants' land.

9. Coöperative organizations of the peasantry, formed for the purpose of improving agricultural production, especially for the purpose of working over agricultural products, improving the peasants' land, maintaining

the handicraft industry, etc., must receive extensive state aid both in finance and in organization.

The Congress recalls that there was never any retreat from the policy of agreement with the middleclass peasantry, either in the decisions of the Party or in the decrees of the Soviet Government. Take, for instance, the most important problem of organizing the Soviet administration in the village. When the Committees of the Poor were created a circular, published under the signature of the President of the Council of People's Commissars and of the People's Commissar for Food, pointed out the necessity of including representatives of the middleclass peasantry in the Committees of the Poor. When the Committees of the Poor were abolished the All-Russian Congress of Soviets again pointed out the necessity of including representatives of the middleclass peasantry in the township Soviets. The policy of the workers' and peasants' government must also in the future be carried out in this spirit of agreement between the proletariat and the poorest peasantry with the middleclass peasantry.

(*Cf.* "The All-Union Communist Party in the Resolutions of its Congresses and Conferences [1898–1926]," pp. 245, 246.)

Kolchak's Declaration on the Land Question, of April 8, 1919

The gallant armies of the Russian Government are moving forward into the territory of European Russia. They are approaching those basic Russian provinces where land is an object of disputes, where no one is convinced of his right to the land and of the possibility of reaping the fruits of his labor.

Our motherland, which was once rich in bread, is now poor and hungry. It is the duty of the Government to create in the agricultural population a sense of calm and firm assurance that the harvest will belong to those who now till the land, who have ploughed and sowed it.

The Government therefore states that everyone who now possesses the land, everyone who sowed it and worked on it, whether he was the owner or the renter, has the right to gather in the harvest. Moreover, the Government will take measures to provide in the future for the landless peasants and for those who have little land, utilizing, first of all, the land of private owners and of the state which has already passed into the actual possession of the peasantry.

Those lands which were formerly tilled entirely or predominantly by the resources of the families of the owners of the land, individual holders and those who separated from the village community, are to be restored to their legal owners.

The measures which have been adopted aim to satisfy the urgent needs of the working population of the villages. The ancient land problem will be finally decided by the National Assembly.

Attempting to assure the peasants land on legal and just principles, the Government emphatically states that in the future no arbitrary seizures of state, public or private land will be permitted, and all who violate the land rights of others will be brought before a court of law.

Legislative acts about the regulation of land relations, about the method of temporarily utilizing land which has been seized, about the subsequent just distribution of such lands, finally, about the conditions of compensating former owners will follow in the near future.

The general objectives of these laws will be: the transfer of the use of land from non-workers to workers, and widespread coöperation in the development of small working households, irrespective of whether these will be based on personal or on community ownership of the land. In order to promote the passing of the land into the possession of working peasant households, the Government will open up wide opportunities for acquiring full property rights in these lands.

The Government carries out this responsible step, which is full of profound historical significance, because it is definitely convinced that only by means of such a decisive measure can it restore, strengthen and guaranty the welfare of the many millions of the Russian peasantry. And the welfare of the peasantry is the healthy and firm foundation on which the fortress of restored free and prosperous Russia will be built.

Omsk, April 8, 1919.

(*Cf.* S. Piontkovsky, "Civil War in Russia: Documents," pp. 301, 302.)

Declarations of General Denikin on the Agrarian and Labor Questions, of April, 1919

DECLARATION ON THE AGRARIAN QUESTION

The benefit of the Russian state imperatively demands the revival and improvement of agriculture.

But life does not wait. The country must be saved from hunger, and the drawing up of a land law for the whole vast expanse of Russia will be the task of the legislative bodies through which the Russian people will express its will.

But life does not wait. The country must be saved from hunger and urgent measures must be taken and put into effect without delay. Therefore the Special Conference* must now proceed to work out and prepare rules for the regions which are under the administration of the Commander-in-chief of the Armed Forces of South Russia.

I consider it necessary to indicate the principles which must be taken as a basis for the rules:

* The Special Conference (*Osoboe Soveschanie*) was a council of military and civilian advisers, attached to General Denikin's Staff, which fulfilled, to some extent, the functions of a Cabinet.—Author.

1. Provision for the interests of the working population.

2. Creation and strengthening of solid small and middle-sized farms at the expense of state and privately owned land.

3. Preservation for proprietors of their right to the land. In each region the amount of land which may be kept in the hands of former owners must be defined and the method by which the remaining agricultural land may pass into the possession of peasants with little land must be established.

These land transfers may be carried out by means of voluntary agreements or by means of compulsory alienation, but payment must always be made.

Land which does not exceed the established limits is given to the new owners on a basis of permanent proprietorship.

4. The lands of Cossacks, allotment lands, forests, land of especially high and valuable agricultural productivity and land which necessarily belongs to mining and other industrial enterprises are not subject to alienation. In the last two cases increased limits are established for each region.

Without awaiting the final working out of agrarian legislation measures must now be taken to facilitate the transfer of land to peasants with small holdings and to raise the productivity of agricultural labor.

DECLARATION ON THE LABOR PROBLEM

Russian industry is completely destroyed, so that Russia's state power is undermined, enterprises are impoverished and millions of working people are deprived of work and bread. I instruct the Special Conference to proceed immediately to the consideration of measures for the restoration of industry and for the working out of labor legislation, taking as the basis of the latter the following propositions:

1. The restoration of the legal rights of the owners of factory undertakings and, along with this, the assurance to the working class of defense of its trade-union interests.

2. The establishment of state control over production, in the interest of the national economic life.

3. Raising of productivity of labor by all means.

4. Establishment of the eight-hour working day in factories.

5. Reconciliation of the interests of the employer and the worker and impartial solution of the disputes which arise between them (arbitration chambers and industrial courts).

6. Further development of workers' insurance.

7. Organization of representation of the workers in connection with the normal development of trade-unions and workers' associations.

8. Efficient protection of the health of the workers, protection of women's and children's labor, arrangement of sanitary inspection in fac-

tories and workshops, improvement of the housing and other living conditions of the working class.

9. Promotion in every possible way of the restoration of old enterprises and the creation of new ones, for the purpose of overcoming unemployment. The adoption of other measures for the achievement of the same end. (Labor exchanges, etc.)

Representatives both of the employers and of the workers must be invited to consider labor legislation. Without waiting for the final working out and realization of labor legislation, the aforesaid basic principles should be applied, so far as possible, in all cases of current life and administrative practise. The state must coöperate especially in providing the workers and their families with the necessaries of life as part of their wages.

LIEUTENANT-GENERAL DENIKIN.

(*Cf.* A. I. Denikin, "Sketches of Russian Turmoil," Vol. V.)

DECLARATION ON HOSTAGES BY GENERAL ROZANOV, KOLCHAK'S GOVERNOR IN YENISEI AND PART OF IRKUTSK PROVINCE, PUBLISHED MAY 25, 1919

The Government troops are carrying on a struggle with robber bands. Criminal elements, the dregs of society, are committing acts of looting, robbery and violence. Bolshevism gave them organization. The outrageous actions which have been committed by the robbers,—the wrecking of passenger trains, the murders of officials and priests, the shootings of the families of peaceful citizens who left the region of insurrection, the acts of violence and cruelty, of which there has been an endless list in the region where the robbers are active—all this compels us to abandon those general moral principles which are applied in relation to the enemy in war. The prisons are full of the chiefs of these murderers. I order the chiefs of the garrisons of the towns in the region under my command to regard the Bolsheviki and the bandits who are kept in the prisons as hostages. Report to me every fact, similar to those which I have mentioned above, and for every crime which is committed in the aforesaid region shoot from three to twenty of the local hostages. This order is to be carried into action by telegraph and is to be widely published.

(Cf. newspaper, *Golos Rabochego,* No. 3, for May 25, 1919.)

ORDER OF GENERAL A. I. DENIKIN, RECOGNIZING THE SUPREME POLITICAL AND MILITARY POWER OF ADMIRAL KOLCHAK, OF JUNE 12, 1919

South Russia has been freed by the marvellous achievements of the Volunteer Armies, of the Kuban, Don and Terek Cossacks and of the Gorsk peoples. The Russian armies move irresistibly forward into the heart of Russia. With bated breath the whole Russian people follows the successes of the Russian armies with faith, hope and love. But, along with the military victories, treachery is developing far in the rear, on the basis of personal ambitions which do not shrink from the mutilation of great and united Russia. The salvation of our Motherland lies in a single Supreme Authority and in a single Supreme Command, inseparable from the former.

Profoundly convinced of this, devoting my life to the service of my warmly beloved Motherland and placing its welfare above everything, I subordinate myself to Admiral Kolchak, as the Supreme Ruler of the Russian State and the Commander-in-chief of the Russian Armies.

May the Lord bless his Way of the Cross and grant salvation to Russia.

(*Cf.* S. Piontkovsky, "Civil War in Russia: Documents," p. 515.)

Admiral Kolchak's Appeal to the Head of the Finnish State, General Mannerheim, of June 23, 1919

In these decisive days of our struggle with destructive and anarchical Bolshevism I should not fulfill my duty to Russia if I did not turn to Your Excellency with an appeal, quite frank and imbued with the deep confidence to which I am inspired by care for the saving of the innumerable human lives which are tormented under the regime of the Bolsheviki.

I proceed from the conviction that everything must be done to crush the Bolsheviki as quickly as possible. Therefore I wish to hope that you will induce the Finnish Government to participate in the common cause and to go over to decisive measures for the liberation of the northern capital of Russia, starting active military operations in the direction of Petrograd.

In the name of the Russian Government I wish to state to you that this is not the time for doubts and waverings, connected with any political questions. Not permitting the idea that in the future there may be unsolved questions, as between liberated Russia and the Finnish nation, I ask you, General, to accept my appeal as a sign of the Russian Army's unchanging recollection of your glorious past in its ranks and of Russia's honest esteem for the national freedom of the Finnish people.

Admiral Kolchak.

(*Cf.* *Krasny Arkhiv,* Vol. 33, p. 128.)

Denikin's Order for the Drive on Moscow, of July 3, 1919

The Armed Forces of South Russia have smashed the armies of the enemy, have captured Tsaritsin and have cleared out the Don Territory, the Crimea and a considerable part of Voronezh, Ekaterinoslav and Kharkov Provinces.

Having as my final goal the seizure of the heart of Russia, Moscow, I order:

1. General Wrangel is to come out on the front Saratov-Rtishevo-Balashov, to replace the Don units in these directions and to continue the offensive on Penza, Ruzaevka, Arzamas and further: Nizhni Novgorod, Vladimir, Moscow.

Immediately send detachments to establish connection with the Ural Army and to clear out the lower valley of the Volga.

2. General Sidorin, with his right wing, until the appearance of the troops of General Wrangel, is to continue the fulfillment of his previous objective: attainment of the front Kamishin-Balashov. His other units are to drive for Moscow in the directions: (*a*) Voronezh, Kozlov, Ryazan and (*b*) N. Oskol, Eletz, Bolovo, Kashira.

3. General Mai-Maevsky is to move on Moscow in the direction: Kursk, Orel, Tula. In order to safeguard himself to the West he is to move to the line of the Dnieper and the Desna, occupying Kiev and the other crossings on the sector Ekaterinoslav-Briansk.

4. General Dobrovolsky is to come out on the Dnieper from Alexandrovsk to the mouth of the river, having in view in the future the occupation of Kherson and Nikolaev.

5. General Tyazhelnikov and General Erdeli are to continue the fulfillment of the tasks which were assigned to them earlier.

6. The Black Sea Fleet is to coöperate in the achievement of the fighting objectives of Generals Tyazhelnikov and Dobrovolsky and to blockade the port of Odessa.

7. Demarcation lines: (*a*) Between the force of General Erdeli and the Caucasian Army, as formerly. (*b*) Between the Caucasian and Don Armies—Kalatch, the boundary of the Don Territory, Balashov, Tambov, Morshansk, all points for the Don Army. (*c*) Between the Don and Volunteer Armies—Slavyanoserbsk, Starobelsk, Valuiki, Korocha, Shigri, Kashira—all points for the Don Army. (*d*) Between the Volunteer Army and the Third Corps—the northern boundary of Tauride Province—Alexandrovsk.

8. The railroad Tsaritsin-Povorino-Balashov is handed over for the joint use of the Caucasian and Don Armies.

LIEUTENANT-GENERAL DENIKIN.

Tsaritsin, June 20, 1919 (Old Style) HP 08878.

(*Cf.* A. I. Denikin, "Sketches of Russian Turmoil," Vol. V.)

MEMORANDUM OF THE TRADE-UNIONS OF SOUTH RUSSIA TO THE PRESIDENT OF THE SPECIAL CONFERENCE, OF THE SUMMER OF 1919

The Bureau of regional branches of the Trade-Unions of South Russia is obliged to make the following statement in connection with the numerous cases of persecutions, arrests and even shootings of responsible officials and rank-and-file members of trade-unions, which have taken place in Kharkov and in a number of other towns in South Russia.

At the end of June in this year N. Vilensky, a member of the district committee of the union of workers of the chemical, porcelain and glass industry, was arrested in Merefa, in Kharkov Province. Notwithstanding repeated appeals to the authorities by representatives of the Bureau of regional branches, who testified that N. Vilensky had no connection either with the Communist Party or with the Soviet regime, it was not only impossible to obtain his liberation, but on July 4 of this year he was killed "while attempting to escape," as the official communication, received by his wife, stated. There is no doubt that this version does not correspond with the truth and that Vilensky was the victim of killing without trial, especially because, according to information in our possession, he was cruelly tortured before his death, being beaten with ramrods and otherwise maltreated.

This case of N. Vilensky was only the most outrageous of a large number of facts which are at the disposal of the Bureau of regional branches. It was not, therefore, an accidental and unique fact. So the president of the committee of the trade-union of municipal workers, Matveenko, was arrested in Kharkov on the night of June 24. At the same time there were arrests of a number of employees of the municipal council (in the departments of water supply, fire protection and electrical streetcar service). These employees, notwithstanding the recommendations of the committee of the union and of the corresponding departments of the municipal administration, have not been freed up to this time.

Polovin, a member of the board of management of the trade-union "Needle," a man who was in no way associated with the Soviet regime or with the Communist Party, was arrested in Kharkov at the end of June. When Polovin was arrested the stamp of the union and about five thousand rubles of union money were taken.

Furthermore, according to the testimony of a member of the union of employees of commerce and industry of Kharkov, N. M. Men, a group of eight or ten officers burst into his apartment on July 1 of this year, searched his apartment and carried off many household goods, without presenting any authorization to make a search. After this, accusing N. M. Men quite falsely of being a commissar and of keeping arms, they pulled him into the courtyard, beat him brutally with ramrods, placed him against the wall and threatened "to cut up all the Yids."

Similar cases occurred also outside of Kharkov. So the chief of the Bakhmut criminal department on June 28 of this year arrested the president of the local trade-union of workers in the chemical, porcelain and glass industry, A. P. Zhitnin, and the member of the same union, Nazar Osipovitch Batashev, at the factory of Lubimov and Solvay at the station Pereezdnaya, in Bakhmut County, Ekaterinoslav Province. Both men after being arrested were sent to Bakhmut. In Konstantinovka, Ekaterinoslav, Province, the instructor of the miners' union, Pecheritz, who had been despatched into the Kadiev and Lozovo-Pavlovsk districts by the union for organization work, was arrested. Union money was taken away from him at the time of his arrest. Of course one could cite many more such facts if difficulties of communication did not deprive the regional centres of connection with their local departments.

Apart from the above mentioned cases of arrests of officials of the trade-union movement there were also incidents of illegal searches in the buildings of the trade-unions and even of attempts to dissolve legally existing workers' organizations. So, on June 15 of this year, agents of the counter-espionage department, in the absence of representatives of the executive committee of the union, opened up the headquarters of the union of workers of the chemical, porcelain and glass industry, on Goryaninovsk Street, No. 13, Apartment 86. After the search all the documents, papers and books of the union were taken away, and part of the papers, according to the testimony of the owner of the building, were burned. This occurred despite the fact that the commandant of Kharkov, in an interview with representatives of the Kharkov council of trade-unions, agreed that searches in the buildings of trade-unions should only be carried out in the presence of representatives of the executive committees of the unions. Another case took place at the factory of M. S. Kuznetzov, in Budi, Kharkov Province. A military detachment of twenty men, under the command of an ensign, appeared here on the 25th of this month and drove out of the headquarters of the factory committee the members of the committee who were present, the members of the executive committee of the local trade-union of workers of the chemical industry and visitors and forbade the factory committee and the executive committee of the trade-union, under a threat of shooting, to continue their activity in the factory building. Incidentally the factory committee possessed the written consent of the factory management to the use of the building by the factory committee and the trade-union.

Such practises in regard to trade-union workers' organizations sharply contradict the declaration of General Denikin on the labor problem on March 24, 1919 (Old Style), in which the working class is assured "organized representation of the workers, in connection with the normal development of the trade-unions and workers' associations" (point 7). They are also inconsistent with the statements which were made by the member of the interdepartmental commission on the labor problem, Y. D. Pryadkin, at a conference on June 26 of this year with the representatives of the regional branches of the trade-unions of South Russia. At a time when the responsible and official representatives of the military and civil authorities make statements about the right of workers' organizations to free existence the agents of authority on the spot in practise place the workers' organizations in such a position that their normal activity and development become completely impossible. Incessant arrests both of responsible officials of the trade-union movement and of rank-and-file members of the trade-unions, which are the result of clearly malicious denunciations and of absolutely unfounded suspicions, completely disorganize the work of the trade-unions, which is carried on with difficulty anyway under the circumstances of civil war and economic breakdown.

Considering that the normal and efficient work of the trade-unions is completely impossible under such circumstances, the Bureau of regional branches states that, unless the policy of the Government in regard to the workers' organization is immediately changed, unless the most urgent measures are taken to remove obstacles to the free activity of these organizations, it cannot regard the above cited facts, which illustrate the attitude of the authorities on the spot toward the trade-union movement, as the isolated result of the accidental deviation of some local officials from the general policy of the Government in regard to workers' organizations. On the contrary it will be compelled to affirm that the general practise of governmental policy toward workers' organizations is clearly inconsistent with its public declarations and statements. Moreover, the Bureau of regional branches, in this case, will be deprived of the possibility of giving organized guidance and leadership to the trade-union movement. It will be compelled to repudiate any responsibility for the possible consequences and to reconsider its former decision that its representatives should participate in the commission on the labor problem, set up by the Special Conference. This decision was taken on the assumption that freedom of action would be granted to the workers' organizations.

(*Cf.* B. Kolesnikov, "The Trade-Union Movement and Counterrevolution," p. 384.)

Outstanding Resolutions on Economic Reconstruction, Adopted by Ninth Congress of the Russian Communist Party, March 29 to April 4, 1920

Immediate Problems of Economic Reconstruction

I. ABOUT THE UPTURN IN LABOR

Recognizing with satisfaction the indisputable signs of an upturn in the labor productivity of the leading classes of the workers, the Congress, however, considers it a duty to warn all the local and central institutions of the Soviet Republic against an exaggerated appraisal of the results which have already been attained.

The labor upturn can make really serious progress only if, first, it will be extended from the leading workers to the millions of toilers in city and village through further efforts of our Party and of the trade-unions in agitation and organization; if, secondly, the central and local economic organizations will take the necessary measures to appraise all the signs of labor upturn both in quantity and in quality, to utilize the available labor force correctly and promptly, to overcome uncoördinated and unorganized efforts, labor partisanism, not suppressing them, but bringing them into the limits of a general state plan.

Along with the forces of the Party all the forces of the Commissariat for Education and of the Political Administration of the Republic must be employed in order to improve the conscientious attitude toward problems of labor and of the scientific organization of industry.

Knowledge of natural science and of technical subjects must be broadly popularized (electrification, scientific agriculture, etc.). Vocational education of all kinds, courses for the preparation of labor instructors and commissars, the publication of textbooks and the production of moving-picture films, etc., must be promoted. All scientific specialists must be called on to work out problems of technique and of the scientific organization of industry. Institutes for scientific research and invention must be created and supported in every possible way.

II. THE UNIFIED ECONOMIC PLAN

The basic condition of the economic recovery of the country is the undeviating carrying out of a *unified economic plan,* reckoning with the next historical period. In view of the profound economic decline and the direct impoverishment of the country the economic plan naturally falls into a series of successive basic problems, which are mutually interdependent:

(*a*) First of all, improvement in the condition of transportation, the shipment and creation of the most necessary reserves of bread, fuel and raw material.

(*b*) Machine building for the benefit of transportation and for the production of fuel, raw material and bread.

(*c*) Intensified development of machine building for the production of articles of mass consumption.

(*d*) Intensified production of articles of mass consumption.

In carrying out the above mentioned plan with the aid of new technical inventions a widespread use of electrical energy must be placed first among the technical problems. This must be adjusted to the fundamental stages of carrying out the general economic plan, as follows:

1. The working out of a plan of electrification of the national economy and the realization of a minimum programme of electrification, *i.e.,* the selection of basic points of electrical supply and the utilization for this purpose both of *existing* electrical stations and of part of the regional central stations which are being built first of all.

2. The construction of the basic regional electrical stations of the first series and of the basic lines of electrical transmission, with a corresponding extension of the activity of factories for the manufacture of electrical equipment.

3. Equipment of district stations of the second series, further development of the network of electrical lines and successive electrification of the most important production processes.

4. Electrification of industry, transportation and agriculture. The economic centres of the Soviet Republic, in their next plans and accounts, must reckon with this unified economic plan, which provides for the nearest future. They must mobilize their main forces and resources first of

all for the solution of the basic problems of each stage of economic development.

Foreign trade, inasmuch as its possibilities open up before the Soviet Republic, must also be entirely subordinated to the requirements of the basic economic plan.

Those industries which contribute to the solution of the basic objective of each stage of economic reconstruction must be developed in line with real necessity. Industries which are not unconditionally necessary for the basic objective of an economic period can be supported only in so far as their work does not obstruct the fulfillment of the basic objective. Therefore the current economic tasks of Soviet economic centres must not represent a simple sum of requirements and needs which have been registered. They must be linked up with iron logicality to the entire economic plan, which reckons in terms of a period of the nearest future.

The realization of the above mentioned plan is possible not by means of separate and single heroic efforts of the leading elements in the working class, but by means of stubborn, systematic, planned labor, which attracts into its sphere larger and larger masses of the workers. The success of such an expanding mobilization and labor education can be assured only if there is a wide and insistent campaign of explanation among the masses of city and village, pointing out the inner meaning of the economic plan, its internal logicality, which assures fruits that will be perceptible to all only after the expiration of a long period, which demands the greatest exertion and the greatest sacrifices.

III. MOBILIZATION OF SKILLED WORKERS

Approving the theses of the Central Committee of the Russian Communist Party on the mobilization of the industrial proletariat, liability to labor service, militarization of economic life and the employment of military units for economic needs, the Congress decides:

The Party organizations must help in every way the trade-unions and the departments of labor to take account of all the skilled workers for the purpose of bringing them into productive work with the same orderliness and the same strictness with which commanders were mobilized for the needs of the Army.

Every skilled worker must return to work at his trade. Exceptions, *i.e.*, the leaving of skilled workers in other Soviet posts, can be permitted only with the consent of the appropriate organs of authority in the centre and in the provinces.

IV. MASS MOBILIZATION FOR LABOR SERVICE

From the very beginning mass mobilizations for labor service must be placed on a correct basis. On every such occasion a precise balance, so far as possible, must be established between the number of persons mobilized, the place of their concentration, the scope of the working task and the number of necessary tools. It is equally important to provide the labor units which are formed out of mobilized persons with technically competent and politically firm instructors and with labor Communist groups, selected earlier through a Party mobilization. In other words we must go along the same road by which we went to the creation of the Red Army.

XIII. FOOD PROBLEMS

In food policy the following objectives are to be pursued:

1. To collect a food fund of some hundreds of millions of poods by the utmost exertion of forces.

2. To distribute it through food bases in the main industrial regions.

3. To make the policy of food distribution more closely and directly serve the cause of the restoration of industry and transport (provisioning, first of all, of the most important industrial enterprises and of transportation; more flexible maneuvering in connection with the changing problems of production; providing for a premium system with necessary products, etc.).

One of the most important objectives both for the restoration of industry and for exchange of goods with foreign countries is the preparation and creation of reserves of raw material. The preparation of raw material must be based on the system of state requisitioning and of compulsory delivery of the raw material according to the requisitions. Along with this a system of payment for the delivered raw material with manufactured and half-manufactured goods at rates which are especially fixed each time must be applied, on the model of the system which has already been employed in the preparation of flax, hemp, etc.

XIV. LABOR ARMIES

The use of military units for labor tasks has both practical economic and socialist education significance. The conditions for effective use of soldiers' labor on a large scale are:

(*a*) The simple character of the work, which can be equally easily performed by all Red Army soldiers.

(*b*) Introduction of the system of tasks, the penalty for nonfulfillment being a reduced ration.

(*c*) Application of the premium system.

(*d*) Participation in the labor on the same working sector of a considerable number of Communists, capable of instilling enthusiasm into the Red Army units by their example.

The utilization for labor of larger military units inevitably yields a higher percentage of Red Army soldiers who are not directly engaged in production. Therefore the use of entire labor armies, with the maintenance of the army commanding staff, can be justified only inasmuch as it is necessary to preserve the army as a whole for military services. As soon as the need for this disappears the overlarge staffs and administrative departments must be dissolved. The best elements from among the skilled workers must be utilized as small labor shock detachments at the most important industrial undertakings.

XV. LABOR DESERTION

In view of the fact that a considerable part of the workers, in search of better food conditions and often for the sake of speculation, leave their enterprises without permission and move about from place to place, thereby dealing further blows to production and worsening the general condition of the working class, the Congress views as one of the urgent problems of the Soviet Government and of the trade-union organizations a systematic, insistent, stern struggle against labor desertion, especially by means of publishing lists of deserters who are liable to punishment, enrolling the deserters in punishment working gangs and, finally, imprisoning them in concentration camps.

XVI. SUBBOTNIKS

Incomparably more attention than has hitherto been the case must be devoted to the subbotniks. Tasks which are close to the local population must be selected for the subbotniks; the latter must take on the character of a collective working effort for the sake of objects which are known in advance and understandable to all. Not only nonparty workers, but the whole local population in general, men and women, must be drawn into them. No less important are the careful thinking out of a technical plan for every subbotnik, a strictly efficient distribution of labor power and a definitely economical use of it. Only under these conditions can the subbotniks enter deeply into life, attracting new masses all the time and making everyday work fruitful with new initiative and fresh enthusiasm.

(*Cf.* "The All-Union Communist Party in the Resolutions of Its Congresses and Conferences [1898–1926]," pp. 267–275.)

Programme of General P. N. Wrangel, of June, 1920

Hear me, Russian People! For What Are We Fighting?

For violated faith and desecrated shrines.

For the liberation of the Russian people from the yoke of the Communists, tramps and criminals, who have completely ruined Holy Russia.

For the cessation of civil war.

So that the peasant, who has acquired the land which he farms as his own property, may engage in peaceful labor.

So that the honest worker may be assured bread in his old age.

So that real freedom and justice may rule in Russia.

So that the Russian people may choose for itself a *master*.

Help me, Russian people, to save the Motherland.

General Wrangel.

(*Cf.* "The Revolution in the Crimea," No. 3, p. 186.)

Decree of the Supreme Economic Council on the Nationalization of Small Industrial Enterprises, of November 29, 1920

1. All industrial enterprises belonging to private persons or companies and employing more than five workers with mechanical power or more than ten workers without mechanical power are declared nationalized.

2. All the property, business assets and capital of the enterprises specified in Paragraph 1, wherever this property may be, and whatever it may consist of, are declared the property of the Russian Socialist Federative Soviet Republic.

3. The provincial economic councils are to begin immediately to take all the undertakings nationalized by this decree with their property under their control and to organize the management, observing all the decisions which have been issued earlier in this connection.

The appropriate departments of the Supreme Economic Council are to watch out for the speediest execution of this decision by their local organs and to give the presidium of the Supreme Economic Council accounts of the course of work of the aforesaid organs and undertakings.

4. From the time of the promulgation of this decree members of the administration, directors, owners and other responsible managers of the enterprises which have been nationalized according to Paragraph 1 remain at their posts until the business is turned over to the Supreme Economic Council or to its representative organization and are responsible to the Soviet Republic both for the integrity and preservation of the undertakings and properties which belong to them and for their correct functioning.

In the event that anyone leaves his post of service without the consent of the proper department of the Supreme Economic Council or in the event of unjustified neglect in the management of the business of the undertaking those who are guilty not only are responsible to the Republic with all their property but also are criminally responsible before the Court of the Republic for destruction of production.

5. The enterprises which have been nationalized according to this decree retain the right to use their current accounts in the People's Bank under the control of the corresponding Economic Councils or their local organs until some other form of financing is adopted. Contracts of the enterprise with customers are to be examined by the appropriate Economic Council and remain valid only with the sanction of the latter.

6. All the technical and working personnel of the enterprise, together with the directors, members of the board of management and persons holding responsible posts, without any exception, are considered as being in the service of the Russian Socialist Federative Soviet Republic and receive remuneration according to the salary scales fixed for specialists.

If members of the administrative and technical personnel of the nationalized enterprise leave their posts without the knowledge of the presidium of the town Economic Council they are strictly liable as labor deserters to prosecution before the Revolutionary Tribunal.

7. Enterprises may be left in the hands of private persons or companies only by virtue of a special decision of the Presidium of the Supreme Economic Council in each case. The Provincial Economic Councils are to decide which of the enterprises may continue to be operated by the owners, and on what conditions this may take place. All decisions of the Provincial Economic Councils according to this Paragraph must be submitted for the approval of the Supreme Economic Council within a period of one week.

Assistant President of the Supreme Economic Council,
V. Milyutin.

(*Cf. Ekonomicheskaya Zhizn,* for December 4, 1920.)

Newspaper Comment, Foreshadowing Application of Red Terror in the Crimea After the Evacuation of Wrangel's Forces: Excerpts from Soviet Newspaper, *Krasni Krim,* of Simferopol

Zemlyachka writes in issue of December 4, 1920:

"We need pitiless, unceasing struggle against the snakes who are hiding in secret. We must annihilate them, sweep them out with an iron broom from everywhere. The great fighter for the great future, the worker-titan, bearing peace to the whole world through a sea of precious blood, shed in the struggle for a bright future, knows neither pity nor neglect."

Margolin writes in issue of December 5, 1920:

"Too many White Guards remain in liberated Crimea. Now they have become quiet, hiding in corners. They await the moment to throw themselves on us again. But No. We pass over to attack.

"With the punishing, merciless sword of Red Terror we shall go over all the Crimea and clear it of all the hangmen, enslavers and tormentors of the working class. We shall take away from them forever the possibility of attacking us."

Demands of the Kronstadt Insurgents, Expressed in the Resolution of the General Meeting of the Crews of the Ships of the Line, Held in Kronstadt on March 1, 1921

Having heard the report of the representatives of the Crews, despatched by the General Meeting of the Crews from the ships to Petrograd in order to learn the state of affairs in Petrograd we decided:

1. In view of the fact that the present Soviets do not represent the will of the workers and peasants, immediately to reëlect the Soviets by secret voting, with free preliminary agitation among all workers and peasants before the elections.

2. Freedom of speech and press for workers, peasants, Anarchists and Left Socialist Parties.

3. Freedom of meetings, trade-unions and peasant associations.

4. To convene, not later than March 1, 1921, a nonparty conference of workers, soldiers and sailors of Petrograd City, Kronstadt and Petrograd Province.

5. To liberate all political prisoners of Socialist Parties, and also all workers, peasants, soldiers and sailors who have been imprisoned in connection with workingclass and peasant movements.

6. To elect a commission to review the cases of those who are imprisoned in jails and concentration camps.

7. To abolish all Political Departments, because no single party may enjoy privileges in the propaganda of its ideas and receive funds from the state for this purpose. Instead of these Departments locally elected cultural-educational commissions must be established and supported by the state.

8. All "cordon detachments" * are to be abolished immediately.

9. To equalize rations for all workers, harmful departments being excepted.

10. To abolish all Communist fighting detachments in all military units, and also various Communist guards at factories. If such detachments and guards are needed they may be chosen from the companies in military units and in the factories according to the judgment of the workers.

11. To grant the peasant full right to do what he sees fit with his land and also to possess cattle, which he must maintain and manage with his own strength, but without employing hired labor.

12. To ask all military units and also our comrades, the military cadets, to associate themselves with our resolutions.

13. We demand that all resolutions be widely published in the press.

14. To appoint a travelling bureau for control.

15. To permit free artisan production with individual labor.

The resolutions were adopted by the Meeting unanimously, with two abstentions.

President of the Meeting, Petrichenko,
Secretary, Perepelkin.

(*Cf.* "The Truth About Kronstadt.")

Ultimatum of the Military Revolutionary Council to the Kronstadt Insurgents, of March 5, 1921

Last warning to the garrison of Kronstadt and the insurgent forts. The Workers' and Peasants' Government has decided:

* The "cordon detachments" were requisitioning detachments which searched passengers on the trains for food.

To bring Kronstadt and the mutinous ships into the possession of the Soviet Republic.

All who have lifted up their hands against the socialist fatherland, lay down their arms immediately. Disarm and hand over to the Soviet authorities those who are stubborn. Immediately set free the arrested commissars and the other representatives of the Soviet regime.

Only those who surrender unconditionally can count on the mercy of the Soviet Republic. At the same time orders have been given to prepare everything for the smashing of the mutiny and the mutineers by arms.

The responsibility for the sufferings which will fall on the peaceful population in this connection rests entirely with the White Guard mutineers.

The present warning is the last.

(*Cf.* N. Kornatovsky, "The Kronstadt Mutiny" [Compilation of documents].)

Radio Message of the Kronstadt Insurgents to the Working Women of the World, of March 8, 1921

To-day is a world holiday, the day of the working women. We, Kronstadters, amid the roar of the cannon and the sound of bursting shells, hurled against us by the enemies of the working people, the Communists, send our brotherly greetings to you, working women of the world. We send greetings from insurgent Red Kronstadt, from the realm of freedom. Let our enemies try to smash us. We are strong, we are invincible.

We hope you will soon gain liberation from all oppression and violence.

Long live the free revolutionary working women!

Long live the world social revolution!

March 8, 1921.

(*Cf. Izvestia Vremennogo Revolutsionnogo Komiteta,* for March 9, 1921.)

Resolution of the Tenth Congress of the Russian Communist Party on the Unity of the Party, of March 8–16, 1921

1. The Congress directs the attention of all members of the Party to the fact that the unity and solidarity of its ranks, the guarantying of complete confidence between members of the Party and of work that is really enthusiastic, that genuinely embodies the unified will of the vanguard of the proletariat is especially necesssary at the present moment, when a number of circumstances increase the waverings among the petty-bourgeois population of the country.

2. On the other hand, even before the general Party discussion about the trade-unions, some signs of fractionalism were manifested in the Party. Groups grew up with special platforms and with a desire to maintain a

separate existence to a certain degree and to create their own group discipline.

All classconscious workers must clearly recognize the harm and impermissibility of any kind of fractionalism, which inevitably leads in fact to the weakening of energetic work and to the strengthening of the repeated attempts of enemies who have crept into the governing Party to deepen the differences and to exploit them for counterrevolutionary purposes.

The ability of the enemies of the proletariat to exploit any departures from a strictly maintained Communist line was most clearly revealed at the time of the Kronstadt mutiny, when the bourgeois counterrevolution and the White Guards in all countries of the world showed their readiness to accept the slogans even of the Soviet regime, only in order to overthrow the dictatorship of the proletariat in Russia, when the Socialist Revolutionaries and the bourgeois counterrevolution in general exploited in Kronstadt the slogans of uprising, as it were, for the sake of the Soviet regime against the Soviet Government in Russia. Such facts furnish clear proof that the White Guards attempt and are able to assume the coloring of Communists and even to pose as more "left" than the Communists, only in order to weaken and overthrow the bulwark of the proletarian revolution in Russia. The Menshevik pamphlets in Petrograd on the eve of the Kronstadt mutiny show in equal measure how the Mensheviki exploited the differences within the Russian Communist Party in order actually to encourage and support the Kronstadt mutineers, Socialist Revolutionaries and White Guards, representing themselves, in words, as opponents of rebellions and adherents of the Soviet regime, only, as it were, with little corrections.

3. Propaganda in this question must consist, on one hand, in a detailed explanation of the harm and danger of fractionalism from the standpoint of the unity of the Party and the realization of the unified will of the vanguard of the proletariat, as the fundamental condition for the success of the proletarian dictatorship; on the other hand, in an exposition of the peculiarity of the latest tactical devices of the enemies of the Soviet regime. These enemies, convinced of the hopelessness of counterrevolution under an openly White Guard banner, now bend all their energies, exploiting the differences within the Russian Communist Party, in order to push forward the counterrevolution by transferring power to the political groupings which are closest externally to the recognition of the Soviet regime.

Propaganda must also set forth the experience of preceding revolutions, when counterrevolution supported the petty-bourgeois groupings which were closest to the extreme revolutionary party, in order to shake and overthrow the revolutionary dictatorship, thereby opening up the road for the further complete victory of the counterrevolution, the capitalists and landlords.

4. Every Party organization must very strictly see to it that the absolutely necessary criticism of the failings of the Party, that any analysis of

the general policy of the Party or appraisal of its practical experience, examination of the fulfilment of its decisions and of means to correct mistakes, etc., should be submitted not for the consideration of groups which have formed on the basis of some "platform," etc., but for the consideration of all the members of the Party. For this purpose the Congress gives instructions to publish the "Discussion Pamphlet" more regularly and to publish special collections of material. Anyone who voices criticism must take account of the position of the Party among the enemies who surround it and must also attempt to correct in practise the mistakes of the Party by participating directly in Soviet and Party work.

5. Commissioning the Central Committee to abolish any kind of fractionalism, the Congress states at the same time that on questions which attract the special attention of members of the Party,—purging of the Party from nonproletarian and unreliable elements, struggle with bureaucratism, development of democracy and of the initiative of the workers, etc.—any practical proposals must be considered with the greatest attention and tested in practical work. All members of the Party must know that, as regards these problems, the Party doesn't realize all the necessary measures, encountering a number of varied obstacles, and that, decisively rejecting impractical and fractional criticism, the Party will continue to test new methods, to fight with all means against bureaucratism for the extension of democratism and initiative, for the discovery, exposure and expulsion of careerists in the Party, etc.

6. The Congress gives instructions that all groups which have been organized on the basis of some platform should be immediately dissolved and commissions all organizations to watch out very closely, so that no fractional demonstrations may be permitted. Nonfulfilment of this decision of the Congress must bring as its consequence unconditional and immediate expulsion from the Party.

(*Cf.* "The All-Union Communist Party in the Resolutions of Its Congresses and Conferences [1898–1926]," pp. 301, 302.)

THE BEGINNING OF THE NEW ECONOMIC POLICY: THE DECREE OF THE ALL-RUSSIAN SOVIET EXECUTIVE COMMITTEE ON THE SUBSTITUTION OF A TAX IN KIND FOR REQUISITIONING

In order to assure an efficient and untroubled economic life on the basis of a freer use by the farmer of the products of his labor and of his economic resources, in order to strengthen the peasant economy and raise its productivity and also in order to calculate precisely the obligation to the state which falls on the peasants, requisitioning, as a means of state collection of food supplies, raw material and fodder, is to be replaced by a tax in kind.

2. This tax must be less than what the peasant has given up to this time through requisitions. The sum of the tax must be reckoned so as to

cover the most essential needs of the Army, the city workers, the non-agricultural population. The general sum of the tax must be diminished inasmuch as the reëstablishment of transportation and industry will permit the Soviet Government to receive agricultural products in exchange for factory and hand-industry products.

3. The tax is to be taken in the form of a percentage or partial deduction from the products raised in the peasant holding, taking into account the harvest, the number of eaters in the holding and the number of cattle.

4. The tax must be progressive; the percentage must be lower for the holdings of middleclass and poorer peasants and of town workers. The holdings of the poorest peasants may be exempted from some and, in exceptional cases, from all forms of the tax in kind.

The industrious peasants who increase the amount of land planted and the number of cattle in their holdings and those who increase the general productivity of their holdings receive privileges in paying the tax in kind.

5. The taxation law must be so framed, and published within such a time limit, that the peasants should be informed as exactly as possible about the amount of their obligations before the beginning of the spring field work.

6. The delivery to the state of the products listed in the tax ends within definite time limits, which are precisely established by the law.

7. The responsibility for paying the tax rests with each individual household and the organs of the Soviet Government are requested to prosecute everyone who does not fulfill his obligation. All-around responsibility is abolished. In order to control the assessment and the payment of the tax, organizations of local peasants are formed, consisting of groups of payers of various rates of the tax.

8. All the reserves of food, raw material and fodder which remain with the peasants after the tax has been paid are at their full disposition and may be used by them for improving and strengthening their holdings, for increasing personal consumption and for exchange for products of factory and hand industry and of agriculture.

Exchange is permitted within the limits of local economic turnover, both through coöperative organizations and through markets.

9. Those farmers who wish to deliver to the state the surplus in their possession after the tax has been paid must receive, in exchange for the voluntary delivery of this surplus, objects of general consumption and agricultural machinery. With this end in view, a steady state reserve fund of agricultural machinery and of objects of general consumption is being created. It includes both domestic products and goods purchased abroad. Part of the state gold reserve and part of the ready raw material are set aside for the purpose of making purchases abroad.

10. The supply of the poorest classes of the agricultural population is arranged by the state according to a special ruling.

11. As a development of the present decree, the All-Russian Soviet Central Executive Committee requests the Council of People's Commissars to issue corresponding detailed instructions within a period of not more than one month.

PRESIDENT OF THE ALL-RUSSIAN SOVIET CENTRAL EXECUTIVE COMMITTEE, M. KALININ,

SECRETARY, ZALUTZKY.

(*Cf. Pravda,* for March 23, 1921.)

To the Peasants of the Russian Socialist Soviet Republic.

The difficult and destructive war which the Soviet Government carried on for three years with Tsarist Generals and landlords, with Russian and foreign capitalists ended in the victory of the workers and peasants. In this war, thanks to the heroism of the Red Army, we saved the land of the peasants from seizure by the landlords, did not permit the manufacturers to return to their factories, did not allow the foreign bourgeois countries to deprive Russia of independence or give them her riches to be robbed. The war was very costly and demanded a great many sacrifices from the workers and peasants. Especially difficult for the peasants was the requisitioning of agricultural products, which the Soviet Government was obliged to take in order to feed the many millions of Red Army soldiers, the workers of the railroads and of the most important industrial enterprises. The Soviet Government knew very well all the burdensomeness of requisitioning for the peasants, the unevenness of its distribution, all its inconveniences for the development of the peasant holdings. But it stood firmly for requisitioning, realizing very well that the working peasants will sooner forgive the Soviet Government all the burdens of requisitioning for the sake of victory over the enemies than the abolition of requisitioning, purchased at the price of the victory of the landlords, the loss of the land, the break-up and destruction of the Red Army.

Now, when the first onset of the capitalists and landlords against the Soviet Government has been repulsed, when Russia has defended its independence from the power of foreign capital in war and speaks on equal terms with the most powerful countries of the world, when mighty England has signed a trade agreement with us, when we are able to send back half of the Red Army to peaceful labor, when by means of foreign trade we can obtain for the peasants products in exchange for part of their own surplus, now the moment has come to decrease the burdens of the peasants without risking the loss of the most precious conquests of the workers' and peasants' revolution.

From now on, by decision of the All-Russian Soviet Central Executive Committee and the Council of People's Commissars, requisitioning is abolished and a tax in kind in agricultural products is introduced in its place.

This tax must be smaller than the requisitions. It must be fixed before the spring planting, so that each peasant may reckon in advance what part of the harvest he must give to the state and what part will remain in his full possession. The tax must be collected without all-around responsibility, *i.e.,* it must fall on the individual household, so that a careful and industrious proprietor will not have to pay for a defaulting fellow-villager. After the tax has been paid the remainder left with the peasant is to be disposed of at his will. He has a right to exchange it for products and machinery which the state will send into the village from abroad and from its own factories; he can use it in exchange for the products which he needs through the coöperatives and through the local markets. At the same time the Soviet Government does not repudiate its duty of supplying with necessary products the poorest classes of the village, which will have no surplus for exchange.

The abolition of grain requisitions and the substitution of a tax in kind will be a great relief for the peasant population and at the same time will strengthen the union of the peasants and workers, on which all the conquests of the Revolution are based.

But the peasants must remember that this measure also is temporary. Only the terrible poverty and disorganization of foreign trade compel the Soviet Government to take part of the peasants' products in the form of a tax, *i.e.,* without any compensation. But as our industry, on the success of which depends the fate of the peasant economy, makes progress and as the importation of foreign goods in exchange for our raw material increases, the amount of the tax in kind, which falls on the peasants, will decrease. In the future we shall achieve such success in the upbuilding of socialist economy that for each pood of peasant grain the Soviet Government will give a product of equal value and one which the village will need.

The time of spring planting is approaching. The All-Russian Soviet Central Executive Committee and the Council of People's Commissars call upon the peasants of Russia to strain all their energy so that not a single *desyatina* of arable land will remain untilled. Every peasant now must know and firmly remember that the more land he plants the greater will be the surplus of grain which will remain in his full possession. But let all Workers' and Peasants' Russia also firmly remember that the Soviet Government is now able to ease the burdens of the peasants only because the heroic Red Army has beaten the enemies of the working people and proved to the whole world that the Workers' and Peasants' state cannot be overthrown. If disagreements should begin in the country between the workers and peasants and among the numerous peoples who are part of our great union of toilers, foreign robbers would always prefer to break their agreements with us, to stop trade, to begin a new war, so as to bring back into power the landlords and capitalists and make out of weakened Russia an easy prey for their robbery and oppression.

Long live our valiant Red Army!

Long live the indestructible union of the workers and peasants!

Long live the invincibility of the Workers' and Peasants' Soviet Government!

Long live Russia's peaceful labor, free from the power of landlords and capitalists!

This appeal must be read in all the villages and stanitsas, in factories and Red Army divisions of the RSFSR.

Signed by Kalinin, Lenin, Yenukidze, all the People's Commissars and all members of the Presidium of the All-Russian Soviet Central Executive Committee.

(*Cf. Pravda,* for March 23, 1921.)

BIBLIOGRAPHY

BOOKS IN THE RUSSIAN LANGUAGE

ABIKH, R. (editor). *Feliks Dzerzhinsky* (Felix Dzerzhinsky) (Collection of articles). Sotsekgiz, Moscow, 1931.

ABOLIN, A. *Syezd X.* (The Tenth Congress). Proletarii, Kharkov, 1930.

AKHUN, M., AND PETROV, V. *Bolsheviki I Armia, 1905–1917* (The Bolsheviki and The Army, 1905–1917). Krasnaya Gazeta, Leningrad, 1929.

AKOLOV, S. *Oktyabr I Uspekhi Natsionalnogo Stroitelstva* (October and The Successes of National Upbuilding). Partizdat, 1932.

ALEKSEENKOV, P. *Kokandskaya Avtonomia* (Autonomous Kokand). Uzbekistan State Publishing Company, Tashkent, 1931.

ALEKSEEV, S. (editor). *Fevralskaya Revolutsia* (The February Revolution) (Compilation of memoirs). Gosizdat, Moscow, 1926.

——*Oktyabrskaya Revolutsia* (The October Revolution) (Compilation of memoirs). Gosizdat, Moscow, 1926.

——*Nachalo Grazhdanskoi Voini* (The Beginning of Civil War) (Compilation of memoirs). Gosizdat, Moscow, 1926.

——*Denikin, Yudenitch, Vrangel* (Denikin, Yudenitch, Wrangel) (Compilation of memoirs). Gosizdat, Moscow, 1927.

——*Grazhdanskaya Voina V Sibirii I Eevernoi Oblasti* (Civil War in Siberia and The Northern Territory) (Compilation of memoirs). Gosizdat, Moscow, 1927.

——*Revolutsia Na Ukraine* (The Revolution in Ukraina) (Compilation of memoirs). Gosizdat, Moscow, 1930.

ANIKST, A. The Organization of Labor Power in 1920. Agitation Editorial Department of the Main Labor Committee and the Commissariat for Labor, Moscow, 1921.

ANISHEV, A. *Ocherki Istorii Grazhdanskoi Voini, 1917–1920* (Sketches of The History of The Civil War, 1917–1920). Gosizdat, Leningrad, 1925.

Antanta I Vrangel (The Entente and Wrangel) (Collection of articles). Gosizdat, Moscow, 1923.

ANTONOV-OVSEENKO, V. *Zapiski O Grazhdanskoi Voine* (Reminiscences of The Civil War) (In four volumes). Gosizdat and Gosudarstvennoe voennoe Izdatelstvo, Moscow, 1933.

ANTONOV-SARATOVSKY, V. *Pod Styagom Proletarskoi Borbi* (Under The Banner of Proletarian Struggle). Gosizdat, Moscow, 1925.

ANTONOV-SARATOVSKY, V. (editor). *Soveti V Epokhe Voennogo Kommunizma* (The Soviets in The Epoch of War Communism) (Collection of documents) (In two volumes). Communist Academy, Moscow, 1928.

ARSHINOV, P. *Istoria Makhnovskogo Dvizhenia* (History of The Makhno Movement). Group of Russian Anarchists in Germany, 1923.

AVDEEV, N. *Revolutsia 1917 Goda* (The Revolution of 1917) (Volumes I and II, January–April and April–May). Gosizdat, Moscow, 1923.

BADAEV, A. *Bolsheviki V Gosudarstvennoi Dume* (The Bolsheviki in The State Duma). Priboi, Leningrad, 1930.

BELENKY, S. AND MANVELOV, A. The 1917 Revolution in Azerbaidjan. Azerbaidjan Istpart, Baku, 1927.

BEZPALOV, V. *Teatri V Dni Revolutsii 1917* (The Theatres in The Days of The Revolution of 1917). Academia, Leningrad, 1927.

BIKOV, P. *Poslednie Dni Romanovikh* (The Last Days of The Romanovs). Uralkniga, Sverdlovsk, 1926.

BOGAT, A. *Zhenschini-Boitsi Krasnoi Armii* (Women-Soldiers of The Red Army). Gosizdat, Moscow, 1930.

BOLDIREV, V. *Sibir, Kolchak, Interventi* (Siberia, Kolchak, Interventionists). Siberian Regional Publishing Company, Novosibirsk, 1925.

Bolshaya Sovetskaya Entsiklopedia (Large Soviet Encyclopedia). Gosizdat, Moscow.

BONCH-BRUEVITCH, V. *Na Boevikh Postakh Fevralskoi I Oktyabrskoi Revolutsii* (On The Fighting Posts of The February and October Revolutions). Federatsia, Moscow, 1930.

Borba Za Petrograd (The Struggle for Petrograd) (Collection of articles). Gosizdat, Moscow, 1923.

BORISENKO, I. *Sovetskie Respubliki Na Severnom Kavkaze V 1918 Godu* (The Soviet Republics in The North Caucasus in 1918) (In two volumes). Severnii Kaykaz, Rostov-on-the-Don, 1930.

BORYAN, B. *Armenia, Mezhdunarodnaya Diplomatia I SSSR* (Armenia, International Diplomacy and The Soviet Union) (In two volumes). Gosizdat, 1929.

BOZHKO, F. *Grazhdanskaya Voina V Tsentralnoi Azii* (Civil War in Central Asia). Uzbek State Publishing Company, Tashkent, 1930.

BUBNOV, A. *VKP (B)* (The All-Union Communist Party (Bolsheviki). Sotsekgiz, Moscow, 1931.

BUBNOV, A., KAMENEV, S., AND EIDEMAN, R. (editors). *Grazhdanskaya Voina, 1918–1921* (The Civil War, 1918–1921) (In three volumes). Voenni Vestnik, Moscow, 1928.

BUDKEVITCH, S. (editor). *Operatsii Na Visle V Polskom Osveshcenii* (The Operations on The Vistula as Described by The Poles). Gosudarstvennoe voennoe izdatelstvo, Moscow, 1931.

CHAIKIN, V. *Kazn 26 Bakinskikh Komissarov* (The Execution of The 26 Baku Commissars). Z. Grzhebin, Moscow, 1922.

CHEMODANOV, G. *Poslednie Dni Staroi Armii.* (The Last Days of The Old Army) Gosizdat, Moscow, 1926.

CHERIKOVER, I. *Antisemitizm I Pogromi Na Ukraine 1917–1918 GG* (Anti-Semitism and Pogroms in Ukraina in 1917–1918).

CHERNISHEV, I. *Selskoe Khozyaistvo Dovoennoi Rossii I SSSR* (The Agriculture of Pre-War Russia and of The Soviet Union). Gosizdat, Moscow, 1926.

CHERNISHEVSKY, N. *Dnevnik* (Diary). Published by Izdatelstvo politkarorzhan, Moscow, 1931.

CHERNOMORDIK, S. *Syezd IX* (The Ninth Congress). Proletarii, Kharkov, 1930.

——*Syezd VII* (The Seventh Congress). Proletarii, Kharkov, 1930.

CHICHERIN, B. N. *Vospominania* (Reminiscences): Vol. I, Moscow University (edited by S. V. Bakhrushin and M. A. Tsyarlovsky). Severs, Moscow, 1929.

CHICHERIN, G. *Vneshnaya Politika Sovetskoi Rossii Za Dva Goda* (Two Years of Foreign Policy of Soviet Russia). Gosizdat, Moscow, 1920.

Communist International (*Vtoroi Kongress: Stenograficheskii Otchet*) (Second Congress: Stenographic Report). Publishing House, Communist International, Petrograd, 1921.

Communist Party (Russian) (Stenographic Reports of Congresses).

——*Syedmoi Syezd* (The Seventh Congress). Gosizdat, Moscow, 1923.

——*VIII Syezd* (The Eighth Congress). Kommunist, Moscow, 1920.

——*Devyatii Syezd* (The Ninth Congress). Gosizdat, Moscow, 1920.

——*Desyatii Syezd* (The Tenth Congress). Gosizdat, Petrograd, 1921.

DAN, F. *Dva Goda Skitanii* (*1919–1921*) (Two Years of Wanderings, 1919–1921). Berlin, 1922.

DE-LAZARI, A. *Grazhdanskaya Voina V Rossii* (*V Skhemakh*) (The Civil War in Russia) (in maps). Gosizdat, Moscow, 1926.

DENIKIN, A. *Ocherki Russkoi Smuti* (Sketches of Russian Turmoil) (In five volumes). Paris and Berlin, 1921–1925.

DENISOV, S. *Vospominania* (Reminiscences). Constantinople, 1921.

DIBENKO, P. *Myatezhniki* (Rebels). Krasnaya Nov, Moscow, 1923.

DRABKINA, E. *Gruzinskaya Kontr-Revolutsia* (The Georgian Counterrevolution). Priboi, Leningrad, 1928.

DROZDOVSKY, M. *Dnevnik* (Diary). Otto Kirchner, Berlin, 1923.

DUBNER, A. *Bakinskii Proletariat V Godakh Revolutsii* (The Baku Proletariat in Years of Revolution). Azerbaidjan State Publishing Company, Baku, 1931.

DUMBADZE, E. *Na Sluzhbye Cheka I Kominterna* (In The Service of The Cheka and The Comintern). Mishen, Paris, 1930.

EGOROV, A. *Razgrom Denikina 1919* (The Smashing of Denikin in 1919). Gosudarstvennoe Voennoe Izdatelstvo, Moscow, 1931.

——*Lvov-Varshava* (Lvov-Warsaw). Gosizdat, Moscow, 1929.

EIDELMAN, B. *Pervii Syezd RSDRP* (The First Congress of The Russian Social-Democratic Labor Party). Moskovskii Rabochii, 1926.

Enborisov, G. *Ot Urala Do Kharbina* (From The Urals to Harbin). Shanghai, 1932.

Erde, D. *Godi Buri I Natiska* (Years of Storm And Stress) (Book One). Gosudarstvennoe Izdatelstvo Ukraini, Kharkov, 1923.

Fedders, G., and Tsvetaev, V. *Grazhdanskaya Voina V Khudozhestvennoi Literature* (The Civil War in Artistic Literature). Gosizdat, Moscow, 1929.

Gai, G. *Na Varshavu* (On to Warsaw). Gosizdat, 1928.

——*Pervii Udar Po Kolchaku* (The First Blow at Kolchak). Military Printing-Shop, War Commissariat, Moscow, 1927.

Galaktionov, M. *Lenin O Religii I Borbe S Nei* (Lenin About Religion and The Struggle with It). Gosizdat, Moscow, 1933.

Gerasimenko, N. *Batko Makhno* (Little Father Makhno). Gosizdat, Moscow, 1928.

Gins, G. *Sibir, Soyuzniki I Kolchak* (Siberia, The Allies and Kolchak). Peking, 1921.

Golochek, V. *Chekhoslovakskie Voiska V Rossii* (The Czecho-Slovak Troops in Russia). Publishing Department of Czecho-Slovak Troops, Irkutsk, 1919.

Golubev, A. *Vrangelevskie Desanti Na Kubani* (Wrangel's Descents in The Kuban). Gosizdat, 1929.

Golubev, A. (editor). *Perekop I Chongar* (Perekop and Chongar). Gosudarstvennoe Voennoe Izdatelstvo, Moscow, 1933.

Gorky, M. *V. I. Lenin* (V. I. Lenin). Gikhl, Moscow, 1932.

Gorn, V. *Grazhdanskaya Voina V Severozapadnoi Rossii* (Civil War in Northwestern Russia). Hamaun, Berlin, 1923.

Grave, B. *Burzhuazia Nakanune Fevralskoi Revolutsii* (The Bourgeoisie on The Eve of The February Revolution) (Collection of documents). Gosizdat, Moscow, 1927.

Gukovsky, A. *Frantsuskaya Interventsia Na Yuge Rossii, 1918–1919* (The French Intervention in South Russia, 1918–1919). Gosizdat, 1928.

Gukovsky, A., Malakhovsky, V., and Melikov, V. (editors). *Razgrom Vrangelya 1920* (The Crushing of Wrangel in 1920). Gosudarstvennoe Voennoe Izdatelstvo, Moscow, 1930.

Gul, R. *Ledyanoi Pokhod* (The Ice March). Gosizdat, 1923.

Gurvich, G. *Istoria Sovetskoi Konstitutsii* (History of The Soviet Constitution). Socialist Academy, Moscow, 1923.

Gurvich, L. (editor). *V Ogne Revolutsii* (In The Fire of Revolution). Ogiz-Molodaya Gvardia, Moscow, 1933.

Gusev, S. *Grazhdanskaya Voina I Krasnaya Armia* (The Civil War and The Red Army). Gosizdat, 1925.

Gusev-Orenburgsky, S. *Kniga O Evreiskikh Pogromakh Na Ukraine V 1919* (A Book About The Pogroms Against The Jews in Ukraina in 1919). Z. Grzhebin, Petrograd.

IGNATIEV, V. *Nekotorie Fakti I Itogi Chetirekh Let Grazhdanskoi Voini* (Some Facts and Results of Four Years of Civil War) (Part I). Gosizdat, Moscow, 1922.

IGNATOV, E. *Moskovskii Sovet Rabochikh Deputatov V 1917 G* (The Moscow Soviet of Workers' Deputies in 1917). Communist Academy, Moscow.

IGRITZKY, I. *1917 in The Village.* Gosizdat, 1929.

ILIN-ZHENEVSKY, A. *Bolsheviki U Vlasti* (The Bolsheviki in Power). Priboi, Leningrad, 1929.

INSTITUTE OF LENIN. *Dati Zhizni I Deyatelnosti Lenina, 1870–1924* (Dates of The Life and Activity of Lenin, 1870–1924). Sotsekgiz, Moscow, 1931.

ISTPART (Commission for The History of The October Revolution and The Russian Communist Party). *25 Let R. K. P. (Bolshevikov), 1898–1923* (25 Years of The Russian Communist Party [Bolsheviki], 1898–1923). Gosizdat, Moscow, 1923.

——*Revolutsia Na Dalnem Vostoke* (Revolution in The Far East), Gosizdat, Moscow, 1923.

——*Revolutsia V Krimu* (Revolution in The Crimea). Krimskoe Gosudarstvennoe Izdatelstvo, 1930.

——*Oktyabrskaya Revolutsia I Grazhdanskaya Voina V Voronezhskoi Gubernii* (The October Revolution and Civil War in Voronezh Province). Voronezhskaya Kommuna, Voronezh.

——*Revolutsia V Srednei Azii* (Revolution in Central Asia) (In two volumes). Pravda Vostoka, Tashkent, 1929.

——*Oktyabr Na Kubani I Chernomore* (October in The Kuban and The Black Sea Province). Burevestnik, Krasnodar, 1924.

——*1905* (Series in six volumes: I—*Predposiliki Revolutsii* [Conditions Preceding The Revolution]; II—*Ot Yanvarya k Oktyabru* [From January to October]; III—*Vooruzhenoe Vosstanie* [Armed Uprising]; IV—*Stachechnoe Dvizhenie* [The Strike Movement]; V—*Armia v pervoi revolutsii* [The Army in The First Revolution]; VI—*Agrarnoe dvizhenie v 1905–1907 gg* [The Agrarian Movement, 1905–1907]). Gosizdat, 1925.

——*Aleksandr Iliyitch Ulyanov I Delo I Marta 1887* (Alexander Ilyitch Ulianov and The Case of March 1, 1887). Gosizdat, 1927.

——*Pervii Legalni Pe-Ka Bolshevikov V 1917 G* (The First Legal Petrograd Committee of The Bolsheviki in 1917). Gosizdat, 1927.

ISTPART VOTSKOGO RAIKOMA VKP (Istpart of The Votsk Regional Committee of The All-Union Communist Party). *Izhevsk V Ogne Grazhdanskoi Voini* (Izhevsk in The Flame of Civil War). Izhevsk, 1927.

IZHEVSKY, V. *Kratkaya Istoria Komitetov Nezamozhnikh Selyan Na Ukraine* (Brief History of The Committees of Poor Peasants in Ukraina). Chervonii Shlyakh, Kiev, 1925.

KACHINSKY, V. *Ocherki Agrarnoi Revolutsii Na Ukraine* (Sketches of The

Agrarian Revolution in Ukraina) (In two parts). Gosudarstvennoe Izdatelstvo Ukraini, Kharkov, 1922 and 1923.

KAGAN, S. *Agrarnaya Revolutsia Na Kievschine* (Agrarian Revolution in Kiev Province). Gosudarstvennoe Izdatelstvo Ukraini, Kiev, 1923.

KAKURIN, N. *Kak Srazhalas Revolutsia* (How The Revolution Fought) (In two volumes). Gosizdat, Moscow, 1925.

KAKURIN, N., AND MELIKOV, V. *Voina S Belopolyakami* (The War With The White Poles). Gosudarstvennoe Voennoe Izdatelstvo, Moscow, 1925.

KALININ, I. *Russkaya Vandeya* (The Russian Vendée). Gosizdat, Moscow, 1926.

——*Pod Znamenem Vrangelya* (Under The Banner of Wrangel). Priboi, Leningrad, 1928.

——*Kak I Potchemu Ispolkom Kominterna Respustil U. K. P.* (How and Why The Executive Committee of the Communist International Dissolved the Ukrainian Communist Party). Proletarii, Kharkov, 1925.

KEDROV, M. *Bez Bolshevistskogo Rukovodstva* (Without Bolshevik Leadership). Krasnaya Gazeta, Petrograd, 1930.

——*Za Sovetsky Sever* (For The Soviet North). Priboi, Leningrad, 1927.

KERZHENTSEV, P. *Zhizn Lenina* (The Life of Lenin). Partizdat, Moscow, 1934.

KHODZHAEV, F. *K Istoria Revolutsii V Bukhare* (History of The Revolution in Bokhara). Uzbekskoe Gosudarstvennoe Izdatelstvo, Tashkent, 1926.

KIN, D. *Denikinschina* (The Denikin System). Priboi, Leningrad.

KLINGER, G. (editor). *Sovetskaya Politika Za Desyat Let Po Nationalnomu Voprosu V RSFSR* (Soviet Policy in The National Question in The RSFSR for Ten Years) (Collection of decrees on nationality problems). Gosizdat, Moscow, 1928.

KLUCHEVSKY, V. *Kurs Russkoi Istorii* (Course of Russian History) (In five volumes).

——*Istoria Soslovii V Rossii* (History of Classes in Russia). Literary-Publishing Department of the Commissariat for Education, Petrograd, 1918.

KLUCHNIKOV, U., AND SABANIN, A. *Mezhdunarodnaya Politika Noveischego Vremeni V Dogovorakh, Notakh I Deklaratsiakh* (Recent International Policy in Treaties, Notes and Declarations). Narkomindel, Moscow, 1926.

KLUEV, L. *Borba Za Tsaritsin* (The Struggle for Tsaritsin). Gosizdat, 1928.

Dopros Kolchaka (The Cross-Examination of Kolchak). Gosizdat, Leningrad, 1925.

KOLEROV (editor). *Kornilovski Dni* (The Kornilov Days). Union of Socialists of People's Army, Petrograd, 1917.

KOLESNIKOV, B. *Professionalnoe Dvizhenie I Kontr-Revolutsia* (The

Trade-Union Movement and Counterrevolution). Gosudarstvennoe Izdatelstvo Ukraini, 1923.

KOLOSOV, E. *Sibir Pri Kolchake* (Siberia Under Kolchak). Biloe, Petrograd, 1923.

KONSTANTINOV, M. M. (editor). *Poslednie Dni Kolchakovschini* (The Last Days of The Kolchak Regime). Gosizdat, 1926.

KORNATOVSKY, N. (editor). *Kolchakovschina* (The Kolchak Regime) Compilation of memoirs). Krasnaya Gazeta, Leningrad, 1930.

——*Kronshtadtski Myatezh* (The Kronstadt Mutiny) (Compilation of articles). Leningrad Regional Publishing-House, 1931.

KOROLKOV, G. *Varshavsko-Ivangorodskaya Operatsiya* (The Warsaw-Ivangorod Operation). Visshi Voennii Redaktionnii Sovet, Moscow, 1923.

KOSTOMAROV, G., AND MALAKHOVSKY, V. *Materiali I Dokumenti* (Materials and Documents) (From The History of The Moscow Workers' Red Guard). Moskovsky Rabochii, Moscow, 1930.

KOVTYUKH, E. *"Zhelezni Potok" V Voennom Izlozhenii* ("The Iron Stream": A Military Exposition). Gosudarstvennoe Voennoe Izdatelstvo, Moscow, 1931.

KOVTYUKH, E. *Ot Kubani Do Volgi I Obratno* (From The Kuban to The Volga and Back). Gosudarstevennoe Voennoe Izdatelstvo, Moscow, 1926.

KOZLOV, T. *Krasnaya Gvardia I Krasnaya Armia V Turkmenistane* (Red Guard and Red Army in Turkmenistan). Askhabad, 1928.

KOZLOVSKY, E. *Za Krasni Turkestan* (For Red Turkestan). Publishing-house of the Central Asiatic Military District, Tashkent, 1926.

KRITZMAN, L. *Geroicheskii Period Velikoi Russkoi Revolutsii* (The Heroic Period of The Great Russian Revolution). Gosizdat, Moscow, 1925.

KRIVTSOV, S. (editor). *Osnovi Istoricheskogo Materializma* (The Bases of Historical Materialism) (Excerpts from the writings of Marx, Engels, Plekhanov, Lenin and others). Sotsekgiz, Moscow, 1931.

KRUPSKAYA, N. *Vospominania O Lenine* (Reminiscences of Lenin). Partizdat, Moscow, 1932.

KUBANIN, M. *Makhnovschina* (The Makhno Movement). Priboi, Leningrad.

KUN, B. *Komintern V Resolutsiakh* (The Communist International in Resolutions). Sverdlov Communist University, Moscow, 1926.

KURGAN, R. *Stranitsa Grazhdanskoi Voini* (A Page of Civil War). Gosudarstvennoe Izdatelstvo Ukraini, 1925.

KURLOV, P. *Konets Russkogo Tsarizma* (The End of Russian Tsarism). Gosizdat, 1923.

KUTYAKOV, I. *Razgrom Uralskoi Beloi Kazachei Armii* (The Smashing of The Ural White Cossack Army). Gosudarstvennoe Voennoe Izdatelstvo, Moscow, 1931.

LEBED, D. *Itogi I Uroki Trekh Let Anarkho-Makhnovschini* (Results and

Lessons of Three Years of Anarcho-Makhnovism). Gosizdat, Kharkov, 1921.

LELEVITCH, G. *Strekopitovschina* (The Strekopitov Mutiny). Gosizdat, Moscow, 1924.

——*Oktyabr V Stavke* (October in The Stavka). Gomelskii Rabochii, 1922.

LENIN, V. *Sobranie Sochinenii* (Collected Works) (in eighteen volumes).

——*Pisma K Rodnim* (Letters to Relatives). Gosizdat, 1930.

——*Pisma Lenina Gorkomu* (Letters of Lenin to Gorky). Partizdat, 1933.

Lenin V Pervie Mesyatsi Sovetskoi Vlasti (Lenin in the First Months of the Soviet Regime) (Collection of articles and reminiscences). Partizdat, 1933.

Leninsky Sbornik (Lenin Collection) (All published volumes up to and including XXIV).

Zapiski Instituta Lenina (Notes of The Lenin Institute).

LEPESHINSKY, P. *Vokrug Ilitcha* (Around Ilyitch). Proletarii, Kharkov, 1926.

——*Prazhskaya Konferentsia* (The Prague Conference). Proletarii, Kharkov, 1930.

——*Syezd I.* (The First Congress). Proletarii, Kharkov, 1930.

——*Syezd II.* (The Second Congress). Proletarii, Kharkov, 1930.

LEVIDOV, M. *K Istorii Soyuznoi Interventsii V Rossii* (Concerning The History of The Allied Intervention in Russia). Priboi, Leningrad, 1925.

LOKSHIN, E. *Kratkii Ocherk Razvitiya Promishlennosti SSSR* (A Brief Sketch of The Development of The Industry of The Soviet Union). Sotsekgiz, Moscow, 1933.

LUBIMOV, I. *Revolutsia 1917* (The Revolution of 1917), Vol. VI, October–December. Gosizdat, 1930.

LUCHINSKAYA, A. *Velikii Provokator* (The Great Provocator). Raduga, Moscow, 1923.

LUKOMSKY, A. *Vospominania* (Reminiscences) (In two volumes). Otto Kirchner, Berlin, 1922.

LYADOV, M., AND POZNER, S. *Leonid Borisovitch Krasin* (Collection of reminiscences, articles and documents). Gosizdat, 1928.

MAISKY, I. *Demokraticheskaya Kontr-Revolutsia* (The Democratic Counterrevolution). Gosizdat, Moscow, 1923.

MAKAROV, P. *Adyutant Generala Mai-Maevskogo* (Adjutant General Mai-Maevsky). Priboi, Leningrad.

MAKSAKOV, V. (editor). *Partizanskoe Dvizhenie V Sibiri* (The Partisan Movement in Siberia). Gosizdat, Moscow, 1925.

MAKSAKOV, V., AND TURUNOV, A. *Khronika Grazhdanskoi Voini V Sibiri, 1917–1918* (Chronicle of The Civil War in Siberia, 1917–1918). Gosizdat, Moscow, 1926.

Malaya Sovetskaya Entsiklopedia (Small Soviet Encyclopedia). Gosizdat, Moscow.

MALITZKY, A. *Cheka I Gpu* (Cheka and Gay-Pay-Oo). Put Prosveschenya, Kharkov, 1923.

MARGOLIN, A. *Ukraina I Politika Antanti* (Ukraina and The Policy of The Entente). S. Efron, Berlin, 1921.

MARGULIES, M. *God Interventsii* (A Year of Intervention) (In three volumes). Z. Grzhebin, Berlin, 1923.

MARTINOV, E. *Tsarskaya Armia V Fevralskoi Revolutsii* (The Tsarist Army in The February Revolution). Printing-Shop of the War Commissariat, Moscow, 1924.

——*Kornilov: Popitka Voennogo Perevorota* (Kornilov: An Attempted Military Coup). Military Printing-Shop of the War Commissariat, Moscow, 1927.

MARUSHEVSKY, V. *Belie V Arkhangelske* (The Whites in Archangel). Priboi, Leningrad, 1930.

MASHKIN, A. (editor). *Sotsialno-Ekonomicheskii Minimum* (Social-Economic Minimum). Put Prosveschenia, Kharkov, 1924.

MELGUNOV, S. *Tragedia Admirala Kolchaka* (The Tragedy of Admiral Kolchak) (In four volumes). Russkaya Tipografia, Belgrade, 1930.

MELIKOV, V. *Marn, Visla, Smirna* (Marne, Vistula, Smyrna). Gosizdat, 1928.

Partia Menshevikov I Denikinschina (The Menshevik Party and The Denikin System). Krasnaya Nov, Moscow, 1923.

MENSHIKOV, A. *Okhrana I Revolutsia* (The Okhrana and The Revolution) (In two parts and three volumes). Izdatelstvo Politkatorzhan, Moscow, 1925 and 1929.

MESCHERAKOV, N. *O Lenine: Sbornik Vospominanii* (A Collection of Reminiscences of Lenin) (In three volumes). Gosizdat, 1925.

MEZHENINOV, S. *Nachalo Borbi S Polyakami Na Ukraine V 1920 Godu* (The Beginning of The Struggle with The Poles in Ukraina in 1920). Gosudarstvennoe Voennoe Izdatelstvo, 1926.

MILYUKOV, P. *Istoria Vtoroi Russkoi Revolutsii* (History of The Second Russian Revolution). Rossiisko-Bolgarskoe Knigoizdatelstvo, Sofia.

MILYUTIN, V. *Istoria Ekonomicheskogo Razvitiya SSSR* (History of The Economic Development of The Soviet Union). Gosizdat, 1927.

MININ, S. *Gorod-Boits* (City-Warrior). Priboi, Leningrad, 1926.

MOTILEV, I. *Khrestomatia Izbrannikh Otrivkov Russkoi Literaturi, 1917–1924* (Selected Excerpts from Russian Literature, 1917–1924). Gosizdat, Moscow.

MOVCHIN, N. *Posledovatelnie operatsii po opitu marni I visli* (Successive Operations According to The Experience of The Marne and The Vistula). Gosizdat, Moscow, 1928.

——*Komplektovanie Krasnoi Armii* (The Recruiting of The Red Army). Military Printing-Shop, Moscow, 1926.

MSTISLAVSKY, S. *Pyat Dnei* (Five Days). Grzhebin, Berlin, Petersburg, Moscow, 1922.

MURTAZIN, M. *Bashkiria I Bashkirskie Voiska V Grazhdanskoi Voine*

(Bashkiria and The Bashkir Troops in The Civil War). Staff of The Red Army, 1927.

N-Sky. *Vtoroi Vserossiiskii Syezd Professionalnikh Soyuzov* (The Second All-Russian Congress of Trade-Unions). Izdanie Vserossiiskogo Tsentralnogo Soveta Professionalnikh Soyuzov, Moscow, 1929.

Nabokov, V. *Vremennoe Pravitelstvo* (The Provisional Government). Novi Mir, Moscow, 1924.

Nadezhni, D. *Na Podstupakh K Petrogradu* (On The Approaches of Petrograd). Gosizdat, Moscow.

Nevsky, V. *Syezd III* (The Third Congress). Proletarii, Kharkov, 1930.

——*Lenin Kak Materialist* (Lenin as a Materialist). Gosizdat, Moscow, 1925.

Nikolaenko, A. *Istoria Rabochego Klassa V Rossii* (History of The Working Class in Russia). Gudok, Moscow, 1926.

Dnevnik Imperatora Nikolaya II (The Diary of The Emperor Nicholas II). Slovo, Berlin, 1923.

Obolensky, V. *Krim Pri Vrangele* (The Crimea Under Wrangel). Gosizdat, Moscow, 1927.

Ol, P. *Inostranni Kapital V Rossii* (Foreign Capital in Russia). Petrograd, 1922.

——*Oktyabrskaya Revolutsia: Pervoe Pyatiletie* (The October Revolution: The First Five Years). Gosudarstvennoe Izdatelstvo Ukraini, Kharkov, 1922.

Olikov, S. *Dezertirstvo V Krasnoi Armii I Borba S Nim* (Desertion in The Red Army and The Struggle with It). Staff of The Red Army, 1928.

Orakhelishvili, M., and Sorin, V. *Dekreti Oktyabrskoi Revolutsii* (Decrees of The October Revolution). Partizdat, Moscow, 1933.

Orlov, N. *Prodovolstvennaya Rabota Sovetskoi Vlasti* (The Provisioning Activity of The Soviet Government). Food Commissariat, Moscow, 1918.

Orlovsky, S. *Velikii God* (The Great Year). Gosizdat, 1930.

——*Kliment Efremovitch Voroshilov.* Krestyanskaya Gazeta, Moscow, 1931.

Oskin, D. *Khozyaistvennaya Rabota Vtoroi Osoboi Armii* (The Economic Work of The Second Special Army). Gosudarstvennoe Voennoe Izdatelstvo, Moscow, 1926.

Padenie Tsarskogo Rezhima (The Fall of The Tsarist Regime) (Stenographic reports of the examinations carried out by the special investigating commission of the Provisional Government; in seven volumes). Gosizdat, Leningrad, 1924–1926.

Papoushek, Y. *Chekhoslovaki I Soveti* (The Czecho-Slovaks and The Soviets). Published by the Author, Prague, 1928.

Parfenov, P. *Grazhdanskaya Voina V Sibiri, 1918–1920* (Civil War in Siberia, 1918–1920). Gosizdat, Moscow, 1923.

——*Borba Za Dalni Vostok* (The Struggle for The Far East). Gosizdat, Moscow.

Pervaya Konnaya V Izobrazhenii Ee Boitsov I Komandirov (The First Cavalry Army, as Depicted by Its Soldiers and Commanders). Gosizdat, Moscow, 1930.

PETROV, P. *Ot Volgi Do Tikhago Okeana* (From The Volga to The Pacific Ocean). Didkovsky, Riga, 1930.

PETROVSKY, D. *Voennaya Shkola V Godi Revolutsii* (The Military School in the Years of Revolution). Visshii Voennii Redaktionnii Sovet, Moscow, 1924.

PILSUDSKY, J. *1920 God* (1920). Voennii Vestnik, Moscow, 1926.

PINEZHSKY, E. *Krasnaya Gvardia* (The Red Guard). Gosizdat, Moscow, 1929.

PIONTKOVSKY, S. *Ocherki Istorii Rossii V XIX–XX Vekakh* (Sketches of Russian History in The 19th and 20th Centuries). Proletarii, Kharkov, 1930.

——*Khrestomatia Po Istorii Oktyabrskoi Revolutsii* (Documents on The History of The October Revolution). Gosizdat, Moscow, 1925.

——*Grazhdanskaya Voina V Rossii (1918–1921): Khrestomatia* (The Civil War in Russia [1918–1921]: Documents). Izdanie Kommunisticheskogo Universiteta Im. Y. M. Sverdlova, Moscow, 1925.

PLATONOV, A. *Stranichka Iz Istorii Eserovskoi Kontr-Revolutsii* (A Page From The History of The S. R. Counterrevolution). Krasnaya Nov, Moscow, 1923.

PLEKHANOV, G. *Istoria Russkoi Obschestvennoi Misli* (History of Russian Social Thought) (In three volumes). Gosizdat, Moscow, 1925.

PODSHIVALOV, I. *Grazhdanskaya Voina Na Urale, 1917–1918* (Civil War in the Urals, 1917–1918). Gosudarstvennoe Voennoe Izdatelstvo, Moscow, 1925.

POKROVSKY, G. *Denikinschina* (The Denikin System). Proletarii, Kharkov, 1926.

POKROVSKY, M. *Russkaya Istoria V Samom Szhatom Ocherke* (Brief History of Russia) (In two volumes). Moskovskii Rabochii, Moscow, 1931.

——(editor) *Ocherki Po Istorii Oktyabrskoi Revolutsii* (Sketches of The History of The October Revolution). Gosizdat, Moscow, 1927.

POKROVSKY, M., AND YAKOVLEV, Y. (editors). *Razlozhenie Armii V 1917 Godu* (The Dissolution of The Army in 1917). Gosizdat, Moscow, 1925.

——*Rabochee Dvizhenie V 1917 Godu* (The Workers' Movement in 1917). Gosizdat, Moscow, 1926.

——*Krestyanskoe Dvizhenie V 1917 Godu* (The Peasant Movement in 1917). Gosizdat, Moscow, 1927.

——*Vtoroi Vserossiiskii Syezd Sovetov* (The Second All-Russian Congress of Soviets). Gosizdat, 1928.

——*Vserossiiskoe Uchreditelnoe Sobranie* (The All-Russian Constituent Assembly). Gosizdat, 1930.

——*Pervii Vserossiiskii Syezd Sovetov* (The First All-Russian Congress of Soviets). Gosizdat, Moscow, 1930.

——*Gosudarstvennoe Soveschanie* (The State Conference). Gosizdat, 1930.

——*Petrogradsky Soviet Rabochikh I Soldatskikh Deputatov* (The Pettrograd Soviet of Workers' and Soldiers' Deputies). Gosizdat, 1925.

POLONSKY, V. *Zhizn M. Bakunina* (The Life of Michael Bakunin). Priboi, Leningrad, 1926.

POLTAVSKY, I. *Geroicheskoe V Russkoi Revolutsii* (The Heroic in The Russian Revolution). L. D. Frankel, Moscow, 1925.

POPOV, N. *Ocherk Istorii VKP* (Sketch of The History of The All-Union Communist Party). Gosizdat, 1929.

——*Ocherk Istorii Kommunisticheskoi Partii Ukraini* (Sketch of The History of The Communist Party of Ukraina). Proletarii, Kharkov, 1931.

POPOV, N., AND YAKOVLEV, Y. *Zhizn Lenina I Leninizm* (The Life of Lenin and Leninism). Krasnaya Nov, Moscow, 1924.

PROKOPOVITCH, S. *Narodnoe Khozyaistvo V Dni Revolutsii* (National Economy in The Days of Revolution). Economic Department of The Co-operative Unions, Moscow, 1918.

RABINOVITCH, S. *Borba Za Armiyu V 1917 G* (The Struggle for The Army in 1917). Gosizdat, Moscow, 1930.

RADEK, K. *Pyat Let Kominterna* (Five Years of The Communist International) (In two volumes). Krasnaya Nov, Moscow, 1924.

——*Germanskaya Revolutsia* (The German Revolution) (In two volumes). Gosizdat, Moscow, 1925.

——*Portreti I Pamphleti* (Portraits and Pamphlets). Gosizdat, Moscow, 1927.

——*Na Sluzhbe Germanskoi Revolutsii* (In The Service of The German Revolution). Gosizdat, Moscow, 1921.

RAEVSKY, A. *Angliiskaya Interventsia I Musavatskoe Pravitelstvo* (British Intervention and The Musavat Government). Krasny Vostok, Baku, 1927.

RAFES, M. *Dva Goda Revolutsii Na Ukraine* (Two Years of Revolution in Ukraina). Gosizdat, Moscow, 1920.

RAKOVSKY, C. *Borba Za Osvobozhdenie Derevni* (The Struggle for The Liberation of The Village). Political Department of The Council of The Ukrainian Labor Army, Kharkov, 1920.

RAKOVSKY, G. *V Stanye Byelikh* (In The Camp of The Whites). Pressa, Constantinople, 1920.

——*Konets Byelikh* (The End of The Whites). Volya Rossii, Prague 1921.

RASKOLNIKOV, F. *Kronshtadt I Piter V 1917 Godu* (Kronstadt and Petersburg in 1917). Gosizdat, 1925.

RAVITCH-CHERKASSKY, M. *Istoria Kommunisticheskoi Partii Ukraini* (History of The Communist Party of Ukraina). Gosudarstvennoe Izdatelstvo Ukraini, Kharkov, 1923.

REISNER, L. *Front* (The Front). Gosizdat, Moscow, 1922.

REZTZOV, L. *Oktyabr V Turkestane* (October in Turkestan). Central Asiatic Publishing Company, 1927.

RIMSHAN, M. *Reid Mamontova* (The Mamontov Raid). Gosudarstvennoe Voennoe Izdatelstvo, Moscow, 1926.

RODZIANKO, A. *Vospominania O Syevero-Zapadnoi Armii* (Reminiscences of The Northwestern Army). Berlin, 1921.

RUDNEV, B. *Makhnovschina* (The Makhno Movement). Knigospilka, Kharkov, 1928.

RYABINSKY, K. *Revolutsia 1917 Goda* (The Revolution of 1917) (Vol. V: October). Gosizdat, 1926.

SAKHAROV, K. *Cheshkie Legioni V Sibiri* (The Czech Legions in Siberia). Berlin, 1930.

SAMOILOV, F. *Malaya Bashkiria* (Little Bashkiria). Starii Bolshevik, Moscow, 1933.

——*Delo Borisa Savinkova* (The Case of Boris Savinkov). Gosizdat, Moscow, 1924.

SAVELEV, M. *Protokoli Tsentralnogo Komiteta RSDRP* (Protocols of The Central Committee of The RSDRP). Gosizdat, Moscow, 1929.

SEF, S. *Pravda O Shamkhore* (The Truth About Shamkhor). Zakavkazkaya Kniga, Tiflis, 1927.

SEMASHKO, N. *Syezd V.* (The Fifth Congress). Proletarii, Kharkov, 1930.

SEMENNIKOV, V. *Monarkhia Pered Krushenie 1914–1917* (The Monarchy Before Downfall, 1914–1917) (From the papers of Nicholas II). Gosizdat, Moscow, 1929.

SERGEEV, E. *Ot Dvini Do Visli* (From The Dvina to the Vistula). Military Editorial Council of the Western Front, Smolensk, 1923.

SHAFIR, Y. *Ocherki Gruzinskoi Zhirondi* (Sketches of The Georgian Gironde). Gosizdat, 1925.

——*Grazhdanskaya Voina V Rossii I Menshevistskaya Gruzia* (Civil War in Russia and Menshevik Georgia). Gosizdat, Moscow, 1921.

SHAPOSHNIKOV, A. *Na Visle* (On The Vistula). Gosizdat, Moscow, 1924.

SHELAVIN, K. *Syezd VI* (The Sixth Congress). Proletarii, Kharkov, 1930.

SHESTAKOV, A. (editor). *Kombedi RSFSR* (The Committees of the Poor in the Russian Socialist Federative Soviet Republic). Gosizdat, Moscow, 1933.

——*Soveti Krestyanskikh Deputatov I Drugie Krestyanskii Organizatsii* (Soviets of Peasant Deputies and Other Peasant Organizations) (In two volumes). Communist Academy, Moscow, 1929.

SHLICHTER, A. (editor). *Chernaya Kniga* (The Black Book) (Collection of articles and material about Entente intervention in Ukraina in 1918–1919). Gosudarstvennoe Izdatelstvo Ukraini, Kharkov, 1925.

SHLYAPNIKOV, A. *Semnadtsatii God* (The Year 1917) (In four volumes). Gosizdat, Moscow, 1925–1931.

SHOTMAN, A. *Lenin V Podpole V 1917 G* (Lenin in Underground in 1917). Gosizdat, 1930.

SHULGIN, V. *Dni* (Days). Priboi, Leningrad, 1925.

——*1920 God* (The Year 1920). Priboi, Leningrad, 1926.

SHVITTAU, G. *Revolutsia I Narodnoe Khozyaistvo V Rossii 1917–1921* (Revolution and Russian National Economy, 1917–1921). Leipzig, 1922.

SIMONOV, B. *Razgrom Denikinschini* (The Crushing of Denikin's Movement). Gosizdat, Moscow, 1928.

SLASCHOV, Y. *Krim V 1920 G* (The Crimea in 1920). Gosizdat, Moscow.

SLEPKOV, A. *Kronshtadtskii Myatezh* (The Kronstadt Rebellion). Moskovskii Rabochii, Moscow, 1928.

SLOBODSKOI, A. *Eto Bilo* (This Was). Proletarii, Kharkov, 1926.

SMIRNOV, I., FLEROVSKY, I., AND GRUNT, Y. (editors). *Borba Za Ural I Sibir* (The Struggle for The Urals and Siberia). Gosizdat, Moscow, 1926.

SOCIETY OF HELP TO THE VICTIMS OF INTERVENTION. *K Desyatiletiu Interventsii* (On The Tenth Anniversary of Intervention) (A collection of articles). Gosizdat, Moscow, 1929.

SOKOLOV, K. *Pravlenie Generala Denikina* (The Government of General Denikin). Rossiisko-Bolgarskoe Knigoizdatelstvo, Sofia, 1921.

SOKOLOV, N. *Ubiistvo Tsarskoi Semi* (The Murder of The Tsarist Family). Slovo, Berlin, 1925.

SOLOVIEV, S. *Istoria Rossii S Drevnyeishcikh Vremen* (The History of Russia From The Most Ancient Times) (In six volumes). Obschestvennaya Polza, St. Petersburg.

SORIN, V. *V. I. Lenin: Kratkaya Biografia* (V. I. Lenin: A Brief Biography). Moskovskii Rabochii, Moscow, 1931.

STALIN, J. *Oktyabrskaya Revolutsia I Taktika Russkikh Kommunistov* (The October Revolution and The Tactics of The Russian Communists). Partizdat, Moscow, 1933.

——*Na Putyakh K Oktyabru* (On The Road to October). Gosizdat, Leningrad, 1925.

——(Collection of Articles on The Occasion of His Fiftieth Birthday). Gosizdat, Moscow, 1929.

STANCHINSKY, A. *Aprelskaya Konferentsia* (The April Conference). Proletarii, Kharkov, 1930.

STEKLOV, U. *Zhizn I Deyatelnost N. G. Chernishevskogo* (The Life and Activity of N. G. Chernishevsky). Krasnaya Gazeta, Leningrad, 1930.

——*A. I. Gertsen* (A. I. Herzen). Krasnaya Gazeta, Leningrad, 1930.

STEPANOV, I. *S Krasnoi Armiei Na Panskuyu Polshu* (With The Red Army Against Noblemen's Poland). Gosizdat, 1920.

STRUMILIN, S. *Zarabotnaya Plata I Proizvoditelnost Truda V Russkoi Promishlennosti V 1913–1922 GG* (Wages and Productivity of Labor in Russian Industry, 1913–1922). Voprosi Truda, Moscow, 1923.

SUBBOTOVSKY, I. *Soyuzniki, Russkie Reaktsioneri I Interventsia* (The Allies, The Russian Reactionaries and Intervention). Leningrad, 1926.

SUKHANOV, N. *Zapiski O Revolutsii* (Reminiscences of The Revolution) (In seven volumes). Z Grezhebin, Berlin and Petrograd, 1919–1922.

SUSLOV, P. V. *Politicheskoe Obezpechenie Sovetsko-Polskoi Kampanii 1920 Goda* (Political Measures in The Soviet-Polish Campaign of 1920). Gosizdat, Moscow-Leningrad, 1930.

SVECHNIKOV, M. *Borba Krasnoi Armii Na Severnom Kavkaze* (The Struggle of The Red Army in The North Caucasus). Gosudarstvennoe Voennoe Izdatelstvo, Moscow, 1926.

TAKHO-GODI, A. *Revolutsia I Kontr-Revolutsia V Daghestane* (Revolution and Counterrevolution in Daghestan). Daghestanskii Nauch.-Issl. Institut, Makatch-Kala, 1927.

TAMARKIN, E., AND POSSE, S. *Uchenie Lenina O Partii* (Lenin's Teaching About The Party). Partizdat, Moscow, 1934.

TANYAEV, A. *Kolchakovschina Na Urale* (The Kolchak Regime in The Urals). Gosizdat, Moscow, 1930.

TEPER, I. *Makhno* (Makhno). Molodoi Rabochii, Moscow, 1924.

TODORSKY, A. *Krasnaya Armia V Gorakh* (The Red Army in The Mountains). Voennii Vestnik, Moscow, 1924.

TROTZKY, L. *Kak Vooruzhalas Revolutsia* (How The Revolution Armed Itself) (In five volumes). Visshi Voennii Redaktionnii Sovet, Moscow, 1923–1925.

——1917 (In two volumes). Gosizdat, 1925.

——*Khozaestvennoe Stroitelstvo Sovetskoi Respubliki* (The Economic Upbuilding of The Soviet Republic). Gosizdat, 1927.

——*Sovetskaya Respublika I Kapitalisticheskii Mir* (The Soviet Republic and the Capitalist World).

TSARINNI, A. *Ukrainskoe Dvizhenie* (The Ukrainian Movement). Berlin, 1925.

TUGAN-BARANOVSKY, M. *Russkaya Fabrika V Proshlom I Nastoyashchem* (The Russian Factory in Past and Present). Proletarii, Kharkov, 1926.

TUN, A. *Istoria Revolutsionnikh Dvizhenii V Rossii* (The History of Revolutionary Movements in Russia). Gosizdat, Leningrad, 1924.

ULYANOV-ELIZAROVA, A. *Vospominania Ob Iliche* (Reminiscences of Ilyitch). Molodaya Gvardiya, Moscow, 1930.

VANAG, N. *Finansovi Kapital V Rossii* (Financial Capital in Russia). Sverdlovsk University, Moscow, 1925.

VARENTSOVA, O. *Syezd IV* (The Fourth Congress). Proletarii, Kharkov, 1930.

VEDENSKY, A. *Tserkov I Gosudarstvo* (Church and State). Gosizdat, Moscow, 1923.

VILENSKY-SIBIRYAKOV, V., CHUZHAK-NASIMOVICH, N., AND SCHELOK, P. (editors). *Tsentrosibirtsi* (Central Siberians). Moskovskii Rabochii, Moscow, 1927.

VISHINSKY, A. *Revolutsionnaya Zakonnost Na Sovremennom Etape, 1917–1933* (Revolutionary Legality in the Contemporary Stage, 1917–1933). Gosizdat, Moscow, 1933.

VLADIMIROVA, V. *God Sluzhbi "Sotsialistov" Kapitalistam* (A Year of Service of "Socialists" to Capitalists). Gosizdat, Moscow, 1927.

——*Revolutsia 1917: Iyun–Iyul* (The Revolution of 1917: June–July). Gosizdat, Moscow, 1923.

——*Revolutsia 1917: Avgust–Sentyabr* (The Revolution of 1917: August–September). Gosizdat, Leningrad, 1924.

VOZNESENSKY, L. *Moskva V 1917 Godu* (Moscow in 1917). Gosizdat, Moscow, 1928.

Vsesoyuznaya Kommunisticheskaya Partiya V Rezolutziakh Ee Syezdov I Konferentsii (The All-Union Communist Party in The Resolutions of Its Congresses and Conferences). Gosizdat, Moscow, 1927.

WOLFSON, M. *Syezd VIII* (The Eighth Congress). Proletarii, Kharkov, 1930.

YAKOVLEV, Y. *Russkii Anarkhizm V Velikoi Russkoi Revolutsii* (Russian Anarchism in The Great Russian Revolution). Gosizdat, Moscow, 1921.

YAKOVLEV, Y. (editor). The War of The Peasants with The Landlords in 1917 (Recollections of peasants). Krestyanskaya Gazeta, Moscow, 1926.

YAKUSHKIN, E., AND POLUNIN, S. *Angliiskaya Interventsia, 1918–1920* (British Intervention, 1918–1920). Gosizdat, 1928.

YAROSLAVSKY, E. *Misli Lenina O Religii* (Lenin's Thoughts About Religion). Gosizdat, Moscow, 1925.

YAROSLAVSKY, E. (editor). *Istoria VKP (B)* (History of The All-Union Communist Party [Bolsheviki]).

YOFFE, A. (editor). *Mirnie Peregovori V Brest-Litovske* (Peace Negotiations in Brest-Litovsk). Commissariat for Foreign Affairs, Moscow, 1920.

YUROVSKY, L. *Denezhnaya Politika Sovetskoi Vlasti, 1917–1927* (The Monetary Policy of The Soviet Regime, 1917–1927). Finantsovoe Izdatelstvo, Moscow, 1928.

Za Pyat Let (For Five Years) (Collection of articles published by the Central Committee of The Russian Communist Party). Krasnaya Nov, Moscow, 1922.

ZASLAVSKY, D., AND KANTOROVITCH, V. *Khronika Fevralskoi Revolutsii*

(Chronicle of The February Revolution) (Vol. I). Biloe, Petrograd, 1924.

ZASULITCH, VERA. *Vospominania* (Reminiscences). Izdatelstvo Politkatorzhan, Moscow, 1931.

ZENZINOV, V. *Gosudarstvenni Pereovorot Admirala Kolchaka* (The *Coup d'Etat* of Admiral Kolchak) (Collection of documents). Paris, 1919.

ZHUKOV, V. *Chernomorskii Flot V Revolutsii 1917–1918 GG* (The Black Sea Fleet in The Revolution of 1917–1918). Molodaya Gvardiya, Moscow, 1931.

ZINOVIEV, G., AND LENIN, N. *Protiv Techeniya* (Against The Tide). Gosizdat, Leningrad, 1925.

ZOLOTAREV, A. *Iz Istorii Tsentralnoi Ukrainskoi Radi* (From The History of The Central Ukrainian Rada). Gosudarstvennoe Izdatelstvo Ukraini, Kharkov, 1922.

BOOKS IN LANGUAGES OTHER THAN RUSSIAN

GRAND DUKE ALEXANDER OF RUSSIA. *Once A Grand Duke.* Farrar and Rinehart, New York, 1932.

BAERLEIN, H. *The March of the Seventy Thousand.* Leonard Parsons, London, 1926.

BENESCH, E. *Der Aufstand der Nationen.* Erich Reiss Verlag, Berlin.

BERKMAN, A. *The Bolshevik Myth.* Boni and Liveright, New York, 1925.

BOTCHARSKY, S. *The Kinsmen Know How to Die.* William Morrow, New York, 1931.

BRESHKOVSKAYA, K. *Hidden Springs of the Russian Revolution.* Stanford University Press, 1931.

BUCHANAN, G. *My Mission to Russia and Other Diplomatic Memories* (In two volumes). Cassell, London, 1923.

BUKHARIN, N. *Historical Materialism.* International Publishers, New York, 1925.

The Bullitt Mission to Russia. B. W. Huebsch, New York, 1919.

BUNYAN, J., AND FISHER, H. *The Bolshevik Revolution.* Stanford University Press, 1934.

CHURCHILL, W. *The World Crisis: The Aftermath.* Thornton Butterworth, London, 1929.

CLEINOW, G. *Neu-Sibirien.* Reimar Hobbing, Berlin, 1928.

DOBB, M. *Russian Economic Development Since the Revolution.* Routledge, London, 1928.

DUKES, P. *Red Dusk and the Morrow.* Doubleday, Page, New York, 1922.

FISCHER, L. *The Soviets in World Affairs* (In two volumes). Jonathan Cape, London, 1930.

FLORINSKY, M. *The End of the Russian Empire.* Yale University Press, New Haven, 1931.

Foreign Relations of the United States: 1918: Russia (In three volumes). Government Printing Office, Washington, 1931.

Fox, R. *Lenin: A Biography*. Gollancz, London, 1933.

Francis, D. *Russia from the American Embassy*. Scribner, New York, 1921.

Golder, F. *Documents of Russian History, 1914–1917*. Century, New York, 1927.

Goldman, E. *My Disillusionment in Russia*. Doubleday, Page, New York, 1923.

——*My Further Disillusionment in Russia*. Doubleday, Page, New York, 1924.

Golovine, N. *The Russian Army in the World War*. Yale University Press, New Haven, 1931.

Graves, W. *America's Siberian Adventure*. Cape and Smith, New York, 1931.

Hard, W. *Raymond Robins' Own Story*. Harper, New York, 1920.

Harrison, M. *Marooned in Moscow*. Doran, New York, 1921.

Heifetz, E. *The Slaughter of the Jews in the Ukraine in 1919*. Seltzer, New York, 1921.

Hoare, S. *The Fourth Seal*. Heinemann, London, 1930.

Hodgson, J. *With Denikin's Armies*. Lincoln Williams, London, 1932.

Hoetsch, O. *Russland. Georg Reimar*, Berlin, 1917.

Kerensky, A. *The Prelude to Bolshevism*. Dodd, Mead, New York, 1919.

Klante, M. *Von der Wolga zum Amur*. Ost-Europa Verlag, Berlin, 1931.

Kornilov, A. *Modern Russian History*. Knopf, New York, 1924.

Lawton, L. *An Economic History of Soviet Russia* (In two volumes). Macmillan, New York and London.

Levine, I. *Stalin*. Blue Ribbon Books, New York, 1931.

Lockhart, R. H. B. *Memoirs of a British Agent*. Putnam, London and New York, 1932.

Martov, J., and Dan, F. *Geschichte der Russischen Sozialdemokratie*. J. H. W. Dietz Nachfolger, Berlin, 1926.

Masaryk, T. *The Spirit of Russia* (In two volumes). Macmillan, New York, 1919.

——*Die Welt-Revolution*. Erich Reiss Verlag, Berlin, 1925.

Mavor, J. *Economic History of Russia* (In two volumes). Dent, London, 1925.

Maynard, C. *The Murmansk Venture*. Hodder and Stoughton, London, 1928.

Milyukov, P. *Russlands Zusammenbruch* (In two volumes). Obelisk Verlag, Berlin, 1926.

Mirsky, D. *Russia: A Social History*. Cresset Press, London, 1930.

——*Lenin*. Little, Brown, Boston, 1931.

Pares, B. *A History of Russia*. Jonathan Cape, London, 1927.

Ponafidine, E. *Russia: My Home*. Bobbs-Merrill, Indianapolis, 1931.

Popoff, G. *The City of the Red Plague*. Dutton, New York, 1925.

PRICE, M. P. *Reminiscences of the Russian Revolution.* Allen and Unwin, 1921.

RANSOME, A. *Russia in 1919.* Huebsch, New York, 1919.

——*The Crisis in Russia.* Allen and Unwin, London, 1921.

REED, J. *Ten Days That Shook the World.* International Publishers, New York, 1926.

RIAZANOV, D. *Karl Marx and Friedrich Engels.* International Publishers, New York, 1927.

ROSENBERG, A. *Geschichte des Bolschevismus.* Rowohlt Verlag, Berlin, 1932.

ROSS, E. A. *The Russian Soviet Republic.* Century, New York, 1923.

SAVINKOV, B. *Memoirs of a Terrorist.* Albert and Charles Boni, New York, 1931.

SKARIÄTINA, I. *A World Can End.* Cape and Smith, New York.

SOKOLNIKOV, G. AND ASSOCIATES. *Soviet Policy in Public Finance.* Stanford University Press, 1931.

SPINKA, M. *The Church and the Russian Revolution.* Macmillan, New York, 1927.

STEWART, G. *The White Armies of Russia.* Macmillan, New York, 1933.

TARASOV-RODIONOV, A. *February 1917.* Covici, Friede, New York, 1931.

TROTZKY, L. *The History of the Russian Revolution* (In three volumes). Simon and Schuster, New York, 1932.

——*Mein Leben.* S. Fischer Verlag, Berlin, 1930.

——*Lenin.* Minton, Balch, New York, 1925.

——*Die Russische Revolution 1905.* Vereinigung Internationaler Verlagsanstalten, Berlin, 1923.

——*Die Wirkliche Lage in Russland.* Avalun Verlag, Dresden, 1928.

VERNADSKY, G. *A History of Russia.* Yale University Press, New Haven, 1929.

——*Lenin: The Red Dictator.* Yale University Press, New Haven, 1931.

VULLIAMY, C. *The Red Archives.* Geoffrey Bles, London, 1929.

YAKHONTOFF, V. *Russia and the Soviet Union in the Far East.* Coward, McCann, New York, 1931.

ZINOVIEV, G. *Geschichte der Kommunistischen Partei Russlands.* Verlag Carl Hoym Nachfolger, Hamburg, 1923.

JOURNALS (SOVIET)

Biloe (The Past).

Bolshevik (Bolshevik).

Istorik-Marksist (Historian-Marxist).

Krasny Arkhiv (Red Archives).

Krasnaya Letopis (Red Chronicle)

Krasnaya Nov (Red Soil).

Letopis Revolutsii (Chronicle of The Revolution).

Novy Mir (New World).

Pravda (The Truth).
Proletarskaya Revolutsia (Proletarian Revolution).

JOURNALS (PUBLISHED BY RUSSIANS ABROAD)

Arkhiv Grazhdanskoi Voini (Archive of The Civil War).
Arkhiv Russkoi Revolutsii (Archive of The Russian Revolution).
Byeloe Dyelo (The White Cause).
Golos Minuvschego na chuzhoi storone (Voice of The Past on Foreign Soil).
Istorik i Sovremennik (Historian and Contemporary).
Revolutsionnaya Rossia (Revolutionary Russia).
Sotsialisticheski Vestnik (Socialist Messenger).
Volya Rossii (Russia's Will).

CHRONOLOGICAL TABLE

OF THE MOST IMPORTANT EVENTS IN RUSSIA FROM MARCH, 1917, UNTIL MARCH, 1921

1917

March 7–11. Strikes and demonstrations of increasing intensity in the workingclass districts of Petrograd; more and more serious clashes with the Police.

March 12. Tsarist regime overthrown in Petrograd; organization of the Committee of the State Duma and the Soviet of Workers' Deputies.

March 15. Formation of first Provisional Government; abdication of Tsar Nicholas II in favor of his brother Michael.

March 16. Abdication of Michael.

March 27. Appeal of Petrograd Soviet to peoples of world on behalf of peace.

April 16. Lenin arrives in Petrograd.

April 20. Publication of his theses, calling for struggle against the Provisional Government and against the War.

May 1. Note of Foreign Minister Milyukov to Allied Governments, affirming Russia's loyalty to treaties concluded during the War.

May 3–5. Hostile demonstrations of soldiers and workers against Milyukov and against Provisional Government in connection with Milyukov's note.

May 10. Resignation of Milyukov.

May 13. Resignation of War Minister, Gutchkov.

May 17. Trotzky arrives in Russia.

May 18. Provisional Government reorganized; number of Mensheviki and Socialist Revolutionaries assume office in new Cabinet.

June 16. First Congress of Soviets opens in Petrograd.

July 1. Huge workers' demonstration in Petrograd, with predominance of Bolshevik slogans and placards.

July 2. Beginning of Russian offensive, which breaks down after a few initial successes as a result of the demoralized condition of the troops.

July 15. Governmental crisis caused by retirement of Cadets.

July 16–18. Unsuccessful uprising of part of Petrograd workers and soldiers, together with Kronstadt sailors, against Provisional Government. Lenin, Zinoviev and some other prominent Bolsheviki go into hiding.

July 21. Organization of new Cabinet, headed by Kerensky.

August 6. Arrest of Trotzky and Lunacharsky.

August 8–16. Sixth Congress of Communist Party held in Petrograd; decides to put aside slogan "All Power to Soviets," in view of changed circumstances.

August 25–27. State Conference in Moscow, attended by representatives of all political groupings in Russia except the Bolsheviki; reveals irreconcilable difference between right-wing and left-wing representatives; Moscow workers carry out strike of protest against allegedly counterrevolutionary character of State Conference.

September 6. General Kornilov, Commander-in-chief of the Russian Army, starts movement of troops on Petrograd, with objectives of crushing the Soviet and bringing about a reorganization of the Provisional government.

September 10. Kornilov's movement collapses, as result of vigorous organization of resistance by the Petrograd Soviet and workers' organization, and of the unwillingness of his own troops to fight.

September 13. Organization of Directory, headed by Kerensky, as temporary substitute for Cabinet, which was disorganized by withdrawal of Cadets. . . . Petrograd Soviet passes its first Bolshevik resolution.

September 19. Voting in Moscow Soviet first time reveals Bolshevik majority.

September 27 to October 5. Democratic Conference in Petrograd.

October 6. Trotzky elected President of Petrograd Soviet.

October 8. New coalition Government, with participation of Cadets.

October 20. Council of the Republic (Pre-Parliament) opens its sessions in Petrograd.

October 23. Bolshevik Party Central Committee in secret session decides to organize armed uprising against the Provisional Government.

October 25. Petrograd Soviet decides to organize Military Revolutionary Committee, which becomes staff for guidance of uprising.

November 3. Breach between Military Revolutionary Committee and Staff of the Petrograd Military District.

November 6. Final preparations for uprising. The Provisional Government mobilizes Junkers and closes Bolshevik newspapers, *Rabochii Put* and *Soldat*.

November 7. Overthrow of the Provisional Government in Petrograd; Kerensky flees. Second Congress of Soviets, with Bolshevik majority, opens in Petrograd.

November 8. Organization of new Government of People's Commissars, consisting exclusively of Bolsheviki; promulgation of decrees nationalizing the land and proposing immediate peace negotiations to all belligerent powers.

November 9. Kerensky starts to move on Petrograd with General Krasnov, who commands a force of a few hundred Cossacks. . . . Beginning of fighting between the forces of the Provisional Government and of the Soviet in Moscow.

November 11. Unsuccessful uprising of Junkers in Petrograd.

November 12. Fighting with Kerensky's troops on the outskirts of Petrograd.

November 14. Flight of Kerensky and capture of Krasnov.

November 15. Victory of the Bolsheviki in Moscow. . . . General Alekseev, former Commander-in-chief of the Russian Army, arrives in the Don Cossack capital, Novo-Cherkassk, and sets about forming the Volunteer Army, which later becomes the most formidable of the anti-Bolshevik military forces.

November 17. Withdrawal of some prominent Communists from the Council of People's Commissars and from the Central Committee of the Communist Party as protest against Lenin's uncompromising attitude toward inclusion of representatives of other Socialist parties in the Government.

November 20. Ukrainian Rada, which has seized power in Ukraina, publishes Third Universal, asserting its right to exercise state power until the convocation of the Constituent Assembly. . . . Soviet Government orders Commander-in-chief Dukhonin to begin peace negotiations.

November 22. Dukhonin dismissed for refusing to obey orders of Soviet Government; Bolshevik Ensign Krilenko appointed Commander-in-chief.

November 26. Decree establishing workers' control over all industrial enterprises.

December 1. Agreement between Bolsheviki and Left Socialist Revolutionaries, as result of which representatives of latter Party enter the Government.

December 2. Kornilov, Denikin and other Generals, imprisoned in Bikov, near Moghilev, for participation in the Kornilov revolt, escape and make for the Don Territory, where they become leaders of Alekseev's Volunteer Army.

December 3. Moghilev, the headquarters of the Stavka (Army General Staff), captured by Krilenko, with a detachment of sailors; Dukhonin is murdered.

December 5. Preliminary armistice agreement signed.

December 15. Conclusion of armistice with Central Powers.

December 17. Soviet Government addresses ultimatum to Ukrainian Rada, demanding that it cease disarming revolutionary troops and permitting Cossack units to pass through Ukraina to the Don.

December 20. Organization of the Cheka—the All-Russian Commission for Combating Counterrevolution, Sabotage and Speculation.

December 22. Beginning of peace negotiations in Brest-Litovsk.

December 26. Organization of Ukrainian Soviet Government, challenging the authority of the Rada, in Kharkov.

December 27. Decree nationalizing the banks.

1918

January 18. The Constituent Assembly opens; reveals an anti-Bolshevik majority.

January 19. Constituent Assembly dispersed by commander of the sailors and soldiers appointed to guard it.

January 23. Congress of "Front Cossacks" in Kamenskaya repudiates Government of Ataman Kaledin.

January 23–31. Third Congress of Soviets.

January 25. Ukrainian Rada issues Third Universal, declaring Ukraina independent.

January 29 to February 3. Bolshevik rebellion in Kiev, finally suppressed by Ukrainian troops.

February 8. Kiev occupied by Red Army under Muraviev.

February 9. Representatives of the Rada sign separate peace with the Central Powers.

February 10. Trotzky, as head of the Soviet peace delegation, issues statement refusing to sign peace, but declaring the war ended and the Russian army demobilized.

February 18. Germans, beginning broad advance, occupy Dvinsk.

February 19. Soviet Government agrees to sign peace.

February 20. Decree for formation of Red Army.

February 22. Soviet Government receives new German peace conditions.

February 23. The Council of People's Commissars and the Bolshevik Party Central Committee agree to sign the peace.

February 25. Rostov and Novo-Cherkassk, the centres of the anti-Bolshevik movement in the Don Territory, occupied by Red Troops; the small Volunteer Army retreats southward and moves into the Kuban Territory.

March 2. German army occupies Kiev, restores Government of the Ukrainian Rada.

March 3. Signature of Peace of Brest-Litovsk.

March 8. The Bolsheviki adopt the name "Communists."

March 12. Government moves from Petrograd to Moscow.

March 13. Trotzky appointed War Commissar.

March 14. Red troops occupy Kuban capital, Ekaterinodar, after flight of the local Cossack Government.

March 15. Fourth Extraordinary Congress of Soviets ratifies the Peace of

Brest-Litovsk. . . . Left Socialist Revolutionaries leave Soviet Government as protest against the signature of the Treaty.

April 6. Japanese descent in Vladivostok.
April 9. Proclamation of the independence of Trans-Caucasia.
April 13. Kornilov killed during unsuccessful attempt to storm Ekaterinodar.
April 23. Decree nationalizing foreign trade.
April 29. Germans dissolve Ukrainian Rada; General Skoropadsky proclaimed Hetman of Ukraina with dictatorial powers.

May 6. Insurgent anti-Soviet Cossacks occupy Novo-Cherkassk.
May 8. Germans and Cossacks occupy Rostov.
May 25. Beginning of open hostilities between the Soviets and the Czecho-Slovaks; the latter occupy Cheliabinsk.
May 26. The Trans-Caucasian Federation breaks up into the three independent states of Georgia, Armenia and Azerbaidjan.
May 28. Czecho-Slovaks seize a number of towns in Eastern Russia and Siberia.
May 29. All-Russian Soviet Executive Committee introduces partial conscription for the Red Army.

June 8. Czecho-Slovaks occupy Samara, making possible creation of anti-Bolshevik Government, headed by Socialist Revolutionary members of the Constituent Assembly. Anti-Bolshevik Government created in Omsk, in Siberia.
June 11. Institution of the Committees of the Poor.
June 17–19. Unsuccessful rebellion against the Soviet regime in Tambov.
June 20. Assassination of prominent Petrograd Communist, Volodarsky, by a Socialist Revolutionary.
June 28. Nationalization of large industries.

July 4–10. Fifth Congress of Soviets in Moscow.
July 6. German Ambassador, Count Mirbach, assassinated by Left Socialist Revolutionaries in Moscow; rebellion of the Left Socialist Revolutionaries. . . . Town of Yaroslavl seized by insurgents acting under the direction of Boris Savinkov.
July 11. Muraviev, commander of Soviet troops on the Volga front, turns against the Bolsheviki and tries to send troops against Moscow; is shot when his troops refuse to follow him.
July 16. The former Tsar and members of his family shot in Ekaterinburg.
July 21. Yaroslavl captured by Soviet troops.
July 30. Left Socialist Revolutionary, Boris Donskoy, mortally wounds General Eichhorn, commander of the German troops in Ukraina, with a bomb.

August 2. Allied occupation of Archangel and organization of anti-Bolshevik Government of North Russia.

August 6. Czecho-Slovaks and anti-Bolshevik Russians capture Kazan, high point of their advance.

August 14. Small British force under General Dunsterville occupies Baku after Bolshevik Soviet regime has been ousted by the population.

August 15. Volunteer Army, under leadership of General Denikin, captures the capital of the Kuban Territory, Ekaterinodar.

August 26. Volunteer Army occupies Novorossisk, gains access to the sea.

August 30. Fanya Kaplan fires at and wounds Lenin; Uritzky, prominent Petrograd Communist, killed by Socialist Revolutionary, Kannegiesser, in Petrograd.

September 4. Soviet Commissar for the Interior, Petrovsky, publishes appeal for "mass terror" against the bourgeoisie.

September 8–23. Representatives of anti-Bolshevik Governments of Siberia and Eastern Russia meet in State Conference at Ufa; agree to create central authority in the form of a Directory of five persons.

September 10. Red Army captures Kazan; turningpoint of campaign on Volga.

September 14. Turks occupy Baku after departure of British; great massacre of Armenians.

September 20. Execution of Twenty-six Baku Commissars in the desert between Krasnovodsk and Askhabad by order of the Trans-Caspian authorities.

October 8. Red Army captures Samara. . . . Death of General Alekseev, organizer of the Volunteer Army.

October 26. Mutiny of commander of North Caucasian Red Army, Sorokin, who kills number of leading Communists and Soviet officials, and is later shot himself.

November 2. Extraordinary tax of ten billion rubles levied on propertied classes of city and village.

November 9. Revolution in Germany.

November 13. Soviet Government annuls Treaty of Brest-Litovsk. . . . Ukrainian nationalists, under leadership of Petlura, raise revolt against Hetman in town of Belaya Tserkov.

November 18. Admiral Alexander Kolchak proclaimed Supreme Ruler, vested with dictatorial powers, after military *coup d'état* in Omsk and arrest of Socialist Revolutionary members of the Directory, Avksentiev and Zenzinov.

November 21. Soviet Government nationalizes internal trade.

November 27. Provisional Soviet Government of Ukraina proclaimed, as first step toward new Bolshevik occupation of Ukraina.

December 14. Ukrainian nationalist troops under Petlura occupy Kiev; Hetman Skoropadsky flees. . . . Red Army, moving westward into former zone of German occupation, occupies Minsk.

1919

January 3. Soviet troops, advancing in western and southern directions, take Riga, capital of Latvia, and Kharkov, the largest city of Eastern Ukraina.

January 6–13. Unsuccessful uprising of Spartacists, German sympathizers with Bolshevism, in Berlin.

February 6. Red Army captures Kiev, capital of the Ukrainian nationalist regime.

February 15. General Krasnov, Ataman of the Don Territory, resigns and is succeeded by General Bogaevsky; withdrawal of Krasnov leaves Denikin in supreme command of anti-Bolshevik forces in southeastern Russia.

March 2–7. First Congress of the Communist International in Moscow.

March 13. Kolchak's army, launching drive toward Volga, captures Ufa.

March 18–23. Eighth Congress of the Communist Party; decision to adopt more conciliatory policy toward middleclass peasants.

March 21. Soviet regime established in Hungary.

April 6. Red Army enters chief Ukrainian port, Odessa, after its evacuation by French forces of occupation.

April 10. Soviet troops, invading Crimean peninsula, occupy Simferopol.

April 26. Kolchak's offensive stopped before reaching Volga as a result of defeats in the Buzuluk and Buguruslan regions.

May 1. Soviet note to Rumania demands immediate evacuation of Bessarabia; despatch of note largely motivated by Soviet desire to come to aid of Hungary.

May 7. Ataman Grigoriev, leader of Soviet troops which were destined for offensive against Rumania, begins rebellion; issues anti-Bolshevik and anti-Semitic manifesto to the population.

May 15–17. Huge pogrom carried out by Grigoriev troops in town of Elizavetgrad.

May 19. Denikin takes offensive against Soviet troops on southeastern front; his cavalry breaks through Red front near Yuzovka.

June 4. Partisan leader Makhno breaks with Red Army command; dissatisfaction among Makhno's followers and other Red troops helps White Army of Denikin to win decisive victories in the Don Territory and in the Donetz coal basin.

June 9. Ufa retaken by Red troops; Kolchak's retreat continues.

June 12. Fort Krasnaya Gorka, near Petrograd, betrayed to Northwestern White Army by its commanding officers.

June 16. Krasnaya Gorka retaken; threat to Petrograd averted.

June 25. Denikin captures Kharkov.

June 30. Continuation of Denikin's advance marked by capture of Tsaritsin and Ekaterinoslav.

July 1. Soviet troops, pushing forward on Eastern Front, take Perm.

July 25. Red Army occupies Cheliabinsk; retreat of Kolchak's troops becomes increasingly disorderly.

July 27. Grigoriev killed by Makhno.

August 1. Fall of Hungarian Soviet Government.

August 10. Denikin's cavalry General, Mamontov, breaks through front, begins long raid in rear of Soviet armies on Southern Front.

August 18–21. Mamontov holds Tambov.

August 23. Denikin seizes Odessa.

August 30. Red Army evacuates Kiev; Petlurists march in.

August 31. Denikin's forces push Petlurists out of Kiev.

September 7. Beginning of peace negotiations between the Soviet Government and Esthonia.

September 25. Anarchists throw bomb into headquarters of Moscow Committee of the Communist Party; a number of Communists killed and wounded.

October 11. Yudenitch starts drive on Petrograd.

October 14. Denikin occupies Orel: high point of his advance.

October 20. Red Army retakes Orel.

October 22. Yudenitch pushed back from suburbs of Petrograd, Tsarskoe Selo and Pavlovsk.

November 9. Makhno, harassing Denikin's rear, captures Ekaterinoslav.

November 14. Red Army takes Kolchak's capital, Omsk.

November 17. Soviet troops on Southern Front occupy Kursk; Denikin's resistance begins to crumble all along the line.

December 12. Red Army captures Kharkov.

December 16. Kiev falls into the hands of the Red troops.

December 27. Radicals and liberals, organized in the so-called Political Centre, create new Government, in opposition to Kolchak, in Irkutsk.

December 30. Red troops take Ekaterinoslav.

1920

January 3. Red Army occupies Tsaritsin.

January 4. Kolchak abdicates as Supreme Ruler in favor of Denikin.

January 8. Red Army captures Rostov, seat of Denikin's Government; Denikin's Army retreats south of the Don.

January 15. Kolchak handed over to the Political Centre in Irkutsk by Czecho-Slovaks who were guarding him.

January 16. Allied Supreme Council raises the blockade of Soviet Russia.

January 18. Revolutionary Committee, in which Bolshevik influence predominates, takes over power from the Political Centre in Irkutsk.

February 1. Revolution in Khiva, with aid of Red Army, leads to establishment of Soviet regime there.

February 2. Signature of Peace with Esthonia.

February 7. Kolchak shot by decision of the Revolutionary Committee in Irkutsk.

February 10. Beginning of organization of "labor armies" with a view to utilizing Red Army soldiers for productive work.

February 19. Fall of Northern Government in Archangel.

March 17. Red Army occupies Kuban capital, Ekaterinodar.

March 27. Soviet troops, pursuing demoralized White Army of Denikin, take port of Novorossisk.

April 4. Denikin resigns command of armed forces of South Russia, nominating General Baron Peter Wrangel as his successor.

April 27. Red Army captures Baku; Azerbaidjan Soviet Government organized.

May 2. Number of distinguished military specialists, including former Commander-in-chief, General Brussilov, enter special council and place their services at the disposal of the Soviet Government in the war against Poland.

May 6. Poles enter Kiev.

May 7. Soviet Government concludes treaty with Georgia, recognizing its independence.

June 6. Wrangel, after reorganizing his army, begins movement northward from the Crimea.

June 8. Budenny's Cavalry Army, raiding in rear of Poles, seizes Berditchev and Zhitomir.

June 12. Red Army retakes Kiev.

July 11. Red Army, on the offensive on the Polish Front, captures Minsk.

July 14. Soviet troops occupy Vilna.

July 31. With view to creating a Soviet regime in Poland a Revolutionary Committee, headed by Communists of Polish origin, is established in Belostok.

August 1. Red Army takes Brest-Litovsk.

August 15. Polish forces south of Warsaw launch counter-offensive.

August 21. Success of Polish counterstroke marked by recapture of Brest-Litovsk and general retreat of Red Army from the Vistula.

September 1. Red Army storms Bokhara; Emir flees.

September 2. Congress of Peoples of the East, designed to stir up revolutionary movements throughout Asia, opens in Baku.

September 21. Beginning of Russo-Polish peace negotiations in Riga.

October 12. Signature of preliminary peace treaty with Poland.

October 20. Beginning of final offensive against Wrangel.

November 2. Wrangel's Army retreats into the Crimea.

November 11. Red Army storms the Isthmus of Perekop, the approach to the Crimea.

November 14. Wrangel evacuates the Crimea.

November 29. Soviet Government issues decree nationalizing small industries.

1921

February 8. Death of famous Anarchist, Prince Kropotkin.

February 27. Soviet regime proclaimed in Georgia, after invasion of the country by Red Army.

March 1–17. Rebellion of the sailors and garrison of the naval fortress of Kronstadt, near Petrograd.

March 8. Lenin announces introduction of the New Economic Policy at first session of the Tenth Party Congress.

March 16. Decree of the Soviet Central Executive Committee, replacing former system of requisitions of the peasants' products with fixed tax in kind. . . . Signature of Anglo-Soviet Trade Agreement.

INDEX

C

D

E

F

L

N

Q

R

S

W

Library of Congress Cataloging-in-Publication Data

Chamberlin, William Henry, 1897–1969.
The Russian revolution, 1917–1921.

Reprint. Originally published: New York : Macmillan, 1954.
Bibliography: p.
Contents: v. 1. From the overthrow of the Tzar to the assumption of power by the Bolsheviks—v. 2. From the civil war to the consolidation of power.
1. Soviet Union—History—Revolution, 1917–1921.
I. Title.
DK265.C43 1987 947.084'1 87-3719
ISBN 0-691-00816-7 (pbk. : set)
ISBN 0-691-05492-4 (v. 1 : alk. paper)
ISBN 0-691-00814-0 (pbk. : v. 1)
ISBN 0-691-05493-2 (v. 2 : alk. paper)
ISBN 0-691-00815-9 (pbk. : v. 2)